Java™ 2 Primer Plus

Steven Haines &
Steve Potts

201 West 103rd St., Indianapolis, Indiana, 46290 USA

Java™ 2 Primer Plus

International Standard Book Number: 0-672-32415-6

Library of Congress Catalog Card Number: 2002102794

Printed in the United States of America

First Printing: December 2002

05   04   03   02   4   3   2   1

Trademarks

All terms mentioned in this book that are known to be trademarks or service marks have been appropriately capitalized. Sams Publishing cannot attest to the accuracy of this information. Use of a term in this book should not be regarded as affecting the validity of any trademark or service mark.

Warning and Disclaimer

Every effort has been made to make this book as complete and as accurate as possible, but no warranty or fitness is implied. The information provided is on an "as is" basis. The author and the publisher shall have neither liability nor responsibility to any person or entity with respect to any loss or damages arising from the information contained in this book.

ASSOCIATE PUBLISHER
Michael Stephens

ACQUISITIONS EDITORS
Todd Green
Michelle Newcomb

DEVELOPMENT EDITOR
Mark Renfrow

MANAGING EDITOR
Charlotte Clapp

PROJECT EDITOR
Andy Beaster

COPY EDITOR
Chip Gardner

INDEXER
Sharon Shock

PROOFREADER
Linda Seifert

TECHNICAL EDITORS
Marc Goldford
Steve Heckler
John Purdum

TEAM COORDINATOR
Lynne Williams

INTERIOR DESIGNER
Gary Adair

COVER DESIGNER
Aren Howell

PAGE LAYOUT
Point 'n Click Publishing, LLC.

GRAPHICS
Oliver Jackson
Tammy Graham

CONTENTS AT A GLANCE

TABLE OF CONTENTS

ABOUT THE AUTHORS

Steve Haines has worked in the enterprise software industry for the past eight years and has been focusing on Java since 1997. He has been filling key architectural roles in the areas of B2B e-commerce, high-speed Internet marketing, application monitoring and diagnosis, and robust client and server-side image layout and management over the past few years. He is currently the J2EE Domain Architect for Quest Software and is responsible for defining the expert rules for tuning and monitoring Enterprise Java applications and application servers.

He is the author of Que Publishing's *Java 2 from Scratch* and has numerous articles on InformIT.com in the areas of Java Swing and Enterprise Java. He shares author credits on *Java Web Services Unleashed*, *C++ Unleashed*, *Sams Teach Yourself C++ in 21 Days*, and *Sams Teach Yourself Java in 21 Days*. He has also worked as a technical editor for Pearson Education in areas of Java, Enterprise Java, Network Communications, C++, and video-game programming. Steve has taught all aspects of Java programming from basic certification training through Database, Web Development, and Enterprise JavaBeans at Learning Tree University (LTU). Steve recently enrolled in a Bachelor's of Biblical Studies at Calvary Chapel Bible College.

Steve Potts is an independent consultant, author, and Java instructor in Atlanta, Georgia. Steve received his Computer Science degree in 1982 from Georgia Tech. He has worked in a number of disciplines during his 20-year career, with manufacturing being his deepest experience. Steve has consulted for such companies as Home Depot, Disney, and IBM. His previous books include *Java Unleashed* and *Java 1.2 How-To*. He can be reached via email at `steve-potts@mindspring.com`.

ABOUT THE TECHNICAL EDITOR

John Purdum is a software engineer for Roche Diagnostics Corporation in Indianapolis, Indiana. He is currently developing both standalone and Web-based Java Applications for the Business Information Warehouse, specializing in reusable component development. Prior to his current job, he was a software engineer consultant specializing in Visual Basic and C++ development for Bank One. Programming with the Java language has been the most enlightening and fulfilling aspect of his career.

DEDICATIONS

To my son Michael and my wife Linda: Michael, you are the greatest son I could have ever prayed for, I love you so much. Linda, your love has shown me that marriage can be a piece of Heaven here on Earth!

—Steve Haines

I would like to dedicate this book to Suzanne, my wife of twenty years. The hours required to produce a book of this size and scope place an additional burden on her in caring for our six children.

—Steve Potts

ACKNOWLEDGMENTS

First of all I would like to thank my personal Lord and Savior Jesus Christ for blessing me so richly and giving me this opportunity. I would like to thank all my friends at Sams Publishing for their belief in me and for helping me build this book: Michelle Newcomb, Todd Green, Mark Renfrow, Andrew Beaster, Chip Gardner, and Heather McNeill. Special thanks to Michelle Newcomb; you are a blessing to work with and have become a great friend over the past few years! Thanks to my family for their support: Elizabeth Haines, Heru Susilo, Cecilia Chandra, Herindarno Heru (Wei Wei), Hernanto Heru (Yong Yong), and my favorite uncle Bing Oei. Thanks to my friends for bearing with my schedule: Jeff and Maria Thornton, Matt Torres, Alex Blank, Henry and Yolanda Jahja. Many thanks to Quest Software's technology staff for their support: Guy Harrison, Eyal Aranoff, and Pat Stephenson. Thanks to my friends in the computer industry that I have worked with and kept in touch with over the last eight years—Canon: Jessie Labayen, Mark An, Jay Tadbiri, Raemonde Olson, Kiyoshi Oka, Julie Lin; Engage: Jyoti Mody, Gary McKenzie, Siobhan Cooper; Wonderware: Robert Asis, Trevor Nguyen, Keyee Hsu, Jay Cook, Rashesh Mody; Rainbow: Anne Barrette; IPNet: Danny Lim, Ryan Saldara, Sean Slavin, Gary Kostalnick, Steve Chuang; and BigBallot: Michael Foo. Thanks to my LTU friends: Mara Scott, Sandy Ock, Brad O'Hearne, and Brian Maslowe. Finally, I would like to thank you the reader—there are many Java books on the market and I am very honored that you chose this one—I won't let you down!

—Steve Haines

I would like to thank all the editors on this book for their contributions. Michelle Newcomb got me involved with the project, and Todd Green helped me stay on schedule. Mark Renfrow has been a big help in keeping me focused on the details. I would also like to thank John Purdum and Marc Goldford, the technical reviewers, for their diligence.

—Steve Potts

TELL US WHAT YOU THINK!

As the reader of this book, *you* are our most important critic and commentator. We value your opinion and want to know what we're doing right, what we could do better, what areas you'd like to see us publish in, and any other words of wisdom you're willing to pass our way.

As an Associate Publisher for Sams, I welcome your comments. You can email or write me directly to let me know what you did or didn't like about this book—as well as what we can do to make our books better.

Please note that I cannot help you with technical problems related to the *topic* of this book. We do have a User Services group, however, where I will forward specific technical questions related to the book.

When you write, please be sure to include this book's title and author as well as your name, email address, and phone number. I will carefully review your comments and share them with the author and editors who worked on the book.

Email: feedback@samspublishing.com

Mail: Michael Stephens, Associate Publisher
            Sams Publishing
            201 West 103rd Street
            Indianapolis, IN 46290 USA

For more information about this book or another Sams title, visit our Web site at www.samspublishing.com. Type the ISBN (excluding hyphens) or the title of a book in the Search field to find the page you're looking for.

INTRODUCTION

Java programming, like all computer programming, requires a dedication to learning and the right study tools. As a Java programmer, I have spent years reading various books on every aspect of Java and analyzing Sun's implementation of it to gain insight into its design philosophies. The Java programming books I have read vary in detail and approach, but something very important is missing.

Several years back, when I was deep into Windows programming, I read Don Box's *Essential COM*, which changed my standards for programming books. COM is a difficult subject to understand, let alone master, but Don's approach was quite different from any other book on the market. He started from the foundation and derived COM feature-by-feature so that the reader truly understood why each design decision was made. By the end of the first chapter I looked at COM from a completely different perspective: It was no longer a crazy mystery, but everything suddenly made sense. Then, when learning the more advanced features of the language, it was just adding details to build on a firmly established foundation.

I have not read a Java book that has taken this approach, which is what differentiates *Java 2 Primer Plus* from any other book. Instead of simply teaching the reader *how* to write Java programs, every effort has been made to teach the reader *why* the language is the way it is. The book also explores the underlying design decisions Java's originators made when creating the language. The goal, therefore, is for the reader to walk away from this book with a solid foundation in the Java programming language so, as new technologies evolve, the reader can easily add the details to his firmly established foundation.

Who Should Read This Book?

Java 2 Primer Plus is geared to the following categories of readers:

- Readers new to computer programming
- Existing programmers new to Java
- Java programmers wanting to gain a deeper understanding of Java

This book starts from the foundation of Java and assumes nothing about the reader. It offers sufficient depth to appeal to both the novice and the seasoned pro. If you are already proficient in another programming language, your focus in the early chapters will be on the specific application of familiar concepts in the Java programming language. If you are new to computer programming in general, the book will guide you through the basic concepts and explain how they are derived.

This book was built not only from my experience as a professional Java programmer, but also from tried-and-true instructional techniques borrowed from the classroom. I have taught a wide variety of students ranging from new computer programmers to Visual Basic experts; from accountants to experienced Java programmers, and have engineered an approach to Java programming that has worked in each specific case. My goal is to transfer this experience to print.

What You Need to Know Before Reading This Book

You do not need to have any programming background to find this book a valuable study aid.

How This Book Is Organized

This book is broken down into five parts:

- Part I: Java Foundations
- Part II: Object-Oriented Programming
- Part III: Graphical User Interfaces
- Part IV: Advanced Topics
- Part V: Java Web Technologies

Part I, "Java Foundations," covers the basics of computer programming as applied to Java programming. It talks about Java's keywords, data types, variables, operators, flow-control, and methods. After reading through Java Foundations, you will understand the major tools you will use to build Java programs later in the book.

Part II, "Object-Oriented Programming," introduces you to the most popular and effective programming paradigm ever seen in computer programming: object-oriented programming. It talks about Java classes, encapsulation, inheritance, and polymorphism. Furthermore, it includes some of the more advanced core features of Java, including interfaces, exception handling, Java's collection classes, and input and output.

Part III, "Graphical User Interfaces," teaches you how to build graphical user interfaces, which are targeted for both applications and applets, using the standard Abstract Window Toolkit as well as advanced user interfaces using Swing. It walks you through a complete derivation of the event-delegation model that drives Java's entire event-handling strategy.

Part IV, "Advanced Topics," brings together the advanced topics that complete what I call the core components of the Java programming language. After this section you should be able to understand any application of Java whether it be applied to the Web, enterprise computing, or mobile computing. The topics include multithreaded programming, Java's introspection and reflection programming interface, the Java Database Connectivity API (JDBC), network programming using raw sockets, and Java's Remote Method Invocation (RMI). The section finishes up with a discussion of best practices and code optimization techniques.

Part V, "Java Web Technologies," discusses the application of the Java programming language in server-side Web programming. It discusses the modest beginnings of servlets, the more recent and easy-to-use JavaServer Pages (JSP), as well as advanced subjects such as building custom tag libraries to supplement your Web programming and handling XML. Finally, it includes a discussion into proper Web application design and the application of the tried-and-true Model-View-Controller (MVC) design pattern applied to Web design. Because Java Web programming is very flexible, its technology can easily be abused and not yield optimal results; this section addresses the need to ensure that your Web applications are scalable and optimally configured.

Conventions Used In This Book

Throughout the book you will see sections named "Problem" this is where you will find the derivation of the contextual topics. These sections define the problems that Java is trying to solve, and walk you through the design process step-by-step to help you understand that process.

Each chapter also has a set of review questions and exercises. These are aimed at reinforcing key concepts in the Java programming language and motivating you to continue your studies further by applying what you have learned to a real project. Learning a programming language is a very proactive exercise; if you want to become proficient in any programming language, you need to do more than read the book[md]you must apply what you have learned into a real example. I encourage you to do the exercises; your ability will improve greatly if you do!

Other features included in this book are

Note

Notes give you comments and asides about the topic at hand, as well as full explanations of certain concepts.

Tip

Tips provide great shortcuts and hints on how to program with Java 2 more effectively.

Caution

Cautions warn you about common pitfalls.

In addition, you'll find various typographic conventions throughout this book:

- URLs, files, methods, functions, events, interfaces, parameters, tags, and so on appear in text in a special `monospaced font`.

- Commands and code you type appear in **boldface type.**

- Placeholders in syntax descriptions appear in *`monospaced italic`* typeface. This indicates that you will replace the placeholder with the actual filename, parameter, or other element that it represents.

PART I

JAVA FOUNDATION

CHAPTER 1

INTRODUCTION TO JAVA

You will learn about the following in this chapter:

- What is Java?
- Setting up a Java programming environment

- Writing your first Java program

Welcome to Java!

This chapter will take you through a brief introduction to the Java language, including all the benefits of the language and answer the question: Why would you want to use Java? It will talk a little about Java's history, and then get you up and running with your first Java application!

What Is Java?

Java is a high-level programming language that has many functions. It is used to develop applets that reside on Web pages, applications that run on your desktop, server-side middleware that are used to communicate between clients and server resources. Java is also used on Web servers and in embedded systems and smart devices, just to name a few of its many functions. The practical applications of Java can be found in Web browser applets and in server-side applications (Web and enterprise-wide).

History

The following is a short history of the Java programming language and the reasons for its inception. In 1991, a research group working as part of Sun Microsystems's "Green" project, was developing software to control consumer electronic devices. The goal was to develop a programming language that could be used to control and network "smart" devices, such as televisions, toasters, and even buildings. These devices would all coexist and communicate with one another.

The first prototype that Sun came out with was a device called the Star7—a device, similar to a remote control, that could communicate with other Star7 devices. The initial intent was to use C++ to control the Star7, but as a result of frustration with that language, Green project member James Gosling developed a new language called Oak to control the Star7. The title Oak came from a tree that Gosling could see from his office window while developing the language. Sun later replaced the name with Java because Oak was already being used.

As a result of Oak, or Java, being designed to run on small appliances, the language had the following inherent benefits:

- It was small, so it could run on the limited memory of small appliances.

- It was efficient and reliable, so it could function as a small appliance—we are all used to computer crashes, but a microwave oven crash is not acceptable.

- It was portable, so it could run on different pieces of hardware.

In 1994, the members of the Green project developed a World Wide Web (WWW) browser completely in Java that could run Java applets to demonstrate the power of the language. The browser was originally called WebRunner, but is now known as HotJava. Java came alive in 1995, however, when Netscape licensed the Java programming language and included support for it in its Navigator product.

In 1997, Sun released the Servlet API, which revolutionized server-side Web development and moved it away from monolithic CGI scripts or proprietary solutions. In 1999, Sun released the first version of the Java 2, Enterprise Edition (J2EE) specification that included JavaServer Pages (JSP) and Enterprise JavaBeans (EJB) in a highly distributed enterprise middleware. Since then the J2EE specification, along with the JSP, Servlet, and EJB specifications, have evolved into a very powerful programming paradigm.

Why Use Java?

You might have heard some of the geeks in your office talking about Java, or maybe you are taking a Java class in school, or perhaps you already know what Java is, but aren't too sure why you would want to use it. Here are some reasons to learn Java, regardless of which category you fall under.

- Java is a truly object-oriented programming language, perfect for modeling the real world and solving real-world problems. It will adapt to the latest design methodologies, and it provides extensibility so that your large project will be manageable.

- Java is platform independent, so the same semicompiled byte code will work on Microsoft Windows, Unix, Apple Macintosh, Linux, and any future Wiz-bang operating system that implements a Java virtual machine.

- Java can add interactivity to your Web pages. Java applets provide much of the functionality you are probably already familiar with, such as menus, data entry forms, and other user interface components as well as some of the neat drawings and animated graphics that are found on most Web pages.

- With increasing CPU speeds, Java is becoming more feasible for building usable applications.

- Java's new SWING libraries rival components you see in the Microsoft Windows operating systems: tree controls, tab controls, list controls, tables, and so on.

- Java has an incredible future in the upcoming decade! There is more and more talk about "intelligent devices" hosting a Java virtual machine that can run Java programs. These devices, such as smart toasters, smart televisions, and smart houses, will be networked together so that your television can tell your VCR to tell your toaster to start toasting! Java is the forefront technology of this exciting, evolving field.

Java has existed in its infancy for the past couple years, demonstrating conceptual leaps and bounds and accomplishing the unthinkable. As it evolves and matures, it is more and more apparent that Java will become the prevalent development language of the future. Learning Java will not only help you develop incredible applets and applications now, it will also prepare you for the future of computer and device programming!

Java Buzzwords

The following buzzwords are associated with Java; this section defines those buzzwords and explains how they are applicable to Java:

- Simple

- Object oriented

- Distributed

- Robust

- Secure

- Architecture neutral

- Portable

- Interpreted

- Multithreaded

Simple

Java is simple to learn and simple to implement. Its syntax is very similar to C++ and C#, and it touts all the standard programming paradigms in an easy-to-use fashion. In fact, one of Java's goals is to enable its developers to be up-and-running fast. Furthermore, it is consistent; when you learn how something works, you can rest assured that it will not change on you as you encounter a similar topic.

Object Oriented

Java is a truly object-oriented programming language that supports objects, inheritance, and polymorphism; this makes it ideal for establishing a good foundation in computer programming. We will discuss objects and object-oriented programming starting in Chapter 6, "Classes," but the main benefit of it is that you can model your Java programs after real-life objects, such as an apple, a car, or a person. This programming paradigm helps bridge the gap between the way a machine thinks and the way you do.

Distributed

Connectivity between components has been a basic tenet of the Java programming language since its inception. Java's developers have remained true to this belief as the technology has evolved. Hence, developing applications that run on multiple machines concurrently and communicate with one another is far easier and efficient using Java than with many other programming languages.

Robust

Java's modest beginnings as a simple mechanism to add interactivity to Web pages and develop simple communication schemes are a distant memory. Today Java boasts a graphical user interface (GUI) library that rivals features of the best operating systems; a Web development solution that surpasses any other offering; a distributed enterprise platform that leads the market; and a rich set of libraries for data input and output, multithreading, advanced imaging, XML document manipulation, and more. Almost any feature you could be searching for in a programming language you will find in Java.

Secure

Remember that Java's inception was designed around the communication between smart devices. This legacy added a set of very strict rules governing what it can and cannot do. Various components of the Java programming language operate in different secure environments. For example, applets running in a Web browser cannot access a Web client's underlying file system or any other Web site other than that from which it originated; a distributed component must be granted access to communicate with other hosts; and all Java programs run in a virtual machine that protects the underlying operating system from harm.

Architecture Neutral

Because Java runs inside of a Virtual Machine (a program written in operative system specific code that provides a common front-end to all operating systems) it in no way depends on the underlying operating system or hardware. Again this was another of the basic tenets of Java's existence: to be able to run on any device.

Portable

Applications developed in Java are compiled into byte-code, which consists of instructions that a Virtual Machine will translate to operating system–specific instructions. Because of this, any Java code that you write and compile into byte-code will run on any operating system for which there exists a compatible Virtual Machine. Hence, the phrase: write once, run anywhere. The joke in the industry used to be write once, debug everywhere, but that is becoming less of a concern, especially in the server-side arenas.

Interpreted

Java is interpreted, which means that it is not compiled into machine-specific code until it is executed. Interpreted code tends to run much slower than fully compiled code, but Java gains some performance because it is partially compiled into byte-code. The partial compilation further benefits Java in that Java applications shipped to customers are not shipped as pure source code that can be easily read, but in a binary form.

Multithreaded

Multithreaded applications have the capability to run multiple things at the same time, for example a multithreaded application can display a graphical user interface to a user while downloading stock quotes from the Internet and computing historical averages. Java's threading model was designed into the language from the beginning and is eloquently implemented, as you will learn later in the book.

Setting Up a Java Programming Environment

Before you can compile and execute a Java application, you must setup a Java programming environment. There are various Java compilers, but the standard is the one distributed on the Sun Web site. You can download the Java 2 SDK, Standard Edition from `http://java.sun.com/j2se/`.

On this page you will see three types of downloads for the latest released version and latest prereleased/release candidate (if available) version of Java. These three downloads are

- Software Developers Kit (SDK)
- Java Runtime Engine (JRE)
- Documentation

The SDK is used to compile and execute Java programs; you will need to download this.

The JRE is used to execute Java programs, but does not contain anything for compiling them. People that use your Java applications will have to download and install JRE; the SDK includes the JRE so you don't need to download it.

The documentation is specifically for users of the SDK. It lists and explains all the public classes in Java. I would highly recommend that you download and install this (it is viewable directly from the Internet). If you are short on disk space, then you can browse through the documentation as you need it.

As of this writing, the latest version of the Java 2, Standard Edition is version 1.4.

There are links to installation instructions presented to you when you download the SDK, but the following sections summarize the installation steps.

Microsoft Windows

The Java SDK for Microsoft Windows is an InstallShield® file that guides you through the installation using wizard-like screens.

1. Download the SDK.

2. Launch the downloaded file.

3. Follow the prompts.

Linux

There are two versions of installation for Linux: a self-extracting binary file, and a binary file containing RPM packages.

Self-Extracting Binary

1. Download the SDK.

2. Copy the file to the directory where you want to install Java.

3. Grant the file execute privileges:

   ```
   chmod a+x filename.bin
   ```

4. Execute the file:

   ```
   ./filename.bin
   ```

5. Follow the onscreen instructions.

RPM

RPM files, which are primarily used on Red Hat Linux, contain detailed installation instructions. RPM files are very easy to install and require little user interaction.

1. Download the SDK.

2. Grant the file execute privileges:

   ```
   chmod a+x filename.rpm.bin
   ```

3. Execute the file:

   ```
   ./filename.rpm.bin
   ```

4. The result of this execution is the creation of a `.rpm` file. Execute the `.rpm` file as follows:

   ```
   rpm -iv filename.rpm
   ```

Writing Your First Java Program

You can never escape the first chapter of a book without writing the traditional "Hello, World" application. Back in the early 1980s there was a book written by Brian Kernighan and Dennis Ritchie called *The C Programming Language* that was and is the de facto standard for C programming. In their book they defined the first example that all computer programming books should have: A program that writes the words "Hello, World" on the screen. Therefore, you will find a standard "Hello, World" example in almost every programming book you encounter. So, as not to break tradition, Listing 1.1 is "Hello, World" a la Java.

LISTING 1.1   `HelloWorld.java`

```
1: public class HelloWorld
2: {
3:     public static void main( String[] args )
4:     {
5:         System.out.println( "Hello, World!" );
6:     }
7: }
```

Compiling Your First Java Program

Create a new file on your computer in a specific folder of your choice. For example, you might create a new file using Windows Notepad in the following folder:

`C:\java`

Enter the complete text of Listing 1.1 into your editor and save it with the following filename (note that case is important —capital "H" and "W" and all the rest of the letters are lowercase):

`HelloWorld.java`

If you are using Notepad, be sure to either enclose the filename in quotes (`"HelloWorld.java"`) or check the filename when you are done, in some cases it likes to append a `.txt` to the end of the filename. If the filename is not correct, please correct it.

Open a command prompt and navigate to the folder where you saved your `HelloWorld.java` file. Using Windows as an example, open a command prompt, or MS-DOS prompt if you are using Windows 95, and enter the following command:

```
c:
cd \java
```

This will ensure that you are on the C: drive and change directory (cd) to the `java` subdirectory. Note that in this example you must have saved the file in this directory. Now you are ready to compile.

Compilation of Java programs is done at the command prompt using a tool that is packaged with the Java 2 SDK: `javac` read java see for Java Compiler. You compile a Java program by passing `javac` the name of the file you want to compile, for example:

`javac HelloWorld.java`

Upon executing the command you will see one of two possible responses: a new command prompt or a set of one or more errors. The most common error that my readers and students have when compiling Java programs has to do with an environment variable that Java depends on called CLASSPATH. The Java CLASSPATH is an interesting concept that often confuses not only new Java programmers, but experienced ones as well. The Java CLASSPATH is a list of folders that contain Java classes that you might want to include in your program, these define where your dependencies are located. If there is no CLASSPATH environment variable defined, the default value is the current folder. If there is one defined, the value must explicitly have the current folder in it if you want to compile from the current folder. To check the value of the CLASSPATH environment variable on your computer do the following:

```
Windows:
echo %CLASSPATH%
```

```
Unix:
echo $CLASSPATH
```

If the result is blank, then any errors you are receiving are not related to your CLASSPATH. If there is a value associated with the CLASSPATH environment variable, you must ensure that it includes the current folder. The CLASSPATH is simply a list of folders delimited by semi-colons (;) on Windows and colons (:) on Unix. The current folder is specified by a period (.), which must appear in the CLASSPATH. To add the current folder to the CLASSPATH, enter the following:

```
Windows:
Add the current folder to the CLASSPATH
set CLASSPATH=.;%CLASSPATH%
```

```
Or to erase the CLASSPATH's value
set CLASSPATH=
```

```
Unix:
CLASSPATH=.:$CLASSPATH; export CLASSPATH
```

At this point your CLASSPATH related errors should go away.

If you have other errors, here is a list of things to check:

- Ensure that your Java code matches Listing 1.1: The case of all words must match identically, for example, `class` must be lowercase and "HelloWorld" must have a capital "H" and "W" and all remaining characters must be lowercase. Note that the formatting of the document does not affect the compilation, for example, if you want to write the entire program on one line or add 20 spaces between each line it would have no affect on the compiler.

- Ensure that the name of your file is `HelloWorld.java`, again check the case of each letter, and if in Windows make sure Notepad did not add a `.txt` to the end of the filename. That can be accomplished by getting a directory of the folder your file is in by issuing a `dir` command (or `ls` in Unix):

  ```
  dir
  ```

- Ensure that you have the Java 2 SDK installed, and that the version you downloaded is the current version. To do so, execute the following command in the PATH:

```
java -version
```

Running Your First Java Program

After the `HelloWorld.java` file is successfully compiled, a new `HelloWorld.class` file is created. This is the file that contains the byte-code that contains instructions for the Java virtual machine to process. Java applications are run using the command-line tool `java`. To run `HelloWorld`, type the following from a command prompt in the folder that holds `HelloWorld.class`:

```
java HelloWorld
```

The result should be the following displayed to the screen:

```
Hello, World
```

If you receive an error, look at your CLASSPATH environment variable (see the discussion in the previous section for details).

Understanding Your First Java Program

It only took 7 lines to print "Hello, World" to the screen, and most of them have only one character each! Let's look at this program line-by-line and see what is happening.

```
1: public class HelloWorld
```

In Java programs, `.java` files are compiled into byte-code with a `.class` extension. `.class` files can be thought of as the program itself. In this first line, a new class called `HelloWorld` is being defined. You can create new classes by using the keyword `class` followed by a name for the class.

Lines 2 and 7, the brace pair { and }, define the body of the `HelloWorld` class. Everything that is included between Lines 2 and 7 is part of the `HelloWorld` class.

```
3:     public static void main( String[] arguments )
```

Line 3 defines a method, or function if you would prefer, that is a member of the `HelloWorld` class called `main`. `main` is a very special function in Java, specifically for applications. `main` is the entry point that the Java Runtime Engine (JRE), or `java.exe`, processes when it starts. When you launch the application later by typing

```
java HelloWorld
```

you are telling the Java Runtime Engine to open the class file `HelloWorld.class` and process the `main` function. Let's break down this function prototype further:

```
public
```

The keyword `public` is known as an access modifier; an access modifier defines who can and cannot see this function (or variable.) There are three possible values for access modifiers:

public, protected, and private, each having their own restrictions, which we will cover later in the book. In this case, it is saying that this function, main, is publicly available to anyone who wants to call it. This is essential for the main function; otherwise the Java Runtime Engine would not be able to access the function, and hence could not launch our application.

static

The static keyword tells the compiler that there is one and only one method (or variable) to be used for all instances of the class. For example, if you have 100 different copies of the HelloWorld class running, there will be only one main function. This functionality will be explained more later when you get a little more Java under your belt, but for now remember that main functions have to be static in a class.

void

The term void refers to the return type. Functions can return values; for example, integers, floating-point values, characters, strings, and more. If a function does not return any value, it is said to return void. In this declaration it is saying that the main function does not return a value.

main

The word main is the name of the function. As previously mentioned, main is a special function that must be defined when writing a Java application. It is the entry-point into your class that the Java Runtime Engine processes when it starts; it will control the flow of your program.

(String[] arguments)

Enclosed in parentheses next to the function name is the parameter list passed to the function. When you write a function, you can pass any type of data for that function to work with. In this case, the main function accepts an array (a collection or set of items) of String objects (text) that represent the command-line arguments the user entered when he launched the application.

java HelloWorld one two three four

The command line then would have four items sent to it: one, two, three, and four. The variable arguments would contain an array of these four strings. Here is how that would be listed:

arguments[0] = "one"

arguments[1] = "two"

arguments[2] = "three"

arguments[3] = "four"

Note that the indexes (0, 1, 2, and 3) start at zero and climb up to one, minus the total number of elements. This zero indexing is common to many programming languages such as C and C++ and programmers refer to the first element in an array as the "0-th element." This book will address arrays in detail a bit later.

Command-line arguments are beneficial because they can give a program additional information about what tasks to perform. For example, if you wanted to create an application that added two numbers and printed the result, you could take the two numbers to add from the command line, for example:

```
java AddApp 5 10
```

In the main function you would read in the numbers 5 and 10, and then print their sum to the screen.

Lines 4 and 6, the brace pair, denote the body of the main function; everything that is written between these braces is part of the main function.

```
5:          System.out.println( "Hello, World" );
```

Now this statement looks a little scary, but don't fret, it is not nearly as intimidating as it looks. Let's break apart this statement a bit:

```
System
```

`System` is actually a class that the Java language provides for you. This class is the focal point that you will use to access the standard input (keyboard), standard output (monitor), and standard error (usually a monitor unless you have a separate error output defined).

> ### Note
>
> Whenever you have questions about a class, you can always refer to the Java SDK documentation. Here is what the Java 2 SDK documentation has to say about the `System` class:
>
> "The `System` class contains several useful class fields and methods. It cannot be instantiated."
>
> Among the facilities provided by the `System` class are standard input, standard output, and error output streams; access to externally defined "properties;" a means of loading files and libraries; and a utility method for quickly copying a portion of an array.

The `System` class has a collection of public attributes, or data members, and a collection of public methods, or functions, that you can access in your program. You access these properties and methods by placing a period (.) after the class name `System`, and then appending to it the method or property name. The "." denotes a hierarchical movement through the object; the object to the left of the dot is the parent of the object to the right. In this example, we are going to access the `System` class's `out` property.

```
out
```

The `System` class's `out` property is defined as follows:

```
public static final PrintStream out
```

As with the `main` function, it is both `public`, meaning that everyone can access it, and `static`, meaning that there is only one copy of it for all instances of the `System` class. The `final` keyword says that this variable cannot change in value.

As I already mentioned, the `out` variable represents the standard output device, typically the monitor. Note that the `out` variable is of type `PrintStream`.

The `PrintSteam` class contains a collection of **print**, **println**, and **write** functions that know how to print different types of variables: Booleans, ints, floats, and so on. This is how **println** can print out so many different types of values.

println

Okay, finally we are down to the function that actually does all the work for us! **println** has multiple definitions, one for each of the native data types (int, Boolean, float, double, String, and so on). The one that we are concerned with is declared as follows:

```
public void println(String x)
```

This version of the **println** function prints a String called **x**, which is what you send it, to an output stream.

You might have noticed that the `PrintSteam` class has both **print** and **println** member functions. The only difference here has to do with the line termination. **print** simply prints text to the screen, whereas **println** prints text to the screen followed by a new line.

```
"Hello, World"
```

Finally, you have the text String that you are telling **println** to print to the standard output device. The text string is enclosed in parentheses and delimited by double quotes ("").

Note that a semicolon terminates the very end of the statement. This is very important in the Java programming language. A semicolon terminates all statements; this is how the Java compiler knows where one statement ends and the next begins.

Summary

This chapter discussed the fundamental concepts that empower Java as a powerful and productive programming language. It discussed the installation procedures and location of the Java 2 SDK Standard Edition, and then finished with writing your first Java program. Most of the discussion of your first Java program is probably still fuzzy, but now that you have a starting point, we will go through the entire Java programming language step-by-step so that this example will become trivial.

The next few chapters help you build a solid foundation into the Java programming language, starting with Chapter 2, "Keywords, Data Types, and Variables."

CHAPTER 2

KEYWORDS, DATA TYPES, AND VARIABLES

In this chapter you will learn:

- Java's keywords

- Data types used in Java

- Java variables

- How memory is organized and how it is interpreted by Java variables

All programming languages define a set of keywords that represent instructions to the programming language compiler; data types that define how memory is allocated for items in memory such as numbers and characters; and variables that are used to name a region of memory. This chapter describes how these concepts are implemented in the Java programming language.

New Programmers

Before you can write a computer program, you must learn a set of rules that define how a computer program can be written. There are two sets of rules: *syntax* and *semantics*. Syntax defines the rules by which a program must adhere to be processed by the compiler. Semantics defines the logical rules that make a computer program do what you want it to.

The Java programming process is as follows:

1. You write a Java program and save it as a text file with the .java file extension.

2. The Java compiler reads your program and ensures that it is syntactically correct according to the rules of the language.

3. The Java compiler generates a new file with a .class file extension that contains byte-code instructions that will be later interpreted by a Java Virtual Machine (JVM).

4. A Java Virtual Machine interprets the byte-code and performs the instructions defined in it.

5. The results of the execution depend on the semantics of your program.

This chapter explains the basics of the Java programming language syntax.

Keywords

Keywords are the words in a program that offer specific instructions to the Java compiler. These words cannot be used as variable names because their presence in your Java program have very distinct meanings and can be thought of as placeholders for specific Java functionality.

The Java keywords are

abstract	else	interface	switch
boolean	extends	long	synchronized
break	false	native	this
byte	final	new	throw
case	finally	null	throws
catch	float	package	transient
char	for	private	true
class	goto	protected	try
const	if	public	void
continue	implements	return	volatile
default	import	short	while
do	instanceof	static	
double	int	super	

Each of these keywords will be discussed in detail as you read through this and the following chapters. For now pay particular attention so that you don't use any of these words as names for your variables.

Data Types

A *data type* is a human-readable tag that represents a specific usage of a computer's memory. When used in a program, it defines the amount of memory that will be used and the valid values that might be placed in that memory.

Java is a *strongly typed* programming language, meaning that all variables used in a Java program must have a specifically defined data type. A *loosely typed* programming language, such as JavaScript or Visual Basic, allows the use of the variable to define its type. For example, if a variable is used as a number, then it is a number, if it is used as a string of characters, then it is a string of characters. Because Java is a strongly typed language, we must define how a variable will be used before it can be defined.

The Computer/Human Communication Problem

Computers and humans speak two different languages. Humans think of things in terms of objects and define things in terms of numbers, letters, and words. Computers think in terms of 1s and 0s, which represent electrical impulses (1 = impulse, 0 = no impulse).

How can we translate our numbers, characters, and words into the 1s and 0s that computers understand?

Because computers do not have any inherent understanding of the number 5 or the letter B, we must define a representation of these using 1s and 0s, and then write rules that govern how certain operations on these values affect them. We can take the electrical signals, let's call them bits, and group them into groups of 8 bits and call those bytes. So a byte will represent 8 bits, which is comprised of 1s and 0s. How might we represent a number with these 8 bits?

Our alphabet has 26 letters (A through Z), but we are now defining a computer's alphabet as having two "letters": 0 and 1. Because we have only two numbers in our numerical alphabet, we must devise a way to count. In our decimal system we have 10 digits: 0, 1, 2, 3, 4, 5, 6, 7, 8, and 9. In decimal we count as follows: 0 1 2 3 4 5 6 7 8 9, and then we start over with a two digit representation: 10 and proceed 11, 12, 13, and so on. If we count with two digits (binary) we start with 0, 1, and suddenly we are out of numbers. Following the decimal example, we now have our ten: 10, which if we are counting in our familiar decimal notation would be two—followed by 11 (or three), and hence we create the sequence: 0 1 10 11 100 101 110 111 1000 (or 1 2 3 4 5 6 7 8).

If we have 8 digits to work with that gives us 256 possible numbers in a single byte. But what about negative numbers? We can designate one bit as representing the sign of the number: Let's say the highest bit (8th in this case) represents the sign (0 is positive and 1 is negative). Now we can represent 128 or 127 negative numbers, zero, and either 127 or 128 positive numbers (we have to count zero as one of our 256 possible numbers). If we were designing Java we would have decided to have 128 negative numbers and 127 positive numbers, thus with one byte, or 8 bits, or 8 electrical signals passing between circuits, we have a mechanism to represent numbers between −128 and +127.

The numbering system we just derived is referred to as binary notation, or base-2, where decimal is base-10. Each bit as we counted up represented a power of 2, see Figure 2.1.

As Figure 2.1 shows, we have a definitive way to convert a stream of 1s and 0s into decimal numbers, and vice versa. What if we need larger numbers than 128? We could group bytes together and have multiple bytes represent one single number. For example, if we grouped two bytes together, which is 16 bits, we could designate the high bit to represent the sign, which leaves us with 15 bits to represent our number. 15 bits enables us to now represent the range of numbers −32768 to 32767. We could extrapolate this out further and represent any arbitrary size number we want.

FIGURE 2.1

Binary numbers.

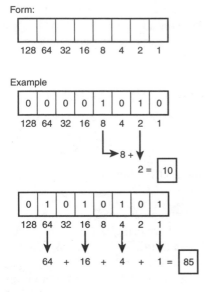

Note that in binary numbers, each successive bit represents double the value that the previous bit represented. That is why that adding an additional 8 bits to our original –128 to 127 range did not simply double the range, but increased it exponentially. This concept of exponential growth is very powerful: Take the entire contents of the Pacific Ocean and dry it up, now start refilling it one drop at a time, doubling the drops each time—1 drop, then 2 drops, then 4 drops, and so on, and by the time you reach the 80th iteration, you have the Pacific Ocean refilled! Powerful stuff!

When we have our bits and bytes, we can define data types, such as numbers and characters, by defining our own interpretation of what these bits mean when associated with a data type. That is all that Java, and every other programming language in the world, has done; only they have involved standards committees to ensure that parts of their interpretation of these bits is global across programming languages. It would be hard to read a text file if Java said that a capital A was one thing and C++ said it was something else.

Primitive Data Types

Java defines eight primitive data types, which define the core data that can be represented in the Java programming language. A data type defines the amount of memory that will be used when defining one of the data types and the valid range of values it can represent.

Integer Data Types

Integers represent whole numbers (numbers without a fractional part), and Java defines four data types that represent integers:

```
byte              short              int              long
```

All integer types are represented as we derived earlier in this chapter: The highest bit represents the sign, whereas the low bits represent the number. The difference between the different integer types is the number of bytes (or bits) grouped together to represent a single number.

Table 2.1 lists the memory usage required for each type and the valid ranges it can represent.

TABLE 2.1   Integer Data Types

Integer Type	Memory Usage	Range of Values
byte	1 byte (8 bits)	-128 to $+127$ (-2^7 to 2^7-1)
short	2 bytes (16 bits)	-2^{15} to $2^{15}-1$int 4 bytes (32 bits) -2^{31} to $2^{31}-1$
long	8 bytes (64 bits)	-2^{63} to $2^{63}-1$

Choose the integer data type based on the type of data you want to represent. For example, a human age might be represented by a byte or a short (not too many people are older than 32767 years old), whereas the national debt might be better represented by a long.

Here's an example, but don't worry about the Java syntax, we'll talk about that shortly:

```
byte b = 50;
short s = 1000;
int i = 500000;
long l = 1000000000000000000000;
```

Floating-Point Types

Now that we have a type that represents whole numbers, we need a type that represents numbers with a fraction part; this category of numbers is referred to as floating-point types.

Floating-point types are represented by the same bytes that represent integer types, but their interpretation is different. A certain number of bits are used to represent the whole part of the numbers, and a certain number of bits are used to represent the fractional part of the number. The mathematical concept of significant digits is applied with these data types: The number of consecutive numerical entries in the number that can be accurately recorded defines the number of significant digits in the number. For example consider:

```
3.1428571
```

This number has eight significant digits. Whereas

```
120,000,000
```

has only two. 0 is not considered a significant digit unless it is surrounded by two nonzero digits. A common way in mathematics, as well as in computer science, to represent floating-point numbers is to provide an exponential representation of a number. This is defined as listing the significant digits with one digit written before the decimal point, and then defining the power of 10 to multiply by the number to generate its real value. So 120 million could be written as

```
1.2 multiplied by 10⁸ or 1.2E+8
```

From this representation, the number of significant digits should be more apparent.

There are two types of floating-point data types, as shown in Table 2.2.

TABLE 2.2   Floating-Point Data Types

Integer Type	Memory Usage	Range of Values
float	4 bytes (32 bits)	+/– 3.40282347E+38 (6–7 significant digits)
double	8 bytes (64 bits)	+/– 1.7976931346231570E+308 (15 significant digits)

The float data type can represent a large amount of numbers, but only to 6 or 7 digits of precision. If you were representing currency, that would be more than adequate, but if you were calculating the amount of light to apply to a surface in a 3-dimensional graphics application, a double would be more appropriate.

Character Type

With numbers out of the way it is time to discuss characters. We use our same set of bits to represent characters, but this time in a tabular lookup form. How much storage is needed to represent characters? In the English language we have 26 uppercase letters, 26 lowercase letters, 10 digits, and an assortment of other characters (+, -, /, *, and so on). But we are very safe in saying that we could represent the English language in 128 characters or less.

But do we arbitrarily give each letter a numerical representation? In the beginning everyone did just that, and it quickly became apparent that machines could not communicate with one another. So, in 1961 Bob Bemer from IBM submitted a numbering scheme that he called the American Standard Code for Information Interchange (ASCII) to the American National Standards Institute (ANSI), a standards body, for approval. In 1968 ASCII was approved as a standard as "ANSI Standardx3.4-1968," and it is the base for our English character set today. Figure 2.2 shows the ASCII table as we know it today.

We were quite efficient in defining a character set to represent the English language, but how do we represent another language? Do we arbitrarily assign numerical values to their alphabet? How do we differentiate between character sets so that we know what language we are reading? How do we deal with a non-Roman alphabet such as Japanese?

The answer is that we need a much larger set of characters so that we can assign every character in every language a unique value. If we can represent the entire English language in 7 bits (128 characters), how many bits will it take to represent all characters in all languages?

Again, different companies haphazardly created values for different languages until the Unicode Consortium released a standard called Unicode in 1988. It has been through a couple revisions and is currently at version 3.0. This standard uses two bytes (16 bits) to represent a character, which yields more than 1 million different characters; this permits unique characters, no matter the platform, the program, or the language. Following its ASCII heritage, the first 128 characters in the Unicode standard are the ASCII standard.

FIGURE 2.2

ASCII table.

Char	Dec	Oct	Hex	Char	Dec	Oct	Hex	Char	Dec	Oct	Hex	Char	Dec	Oct	Hex
(nul)	0	0000	0x00	(sp)	32	0040	0x20	@	64	0100	0x40	`	96	0140	0x60
(soh)	1	0001	0x01	!	33	0041	0x21	A	65	0101	0x41	a	97	0141	0x61
(stx)	2	0002	0x02	"	34	0042	0x22	B	66	0102	0x42	b	98	0142	0x62
(etx)	3	0003	0x03	#	35	0043	0x23	C	67	0103	0x43	c	99	0143	0x63
(eot)	4	0004	0x04	$	36	0044	0x24	D	68	0104	0x44	d	100	0144	0x64
(enq)	5	0005	0x05	%	37	0045	0x25	E	69	0105	0x45	e	101	0145	0x65
(ack)	6	0006	0x06	&	38	0046	0x26	F	70	0106	0x46	f	102	0146	0x66
(bel)	7	0007	0x07	'	39	0047	0x27	G	71	0107	0x47	g	103	0147	0x67
(bs)	8	0010	0x08	(	40	0050	0x28	H	72	0110	0x48	h	104	0150	0x68
(ht)	9	0011	0x09	)	41	0051	0x29	I	73	0111	0x49	i	105	0151	0x69
(nl)	10	0012	0x0a	*	42	0052	0x2a	J	74	0112	0x4a	j	106	0152	0x6a
(vt)	11	0013	0x0b	+	43	0053	0x2b	K	75	0113	0x4b	k	107	0153	0x6b
(np)	12	0014	0x0c	,	44	0054	0x2c	L	76	0114	0x4c	l	108	0154	0x6c
(cr)	13	0015	0x0d	-	45	0055	0x2d	M	77	0115	0x4d	m	109	0155	0x6d
(so)	14	0016	0x0e	.	46	0056	0x2e	N	78	0116	0x4e	n	110	0156	0x6e
(si)	15	0017	0x0f	/	47	0057	0x2f	O	79	0117	0x4f	o	111	0157	0x6f
(dle)	16	0020	0x10	0	48	0060	0x30	P	80	0120	0x50	p	112	0160	0x70
(dc1)	17	0021	0x11	1	49	0061	0x31	Q	81	0121	0x51	q	113	0161	0x71
(dc2)	18	0022	0x12	2	50	0062	0x32	R	82	0122	0x52	r	114	0162	0x72
(dc3)	19	0023	0x13	3	51	0063	0x33	S	83	0123	0x53	s	115	0163	0x73
(dc4)	20	0024	0x14	4	52	0064	0x34	T	84	0124	0x54	t	116	0164	0x74
(nak)	21	0025	0x15	5	53	0065	0x35	U	85	0125	0x55	u	117	0165	0x75
(syn)	22	0026	0x16	6	54	0066	0x36	V	86	0126	0x56	v	118	0166	0x76
(etb)	23	0027	0x17	7	55	0007	0x37	W	87	0127	0x57	w	119	0167	0x77
(can)	24	0030	0x18	8	56	0070	0x38	X	88	0130	0x58	x	120	0170	0x78
(em)	25	0031	0x19	9	57	0071	0x39	Y	89	0131	0x59	y	121	0171	0x79
(sub)	26	0032	0x1a	:	58	0072	0x3a	Z	90	0132	0x5a	z	122	0172	0x7a
(esc)	27	0033	0x1b	;	59	0073	0x3b	[	91	0133	0x5b	{	123	0173	0x7b
(fs)	28	0034	0x1c	<	60	0074	0x3c	\	92	0134	0x5c	|	124	0174	0x7c
(gs)	29	0035	0x1d	=	61	0075	0x3d	]	93	0135	0x5d	}	125	0175	0x7d
(rs)	30	0036	0x1e	>	62	0076	0x3e	^	94	0136	0x5e	~	126	0176	0x7e
(us)	31	0037	0x1f	?	63	0077	0x3f	_	95	0137	0x5f	(del)	127	0177	0x7f

Java represents all characters in Unicode (again 2 bytes), so all programs that you write will be ready for translation into any other language without requiring you to rewrite the framework of your application.

Characters can be represented in their Unicode form as:

```
\uXXXX
Where XXXX is a number in the range of 0000 to FFFF (hexadecimal)
```

Or as their English equivalents delimited by single quotes:

```
'a'
'Z'
'n'
```

Because characters are delimited by single quotes, Strings (as we will soon learn) are delimited by double quotes, and there are various unprintable characters, Java defines a set of special characters, shown in Table 2.3.

TABLE 2.3   Java Special Characters

Character	Meaning	Unicode Equivalent
\b	Backspace	\u0008
\t	Tab	\u0009
\n	Linefeed	\u000a
\r	Carriage Return	\u000d
\"	Double quote	\u0022
\'	Single quote	\u0027
\\	Backslash	\u005c

Characters in Java are represented by the datatype `char`.

Boolean Data Type

Up to this point we have learned to represent whole numbers, fractional numbers, and characters, so what is left?

The last primitive data type in the Java programming language is the `boolean` data type. A `boolean` data type has one of two values: `true` or `false`. These are not strings, but keywords in the Java programming language.

Programming languages need to have boolean types so that they can perform specific actions based on predetermined conditions. For example, a program running a traffic light might have a sensor that tells it when people are waiting at the light. If people are waiting at the light (`true`), the light should prepare itself to change, otherwise it should remain unchanged (`false`).

Variables

Data types define the storage capacity and usage for a region in memory, but how is that memory accessible? Memory itself has a numerical address associated with it that, when accessed, references its value. If you think of memory linearly starting from 0 and ascending one value per byte you might represent your data as shown in Figure 2.3.

Figure 2.3 shows a simplistic view of how you might have a `char`, two `int`s, and a `short` stored in memory. Consider computing the sum of the two `int`s, how would you do it? Take the integer value stored in memory location 2–5 and add that to the integer value stored in memory location 8–11. Now let's give them real-world meaning: Call the first integer the students in classroom 1, and the second integer the students in classroom 2. How many students are there in the two classrooms?

FIGURE 2.3

Data in memory.

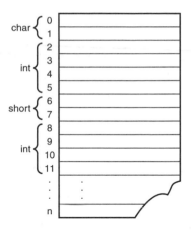

The answer is the sum of the integer value stored in memory location 2–5, and the integer value stored in memory at location 8–11. Not only is reading that unfriendly, I would venture to say that it is completely unusable! What are we to do?

Wouldn't it be nice to associate a meaningful identifier with the portion of memory it refers to? For example we could call the memory location 2–5 `classroomA`, and the memory location 8–11 `classroomB`. Then, when asked for the total number of students we could answer with the following:

```
classroomA + classroomB
```

That is much easier to read and far more understandable.

In Java when you assign a meaningful identifier to a region of memory, that identifier is called a *variable*. Furthermore, you do not have to concern yourself with the actual location in memory that variable represents, that task can be delegated to the virtual machine, you only need to specify the data type and the variable name.

The act of creating a variable is called *declaring* a variable, and it has the following form:

```
datatype variableName;
```

The first thing you specify is the data type, which is one of the data types you learned about earlier in this chapter. Next is a meaningful name for your variable; you are free to use any name you want, with the following restrictions:

- It must start with an alphabetic character (a through z, A through Z, or any Unicode character that denotes a letter in a language), an underscore, or the dollar sign.

- It can have any alphabetic or numeric value as well as an underscore anywhere in its name.

- It can be of unlimited length.

- It cannot have any spaces or non-alphanumeric characters, such as + or -, in it.

- It cannot be a Java keyword.

- It is case sensitive (the case of a letter—uppercase or lowercase—has meaning, for example, myBook is not the same as myBooK.

The convention adopted by the Java world in naming variable is to start with a lowercase letter, and if the name has multiple words, capitalize the first letter of every word. For example:

- `thisIsMyVariableName`

- `classroomA`

- `totalNumberOfStudents`

Finally, all variable declarations are terminated by a semicolon.

As an example consider the following variable declarations:

```
char c;
int numberOfStudentsInClassroom1;
float bankAccountBalance;
```

After a variable as been declared, a value can be assigned to it. Remember that its data type defines the valid values for a variable. Java defines an assignment operator for assigning values to variables: the equal sign (=). For example:

```
int myAge;
myAge = 30;
```

A line of Java code is called a *statement*, and a semicolon terminates each statement in Java. Another more common method of initializing a variable is to do so during its declaration. For example:

```
int myAge = 30;
```

This statement reads: define a variable named *myAge* that represents a 4-byte integer in memory and assign it the value 30.

Literals

A literal represents an actual character, string, or number and not a variable referencing, a character, string, or number in memory. The following are examples of literals:

```
1.0
'c'
"Happy"
7
```

In an expression (detailed in the next chapter) you might add 5 to an integer variable:

```
int n = a + 5;
```

In this case `a` is a variable and 5 is a literal value.

When defining numeric literals there are circumstances where you will have to tell the Java compiler how to interpret the value (what data type it is). When defining a floating-point number such as 1.0, the compiler automatically interprets the value as a **double**—if you want it to be interpreted as a **float**, you would have to append an f to it. For example:

```
float f = 1.0f
```

A failure to do so would result in a compilation error stating that you might lose precision in the assignment (because a double is represented by eight bytes and a float is only represented by four).

Conversion Between Numeric Types

Variables in Java can be participants in various operations including, but not limited to, addition, subtraction, multiplication, and division. These operations will be discussed in detail in the next chapter, but to complete the discussion of variables you need to know the general form. The general form of a mathematical operation in Java is

```
operand operator operand
```

Where a variable or a value is an operand and all mathematical operators are included as operators. Consider the following:

```
myApples + yourApples
```

The result is usually assigned to another variable using the assignment operator (=). The following adds **myApples** and **yourApples** and assigns them to the new integer **totalApples**:

```
int totalApples = myApples + yourApples;
```

When using numeric variables (variables defined to be **int**s, **float**s, and so on) the type does not necessarily have to be the same; in other words you can add an **int** to a **byte**. But what happens when you add an **int** to a **byte**? Remember that an **int** is 4 bytes, and a **byte** is just 1 byte. Take for example a **byte** with the value 100 and add an **int** with the value 1000 to it. The result is 1100, but how do we represent that in a byte? There simply are not enough bits to do it!

The answer is to convert the **byte** to be an **int**. This is referred to as *arithmetic promotion*. But what if we add a **long**, an **int**, and a **byte**? Should they all be promoted to a **long**?

All mathematical operations in Java are performed by promoting each operand in the operation to a specific data type, following these rules in this order:

1. If any of the operands is of type **double**, the other one will by converted to a **double**.
2. If any of the operands is of type **float**, the other one will be converted to a **float**.
3. If any of the operands is of type **long**, the other one will be converted to a **long**.
4. Otherwise all operands will be converted in **int**s.

The promotion, or conversion, of a *narrower* type (fewer number of bytes) to a *wider* type (greater number of bytes), such as the conversion of a **short** to an **int**, is accomplished by prepending the narrower type with enough bytes to be the same size as the wider type, and ensuring that the values are identical. For example, converting the **byte** 10 (written in binary):

```
0000 1010
```

To a short would result in the following:

```
0000 0000 0000 1010
```

Negative value conversions would be a little more complicated because the sign would have to maintained, but Java takes care of that for you.

These rules ensure that all operations resolve to the widest type (in number of bytes) in the operation. Thus, the result of the following operation is a long:

```
long l = 10;
int i = 10;
byte b = 10;
long result = l + i + b;
```

The int and byte are promoted to be longs before the operation is performed.

Conversion Through Assignment

You might have noticed that short and byte variables are promoted to ints during operations, even if there are no ints in the operation. Thus, the following statement would generate an unexpected error:

```
byte b1 = 10;
byte b2 = 10;
byte result = b1 + b2;
```

The Java compiler would complain about this operation saying that there is a "possible loss of precision" because although b1 and b2 are both bytes, they are promoted to ints before assigning the result to result. A byte has 1 byte, whereas an int has 4 bytes, so assigning an int to a byte loses the top 3 bytes during the assignment. Consider the integer 512, it is represented in binary as

```
0000 0000 0000 0000 0000 0010 0000 0000
```

If you remove the top 3 bytes, you have the following left:

```
0000 0000
```

Which is zero! That is why the compiler disallows the assignment of an int to a byte.

The rule for conversion between primitive numeric types is that a type can be assigned to a *wider* type (one with more bytes), but not a *narrower* type (one with less bytes). So, the following conversions are permissible by the compiler:

1. byte—short, int, long, float, double

2. short—int, long, float, double

3. int—long, float, double

4. long—float, double

5. `float—double`

6. `char—int`

For example:

```
int i = 10;
long l = i; // legal
double d = i; // legal
short s = i; // Illegal!
```

Casting Between Data Types

Does this mean that the result of your operations must be the data type of the largest data type in the operation? What if you, as the programmer, have knowledge of the nature of the data and can ensure that the data will not be lost?

Java offers a mechanism for overriding the compiler called *casting*. Casting tells the compiler to convert the data to the specified type even though it might lose data. By casting you are assuring the compiler that either data will not be lost, or if it is, that you will not care. Casting is performed by prefixing the variable or value by the desired data type enclosed in parentheses:

```
datatype variable = ( datatype )value;
```

For example:

```
int i = 10;
short s = ( short )i;

long l = 100;
byte b = ( byte )l;
```

Be sure that you do this with caution because the side effect of casting a variable to a narrower data type can result in the loss of data as you saw earlier.

Constants

Now that you have data types that represent memory in a specific way and variables as a convention to refer to that memory, how would you represent values that do not change, for example pi? You could define a variable named pi as follows:

```
double pi = 3.14285
```

When you need to use it, you could simply reference it in an equation:

```
double r = 10;
double area = pi * r * r;
```

Variables can, as their name implies, contain variable data. But because variables such as pi really cannot change, you must prevent the user from doing the following:

```
pi = pi / 2;
```

This is perfectly legal in Java, but violates the property of pi.

The answer is that we can declare a variable to be a *constant*, or not changing. Java uses the keyword *final* to denote that a variable is in fact a constant. Now you can preface your declaration of pi with the keyword `final` and ensure that its value cannot change:

```
final double pi = 3.14285
```

When you try to compile a statement that modifies a constant value, such as

```
final double pi = 3.14285
pi = pi / 2;
```

The compiler generates an error saying that you cannot assign a value to a final variable.

By convention, programmers usually capitalize all the letters in a constant's name so that it can be found with only a casual glance of the source code. Pi, therefore, would be declared as follows:

```
final double PI = 3.14285;
```

Summary

This chapter introduced you to some of the plumbing of the Java programming language: its keywords, the data types it supports, and the concept of named variables. The next couple chapters will build on this foundation and start getting you productive in your Java programming. When you are building a house you need both the tools and a set of plans to ensure that your house is built properly and does not fall down. Similarly in any programming language you need the tools—your keywords, data types, variables, operators, and so on—as well as the plans, a set of rules (syntax and semantics) to ensure that your program runs successfully.

Review Questions

1. Which of the following is not a keyword in Java?

    a. int

    b. label

    c. continue

    d. byte

2. What is the difference between syntax and semantics?

3. How do computers represent data?

4. What are data types? What do they do?

5. What is the difference between a `short` and an `int`?

6. Are the following statements legal? Why or why not?

```
short s1 = 10;
short s2 = 10;
short result = s1 + s2;
```

7. What is arithmetic promotion?

8. What types can you assign a short to without explicit casting?

9. What is casting and how do you do it?

10. How do you designate a variable to be a constant?

CHAPTER 3

OPERATORS

You will learn about the following in this chapter:

- All Java operators: what they are and how they are used.
- Java Operator Precedence: what operators are evaluated first?

*I*n the previous chapter you learned that computers think in terms of 1s and 0s, and that you can use those 1s and 0s to represent numbers, characters, and booleans. Then you learned that through Java you could create meaningful names that refer to regions of memory using variables. The next step is to take those variables and do something meaningful with them. In this chapter, you will address all the mathematical operations you can perform in Java on primitive data types.

Operators work in conjunction with operands, or the literal values or variables involved in the operation. There are unary operators, which are operators that operate on a single operand, as well as operators that operate on two or more variables.

Arithmetic Operators

Arithmetic operators refer to the standard mathematical operators you learned in elementary school: addition, subtraction, multiplication, and division.

Addition

Addition, as you would expect, is accomplished using the plus sign (+) operator. The form of an addition operation is

```
operand + operand
```

For example:

```
// Add two literal values
int result = 5 + 5;
```

```
// Add two variables
int a = 5;
int b = 6;
int result = a + b;

// Add two variables and a literal
int result = a + b + 15;
```

An addition operation, can add two or more operands, whereas an operand can be a variable, a literal, or a constant.

Subtraction

Subtraction, again as, you would expect, is accomplished using the minus sign (–) operator. The form of a subtraction operation is

```
operand - operand
```

For example:

```
// Subtract a literal from a literal; the result is 5
int result = 10 - 5;

// Subtract a variable from another variable; the result is -1
int a = 5;
int b = 6;
int result = a - b;

// Subtract a variable and a literal from a variable
// The result is 5 - 6 - 15 = -1 - 15 = -16
int result = a - b - 15;
```

A subtraction operation can compute the difference between two or more operands, where an operand can be a variable, a literal, or a constant.

Multiplication

Multiplication is accomplished using the asterisk (*) operator. The form of a multiplication operation is

```
operand * operand
```

For example:

```
// Multiply two literal values; result is 25
int result = 5 * 5;

// Multiply two variables; result is 30
int a = 5;
int b = 6;
int result = a * b;

// Multiply two variables and a literal
// The result is 5 * 6 * 15 = 30 * 15 = 450
int result = a * b * 15;
```

A multiplication operation can multiply two or more operands, where an operand can be a variable, a literal, or a constant.

Division

Division is accomplished using the forward slash (/) operator. The form of a division operation is

```
operand / operand
```

For example:

```
// Divide a literal by a literal; result is 5
int result = 10 / 2;

// Divide a variable by another variable; result is 3
int a = 15;
int b = 5;
int result = a / b;
```

When dividing integer types, the result is an integer type (see the previous chapter for the exact data type conversions for mathematical operations). This means that if you divide an integer unevenly by another integer, it returns the whole number part of the result; it does not perform any rounding. For example, consider the following two operations that both result to 1.

```
int result1 = 10 / 6; // Float value would be 1.6666
int result2 = 10 / 9; // Float value would be 1.1111
```

Both `result1` and `result2` resolve to be 1, even though `result1` would typically resolve to 2 if you were rounding off the result. Therefore, be cognizant of the fact that integer division in Java results in only the whole number part of the result, any fractional part is dropped.

When dividing floating-point variables or values, this caution can be safely ignored. Floating-point division results in the correct result: The fractional part of the answer is represented in the floating-point variable.

```
float f = 10.0f / 6.0f;  // result is 1.6666
double d = 10.0 / 9.0; // result is 1.1111
```

Note the appearance of the `f` following each literal value in the first line. When creating a floating-point literal value (a value that has a fractional element), the default assumption by the compiler is that the values are `double`. So, to explicitly tell the compiler that the value is a `float` and not a `double`, you can suffix the value with either a lowercase or uppercase F.

Modulus

If integer division results in dropping the remainder of the operation, what happens to it? For example if you divide 10 by 6:

```
int i = 10 / 6;
```

The Java result is 1, but the true result is 1 Remainder 4. What happened to the remainder 4?

Java provides a mechanism to get the remainder of a division operation through the modulus operator, denoted by the percent character (%). Although the previous example had a result of 1, the modulus of the operation would give you that missing 4. The form of a modulus operation is

```
operand % operand
```

For example:

```
int i = 10 / 6; // i = 1
int r = 10 % 6; // r = 4
```

Similar to the other arithmetic operators in this chapter, the modulus of an operation can be performed between variables, literals, and constants.

Increment and Decrement Operators

In computer programming it is quite common to want to increase or decrease the value of an integer type by 1. Because of this Java provides the increment and decrement operators that add 1 to a variable and subtract 1 from a variable, respectively. The increment operator is denoted by two plus signs (++), and the decrement operator is denoted by two minus signs (--). The form of the increment and decrement operators is

```
variable++;
++variable;
variable--;
--variable;
```

For example:

```
int i = 10;
i++; // New value of i is 11
```

You might notice that the variable could either be prefixed or suffixed by the increment or decrement operator. If the variable is always modified appropriately (either incremented by 1 or decremented by 1), then what is the difference? The difference has to do with the value of the variable that is returned for use in an operation.

Prefixing a variable with the increment or decrement operator performs the increment or decrement, and then returns the value to be used in an operation. For example:

```
int i = 10;
int a = ++i; // Value of both i and a is 11
i = 10;
int b = 5 + --i; // Value of b is 14 (5 + 9) and i is 9
```

Suffixing a variable with the increment or decrement operator returns the value to be used in the operation, and then performs the increment or decrement. For example:

```
// Value of i is 11, but the value of a is 10
// Note that the assignment preceded the increment
int i = 10;
int a = i++;
```

```
// Value of i is 9 as before, but the value of b is 15 (5 + 10)
i = 10;
int b = 5 + i--;
```

Pay particular attention to your code when you use prefix and postfix versions of these operators and be sure that you completely understand the difference. That difference has led many programmers on a search for unexplained behavior in their testing!

Relational Operators

A very necessary part of computer programming is performing certain actions based off the value of a variable; for example if the nuclear reactor is about to blow up, then shut it down. The next chapter will speak at length about the mechanism for implementing this type of logic, but this section addresses the mechanism for comparing two variables through a set of relational operators.

Relational operators compare the values of two variables and return a `boolean` value. The general form of a relation operation is

```
LeftOperand RelationalOperator RightOperand
```

Table 3.1 shows all the relational operators.

TABLE 3.1 Relational Operators

Operator	Description
==	Is Equal; returns a true value if the two values are equal
!=	Not Equal; returns a true value if the two values are not equal
<	Less than; returns a true value if the left operand has a value less than the that of the right operand
>	Greater than; returns a true value if the left operand has a value greater than that of the right operand
<=	Less than or equal; returns a true value if the left operand has a value less than or equal to that of the right operand
>=	Greater than or equal; returns a true value if the left operand has a value greater than or equal to that of the right operand

For example:

```
int a = 10;
int b = 10;
int c = 20;
boolean b1 = a == c; // false, 10 is not equal to 20
```

```
boolean b2 = a == b; // true, 10 is equal to 10
boolean b3 = a < c; // true, 10 is less than 20
boolean b4 = a < b; // false, 10 is not less than 10
boolean b5 = a <= b; // true, 10 is less than or equal to 10 (equal to)
boolean b6 = a != c; // true, 10 is not equal to 20
```

Bit-Wise Operators

Remember the discussion about data types and memory from Chapter 2, "Keywords, Data Types, and Variables," in which you learned that computers think in terms of 1s and 0s, and that data types really only define the grouping and interpretation of these 1s and 0s. These 1s and 0s can be traced back to the underlying hardware implementation of computers and the principals of electrical engineering. At the very rudimentary levels of computer architecture, decisions have to be made based on two signals and whether or not they have a charge. Figure 3.1 shows this graphically.

FIGURE 3.1
Electrical engineering decision circuit.

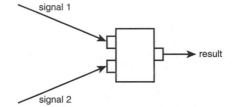

Figure 3.1 shows that a circuit makes its decision as to whether or not to send a charged signal based on the two input signals. Specific rules inside the circuit define whether the signal is charged (1) or not charged (0). These decisions can be summarized by a *truth table*. A truth table lists all the possible values and the required result. In the case of two signals that can be charged (1) or not charged (0), there are four possible combinations, as shown in Table 3.2.

TABLE 3.2 Truth Table Components

Signal A	Signal B	Result
0	0	
1	0	
0	0	
1	1	1

Table 3.2 tells you that if you have no charge on Signal A (0) and a charge on signal B (1), do not send a charge (0) (second row). But if you have a charge on signal A (1) and a charge on signal B (1), send a charge (the last row).

The operators covered thus far in this chapter have been manipulating the interpreted values of these bits (for example, if a was an int with the value 10, a + 1 is equal to 11), but there are some things that can be done directly with those 1s and 0s. Java provides a set of bit-wise operators that looks at each bit in two variables, performs a comparison, and returns the result. The nature of the operator is defined by its truth table.

For the examples in this section, consider the following two bytes:

```
byte a = 10;
byte b = 6;
```

Recall from Chapter 2 that the bits for these values are

```
a = 0000 1010
b = 0000 0110
```

The bit-wise operators are going to define rules in the form of truth tables to apply to these two values for the purpose of building a result. The general form of a bit-wise operation is

```
result = operandA bit-wise-operator operandB
```

The valid bit-wise operators are shown in Table 3.3.

TABLE 3.3   Bit-Wise Operators

Operator	Description
&	AND
|	OR
^	XOR (Exclusive OR)
~	NOT

AND

The AND operator (&) defines a bit-wise comparison between two variables according to the truth table shown in Table 3.4.

TABLE 3.4   AND Bit-Wise Operator

Signal A	Signal B	Result
0	0	0
0	1	0
1	0	0
1	1	1

The AND operator specifies that both Signals A *and* B must be charged for the result to be charged. Therefore, AND-ing the bytes 10 and 6 results in 2, as follows:

```
a = 0000 1010 (10)
b = 0000 0110 (6)
    ---- ----
r = 0000 0010 (2)
```

OR

The OR operator (|) defines a bit-wise comparison between two variables, according to the truth table shown in Table 3.5.

TABLE 3.5   OR Bit-Wise Operator

Signal A	Signal B	Result
0	0	0
0	1	1
1	0	1
1	1	1

The OR operator specifies that the result is charged if either Signals A *or* B are charged. Therefore, OR-ing the bytes 10 and 6 results in 14, as follows:

```
a = 0000 1010 (10)
b = 0000 0110 (6)
    ---- ----
r = 0000 1110 (14)
```

Exclusive OR

The Exclusive OR (XOR) operator (^) defines a bit-wise comparison between two variables according to the truth table shown in Table 3.6.

TABLE 3.6   XOR Bit-Wise Operator

Signal A	Signal B	Result
0	0	0
0	1	1
1	0	1
1	1	0

The XOR operator specifies that the result is charged if Signal A or B is charged, but Signal A and B aren't both charged. It is called exclusive because it is charged only if one of the two is charged. Therefore, XOR-ing the bytes 10 and 6 results in 12, as follows:

```
a = 0000 1010 (10)
b = 0000 0110 (6)
    ---- ----
r = 0000 1100 (12)
```

NOT Operator

The NOT operator (~), also referred to as the bit-wise complement, flips the values of all the charges. If a bit is set to 1, it changes it to 0; if a bit is 0 it changes to 1.

Practical Application

At this point you are probably telling yourself that this is a neat thing you can do, but asking yourself the inevitable question: "Who cares!?"

The primary use for bit-wise operations originated in the data compression and communication applications. The problem was that you needed to either store or transmit the state of several different things. In the past, data storage was not as cheap as it is today and communication mechanisms were not over T3 or even a cable modem, but more like speeds of 1200 or 300 baud. To give you an idea about the difference in speed, cable modem and DSL companies tout that they achieve speeds about 20 times faster than 56K modems, but 56K modems are about 45 times faster than 1200-baud modems, and 180 times faster than 300-baud modems. So early communications were 3600 times slower than your cable modem. Thus, there was the need to compact data as much as possible!

If you have 8 different states to send to someone, you can simply assign a bit in a byte to each of the 8 states: 1 is defined to be true and 0 false (or on/off, and so on). Consider reporting the state of 8 different factory devices where devices 0 and 3 are active:

```
Device byte: 0000 1001 (9)
```

To determine whether device 3 is active, a Boolean expression can be determined with the following statement:

```
boolean is3Active = ( deviceByte & 8 ) == 8;
```

AND-ing the deviceByte (0000 1001) with the number 8 (0000 1000) returns 8, as the first bit is 0 (1 & 0 = 0), and using the equality operator it can be compared to 8 to see if that bit is set.

You should understand how bit-wise operators work (they are covered in Java certification exams) and, depending on what area of Java programming you delve into, you might use them in the future.

Logical Operators

Comparison operators enable you to compare two variables to determine whether they are equal or if one is greater than the other, and so on. But what happens when you want to check to see if a variable is in between a range of values? For example, consider validating that someone entered a correct value for an age field in your user interface. You might want to validate that the user is between the ages of 18 and 120; if someone claims to be 700 years old, you might want to check your calendar, prepare for rain, and see if anyone is building an ark! Furthermore, you might want to target a product to children and senior citizens, and therefore validate that the user's age is less than 8 or greater than 55.

To address this need, Java has provided a set of logical operators that enable you to make multiple comparisons and group the result into a single boolean value. Table 3.7 lists the logical operators.

TABLE 3.7   Logical Operators

Operator	Description
&&	AND
||	OR

AND

The AND logical operator (&&) returns a true value if both of the variables it is comparing are true. The form of an AND operation is

```
boolean1 && boolean2
```

It compares two Boolean variables and returns true only if both of the Boolean variables are true. For example, consider verifying that someone is of age:

```
boolean isAdult = (age >= 18 ) && (age <= 120)
```

If the age is 20, then 20 is greater than 18 and less than 120, so isAdult is true. If the age is 17, then 17 is not greater than or equal to 18 although it is less than 120; both conditions are not satisfied, so isAdult is false.

OR

The OR logical operator (||) returns a true value if either of the variables it is comparing are true. The form of an OR operation is

```
boolean1 && boolean2
```

It compares two Boolean variables and returns true if either of the Boolean variables are true. For example, consider verifying that someone is either a child or a senior citizen:

```
boolean isChildOrSenior = (age <= 10 ) || (age >= 55)
```

If the age is 7, then 7 is less than 18, so `isChildOrSenior` is `true`. If the age is 17, then 17 is not less than or equal to 10, and it is not greater than or equal to 55; neither condition is satisfied, so `isChildOrSenior` is `false`.

Not that this is an inclusive `OR`, not an exclusive `OR`; if either or both of the values are true, the result is true.

Short-Circuit Operators

One notable side effect of the logical `AND` and `OR` operators is referred to as *short circuiting*. This means that you are not guaranteed that both Boolean expressions will be evaluated. Consider the previous adult age verification example:

```
boolean isAdult = (age >= 18 ) && (age <= 120)
```

If the user's age is 10, you know that the first expression (age >= 18) is false. The `AND` operation dictates that both conditions must be true, so if the first one is false, what is the purpose of verifying the second one? If `false`, `AND` anything is always `false`, there is no point in evaluating the second expression. This Java shortcut has caught programmers off guard who attempt to perform operations in these expressions instead of simply evaluating the expression. For example, you might write a method that checks to see if a person is already in a database. The method returns true if the person is in the database or false if the user is not in the database, but it adds the person to the database if he is not already there. If for some reason this method is evaluated second in an `AND` operation and the first expression is false, this method will never be called and, hence, the person will not be added to the database. Adding the user to the database is considered a side effect of the method. Be sure to name methods exactly what they do so that you do not run into this problem.

Likewise, consider the `OR` operation:

```
boolean isChildOrSenior = (age <= 10 ) || (age >= 55)
```

If the user is 8-years-old, the first condition is true. The `OR` operator dictates that if either or both of the conditions are true, the expression evaluates to true. Again, what is the purpose in evaluating the second expression?

Be sure to understand this optimization made on behalf of the compiler and never write code that is evaluated in a logical expression that does anything except compute the value to be compared!

Shift Operators

After looking at the structure of memory and all the 1s and 0s with their binary assignment, you might notice something interesting. What happens if you move all the bits in your variable to the left? Consider the following:

```
0000 1010 = 8 + 2  = 10
0001 0100 = 16 + 4 = 20
0010 1000 = 32 + 8 = 40
```

Now take that value and move it to the right:

```
0010 1000 = 32 + 8 = 40
0001 0100 = 16 + 4 = 20
0000 1010 = 8 + 2  = 10
0000 0101 = 4 + 1  = 5
0000 0010 = 2
```

The basic properties of the binary numbering system demonstrates that moving the bits to the left multiplies the value by two and moving the bits to the right divides the value by two. That is interesting and all, but what is the value in that?

Today video cards have high-performance, floating-point arithmetic chips built into them that can perform high-speed mathematical operations, but that was not always the case. In the early days of computer game programming, every ounce of performance had to be squeezed out of code to deliver a decent performing game. To understand just how much math is behind computer animation in game programming, consider a rudimentary flight simulator. From the cockpit we had to compute the location of all objects in sight and draw them. All the objects in the game were drawn with polygons or in some cases, triangles. Some objects in the game could have 50,000 triangles, which results in 150,000 lines, and to maintain 30 frames per second that requires 4,500,000 lines drawn per second. Whoa! How fast can you draw a line? If you can shave off 100 nanoseconds from the line drawing algorithm, that would result in a savings of

```
100ns * 4,500,000 lines = 450,000,000ns = .45 second
```

So, an increase of just 100 nanoseconds results in almost a half a second of savings per second! The bottom line is that every tiny bit of performance that can be improved can have dramatic results.

Okay, fine, now that you have a background on drawing lines, how does this relate to moving bits around?

It turns out that moving bits is exceptionally fast, whereas multiplication and division are very slow. Combine these two statements and what do you get? It would sure be better to make use of the fact that shifting bits can perform multiplication and division instead of using the multiplication and division operators!

That works great for multiplication by two, but how do you handle multiplications by other numbers?

It turns out that addition is also a very inexpensive operation, so through a combination of shifting bits and adding their results can substitute for multiplication in a much more efficient manner. Consider multiplying a value by 35: this is the same as shifting it 5 bits to the left (32), adding that to its value shifted 1 bit to the left (2), and adding that to its unshifted value (1). For more information on this peruse the selection of video game–programming books at your local bookstore.

Java supports three types of shifting, as shown in Table 3.8.

TABLE 3.8   Shift Operators

Operator	Description
<<	Left Shift
>>	Right Shift
>>>	Right Shift (fill with 0s)

Shift Left Operator

Shifting a value to the left (<<) results in multiplying the value by a power of two. The general form of a left shift operation is

```
value << number-of-bits
```

The number of bits specifies how many bits to shift the value over; it has the effect shown in Table 3.9.

TABLE 3.9   Left Shift Bits to Value

Number of Bits	Multiplication Result
1	2
2	4
3	8
4	16
5	32
...	...

Or stated more simply shifting a value, n bits, is the same as multiplying it by 2^n. For example:

```
int i=10;
int result = i << 2; // result = 40
```

Shift Right

Shifting a value to the right (>>) is the same as dividing it by a power of two. The general form of a right shift operation is

```
value >> number-of-bits
```

For example:

```
int i = 20;
int result = i >> 2; // result = 5
int j = -20;
int result2 = j >> 2; // result = -5
```

Shift Right (Fill with 0s)

Shifting a value to the right has the effect of dividing a value by a power of two, and as you just saw, it preserved the sign of the negative number. Recall that this highest bit in each of Java's numeric data types specified the sign. So, if a right shift operator truly did shift the bits, it would move the sign bit to the right, and hence the number would not be equivalent to a division by a power of 2. The right shift operator performs the function that you would expect it to, but does not actually do a true shift of the value.

If your intent is not to perform division but to perform some true bit operations, this side effect is not desirable. To address this, Java has provided a second version of the right shift operator (>>>) that shifts the bits to the right and fills the new bits with zero.

Therefore, the right-shift operator (>>>) can never result in a negative number because the sign bit will always be filled with a zero.

Operator Precedence

There are all these operators and the good news is that they can all be used together. Consider multiplying a value by 10 and adding 5 to it:

```
int result = a * 10 + 5;
```

But what happens when you want to add 5 to a value, and then multiply it by 10? Does the following work?

```
int result = a + 5 * 10;
```

Consider for a moment that in the compiler it performs its calculations left to right, now how would you add 5 multiplied by 10 to a?

```
int result = 5 * 10 + a;
```

This is starting to get confusing and complicated! Furthermore it is not intuitive! When you study mathematics, you learn that certain operations are reflective, meaning that they can be performed in any order and offer the same result. Thus, the following two statements are equivalent:

```
int result = a + 5 * 10;
int result = 5 * 10 + a;
```

The confusion between these two statements is what operation to perform first; the multiplication or the division? How would you solve this in your math classes? You would simply instrument the statements with parentheses to eliminate the confusion:

```
int result = ( a + 5 ) * 10;
int result = ( 5 * 10 ) + a;
```

These statements are now read as follows: add 5 to **a**, and then multiply the result by 10; and multiply 5 by 10, and then add **a** to the result, respectively. In mathematics, the operation enclosed in parentheses is completed before any other operation.

The same mechanism can be implemented in Java, and it is! To qualify what operations to perform first, you can eliminate all ambiguity by explicitly using parentheses to denote what operations are grouped together. But that does not solve the problem of how to handle a statement without parentheses. What is the result of the following operation?

```
int result = 8 + 5 * 10;
```

Is the result 130 or 58?

The answer is that there needs to be a set of rules that defines the order of operation execution. This is defined by what is called the *operator precedence*. The operator precedence defines what operators take precedence over other operators, and hence get executed first. All programming languages define an operator precedence, which is very similar between programming languages, and you must be familiar with it.

Java Operator Precedence

Table 3.10 defines the operator precedence for Java. Precedence is determined by reading Table 3.10 from top to bottom, left to right.

TABLE 3.10   Operator Precedence

Type	Operators
Unary	! ~ ++ -- + - () new
Arithmetic	* / % + -
Shift	<< >> >>>
Comparison	< <= > >= instanceof == !=
Bitwise	& ^	
Short-circuit	&& ||
Ternary	?:
Assignment	= "op=" (for example, *=, +=, %=, ^=)

Unary operators are those operators that operate on a single variable, such as increment and decrement (++), positive and negative signs (+ −), the bit-wise **NOT** operator (~), the logical **NOT** operator (!), parentheses, and the new operator (to be discussed later).

Arithmetic operators are those operators used in mathematical operations. Here it is important to note that this table is read from left to right, therefore multiplication and division have greater precedence than addition and subtraction. Thus the answer to the aforementioned question:

```
int result = 8 + 5 * 10;
```

The result is 58; multiplication has a higher precedence than addition, so the multiplication is performed first followed by the addition. So, the compiler reads this as multiply 5 by 10 (50) and add 8 to the result (50 + 8 = 58).

Shift operators refer to the bit-wise shift left, shift right, and shift right and fill with zeros operators.

The logical *comparison* operators follow with the familiar greater than, less than, and equality variations. Comparison operators return a boolean value, so there is one additional operator added: `instanceof`; this operator will be addressed later when you have a little more Java under your belt.

Next are the bitwise `AND`, `OR`, and `XOR` operators followed by the logical `AND` and `OR` (&& ||), referred to as the *short-circuit* operators.

Next is a new category of operators in the *ternary* operators; the sole operator in this category is referred to as ternary because it uses three operands when computing its result. It is the following form:

```
a ? b : c;
```

This statement is read as follows: If **a** is true, then the result of this operation is **b**, otherwise the result is **c**. The ternary operator does not have to be comprised of single values, the only requirement is that the first value or operation resolves to be a boolean. Consider the following examples:

```
int result = ( 5 > 3 ) ? 2 : 1; // result is 2
int result = ( 5 < 3 ) ? 2 : 1; // result is 1
```

In the first example 5 is greater than 3, therefore the result is 2; in the second example 5 is not less than 3, so the result is 1. So more clearly written, the form of the ternary operator is

```
(boolean expression) ? (return if true) : (return if false)
```

The ternary operator is rarely used, and is mainly inherited from Java's initial syntactical base from C/C++. It is a somewhat cryptic shortcut, but is perfectly legal, so be sure to understand how it is used.

The final sets of operators in the operator precedence hierarchy are the *assignment* operators. The assignment operators include the familiar assignment (=) operator as well as a set of additional assignment operators referred to generically as `op=` (operator equal). These new operators are shortcut operators used when performing an operation on a variable and assigning the result back to that variable. Consider adding 5 to the variable **a**; this could be accomplished traditionally as follows:

```
a = a + 5;
```

Because this is such a common operation Java provides a shortcut for it:

```
a += 5;
```

This is read: **a** plus equal 5, or explicitly **a** equals **a** plus 5. The *operator equal* operator can be applied to all the arithmetic, shift, and bit-wise operators.

Finally, whenever there is ambiguity or you desire a higher degree of readability, you can use parentheses to explicitly qualify the operator precedence yourself.

Summary

This chapter discussed the operators that you can use in Java to manipulate the values of variables. It included all the standard arithmetic operators, the increment and decrement operators, the relational operators, the bit-wise operators, and the shift operators. Finally it discussed the concept of operator precedence that defined the rules by which the order of operators is evaluated.

At this point Java is little more than a glorified calculator, so in the next chapter you will learn about flow control so that you can programmatically make decisions in your programs.

Review Questions

1. What is modulus operator, and how is it used?

2. What is the difference between the following operators: && and &?

3. What is a truth table, and what does it tell you?

4. What is the result of 21 & 3?

5. What is the result of 21 | 3?

6. What is the result of 21 ^ 3?

7. What is the difference between the following operators: >> and >>>?

8. What is the result of 5 * 5 + 5?

9. What is the result of 5 + 5 * 5?

10. What is the result of the following code fragment?

    ```
    int a = 5;
    a += 6 * ++a / 2 - 6 * 9 + 2
    ```

CHAPTER 4

FLOW CONTROL

You will learn about the following in this chapter:

- `if-then-else` statements
- `switch` statements
- `while` loops
- `do` loops
- `for` loops

T his chapter addresses two new categories of statements: conditional and loop. *Conditional statements* enable you to execute a subset of your code depending on specific criteria, and *loop statements* enable you to execute a subset of your code multiple times.

Conditional Statements

Consider drawing a graph in a Java application that displays the pressure level of a nuclear plant with requirements that normal values are green, warning values are yellow, and dangerous values are red. Assign the following values to these conditions:

- Pressure levels of 0% to 70% are displayed as normal

- Pressure levels of 71% to 90% are displayed as a warning

- Pressure levels greater than 90% are displayed as dangerous

Conditional statements enable you to look at the value of a variable, and then decide on the statements of code that you would like to execute. Java provides support for conditional statements through the following two mechanisms: `if-then-else` statements and `switch` statements

The if-then-else Statements

If statements are the most simple and straightforward mechanism for implementing a conditional statement. In its simplest form you ask the question of whether some conditional value is true, and if so, you execute a set of code. The general form of an if statement is

```
if( boolean_value ) {
    // Execute these statements
}
```

The if statement accepts a Boolean value, or an expression that evaluates to a Boolean value, and executes the code enclosed in the following braces if that value is true. If that value is false, the program continues executing the program at the first statement following the if statement's closing brace. Consider the following example:

```
System.out.println( "I will examine your age" );
if( age < 18 ) {
    System.out.println( "You are a child - kids rule!" );
}
System.out.println( "Let's continue" );
```

If age is defined to be 10, you will see the following output:

```
I will examine your age
You are a kid - kids rule!
Let's continue
```

If age is defined to be 20, you will only see the following output:

```
I will examine your age
Let's continue
```

That served well for executing a set of code only if a specific condition was true, but how could you execute code if a condition was true, and then execute different code if the condition was false? Looking at the structure of the if statement, you could do the following:

```
if( age < 18 ) {
    System.out.println( "You are a child - kids rule!" );
}
if( age >= 18 ) {
    System.out.println( "You are an adult - adults are alright!" );
}
```

Writing two if statements, each checking for different values is perfectly legal and effective, but it is not very efficient. From the first if statement, the program knows what age is and whether it is less than or greater than 18, so how can the compiler make use of this information? The answer is through another keyword: else. else accepts no parameters and follows an if statement block. For example:

```
if( age < 18 ) {
    System.out.println( "You are a child - kids rule!" );
}
else {
```

```
    System.out.println( "You are an adult - adults are alright!" );
}
```

The `else` statement that follows the `if` statement block says that if the condition in the preceding `if` evaluates to `false`, execute the `else` statement block.

Now consider that you would like to differentiate between children, adults, and seniors. The `if` statement's `else` clause offers the ability to perform additional comparisons. The complete form of the `if` statement is as follows:

```
if( condition ) {
    // statements;
}
else if( another_condition ) {
    // statements;
}
else if( some other condition ) {
    // statements;
}
else {
    // statements;
}
```

Between the `if` and `else` clauses can appear any number of `else if` clauses. These `else if` clauses, like the `if` clause, accepts conditions that if evaluated to true cause that block of code to be execute. Furthermore, when a true condition is met, the rest of the conditions are not evaluated and the `if` statement is completed.

```
if( age < 18 ) {
    System.out.println( "You are a child - kids rule!" );
}
else if( age < 55 ) {
    System.out.println( "You are an adult - adults are alright!" );
}
else {
    System.out.println( "You are a senior - seniors are great!" );
}
```

Before leaving this section, here is the solution to the aforementioned nuclear plant example using `if` statements:

```
if( pressure < 70 ) {
    System.out.println( "Normal - green" );
}
else if( pressure < 90 ) {
    System.out.println( "Warning - yellow" );
}
else {
    System.out.println( "Danger - red - hit the ground!" );
}
```

Blocks of Statements

You might have noticed that each of the aforementioned `if` statements had blocks of statements that were executed based on the result of the condition. Although the braces that denote a block of statements is readable and offers support for multiple lines of Java code to be executed, the braces are not necessary. This is only true if a single statement is to be executed. In this case the braces can be omitted, as follows:

```
if( condition )
    // true statement;
else
    // false statement;
```

Understand that if you have multiple statements to execute then this shortcut will not work. Consider the following:

```
if( condition )
    // true statement 1;
    // true statement 2;
else
    // false statement 1;
    // false statement 2;
```

When there are no braces, the compiler executes a single statement, and then it considers the `if` statement complete. Here is how the compiler would add braces to this example:

```
if( condition ) {
    // true statement 1;
}

// true statement 2;
else  // compiler error!
// false statement 1;
// false statement 2;
```

Note that the `else` statement generates a compiler error because it is not considered part of the previous `if` statement. Thus, you would have to do the following:

```
if( condition ) {
    // true statement 1;
    // true statement 2;
}
else {
    // false statement 1;
    // false statement 2;
}
```

Ternary Operator

You might have already made the association between the ternary operator and the `if-then-else` statement, and you are right, it has very similar behavior to a simple `if-else` block. To review, the form of the ternary operator is

```
condition ? true statement : false statement;
```

The `condition` is evaluated and if it is true, the true statement is executed; or if it is false, the false statement is executed. This could be expressed using the `if` statement as follows:

```
if( condition ) {
   // true statement(s);
}
else {
   // false statement(s);
}
```

The ternary operator presents this same functionality, but its intention is based on returning or computing a value to be returned to the caller based on a condition. For example:

```
boolean letIntoClub = ( age >= 18 ) ? true : false;
```

The ternary operator is functionally similar to a simple `if` statement, but each has a distinct purpose.

The `switch` Statement

The `if` statement is very useful, but what happens when you have several values that you want to work with? Consider defining the column names for a table: id, name, address, and phone number. Assign values to these columns starting with 0 and counting up to 3. Using an `if` statement, this would be accomplished as follows:

```
if( col == 0 ) {
  System.out.println( "id" );
}
else if( col == 1 ) {
  System.out.println( "name" );
}
else if( col == 2 ) {
  System.out.println( "address" );
}
else if( col == 3 ) {
  System.out.println( "phone number" );
}
else {
  System.out.println( "unknown" );
}
```

In Java programming performing certain actions based on specific numeric values is quite common, so common in fact that there is another construct in the language defined to handle it. The `switch` statement enables you to make a choice between multiple alternative execution paths based on an integer value (or any value that can be converted to an integer). The general form of the `switch` statement is

```
switch( variable ) {
case value_1:
   // statements
   break;
case value_2:
   // statements
```

```
   break;
...
default:
   // default statements
}
```

The `variable` must be an `int` or be able to be converted to an `int`. The new keywords in the `switch` statement are

- `switch`: Denotes the start of the `switch` statement and uses the variable passed to it through its parentheses for all comparisons

- `case`: Notes the comparison of the `variable` to the specified `value`

- `break` (optional): Causes execution to continue at the statement immediately following the `switch` block

Consider the aforementioned table column example and convert it to use a `switch` statement:

```
switch( col ) {
case 0:
   System.out.println( "id" );
   break;
case 1:
   System.out.println( "name" );
   break;
case 2:
   System.out.println( "address" );
   break;
case 3:
   System.out.println( "phone" );
   break;
default:
   System.out.println( "unknown" );
}
```

The `switch` statement converts `col` to an `int`, if it is not one already, and then compares its value to the values specified in each of the four case statements. If the value of `col` is 0 it prints id, if it is 1 it prints name, and so on. If the value of `col` does not match any of the cases, it executes the statements following the `default` statement.

The next question you must have concerns the `break` statement. The `break` statement causes execution to continue at the statement immediately following the `switch` block, but what happens if the `break` statement is omitted? The answer is that the execution continues with the next statement, which might be a statement for another `case` value. Consider omitting the `break` statements in the previous example:

```
switch( col ) {
case 0:
   System.out.println( "id" );
case 1:
   System.out.println( "name" );
case 2:
   System.out.println( "address" );
```

```
case 3:
   System.out.println( "phone" );
default:
   System.out.println( "unknown" );
}
```

Consider the output for `col` with a value of 1. The first statement executed would be to print `name`, the next statement is not a `break`, so it continues and prints `address`, `phone`, and finally `unknown`:

```
Output:
name
address
phone
unknown
```

This effect is referred to as *falling through*, and can be useful if there are several values that should perform the same function. Consider the following example:

```
switch( number ) {
case 2:
case 4:
case 6:
case 8:
case 10:
   System.out.println( "Even" );
   break;
case 1:
case 3:
case 5:
case 7:
case 9:
   System.out.println( "Odd" );
   break;
default:
   System.out.println( "Number is not between 1 and 10" );
```

If `number` is an even number between 1 and 10 the `switch` statement prints `"Even"`, if `number` is an odd number between 1 and 10 the `switch` statement prints `"Odd"`, else it prints `"Number is not between 1 and 10"`. In this case the fall through effect was very beneficial! You can still add statements in the body of one case statement, and let it fall through to the results.

Loop Constructs

It is quite common in computer programming to want to perform a task a specific number of times or until some condition is satisfied. Java provides three loop constructs that facilitate this: the `while` statement, `do-while` statement, and `for` statement.

The while Statement

The while statement tells the compiler to repeatedly execute a set of code until a condition is satisfied. The general form of the while statement is

```
while( boolean_condition ) {
   //statements;
}
```

The statements contained within the braces will be executed as long as the **boolean** condition is **true**. When the **boolean** becomes **false**, the while loop ceases executing these statements and continues execution at the statement immediately following the while statement block. Consider displaying the numbers between 1 and 10, see Listing 4.1.

LISTING 4.1   WhileExample.java

```
1: public class WhileExample {
2:    public static void main( String[] args ) {
3:       int i=1;
4:       while( i <= 10 ) {
5:          System.out.println( "i=" + i );
6:          i++;
7:       }
8:    }
9: }
```

Listing 4.1 defines a new class named WhileExample. Line 3 creates an **int** and initializes it to 1. Line 4 defines a while loop that repeats the statements in lines 5 and 6, while i is less than or equal to 10. Line 3 initializes i to 1, and line 6 increments i.

If you were to forget to increment i, what would happen? The **boolean** value that the while statement is evaluating would never become false (i would remain at 1 indefinitely), and hence line 5 would be executed indefinitely. This is referred to as an *infinite loop* and is a programming error. Be sure that the condition in your loops will eventually change and cause the while statement to cease!

There is one alternative to breaking out of the while loop before the condition becomes false: the **break** statement. Not only does the **break** statement enable you to skip over cases in a **switch** statement, its full purpose is to stop execution and continue at the first statement following the block of code (delimited by braces) that contains it. Thus, **break** enables you to continue execution after the while loop.

The do Statement

Are the statements in a while loop guaranteed to be executed at least once? Consider the following example:

```
int i = 10;
while( i < 10 ) {
   System.out.println( "i is less than 10" );
}
```

The while loop evaluates the **boolean** condition and if it is true it executes the statements in its body; then it reevaluates the condition—this process continues until the condition is false. Because you sometimes would like to be assured that the code in your loop will execute at least once, Java has defined a **do while** statement. It has the general form:

```
do {
    // statements;
} while( boolean_condition );
```

The **do while** statement executes the statements in its body, and then evaluates the **boolean** condition, as opposed to the **while** statement evaluating the **boolean** condition prior to executing the statements in its body. The **do while** statement ensures that the statements in the body are executed at least once.

Listing 4.2 shows an example using the **do while** statement.

LISTING 4.2   DoWhileExample.java

```
1: public class DoWhileExample {
2:     public static void main( String[] args ) {
3:         int a = 0;
4:         do {
5:           System.out.println( "a=" + a );
6:             a += 2;
7:         } while( a <= 10 );
8:     }
9: }
```

Listing 4.2 is very similar in functionality to Listing 4.1 (the while loop). Line 3 creates a new **int** named **a** and initializes it to 0. The **do** loop prints the value of **a** in line 5, increases its value by 2 in line 6, and then evaluates its value in line 7. The output for the **DoWhileExample** class is

```
0
2
4
6
8
10
```

If **a** was 20, lines 5 and 6 would be executed before the **while** in line 7 could stop its execution. The output would be

```
10
```

do while and **while** statements are very similar with the sole difference that **do while** ensures the body of the loop will be executed at least once, and the **while** loop might never execute its body. In practice programmers tend to use **while** loops over **do while**, but the choice will be made based on the problem you are trying to solve.

The `for` Statement

To this point the `while` and `do while` statements have been used to iterate over a variable (`i` and `a`) and perform some function on the interim value. `while` and `do while` statements are not only used for counting, but for any function that can resolve to a `boolean` value. If you have the need to iterate a specific number of times Java provides the `for` statement. The `for` statement is typically used for counting or repeating code executions a specific number of times. There are other uses as you will see, but counting is the typical case. The general form of the `for` statement is

```
for( initialization_statement; boolean_condition; iteration_statement ) {
   // statements;
}
```

The *initialization* statement is executed before the loop starts and is used to initialize the variable or variables that will be used in the loop. Next the *boolean condition* is evaluated—if it is true, the body of the `for` loop will be executed. Finally, the *iteration statement* will be executed, and the `boolean` condition will be evaluated again, ad infinitum. Looking at the `while` loop, this is really what the examples did:

```
1: public class WhileExample {
2:    public static void main( String[] args ) {
3:       int i=1; // Initialization statement
4:       while( i <= 10 ) {  //  Boolean comparison
5:          System.out.println( "i=" + i ); // Body
6:          i++; // Iteration statement
7:       }
8:    }
9: }
```

Listing 4.3 shows how this example can be rewritten using a `for` statement.

LISTING 4.3   ForExample.java

```
public class ForExample {
   public static void main( String[] args ) {
      for( int i=1; i<= 10; i++ ) {
         System.out.println( "i=" + i );
      }
   }
}
```

The result of Listing 4.3, as you would expect, is

```
1
2
3
4
5
6
7
8
9
10
```

Before leaving the `for` loop there are some specific rules that you need to know:

- The examples in this section have declared and defined a new variable in the initialization section of the `for` statement; this is permissible and encouraged, but not required. The requirement is only the initialization of the variable, not necessarily its creation. Thus, the following is legal:

```
int i = 0;
for( int i=0; i<10; i++ ) {
    // statements;
}
```

- Furthermore because you are managing the variables and Boolean condition in the `for` statement, you do not have to do anything in the initialization section. Thus, the following is also legal:

```
int i = 0;
for( ; i<10; i++ ) {
    // statements;
}
```

Scope

Programmers found that they often needed a variable for the sole purpose of iterating through a loop; this variable is commonly referred to as the *loop control variable*. Because of this, most programming languages, including Java, offered programmers the ability to declare and initialize one or more variables in the initialization section of the `for` loop. There is however, a set of scoping rules that define where that variable is visible. Any variable declared in the initialization section of a `for` loop is only visible inside that `for` loop's code block.

The region of code where a variable is visible and accessible is referred to as that variable's *scope*. In the `for` loop, the braces that follow the `for` statement define a *block* of code; in this case this is the *body* of the `for` loop. The scope of all variables defined in the initialization section of a `for` loop is the body of the `for` loop. What does this mean practically? Consider the following examples:

```
1: int i = 1;
2: System.out.println( "a=" + a ); // error; a is not visible (out of scope)
3: for( int a=0; a<10; a++ ) {
4:     System.out.println( "a=" + a ); // a is visible (in scope)
5:     System.out.println( "i=" + i ); // i is visible (in scope)
6: }
7: System.out.println( "a=" + a ); // error; a is not visible (out of scope)
8: System.out.println( "i=" + i ); // i is visible (in scope)
```

The `for` loop encompasses lines 3–6, and `a` is the loop control variable. `a` is therefore visible in the `for` statement and between the braces that define the body of the `for` loop (lines 3–6). Any attempt to access `a` outside of the body of the `for` loop will result in a compilation error, which is shown in lines 2 and 7.

The variable `i`, on the other hand, is defined outside the body and initialization section of the `for` loop and therefore is visible outside the `for` loop (line 8) as well as inside the `for` loop (line 5). You will learn more about the scoping rule later in the book, but a standard rule of thumb is that a variable is visible in its code block after its declaration and in child code blocks, but it is not visible outside its code block. Consider the following:

```
// Visible: none, Not Visible: a, b, c, d
int a = 10;
// Visible: a, Not Visible: b, c, d
for( int b=0; b<10; b++ ) {
    // Visible: a, b, Not Visible: c, d
    while( b<5 ) {
        int c = a*b;
        // Visible: a, b, c, Not Visible: d
    }
    while( b>5 {
        int d = b-a;
        // Visible: a, b, d, Not Visible: c
    }
    // Visible: a, b Not Visible: c, d
}
// Visible: a, Not Visible: b, c, d
```

This set of rules is referred to as *block scoping rules* because it defines the visibility, or scope, of variable based on the code block to which it belongs.

Multiple Variables

You are not restricted to defining a single variable in the initialization section of the `for` loop, you can define multiple variables. The only restriction is that they must all be of the same type. You might also update multiple variables in the iteration statement. The key is to separate the operations by commas, see Listing 4.4.

LISTING 4.4   ForMultipleExample.java

```
1: public class ForMultipleExample {
2:     public static void main( String[] args ) {
3:         for( int i=1, j=10; i<=10; i++, j— ) {
4:             System.out.println( "i=" + i );
5:             System.out.println( "j=" + j );
6:             System.out.println( "i*j=" + i*j );
7:         }
8:     }
9: }
```

Listing 4.4 shows the creation of two integers, `i` and `j`, in the initialization section of the `for` loop in line 3. Note that a comma separates the initialization of the two variables. The iteration statement in the `for` loop modifies both variables: it increments `i` and decrements `j`. Both `i` and `j` are visible inside the body of the `for` loop as well as in all parts of the `for` loop statement (initialization, comparison, and iteration statements).

Breaking Out of Loops

As you learned earlier in this chapter, there are some occasions when you want to exit a loop early; this is facilitated by the **break** statement. The **break** statement is not only applicable to the **while** loop, but to all of our loops, including the **for** loop.

The **break** statement causes the execution of the program to break from the point of the **break** statement and continue at the statement immediately following the code block that contains it. Listing 4.5 demonstrates how the **break** statement is used.

LISTING 4.5   BreakExample.java

```
1:  public class BreakExample {
2:     public static void main( String[] args ) {
3:        for( int i=1; i<= 10; i++ ) {
4:           if( i == 5 ) {
5:              break;
6:           }
7:           System.out.println( "i=" + i );
8:        }
9:        System.out.println( "Done" );
10:    }
11: }
```

The output from Listing 4.5 is

```
i=1
i=2
i=3
i=4
Done
```

The **for** loop defined by lines 3–8 counts from 1 to 10 and prints the value out to the screen. Line 4 defines an **if** statement that checks whether **i** is equal to 5, and if it is it subsequently issues the **break** statement in line 5. At this point the program execution skips over line 7 (it does not print **i=5**) and continues with the statement immediately following the **for** loop— line 9 and prints **Done**. The output demonstrates this.

Continuing Execution in a Loop

How would you implement a **for** loop that printed all of the values between 1 and 10 except for 5 and 7? Using the **break** statement you could print the values from 1 to 4, and then break out of the loop, but the requirement is after you skip 5 that you skip over this iteration of the loop and continue with the next iteration.

Java provides this functionality through the **continue** statement. It causes the execution of the current iteration of the loop to cease, and then continue at the next iteration of the loop. Listing 4.6 shows how to solve this problem using the **continue** statement.

LISTING 4.6   ContinueExample.java

```
1:  public class ContinueExample {
2:     public static void main( String[] args ) {
3:        for( int i=1; i<= 10; i++ ) {
4:           if( i == 5 || i == 7 ) {
5:              continue;
6:           }
7:           System.out.println( "i=" + i );
8:        }
9:        System.out.println( "Done" );
10:    }
11: }
```

The output of Listing 4.6 is

```
i=1
i=2
i=3
i=4
i=6
i=8
i=9
i=10
Done
```

The **for** loop, defined by lines 3–8 of Listing 4.6, counts from 1 to 10 and prints the value (line 7). Line 4 however, checks the value of **i** to see if it is 5 or 7; if it is, it issues the **continue** statement in line 5. The **continue** statement tells the compiler to skip over the rest of this iteration of the **for** loop (line 7) and continue with the next iteration (execute the iteration statement in the **for** loop, and then the comparison). From the output you can see that when line 4 encountered the values 5 and 7 it skipped over line 7 and did not print the value of **i**, but continued with the next iteration of the **for** loop.

Labels

The **break** and **continue** statements are great for breaking out of, or continuing out of, a single loop, but they do not provide support for multiple nested loops. Consider building a mathematical Times Table from 1 to 10, a possible solution is to use *nested* **for** loops. A nested loop is a loop that is contained within the body of another loop. Listing 4.7 shows code that generates a Times Table.

LISTING 4.7   TimesTableExample.java

```
1:  public class TimesTableExample {
2:     public static void main( String[] args ) {
3:        for( int i=1; i<=10; i++ ) {
4:           for( int j=1; j<=10; j++ ) {
5:              System.out.print( (i*j) + "\t" );
6:           }
7:           System.out.println();
8:        }
9:     }
10: }
```

The output from Listing 4.7 is

1	2	3	**4**	5	6	7	8	9	10
2	4	6	8	10	12	14	16	18	20
3	6	9	12	15	18	21	24	27	30
4	8	12	16	20	24	28	32	36	40
5	10	15	20	25	30	35	40	45	50
6	12	18	**24**	30	36	42	48	54	60
7	14	21	28	35	42	49	56	63	70
8	16	24	32	40	48	56	64	72	80
9	18	27	36	45	54	63	72	81	90
10	20	30	40	50	60	70	80	90	100

Thus, if you look at any value in the top row and multiply it by the value found in left column, you find the answer where the row and column intersect. Consider 4 times 6: The first row number, 4, multiplied by the sixth row number, 6, results in 24, which is where they intersect (row 6, column 4).

The generation of this Times Table is accomplished in Listing 4.7 by defining a `for` statement for lines 3 to 8 that counts from 1 to 10, and then defining a nested `for` loop from lines 4 to 6 that also counts from 1 to 10. Line 5 multiplies the value from the outer loop by the value of the nested, or inner, loop, and thus the Times Table is generated. To this point you have been using the `System.out.println()` call to print a value to the screen, but in this case line 5 uses `System.out.print` instead. The difference is that `println()` prints a carriage return and line-feed after printing the value, whereas `print()` prints the value and leaves the output at the end of the print without adding a carriage return or line feed.

Now consider building this Times Table, but when you reach a product of 25, stop completely. Java enables you to define a point in your code that `break` and `continue` statements can be anchored to, called a *label*, so their functionality will be tied to that specific location in code. With a label defined, you can tell the `break` or `continue` statements to break or continue to that label by passing them the label's name.

A label is defined by a string of text (same rules apply to defining a label name as to defining a variable name) followed by a colon. The following loop defines the location that `break` and `continue` statements can be sent to. The `break` and `continue` statements can either break out of or continue to the current loop (as you have seen), or specify a specific label to break out of. This is accomplished by passing the `break` or `continue` statement the label. The general form for this operation is

```
mylabel:
   for( int a=0; a<10; a++ ) {
      for( int b=0; b<10; b++ ) {
         break mylabel;
      }
   }
```

Listing 4.8 shows the solution to the partial Times Table example.

LISTING 4.8   TimesTableExample2.java

```
1:  public class TimesTableExample2 {
2:     public static void main( String[] args ) {
3:        outer:
4:        for( int i=1; i<=10; i++ ) {
5:           for( int j=1; j<=10; j++ ) {
6:              if( ( i*j ) == 25 ) {
7:                 break outer;
8:              }
9:              System.out.print( (i*j) + "\t" );
10:          }
11:          System.out.println();
12:       }
13:       System.out.println( "Done" );
14:    }
15: }
```

The output from Listing 4.8 is

1	2	3	4	5	6	7	8	9	10
2	4	6	8	10	12	14	16	18	20
3	6	9	12	15	18	21	24	27	30
4	8	12	16	20	24	28	32	36	40
5	10	15	20	Done					

Line 3 defines the label outer, and then line 7 issues a break statement passing it the label name outer. When line 6 finds two numbers where the product is 25 it breaks out of both loops and continues at the statement immediately following the loop associated with the label.

Summary

This chapter was all about flow control: How to conditionally execute sections of code, and how to execute sections of code multiple times. This chapter discusses the if and if-then-else statements for general conditional statements, and the switch statement for a specific variety of conditional statements. Iterative statements were discussed in the form of while, do while, and for statements.

Now Java is more than just a glorified calculator, you now have the ability to programmatically make decisions and do some real computations.

The next chapter will take what you have learned thus far to the next level and enable you to create reusable methods that perform specific sets of functionality.

Review Questions

1. What is the general form of an `if` statement?

2. What is the function of the `else` clause for an `if` statement?

3. How many `else if` statements can follow an `if` statement?

4. The `switch` statement only evaluates what type of values?

5. Which loop ensures that the body of the loop is evaluated at least once?

6. What is an infinite loop?

7. What is the most popular type of loop for iterating over a variable or set of variables?

8. How do you skip the statements in the current iteration of a loop?

9. How do you stop executing the statements in a loop and continue at the first line following the loop?

10. How do you break out of multiple nested loops?

Exercises

1. Write a program that displays the temperatures from 0 degrees Celsius to 100 degrees Celsius and its Fahrenheit equivalent.

   Note that the conversion from Celsius to Fahrenheit uses the following formula:

   ```
   F = C * 9/5 + 32;
   ```

2. Write a program that displays all prime numbers from 1 to 100.

   Note that a prime number is a number that is only divisible by itself and 1. For example the number 7 is prime, but the number 6 is not:

   ```
   6 = 6*1 and 2*3
   ```

CHAPTER 5

METHODS

In this chapter you will learn:

- The concept of divide-and-conquer
- The format of a Java method
- How to implement methods
- How to call methods
- Method access modifiers

- Variable scoping rules with respect with methods
- Recursion versus iteration
- Overloading methods
- Introduction to Java class libraries

A t this point in your arsenal of Java programming knowledge, you can create variables of differing types and manipulate them. For more complex operations you can modify them conditionally or derive values through iterative means.

Assuming you completed the exercises in the previous chapter, you have a good set of code that computes prime numbers, but what happens when you need to compute prime numbers again in another application? It would be nice to package that piece of code you wrote to determine whether a number is prime in such a way that you can reuse it.

Divide and Conquer

Not that I am endorsing this, or suggesting that you even try it, but how much effort do you think it would be to rip this book in half? There are approximately 1,000 pages in this book, so if you grab the top with your left hand and the bottom with your right hand and pull, can you rip the book?

Okay, I have seen those muscle men shows on television in the middle of the night when someone actually rips a phone book in half, but for the average man it is just too hard! Do you have any ideas about how you could rip the book in half without trying to do it all at once? Can you rip one page in half? Surely! How about ten? Probably.

So, if you divide the book up into one hundred, ten page segments, ripping the book in half is not a problem. What you have just done is called *divide and conquer*.

Whether it is in war or computer programming, the concept of dividing a difficult problem into smaller manageable problems is powerful. Computer programming divides a problem into modules called *methods* that perform a set of very specific functionality. Your programs will then be built from methods that you write, and methods that Java provides for you.

The Format of a Method

The general form of a Java method is

```
return_type method_name( parameter_list )
{
    declarations and statements...
}
```

The `method_name` is any valid identifier and has the same naming rules as variables.

The `return_type` is the data type of the result returned from the method to the caller; if your method was defined to square an `int`, note that the method returns an `int` here.

The `parameter_list` is a comma-separated list containing the declarations of values passed to the method. Again, if you were writing a method to square an integer you would need to specify that the method receives one `int` and give it a name that you can reference from within the method.

The method name, return type, and parameter list define what is referred to as the method's *signature*: A method *signature* uniquely identifies a method.

Enclosed between the parentheses is the *body* of the method; this is where all the work takes place. The parentheses denote a *block* of code; variables can be declared in a block and blocks can contain other blocks. When the method has completed all the work it has to do, there are three ways it can return control back to the caller:

1. Control passes back at the closing brace of the method if the method does not return a result.

2. Manually return with no value:

   ```
   return;
   ```

3. Return a value:

   ```
   return expression;
   ```

Note

Note that for a method to return without passing a result back to the caller, the method must be declared with a return type of `void`. `void` specifies that the method will not return any value.

The following code snippet shows a method that squares an integer:

```
public static int square( int i ) {
    return i*i;
}
```

The `square` method is `publicly` available to anyone who wants to call it (described in the next section). It is `static` (similar to the `main` method you are already used to) meaning that there is only one instance of the method for all classes (discussed in the next chapter). The `square` method returns an `int` and accepts as its parameter list one `int` that is labeled `i`. The body of the method simply returns `i*i`, or the square of `i`.

The breakdown of the method components for the `square` method follow:

- Method name: `square`
- Return Type: `int`
- Parameter List: `int i`
- Return Expression: `i*i`
- Return Statement: `return i*i`

The signature of the method, which uniquely identifies it, is

```
public static int square( int i )
```

In this class there can only be one method named `square` that accepts a single `int` as its parameter list.

The body of the method is

```
    return i*i;
```

Many of the terms described here will make more sense in the next chapter, but they are needed to make the example in the next section work.

Calling a Method

After a method is defined, you can call it in your program. In this case the method is publicly available to everyone, so it can be directly referenced inside the `main` method. The mechanism to call a method is as follows:

```
return_datatype variable = method_name( parameter_list );
```

If the method returns a value (the return type is not null), you can assign the result to a variable or use it in any expression that the data type returned by the method is usable. For example, you can use the result of the `square` method anywhere you can use an `int`:

```
int result = 5 * square( 10 ); // result is 5 * 100 = 500
```

Listing 5.1 shows an example that defines the `square` method and calls it in a complete Java application.

LISTING 5.1   `Math.java`

```
 1:  public class Math {
 2:    public static int square( int i ) {
 3:      return i*i;
 4:    }
 5:
 6:    public static void main( String[] args ) {
 7:      for( int i=1; i<=10; i++ ) {
 8:        System.out.println( "i=" + i + ", i*i=" + square( i ) );
 9:      }
10:    }
11: }
```

Line 1 creates a new class named `Math`.

Lines 2–4 define the `square` method described in the previous section.

Lines 6–10 define the `main` method for the `Math` application. The `main` method uses a `for` loop to count from 1 to 10 and prints the current value and the square of the value. The `square` method invocation is hidden inside the `println` method call.

The output from the `Math` application is

```
i=1, i*i=1
i=2, i*i=4
i=3, i*i=9
i=4, i*i=16
i=5, i*i=25
i=6, i*i=36
i=7, i*i=49
i=8, i*i=64
i=9, i*i=81
i=10, i*i=100
```

The `println` method call is pretty busy and could be broken down further and written as follows for clarity:

```
int iSquared = square( i );
String output = "i=" + i + ", i*i=" + iSquared;
System.out.println( output );
```

In this example you can see the value returned by the `square` method call assigned to a variable, and then used. In Listing 5.1 you see that the value returned by the `square` method is used in a normal expression.

If the method does not return any value then the method call cannot be assigned to a variable or used in an expression. Consider the following method:

```
public static void printNumber( int n ) {
   System.out.println( "The number is " + n );
}
```

Because the method is defined to return **void**, there is no return type for the method. It could be called as follows:

```
int n = 10;
printNumber( n ); // Note the result in not assigned to anything
```

Complex Class Methods

Your classes are not limited to defining a single method, on the contrary you will define multiple methods in most of your classes. Consider a more complete mathematics class, you might want to have methods not only to square a number, but also cube a number or raise a number to any particular power. Furthermore, you might want to add in your prime number checker, a factorial method, or a square root method.

Listing 5.2 defines a class with a more complex and complete set of methods.

LISTING 5.2   `Math2.java`

```
1:  public class Math2 {
2:    public static int square( int n ) {
3:      return n*n;
4:    }
5:
6:    public static int cube( int n ) {
7:      return n*n*n;
8:    }
9:
10:   public static int toThePower( int n, int power ) {
11:     int result=n;
12:     for( int i=0; i<power; i++ ) {
13:       result *= n;
14:     }
15:     return result;
16:   }
17:
18:   public static int factorial( int n ) {
19:     int result = n;
20:     for( int i=n-1; i>0; i— ) {
21:       result *= i;
22:     }
23:     return result;
24:   }
25:
26:   public static boolean isPrime( int n ) {
27:     // This will left as one of your exercises
28:     return false;
29:   }
30:
31:   public static void showNumber( String operation, int n ) {
32:     System.out.println( "The result of the " + operation + " is " + n );
```

LISTING 5.2   Continued

```
33:    }
34:
35:    public static void main( String[] args ) {
36:       int a = 5;
37:       showNumber( "Square", square( a ) );
38:       showNumber( "Cube", cube( a ) );
39:       showNumber( "To The Power", toThePower( a, 4 ) );
40:       showNumber( "Factorial", factorial( a ) );
41:    }
42: }
```

Listing 5.2 defines six methods:

- square

- cube

- toThePower

- factorial

- isPrime

- showNumber

The first five methods are mathematical and the last is a convenience method so that you don't have to manually type the output each time. `square`, `cube`, and `toThePower` should be self-explanatory; note however that `toThePower` has a parameter list with two values: the number to raise to the specified power (`n`), and the power to raise that number to (`power`).

In mathematics there is the concept of *factorial*, denoted in mathematical notation (but not Java notation) by an exclamation point (!), which is a number multiplied by every integer number from 1 to the number itself. In this example, the 5 factorial is

```
5! = 5*4*3*2*1 = 120
```

The `factorial` method in Listing 5.2 shows an iterative approach to solving this problem.

The `isPrime` method, because it is an exercise question, is left for you to do at the end of this chapter.

The `main` method defines an `int` variable named `a`, assigns it the value 5, and then calls each of the mathematical methods on it, passing the result to `showNumber` for output.

Variable Scope

The Chapter 4, "Flow Control," started discussing *scope* and *scoping* rules, but now you have enough knowledge to formalize these concepts.

The *scope* of an identifier for a variable, reference, or method is the portion of the program in which the identifier can be referenced.

There are three types of scope defined in Java:

- *Class Scope*: Available to all methods in the class
- *Block Scope*: Available only with the block it is declared to, or within nested blocks
- *Method Scope*: Special type for labels used with break and continue statements

Listing 5.3 shows a sample application with variables at differing scopes.

LISTING 5.3   Scope.java

```java
public class Scope {
  static int x = 5;

  public static int timesX( int n ) {
    int result = n*x;
    return result;
  }

  public static void main( String[] args ) {
    int m = 10;
    System.out.println( "m times x = " + timesX( m ) );
  }
}
```

In Listing 5.3 there are 3 variables: x, n, and m. Table 5.1 lists the type of scope they have and to which method (if applicable).

TABLE 5.1   Scope.java Variable Scoping

Variable	Scope	Relation
x	Class Scope	The entire Scope class
n	Local/Block	The timesX method
m	Local/Block	The main method

x is a variable defined outside of a method and inside the class **Scope**, so it is said to have class scope, and is therefore visible from all methods in the class. m is defined inside the **main** method, so it has local or block scope to the **main** method. n is declared inside the parameter list of the **timesX** method, so it has local or block scope to the **timesX** method.

A *local variable* declared in a block can only be used in that block or nested blocks within that block.

Recursion

Thus far the methods in this chapter have been self-sufficient; they represented a single set of functionality and returned the result of that functionality. Methods are very capable of calling other methods to help solve their problems, but there is another domain of methods that relies on multiple calls to itself. If a method calls itself, that act is referred to as *recursion*.

Recursive programming can solve some very interesting problems in a very natural and intuitive manner. Consider the factorial example from earlier in the chapter. The result of the factorial operation on a number is the product of that number with all numbers between 1 and the number. The way that that problem was solved in an iterative fashion in Listing 5.2 was to create an intermediate result value equal to the number, and then iterate from that number to 1, multiplying the numbers to the result to get the answer:

```java
public static int factorial( int n ) {
  int result = n;
  for( int i=n-1; i>0; i-- ) {
    result *= i;
  }
  return result;
}
```

Consider passing the number 4 to this method:

```java
int result = 4;
for( int i=3; i>0; i-- ) {
  result *= i;
}
```

Or

```java
int result = 4; // result is 4
result *= 3; // result is 12
result *= 2; // result is 24
result *= 1; // result is 24
```

This is a *brute force* (manually do every computation) way of solving this problem, but there is an elegant, recursive way of solving it. Listing 5.4 shows this recursive solution.

LISTING 5.4   FactorialRecursive.java

```java
public class FactorialRecursive {
  public static int factorial( int n ) {
    if( n == 1 ) return 1;
    return n * factorial( n-1 );
  }

  public static void main( String[] args ) {
    System.out.println( "5 factorial = " + factorial( 5 ) );
  }
}
```

Listing 5.4 defines the `factorial` method to return 1 if 1 is passed to it (`1! = 1`), otherwise it returns the product of the number passed to it with the factorial of the number minus 1. The calls for this solution would look as follows:

```
factorial( 5 ) = 5 * factorial( 4 )
factorial( 4 ) = 4 * factorial( 3 )
factorial( 3 ) = 3 * factorial( 2 )
factorial( 2 ) = 2 * factorial( 1 )
factorial( 1 ) = 1
```

You will see the following after unwinding the call stack.

```
1 * 2 * 3 * 4 * 5 = 120
```

The key to using recursion is that you must define a stopping point otherwise the recursion will repeat indefinitely. Recursion takes a lot of forethought and planning, but once a solution is found there is usually not too much code and the solution is very elegant.

Recursion Versus Iteration

Just looking at the factorial example you can see that both solved the same problem but in quite different ways. I am sure that after you spend some time meditating over the recursive code you will agree that the solution is more elegant.

All recursive problems can be solved through iteration, although not as "pretty," but when would you choose one over the other? From a performance standpoint the answer to this question is obvious after you understand how method calls work (back to the 1s and 0s).

Method calls in Java require the allocation of a section of memory to hold all the method parameters passed to it, plus if the method is not static, a copy of the method executable that will process the invocation. Iterative methods on the other hand, setup the memory for the method call once, and then reference variables in memory for both conditional and increment statements. The end result is that calling methods is far more expensive in terms of memory and CPU time than iteratively checking and incrementing variables in memory.

If performance is of the utmost importance to you, be sure to solve your problems iteratively, not recursively. On the other hand, if you are more concerned with understanding and maintaining your code, you might consider recursive programming.

Method Overloading

Consider defining a method called `square` that returns the square of two numbers, which has been done repeatedly in this chapter. The examples thus far have worked on `int`s, but what happens when we want to square a `long` or a `double`? Do you create different methods with different names to solve the problem?

```
int squareInt( int i )
long squareLong( long l )
double squareDouble( double d )
```

That is perfectly legal, but when you are writing your code, and subsequently reading it back later, do you care whether you are squaring an `int` or a `long`? It would be nice to have the method `square` return the square of all the previous types.

Unfortunately, because of how variables are stored in memory, there is no way to write a single method that handles all these cases, but Java enables you to reuse the same method name. Remember that a method is defined by its signature; the signature includes the method name and its parameter list. As long as methods differ in their signature, the compiler treats them as different methods.

This means that you are free to define methods with the same name as long as their parameter list is different. Here are three `square` methods that solve this problem:

```
int square( int i )
long square( long l )
double square( double d )
```

All three methods are named `square`, but their parameter lists are different: the first is a single `int`, the second is a `long`, and the last is a `double`. The rules are satisfied and the compiler will treat these three methods differently. The process of defining multiple methods with the same name but differing signatures is referred to as *method overloading*. Listing 5.5 shows a complete example of these three methods.

LISTING 5.5   SquareOverload.java

```java
public class SquareOverload {
  public static int square( int n ) {
    System.out.println( "Integer Square" );
    return n*n;
  }

  public static long square( long l ) {
    System.out.println( "Long Square" );
    return l*l;
  }

  public static double square( double d ) {
    System.out.println( "Double Square" );
    return d*d;
  }

  public static void main( String[] args ) {
    int n = 5;
    long l = 100;
    double d = 1000.0;
    System.out.println( "n squared=" + square( n ) );
    System.out.println( "l squared=" + square( l ) );
    System.out.println( "d squared=" + square( d ) );
  }
}
```

When the compiler sees the three different versions of `square` in Listing 5.5, it treats them as separate methods.

Note

A final note about method signatures is that although the return value is part of the signature, it cannot be the differentiating factor that results in overloaded methods. The following two methods cannot be defined in the same Java class:

```
public int square( long l ) { ... }
public long square( long l ) { ... }
```

The compiler only looks at the method name and parameter list, and does not consider the return type.

Java Class Libraries

This chapter began discussion about the idea of divide and conquer, and how you can create reusable methods that encapsulate the functionality you might want to use in the future. From this concept you are going to develop a set of methods over the next few years that other people are probably developing as well. Because everyone is going to need a `square` method, would it be nice if someone created this method and published it for everyone to use?

After you understand the basic syntax and semantics of the Java programming language, a big part of the learning curve is locating all the prebuilt classes and methods that you have been created for you. Java has implemented most of the basic functionality that you could ever think of developing on your own. The Java 2 SDK contains classes that will do much of your work for you!

The best resource you can have as a Java programmer is a link to Java's Documentation, referred to as Javadoc. Javadoc is a set of HTML-based documentation for the Java 2 SDK—and through a mechanism you will learn about later, you can document your own classes and methods to share with others (and to understand six months from now when you have completely forgotten what a method does).

The Javadoc for the Java 2 SDK can be found at `http://java.sun.com/docs/index.html`.

Find the version of the SDK you are using and follow the links to see the documentation for your version. You can also download a copy of the documentation to install on you own computer, which is highly recommended if you have the space.

There are hundreds of classes you can look at, but because of the heavy focus on mathematical operations in this chapter, this section will present Java's `Math` class. The `Math` class defines two very important fields: E and PI, so if you are computing natural logarithms or need to use PI you can access them by referencing the explicit name of the `Math` class, appending a period to it, and then referencing the field you are interested in, as follows:

```
int radius = 5;
float area = Math.PI * square( radius );
```

The `Math` class also defines a set of methods, as shown in Table 5.2.

TABLE 5.2 Math Methods

Method	Description
double abs(double a)	Returns the absolute value of a double value.
float abs(float a)	Returns the absolute value of a float value.
int abs(int a)	Returns the absolute value of an int value.
long abs(long a)	Returns the absolute value of a long value.
double acos(double a)	Returns the arc cosine of an angle, in the range of 0.0 through pi.
double asin(double a)	Returns the arc sine of an angle, in the range of –pi/2 through pi/2.
double atan(double a)	Returns the arc tangent of an angle, in the range of –pi/2 through pi/2.
double atan2(double a, double b)	Converts rectangular coordinates (b, a) to polar (r, theta).
double ceil(double a)	Returns the smallest (closest to negative infinity) double value that is not less than the argument and is equal to a mathematical integer.
double cos(double a)	Returns the trigonometric cosine of an angle.
double exp(double a)	Returns the exponential number e (that is, 2.718…) raised to the power of a double value.
double floor(double a)	Returns the largest (closest to positive infinity) double value that is not greater than the argument and is equal to a mathematical integer.
double IEEEremainder(double f1, double f2)	Computes the remainder operation on two arguments as prescribed by the IEEE 754 standard.
double log(double a)	Returns the natural logarithm (base e) of a double value.
double max(double a, double b)	Returns the greater of two double values.
float max(float a, float b)	Returns the greater of two float values.
int max(int a, int b)	Returns the greater of two int values.
long max(long a, long b)	Returns the greater of two long values.
double min(double a, double b)	Returns the smaller of two double values.

TABLE 5.2   Continued

Method	Description
float min(float a, float b)	Returns the smaller of two float values.
int min(int a, int b)	Returns the smaller of two int values.
long min(long a, long b)	Returns the smaller of two long values.
double pow(double a, double b)	Returns of value of the first argument raised to the power of the second argument.
double random()	Returns a double value with a positive sign, greater than or equal to 0.0 and less than 1.0.
double rint(double a)	Returns the double value that is closest in value to a and is equal to a mathematical integer.
long round(double a)	Returns the closest long to the argument.
int round(float a)	Returns the closest int to the argument.
double sin(double a)	Returns the trigonometric sine of an angle.
double sqrt(double a)	Returns the correctly rounded positive square root of a double value.
double tan(double a)	Returns the trigonometric tangent of an angle.
double toDegrees(double angrad)	Converts an angle measured in radians to the equivalent angle measured in degrees.
double toRadians(double angdeg)	Converts an angle measured in degrees to the equivalent angle measured in radians.

All these methods are `static`, so you do not need to create an instance of the `Math` class to use them, simply reference them as `Math-period-method_name`, for example:

```
double result = Math.tan( angle );
```

Spend some time looking through these methods, experiment, and see what you can come up with.

Summary

This chapter discussed one of the foundational concepts in computer programming: divide and conquer. Just as you could not rip this book in half all at once (again, please do not actually try to rip your book in half), tackling computer programming programs can be a daunting task until you break the problem into manageable pieces. Java enables you to do this by defining methods that solve parts of the problem. Your computer program combines these methods as well as the Java provided methods to solve the actual problem.

This chapter discussed solving computer-science problems iteratively and recursively and the pros and cons of each. Finally, this chapter concluded with a discussion of the classes provided to you in the Java 2 SDK and took a close look at the Math class.

The next chapter leaves the introductory syntax/semantics section of the book and dives into the core concepts of object-orientation that gives Java its true power!

Review Questions

1. Define the concept of divide and conquer in your own words.

2. Describe the parts of a method definition.

3. What constitutes the signature of a method?

4. How do you specify that a method is not going to return a value?

5. What are the three types of scope and how do they differ?

6. Describe the computer-programming concept of recursion.

7. When would you use recursion and when would you use iteration?

8. What is method overloading?

9. Can the following two methods exist in the same class? Why or why not?

```
public int cube( int n ) { ... }
public long cube( long l ) { ... }
```

10. How do you access the Math class's methods?

Exercises

1. Implement the isPrime method mentioned in the chapter and test it from your main method.

2. Write a method that computes the area of a circle. Note the area formula is

```
area = PI * r * r
```

3. Write a series of methods that compute the area of a rectangle for int, long, and double values.

PART II

OBJECT-ORIENTED PROGRAMMING

CHAPTER 6

CLASSES

A t this point in the book you have learned all the basic tools required to build computer programs: data types, variables, operators, conditional statements, iterative statements, and methods. You learned how a large problem can be broken down into smaller sub-problems that are easier to solve through a technique called divide and conquer. Divide and conquer was successful in solving a specific set of problems, but now I want to turn your attention toward solving a generic set of problems.

With the techniques discussed thus far, how could you represent a car in Java? What are the attributes of a car? What are the types of actions you can perform on or with a car?

The attributes of a car can represent both physical properties as well as the state of the car (see Tables 6.1 and 6.2).

TABLE 6.1   Physical Attributes of a Car

Attribute	Description
Engine	The type of engine
Wheels	Four wheels—these could have attributes of their own: remaining tread, temperature, amount of air
BodyType	The type of the body: coupe, convertible, targa top
Windshield	The type and style of windshield
Doors	Four doors
Radiator	The car's radiator
TopSpeed	How fast can the car go?
Gas cap	You get the point…

TABLE 6.2   State Attributes of a Car

Attribute	Description
Running	Is the car running?
CurrentSpeed	What is the current speed of the car?
CurrentOil	How much oil does the car have?
CurrentFuel	How much gas does the car have?
Direction	What direction is the car facing?
GlobalLocation	The location of the car (using a GPS system)

Tables 6.1 and 6.2 show a small subset of all the attributes that could describe a car or its state.

Now consider the actions that a car can perform or that you can perform with a car (see Table 6.3).

TABLE 6.3   Car Actions

Action	Description
TurnOn	Start the car
TurnOff	Turn off the car

TABLE 6.3   Continued

Action	Description
Accelerate	Accelerate the car
Decelerate	Decelerate the car
Turn	Change the car's direction (right or left)
AddGas	Increase the car's fuel
AddOil	Add oil to the car

With all these attributes and actions defined for a car, how might a car be represented in a Java program? The physical and state attributes could be represented by variables, and the actions could be represented by methods (see Listing 6.1).

LISTING 6.1   CarTest.java

```java
public class CarTest {
  static final int COUPE = 1;
  static final int CONVERTIBLE = 2;
  static final int T_TOP = 3;

  static final int V4 = 1;
  static final int V6 = 2;
  static final int V8 = 3;
  static final int V10 = 4;

  static int engineType;
  static int bodyType;
  static int topSpeed;
  static int gas;
  static int oil;
  static boolean isRunning;
  static int currentSpeed;

  public static void turnOn() {
    isRunning = true;
  }

  public static void turnOff() {
    isRunning = false;
  }

  public static void accelerate() {
    switch( engineType ) {
    case V4:
      speedUp( 2 );
      break;
    case V6:
```

LISTING 6.1   Continued

```
        speedUp( 3 );
        break;
      case V8:
        speedUp( 4 );
        break;
      case V10:
        speedUp( 5 );
        break;
    }
  }

  public static void speedUp( int amount ) {
    if( isRunning == false ) {
      // Do nothing - car is not running!
      return;
    }

    if( ( currentSpeed + amount ) >= topSpeed ) {
      currentSpeed = topSpeed;
    }
    else {
      currentSpeed += amount;
    }
  }

  public static void decelerate() {
    if( isRunning == false ) {
      // Do nothing - car is not running!
      return;
    }

    if( ( currentSpeed - 5 ) <= 0 ) {
      currentSpeed = 0;
    }
    else {
      currentSpeed -= 5;
    }
  }

  public static void main( String[] args ) {
    // Define the attributes of the car
    engineType = V10;
    bodyType = CONVERTIBLE;
    topSpeed = 185;
    isRunning = false;
    currentSpeed = 0;

    // Do some things with the car
    turnOn();
    for( int i=0; i<10; i++ ) {
      accelerate();
      System.out.println( "Current Speed: " + currentSpeed );
```

LISTING 6.1   Continued

```
      }

    for( int i=0; i<5; i++ ) {
      decelerate();
      System.out.println( "Current Speed: " + currentSpeed );
    }
    turnOff();
  }
}
```

The `CarTest` class defines several class variables and static methods that manipulate those variables; this effectively represents a car. Now what would happen if you want to represent two cars?

Using the techniques presented thus far you are forced to define a new set of variables and methods for the second car; for example, `accelerate2()`, `speedUp2()`, and so on. This creates considerably more work, but most of it revolves around copying the methods and renaming them—it is not desirable but feasible.

Finally, what happens when you want to represent an arbitrary number of cars? These techniques cannot solve this problem!

The next evolutionary step in software development history was to group attributes into what are referred to as *data structures*. Data structures can contain multiple attributes, used to represent real-world objects such as a car. In Java a data structure is referred to as a *class*. Thus, you can define a `Car` class that contains all the attributes of a car, and then create methods that operate on a generic car. Listing 6.2 displays the code that represents a `Car`, and Listing 6.3 defines a new class `CarTest2` that uses the `Car` class.

LISTING 6.2   Car.java

```
public class Car {
  public static final int COUPE = 1;
  public static final int CONVERTIBLE = 2;
  public static final int T_TOP = 3;

  public static final int V4 = 1;
  public static final int V6 = 2;
  public static final int V8 = 3;
  public static final int V10 = 4;

  public int engineType;
  public int bodyType;
  public int topSpeed;
  public int gas;
  public int oil;
  public boolean isRunning;
  public int currentSpeed;
}
```

LISTING 6.3   CarTest2.java

```java
public class CarTest2 {
    public static void turnOn( Car c ) {
      c.isRunning = true;
    }

    public static void turnOff( Car c ) {
      c.isRunning = false;
    }

    public static void accelerate( Car c ) {
      switch( c.engineType ) {
      case Car.V4:
        speedUp( c, 2 );
        break;
      case Car.V6:
        speedUp( c, 3 );
        break;
      case Car.V8:
        speedUp( c, 4 );
        break;
      case Car.V10:
        speedUp( c, 5 );
        break;
      }
    }

    public static void speedUp( Car c, int amount ) {
      if( c.isRunning == false ) {
        // Do nothing - car is not running!
        return;
      }

      if( ( c.currentSpeed + amount ) >= c.topSpeed ) {
        c.currentSpeed = c.topSpeed;
      }
      else {
        c.currentSpeed += amount; }
    }

    public static void decelerate( Car c ) {

      if( c.isRunning == false ) {
        // Do nothing - car is not running!
        return;
      }

      if( ( c.currentSpeed - 5 ) <= 0 ) {
        c.currentSpeed = 0;
      }
      else {
        c.currentSpeed -= 5;
      }
```

LISTING 6.3   Continued

```java
  }

  public static void main( String[] args ) {
    // Define the attributes of the car
    Car c1 = new Car();
    c1.engineType = Car.V10;
    c1.bodyType = Car.CONVERTIBLE;
    c1.topSpeed = 185;
    c1.isRunning = false;
    c1.currentSpeed = 0;

    // Do some things with the car
    turnOn( c1 );
    for( int i=0; i<10; i++ ) {
      accelerate( c1 );
      System.out.println( "Current Speed: " + c1.currentSpeed );
    }

    for( int i=0; i<5; i++ ) {
      decelerate( c1 );
      System.out.println( "Current Speed: " + c1.currentSpeed );
    }
    turnOff( c1 );
  }

}
```

Listing 6.2 defines a new class named Car, which contains all the attributes that were defined as class variables in the CarTest example. Listing 6.3 defines a new class named CarTest2, which defines a main method that creates a new *instance* of the Car class and sends that Car instance to its set of methods.

To compile these two classes, put the contents of the Car class into a file named Car.java, and the contents of the CarTest2 class into a file named CarTest2.java and place both files in the same directory. You can then compile the classes individually:

```
javac Car.java
javac CarTest2.java
```

Or, you can compile the CarTest2 class and it will find the Car class for you. Remember that you can only launch classes that have a main method in them, so you cannot launch the Car class directly; you can however launch the CarTest2 class and it will reference the Car class for you:

```
java CarTest2
```

Looking at the code for the CarTest2 class, class instances are created using the Java keyword *new*. The general form of the *new* keyword is

```
ClassName var = new ClassName();
```

Thus, the data type of var is ClassName and it is assigned the value of a new instance of ClassName. This is accomplished in CarTest2 as follows:

```
Car c1 = new Car();
```

So, c1 is a Car and is assigned the value of a new instance of a Car. Just like you can use a variable that is an int or a char, you can use a Car variable. Classes are a little different from primitive data types such as ints and chars in that they have attributes that can be accessed using the dot (.) operator. To access the car's engineType attribute, you reference the Car instance variable, append a dot to it, and then reference the attribute by name:

```
c1.engineType = Car.V10;
```

This statement accesses c1's engineType attribute and assigns it the value Car.V10. The Car class defines a set of constants that represent engine type values that are static. Remember that there is only one instance of all static variables and methods for all instances of a class. Therefore, the V10 attribute can be accessed by specifying the class name Car and the attribute V10 without using the Car instance c1. The attributes however, are not static and are thus associated with a specific instance of the Car class. If you define two Car instances, they will share the same static constant values, but they will have their own engine type, body type, and top speed.

All the methods in the CarTest2 class are defined to accept an instance of the Car class as the first parameter—these methods manipulate the attributes of a Car instance. You can therefore create one hundred different instances of the Car class and pass each one to any of these methods, and they would know how to manipulate the car.

Classes used as data structures solve a vast array of problems. They are an abstraction of disparate data types combined to represent a real-world object. Until the early '90s this is how almost all programming problems were solved, but there is still one set of problems. The accelerate method works great for a Car, but what about accelerating a Truck or a Motorcycle? What does a Truck's attribute care about a method that can manipulate a Car? If a Car's accelerate method is going to exclusively operate on a Car, why is it in a global area that everyone can see and not directly associated with a Car?

The answer lies in a development paradigm that appeared in the mainstream in the early '90s called *object-oriented programming*.

Object-Oriented Programming

After years of developing applications using data structures and the divide and conquer technique, a new thought-pattern emerged that modeled computer programs after real-world objects. The thought is that you do not think of a car as a set of attributes, and then define methods to manipulate those attributes. You instead think of a car in terms of both attributes and behavior: a car has an engine, four wheels, and two doors and you can turn it on, accelerate it, put it in reverse, and turn it off. Because real-world objects do not decouple the interaction between attributes and actions (behavior), why should computer programs?

When you accelerate a car you don't need to think about a fuel tank firing gas into a combustion chamber, which generates heat and eventually turns the wheels; you just press the gas pedal and the car goes—the things happening internally do not concern you!

A *class* represents an object in Java. Thus, when analyzing your problem and designing your classes you can start thinking in terms of objects that can be used to solve your problem. And, if you do a good enough job, you can define an object that you can reuse later in a different application.

Encapsulation

When properly designed, Java objects can act as black boxes. Which means you know the information that you pass to the object, and you know the expected result from invoking methods, but you do not know anything about the internal implementation of those methods. This is a powerful programming paradigm because it enables you, as the object developer, to change the underlying implementation without affecting the applications that are using your objects. This object-oriented principal is referred to as *encapsulation*. Your Java classes are encapsulating data and attributes in such a way that they provide a programmatic interface that enables you to use the object without knowing the underlying implementation.

Information Hiding

A very similar object-oriented concept to encapsulation is *information hiding*. When building your objects you choose the information that you want to publish to consumers of your objects, and the information that you want to keep private to your implementation. In the car example you might want to expose the method `accelerate`, but hide the `speedUp` method. It is an internal method that `accelerate` needs, but it should never be accessed by applications using the `Car` class.

Classes

Now that you have an idea about what objects and classes are, let's formalize some terms:

- Objects in Java are implemented as *classes*; they are sometimes referred to as *user-defined data types* or *programmer defined data types*

- Object attributes are implemented as *class variables* or *instance variables*

- Behaviors are implemented as *class methods*

CarObject Class

Listing 6.4 shows an object-oriented implementation of the `CarObject` class, and Listing 6.5 shows a new test application, `CarTest3`, which uses the new `CarObject` class.

LISTING 6.4   CarObject.java

```java
public class CarObject {
  public static final int COUPE = 1;
  public static final int CONVERTIBLE = 2;
  public static final int T_TOP = 3;

  public static final int V4 = 1;
  public static final int V6 = 2;
  public static final int V8 = 3;
  public static final int V10 = 4;

  private int engineType;
  private int bodyType;
  private int topSpeed;
  private int gas;
  private int oil;
  private boolean running;
  private int currentSpeed = 0;

  public CarObject() {
  }

  public CarObject( int engineType,
                    int bodyType,
                    int topSpeed ) {
     this.engineType = engineType;
     this.bodyType = bodyType;
     this.topSpeed = topSpeed;
  }

  public int getEngineType() {
     return this.engineType;
  }

  public void setEngineType( int engineType ) {
     if( engineType >= V4 && engineType <= V10 ) {
        this.engineType = engineType;
     }
  }

  public int getBodyType() {
     return this.bodyType;
  }

  public void setBodyType( int bodyType ) {
     if( bodyType >= COUPE && bodyType <= T_TOP ) {
        this.bodyType = bodyType;
     }
  }

  public int getTopSpeed() {
     return this.topSpeed;
  }

  public void setTopSpeed( int topSpeed ) {
```

LISTING 6.4   Continued

```
        if( topSpeed > 0 ) {
            this.topSpeed = topSpeed;
        }
    }

    public boolean isRunning() {
        return this.running;
    }

    public int getCurrentSpeed() {
        return this.currentSpeed;
    }

    public void turnOn() {
      running = true;
    }

    public void turnOff() {
      running = false;
    }

    public void accelerate() {
      switch( engineType ) {
      case V4:
        speedUp( 2 );
        break;
      case V6:
        speedUp( 3 );
        break;
      case V8:
        speedUp( 4 );
        break;
      case V10:
        speedUp( 5 );
        break;
      }
    }

    private void speedUp( int amount ) {
      if( running == false ) {
        // Do nothing - car is not running!
        return;
      }

      if( ( currentSpeed + amount ) >= topSpeed ) {
        currentSpeed = topSpeed;
      }
      else {
        currentSpeed += amount;
      }
    }

    public void decelerate() {
      if( running == false ) {
```

LISTING 6.4   Continued

```
        // Do nothing - car is not running!
        return;
    }

    if( ( currentSpeed - 5 ) <= 0 ) {
      currentSpeed = 0;
    }
    else {
      currentSpeed -= 5;
    }
  }
}
```

LISTING 6.5   CarTest3.java

```
public class CarTest3 {
    public static void main( String[] args ) {
        // Define the attributes of the car
        CarObject car = new CarObject( CarObject.V10,
                                       CarObject.CONVERTIBLE,
                                       185 );

        // Do some things with the car
        car.turnOn();
        for( int i=0; i<10; i++ ) {
            car.accelerate();
            System.out.println( "Current Speed: " + car.getCurrentSpeed() );
        }

        for( int i=0; i<5; i++ ) {
            car.decelerate();
            System.out.println( "Current Speed: " + car.getCurrentSpeed() );
        }
        car.turnOff();
    }
}
```

Component Attributes

The CarObject has the component, or physical attributes defined in Table 6.4—this is a subset of the attributes defined in Table 6.1.

TABLE 6.4   CarObject Component Attributes

Attribute	Description
engineType	The car's engine type; one of the constants defined in the class: V4, V6, V8, V10
bodyType	The car's body type; one of the constants defined in the class: COUPE, CONVERTIBLE, T_TOP
topSpeed	The car's top speed

The component attributes are those attributes that define physical properties of an object; this could include things such as an engine object, wheels, doors, horsepower, and so on.

State Attributes

The `CarObject` has the state attributes defined in Table 6.5—this is a subset of the attributes defined in Table 6.2.

TABLE 6.5 `CarObject` State Attributes

Attribute	Description
gas	The amount of gas in the car's gas tank
oil	The amount of oil in the car's oil tank
currentSpeed	How fast is the car currently going
running	Is the car running

The state attributes define those attributes that change over time.

There is not a functional difference between component and state attributes, just a logical difference. It is given here as an illustration to encourage your thought process in defining your objects.

Behavior (Methods)

Table 6.6 defines the `CarObject`'s behavioral methods.

TABLE 6.6 `CarObject` State Attributes

Method	Description
turnOn	Turns the car on
turnOff	Turns the car off
accelerate	Accelerates the car; increases the current speed
decelerate	Decelerates the car; decreases the current speed

The behavioral methods are defined to control the object and cause the object to perform some action. In this case the `accelerate` and `decelerate` methods, along with changing the current speed of the car, also perform validation checks to see if the car is running, and if accelerating or decelerating the car has an impact on the current speed.

Get/Set Methods

Why provide methods to get and set the values of attributes rather than allow them to be modified directly?

There are actually a two answers to this question:

1. They enable you to validate the value being assigned to the attribute. In this example the engineType can have only one of four values, but because it is an int, if the user had access to the attribute directly, what is stopping him from setting it to 1000? The compiler will enforce the valid range of integers, but knows nothing about the limitation we are imposing in this class.

2. Some values might be read only—in this example the currentSpeed is read only—the accelerate and decelerate methods can modify the current speed, and the user can query the car for the current speed but cannot access it directly.

Validating values being assigned to attributes is an essential function of the encapsulation object-oriented concept. Consider a Fraction class, see Listing 6.6.

LISTING 6.6   Fraction.java

```java
public class Fraction
{
    private int numerator = 1;
    private int denominator = 1;

    public Fraction( int numerator,
                     int denominator ) {
        this.numerator = numerator;
        if( denominator != 0 ) {
            this.denominator = denominator;
        }
    }

    public int getNumerator() {
        return this.numerator;
    }

    public void setNumerator( int numerator ) {
        this.numerator = numerator;
    }

    public int getDenominator() {
        return this.denominator;
    }

    public void setDenominator( int denominator ) {
        if( denominator != 0 ) {
            this.denominator = denominator;
        }
    }
```

LISTING 6.6   Continued

```
    public float getFraction() {
        return ( float )numerator / ( float )denominator;
    }

    public static void main( String[] args ) {
        Fraction f = new Fraction( 3, 4 );
        System.out.println( "3/4 = " + f.getFraction() );
    }
}
```

Note the **setDenominator** method in Listing 6.6. It validates that the value set in the denominator is not zero before making the assignment. If this value was not validated, or if the **denominator** value was publicly accessible, then every use of the **denominator** would have to be checked for zero. At this point you control the valid values that the denominator can be set to, so you can program your class assuming that the value is valid, knowing that you will not allow it to ever become invalid.

The **Car** class controls access to all its attributes; **currentSpeed** and **running** are read only, the **engineType** and **bodyType** are restricted to a limited subset of integer values, and **topSpeed** is restricted to positive integer values.

Constructors

There are two suspicious looking methods in the **CarObject** class: **CarObject()** and **CarObject(...)**. These methods have names that match the class name and have no return values.

These methods are referred to as *constructors* and define initialization information to use when constructing the class. Classes are constructed using the **new** operator that has this form:

```
CarObject myCar = new CarObject();
CarObject myOtherCar = new CarObject( CarObject.V6, CarObject.COUPE, 120 );
```

Recall that primitive types are built as follows:

```
int n = 5;
```

This definition allocated enough memory to hold an integer and assigned the value 5 to that memory location. When classes are constructed, the following steps are performed:

1. Allocate memory for the class

2. Create and initialize the class variables (in this case they are all primitive types)

3. Call the appropriate constructor for additional initialization

4. Return a reference to the memory location allocated in step 1

Both **myCar** and **myOtherCar** are references to **CarObject**'s in memory. **myCar** uses the *default constructor*, or the constructor that does not take any parameters, and **myOtherCar** uses the constructor that accepts three parameters. Constructors, just like methods, can be overloaded as many times as you want, as long as the signature is different between each constructor. After both cars are constructed, `myOtherCar` has a body type of `CarObject.COUPE`, but what about `myCar`?

When class variables are created, but not initialized they have the default values shown in Table 6.7.

TABLE 6.7   Class Variable Default Values

Data Type	Default Value
Numeric	0
boolean	false
char	0
Object	null

All numeric types (`int`, `float`, `long`, and so on) and `char` are assigned an initial value of 0. All `boolean`s are initialized to `false`, and all objects (classes) are initialized to `null`.

So `myCar` has an initial body type of 0, which coincidentally is not valid!

Note

One last note about default constructors: If you do not specify any constructor, a default constructor that accepts no parameters and does not do anything, is provided for you. But if you provide one or more constructors, if you want a default constructor, you must define one yourself.

Class Scope

A class's variables and methods belong to that class's *scope*; they are available inside methods in that class by their name. Publicly available variables are accessible outside the class through a *handle*; the instance variable name followed by a dot, followed by the variable or method name:

```
CarObject myCar = new CarObject();
myCar.setEngineType( CarObject.V10 );
```

Or more generically:

```
objectReferenceName.objectMemberName
```

Controlling Access to Members

Java enables you to control access to methods and attributes using *access modifiers*. A method or attribute can be defined to be `public`, which enables it to be accessed by external classes or be defined to be `private` to ensure that only methods internal to the class can access them.

The CarObject class defines all attributes to be private, and thus not accessible from outside the class. It defines a set of public methods that act as a public interface by which external classes can use the car: turnOn, accelerate, isRunning, and so on.

this Variable

All class variables are available by name in each method in the class. If a method's parameter list contains a variable with the same name as a class variable, how are the two variables differentiated? Why would you want to do this?

Each class instance has an implicit this variable that can access all class information: both class variables and class methods. Class variables and class methods can be accessed by prefacing the variable or method name with the keyword this followed by a dot. The setTopSpeed method differentiates between the parameter variable topSpeed and a class variable topSpeed in the following code segment:

```
public void setTopSpeed( int topSpeed ) {
    if( topSpeed > 0 ) {
        this.topSpeed = topSpeed;
    }
}
```

Because of the this keyword, you can qualify the variable you are referencing explicitly, so you do not have to devise a different naming convention to differentiate between parameter and class variables. There are conventions that are commonly used in other programming languages, for example C++ has two: precede class variables with an underscore, _topSpeed or precede class variables with an m_, for example m_topSpeed. These conventions are perfectly acceptable, but it makes the code a little more cryptic to read. The Java programming guidelines recommend that you use the explicit this referencing for class variables when there is a naming conflict.

Constants

As previously discussed, class-level constants can be defined by using the final keyword. Typically, constants are public so that other classes can see the values. They are usually associated with a class attribute, and constants are usually static, meaning that there is only one for all instances of a class—if the value cannot change, why create multiple versions of it in memory?

The CarObject class defines a set of constant values for its engine and body types:

```
public static final int COUPE = 1;
public static final int CONVERTIBLE = 2;
public static final int T_TOP = 3;

public static final int V4 = 1;
public static final int V6 = 2;
public static final int V8 = 3;
public static final int V10 = 4;
```

Note

Java constants have a type associated with them; in the `CarObject` they are all defined to be `int`s. This is important because the constants have the same properties in numerical computations and comparisons as their variable equivalents. Many programming languages do not enforce this constraint, and therefore constants can be misused or generate unexpected results in computations; Java protects you from this.

Composition

All the attributes of the `CarObject` class are primitive types, but there is nothing stopping the `CarObject` from having attributes that are of object types. Consider defining an `Engine` class and creating an instance of that `Engine` inside the `CarObject` class:

```
public class Engine {
  ...
}

public class Car {
  private Engine myEngine;
}
```

The concept of a class containing another class is *composition*, a class can be composed of other classes. This is powerful object-oriented programming paradigm because it enables you to create a class, such as `Engine`, and reuse it—after you have built it once, for a `CarObject` for example, you never have to rebuild it, for a `TruckObject` for example.

Garbage Collection

What happens in Java when an object is no longer needed? In C++, when you are done using an object you must explicitly delete that object—if you forget, the memory used by that object will be lost until the program is shutdown. The designers of Java saw this as a major headache and an overhead step that programmers should not be burdened with, so they devised a new programming paradigm revolving around a process known as the garbage collector. When you no longer need a variable in Java, you can assign it a `null` value, enable it to reference a different region in memory (either by assigning it to another object or creating a new object), or let the variable go *out of scope* (leave the block of code that the variable is defined in).

When there is a region in memory that is no longer accessible, it is eligible for garbage collection. Java has a process running in the background that looks for these objects, but only when the application is running low on memory. When that region of memory is *orphaned*, it might be reclaimed by the system immediately, or in a few minutes. Or, if the system has ample memory, it might only be reclaimed when the application shuts down. Java manages all your memory for you.

```
System.gc()
```

If you want to request garbage collection, you can make a call to the `System` class's `gc()` static method. This method call requests that garbage collection run, but it in no way forces the Java Virtual Machine to perform garbage collection.

Finalizers

If Java is managing your memory, can you do anything to cleanup your objects before they are deleted from memory? This question is derived from my C++ background, and a C++ programming practice known as *smart objects*. The general concept is that you create a smart object that wraps any resource you are using, for example a handle to file; you open the file in the constructor, and then close the file in the *destructor* (the C++ class method that is called when an object is deleted). This programming paradigm ensures that resources are never lost; a file that is opened is always closed.

Java does not have destructors, per se, but it does have a similar construct known as a *finalizer*. Classes can define a `finalize` method that can be called when an object is deleted from memory. Finalization must be explicitly enabled by calling the `System` class's `runFinalization()` method. This method call only suggests that the garbage collector call the `finalize` method on objects that are targeted for garbage collection before reclaiming memory.

The bottom line is that you cannot control when garbage collection is run, or if the finalizer is ever called. If you are coming from C++ and enjoyed writing smart objects, this is one limitation of the Java programming language. But do not get discouraged, I have been enveloped into the deepest regions of Java programming and this is really the only limitation that I have found that I dislike about the language. Considering that you do not have to worry about memory management in anyway, it is a good trade-off.

Before leaving garbage collection and finalizers, here is a rough outline of the lifecycle of a Java object:

1. Memory is allocated for the object

2. Attributes are initialized

3. The appropriate constructor is called

4. The object is used in your program

5. The reference to the object is disassociated with object in memory

6. At some point Java's garbage collection runs and sees that the memory is no longer being used

7. The garbage collector optionally calls the object's `finalize` method

8. The garbage collector frees the memory

Static Class Members

Remember that there is only one instance of static variables or methods that are defined for a class. Therefore, if you were to have 100 instances of the `CarObject` class, there would be only one `COUPE` variable in memory, shared by all the instances. Static variables are good to use for constants and those variables that are global to all instances of your class; they are sometimes used to count class instances. Personally, I reserve static variables for defining constants.

Static methods are useful because they do not require an instance of your class to be created; that is why you can call `System.out.println()` without having to create an instance of the `System` class. The `out` variable is static to the `System` class so you can access it as `System.out`.

Inner Classes

Classes can be defined inside of other classes; these are called *inner classes*. Fundamentally inner classes are the same as any other class except that they are defined inside the body of another class. For example:

```
public class Outer {
    public class Inner {
        private int i;
        public void myMethod(){ … }
    }
}
```

Scope

An inner class defined outside a method belongs to the class and has class scope (similar to member variables). Instances of the inner class can be created in any method of the outer class.

Inner classes can also be defined inside a method; an inner class declared inside a method belongs to the method and has local (method) scope (similar to automatic variables). That method can create instances of that class, but other methods of the outer class cannot see this inner class.

Inner classes defined inside a method have some limitations:

- They cannot be declared with an access modifier

- They cannot be declared static

- Inner classes with local scope can only access variables of the enclosing method that are declared final, referring to a local variable of the method or an argument passed into the enclosing method

Inner classes have full visibility to their outer classes' variables and methods. Listing 6.7 demonstrates this.

LISTING 6.7   `Outer.java`

```
public class Outer
{
    private int a = 5;
    public class Inner {
        private int i=1;
        public void myMethod() {
            System.out.println( "a=" + a + ", i=" + i );
        }
    }

    public static void main( String[] args ) {
        Outer.Inner innerClass = new Outer().new Inner();
        innerClass.myMethod();
    }
}
```

The inner class, `Inner`, can access its own member variable `i` as well as the outer class `Outer`'s member variable `a`, even though it is private.

Access Modifiers

Because inner classes defined outside a method behave similar to member variables, the access modifier that you choose to assign to that class controls whether that class can be accessed outside of the outer class. If you declare the inner class to be public, it can be accessed by prefixing the inner class name with the outer class name. An instance of the outer class must exist for this to be possible. For example:

```
Outer outer = new Outer();
Outer.Inner inner = o.new Inner()
```

Or:

```
Outer.Inner inner = new Outer().new Inner();
```

Static Inner Classes

Inner classes, such as class variables and methods, can be declared to be **static**. Because they are static, they are not associated with an instance of an outer class. This means that you can create an instance of the inner class without having to create an instance of the outer class. Static inner classes have some limitations regarding accessing the outer class's methods:

- Methods of a static inner class cannot access instance variables of the outer class
- Methods of a static inner class can only access static variables of the outer class

Listing 6.8 demonstrates these two limitations.

LISTING 6.8   `OuterTest.java`

```java
public class OuterTest
{
    public static int outerInt = 5;

    public static class StaticInner {
        public static int doubleVal( int n ) {
            System.out.println( "outerInt=" + outerInt );
            return 2*n;
        }
    }

    public void testInner() {
        int a = 5;
        System.out.println( "a=" + a + ", doubleVal=" +
                            StaticInner.doubleVal( a ) );
    }

    public static void main( String[] args ) {
        int n = 7;
        System.out.println( "n=" + n + ", doubleVal=" +
                            OuterTest.StaticInner.doubleVal( n ) );
        OuterTest out = new OuterTest();
        out.testInner();
    }
}
```

The inner class, `StaticInner`, accesses the outer class `OuterTest`'s static variable `outerInt` in the `doubleVal` method call. If `outerInt` was not defined to be `static`, the `StaticInner` class could not access it. The `main` method demonstrates that you do not need to create an instance of the outer class to access a `static` inner class when it makes the following call:

```java
OuterTest.StaticInner.doubleVal( n )
```

Anonymous Inner Classes

There is a category of inner classes that will be discussed extensively in Chapter 14, "Event Delegation Model," called *anonymous classes*. They have the following properties:

- Created with no name
- Defined inside a method
- Have no constructor
- Declared and constructed in the same statement
- Useful for event handling (Chapter 14)

Chapter 14 will show a complete example demonstrating common usage.

Understanding Object References

When you create a variable that is an instance of a class, you are actually creating a reference to that class instance. The reference is defined to know how to access its class, but not to be tightly coupled with any particular instance. If you were to create two instances of a class, and then assign one to the other, both variables will be referencing the same object. Listing 6.7 demonstrates this.

LISTING 6.7   Number.java

```java
public class Number {
    private int number;

    public Number( int number ) {
        this.number = number;
    }

    public int getNumber() {
        return this.number;
    }

    public void setNumber( int number ) {
        this.number = number;
    }

    public static void main( String[] args ) {
        Number one = new Number( 1 );
        Number two = new Number( 2 );
        System.out.println( "Beginning: " );
        System.out.println( "One = " + one.getNumber() );
        System.out.println( "Two = " + two.getNumber() );

        // Assign two to one
        two = one;
        System.out.println( "\nAfter assigning two to one: " );
        System.out.println( "One = " + one.getNumber() );
        System.out.println( "Two = " + two.getNumber() );

        // Change the value of two
        two.setNumber( 3 );
        System.out.println( "\nAfter modifying two: " );
        System.out.println( "One = " + one.getNumber() );
        System.out.println( "Two = " + two.getNumber() );
    }
}
```

The output of the Number class is

```
Beginning:
One = 1
Two = 2
```

LISTING 6.7   Continued

```
After assigning two to one:
One = 1
Two = 1

After modifying two:
One = 3
Two = 3
```

From this output you can see that assigning the `Number` variable `two` to the `Number` variable `one` actually made `two` point to the same memory as `one`. Then, when `two` was modified, it affected the value of `one`.

Therefore, when you pass an object reference to a method, it is passed to that method *by reference*. If the method modifies the object, the original object is also modified. This is a powerful feature for performance because the Java Runtime Engine does not have to make a copy of the class when passing it to a method, but be aware of the potential side effects!

Summary

This chapter covered quite a bit of material. It discussed the basics of object-oriented programming, the use of Java classes, Java Constructors, and scoping rules. It discussed access modifiers, the `this` variables, how garbage collection works, inner classes, and finally the way that Java references objects.

In the next chapter we will continue down the path of object-oriented concepts and jump into inheritance.

Review Questions

1. Define encapsulation.

2. What is the purpose of the get/set methods?

3. What is a constructor? When is it called?

4. What is the difference between a `public` variable and a `private` variable?

5. What is the `this` variable, and what is it used for?

6. What is composition?

7. What is garbage collection, and when is it run?

8. What is an inner class, and what types of inner classes can you create?

9. What does "pass by reference" mean?

10. What is significant about the fact that object variables are really references to objects?

Exercises

1. In the chapter we modeled a car and created a `CarObject` class. Create a `Dog` class and a `Cat` class; be sure to include functionality such as eating and speaking.

2. Create a class named `Calculator` with a static inner class named `Math` that provides methods such as `add`, `subtract`, `multiply`, `divide`, and `modulus`.

CHAPTER 7

INHERITANCE

You will learn the following in this chapter:

- The object-oriented concept of inheritance
- Java's implementation of inheritance
- Superclasses and subclasses
- Abstract classes
- Final classes
- Guidelines to using inheritance

*I*n the previous chapter you learned about creating objects called classes that represent real-world objects. In this chapter you will learn another powerful concept in the object-oriented arena called *inheritance*.

Problem Derivation

In the previous chapter we created a `CarObject` class that represented a car, but now I want to create two specific types of cars: a Porsche and a Pinto. Before diving into the differences between these two types of cars, which my students have greatly enjoyed, I want to preface this discussion by telling you that when I was a child my grandparents replaced my mother's Chevy Super Sport with a Ford Pinto. All the presuppositions you might have about Pintos are quite true: max speeds reaching close to 60 mph on a downhill, and, yes, you do have to push the car up hills. So, before emailing me in opposition to the humorous comparison between a Porsche and a Pinto, rest assured that I am speaking from my own personal experience.

Let's comprise a list of all the attributes we can think of specifically related to highly tuned Porsches. This list could include

- Horse power: about 450
- Maximum speed: 220 mph
- Acceleration: 0–60 in 3.5 seconds

- Doors: 2

- Paint: red or yellow, take your pick

- Turbos: 2 (twin turbo)

- Gas

- Oil

- Transmission: Tiptronic

- Nitrous Oxide System (NOS)

The following could be methods that we could apply to the Porsche class:

- Start

- Stop

- Accelerate

- Decelerate

- Engage turbos

- Turn on NOS

- Turn off NOS

Listing 7.1 shows a partial implementation of the code for the `Porsche` class.

LISTING 7.1   Porsche.java

```java
public class Porsche
{
    public static final int TIPTRONIC = 1;

    // Attributes
    private int horsePower = 450;
    private int maximumSpeed = 220;
    private int numberOfDoors = 2;
    private String paint = "Yellow";
    private int turbos = 2;
    private int gasCapacity = 15;
    private int oilCapacity = 5;
    private int transmission = TIPTRONIC;
    private boolean nos;

    // State attributes
    private boolean turbo1Engaged = false;
    private boolean turbo2Engaged = false;
    private boolean nosEnabled = false;
    private boolean running = false;
    private int currentSpeed;
```

LISTING 7.1   Continued

```java
private int currentGas;
private int currentOil;

public Porsche()
{
}

public void start()
{
    running = true;
}

public void stop()
{
    running = false;
}

public boolean isRunning()
{
    return running;
}

public void accelerate()
{
    // Check to see if we are running or not
    if( running == false )
    {
        return;
    }

    // Create a variable representing how much we are going to
    // accelerate this second
    int increment = 15;

    // Check the turbos; they add 5mph per second acceleration
    if( turbo1Engaged )
    {
        increment += 5;
    }
    if( turbo2Engaged )
    {
        increment += 5;
    }

    // Check the NOS; it represents 15mph per second
    if( nos )
    {
        increment += 15;
    }

    // Increment the current speed
    currentSpeed += increment;
```

LISTING 7.1   Continued

```java
        if( currentSpeed > maximumSpeed ) currentSpeed = maximumSpeed;
    }

    public void decelerate()
    {
        currentSpeed -= 20;
        if( currentSpeed < 0 ) currentSpeed = 0;
    }

    public void engageTurbos()
    {
        turbo1Engaged = true;
        turbo2Engaged = true;
    }

    public void disengageTurbos()
    {
        turbo1Engaged = false;
        turbo2Engaged = false;
    }

    public void engageNOS()
    {
        nos = true;
        maximumSpeed += 50;
    }

    public void disengageNOS()
    {
        nos = false;
        maximumSpeed -= 50;
    }

    public int getCurrentSpeed()
    {
        return currentSpeed;
    }

    public String toString()
    {
        return "A shiny new " + paint + " Porsche!";
    }

    public static void main( String[] args )
    {
        Porsche p = new Porsche();
        System.out.println( "My new car: " + p );
        p.start();
        System.out.println( "Current speed: " + p.getCurrentSpeed() );
        for( int i=0; i<20; i++ )
        {
            if( i == 5 )
```

LISTING 7.1   Continued

```
            {
                p.engageTurbos();
            }
            else if( i == 14 )
            {
                p.engageNOS();
            }
            p.accelerate();
            System.out.println( "Current speed: " + p.getCurrentSpeed() );
        }
        p.disengageNOS();
        p.disengageTurbos();
        while( p.getCurrentSpeed() > 0 )
        {
            p.decelerate();
            System.out.println( "Current speed: " + p.getCurrentSpeed() );
        }
        p.stop();
    }
}
```

The output of Listing 7.1 should be similar to the following:

```
My new car: A shiny new Yellow Porsche!
Current speed: 0
Current speed: 15
Current speed: 30
Current speed: 45
Current speed: 60
Current speed: 75
Current speed: 100
Current speed: 125
Current speed: 150
Current speed: 175
Current speed: 200
Current speed: 220
Current speed: 220
Current speed: 220
Current speed: 220
Current speed: 260
Current speed: 270
Current speed: 270
Current speed: 270
Current speed: 270
Current speed: 270
Current speed: 250
Current speed: 230
Current speed: 210
Current speed: 190
Current speed: 170
Current speed: 150
Current speed: 130
```

```
Current speed: 110
Current speed: 90
Current speed: 70
Current speed: 50
Current speed: 30
Current speed: 10
Current speed: 0
```

The `main()` method creates a new `Porsche`, starts it, accelerates it for five seconds, engages the turbos, accelerates for another nine seconds, and then kicks in the NOS. Finally, it turns off the turbos and the NOS and decelerates until the car stops. The code in the `Porsche` class is fairly self-explanatory, but there is one helpful method added called `toString()`. You might have noticed in the `main()` method that we printed the `Porsche` instance p:

```
System.out.println( "My new car: " + p );
```

Whenever a class is used as a `String`, its `toString()` method is called, and the result of that method is added to the `String`. Thus, when we implement the `toString` method we can return a meaningful textual representation of our class; in this case:

`A shiny new Yellow Porsche!`

Now, on the other end of the spectrum we have the Pinto. The following could be attributes of the Pinto class:

- Horse power: about 50

- Maximum Speed: 60 mph

- Acceleration: 0–60 in 35 seconds

- Doors: 5

- Hatchback door

- Paint: two-tone

- Gas

- Oil

- Transmission: manual

And the following could be methods of the Pinto class:

- Start: Turn the car on

- Stop: Turn the car off

- Accelerate: increase the speed

- Decelerate: decrease the speed

- Open hatchback

- Close hatchback

- Push up hill

- Roll start

Listing 7.2 shows a partial implementation of the code for the `Pinto` class.

LISTING 7.2   `Pinto.java`

```java
public class Pinto
{
    public static final int MANUAL = 2;

    // Attributes
    private int horsePower = 50;
    private int maximumSpeed = 60;
    private int numberOfDoors = 5;
    private String paint = "Two-tone";
    private int gasCapacity = 15;
    private int oilCapacity = 5;
    private int transmission = MANUAL;

    // State attributes
    private boolean running = false;
    private int currentSpeed;
    private int currentGas;
    private int currentOil;
    public boolean hatchBackDoorOpen = false;

    public Pinto()
    {
    }

    public void start()
    {
        // It isn't going to start ;)
        running = false;
    }

    public void stop()
    {
        running = false;
    }

    public boolean isRunning()
    {
        return running;
    }

    public void accelerate()
    {
        // Check to see if we are running or not
        if( running == false )
        {
```

LISTING 7.2   Continued

```java
            return;
        }

        currentSpeed += 4;
        if( currentSpeed > maximumSpeed )
        {
            currentSpeed = maximumSpeed;

            // The high speed knocked the door open!
            openHatchBack();
        }
    }

    public void decelerate()
    {
        currentSpeed -= 5;
        if( currentSpeed < 0 ) currentSpeed = 0;
    }

    public int getCurrentSpeed()
    {
        return currentSpeed;
    }

    public void rollStart()
    {
        running = true;
    }

    public void pushUpHill()
    {
        System.out.println( "Ouch, this thing is heavy!" );
    }

    public void openHatchBack()
    {
        hatchBackDoorOpen = true;
    }

    public void closeHatchBack()
    {
        hatchBackDoorOpen = false;
    }

    public boolean isHatchBackDoorOpen()
    {
        return hatchBackDoorOpen;
    }

    public String toString()
    {
        return "A rusty old " + paint + " Pinto";
```

LISTING 7.2   Continued

```
    }

    public static void main( String[] args )
    {
        Pinto p = new Pinto();
        System.out.println( "My car: " + p );
        p.start();
        if( p.isRunning() == false )
        {
            System.out.println( "Starter failed, let's roll start it!" );
            p.rollStart();
        }
        System.out.println( "Current speed: " + p.getCurrentSpeed() +
                            ", Hatchback open = " + p.isHatchBackDoorOpen() );
        for( int i=0; i<20; i++ )
        {
            p.accelerate();
            System.out.println( "Current speed: " + p.getCurrentSpeed() +
                                ", Hatchback open = " + p.isHatchBackDoorOpen() );
        }
        while( p.getCurrentSpeed() > 0 )
        {
            p.decelerate();
            System.out.println( "Current speed: " + p.getCurrentSpeed() +
                                ", Hatchback open = " + p.isHatchBackDoorOpen() );
        }
        p.stop();
        if( p.isHatchBackDoorOpen() )
        {
            System.out.println( "Have to close the hatchback!" );
            p.closeHatchBack();
        }
    }
}
```

The output of Listing 7.1 should be similar to the following:

```
My car: A rusty old Two-tone Pinto
Starter failed, let's roll start it!
Current speed: 0, Hatchback open = false
Current speed: 4, Hatchback open = false
Current speed: 8, Hatchback open = false
Current speed: 12, Hatchback open = false
Current speed: 16, Hatchback open = false
Current speed: 20, Hatchback open = false
Current speed: 24, Hatchback open = false
Current speed: 28, Hatchback open = false
Current speed: 32, Hatchback open = false
Current speed: 36, Hatchback open = false
Current speed: 40, Hatchback open = false
Current speed: 44, Hatchback open = false
Current speed: 48, Hatchback open = false
```

```
Current speed: 52, Hatchback open = false
Current speed: 56, Hatchback open = false
Current speed: 60, Hatchback open = false
Current speed: 60, Hatchback open = true
Current speed: 60, Hatchback open = true
Current speed: 60, Hatchback open = true
Current speed: 60, Hatchback open = true
Current speed: 60, Hatchback open = true
Current speed: 55, Hatchback open = true
Current speed: 50, Hatchback open = true
Current speed: 45, Hatchback open = true
Current speed: 40, Hatchback open = true
Current speed: 35, Hatchback open = true
Current speed: 30, Hatchback open = true
Current speed: 25, Hatchback open = true
Current speed: 20, Hatchback open = true
Current speed: 15, Hatchback open = true
Current speed: 10, Hatchback open = true
Current speed: 5, Hatchback open = true
Current speed: 0, Hatchback open = true
Have to close the hatchback!
```

The main() method creates a new Pinto instance, tries to start it, and when it fails, it roll starts the car. Then, it accelerates for 16 seconds to get to 60 miles per hour (I think I was quite generous) when the hatchback flies open. Finally, it decelerates to zero, and then closes the hatchback.

The Solution: Interfaces

Aside from being a fun exercise, designing our dream Porsche and completely ripping apart any integrity that the Pinto might have had, you might have noticed a lot of similarities between the Porsche class and the Pinto class. Yes, all the performance metrics are different, but each shares similar attributes and methods. The common attributes are

- horsePower

- maximumSpeed

- numberOfDoors

- paint

- gasCapacity

- oilCapacity

- transmission

- running

- currentSpeed

- currentGas

- currentOil

And the following methods are common:

- start

- stop

- accelerate

- decelerate

- isRunning

- getCurrentSpeed

What happens when we want to create a `Corvette` class? Or an `Accord` class? Do we have to duplicate all this common functionality in all the car classes that we build?

The answer is no, and theobject-oriented concept that will help us is called *inheritance*. The idea is that you can group all the common functionality into a class called `Car`; create specializations of that `Car` that *inherit* all that common functionality; and then add all the special features that make it unique. For example, you can create a `Porsche` from a `Car`.

Listing 7.3 shows the code for the `Car` class.

LISTING 7.3   `Car.java`

```java
public class Car
{
    // Transmission types
    public static final int AUTOMATIC = 0;
    public static final int TIPTRONIC = 1;
    public static final int MANUAL = 2;

    // Attributes
    protected String typeOfCar;
    protected int horsePower;
    protected int maximumSpeed;
    protected int numberOfDoors;
    protected String paint;
    protected int gasCapacity;
    protected int oilCapacity;
    protected int transmission;

    // State attributes
    protected boolean running = false;
    protected int currentSpeed;
    protected int currentGas;
    protected int currentOil;

    public Car( String typeOfCar,
                int horsePower,
                int maximumSpeed,
                int numberOfDoors,
```

LISTING 7.3   Continued

```
                   String paint,
                   int gasCapacity,
                   int oilCapacity,
                   int transmission )
        {
            this.typeOfCar = typeOfCar;
            this.horsePower = horsePower;
            this.maximumSpeed = maximumSpeed;
            this.numberOfDoors = numberOfDoors;
            this.paint = paint;
            this.gasCapacity = gasCapacity;
            this.oilCapacity = oilCapacity;
            this.transmission = transmission;
        }

        public void start()
        {
            running = true;
        }

        public void stop()
        {
            running = false;
        }

        public boolean isRunning()
        {
            return running;
        }

        public void accelerate()
        {
            currentSpeed += 5;
        }

        public void decelerate()
        {
            currentSpeed -= 5;
        }

        public int getCurrentSpeed()
        {
            return currentSpeed;
        }

        public String toString()
        {
            return typeOfCar;
        }
    }
```

The Car class contains all the common functionality that we found between the Porsche, the Pinto, and other cars that we might want to build in the future. It provides default implementation for starting and stopping the car, returning the current speed, checking whether it is running, and accelerating and decelerating the car. One change that you will notice to the attributes in the Car class is that now instead of being private, they have a new access modifier called protected. The protected access modifier offers the same level of protection that private offers to classes outside of the Car class, but enables them to be publicly accessible by all new classes that specialize the Car class (more on that in a minute).

The acceleration and deceleration implementations differ dramatically between the cars, but we'll address that in a minute. The next order of business is to create a Porsche and a Pinto from the car we just created. The process of creating a new class from an existing class is called *extending*; the new class *extends* the old class. Java facilitates this through the keyword: extends.

Listing 7.4 shows the new code for the Porsche2 class that extends the Car class.

LISTING 7.4   Porsche2.java

```java
public class Porsche2 extends Car
{
    // Attributes
    private int turbos = 2;
    private boolean nos;

    // State attributes
    private boolean turbo1Engaged = false;
    private boolean turbo2Engaged = false;
    private boolean nosEnabled = false;

    public Porsche2()
    {
        super( "Porsche",
               450,
               220,
               2,
               "Yellow",
               15,
               5,
               Car.TIPTRONIC );
    }

    public void accelerate()
    {
        // Check to see if we are running or not
        if( running == false )
        {
            return;
        }

        // Create a variable representing how much we are going to
```

LISTING 7.4   Continued

```
    // accelerate this second
    int increment = 15;

    // Check the turbos; they add 5mph per second acceleration
    if( turbo1Engaged )
    {
        increment += 5;
    }
    if( turbo2Engaged )
    {
        increment += 5;
    }

    // Check the NOS; it represents 15mph per second
    if( nos )
    {
        increment += 15;
    }

    // Increment the current speed
    currentSpeed += increment;
    if( currentSpeed > maximumSpeed ) currentSpeed = maximumSpeed;
}

public void decelerate()
{
    currentSpeed -= 20;
    if( currentSpeed < 0 ) currentSpeed = 0;
}

public void engageTurbos()
{
    turbo1Engaged = true;
    turbo2Engaged = true;
}

public void disengageTurbos()
{
    turbo1Engaged = false;
    turbo2Engaged = false;
}

public void engageNOS()
{
    nos = true;
    maximumSpeed += 50;
}

public void disengageNOS()
{
    nos = false;
    maximumSpeed -= 50;
```

LISTING 7.4   Continued

```java
    }

    public String toString()
    {
        return "A shiny new " + paint + " Porsche!";
    }

    public static void main( String[] args )
    {
        Porsche2 p = new Porsche2();
        System.out.println( "My new car: " + p );
        p.start();
        System.out.println( "Current speed: " + p.getCurrentSpeed() );
        for( int i=0; i<20; i++ )
        {
            if( i == 5 )
            {
                p.engageTurbos();
            }
            else if( i == 14 )
            {
                p.engageNOS();
            }
            p.accelerate();
            System.out.println( "Current speed: " + p.getCurrentSpeed() );
        }
        p.disengageNOS();
        p.disengageTurbos();
        while( p.getCurrentSpeed() > 0 )
        {
            p.decelerate();
            System.out.println( "Current speed: " + p.getCurrentSpeed() );
        }
        p.stop();
    }
}
```

Listing 7.4 requires some discussion. The `Porsche2` extends the `Car` class using the `extends` keyword in the following line:

```java
public class Porsche2 extends Car
```

Next it defines the attributes that are specific to a Porsche: its turbo and Nitrous Oxide System.

The constructor does something interesting; its first line is a call to the `super` method. The `Car` class, in this example, is referred to as the *super class*, or *base class*, and the `Porsche2` is referred to as the *subclass*, or *derived* class. This relationship denotes that the `Porsche2` class inherits all the functionality from the `Car` class, not vice versa. Because the relationship is super class to subclass, subclasses have a variable in them similar to the `this` variable called the *super* variable. Although the `this` variable refers to this instance of a class, the `super` variable refers to the instance of the super class. Similar to the way you can reference a class's own methods and variables by prefacing the method or variable with `this`. You can reference the super class's methods and variables by prefacing the method or variable with `super`.

Along with the `super` variable, there is also a `super` method that is used to invoke one of the super class's constructors. The way that the Java Runtime Engine handles the creation of classes with inheritance is by following these steps:

1. Create the class

2. Initialize all the super class's class variables

3. Initialize all the subclass's class variables

4. Execute the super class's constructor

5. Execute the subclass's constructor

The `super` method is the way that your subclass can decide which of the super class's constructors will be executed. The constraint is that because the super class's constructor is executed before the subclass's constructor, the `super` method, if used, must be the first statement in the subclass's constructor. If no `super` method is provided in the subclass's constructor, the default constructor is used. Recall that the default constructor is one that does not accept any parameters. If there is not a default constructor in the super class, you must specify which constructor to execute by using the `super` method.

The `Porsche2` class's constructor calls the only constructor defined in the car class using the `super` method:

```
super( "Porsche",
       450,
       220,
       2,
       "Yellow",
       15,
       5,
       Car.TIPTRONIC );
```

This passes the relevant data to the `Car` class to initialize its variables.

The `Porsche2` class then *overloads* the `accelerate` and `decelerate` methods. The term *overloading* means that the subclass provides a method with the exact same signature as a method in the super class, and it is executed instead of the super class's method. In this case, the `Porsche2` class's `accelerate` method is executed instead of the `Car` class's accelerate method. This is a powerful concept because the `Car` class can provide a default implementation, but any of the subclasses are free to overload it and provide a custom implementation. The implementations of the `accelerate` and `decelerate` methods are the same as the ones from the original `Porsche` class.

The rest of the class implements the custom `Porsche2` methods.

Listing 7.5 shows the updated Pinto class: `Pinto2`.

LISTING 7.5   `Pinto2.java`

```java
public class Pinto2 extends Car
{
    // State attributes
    public boolean hatchBackDoorOpen = false;

    public Pinto2()
    {
        super( "Pinto",
                50,
                60,
                5,
                "two-tone",
                15,
                5,
                Car.MANUAL );
    }

    public void accelerate()
    {
        // Check to see if we are running or not
        if( running == false )
        {
            return;
        }

        currentSpeed += 4;
        if( currentSpeed > maximumSpeed )
        {
            currentSpeed = maximumSpeed;

            // The high speed knocked the door open!
            openHatchBack();
        }
    }

    public void decelerate()
    {
        currentSpeed -= 5;
        if( currentSpeed < 0 ) currentSpeed = 0;
    }

    public void rollStart()
    {
        running = true;
    }

    public void pushUpHill()
    {
        System.out.println( "Ouch, this thing is heavy!" );
    }

    public void openHatchBack()
```

LISTING 7.5   Continued

```java
    {
        hatchBackDoorOpen = true;
    }

    public void closeHatchBack()
    {
        hatchBackDoorOpen = false;
    }

    public boolean isHatchBackDoorOpen()
    {
        return hatchBackDoorOpen;
    }

    public static void main( String[] args )
    {
        Pinto2 p = new Pinto2();
        System.out.println( "My car: " + p );
        p.start();
        if( p.isRunning() == false )
        {
            System.out.println( "Starter failed, let's roll start it!" );
            p.rollStart();
        }
        System.out.println( "Current speed: " + p.getCurrentSpeed() +
                            ", Hatchback open = " + p.isHatchBackDoorOpen() );
        for( int i=0; i<20; i++ )
        {
            p.accelerate();
            System.out.println( "Current speed: " + p.getCurrentSpeed() +
                                ", Hatchback open = " + p.isHatchBackDoorOpen() );
        }
        while( p.getCurrentSpeed() > 0 )
        {
            p.decelerate();
            System.out.println( "Current speed: " + p.getCurrentSpeed() +
                                ", Hatchback open = " + p.isHatchBackDoorOpen() );
        }
        p.stop();
        if( p.isHatchBackDoorOpen() )
        {
            System.out.println( "Have to close the hatchback!" );
            p.closeHatchBack();
        }
    }
}
```

The `Pinto2` class is very similar to the `Porsche2` class in that it extends the `Car` class, calls the similar `Car` class constructor using the **super** method, overrides the `accelerate` and `decelerate` methods, and provides its own custom methods.

The inheritance relationship is sometimes referred to as the *is-a* relationship because a Porsche *is-a* car and a Pinto *is-a* car.

When to Use Inheritance

Inheritance is a great tool when used properly, therefore, you need to understand when to use it. The thought process is to look at all the objects you are designing collectively and identify both the attributes and behaviors that are common between the objects as well as those that differentiate the individual objects.

Attributes and behaviors that are common between objects are called *generalizations*, and they belong in common super classes. In this case we moved the functionality common to both the `Pinto` and `Porsche` objects to the `Car` object. Attributes and behaviors that differentiate objects are called *specializations*, and they belong in different subclasses.

Guidelines for Inheritance Relationships

The following is a list of guidelines to keep in mind when designing your inheritance relationships.

- Always make a subclass capable of doing everything a super class can do

- Ensure that a subclass holds all information that the super class holds

- Add attributes and behavior to the subclass to define behavior that is more specialized than what is found in the super class

- Move common characteristics to the super classes

- Allow different subclasses of the same super class to do the same thing, but differently

Tree Diagrams

Inheritance relationships are usually displayed graphically in a tree diagram (see Figure 7.1).

Figure 7.1 shows that the root of all the classes, or the top-level super class, is `Car`. The `Car` has three subclasses: `Porsche`, `Pinto`, and `Corvette`. In this tree, the `Pinto` and `Corvette` do not have any subclasses and are referred to as *leafs* of the tree. The `Porsche` has two subclasses: `911` and `944`. To these subclasses, the `Porsche` is the super class—thus, the `Porsche` is a subclass of `Car` and a super class to `911` and `944`. Finally, the `TwinTurbo` class is a subclass of `911`.

These diagrams will greatly help you understand the relationships between your classes.

FIGURE 7.1
Car tree diagram.

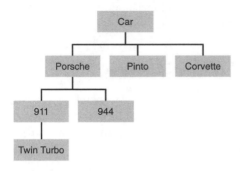

Syntax

As previously discussed, the term used for deriving a subclass from a super class is *extending* because of the Java keyword `extends`. The formal syntax for the `extends` keyword is as follows:

```
[public] [qualifiers] class subclass extends superclass
```

- `public`—this can have the value `public` or no value, which identifies *package* access and is discussed later

- `qualifiers`—valid qualifiers are `final`, `abstract`, `static`, or nothing at all

Final Classes

Defining a class to be final means that it cannot be subclassed—you cannot extend it. Use the keyword `final` to declare a class to be final, for example:

```
public final class MyClass {
}
```

Typically, you'll want to define classes to be final when you do not want anyone else extending them. This can be either when they encapsulate all the functionality they will ever need, or if they contain core pieces of functionality that you do not want to expose for use by anyone else in any other capacity than how you intend.

Abstract Classes

Defining a class to be abstract means that it must be subclassed—it cannot be instantiated on its own. An abstract class is defined using the `abstract` keyword, for example:

```
public abstract class Car {
}
```

Abstract classes typically contain at least one abstract method. Abstract methods are identified by the `abstract` keyword in their declaration, and they do not contain a method body. Instead, a semicolon terminates the declaration, for example:

```
public abstract void accelerate();
```

The `Car` class might be declared to be abstract because you cannot create a generic car. You must have a specialization of a car, and some methods do not have any good default implementation. The `Car` class, for example, should not provide a default implementation for the `accelerate()` and `decelerate()` methods because they are too specific to the subclasses that implement them. Listing 7.6 defines a new version of the car class that is abstract: `Car2`.

LISTING 7.6 `Car2.java`

```java
public abstract class Car2
{
    // Transmission types
    public static final int AUTOMATIC = 0;
    public static final int TIPTRONIC = 1;
    public static final int MANUAL = 2;

    // Attributes
    protected String typeOfCar;
    protected int horsePower;
    protected int maximumSpeed;
    protected int numberOfDoors;
    protected String paint;
    protected int gasCapacity;
    protected int oilCapacity;
    protected int transmission;

    // State attributes
    protected boolean running = false;
    protected int currentSpeed;
    protected int currentGas;
    protected int currentOil;

    public Car( String typeOfCar,
                int horsePower,
                int maximumSpeed,
                int numberOfDoors,
                String paint,
                int gasCapacity,
                int oilCapacity,
                int transmission )
    {
        this.typeOfCar = typeOfCar;
        this.horsePower = horsePower;
        this.maximumSpeed = maximumSpeed;
        this.numberOfDoors = numberOfDoors;
        this.paint = paint;
        this.gasCapacity = gasCapacity;
        this.oilCapacity = oilCapacity;
        this.transmission = transmission;
    }

    public void start()
    {
```

LISTING 7.6   Continued

```
            running = true;
        }

        public void stop()
        {
            running = false;
        }

        public boolean isRunning()
        {
            return running;
        }

        public abstract void accelerate();

        public abstract void decelerate();

        public int getCurrentSpeed()
        {
            return currentSpeed;
        }

        public String toString()
        {
            return typeOfCar;
        }
    }
```

Car2 cannot be instantiated itself and all classes that subclass it must either provide an implementation of both the accelerate and decelerate methods or be declared to be abstract. If you declare a class that extends the Car2 class and do not implement both accelerate and decelerate, a compilation error will result. Consider Listing 7.7, it defines a new class: BadCar, that extends Car2 and does not implement its abstract methods.

LISTING 7.7   BadCar.java

```
public class BadCar extends Car2  {
}
```

Upon compilation you should receive the following error:

```
BadCar.java:1: BadCar should be declared abstract; it does not
                define decelerate
() in Car2
public class BadCar extends Car2
       ^
1 error
```

Access Specifiers

In previous chapters you have been exposed to two access modifiers: `public` and `private`. This chapter has presented a new hybrid access modifier: `protected`. `public` methods and variables are available both from within the class and outside the class. `private` methods and variables are only available from within the class and not from the outside `protected` methods and variables are available within the class and within any subclass, but not outside the class.

The end result of this is that if you declare your methods and variables to be `public`, they will be available to anyone who wants to use them, including your subclasses. If you define them to be `private`, they will not be available to anyone outside your class, including your sub-classes. So, Java defined an access modifier specifically to support data that you want available in subclasses, but nowhere else: `protected`.

Class Finalizers

Inherited constructors were already discussed: A super class's constructor is always called before a subclass's constructor, but the same is not true of finalizers. A super class's finalizer is not executed unless the subclass's finalizer explicitly calls it. Furthermore, it must be the last method called by subclass's finalizer. To invoke the super class's constructor you access it through the `super` variable, for example:

```
public class MyClass extends MySuperClass {
   protected void finalize() {
      // Clean up this class
      super.finalize();
   }
}
```

Thus, if `MyClass`'s finalizer is invoked, the last thing it does is call `MySuperClass`'s `finalize` method.

Overridding Methods

Subclasses can redefine inherited methods as well as define new ones. The process of redefining methods that a subclass would otherwise inherit is called *overriding* methods. The signature and the return type of the method must be identical in both the super class and the subclass.

The subclass's overridden method's access modifier must be the same or less restrictive than in the super class. Thus, the subclass can make a `protected` method `public`, but it cannot make it `private`.

The final constraint for overridden methods is that they can and must override the super class's abstract methods (unless the subclass is defined to be abstract as well).

Dynamic Binding and Polymorphism

Object-orientation is defined by three key concepts: encapsulation, inheritance, and polymorphism. The previous chapter dealt with encapsulation, and thus far in this chapter we have been talking about inheritance, but the final key concept is *polymorphism*. The term literally means many shapes and refers to one object being used in multiple differing ways.

Consider a car for a moment. If you have a driver's license, do you need any knowledge specific to a specialization of a car to drive it? If you know how to drive a Porsche, can you still drive a Pinto? Would you want to?

The last question might be no, but the real answer is that if you know how to drive a Porsche, you should have no problem at least understanding how to drive a Pinto. If you write a new class **Driver**, how would you ask it to drive one of your cars? Listing 7.8 shows the code for a potential driver.

LISTING 7.8   Driver1.java

```java
public class Driver1
{
    public void drivePorsche( Porsche2 p )
    {
        System.out.println( "Driving: " + p );
        p.start();
        for( int i=0; i<10; i++ )
        {
            p.accelerate();
            System.out.println( "Current speed: " + p.getCurrentSpeed() );
        }
        for( int i=0; i<5; i++ )
        {
            p.decelerate();
            System.out.println( "Current speed: " + p.getCurrentSpeed() );
        }
        p.stop();
    }

    public void drivePinto( Pinto2 p )
    {
        System.out.println( "Driving: " + p );
        p.start();
        for( int i=0; i<10; i++ )
        {
            p.accelerate();
            p.rollStart();
            System.out.println( "Current speed: " + p.getCurrentSpeed() );
        }
        for( int i=0; i<5; i++ )
        {
            p.decelerate();
            System.out.println( "Current speed: " + p.getCurrentSpeed() );
```

LISTING 7.8   Continued

```
        }
        p.stop();
    }

    public static void main( String[] args )
    {
        Driver1 d = new Driver1();

        Porsche2 porsche = new Porsche2();
        d.drivePorsche( porsche );
        Pinto2 pinto = new Pinto2();
        d.drivePinto( pinto );
    }
}
```

The `Driver1` class defines two methods that drive cars: `drivePorsche` and `drivePinto`. If you look closely, the methods are the same except they accept different types of cars, a Porsche and a Pinto, respectively.

If we apply the earlier principal that a driver really knows how to drive any type of car to object-oriented programming, we can leverage the fact that both Pinto and Porsche share a common super class. We define a `Driver` class method that knows how to drive a `Car`, and then pass instances of the `Porsche2` and `Pinto2` to it. Thus, the `Porsche2` and `Pinto2` classes can be used in different ways: as a `Car` and as their specialized classes. Thus, defines the term *polymorphism*.

The limitation of using a `Porsche2` as a `Car` is that you can only access the methods defined in the `Car` class. You cannot access `Porsche2` specific methods such as `engageTurbos` and `engageNOS`.

Listing 7.9 shows this concept in action.

LISTING 7.9   Driver2.java

```
public class Driver2
{
    public void drive( Car c )
    {
        System.out.println( "Driving: " + c );
        c.start();
        for( int i=0; i<10; i++ )
        {
            c.accelerate();
            System.out.println( "Current speed: " + c.getCurrentSpeed() );
        }
        for( int i=0; i<5; i++ )
        {
            c.decelerate();
            System.out.println( "Current speed: " + c.getCurrentSpeed() );
        }
```

LISTING 7.9   Continued

```
        c.stop();
    }

    public static void main( String[] args )
    {
        Driver2 d = new Driver2();

        Porsche2 porsche = new Porsche2();
        d.drive( porsche );
        Pinto2 pinto = new Pinto2();
        d.drive( pinto );
    }
}
```

The `Driver2` class defines a single `drive` method that, because of polymorphism, can accept either a `Porsche2` or a `Pinto2` instance. When there are two implementations of a method, for example the `Porsche2` class overrides the `Car`'s `accelerate` method, how does the compiler know to use the `Porsche2`'s instance instead of the `Car`'s instance? It is, after all, using the `Porsche2` instance as a `Car`.

The answer to this a term that goes hand in hand with polymorphism called *dynamic binding*. Dynamic binding means that the Java Runtime Engine will resolve the implementation at run-time, not at compile time (when the `Driver2` class is being compiled). This means that the `Driver2` class will know how to `drive` any new car that you define in the future.

Summary

This chapter completed the basic concepts of object-oriented programming that were started in the previous chapter by defining inheritance and polymorphism. Inheritance enables you to create new specialized versions of classes based on existing classes. The design process enables you to create an inheritance hierarchy based on common functionality and object specialization. Polymorphism enables you to leverage that inheritance hierarchy to write methods that operate on super classes in the hierarchy and pass subclasses to those methods.

The next chapter looks at a Java-specific mechanism used to enhance polymorphism and facilitate some rather interesting new functionality called interfaces.

Review Questions

1. Define the term override with respect to Java inheritance.

2. How do you define a class that must be extended?

3. How do you define a class that cannot be extended?

4. Define polymorphism.

5. Where does specialized functionality belong in the inheritance hierarchy?

6. Where does generalized functionality belong in the inheritance hierarchy?

7. Is the super class or subclass constructor called first?

8. What is the keyword `super`, and what does it offer you?

9. What is the `super()` method?

10. How is finalization accomplished for super classes?

Exercises

Define the following classes in an inheritance hierarchy:

- Animal
- Dog
- Wolf
- Coyote
- Cat
- Tiger
- Lion

Where wolves and coyotes are specializations of dogs, tigers and lions are specializations of cats, and dogs and cats are specializations of animals. Think about the different attributes and behavior of each animal and move common functionality up the inheritance hierarchy and specialized functionality down the inheritance hierarchy.

CHAPTER 8

INTERFACES

In this chapter you will learn:

- The Java concept of interfaces
- When and how to use interfaces
- The properties of interfaces

The previous chapter completed the standard object-oriented conceptual discussion. As a review, the three tenants of object-oriented programming are encapsulation, inheritance, and polymorphism.

This chapter builds on those object-oriented programming concepts with a Java-specific concept called an *interface*, to solve a new category of problem thus far not addressed.

Problem Derivation

In the past couple of chapters we defined two primary types of cars: Pintos and Porsches. During their creation we found that they had a lot of common attributes and behaviors, so we used the concept of inheritance to move all that common functionality to a super class named `Car`. Then we made the `Porsche` and `Pinto` classes extend the `Car` class. Thus, the `Porsche` and `Pinto` classes contained only the attributes and behaviors unique to them.

Now consider another piece of functionality that we want to add to these cars: maintainability. When these cars require service, the owners take them to a mechanic that does standard maintenance: change the oil, rotate the tires, tune up the engine, and so on. In Java we can represent this through the creation of a `Mechanic` class, which invokes methods on the `Porsche` and `Pinto` class instances. Tuning up a `Porsche` is different from tuning up a `Pinto`, so that functionality should reside in the individual subclasses. We'll take what we learned while building the `Driver` class in the previous chapter and avoid writing both `tuneUpPorsche()` and `tuneUpPinto()` methods. Instead, we'll write a single `tuneUp` class that knows how to tune up a `Car`; this is facilitated by defining the functionality abstractly to the `Car` super class.

Listing 8.1 shows the modifications to the `Car` class. Listing 8.2 shows the modifications to the `Pinto` class. Listing 8.3 shows the modifications to the `Porsche` class.

LISTING 8.1   `Car.java`

```java
public abstract class Car
{
    ...

    public abstract void tuneUp();

    public abstract void changeOil();
}
```

The `Car` class has added two abstract methods to facilitate servicing a car: `tuneUp()` and `changeOil()`. Recall that **abstract** methods require all nonabstract subclasses to implement them.

LISTING 8.2   `Pinto.java`

```java
public class Pinto extends Car
{
    ...

    public void tuneUp()
    {
        System.out.println( "Tuning up a pinto..." );
    }

    public void changeOil()
    {
        System.out.println( "Changing a pinto's oil..." );
    }

    ...
}
```

The `Pinto` class has been modified to implement both of the new abstract `Car` methods in a Pinto-centric way.

LISTING 8.3   `Porsche.java`

```java
public class Porsche extends Car
{
    ...

    public void tuneUp()
    {
        System.out.println( "Tuning up a porsche..." );
    }
```

LISTING 8.3   Continued

```
    public void changeOil()
    {
        System.out.println( "Changing a porsche's oil..." );
    }

    ...
}
```

The `Porsche` class has been modified to implement both of the new abstract `Car` methods in a Porsche-centric way.

Finally, Listing 8.4 shows the implementation of the first mechanic class: `Mechanic1`.

LISTING 8.4   `Mechanic1.java`

```
public class Mechanic1
{
    public void service( Car car )
    {
        car.changeOil();
        car.tuneUp();
    }

    public static void main( String[] args )
    {
        Porsche porsche = new Porsche();
        Pinto pinto = new Pinto();
        Mechanic1 mechanic = new Mechanic1();
        mechanic.service( porsche );
        mechanic.service( pinto );
    }
}
```

The `Mechanic1` class defines a single method of interest:

```
    public void service( Car car )
```

This `service()` method accepts as its parameter a `Car` through which it calls the abstract `changeOil()` and `tuneUp()` methods.

That actually worked very well; we now have a mechanic that knows how to service cars. All future cars that we create need only extend the `Car` super class and implement the abstract methods, and presto, the mechanic can service them!

But now what happens when we need to service a truck or a motorcycle? Do we need a new mechanic? If a mechanic knows how to change the oil of a car, he can probably change the oil of a truck and a motorcycle, this does not fit into the inheritance hierarchy we have established. Furthermore, when you think conceptually about a car, or any vehicle, you do not think of servicing it as a property of the car itself, but as a function that the mechanic performs on the car. The car supports the capability to be serviced, but it does not perform the service itself (except maybe for some of the new self-tuning BMWs, but let's ignore those for the time being.)

The answer to these problems is that we want a mechanism external to the car itself that provides the functionality required to service a vehicle. Any vehicle that can be serviced can provide this functionality regardless of the inheritance hierarchy to which it belongs and our mechanic can service it.

Java provides the mechanism for doing this through *interfaces*. An interface defines a set of public methods that is implemented by all classes that want to offer a set of functionality. Then, classes that want to access that functionality can do so by referencing class instances through that interface. The first step in solving this problem is to externalize the desired functionality into an interface. An interface looks like a class, but it uses the keyword `interface` and all its methods must be abstract; you cannot provide any default behavior.

Listing 8.5 shows the definition for a new interface called `Serviceable`.

LISTING 8.5 Serviceable.java

```
public interface Serviceable
{
    public void changeOil();
    public void tuneUp();
}
```

Similar to classes, interfaces are defined with a `java` extension. The keyword `interface` is used in place of `class` and methods do not contain any implementation. Because interfaces are abstract and all their methods are abstract by nature, you do not need to use the `abstract` keyword.

The `Car` class has been replicated to `Car2` for this example and the two abstract serviceable methods, `tuneUp()` and `changeOil()`, have been removed.

Listing 8.6 shows excerpts from the new `Porsche` class, named `Porsche2` for clarity.

LISTING 8.6 Porsche2.java

```
public class Porsche2 extends Car implements Serviceable
{
    ...

    public void tuneUp()
    {
        System.out.println( "Tuning up a porsche..." );
    }

    public void changeOil()
    {
        System.out.println( "Changing a porsche's oil..." );
    }

    ...
}
```

The `Porsche2` class implements the `Serviceable` interface by using the keyword `implements`:

```
public class Porsche2 extends Car implements Serviceable
```

A class can extend only one super class, but it can implement as many interfaces as is required. Implementing interfaces involves using the keyword, `implements`, following any extension followed by a comma-separated list of interfaces that it is implementing.

Implementing an interface is like signing a contract; it requires that you implement all methods defined in the interface. If you implement `Serviceable`, you must provide implementations for both `changeOil()` as well as `tuneUp()`.

Listing 8.7 shows an excerpt from the new `Pinto` class: `Pinto2`.

LISTING 8.7   `Pinto2.java`

```
public class Pinto2 extends Car implements Serviceable
{
    ...

    public void tuneUp()
    {
        System.out.println( "Tuning up a pinto..." );
    }

    public void changeOil()
    {
        System.out.println( "Changing a pinto's oil..." );
    }

    ...
}
```

The `Pinto2` class, similar to the `Porsche2` class, implements the `Serviceable` interface and provides implementations for both `Serviceable` methods: `changeOil()` and `tuneUp()`.

Now that both of the cars implement a common `Serviceable` interface, we can define a mechanic that can service them. Listing 8.8, called `Mechanic2`, defines a new mechanic.

LISTING 8.8   `Mechanic2.java`

```
public class Mechanic2
{
    public void service( Serviceable s )
    {
        s.changeOil();
        s.tuneUp();
    }
```

LISTING 8.8   Continued

```
public static void main( String[] args )
{
    Porsche porsche = new Porsche();
    Pinto pinto = new Pinto();
    Mechanic1 mechanic = new Mechanic1();
    mechanic.service( porsche );
    mechanic.service( pinto );
}
}
```

Like `Mechanic1`, `Mechanic2` defines a single method `service`. Instead of working `Car` classes and their derivatives, it works on classes implementing the `Serviceable` interface. Thus, its signature is as follows:

```
public void service( Serviceable s )
```

Thus, you can create an instance of a class that implements `Serviceable` and pass it to the mechanic's `service` method. That is precisely what is done in the mechanic's `main` method: A `Porsche2` and a `Pinto2` are created and passed to the `Mechanic2` class's `service` method.

When you define a method that accepts an interface, you are limited to calling only those methods that are defined in the interface; you cannot make calls to other methods implemented by the class. For example, you can call the `changeOil` and `tuneUp` and methods of the `Porsche2` class, but you cannot call its `engageTurbos` method.

Multiple Inheritance

Assuming the behavior of multiple different objects is accomplished in many programming languages through *multiple inheritance*, or inheriting the functionality of more than one super class. There is a danger in multiple inheritance known as diamond inheritance, see Figure 8.1.

FIGURE 8.1
Diamond inheritance
diagram.

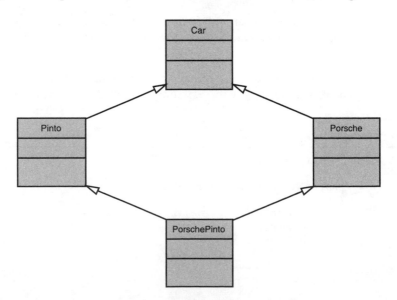

In Figure 8.1, we have created a new `PorschePinto` hybrid car (scary huh?). You can see that the `PorschePinto` extends both `Porsche` and `Pinto`, which both extend `Car`. Numerous questions arise as to which implementation of a method is executed when it is called on the `PorschePinto` class. Consider the `accelerate` method: If the `PorschePinto` does not implement the `accelerate` method itself, does it accelerate like a `Pinto` or a `Porsche`? Furthermore, if you think about the creation process of classes in an inheritance hierarchy, all super classes must be created prior to their subclasses. In this scenario, there will be two instances of the `Car` class in memory for the `PorschePinto`. Now, if you start the `PorschePinto` by calling its `start` method, which instance of the two `Car` parents actually has its `running` variable set to `true`?

Because of all these questions and problems, Java has opted not to include support for multiple inheritance. Java supports single inheritance (one super class), and then works around the problem by allowing you to implement as many interfaces as you need. Because interfaces cannot provide any implementation, there is no ambiguity in which implementation of a method to execute. In some situations you might have to write more code because of this restriction, but it does solve a lot of problems.

Interface Syntax

The general syntax for defining interfaces is as follows:

```
[public] interface iname [extends i2name]
```

- Can include the keyword `abstract`, but it is implied
- Can include the keyword `public`, but it is implied
- Can include `static` and `final` for fields, but they are implied

All interfaces are public and abstract and if they contain any attributes, those attributes are static and final.

Implementing Interfaces

Classes implement interfaces using the keyword `implements`:

```
[public] [qualifiers] class classname implements iname [,i2name]
```

- Classes can implement any number of interfaces
- Classes can be abstract and/or final
- Classes can extend a class and still implement any number of interfaces

Interfaces Used for Multiple Inheritance Reasons

Interfaces can be used for a couple different reasons, one of which is to work around Java's lack of support for multiple inheritance. The classic example to describe multiple inheritance is the mythical creature Pegasus. Pegasus was a horse that had wings and could fly like a bird. Thus, if you wanted to create a Pegasus class, would you derive it from horse or from bird? It has the abilities of both.

In Java, the best way to implement the Pegasus class is to define two interfaces that encapsulate the functionality of a horse and of a bird: `HorseLike` and `BirdLike`. Then, define the `Pegasus` class to implement both interfaces. Listing 8.9 and 8.10 show the definition of the `HorseLike` and `BirdLike` interfaces, respectively.

LISTING 8.9   HorseLike.java

```
public interface HorseLike
{
    public void winee();
    public void gallop();
}
```

LISTING 8.10   BirdLike.java

```
public interface BirdLike
{
    public void chirp();
    public void fly();
}
```

Listing 8.11 shows the implementation of the `Pegasus` class.

LISTING 8.11   Pegasus.java

```
public class Pegasus implements HorseLike, BirdLike
{
    public void winee() {
        System.out.println( "winee!" );
    }
    public void gallop() {
        System.out.println( "I can run fast!" );
    }
    public void chirp() {
        System.out.println( "Chirp, chirp!" );
    }
    public void fly() {
        System.out.println( "Look at me, I'm a flying horse!" );
    }
}
```

Listing 8.11 shows the Pegasus class implementing both interfaces and providing implementations of all the methods defined by both interfaces.

Interfaces Used to Add External Capabilities to a Class

Another common use of interfaces is to add external capabilities to an existing class, as we did by making the car classes serviceable. This is more of a conceptual differentiator when deciding what functionality to add to a class and what functionality to put into an interface, but from a strict object-oriented perspective, you want to keep your classes pure.

You should design your classes so that they encapsulate the attributes and behaviors of the object they are representing. Functionality that resides external to the object can be implemented through interfaces. This is only a conceptual distinction, but if you follow it you will find your classes to be more reusable, and the methods you use to service interfaces infinitely more versatile.

Interfaces Versus Abstract Classes

Sometimes there is some confusion about when to use interfaces and when to simply create abstract methods and place them in a super class. Here are a few guidelines:

- Use an abstract base class method when the functionality is tightly coupled with the object itself

- Use an interface when the functionality is auxiliary to the object

- Use an interface when the functionality can be applied globally to other unrelated objects

Summary

This chapter introduced you to Java's concept of interfaces. Interfaces are defined much the same way as classes, but with the interface keyword. Other differences are that all methods are public and abstract by default. You can define attributes to interfaces, but they must be static and final.

The big difference between classes and interfaces comes in how you use them. This chapter dedicated a lot of space to help you make this differentiation.

The next chapter will introduce you to Java's implementation of exception handling.

Review Questions

1. Can you define a private interface?

2. Can you provide a default implementation for any methods defined in an interface?

3. How do you implement an interface?

4. What is multiple inheritance?

5. What is the danger of multiple inheritance?

6. Should functionality that is representative of an object go into that object's class or an interface?

7. When would you use an interface, and when would you use an abstract class?

8. Describe diamond inheritance.

Exercises

Extend the animal classes you built in the previous chapter to include two interfaces: `Eating` defines one method `eat()`, and `Playing` that defines one method `play()`. Each animal should implement these interfaces in a way that is most appropriate for them.

Create a `ZooKeeper` class that goes to each animal and plays with it, and then feeds it.

CHAPTER 9

EXCEPTION HANDLING

You will learn about the following in this chapter:

- Problem derivation

- Definitions

- Rethrowing an exception

- Passing an exception through your method

- Custom exception example

A t this point in the book you have learned all the basic syntax of Java, as well as the object-oriented programming concepts that make it powerful. This chapter will expand on that knowledge to include Java's way of handling errors.

Problem Derivation

The car examples we have discussed up until now have assumed that everything in the methods went well. The car class defined attributes such as the amount of oil left in the engine and the amount of gas left in the tank, but the code did not make use of them. How could you handle error conditions with the Java tools currently available to you?

Consider the car's `accelerate` method, which currently returns `void`. It could, however, be modified to return a `true` value if it succeeds, and `false` if it fails. Then, the code to handle it would look something like this:

```
Porsche porsche = new Porsche();
porsche.start();
for( int n=0; n<10; n++ ) {
   if( porsche.accelerate() ) {
      System.out.println( "Accelerate successful!" );
   }
   else {
      System.out.println( "Accelerate failed!" );
   }
}
```

It is good to know whether the method succeeded or failed, but now how do we fix the problem? Or more importantly what is the problem? Is the car out of gas? Is it out of oil?

The `accelerate` method can be further refined to return an integer value. See the values in Table 9.1.

TABLE 9.1   `accelerate` Method Return Values

Value	Description
0	accelerate successful
−1	Out of oil
−2	Out of gas
−3	Car is not started
−4	General failure

Typically, negative values have been associated with error codes, whereas zero or a positive value denotes a success. For example, the `accelerate` method could be defined to return the current speed of the car—this would not interfere with diagnosing the error condition. The following code checks for an error condition:

```
Porsche porsche = new Porsche();
porsche.start();
for( int n=0; n<10; n++ ) {
   int returnCode = porsche.accelerate();
   if( returnCode >= 0 ) {
      System.out.println( "Accelerate successful!" );
   }
   else {
      System.out.println( "Accelerate failed!" );
   }
}
```

Recall, though, that the point of having these error conditions is to respond to and handle errors. Thus, the code might be better written as follows:

```
Porsche porsche = new Porsche();
porsche.start();
for( int n=0; n<10; n++ ) {
   int returnCode = porsche.accelerate();
   switch( returnCode ) {
   case 0:
      System.out.println( "Accelerate successful!" );
      break;
   case -1:
      System.out.println( "Out of oil, time to change!" );
      break;
```

```
    case -2:
       System.out.println( "Out of gas, time to fuel up!" );
       break;
    case -3:
       System.out.println(
            "Car is not started, insert the key and turn!" );
       break;
    case -4:
       System.out.println(
            "Whoops! General failure, time to pay the big bucks!" );
       break;
    default:
       System.out.println( "Unknown error condition" );
    }
}
```

That was much more informative and easier to debug, but a lot of code! Now consider a method that you have to call the accelerate method multiple times outside of a loop:

```
public void race( Porsche p ) {
    p.start();
    p.accelerate();
    p.accelerate();
    p.decelerate();
    p.turnRight();
    p.accelerate();
    p.accelerate();
    p.decelerate();
    p.turnLeft();

    // Straight away!
    p.engageTurbos();
    p.accelerate();
    p.engageNOS();

    // Cross the finish line
    while( p.getCurrentSpeed() > 0 ) {
        p.decelerate();
    }
    p.stop();
}
```

The previous code block represents a short race course, but it illustrates that you would have to repeatedly call the **accelerate** and **decelerate** methods. To properly handle all the errors that would occur during each call to **accelerate**, you would have to add the 20 lines of code that handled the error to each **accelerate** invocation. That would add 100 lines of code to this method simply to identify errors—we haven't added error handling to **decelerate**, **engageTurbos**, and **engageNOS** yet! Suddenly a seemingly harmless little 20-line method could grow to a convoluted 200-line method, where 80% of the code is handling error conditions. There must be a better way!

Consider writing your method as follows. Assume that everything will work correctly, but if some exceptional circumstance occurs (an error), add code to handle it at the end of your method. This enables you to write the error-handling code in one place and, by writing the method expecting it to work, it will be clear and understandable.

In Java you define a set of code that you would want to *try* to execute. In the code, one or more methods could raise an exceptional circumstance and *throw* an exception. At the end of the code block you can *catch* that exception and handle it if an error occurred, otherwise continue as usual.

Thus, the code could be rewritten as follows:

```java
public void race( Porsche p ) {
   try {
      p.start();
      p.accelerate();
      p.accelerate();
      p.decelerate();
      p.turnRight();
      p.accelerate();
      p.accelerate();
      p.decelerate();
      p.turnLeft();

      // Straight away!
      p.engageTurbos();
      p.accelerate();
      p.engageNOS();

      // Cross the finish line
      while( p.getCurrentSpeed() > 0 ) {
         p.decelerate();
      }
      p.stop();
   }
   catch( CarException e ) {
      int returnCode = e.getReturnCode();
      switch( returnCode ) {
      case 0:
         System.out.println( "Car race was successful!" );
         break;
      case -1:
         System.out.println( "Out of oil, time to change!" );
         break;
      case -2:
         System.out.println( "Out of gas, time to fuel up!" );
         break;
      case -3:
         System.out.println(
            "Car is not started, insert the key and turn!" );
         break;
      case -4:
         System.out.println(
            "Whoops! General failure, time to pay the big bucks!" );
         break;
```

```
        default:
            System.out.println( "Unknown error condition" );
        }
    }
}
```

Java calls this process *exception handling*.

Exception Definitions

As you can see from the verbiage in the last section, there are a lot of terms associated with exception handling that need to be defined. The following is a list of exception terms and definitions:

- **Exceptions**—An *exception* is a representation of an error condition, or any situation that is not the expected result of a method.

- **Throwing an Exception**—The act of detecting an abnormal condition and generating an exception is called *throwing an exception*.

- **Catching an Exception**—When an exception is thrown it can be *caught* by a *handler*. This is referred to as *catching an exception*.

- **Handling an Exception**—The entire process is called *handling the exception*.

Try Blocks

A `try` block is a Java programming language construct that encloses one or more statements that can throw an exception; it uses the keyword `try`. The `try` block starts with the `try` keyword, and then has a body (enclosed by braces) that contains code that can generate an exception. The general form is

```
try {
    // Some code in here can throw an exception!
}
```

Any method that can throw an exception must be called within the context of a `try` block.

Catch Blocks

Exceptions that are thrown are caught inside `catch` blocks. A `try` block can be followed by zero or more `catch` blocks (if there are zero then there must be a `finally` block—see the next section), each catching and handling a different exception; `catch` blocks use the keyword `catch`. The `catch` block starts with the `catch` keyword followed by a parentheses-delimited, exception-class instance variable (that was thrown by the offending method), and, finally, a brace-delimited body that handles the exception. The general form is

```
catch( ExceptionClassName exception ) {
    // Code to get information out of e and handle the exception
}
```

`exception` is an instance of the exception class `ExceptionClassName`; it has methods and attributes that you can access just like any other class. It should, however, give you insight to the cause of the error condition.

Finally Block

A `catch` or `try` block can be followed by a single `finally` block. The compiler always executes the statements inside a `finally` block regardless of whether an exception is thrown and caught or never thrown. The `finally` block follows the `try` block if there are no `catch` blocks, otherwise, it follows the last `catch` block. `finally` blocks are denoted by the keyword `finally`, followed by a brace-delimited body of code to execute.

The purpose of the `finally` block is to define code that you want executed regardless of whether the code in the `try` block succeeds or fails. One of the most practical applications of this is with regard to resource management; if you allocate a resource in your try block, you want to release it if your code succeeds or fails. It has the general form:

```
try {
}
catch( ... ) {
}
finally {
    // Release your resources
}
```

Exception Syntax

Putting all these exception-handling constructs together we have the following form:

```
try {
    // One or more statements that can throw an exception
}
catch( ExceptionType1 e1 ) {
    // Handle an exception that can be thrown in the try block
}
catch( ExceptionType2 e2 ) {
    // Handle an exception that can be thrown in the try block
}
finally {
    // Do any cleanup
}
```

Any method call that can throw an exception must be contained within a `try` block, and there must be a `catch` block to catch that exception class or a superclass of that exception class. Exception classes are built on an inheritance hierarchy and if `catch` blocks specify a class higher in the inheritance hierarchy (one of the exception class's superclasses), it will handle all the exception's subclasses. The key to appropriately handling an exception is to define the more specific exceptions in earlier `catch` blocks, and the more general exceptions in the later `catch` blocks.

A `try` block must be followed by either a catch block, a `finally` block, or both; it cannot be alone. If an exception occurs, the exception that is thrown is evaluated against each of the `catch` blocks in turn, starting from the top of the code until the exception class is found or a superclass of the exception class is found. At that point the body of the matching `catch` block is executed and, if there is a `finally` block, it is executed.

For example consider the exception hierarchy defined in Figure 9.1.

FIGURE 9.1

Example exception hierarchy class diagram.

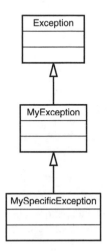

MySpecificException is a subclass of MyException, which is a subclass of Exception. Note that inheritance is specified in class diagrams by drawing an arrow pointing from the subclass to the superclass. If you want to handle each one of these exceptions, you would need to write your `catch` blocks starting with the most specialized class and moving to the most general class. For example:

```
try {
    // Statement that can throw an exception
}
catch( MySpecificException mse ) {
  // do something
}
catch( MyException me ) {
  // do something
}
catch( Exception e ) {
  // do something
}
```

Thus, if a MySpecificException instance is thrown, the first `catch` block handles it. If a MyException instance is thrown, the first catch block is skipped, and the second one handles the exception.

Now, if you reversed the order of the `catch` blocks you would be in trouble.

```
try {
    // Statement that can throw an exception
}
catch( Exception e ) {
  // do something
}
catch( MyException me ) {
  // do something
}
catch( MySpecificException mse ) {
  // do something
}
```

In this case if a `MySpecificException` instance is thrown, the first catch block, or specifically the `Exception` catch block, would handle the exception; the `MySpecificException` catch block that you intended to handle it would never receive the exception. Furthermore, Java will give you a compilation error if you try to do this.

Exception Classes

Exceptions are classes just like any other class, except that all exceptions must directly or indirectly extend the `java.lang.Throwable` class. Typically, your custom exceptions will extend one of the `java.lang.Throwable` class's subclasses: `java.lang.Exception`. Figure 9.2 shows the inheritance hierarchy of the three main types of exceptions: Exceptions, Errors, and Runtime Exceptions.

FIGURE 9.2
Exception hierarchy class diagram.

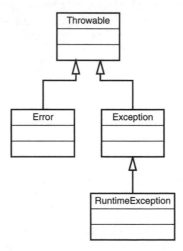

The `java.lang.Exception` class is used for most exceptions in Java and is the base class for most user-defined exceptions. This class of exception requires that methods throwing it explicitly publish that it can be thrown. It also encompasses all your database exceptions, input- and output-based exceptions, as well as a hoard of other Java exceptions.

The `java.lang.Error` class is another extension of the `Throwable` class and indicates a serious problem in the system. Most errors are abnormal conditions such as the death of a thread or a problem with the Java Virtual Machine. Methods that throw errors do not have to explicitly publish them; therefore, callers of that method are not required to catch them.

The `java.lang.RuntimeException` class represents a set of errors that can occur during the normal operation of a program, but they are so common that you are not required to explicitly handle them. The best example of a runtime exception is the `java.lang.NullPointerException` class, which states that you tried to call a method on an object that was not initialized (so the variable was not referencing anything). If you were required to explicitly handle this case, you would have to enclose all statements that ever used objects (all nonprimitive types) in a `try` block. Java realized that this request was too unreasonable for programmers and saw fit to provide a class of exceptions that can occur normally, but that you are not required to handle.

Throwable Class

The `java.lang.Throwable` class provides a familiar set of core methods that its subclasses use. These methods are shown in Table 9.2.

TABLE 9.2   `Throwable` Class Methods

Value	Description
Throwable fillInStackTrace()	Fills in the execution stack trace
String getLocalizedMessage()	Creates a localized description of this throwable
String getMessage()	Returns the error message string of this throwable object
void printStackTrace()	Prints this throwable, and its backtrace to the standard error stream
void printStackTrace(PrintStream s)	Prints this throwable, and its backtrace to the specified print stream
void printStackTrace(PrintWriter s)	Prints this throwable, and its backtrace to the specified print writer
String toString()	Returns a short description of this throwable object

The two methods that are the most interesting to you as a Java developer are the `getMessage()` method, because it tells you what circumstances caused the exception to occur, and the `printStackTrace()` variations. As methods are called, each method call is stored in what is referred to as a *call stack*. When an exception occurs, the throwable class provides you with a mechanism to review that call stack to help determine the cause of a problem. For example, consider the following code:

```
1:  public class Test {
2:    public void methodA() {
3:        methodB();
4:    }
5:    public void methodB() {
6:        methodC();
7:    }
8:    public void methodC() {
9:        // Do something that causes an exception!
10:   }
11:   public static void main( String[] args ) {
12:       Test test = new Test();
13:       test.methodA();
14:   }
15:}
```

In this sample code, the `main()` method creates an instance of the `Test` class and calls its `methodA()` method. `methodA()` in turn calls `methodB()`, which in turn calls `methodC()`, which throws an exception. At the point of the exception, line 9 of the program, the call stack looks as follows:

```
Line 9: Test.methodC() threw an exception: body of the message
Line 6: Test.methodB() called Test.methodC()
Line 3: Test.methodA() called Test.methodB()
Line 13: main() called Test.methodA();
```

If you call one of the `printStackTrace()` methods, you will not only see the message describing the exception, but also the exact path through the code that caused the exception. This is extremely useful because sometimes your exception can occur inside one of the Java classes because of a parameter that you passed it. The context of the exception in and of itself is not useful without knowing how you got there.

Throwing Exceptions

These three steps are involved in throwing exceptions:

1. Publish a list of exceptions that your method can throw

2. Create an instance of the exception class that describes your error

3. Throw that exception

Publishing an Exception List

If a method can potentially throw an exception, it must publish it to all parties that call it. This is accomplished by appending the `throws` clause to the signature of the method. For example:

```
public void myMethod() throws MyException
```

This statement says that `myMethod()` can throw the exception `MyException`, so anyone that calls `myMethod` must explicitly handle `MyException`. In other words, if you call `myMethod()`, you must call it within a `try` block and provide a `catch` block that catches `MyException` or one of its superclasses. If you don't, the compiler will generate an error.

Your method can throw more than one exception, but it must then list all the possible exceptions it can throw in a comma-separated list. For example, if your method can throw `MyException1`, `MyException2`, and `MyException3`, its signature would look as follows:

```
public void myMethod throws MyException1, MyException2, MyException3
```

Creating an Instance of an Exception

You must define a new class, such as `MyException1`, for your exception and then create an instance of it when appropriate. Thus, if your method detects an error condition that is represented by `MyException1`, you create an instance of it in your code:

```
...
if( badCondition ) {
    // Create and initialize MyException1
    MyException1 e =
      new MyException1( "You did not enter the correct value" );
    e.setValueEntered( value );
    e.setRangeExpected( 1, 10 );
}
```

Because exceptions are normal classes that extend `Exception`, you can add properties and methods freely. In this example, the `MyException1` class has a constructor that accepts a `String` describing the exception, two methods for setting the value that the user entered, and a range of valid values. I will show you a concrete example of creating a custom exception in the "Creating a Custom Exception," section later in the chapter.

Throwing the Exception

When you have an instance of an `Exception` created, you can throw it using the `throw` keyword. The `throw` keyword stops the execution of the method at the point that the `throw` is called and throws the exception to the caller. For example:

```
public void myMethod() throws MyException1
...
if( badCondition ) {
    // Create and initialize MyException1
    MyException1 e = new MyException1(
        "You did not enter the correct value" );
    e.setValueEntered( value );
    e.setRangeExpected( 1, 10 );
    throw e;
}
// Do something
int i=10;
...
}
```

The exception e is thrown using the `throw` keyword, and then execution of the method stops; all the statements after the `throw` statement are not executed. In this case the creation of the integer i is never executed if `badCondition` evaluates to `true`.

Rethrowing an Exception

When you catch an exception, you do not necessarily have to resolve the problem: You can catch the exception, examine it, and then rethrow it. This is accomplished by catching the exception using a `catch` block, but in the body of the `catch` block, throwing the exception using the `throw` command. The method must declare that it can throw the exception using the `throws` keyword in the signature of the method. For example:

```
public void myOtherMethod() throws MyException1 {
   try {
      myMethod();
   }
   catch( MyException1 e ) {
      e.printStackTrace();
      throw e;
   }
}
```

In this example, the call to `myMethod()` can throw `MyException1`. If it does, `myOtherMethod()` catches it, prints its stack trace, and then rethrows it.

Passing an Exception Through Your Method

Not only can you catch and rethrow an exception, you can ignore it altogether by adding the exception class to your method's exception list. This way if an exception of a certain type occurs, it can be passed directly to the method that called you. Eventually someone will have to catch the exception and deal with it, but you can defer that to the calling method. If we were to skip printing the stack trace for the exception in the previous example and let the exception pass through to our caller, we can rewrite `myOtherMethod()` as follows:

```
public void myOtherMethod() throws MyException1 {
   myMethod();
}
```

Thus, if `myMethod()` throws a `MyException1` exception, it is passed to the caller of `myOtherMethod()`.

Creating a Custom Exception

Consider the `Car` example discussed at the beginning of the chapter. We defined methods in the `Car` class that have potential error conditions for which we want to check. For example, when you accelerate a car you must ensure that it is currently running, that it is in drive (or in a gear for a manual transmission car), and that it has the appropriate amount of fluids (gas and oil) before increasing the speed. If any of these conditions are not valid, you will want to throw an exception.

Let's first define a custom exception named `CarException`, as in Listing 9.1.

LISTING 9.1   `CarException.java`

```java
public class CarException extends Exception {
  private boolean engineRunning = true;
  private boolean gas = true;
  private boolean oil = true;

  public CarException() {
    super();
  }

  public CarException( String message ) {
    super( message );
  }

  public void setEngineRunning( boolean engineRunning ) {
    this.engineRunning = engineRunning;
  }

  public boolean isEngineRunning() {
    return this.engineRunning;
  }

  public void setGas( boolean gas ) {
    this.gas = gas;
  }

  public boolean hasGas() {
    return this.gas;
  }

  public void setOil( boolean oil ) {
    this.oil = oil;
  }

  public boolean hasOil() {
    return this.oil;
  }
}
```

The `CarException` class extends the `Exception` superclass and provides the settings for three additional parameters: the engine state, the oil state, and the gas state. Thus, a class that throws a car exception can alert the caller to the nature of the problem—is the engine turned off, is the car out of oil, or is the car out of gas?

The `Car` class has been revamped to throw exceptions when errors occur and has been renamed to `NewCar`, so as not to create any naming conflicts. Listing 9.2 shows the code for the `NewCar` class.

LISTING 9.2   `NewCar.java`

```java
public abstract class NewCar
{
    // Transmission types
    public static final int AUTOMATIC = 0;
    public static final int TIPTRONIC = 1;
    public static final int MANUAL = 2;

    // Attributes
    protected String typeOfCar;
    protected int horsePower;
    protected int maximumSpeed;
    protected int numberOfDoors;
    protected String paint;
    protected int gasCapacity;
    protected int oilCapacity;
    protected int transmission;

    // State attributes
    protected boolean running = false;
    protected int currentSpeed;
    protected int currentGas;
    protected int currentOil;

    public NewCar( String typeOfCar,
                   int horsePower,
                   int maximumSpeed,
                   int numberOfDoors,
                   String paint,
                   int gasCapacity,
                   int oilCapacity,
                   int transmission ) {
        this.typeOfCar = typeOfCar;
        this.horsePower = horsePower;
        this.maximumSpeed = maximumSpeed;
        this.numberOfDoors = numberOfDoors;
        this.paint = paint;
        this.gasCapacity = gasCapacity;
        this.oilCapacity = oilCapacity;
        this.transmission = transmission;
    }

    public void start() throws CarException {
        if( this.running == true )
        {
            CarException e = new CarException(
              "Car is already running --- nasty grinding noise!" );
```

LISTING 9.2 Continued

```
                e.setEngineRunning( true );
                throw e;
        }
        running = true;
    }

    public void stop() throws CarException {
        if( this.running == false )
        {
            CarException e = new CarException( "Car is not running!" );
            e.setEngineRunning( false );
            throw e;
        }
        running = false;
    }

    public boolean isRunning() {
        return running;
    }

    public abstract void accelerate() throws CarException;

    public abstract void decelerate() throws CarException;

    public abstract void tuneUp();

    public abstract void changeOil();

    public int getCurrentSpeed() {
        return currentSpeed;
    }

    public String toString() {
        return typeOfCar;
    }
}
```

From Listing 9.2 you can see that the **start**, **stop**, **accelerate**, and **decelerate** methods are each declared to throw the **CarException**. The **start** and **stop** methods are implemented in the **NewCar** class and handle the logic for throwing the **CarException**. The **accelerate** and **decelerate** methods are both declared to be abstract, but for a subclass to throw an exception from a method it must be declared to be throwable in the superclass. A subclass can remove an exception from the exception list, but it cannot add anything that is not already declared in the superclass. One technique for addressing this issue is to declare that a method can throw the **exception** or **throwable** class so that a subclass is free to throw any exception it wants. Although this workaround is functional, it is often bad programming practice because you will want to define specifically what exceptions subclasses of your superclass can throw. Thus, the **accelerate** and **decelerate** methods are declared to throw the **CarException**.

Listing 9.3 shows the code for the modified Porsche class.

LISTING 9.3   Porsche.java

```java
public class Porsche extends NewCar
{
    // Attributes
    private int turbos = 2;
    private boolean nos;

    // State attributes
    private boolean turbo1Engaged = false;
    private boolean turbo2Engaged = false;
    private boolean nosEnabled = false;

    public Porsche()
    {
        super( "Porsche",
               450,
               220,
               2,
               "Yellow",
               15,
               5,
               NewCar.TIPTRONIC );
    }

    public void accelerate() throws CarException
    {
        // Check to see if we are running or not
        if( running == false )
        {
        CarException e = new CarException(
            "Car is not running, cannot accelerate!" );
            e.setEngineRunning( false );
            throw e;
        }

        // Create a variable representing how much we are going to
        // accelerate this second
        int increment = 15;

        // Check the turbos; they add 5mph per second acceleration
        if( turbo1Engaged )
        {
            increment += 5;
        }
        if( turbo2Engaged )
        {
            increment += 5;
        }

        // Check the NOS; it represents 15mph per second
        if( nos )
        {
            increment += 15;
```

LISTING 9.3   Continued

```
        }

        // Increment the current speed
        currentSpeed += increment;
        if( currentSpeed > maximumSpeed ) currentSpeed = maximumSpeed;
    }

    public void decelerate() throws CarException
    {
        // Check to see if we are running or not
        if( running == false )
        {
        CarException e = new CarException(
            "Car is not running, cannot decelerate!" );
            e.setEngineRunning( false );
            throw e;
        }
        currentSpeed -= 20;
        if( currentSpeed < 0 ) currentSpeed = 0;
    }

    public void tuneUp()
    {
        System.out.println( "Tuning up a porsche..." );
    }

    public void changeOil()
    {
        System.out.println( "Changing a porsche's oil..." );
    }

    public void engageTurbos()
    {
        turbo1Engaged = true;
        turbo2Engaged = true;
    }

    public void disengageTurbos()
    {
        turbo1Engaged = false;
        turbo2Engaged = false;
    }

    public void engageNOS()
    {
        nos = true;
        maximumSpeed += 50;
    }

    public void disengageNOS()
    {
        nos = false;
```

LISTING 9.3   Continued

```java
            maximumSpeed -= 50;
    }

    public String toString()
    {
        return "A shiny new " + paint + " Porsche!";
    }

    public static void main( String[] args )
    {
        Porsche p = new Porsche();
        System.out.println( "My new car: " + p );
        try
        {
            //p.start();
            System.out.println( "Current speed: " + p.getCurrentSpeed() );
            for( int i=0; i<20; i++ )
            {
                if( i == 5 )
                {
                    p.engageTurbos();
                }
                else if( i == 14 )
                {
                    p.engageNOS();
                }
                p.accelerate();
                System.out.println( "Current speed: " + p.getCurrentSpeed() );
            }
            p.disengageNOS();
            p.disengageTurbos();
            while( p.getCurrentSpeed() > 0 )
            {
                p.decelerate();
                System.out.println( "Current speed: " + p.getCurrentSpeed() );
            }
            p.stop();
        }
        catch( CarException ce )
        {
            ce.printStackTrace();
        }
    }
}
```

From Listing 9.3 you can see that the **accelerate** and **decelerate** methods are declared to throw the **CarException** and, in fact, check to see whether the car is running before performing its function, and if not it throws the **CarException**. In a more robust implementation it would also check the fluids and throw a **CarException** if the Porsche was out of gas or oil. Not only do the **accelerate** and **decelerate** methods set the text of the exception to describe the problem, they also call the **CarException**'s **setEngineRunning** method to inform the caller that the engine is not running.

The `Porsche`'s `main` method executes all the `Porsche`'s methods inside of a `try` block and prints a stack trace if the `CarException` is thrown. Initially, the `main` method does not call the `Porsche`'s start method, causing the subsequent `accelerate` method to fail and an exception to be thrown. If you uncomment the call to the `start` method, the output will look similar to that in the previous chapter. However, with the `start` method commented out, the result should look something similar to the following:

```
My new car: A shiny new Yellow Porsche!
Current speed: 0
CarException: Car is not running, cannot accelerate!
        at Porsche.accelerate(Porsche.java:29)
        at Porsche.main(Porsche.java:129)
```

Remember that the stack trace shows you every method that was called in the reverse order that it was called. If you read the `CarException` backward you'll see that the `Porsche`'s main method called the `Porsche`'s `accelerate` method, and then the `accelerate` method threw a `CarException` with the message body `Car is not running, cannot accelerate!` Furthermore, if we were to call the `CarException`'s `isEngineRunning` method it would return false.

Summary

This chapter walked you through Java's error-handling mechanism called exception handling. You learned what an exception was, how an exception is thrown, and how to catch an exception. Furthermore, you learned how to create a custom exception of your own and throw it from within your own code.

Java uses exceptions throughout its classes, so a strong foundation in exception handling is essential to using the Java programming language. Some languages facilitate exception handling, but do not enforce it. Java on the other hand forces you to use exceptions.

From this chapter you are ready to use Java's prebuilt classes, which will be discussed in the next chapter.

Review Questions

1. How do you throw an exception?

2. How do you handle an exception?

3. Describe the keyword `try` and how it is used.

4. What is the root class for all exceptions?

5. What type of exceptions require the caller to explicitly handle them?

6. What type of exceptions do not require that the caller explicitly handle them?

7. Can a subclass method throw an exception that its superclass method does not explicitly declare?

8. What is the `throws` keyword, and how does it differ from the `throw` keyword?

9. Describe all the steps required to create a custom exception, and throw it from your own code.

10. Why are exceptions Java classes as opposed to some other structure and how does that benefit you?

Exercises

1. In the previous chapter you created a set of animals that followed an inheritance hierarchy. In this chapter, I want you to modify the animals created in the previous chapter and add a new custom exception called `too tired`. Because each animal implements a `play` method, you should add a `too tired` exception to the `play` method's exception list. In each animal that plays, try to maintain their energy level. Upon each invocation of the `play` method, decrement the energy level. When the energy level reaches 0, throw a `too tired` exception. Modify your animal trainer source code to generate a `too tired` exception in one or more of your animals.

CHAPTER 10

JAVA CLASSES

> **In this chapter, you will learn the following:**
> - An introduction to JavaDoc
> - Using Java's Wrapper classes
> - Using String classes

Now that you know how to build your own classes, it's time to learn about the classes provided by Sun when you download Java. A core set of functionality exists in every programming language, and in Java it is exposed through prebuilt classes.

Introduction to JavaDoc

To effectively use Java's prebuilt classes you need to know what they can do and how to find the ones you want. Therefore there has to be a mechanism you can use to learn each class's methods, the parameters that they accept, the values that they return, and, most importantly, what the method does. Some classes are documented using the tool called JavaDoc, which parses Java source files looking for comments preceding methods that have a very special format and core tags.

Sun's methods are all documented using JavaDoc, and you'll find that your users will be able to effectively use your classes if you comment your methods using this standard instead of generating your own JavaDoc documentation. Before I show you all the intricate details of commenting your code for use with JavaDoc, take a look at Figure 10.1 to see the results. At the time of this writing you can access the following JavaDocs at `http://java.sun.com/apis.html`.

FIGURE 10.1

Sun's JavaDoc classes

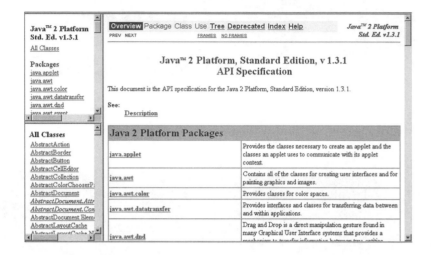

Looking at Figure 10.1, the upper-left corner shows all the available packages from which you can explore their classes. Java allows you to group similar classes into packages for both organizational purposes as well as some special security settings. The lower-left corner shows all the classes available to you. If you select a package from the upper-left corner, only its classes will appear in the lower-left corner. The right side of Figure 10.1 shows the details of all the packages shipped with the Sun SDK. When you click a package you'll see a description of the classes contained within the package. When you click an individual class you'll see a description of the class, a list of all its attributes, a summary of all its methods, and a detailed list of its methods, including usage.

To add JavaDoc comments to your classes, the general form of a comment is as follows:

```
/**
 * This is the description part of a doc comment
 *
 * @tag     Comment for the tag
 */
```

The comment starts with a forward slash followed by two asterisks, and ends with a single asterisk followed by a forward slash. You can place JavaDoc comments at the beginning of a class (preceding the class declaration) to provide a description of the class's functionality, or at the beginning of the method (preceding the method declaration) to provide a description of the method's functionality. Furthermore you can place comments before public constants and variable declarations.

JavaDoc defines a specific set of tags that have meaning dependent on their context (see Table 10.1).

TABLE 10.1 JavaDoc Tag Definitions

Tag	Description
@author	Denotes the author of the class (classes and interfaces only, required)
@version	Denotes the version of the class (classes and interfaces only, required)
@param	One parameter tag is specified for each parameter that is passed to the method (methods and constructors only)
@return	Describes the return value of the method (methods only)
@exception	One throws/exception tag is listed for each exception that the method can throw (@throws is a synonym added in JavaDoc 1.2)
@see	References another class or method
@since	Defines the version of the API that this method/class has been defined since
@serial	Documents serializable fields in this method (or @serialField or @serialData)
@deprecated	Notes that this method has been deprecated, which means that it can possibly be removed at some future time and users of your class should make notes and stop using this method

For example:

```
/**
 * Doubles an integer
 *
 * @param i     The integer to double
 * @return      An integer containing the doubled value
 */
public int double( int i ) {
  return 2*i;
}
```

refers to the following URL for complete documentation on using JavaDoc:

```
http://java.sun.com/javadoc
```

Using Java's Wrapper Classes

As you previously learned, all classes are derived from the `java.lang.Object` class. This is true for all types in the Java language except for primitive types, which include `int`, `boolean`, `float`, `double`, and so on. For the primitive types, the Java class libraries provide classes called wrapper classes. There is an `Integer` class that holds `int`s, there is a `Boolean` class that holds `boolean`s, and there is a `Float` class that holds `float`s. Wrapper classes are important when passing objects across distributed boundaries; distributed objects must all implement the serializable interface; there is no way for a primitive type to be serializable. But we can accomplish the same thing by creating a serializable wrapper around the object.

The wrapper classes have a very unique characteristic in that they are immutable. By definition, the value contained within one of the wrapper classes cannot be altered. Thus, you can be assured that any value you assign to the wrapper class will never change. The drawback to this feature is that if you want to modify the value contained within a wrapper class, you must first extract the value, modify the value, and then create a new wrapper class to hold the modified value. For example, consider the following:

```
// Create a new Integer
int n = 5;
Integer myInteger = new Integer( n );

// Increment n
int a = myInteger.intValue();
myInteger = new Integer( ++a );
```

Effectively, this means that to modify an `Integer`, you must create a new `Integer` instance and orphan the old one in memory. So, you gain the ability to pass objects across distributed boundaries, but at a price.

Although the wrapper classes are all directly derived from the object class, and there is no unique shared-base class, there is a pattern that you will notice when looking at the wrapper class methods. They all have methods of the following form:

- `xxxValue`—This method returns the associated primitive type

- `getXXX`—This method reads the system properties looking for the `String` value passed to this method and converts that value to the associated primitive type

- `valueOf`—This method converts a `String` value to a wrapper class instance

Furthermore, they all provide two constructors: one to build an instance of the class from its associated primitive type, and one to build an instance of the class from a string that will be converted into its associated primitive type.

The `Boolean` Class

The `Boolean` class wraps the `boolean` datatype. The constructors for the `Boolean` class are shown in Table 10.2.

TABLE 10.2   `Boolean` Constructors

Constructor	Description
`Boolean(boolean value)`	Allocates a `Boolean` object representing the `value` argument.
`Boolean(String s)`	Allocates a `Boolean` object representing the value `true` if the `string` argument is not `null` and is `equal`, ignoring case, to the string `true`.

From Table 10.2 you can see that a `Boolean` wrapper class instance can be built from either a `boolean` variable or from a `String` containing either the value `true` or `false`.

Table 10.3 shows some of the more useful methods provided by the `Boolean` class.

TABLE 10.3   Boolean Method Summary

Constructor	Description
`boolean booleanValue()`	Returns the value of this `Boolean` object as a `boolean` primitive.
`boolean equals(Object obj)`	Returns `true` if and only if the argument is not `null`, and is a `Boolean` object that represents the same `boolean` value as this object.
`static boolean getBoolean(String name)`	Returns `true` if and only if the system property named by the argument exists and is equal to the string `true`.
`String toString()`	Returns a `String` object representing this `Boolean`'s value
`static Boolean valueOf(String s)`	Returns a `Boolean` with a value represented by the specified `String`.

The `Boolean` class provides the aforementioned methods (`booleanValue()`, `getBoolean()`, and `valueOf()`) customized for working with the Boolean datatype. In addition, it has a couple more helper methods for converting the `Boolean` to a `String` and comparing to `Boolean`s for equality.

The `Byte` Class

The `Byte` class wraps the `Byte` datatype. The constructors for the `Byte` class are shown in Table 10.4.

TABLE 10.4   Byte Constructors

Constructor	Description
`Byte(byte value)`	Constructs a `Byte` object initialized to the specified `byte` value.
`Byte(String s)`	Constructs a `Byte` object initialized to the value specified by the `String` parameter.

From Table 10.4 you can see that you can build a `Byte` wrapper class instance from either a `byte` variable or from a `String` containing the decimal value (base 10).

Table 10.5 shows some of the more useful methods provided by the `Byte` class.

TABLE 10.5 Byte Method Summary

Method	Description
byte byteValue()	Returns the value of this `Byte` as a byte.
int compareTo(Byte anotherByte)	Compares two `Byte`s numerically.
int compareTo(Object o)	Compares this `Byte` to another `Object`.
static Byte decode(String nm)	Decodes a `String` into a `Byte`.
double doubleValue()	Returns the value of this `Byte` as a double.
boolean equals(Object obj)	Compares this `Object` to the specified `Object`.
float floatValue()	Returns the value of this `Byte` as a float.
int intValue()	Returns the value of this `Byte` as an int.
long longValue()	Returns the value of this `Byte` as a long.
static byte parseByte(String s)	Assuming the specified `String` represents a byte, returns that byte's value (base 10).
static byte parseByte(String s, int radix)	Assuming the specified `String` represents a byte, returns that byte's value.
short shortValue()	Returns the value of this `Byte` as a short.
String toString()	Returns a `String` object representing this `Byte` value.
static String toString(byte b)	Returns a new `String` object representing the specified `Byte`.
static Byte valueOf(String s)	Assuming the specified `String` represents a byte, returns a new `Byte` object initialized to that value.
static Byte valueOf(String s, int radix)	Assuming the specified `String` represents a byte, returns a new `Byte` object initialized to that value.

As you can see from Table 10.5, the `Byte` class is much more sophisticated than the `Boolean` class because a byte can be interpreted in many ways. The `Byte` class provides methods to convert the byte to a `short`, an `int`, a `long`, or `double` value. It provides a set of methods for converting a string to a byte, but to do this it must know the radix of the string value (for example, decimal equals 10, hexadecimal equals 16). Furthermore, it provides two methods for comparing one byte to another byte.

The `Character` Class

The `Character` class wraps the `char` datatype. The constructor for the `Character` class is shown in Table 10.6.

TABLE 10.6   `Character` Constructor

Constructor	Description
`Character(char value)`	Constructs a `Character` object and initializes it so that it represents the primitive value argument.

From Table 10.6 you can see that the `Character` class is an exception to the two constructor summaries described earlier. A character only represents a single character and not a string of characters; therefore, it is not necessary to provide a constructor that accepts a string of characters. Hence, the `Character` class only provides a constructor that accepts a `char` datatype.

Table 10.7 shows some of the more useful methods provided by the `Character` class.

TABLE 10.7   `Character` Method Summary

Method	Description
`char charValue()`	Returns the value of this `Character` object.
`int compareTo(Character anotherCharacter)`	Compares two `Character` objects numerically.
`int compareTo(Object o)`	Compares this `Character` to another `Object`.
`static int digit(char ch, int radix)`	Returns the numeric value of the character ch in the specified radix.
`boolean equals(Object obj)`	Compares this `Object` against the specified `Object`.
`static char forDigit(int digit, int radix)`	Determines the character representation for a specific `digit` in the specified `radix`.
`static int getNumericValue(char ch)`	Returns the Unicode numeric value of the character as a non-negative integer.
`static int getType(char ch)`	Returns a value indicating a character category.
`static boolean isDefined(char ch)`	Determines if a character has a defined meaning in Unicode.
`static boolean isDigit(char ch)`	Determines if the specified character is a digit.

TABLE 10.7 Continued

Method	Description
`static boolean isIdentifierIgnorable(char ch)`	Determines if the specified character should be regarded as an ignorable character in a Java identifier or a Unicode identifier.
`static boolean isISOControl(char ch)`	Determines if the specified character is an ISO control character.
`static boolean isJavaIdentifierPart(char ch)`	Determines if the specified character can be part of a Java identifier other than the first character.
`static boolean isJavaIdentifierStart(char ch)`	Determines if the specified character is permissible as the first character in a Java identifier.
`static boolean isLetter(char ch)`	Determines if the specified character is a letter.
`static boolean isLetterOrDigit(char ch)`	Determines if the specified character is a letter or digit.
`static boolean isLowerCase(char ch)`	Determines if the specified character is a lowercase character.
`static boolean isSpaceChar(char ch)`	Determines if the specified character is a Unicode space character.
`static boolean isTitleCase(char ch)`	Determines if the specified character is a titlecase character.
`static boolean isUnicodeIdentifierPart(char ch)`	Determines if the specified character can be part of a Unicode identifier as other than the first character.
`static boolean isUnicodeIdentifierStart(char ch)`	Determines if the specified character is permissible as the first character in a Unicode identifier.
`static boolean isUpperCase(char ch)`	Determines if the specified character is an uppercase character.
`static boolean isWhitespace(char ch)`	Determines if the specified character is white space according to Java.
`static char toLowerCase(char ch)`	The given character is mapped to its lowercase equivalent; if the character has no lowercase equivalent, the character itself is returned.

TABLE 10.7   Continued

Method	Description
`String toString()`	Returns a `String` object representing this character's value.
`static char toTitleCase(char ch)`	Converts the character argument to titlecase.
`static char toUpperCase(char ch)`	Converts the character argument to uppercase.

Characters can be difficult to work with because they do not necessarily represent a single letter or digit, but can also represent a Unicode character. The `Character` class provides a plethora of methods for testing, the value and type of a character, as well as methods to manipulate the value of a character. Review Table 10.7 and refer to JavaDoc documentation for additional information.

The `Double` Class

The `Double` class wraps the `double` datatype. The constructors for the `Double` class are shown in Table 10.8.

TABLE 10.8   `Double` Constructors

Constructor	Description
`Double(double value)`	Constructs a newly allocated `Double` object that represents the primitive double argument.
`Double(String s)`	Constructs a newly allocated `Double` object that represents the floating-point value of type double represented by the `String`.

As you can see from Table 10.8, `Double` class follows the pattern I mentioned earlier: It contains two constructors, one that accepts a double-primitive type and one that accepts a string.

Table 10.9 shows some of the more useful methods provided by the `Double` class.

TABLE 10.9   `Double` Method Summary

Method	Description
`byte byteValue()`	Returns the value of this `Double` as a `byte` (by casting to a `byte`).
`int compareTo(Double anotherDouble)`	Compares two `Double` classes numerically.
`int compareTo(Object o)`	Compares this `Double` to another `Object`.

TABLE 10.9 Continued

Method	Description
`static long doubleToLongBits(double value)`	Returns a representation of the specified floating-point value according to the IEEE 754 floating-point "double format" bit layout.
`static long doubleToRawLongBits(double value)`	Returns a representation of the specified floating-point value according to the IEEE 754 floating-point "double format" bit layout.
`double doubleValue()`	Returns the double value of this `Double`.
`boolean equals(Object obj)`	Compares this `Object` against the specified `Object`.
`float floatValue()`	Returns the float value of this `Double`.
`int intValue()`	Returns the integer value of this `Double` (by casting to an int).
`boolean isInfinite()`	Returns true if this `Double` value is infinitely large in magnitude.
`static boolean isInfinite(double v)`	Returns `true` if the specified number is infinitely large in magnitude.
`boolean isNaN()`	Returns `true` if this Double value is the special Not-a-Number (NaN) value.
`static boolean isNaN(double v)`	Returns `true` if the specified number is the special Not-a-Number (NaN) value.
`static double longBitsToDouble(long bits)`	Returns the double-float corresponding to a given bit representation.
`long longValue()`	Returns the long value of this `Double` (by casting to a long).
`static double parseDouble(String s)`	Returns a new `Double` initialized to the value represented by the specified `String`, as performed by the `valueOf` method of `Double` class.
`short shortValue()`	Returns the value of this `Double` as a short (by casting to a short).
`String toString()`	Returns a `String` representation of this `Double` object.
`static String toString(double d)`	Creates a `String` representation of the `Double` argument.
`static Double valueOf(String s)`	Returns a new `Double` object initialized to the value represented by the specified `String`.

As shown in Table 10.9 the `Double` class provides a set of methods for converting a `Double` to another primitive type (`byte`, `int`, `long`, `float`), modifying the bit structure/interpretation, and a couple methods used for determining the validity of the double value. The `isNAN()` method returns `true` if the double value contained in the `Double` class is a valid number, and the `isInfinite()` method returns `true` if the value of the double is equivalent to infinity. A careful point to note about the conversion methods in the `Double` class is that they perform a cast to the destination primitive type. You always run the risk of losing some of the value when going from a wide type to a narrow type.

The `Float` Class

The `Float` class wraps the `float` datatype. The constructors for the `Float` class are shown in Table 10.10.

TABLE 10.10   Float Constructors

Constructor	Description
`Float(double value)`	Constructs a newly allocated `Float` object that represents the argument converted from a double to a `float`.
`Float(float value)`	Constructs a newly allocated `Float` object that represents the primitive `float` argument.
`Float(String s)`	Constructs a newly allocated `Float` object that represents the floating-point value of type `float` represented by the `String`.

As you can see from Table 10.10, the `Float` class contains three constructors: one that converts a `double` to a `float`, one that accepts a `float`, and one that accepts a `String`.

Table 10.11 shows some of the more useful methods provided by the `Float` class.

TABLE 10.11   Float Method Summary

Method	Description
`byte byteValue()`	Returns the value of this `Float` as a byte (by casting to a byte).
`int compareTo(Float anotherFloat)`	Compares two `Float` classes numerically.
`int compareTo(Object o)`	Compares this `Float` to another `Object`.
`double doubleValue()`	Returns the double value of this `Float` object.
`boolean equals(Object obj)`	Compares this `Object` against some other `Object`.
`static int floatToIntBits(float value)`	Returns the bit represention of a single-float value.

TABLE 10.11   Float Method Summary

Method	Description
static int floatToRawIntBits(float value)	Returns the bit represention of a single-float value.
float floatValue()	Returns the float value of this Float object.
static float intBitsToFloat(int bits)	Returns the single float corresponding to a given bit representation.
int intValue()	Returns the integer value of this Float (by casting to an int).
boolean isInfinite()	Returns true if this Float value is infinitely large in magnitude.
static boolean isInfinite(float v)	Returns true if the specified number is infinitely large in magnitude.
boolean isNaN()	Returns true if this Float value is Not-a-Number (NaN).
static boolean isNaN(float v)	Returns true if the specified number is the special Not-a-Number (NaN) value.
long longValue()	Returns the long value of this Float (by casting to a long).
static float parseFloat(String s)	Returns a new float initialized to the value represented by the specified String, as performed by the valueOf method of the Double class.
short shortValue()	Returns the value of this Float as a short (by casting to a short).
String toString()	Returns a String representation of this Float object.
static String toString(float f)	Returns a String representation for the specified float value.
static Float valueOf(String s)	Returns the floating-point value represented by the specified String.

The Float class provides methods for converting its float value to other data types (byte, short, int, long, double), as well as converting a string of two floats and converting a float to a string. Other methods include validation of the float value to see if it is a number or if it is infinity.

The `Integer` Class

The `Integer` class wraps the `int` datatype. The constructors for the `Integer` class are shown in Table 10.12.

TABLE 10.12   Integer Constructors

Constructor	Description
`Integer(int value)`	Constructs a newly allocated `Integer` object that represents the primitive `int` argument.
`Integer(String s)`	Constructs a newly allocated `Integer` object that represents the value represented by the `String`.

The `Integer` class provides the two standard constructors: one that accepts an `int` value, and one that accepts a `string` and converts it to an `Integer`.

Table 10.13 shows some of the more useful methods provided by the `Integer` class.

TABLE 10.13   Integer Method Summary

Method	Description
`byte byteValue()`	Returns the value of this `Integer` as a `byte`.
`int compareTo(Integer anotherInteger)`	Compares two `Integer` objects numerically.
`int compareTo(Object o)`	Compares this `Integer` to another `Object`.
`static Integer decode(String nm)`	Decodes a `String` into an `Integer`.
`double doubleValue()`	Returns the value of this `Integer` as a `double`.
`boolean equals(Object obj)`	Compares this `Object` to the specified `Object`.
`float floatValue()`	Returns the value of this `Integer` as a `float`.
`static Integer getInteger(String nm)`	Determines the `Integer` value of the system property with the specified name.
`static Integer getInteger(String nm, int val)`	Determines the Integer value of the system property with the specified name.
`static Integer getInteger(String nm, Integer val)`	Returns the `Integer` value of the system property with the specified name.
`int intValue()`	Returns the value of this `Integer` as an `int`.
`long longValue()`	Returns the value of this `Integer` as a `long`.

TABLE 10.13   Continued

Method	Description
`static int parseInt(String s)`	Parses the `String` argument as a signed decimal integer.
`static int parseInt(String s, int radix)`	Parses the `String` argument as a signed integer in the radix specified by the second argument.
`short shortValue()`	Returns the value of this `Integer` as a `short`.
`static String toBinaryString(int i)`	Creates a `String` representation of the `Integer` argument as an unsigned Integer in base 2.
`static String toHexString(int i)`	Creates a `String` representation of the `Integer` argument as an unsigned integer in base 16.
`static String toOctalString(int i)`	Creates a `String` representation of the integer argument as an unsigned integer in base 8.
`String toString()`	Returns a `String` object representing this `Integer`'s value.
`static String toString(int i)`	Returns a new `String` object representing the specified integer.
`static String toString(int i, int radix)`	Creates a `String` representation of the first argument in the `radix` specified by the second argument.
`static Integer valueOf(String s)`	Returns a new `Integer` object initialized to the value of the specified `String`.
`static Integer valueOf(String s, int radix)`	Returns a new `Integer` object initialized to the value of the specified `String`.

The `Integer` class provides the same methods for converting its `int` value to the other primitive types (`byte`, `short`, `long`, `float`, `double`, and so on), as well as methods to convert the `int` to a `string` and a `string` to an int. It provides some very useful methods for converting an `Integer` from its natural decimal value to a different radix base: `binary`, `octal`, `hexadecimal`. Remember that these methods exist because doing the conversion manually is very tedious, especially when someone has already done it for you.

The Long Class

The `Long` class wraps the `long` datatype. The constructors for the `Long` class are shown in Table 10.14.

TABLE 10.14   Long Constructors

Constructor	Description
Long(long value)	Constructs a newly allocated Long object that represents the primitive long argument.
Long(String s)	Constructs a newly allocated Long object that represents the value represented by the String in decimal form.

The Long class provides the two standard constructors: one that accepts a long value, and one that accepts a string and converts it to a Long.

Table 10.15 shows some of the more useful methods provided by the Long class.

TABLE 10.15   Long Method Summary

Method	Description
byte byteValue()	Returns the value of this Long as a byte.
int compareTo(Long anotherLong)	Compares two Long objects numerically.
int compareTo(Object o)	Compares this Long to another Object.
static Long decode(String nm)	Decodes a String into a Long.
double doubleValue()	Returns the value of this Long as a double.
boolean equals(Object obj)	Compares this Object against the specified Object.
float floatValue()	Returns the value of this Long as a float.
static Long getLong(String nm)	Determines the Long value of the system property with the specified name.
static Long getLong(String nm, long val)	Determines the Long value of the system property with the specified name.
static Long getLong(String nm, Long val)	Returns the Long value of the system property with the specified name.
int intValue()	Returns the value of this Long as an int.
long longValue()	Returns the value of this Long as a long value.
static long parseLong(String s)	Parses the String argument as a signed decimal long.
static long parseLong(String s, int radix)	Parses the String argument as a signed long in the radix specified by the second argument.

TABLE 10.15   Continued

Method	Description
`short shortValue()`	Returns the value of this `Long` as a `short`.
`static String toBinaryString(long i)`	Creates a `String` representation of the `long` argument as an unsigned integer in base 2.
`static String toHexString(long i)`	Creates a `String` representation of the `Long` argument as an unsigned integer in base 16.
`static String toOctalString(long i)`	Creates a `String` representation of the `long` argument as an unsigned integer in base 8.
`String toString()`	Returns a `String` object representing this `Long`'s value.
`static String toString(long i)`	Returns a new `String` object representing the specified integer.
`static String toString(long i, int radix)`	Creates a `String` representation of the first argument in the `radix` specified by the second argument.
`static Long valueOf(String s)`	Returns a new `Long` object initialized to the value of the specified `String`.
`static Long valueOf(String s, int radix)`	Returns a new `Long` object initialized to the value of the specified `String`.

The `Long` class is virtually identical to the `Integer` class except that it uses long value-sensitive integer values. It provides methods for converting its long value to the other primitive types (`byte`, `short`, `int`, `float`, `double`), as well as methods to convert the `long` to a `string` and a `string` to a `long`. It provides the same methods for converting a long from its natural decimal value to a different radix base: `binary`, `octal`, `hexadecimal`.

The `Short` Class

The `Short` class wraps the `short` datatype. The constructors for the `Short` class are shown in Table 10.16.

TABLE 10.16   Short Constructors

Constructor	Description
`Short(short value)`	Constructs a `Short` object initialized to the specified short value.
`Short(String s)`	Constructs a `Short` object initialized to the value specified by the `String` parameter.

The Short class provides the two standard constructors: one that accepts a short value and one that accepts a String and converts it to a Short.

Table 10.17 shows some of the more useful methods provided by the Short class.

TABLE 10.17 Short Method Summary

Method	Description
byte byteValue()	Returns the value of this Short as a byte.
int compareTo(Object o)	Compares this Short to another Object.
int compareTo(Short anotherShort)	Compares two Shorts numerically.
static Short decode(String nm)	Decodes a String into a Short.
double doubleValue()	Returns the value of this Short as a double.
boolean equals(Object obj)	Compares this Object to the specified Object.
float floatValue()	Returns the value of this Short as a float.
int intValue()	Returns the value of this Short as an int.
long longValue()	Returns the value of this Short as a long.
static short parseShort(String s)	Assuming the specified String represents a Short, returns that Short's value.
static short parseShort(String s, int radix)	Assuming the specified String represents a short, returns that short's value.
short shortValue()	Returns the value of this Short as a short.
String toString()	Returns a String object representing this Short's value.
static String toString(short s)	Returns a new String object representing the specified Short.
static Short valueOf(String s)	Assuming the specified String represents a short, returns a new Short object initialized to that value.
static Short valueOf(String s, int radix)	Assuming the specified String represents a short, returns a new Short object initialized to that value.

The Short class is virtually identical to the Integer and Long classes except that it uses a short value: It provides methods for converting its short value to the other primitive types (byte, int, long, float, double), as well as methods to convert the short to a string and a string to a short.

Using String Classes

Java provides support for strings using the String class. A String is a collection of characters that presumably represents some meaningful value. Characters are delimited by single quotes, but a string is delimited by double quotes. For example:

```
String name = "Michael";
```

Java manages strings differently than other primitive data types. It maintains a string table, which holds all strings that are in memory at any given time. Similar to the wrapper classes, the String class is immutable, which means you cannot modify the value of the string, but you must create a new string to hold a new value. If you create a new string matching a value that is already in the string table, your string will simply reference the existing one.

Java implemented this as an optimization to minimize the duplication of string values that tend to exist so frequently in software programs. So how does this affect you?

From the surface this appears to be a nice optimization provided by Java, but insignificant to the programmer. Most beginning Java programmers do not understand that strings are immutable, nor do they know of the existence of the string table.

The impact of string immutability is that the modification of the string actually results in the creation of a new entry into the string table. The String class is special because the addition operator is overloaded. For example:

```
String greeting = "Hello";
greeting += ", ";
greeting += "World!";
System.out.println( greeting );
```

If you were to run this code snippet, it would print out:

```
Hello, World!
```

This is exactly what you'd expect, but what is happening in memory? If we applied the principles of immutability combined with the concept of a string table to the string greeting, there must be a new "Hello" entry added to the string table on the creation of the greeting variable. When the comma is appended to the greeting, the original "Hello" string cannot be modified, so there must be a new entry added to the string table with the value "Hello, ". Furthermore, with the addition of the "World!" string, there must be yet another string created and added to the string table; this time with the value "Hello, World!". Thus, the string table's memory has been littered with two unused strings. It must have the following values:

```
Hello
Hello,
Hello, World
```

Eventually the garbage collector will clean the orphaned memory, but this program inadvertently generated the need to do so. This example might not seem extreme, but consider the following pseudo code that reads a text file character by character:

```
String value;
while( notEndOfFile ) {
  value += nextCharacter;
}
```

And also consider that the file looks as follows:

abcdefg

The resultant string table will look as follows:

a
ab
abc
abcd
abcde
abcdef
abcdefg

What if the file were several hundred kilobytes? Now this becomes a significant problem. Because of the limitation of immutable strings, Java has provided a class to manipulate strings in memory that bypasses the string table—the `StringBuffer` class. The `StringBuffer` class maintains a collection of characters and enables you to insert and append characters or strings to it. You can build a `StringBuffer` from a `String`, and you can convert a `StringBuffer` to a `String`. Therefore, it is very typical to see a string manipulated by using the `StringBuffer` class. Between the `String` class and the `StringBuffer` class, you will find most every function is string manipulation that you could want.

The `String` Class

The `String` class provides methods to help you manipulate and modify strings (see Table 10.18).

TABLE 10.18   `String` Method Summary

Method	Description
`char charAt(int index)`	Returns the character at the specified index.
`int compareTo(Object o)`	Compares this `String` to another `Object`.
`int compareTo(String anotherString)`	Compares two strings lexicographically.
`int compareToIgnoreCase(String str)`	Compares two `Strings` lexicographically, ignoring case considerations.
`String concat(String str)`	Concatenates the specified `String` to the end of this `String`.
`static String copyValueOf(char[] data)`	Returns a `String` that is equivalent to the specified character array.

TABLE 10.18   Continued

Method	Description
`static String copyValueOf(char[] data, int offset, int count)`	Returns a `String` that is equivalent to the specified character array.
`boolean endsWith(String suffix)`	Tests if this `String` ends with the specified suffix.
`boolean equals(Object anObject)`	Compares this `String` to the specified object.
`boolean equalsIgnoreCase(String anotherString)`	Compares this `String` to another `String`, ignoring case considerations.
`byte[] getBytes()`	Converts this `String` into bytes according to the platform's default character encoding, storing the result into a new `byte` array.
`byte[] getBytes(String enc)`	Converts this `String` into bytes according to the specified character encoding, storing the result into a new byte array.
`void getChars(int srcBegin, int srcEnd, char[] dst, int dstBegin)`	Copies characters from this `String` into the destination character array.
`int indexOf(int ch)`	Returns the index within this `String` of the first occurrence of the specified character.
`int indexOf(int ch, int fromIndex)`	Returns the index within this `String` of the first occurrence of the specified character, starting the search at the specified index.
`int indexOf(String str)`	Returns the index within this string of the first occurrence of the specified substring.
`int indexOf(String str, int fromIndex)`	Returns the index within this `String` of the first occurrence of the specified substring, starting at the specified index.
`String intern()`	Returns a canonical representation for the `String` object.
`int lastIndexOf(int ch)`	Returns the index within this `String` of the last occurrence of the specified character.
`int lastIndexOf(int ch, int fromIndex)`	Returns the index within this `String` of the last occurrence of the specified character, searching backward starting at the specified index.
`int lastIndexOf(String str)`	Returns the `index` within this `String` of the right-most occurrence of the specified substring.
`int lastIndexOf(String str, int fromIndex)`	Returns the `index` within this `String` of the last occurrence of the specified substring.

TABLE 10.18   Continued

Method	Description
`int length()`	Returns the `length` of this `String`.
`boolean regionMatches(boolean ignoreCase, int toffset, String other, int ooffset, int len)`	Tests if two `string` regions are equal.
`boolean regionMatches(int toffset, String other, int ooffset, int len)`	Tests if two `String` regions are equal.
`String replace(char oldChar, char newChar)`	Returns a new `String` resulting from replacing all occurrences of `oldChar` in this string with `newChar`.
`boolean startsWith(String prefix)`	Tests if this `String` starts with the specified `prefix`.
`boolean startsWith(String prefix, int toffset)`	Tests if this `String` starts with the specified prefix beginning a specified index.
`String substring(int beginIndex)`	Returns a new `String` that is a substring of this string.
`String substring(int beginIndex, int endIndex)`	Returns a new `String` that is a substring of this `String`.
`char[] toCharArray()`	Converts this `String` to a new character array.
`String toLowerCase()`	Converts all the characters in this `String` to lower-case using the rules of the default locale, which is returned by `LocalegetDefault`.
`String toLowerCase(Locale locale)`	Converts all the characters in this `String` to lower-case using the rules of the given `Locale`.
`String toString()`	This object (which is already a `String`!) is itself returned.
`String toUpperCase()`	Converts all the characters in this `String` to upper-case using the rules of the default `locale`, which is returned by `LocalegetDefault`.
`String toUpperCase(Locale locale)`	Converts all the characters in this `String` to upper-case using the rules of the given `locale`.
`String trim()`	Removes white space from both ends of this `String`.
`static String valueOf(boolean b)`	Returns the `String` representation of the `boolean` argument.

TABLE 10.18   Continued

Method	Description
static String valueOf(char c)	Returns the String representation of the char argument.
static String valueOf(char[] data)	Returns the String representation of the char array argument.
static String valueOf(char[] data, int offset, int count)	Returns the string representation of a specific subarray of the char array argument.
static String valueOf(double d)	Returns the String representation of the double argument.
static String valueOf(float f)	Returns the String representation of the float argument.
static String valueOf(int i)	Returns the String representation of the int argument.
static String valueOf(long l)	Returns the String representation of the long argument.
static String valueOf(Object obj)	Returns the String representation of the Object argument.

Strings can be compared by both considering case and ignoring case; there are a pair of methods defined for comparing and testing the equality of two strings ignoring case and paying attention to case.

For example:

```
String s1 = "Hello";
String s2 = "hello";

if( s1.equals( s2 ) ) {
   System.out.println( "Strings are exactly equal - including case" );
}
else if( s1.equalsIgnoreCase( s2 ) ) {
   System.out.println( "Strings are equal - ignoring case" );
}
else {
   System.out.println( "Strings are not equal" );
}
```

In this case, the output will be "**Strings are equal — ignoring case**".

Strings have characters that are accessible via a zero-based index:

```
String s1 = "Hello";
System.out.println( "Index 1 = " + s1.charAt( 1 ) ); // prints "e"
```

This will be important for all string searches and substring extractions/modifications.

Other methods are provided to test the value of the beginning at the end of a string:

```
String greeting = "Hello, World";
if( greeting.startsWith( "Hello" ) ) {
  System.out.println( "String starts with Hello" );
}
if( greeting.endsWith( "World" ) ) {
  System.out.println( "String ends with World" );
}
```

The `String` class also provides a set of substring methods to extract parts of the string:

```
String action = "Feed the baby";
System.out.println( action.substring( 5 ) ); // Prints "the baby"
System.out.println( action.substring( 5, 8 ) ); // Prints "the"
```

An important facet of extracting a substring is to remember that the first value, or the beginning index, is an inclusive value, whereas the second value, or the end the index, is an exclusive value. So, the first value must be the zero-based index of the first letter of the substring that you want to extract, and the second value must be one plus the zero-based index of the last letter of the substring that you want to extract.

There are two methods to return a string with a modified case:

```
String greeting = "Hello, World";
System.out.println( greeting ); // "Hello, World"
System.out.println( greeting.toLowerCase() ); // "hello, world"
System.out.println( greeting.toUpperCase() ); // "HELLO, WORLD"
```

There also methods for locating substrings within string:

```
String number = "one two one three one four";

// Prints "0"
System.out.println( "First index of 'one': " + number.indexOf( "one" ) );

// Prints "8"; look for "one" starting at index 1
System.out.println( "Next index of 'one': " + number.indexOf( "one", 1 ) );

// Prints "18"; look for "one" starting at end of the string and look backwards
System.out.println( "Next index of 'one': " + number.lastIndexOf( "one" ) );
```

Read through the JavaDoc and familiarize yourself with the other methods provided by the `String` class.

The `StringBuffer` Class

As I mentioned earlier, the `String` class is immutable and, therefore, you should not attempt to modify the value of a `String`. The `StringBuffer` class provides you a good interface to modify `String` values, and in the end convert the value back to a `String` class.

`StringBuffer` classes can be constructed initially empty, empty but with a specified starting size, or from an existing `String` (see Table 10.19).

TABLE 10.19 StringBuffer Method Summary

Method	Description
StringBuffer append(boolean b)	Appends the string representation of the boolean argument to the StringBuffer.
StringBuffer append(char c)	Appends the string representation of the char argument to this StringBuffer.
StringBuffer append(char[] str)	Appends the string representation of the char array argument to this StringBuffer.
StringBuffer append(char[] str, int offset, int len)	Appends the string representation of a subarray of the char array argument to this StringBuffer.
StringBuffer append(double d)	Appends the String representation of the double argument to this StringBuffer.
StringBuffer append(float f)	Appends the string representation of the float argument to this StringBuffer.
StringBuffer append(int i)	Appends the string representation of the int argument to this StringBuffer.
StringBuffer append(long l)	Appends the string representation of the long argument to this StringBuffer.
StringBuffer append(Object obj)	Appends the string representation of the Object argument to this StringBuffer.
StringBuffer append(String str)	Appends the String to this StringBuffer.
int capacity()	Returns the current capacity of the StringBuffer.
char charAt(int index)	The specified character of the sequence currently represented by the StringBuffer, as indicated by the index argument, is returned.
StringBuffer delete(int start, int end)	Removes the characters in a substring of this StringBuffer.
StringBuffer deleteCharAt(int index)	Removes the character at the specified position in this StringBuffer (shortening the StringBuffer by one character).
void ensureCapacity (int minimumCapacity)	Ensures that the capacity of the StringBuffer is at least equal to the specified minimum.
void getChars(int srcBegin, int srcEnd, char[] dst, int dstBegin)	Characters are copied from this StringBuffer into the destination character array dst.
StringBuffer insert(int offset, boolean b)	Inserts the string representation of the Boolean argument into this StringBuffer.

TABLE 10.19 Continued

Method	Description
`StringBuffer insert(int offset, char c)`	Inserts the `String` representation of the char argument into this `StringBuffer`.
`StringBuffer insert(int offset, char[] str)`	Inserts the String representation of the char array argument into this `StringBuffer`.
`StringBuffer insert(int index, char[] str, int offset, int len)`	Inserts the string representation of a subarray of the str array argument into this `StringBuffer`.
`StringBuffer insert(int offset, double d)`	Inserts the string representation of the double argument into this StringBuffer.
`StringBuffer insert(int offset, float f)`	Inserts the string representation of the `float` argument into this `StringBuffer`.
`StringBuffer insert(int offset, int i)`	Inserts the string representation of the second int argument into this `StringBuffer`.
`StringBuffer insert(int offset, long l)`	Inserts the string representation of the long argument into this `StringBuffer`.
`StringBuffer insert(int offset, Object obj)`	Inserts the string representation of the `Object` argument into this `StringBuffer`.
`StringBuffer insert(int offset, String str)`	Inserts the `String` into this `StringBuffer`.
`int length()`	Returns the length (character count) of this `StringBuffer`.
`StringBuffer replace(int start, int end, String str)`	Replaces the characters in a substring of this `StringBuffer` with characters in the specified `String`.
`StringBuffer reverse()`	The character sequence contained in this `StringBuffer` is replaced by the reverse of the sequence.
`void setCharAt(int index, char ch)`	The character at the specified index of this `StringBuffer` is set to ch.
`void setLength(int newLength)`	Sets the length of this `StringBuffer`.
`String substring(int start)`	Returns a new `String` that contains a subsequence of characters currently contained in this `StringBuffer`. The substring begins at the specified index and extends to the end of the `StringBuffer`.
`String substring(int start, int end)`	Returns a new `String` that contains a subsequence of characters currently contained in this `StringBuffer`.
`String toString()`	Converts to a `String` representing the data in this `StringBuffer`.

The `StringBuffer` class provides methods to append values to the end of the `StringBuffer`, insert values somewhere inside the `StringBuffer`, and delete values randomly within the `StringBuffer`. Now consider the previous example of reading seven characters from a text file:

```
File:
abcdefg

Pseudo Code:
StringBuffer sb = new StringBuffer();
while( notEndOfFile ) {
  sb.append( nextCharacter );
}
String value = sb.toString();
```

Comparing this to the earlier example, the variable value still has the value `abcdefg`, but the string table does not have any of the intermediate values.

Aside from having the capability to modify a `String`, the `StringBuffer` class provides you with the substring functionality as well as two new methods: reverse and replace. We are free to modify the value of a string because a string table doesn't limit us. Therefore, the `reverse` and `replace` methods are nice enhancements.

The `StringTokenizer` Class

The last category of string utility classes that I want to describe to you is the `StringTokenizer` class. The `StringTokenizer` class enables you to break a string into components called *tokens*. A prime example of using this would be reading a comma-separated value (CSV) file; it is fairly common to export data from the spreadsheets or a database into a flat-text file that has all the column values separated by commas. Consider the following string:

```
1,2,3,4,5,6,7,8,9
```

You might want to pull out all the values one by one, excluding the commas. The `StringTokenizer` class is constructed from a string that you want to tokenize and, optionally, a list of tokens and the Boolean stating whether to return each token. Table 10.20 lists the `StringTokenizer` constructors.

TABLE 10.20   `StringTokenizer` Constructors

Method	Description
`StringTokenizer(String str)`	Constructs a `StringTokenizer` for the specified string.
`StringTokenizer(String str, String delim)`	Constructs a `StringTokenizer` for the specified string.
`StringTokenizer(String str, String delim, boolean returnDelims)`	Constructs a `StringTokenizer` for the specified string.

Table 10.21 shows that methods of the `StringTokenizer` class.

TABLE 10.21   `StringTokenizer` Methods

Method	Description
int countTokens()	Calculates the number of times that this tokenizer's nextToken method can be called before it generates an exception.
boolean hasMoreElements()	Returns the same value as the hasMoreTokens method.
boolean hasMoreTokens()	Tests if there are more tokens available from this tokenizer's string.
Object nextElement()	Returns the same value as the nextToken method, except that its declared return value is Object rather than String.
String nextToken()	Returns the next token from this StringTokenizer.
String nextToken(String delim)	Returns the next token in this StringTokenizer's string.

Here is an example using the `StringTokenizer` class to parse the aforementioned comma-separated value string:

```
String source = "1,2,3,4,5,6,7,8,9";
StringTokenizer st = new StringTokenizer( source, ",", false );
while( st.hasMoreTokens() ) {
  String value = st.nextToken();
  System.out.println( value );
}
```

The output of this code snippet is

```
1
2
3
4
5
6
7
8
9
```

Summary

Java provides objects that wrap all primitive types available in the Java programming language; these are referred to as wrapper classes. The numeric wrapper classes provide methods for converting strings to numbers and numbers to strings, and for converting one primitive data type to another.

The String class is a specialized class that shares the common characteristic of immutability with wrapper classes. Furthermore, Java maintains strings in a string table to optimize the amount of text storage in a program, but constructing and modify strings have the strange side effect of inadvertently creating unwanted temporary strings. To combat this, Java provides the StringBuffer class to manipulate strings outside of the string table. Java provides prewritten string utility classes to help you.

The next chapter looks at more predefined classes and in particular those used for storing and maintaining data.

Review Questions

1. Why would you want to use and object wrapper rather than a primitive type?

2. How could you convert a String to an Integer?

3. What is immutability?

4. How does immutability affect strings?

5. What is the string table?

6. What is the difference between the String class and the StringBuffer class?

7. How can you reverse a string?

8. What is the StringTokenizer class?

9. What is the difference between a token and the delimiter?

10. Why would you want to use a StringTokenizer class?

Exercises

1. Use the StringTokenizer class to parse a comma-separated value file and display each token on its own line.

2. Use the StringBuffer class to read text from the standard input (System.in) and then print a String once the user presses Enter.

CHAPTER 11

COLLECTION CLASSES

You will learn about the following in this chapter:

- Data structure concepts

- The benefits/trade-offs of each data structure type

- Java's implementation of data structure classes

The Problem Collection Classes Solve

Up to this point, we have created various objects, and you have learned the intricacies of object-oriented programming: encapsulation, inheritance, and polymorphism. After we have our objects defined we're going to have to do something meaningful with them.

Consider, for example, storing a collection of employees where the unique differentiator is the employee's Social Security number. We can store each employee in sequential order by his Social Security number, but what is that going to look like in memory? Are we going to block out enough memory to store 1,000 employees, and then insert them in sequential order? What happens when we have 500 records filled, and we have a new employee with a low Social Security number, are we going to move all 500 records down in memory and insert the new record at the beginning? Or, do we create a mapping that knows the location of each object? These are some of the questions we are going to have to answer when determining how to store collections of objects.

When considering the operations we will have to perform on a collection of objects, the main three are

- Adding a new object

- Removing an object

- Finding an object

We must determine how a new object will be added to the collection. It can be added at the end of the collection, at the beginning, or at some logical location in the middle.

After we remove an object from our collection, how does that affect the existing objects in the collection? Memory might have to be shifted around, or we can just leave an empty hole where the existing objects used to reside.

After we have a collection of objects in memory, we must determine how we are going to locate a specific object. We might have a mechanism to go directly to the object we want based on some search criteria (such as a security number), or we might need to traverse every object in the collection until we find the one we are looking for.

To answer each of these questions, computer scientists have designed containers that hold objects in different forms.

Introduction to Data Structures

Data structures at their core are nothing more than containers that hold objects and provide mechanisms to add objects, remove objects, and find objects. After careful consideration, there are a multitude of different implementations of containers, each serving a very specific purpose. Some are very fast at inserting objects, whereas others are slow inserting objects, but very fast at finding objects. The key is to identify how you will be using the data stored in these collections.

The following sections describe the more common data structures and explain how each addresses the issues of inserting objects, removing objects, and finding objects.

The Array Data Structure

The simplest data structure is probably the array. An array is a fixed-size container that provides direct access to each element in the container through a 0-based index; there is no sorting of elements or management functions to add a remove objects. Figure 11.1 shows what an array looks like in memory.

FIGURE 11.1
Sample array.

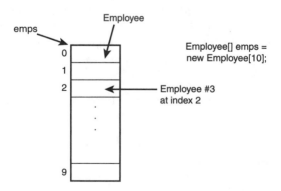

In memory an array is a sequential list of objects, one following another, with each cell the exact size to hold the object type (or in the case of the true object and not a primitive type, the object reference).

An array is created in Java as follows:

```
// Create an array that will hold 10 employees:
Employee[] employees = new Employee[ 10 ];
```

employees is of the type Employee[] that represents an array of the type Employee. It is initialized to hold 10 Employee instances using the keyword new and specifying the size within the brackets. At this point employees has allocated enough memory to hold 10 Employee references.

To add a new employee to the beginning of the array, you must first create an instance of an Employee and assign it to the first elements in the employees array, for example:

```
// Set the first employee to be "Steve"
Employee steve = new Employee( "Steve" );
cmployees[ 0 ] = steve;
```

Array elements are accessed via a 0-based index, so the first elements in the array have index 0, the second elements of the array have index 1, and so on. So, in this case we created an instance of the hypothetical Employee class passing it to a name, and then we assign that instance to the first elements of the employees array.

To search through an array of an element there is no simple mechanism to instantly find the element you are looking for, you must instead use a brute-force traversal of every element in the array. For example:

```
// Find Steve:
for( int index=0; index<employees.length; index++ ) {
  if( employees[ index ].getName().equalsIgnoreCase( "Steve" ) ) {
    System.out.println( "Steve is employee at index: " + index );
    break;
  }
}
```

Here we start at an index of 0 and iterate through the list of employees until we reach the index employees.length. Arrays define a property named length that returns the size of the array, which in this example would be 10. Thus, the worst-case time required to locate an object in an array can be equal to accessing and comparing every element in the array.

Removing an element from an array after you know the index of the element to remove is as simple as overwriting the element or assigning it the null value. For example:

```
// Remove Steve:
employees[ 0 ] = null;
```

Arrays provide a simple mechanism for grouping similar objects in a sequential fashion, but they do not provide any inherent functionality to add, remove, or search for an object. When you use arrays, the burden of these tasks is on you.

Arrays are very simple and because of this simplicity have a set of strong limitations:

- An array has a fixed size, meaning that if you want to add an additional element to a full array you cannot.

- Upon the deletion of an element from the array, the array has no inheritance mechanism to shift the existing elements up in the array to fill in the missing gap; this means that your search implementation must search through meaningful data as well as null data.

- The burden of defining all functionality, except obtaining the length of an array, is on the developer.

The Linked List Data Structure

A linked list solves the fixed-length problem with arrays and has an interesting approach to inserting and removing objects. A linked list is a set of nodes in which each node contains an object and a reference to the next node in the linked list (see Figure 11.2).

FIGURE 11.2
A linked list.

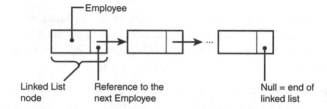

Figure 11.2 shows that the linked list node contains an `Employee` (or a reference to `Employee` rather), and then a reference to the next node in the linked list. The end of a linked list is signified by a null reference to the next node field. Because each node is linked to the next node the length of the linked list can be infinite.

Adding a new element to the end of the list is a simple matter of assigning the next node reference in the end of the list (often referred to as the tail of the list) to the new element. Then, assigning the next node reference in the new elements to null (see Figure 11.3).

FIGURE 11.3
Adding an element to a linked list.

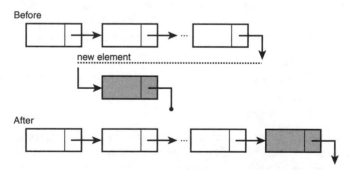

Removing an object from a linked list is a more complicated procedure, but not significantly. After you identify the node to remove, it is a simple matter of reassigning the next node element of the previous node to the next node element of the node being removed. This is much better illustrated graphically, so refer to Figure 11.4.

FIGURE 11.4
Removing an element from a linked list.

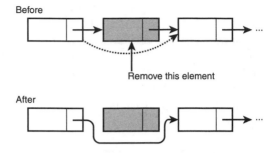

FIGURE 11.5
Inserting an element in a linked list.

Finally, inserting an element into a linked list involves breaking the next node reference at the insertion point, referencing it to the new node, and assigning the next node element of the new node to the next node in the list. Again, this is much better illustrated graphically, so refer to Figure 11.5.

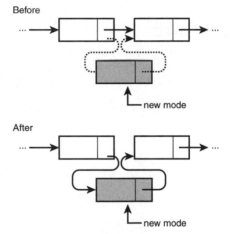

Technically, this is how linked lists are implemented, but luckily Java has already implemented a linked list for you through its `java.util.LinkedList` class. But, before delving into the intricacies of using that class let's step back a moment and analyze the performance of using linked lists.

The insertion of an element into a linked list involves

- Creating a new linked list node

- Reassigning two next element references

Thus, the operation is quite fast.

The removal of an element from a linked list involves the deletion of a linked list node and then reassigning one next element reference. Thus, this operation is quite fast.

Searching for an element in a linked list, however, is a very slow operation and can involve examining each element in the linked list. There is no random access of elements in the list and common implementations can only reference the beginning of the list (referred to as the head) and the end of the list (referred to as the tail). The search for an element involves the examination of the node, then following its next element reference to the next node and examining it, and so on. Some implementations attempt to optimize this by sorting the elements in the linked list and providing links to nodes in both directions; this is referred to as a *doubly linked list*. But still the search is slow (see Figure 11.6).

FIGURE 11.6
A doubly linked list.

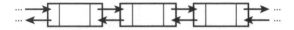

Linked lists are, therefore, good when you need to rapidly insert and/or remove items from a list, but not when you need to search for objects or display different sorted orders of those objects.

The Stack Data Structure

A *stack* is a data structure that can be described by comparing it to a stack of books: you place a book on a table, then another on top of it, and another on top of that, and so on. After you have this stack of books there are a limited list of things you can do with it:

- You can add another book on top of it, but not randomly in the stack.

- You can look at the top book on the stack, but you cannot see the books below the top one.

- You can take the book off the top of the stack, but you cannot take one from the middle.

A stack, as a data structure, has the same functionality, but with some key terminology:

- You can "push" an object onto the top of the stack

- You can "peek" at the object on the top of the stack

- You can "pop" an object off the top of the stack

Figure 11.7 shows this graphically.

FIGURE 11.7
A stack.

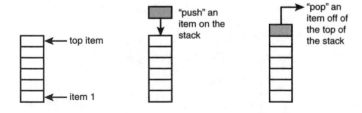

It turns out that stacks work very well for mathematical operations and for developing computer compilers, but aside from that they offer very poor performance for the operations we have been reviewing. Adding an item to the stack is very fast, but inserting an item into the stack involves popping all the items off the stack to the point of insertion, pushing the new item onto the stack, and then pushing the popped objects back on; therefore, it is very slow. Removing an object from the stack similarly requires popping all items from the stack to the deletion point, and then pushing the popped items back onto the stack. Finally, searching for an item requires popping each item off the stack until the desired object is found, and then repushing all objects back on the stack.

From this discussion you can see that a stack is not good to use except for very specific functions.

The Queue Data Structure

A *queue* is a data structure that can be likened to a line in a supermarket: Everyone gets in line and unless someone is very rude, the person at the front of the line is waited on first, and then each subsequent person is waited on in order. Under normal circumstances a person cannot go to the front of the line, or anywhere in the middle of the line, he must go to the back of the line and wait his turn.

A queue, as a data structure, follows a similar pattern:

- An item can be *enqueued*, or added, to the end of the queue.

- An item can be *dequeued*, or removed, from the front of the queue.

Figure 11.8 displays this graphically.

FIGURE 11.8
A queue.

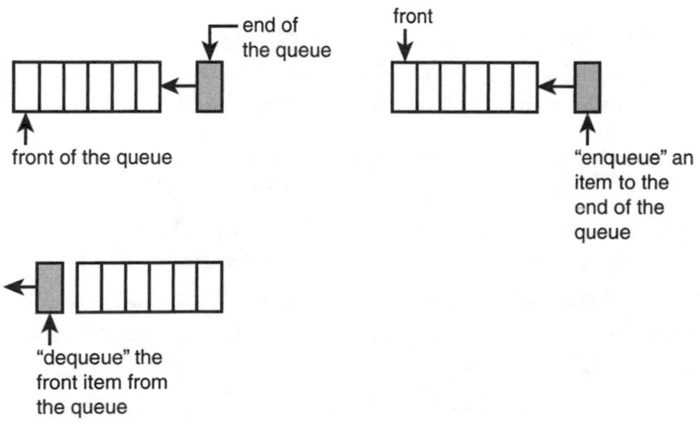

Queues are very good when you need to service requests as they arrive and are very popular when handling events and handling messages, but you can extrapolate out its functionality to see that it does not fit very cleanly into our insert, remove, and search operations.

The Hash Table Data Structure

A hash table is a data structure that computes a numerical value for an item, and then references that item by that numerical value in a table. The table has two columns: the hash code and the item itself (see Figure 11.9).

FIGURE 11.9

A hash table.

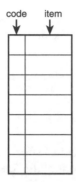

Insertion into the table involves computing a "hash code" for the object, and then inserting the object at that index of the hash table. Finding an object is very simple, compute the hash code, and then it is a direct lookup, you do not need to traverse all the items in the hash table to find the one you are looking for, as with arrays. This works great if you can ensure that you can always compute unique hash codes in the range supported by the hash table. But, if two objects compute to the same hash code, then you have a *collision*. Hash tables are usually defined with a size about 20% greater than the largest amount of data they can hold to avoid collisions, but collisions can occur nonetheless.

When two objects collide in the hash table, the collision must be *resolved*. Different implementations of hash code algorithms do different things, ranging from the simple "move to the next slot until you find an opening," to a more complex computation of another hash code value. Figure 11.10 shows a simple example of hash code collision resolution.

In this example, we use **Integer** objects and define the hash code algorithm to use the leading number of the **Integer** as the index into the hash table. Thus, the hash code of 3 would be 3, and the hash code for 30 would be 3. Figure 11.10 shows the simple resolution of moving to the next open slot. Figure 11.10 also shows the insertion of 31, which resolves to 3, and would require the examination of slot 4, then 5, and then, finally, 6. But instead this implementation uses another hash algorithm to compute a second hash code; in this case it uses the second digit of the **Integer** value, so I'(31) would be 1. Most competent hash code algorithms use a resolution algorithm that, as long as the size of the hash table is sufficient, guarantees that at most two resolution hash codes will be computed before finding a unique slot.

The implementation of hash code algorithms is beyond the scope of this book, but I encourage you to do more research if you are interested.

FIGURE 11.10

Hash code collision.

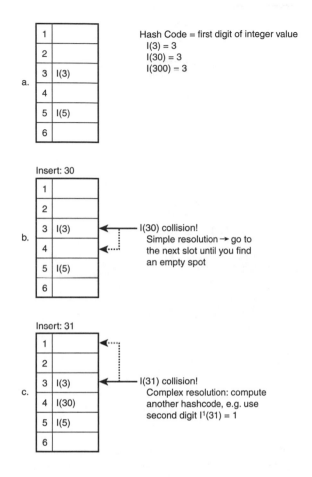

The Tree Data Structure

Trees provide a very sophisticated mechanism for storing data; each node in a tree assumes a role: it is either the parent to other nodes, a child to a node, or both. Figure 11.11 shows an example of a tree.

In computer science there are two types of trees: binary trees and B-Trees. A binary tree restricts each node to having at most two children, whereas a B-Tree removes this restriction. For the purposes of this discussion when referring to trees I will be talking about binary trees.

From Figure 11.11 you can see that node values are placed in a tree in a very specific way. The root of the binary tree in Figure 11.11 has the value 7. The values of all nodes to the left of the root have a value less than 7, whereas all nodes to the right have a value greater than 7. This same relationship is true of every node in a tree: The node with a value 5 has a child to its left with the value 4 and a child to its right with the value 6.

Searching a tree for a node after you know the node's value is very fast and almost a trivial operation. Figure 11.12 shows an example of locating the node with value 6.

FIGURE 11.11

A visual depiction of a tree.

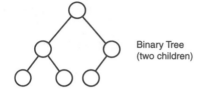

Binary Tree
(two children)

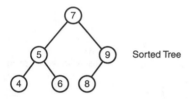

Sorted Tree

FIGURE 11.12

Searching a binary tree for the value 6.

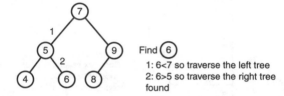

Find (6)
1: 6<7 so traverse the left tree
2: 6>5 so traverse the right tree
found

The search algorithm first looks at the root and sees that the value is 7, which is greater than 6, so it traverses the left subtree. Next, it looks at the root of this subtree and sees that the value is 5, which is less than 6, so it traverses the right subtree. On the third search it finds the node for which it's looking, and the search is complete.

The nature of trees exhibits this sorted property and insertion algorithms ensure that the tree stays *balanced*. A balanced tree has the property that each subtree to the left of the node has approximately the same number of elements as the subtree to the right of the node. Because this is enforced, the average time to find a node in the tree is the natural logarithm of the number of elements in the tree. So, for example, if the tree had 25 elements, the average number of nodes that have to be examined before finding any elements in the tree is ln(25) = 3.22. If you extrapolate this to hundreds of nodes, or even thousands of nodes, the search time has incredible performance.

Inserting the item into a tree is not quite as simple of an operation. The property that gives trees such rapid search capabilities is a direct result of insertion and removal functionality keeping the tree balanced. This means that when you insert an element into the tree you might have to adjust the very nature of the tree itself (see Figure 11.13).

FIGURE 11.13

Inserting a 7 into the tree.

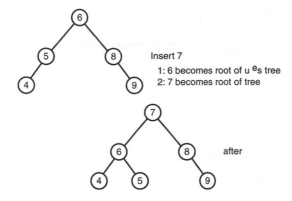

From Figure 11.13 you can see that inserting the 7 node requires restructuring the architecture of the tree. The algorithm displayed in Figure 11.13 required that the 7 become the root of the tree and, thus, the current root had to be shifted down and its children moved around to keep it balanced. The insertion operation can be much slower than the insertion into other data structures such as a linked list, and it is most appropriate when insertions and removals will be minimized and searches will be frequent.

Figure 11.14 shows an example of removing an object from the tree.

FIGURE 11.14

Removing a node from the tree.

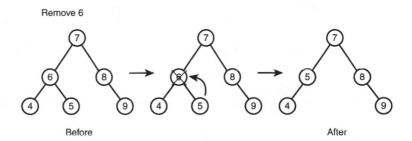

You can see that removing the 6 node requires the 5 node to shift up and take its place. A more complicated example might be removing the 7 node, or root node, from the tree. The end result is that to maintain the balance of the tree another node must be elevated and assume the root responsibility. (This can be a direct child of the root node, or it can be a leaf somewhere in the tree that is the optimal choice for balancing the tree.)

Algorithms for inserting or removing objects from the tree is beyond the scope of this chapter, but further study is encouraged. For the purposes of this discussion, you should understand the operations that must take place and the associated cost of those operations.

To summarize the use of a tree, consider the nature of your data and how will be manipulated. If you need to rapidly add and remove objects from your data structure, a tree is not your best solution. But, if you are going to sparingly add and remove objects from the data structure, and need to search the data structure frequently, a tree is your best bet.

Collection Concepts

Now that you understand some of the essentials in the underlying implementation of data structures, this section describes some of the key concepts in Java's implementation of collection classes.

Lists

Java defines an interface called `java.util.List`, which is implemented by various collection classes that are responsible for presenting an ordered collection of data. These classes are summarized in Table 11.1.

TABLE 11.1   List Classes

List Class	Description
ArrayList	An `ArrayList` is similar in concept to an array in that it presents an indexed collection of elements; the distinguishing factor is that an array list does not have a predetermined size and can grow as needed.
Vector	A `Vector` is almost identical to an `ArrayList`, but it is considered safe to use in multithreaded applications.
LinkedList	A `LinkedList`, as its name implies, implements the functionality of a linked list; you can add, remove, or get the element at the beginning or end of the list. Furthermore, it permits functionality described in the queue data structure.
Stack	A `Stack` is a variation of a `Vector` that implements the functionality of the stack data structure.

Set Interface

Although a list is an ordered collection of elements, a set is a collection of unique elements. A set models the mathematical set abstraction. Furthermore, a set can have at most one null value. Two classes implement the Set interface and are.

- `HashSet`: As its name implies a `HashSet` is a set backed by a hash table, so the data in a hash set is not ordered. It can contain the null value and the order of the elements retrieved from the set, but is not guaranteed to be consistent.

- `TreeSet`: As its name implies a `TreeSet` is a set backed by a tree, so the data in a `TreeSet` is ordered. The order of the elements retrieved from a tree set is guaranteed to be in ascending order.

Map Interface

A map is an object that maps keys to values; all keys must be unique. The two main classes that implement the Map interface are

- `HashMap`: The hash map class maintains its collection of keys in a hash table; the order of the keys is in no particular order, and might not be consistent over time.

- `TreeMap`: The tree map class maintains its collection of keys in a tree; the order of the keys is guaranteed to be in ascending natural order.

At any time the keys from a map can be obtained as a class implementing the Set interface.

Iterators

An `Iterator` is an interface used for traversing a collection. Each collection class has a method called `iterator()` that returns an instance of the `Iterator` class. The `Iterator` class has three methods:

- `hasNext()`: The `hasNext()` method returns true if there are more elements in the collection.

- `next()`: The `next()` method returns the next element in the collection.

- `remove()`: The `remove()` method removes the last element returned by the iterator.

Although each collection class provides a proprietary mechanism for accessing its data, each supports iterators. This enables you to use any collection class in one consistent mechanism.

Collection Classes

This section describes the main collection classes provided by Java in the `java.util` package. It lists the classes in increasing order of complexity:

- `ArrayList`

- `Vector`

- `LinkedList`

- `Stack`

- `HashSet`

- `TreeSet`

- `HashMap`

- `TreeMap`

Figure 11.15 displays the collection class/interface hierarchy.

FIGURE 11.15

Collection class hierarchy.

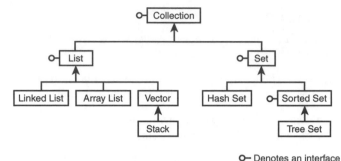

Figure 11.15 shows four interfaces:

- Collection: All collection classes must directly or indirectly implement the Collection interface.

- List: Derives from Collection and provides common functionality for the "list" data structures: `LinkedList`, `ArrayList`, `Vector`, and `Stack`.

- `Set`: Derives from Collection and provides common functionality for the "set" data structures: `HashSet` and `TreeSet`.

- `SortedSet`: Derives from Set and provides the common functionality for "sorted sets," which currently consists of only `TreeSet`.

Figure 11.16 shows the Map class hierarchy.

FIGURE 11.16

Map class hierarchy.

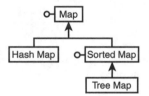

Because maps map a key to a value, they do not fit nicely into the collection paradigm as a single unit. They do, however, present a collection of keys that map to a collection of values, so you can think of maps as a composite of two collection implementations. Figure 11.16 shows two interfaces:

- Map: Root of all Map classes: `HashMap` and `TreeMap`.

- SortedMap: Derives from Map and defines maps that have a sorted key set.

ArrayList

The `java.util.ArrayList` class implements a growable array that has elements that are accessible via a 0-based index. An `ArrayList` can be initialized to hold a specific number of elements or be empty, but is free to grow to hold additional load. Furthermore, it can be initialized with the values contained in another `java.util.Collection` derivative.

The primary methods needed to use the `ArrayList` class are

- `add( Object o )`: Adds an object to the end of the list.
- `add( int index, Object o )`: Inserts an element at a specific index.
- `clear()`: Removes all elements from the list.
- `contains( Object o )`: Returns true if the specified object exists in the list, false otherwise.
- `get( int index )`: Returns the element at the specified index.
- `remove( int index )`: Removes the element at the specified index.
- `set( int index, Object o )`: Sets the element at the specified index.
- `size()`: Returns the number of elements in the list.

Listing 11.1 shows how to use the most common functionality of an `ArrayList`.

LISTING 11.1   ArrayListExample.java

```java
import java.util.ArrayList;
import java.util.Iterator;

public class ArrayListExample
{
    public static void main( String[] args )
    {
        // Create a new ArrayList
        ArrayList al = new ArrayList();

        // Add Items to the array list
        al.add( new Integer( 1 ) );
        al.add( new Integer( 2 ) );
        al.add( new Integer( 3 ) );
        al.add( new Integer( 4 ) );
        al.add( new Integer( 5 ) );
        al.add( new Integer( 6 ) );
        al.add( new Integer( 7 ) );
        al.add( new Integer( 8 ) );
        al.add( new Integer( 9 ) );
        al.add( new Integer( 10 ) );

        // Use ArrayList specific methods to display the values
        for( int i=0; i<al.size(); i++ )
        {
            System.out.println( i + " = " + al.get( i ) );
        }

        // Remove the element at index 5 (value=6)
        al.remove( 5 );
```

LISTING 11.1   Continued

```
        // Set the value at index 5, this overwrites the value 7
        al.set( 5, new Integer( 66 ) );

        // Use iterator to display the values
        for( Iterator i=al.iterator(); i.hasNext(); )
        {
            Integer integer = ( Integer )i.next();
            System.out.println( integer );
        }
    }
}
```

Listing 11.1 starts by creating an empty `ArrayList` and adding values to it using its `add()` method. Next, it displays the list values using the `ArrayList` proprietary methods:

- `size()`: Returns the number of elements in the list.

- `get( int index )`: Returns the element at the specified index.

Next, it removes the element at index 5, which is the `Integer` 6 using the `remove()` method. Then, it sets the value of the element at the new position 5 to 66. Finally, it displays the new list using the `Iterator` construct. The output should look something like the following:

```
0 = 1
1 = 2
2 = 3
3 = 4
4 = 5
5 = 6
6 = 7
7 = 8
8 = 9
9 = 10
1
2
3
4
5
66
8
9
10
```

Vector

Like the `java.util.ArrayList`, the `java.util.Vector` class implements a growable array that has elements, which are accessible via a 0-based index. A `Vector` can be initialized to hold a specific number of elements, and an optional growth rate can be specified or can be initialized empty, but it is free to grow to hold additional load. Furthermore, it can be initialized with the values contained in another `java.util.Collection` derivative.

The primary methods needed to use the `Vector` class are

- `add( Object o )`: Adds an object to the end of the vector.

- `add( int index, Object o )`: Inserts an element at a specific index.

- `clear()`: Removes all elements from the list.

- `contains( Object o )`: Returns true if the specified object exists in the list, false otherwise.

- `elementAt( int index )`: Returns the element at the specified index.

- `get( int index )`: Returns the element at the specified index.

- `indexOf( Object o )`: Returns the numeric index of the specified object in the vector.

- `insertElementAt( Object o, int index )`: Inserts an element at a specific index.

- `isEmpty()`: Returns true if the vector is empty

- `remove( int index )`: Removes the element at the specified index.

- `set( int index, Object o )`: Sets the element at the specified index.

- `setElementAt( Object o, int index )`: Sets the element at the specified index.

- `size()`: Returns the number of elements in the list.

Listing 11.2 shows how to use the most common functionality of a Vector.

LISTING 11.2   VectorExample.java

```java
import java.util.Vector;
import java.util.Iterator;

public class VectorExample
{
    public static void main( String[] args )
    {
        // Create a new Vector
        Vector vector = new Vector();

        // Add Items to the Vector
        vector.add( new Integer( 1 ) );
        vector.add( new Integer( 2 ) );
        vector.add( new Integer( 3 ) );
        vector.add( new Integer( 4 ) );
        vector.add( new Integer( 5 ) );
        vector.add( new Integer( 6 ) );
        vector.add( new Integer( 7 ) );
        vector.add( new Integer( 8 ) );
        vector.add( new Integer( 9 ) );
        vector.add( new Integer( 10 ) );
```

LISTING 11.2   Continued

```
// Use Vector specific methods to display the vvectores
for( int i=0; i<vector.size(); i++ )
{
    Integer integer = ( Integer )vector.elementAt( i );
    System.out.println( i + " = " + integer );
}

// Remove the element at index 5 (vvectore=6)
vector.remove( 5 );

// Set the vvectore at index 5, this overwrites the vvectore 7
vector.setElementAt( new Integer( 66 ), 5 );

// Use iterator to display the vvectores
for( Iterator i=vector.iterator(); i.hasNext(); )
{
    Integer integer = ( Integer )i.next();
    System.out.println( integer );
}
    }
}
```

Listing 11.2 starts by creating an empty `Vector` and adding values to it using its `add()` method. Next, it displays the list values using the `Vector` proprietary methods:

- `size()`: Returns the number of elements in the list.

- `elementAt( int index )`: Returns the element at the specified index.

Next, it removes the element at index 5, which is the `Integer` 6 using the `remove()` method. Then, it sets the value of the element at the new position 5 to 66 using the `setElementAt()` method. Finally, it displays the new list using the `Iterator` construct. The output should look something like the following (the same as the `ArrayList`):

```
0 = 1
1 = 2
2 = 3
3 = 4
4 = 5
5 = 6
6 = 7
7 = 8
8 = 9
9 = 10
1
2
3
4
5
66
8
9
10
```

LinkedList

The `java.util.LinkedList` class implements a linked list a la the previous linked list discussion in this chapter. A `LinkedList` can be initialized either empty or from an existing collection.

The primary methods needed to use the `LinkedList` class are

- `add( Object o )`: Adds an object to the end of the list.
- `add( int index, Object o )`: Inserts an element at a specific index.
- `addFirst( Object o )`: Adds an object to the beginning of the list.
- `addLast( Object o )`: Adds an object to the end of the list.
- `clear()`: Removes all elements from the list.
- `contains( Object o )`: Returns true if the specified object exists in the list, false otherwise.
- `elementAt( int index )`: Returns the element at the specified index.
- `get( int index )`: Returns the element at the specified index.
- `getFirst()`: Returns the first element in the list.
- `getLast()`: Returns the last element in the list.
- `indexOf( Object o )`: Returns the numeric index of the specified object in the vector.
- `insertElementAt( Object o, int index )`: Inserts an element at a specific index.
- `isEmpty()`: Returns true if the vector is empty.
- `remove( int index )`: Removes the element at the specified index.
- `removeFirst()`: Removes and returns the first element in the list.
- `removeLast()`: Removes and returns the last element in the list.
- `set( int index, Object o )`: Sets the element at the specified index.
- `size()`: Returns the number of elements in the list.

Note that although the `java.util.List` functionality is provided that offers random access to the elements in the list, the underlying implementation still must traverse the list to locate the randomly accessed object; thus the performance is still impacted.

Listing 11.3 shows how to use the most common functionality of a `List`.

LISTING 11.3 `LinkedListExample.java`

```java
import java.util.LinkedList;
import java.util.Iterator;
```

LISTING 11.3   Continued

```java
public class LinkedListExample
{
    public static void main( String[] args )
    {
        // Create a new LinkedList
        LinkedList list = new LinkedList();

        // Add Items to the array list
        list.add( new Integer( 1 ) );
        list.add( new Integer( 2 ) );
        list.add( new Integer( 3 ) );
        list.add( new Integer( 4 ) );
        list.add( new Integer( 5 ) );
        list.add( new Integer( 6 ) );
        list.add( new Integer( 7 ) );
        list.add( new Integer( 8 ) );
        list.add( new Integer( 9 ) );
        list.add( new Integer( 10 ) );

        // Use iterator to display the values
        for( Iterator i=list.iterator(); i.hasNext(); )
        {
            Integer integer = ( Integer )i.next();
            System.out.println( integer );
        }

        // Remove the element at index 5 (value=6)
        list.remove( 5 );

        // Set the value at index 5, this overwrites the value 7
        list.set( 5, new Integer( 66 ) );

        // Use the linked list as a queue:
        //   add an object to the end of the list (queue)
        //   remove an item from the head of the list (queue)
        list.add( new Integer( 11 ) );
        Integer head = ( Integer )list.removeFirst();
        System.out.println( "Head: " + head );

        // Use iterator to display the values
        for( Iterator i=list.iterator(); i.hasNext(); )
        {
            Integer integer = ( Integer )i.next();
            System.out.println( integer );
        }
    }
}
```

Listing 11.3 starts by creating an empty **LinkedList** and adding values to it using its **add()** method. Next, it displays the list values using the **Iterator** construct.

Next, it removes the element at index 5, which is the `Integer` 6 using the `remove()` method. Then, it sets the value of the element at the new position 5 to 66 using the `set()` method.

Next, it starts using the list as a queue by adding an element to the end of the list (enqueueing) using the `addLast()` method, and then removing the first element of the list (dequeueing) using the `removeFirst()` method.

Finally, it displays the contents of the list using the `Iterator` construct.

The `Stack` Class

The `Stack` class implements the previously discussed stack data structure. It can only be created empty and cannot be initialized from an existing collection as the other collections discussed so far could.

The primary methods needed to use the `Stack` class are

- `empty()`: Returns true if the stack is empty.
- `peek()`: Returns the object on the top of the stack without removing it from the stack.
- `pop()`: Removes and returns the object on the top of the stack.
- `push( Object o )`: Adds an object to the top of the stack.

Listing 11.4 shows how to use the most common functionality of a `Stack`.

LISTING 11.4   `StackExample.java`

```java
import java.util.Stack;

public class StackExample
{
    public static void main( String[] args )
    {
        // Create a new LinkedList
        Stack stack = new Stack();

        // Add Items to the array list
        stack.push( new Integer( 1 ) );
        stack.push( new Integer( 2 ) );
        stack.push( new Integer( 3 ) );
        stack.push( new Integer( 4 ) );
        stack.push( new Integer( 5 ) );
        stack.push( new Integer( 6 ) );
        stack.push( new Integer( 7 ) );
        stack.push( new Integer( 8 ) );
        stack.push( new Integer( 9 ) );
        stack.push( new Integer( 10 ) );

        // Pop everything out of the stack and display the values
        while( !stack.empty() )
```

LISTING 11.4   Continued

```
        {
            Integer element = ( Integer )stack.pop();
            System.out.println( "Element: " + element );
        }
    }
}
```

Listing 11.4 creates an empty stack, and then pushes 10 Integers on to the stack. Next, it iterates through all the elements in the stack until the stack is empty and removes them using the `pop()` method.

HashSet

The `java.util.HashSet` class implements the mathematical concept of a Set that contains unique elements. A `HashSet` can be initialized by an existing collection, it can be initialized to a specific size with an optional load factor (how much to grow when needed), or it can be initialized empty.

The primary methods needed to use the `HashSet` class are

- `add( Object o )`: Adds an element to the set.
- `clear()`: Removes all the elements from the set.
- `contains( Object o )`: Returns true if the specified object exists in the set.
- `isEmpty()`: Returns true if the set is empty.
- `iterator()`: Returns an iterator that will iterate over the values in the set.
- `remove( Object o )`: Removes the specified element from the set.
- `size()`: Returns the number of elements in the set.

Listing 11.5 shows how to use the most common functionality of a `HashSet`.

LISTING 11.5   HashSetExample.java

```
import java.util.Set;
import java.util.HashSet;
import java.util.Iterator;

public class HashSetExample
{
    public static void main( String[] args )
    {
        // Create a new HashSet
        Set set = new HashSet();

        // Add Items to the HashSet
        set.add( new Integer( 1 ) );
```

LISTING 11.5   Continued

```
        set.add( new Integer( 2 ) );
        set.add( new Integer( 3 ) );
        set.add( new Integer( 4 ) );
        set.add( new Integer( 5 ) );
        set.add( new Integer( 6 ) );
        set.add( new Integer( 7 ) );
        set.add( new Integer( 8 ) );
        set.add( new Integer( 9 ) );
        set.add( new Integer( 10 ) );

        // Use iterator to display the vsetes
        System.out.println( "HashSet Before: " );
        for( Iterator i=set.iterator(); i.hasNext(); )
        {
            Integer integer = ( Integer )i.next();
            System.out.println( integer );
        }

        // Remove the integer 6
        System.out.println( "\nRemove integer 6" );
        set.remove( new Integer( 6 ) );

        // Use iterator to display the vsetes
        System.out.println( "\nHashSet After: " );
        for( Iterator i=set.iterator(); i.hasNext(); )
        {
            Integer integer = ( Integer )i.next();
            System.out.println( integer );
        }
    }
}
```

Listing 11.5 starts by creating an instance of the **HashSet** class. Note that the variable it is assigned to is not a **HashSet**, but rather is a **Set**; this was done purposely so that if the requirements regarding the data change later, the *implementation* of the set can change while the code that uses the set remains unchanged. Next, the set is loaded with 10 **Integers** using the **add()** method. The program then displays the contents of the set using an **Iterator**.

Next, the **Integer** 6 is removed from the set using the **remove()** method, and, finally, the contents are again displayed using an **Iterator**. The output of this program should look as follows:

```
HashSet Before:
10
9
8
7
6
5
4
3
2
1
```

```
Remove integer 6

HashSet After:
10
9
8
7
5
4
3
2
1
```

Recall that there is no order implied in a hash table, so the iteration over the elements just happened to return the values in descending order.

TreeSet

The `java.util.TreeSet` class implements the mathematical concept of a Set that contains unique elements. A `TreeSet` can be initialized by an existing collection, it can be initialized to contain the values of another `SortedSet` (a derivation of a set that sorts its values), it can be initialized using a `Comparator` (a class implementing this interface defines how to compare two objects during sorting), or it can be initialized empty.

The primary methods needed to use the `TreeSet` class are

- `add( Object o )`: Adds an element to the set.

- `clear()`: Removes all the elements from the set.

- `contains( Object o )`: Returns true if the specified object exists in the set.

- `first()`: Returns the element with the lowest value in the set.

- `isEmpty()`: Returns true if the set is empty.

- `iterator()`: Returns an iterator that will iterate over the values in the set.

- `last()`: Returns the element with the highest value in the set.

- `remove( Object o )`: Removes the specified element from the set.

- `size()`: Returns the number of elements in the set.

Listing 11.6 shows how to use the most common functionality of a `TreeSet`.

LISTING 11.6   TreeSetExample.java

```java
import java.util.Set;
import java.util.TreeSet;
import java.util.Iterator;

public class TreeSetExample
```

LISTING 11.6   Continued

```
{
    public static void main( String[] args )
    {
        // Create a new TreeSet
        Set set = new TreeSet();

        // Add Items to the TreeSet
        set.add( new Integer( 1 ) );
        set.add( new Integer( 2 ) );
        set.add( new Integer( 3 ) );
        set.add( new Integer( 4 ) );
        set.add( new Integer( 5 ) );
        set.add( new Integer( 6 ) );
        set.add( new Integer( 7 ) );
        set.add( new Integer( 8 ) );
        set.add( new Integer( 9 ) );
        set.add( new Integer( 10 ) );

        // Use iterator to display the vsetes
        System.out.println( "TreeSet Before: " );
        for( Iterator i=set.iterator(); i.hasNext(); )
        {
            Integer integer = ( Integer )i.next();
            System.out.println( integer );
        }

        // Remove the integer 6
        System.out.println( "\nRemove Integer 6" );
        set.remove( new Integer( 6 ) );

        // Use iterator to display the vsetes
        System.out.println( "\nTreeSet After: " );
        for( Iterator i=set.iterator(); i.hasNext(); )
        {
            Integer integer = ( Integer )i.next();
            System.out.println( integer );
        }
    }
}
```

Listing 11.6 starts by creating an instance of the TreeSet class. Similar to the HashSet example, the TreeSet example defines a TreeSet, but assigns it to a Set variable. The set is next loaded with 10 Integers using the add() method. The program then displays the contents of the set using an Iterator.

Next, the Integer 6 is removed from the set using the remove() method, and, finally, the contents are again displayed using an Iterator. The output of this program should look as follows:

```
TreeSet Before:
1
2
3
4
5
6
7
8
9
10

Remove Integer 6

TreeSet After:
1
2
3
4
5
7
8
9
10
```

Recall that trees have an inherent order implied and, thus, iterating over the values in a `TreeSet` returns the values in ascending order.

HashMap

The `java.util.HashMap` class implements a mapping of keys to values. A `HashMap` can be initialized to an existing `Map`, it can be initialized to a specific size with an optional load factor (how much to grow when needed), or it can be initialized empty.

The primary methods needed to use the `HashMap` class are

- `clear()`: Removes all the elements from the map.
- `containsKey( Object key )`: Returns true if the map contains the specified key.
- `containsValue( Object value )`: Returns true if the map contains the specified value.
- `get( Object key )`: Returns the value associated with the specified key.
- `isEmpty()`: Returns true if the map is empty.
- `keySet()`: Returns the keys in the map as a Set.
- `put( Object key, Object value )`: Adds the key-value pair to the map.
- `remove( Object key )`: Removes the key-value pair from the map for the specified key.
- `size()`: Returns the number of key-value pairs in the map.

Listing 11.7 shows how to use the most common functionality of a `HashMap`.

LISTING 11.7   HashMapExample.java

```java
import java.util.Set;
import java.util.Map;
import java.util.HashMap;
import java.util.Iterator;

public class HashMapExample
{
    public static void main( String[] args )
    {
        // Create a new HashMap
        Map map = new HashMap();

        // Add Items to the HashMap
        map.put( new Integer( 1 ), "One" );
        map.put( new Integer( 2 ), "Two" );
        map.put( new Integer( 3 ), "Three" );
        map.put( new Integer( 4 ), "Four" );
        map.put( new Integer( 5 ), "Five" );
        map.put( new Integer( 6 ), "Six" );
        map.put( new Integer( 7 ), "Seven" );
        map.put( new Integer( 8 ), "Eight" );
        map.put( new Integer( 9 ), "Nine" );
        map.put( new Integer( 10 ), "Ten" );

        // Use iterator to display the keys and associated values
        System.out.println( "Map Values Before: " );
        Set keys = map.keySet();
        for( Iterator i=keys.iterator(); i.hasNext(); )
        {
            Integer key = ( Integer )i.next();
            String value = ( String )map.get( key );
            System.out.println( key + " = " + value );
        }

        // Remove the entry with key 6
        System.out.println( "\nRemove element with key 6" );
        map.remove( new Integer( 6 ) );

        // Use iterator to display the keys and associated values
        System.out.println( "\nMap Values After: " );
        keys = map.keySet();
        for( Iterator i=keys.iterator(); i.hasNext(); )
        {
            Integer key = ( Integer )i.next();
            String value = ( String )map.get( key );
            System.out.println( key + " = " + value );
        }
    }
}
```

Listing 11.7 starts by creating an instance of the HashMap class. Similar to the Set examples, the variable assigned to HashMap is not a HashMap, but rather is a Map. Ten key-value pairs are added to the map through the `put()` method. Next, it displays the contents of the map by iterating over a `Set` of the keys in the map (obtained through a call to `keySet()`), and then calling the map's `get()` method to retrieve the key's associated value.

Next, the value with the key `Integer` 6 is removed from the map using the `remove()` method. Finally, the contents are again displayed using the aforementioned construct. The output of this program should look as follows:

```
Map Values Before:
10 = Ten
9 = Nine
8 = Eight
7 = Seven
6 = Six
5 = Five
4 = Four
3 = Three
2 = Two
1 = One

Remove element with key 6

Map Values After:
10 = Ten
9 = Nine
8 = Eight
7 = Seven
5 = Five
4 = Four
3 = Three
2 = Two
1 = One
```

Recall that there is no order implied in a hash table, so iterating over the key set elements just happened to return the values in descending order.

TreeMap

The `java.util.TreeMap` class implements a mapping of keys to values. A `TreeMap` can be initialized to an existing map, it can be initialized to contain the values of another `SortedMap` (a derivation of a map that sorts its keys), it can be initialized using a `Comparator` (a class implementing this interface defines how to compare two keys during sorting), or it can be initialized empty.

The primary methods needed to use the `TreeMap` class are

- `clear()`: Removes all the elements from the map.
- `containsKey( Object key )`: Returns true if the map contains the specified key.
- `containsValue( Object value )`: Returns true if the map contains the specified value.
- `get( Object key )`: Returns the value associated with the specified key.

- `isEmpty()`: Returns true if the map is empty.

- `keySet()`: Returns the keys in the map as a Set.

- `put( Object key, Object value )`: Adds the key-value pair to the map.

- `remove( Object key )`: Removes the key-value pair from the map for the specified key.

- `size()`: Returns the number of key-value pairs in the map.

Listing 11.8 shows how to use the most common functionality of a `TreeMap`.

LISTING 11.8   TreeMapExample.java

```java
import java.util.Set;
import java.util.Map;
import java.util.TreeMap;
import java.util.Iterator;

public class TreeMapExample
{
    public static void main( String[] args )
    {
        // Create a new TreeMap
        Map map = new TreeMap();

        // Add Items to the TreeMap
        map.put( new Integer( 1 ), "One" );
        map.put( new Integer( 2 ), "Two" );
        map.put( new Integer( 3 ), "Three" );
        map.put( new Integer( 4 ), "Four" );
        map.put( new Integer( 5 ), "Five" );
        map.put( new Integer( 6 ), "Six" );
        map.put( new Integer( 7 ), "Seven" );
        map.put( new Integer( 8 ), "Eight" );
        map.put( new Integer( 9 ), "Nine" );
        map.put( new Integer( 10 ), "Ten" );

        // Use iterator to display the keys and associated values
        System.out.println( "Map Values Before: " );
        Set keys = map.keySet();
        for( Iterator i=keys.iterator(); i.hasNext(); )
        {
            Integer key = ( Integer )i.next();
            String value = ( String )map.get( key );
            System.out.println( key + " = " + value );
        }

        // Remove the entry with key 6
        System.out.println( "\nRemove element with key 6" );
        map.remove( new Integer( 6 ) );

        // Use iterator to display the keys and associated values
```

LISTING 11.8   Continued

```
        System.out.println( "\nMap Values After: " );
        keys = map.keySet();
        for( Iterator i=keys.iterator(); i.hasNext(); )
        {
            Integer key = ( Integer )i.next();
            String value = ( String )map.get( key );
            System.out.println( key + " = " + value );
        }
    }
}
```

Listing 11.8 starts by creating an instance of the `TreeMap` class. Similar to the `HashMap` example, the variable assigned to the `TreeMap` is not a `TreeMap`, but rather is a `Map`. Ten key-value pairs are added to the map through the `put()` method. Next, it displays the contents of the map by iterating over a `Set` of the keys in the map (obtained through a call to `keySet()`), and then calling the map's `get()` method to retrieve the key's associated value.

Next, the value with the key `Integer` 6 is removed from the map using the `remove()` method. Finally, the contents are again displayed using the aforementioned construct. The output of this program should look as follows:

```
Map Values Before:
1 = One
2 = Two
3 = Three
4 = Four
5 = Five
6 = Six
7 = Seven
8 = Eight
9 = Nine
10 = Ten

Remove element with key 6

Map Values After:
1 = One
2 = Two
3 = Three
4 = Four
5 = Five
7 = Seven
8 = Eight
9 = Nine
10 = Ten
```

Trees have an inherent order implied and, thus, iterating over the key set values in a `TreeMap` returns the values in ascending order.

Summary

This chapter introduced you to data structures and the concepts of

- Arrays

- Linked lists

- Stacks

- Queues

- Hash tables

- Trees

It made comparisons of the performance trade-offs of each with respect to adding items, removing items, searching for items, and displaying the contents of the data structure.

Next, it introduced additional collection class concepts:

- Lists

- Sets

- Maps

- Iterators

Finally, the chapter walked you through the Java collection class implementations including an overview of the top methods in each class and an example.

Managing data is a vital part of any computer program, and the Java collection classes provide you with the ability to do this. The next chapter moves to another vital part of computer programming: input and output, or retrieving data and sending data.

Review Questions

1. How does an `Array` differ from an `ArrayList`?

2. What is the difference between an `ArrayList` and a `Vector`?

3. Under what circumstances would you want to use a hash table over a tree to maintain your data?

4. What is a hash table collision, and how is it resolved?

5. Why is the search operation on trees fast?

6. Can a set have duplicate values?

7. What is the functional difference between the iterated output of a `HashMap` and a `TreeMap`?

8. Describe a stack.

9. What is the difference between a stack and a queue?

10. Describe the function of an iterator and the methods it provides.

CHAPTER 12

USING JAVA'S INPUT AND OUTPUT CLASSES

You will learn about the following in this chapter:

- How to read and write byte-oriented data

- How to read and write character-oriented data

- How to read and write to and from files

- How to read from a data source in tokens

This chapter begins by discussing the need for a common interface to read data from and write data to various resources such as files, the standard input and output, and the Internet. Then, it discusses the byte-oriented stream classes and the character-oriented stream classes.

Problem Derivation

If you have ever had to deal with gathering data from a file, from the Internet, and from the user, you had to write three different mechanisms to obtain this data. Traditionally, each input and output device had its own proprietary interface. This was necessary because although the underlying data might be the same, one is loaded from tracks on a physical disc, one is loaded by opening a socket connection to a server, and the other is read from a keyboard. Different devices meant that the mechanism to obtain the data had to be different.

What can be done in an environment that promotes hardware independence? Can that notion be extrapolated to include different input and output devices? With Java's support for interfaces, the answer is, yes we can.

Consider the nature of interfaces: A class that implements an interface provides prescribed functionality that is made available through a set of methods, but the underlying implementation is irrelevant. We can, therefore, create an interface called *Input* and an interface called *Output,* and define classes that implement these that access different devices:

```
public interface Input {
  public Stuff readStuff();
}

public interface Output {
  public void writeStuff( Stuff s );
}

public class FileInput implements Input {
  public Stuff readStuff() {
    return getStuffFromFile();
  }
}

public class KeyboardInput implements Input {
  public Stuff readStuff() {
    return getStuffFromKeyboard();
  }
}

public class InternetInput implements Input {
  public Stuff readStuff() {
    return getStuffFromInternet();
  }
}
```

These classes are obviously written in a Java pseudo-code, but the notion is apparent: each class provides a unique implementation for a common set of functionality. When a new requirement arises that asks for data read from a dial-up proprietary connection (such as a Value Added Network (VAN)), then a new *VANInput* class can be created that implements the *Input* interface. Now all the code that can read a file can also read the data from a VAN.

The versatility of interfaces and interface-based programming allows for this to succeed. The concept is that code is written against an interface instead of a class so that you are free at any time to change the underlying implementation.

Streams As Input and Output Data Sources

Java defines the concept of a stream as an interface to a data source; it comes in two forms:

- Input Streams
- Output Streams

Input streams represent sources that you can read data from and output streams represent sources that you can write data to. To further subdivide the types of data that can be read from streams Java defines streams that read byte data and streams that read character data. Byte data would represent binary data such as images, whereas character data would represent readable text such as HTML pages or text files.

Byte-Oriented Stream Classes

Byte-oriented stream classes all implement the `java.io.InputStream` or `java.io.OutputStream` interface. The `java.io.InputStream` interface provides the methods shown in Table 12.1. These methods provide information to manage streams: read data from the stream, find out how much data is available in the stream, advance to a new place in the stream, and close the stream.

TABLE 12.1   `java.io.InputStream` Methods

Method	Description
`int available()`	Returns the number of bytes that can be read (or skipped over) from this input stream without blocking by the next caller of a method for this input stream.
`void close()`	Closes this input stream and releases any system resources associated with the stream.
`void mark(int readlimit)`	Marks the current position in this input stream.
`boolean markSupported()`	Tests if this input stream supports the mark and reset methods.
`abstract int read()`	Reads the next byte of data from the input stream.
`int read(byte[] b)`	Reads some number of bytes from the input stream and stores them into the buffer array b.
`int read(byte[] b, int off, int len)`	Reads up to len bytes of data from the input stream into an array of bytes.
`void reset()`	Repositions this stream to the position at the time the mark method was last called on this input stream.
`long skip(long n)`	Skips over and discards n bytes of data from this input stream.

All the input stream classes have these methods available to them as a minimum, so it is good for you to see them now.

The `java.io.OutputStream` class provides the methods shown in Table 12.2; output streams are concerned with writing data to a stream, flushing data that is in the stream out to its destination, and closing the stream.

TABLE 12.2   `java.io.OutputStream` Methods

Method	Description
`void close()`	Closes this output stream and releases any system resources associated with this stream.
`void flush()`	Flushes this output stream and forces any buffered output bytes to be written out.
`void write(byte[] b)`	Writes b.length bytes from the specified byte array to this output stream.
`void write(byte[] b, int off, int len)`	Writes len bytes from the specified byte array starting at offset off to this output stream.
`abstract  void write(int b)`	Writes the specified byte to this output stream.

Now that we have this common functionality, the next thing to do is see the destinations and the type of data that we can read data from and write data to. The rest of this section discusses the various classes that implement the **InputStream** and **OutputStream** interfaces as well as the particulars of their implementations. Figure 12.1 shows the hierarchy of **InputStream** and **OutputStream** classes.

FIGURE 12.1
InputStream and
OutputStream Hierarchy.

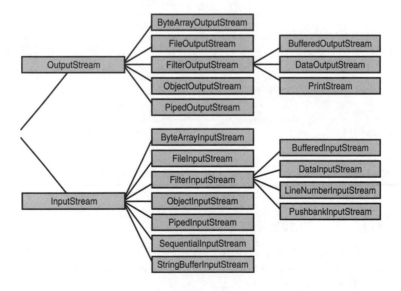

Predefined Stream Objects

Java has some predefined input and output streams that you are already familiar with:

- `System.in (java.io.BufferedInputStream)`

- `System.out (java.io.PrintStream)`

- `System.err (java.io.PrintStream)`

Because you are already familiar with printing messages out to the screen via a `System.out.println()` or `System.out.print()`, you can now work with streams to anything!

Filtered Streams

Java provides a series of what *Filter Streams* that help you work with streams; specifically, they provide extra functionality to preprocess output before actually writing the data to an output stream or postprocess input after data has been read. To define in more practical terms what this means, consider `System.out` in light of `java.io.OutputStream`. Writing text-readable characters to an output stream involves writing a collection of bytes, not a collection of characters, so the `PrintStream` class is provided that enables you to write characters to it and it writes bytes to the destination.

For example:

```
FileOutputStream fos = new FileOutputStream( "myfile.txt" );
PrintStrem ps = new PrintStream( fos );
ps.println( "Here is some text" );
fos.close();
```

The way that filtered streams work is that you pass an output stream to the constructor of a filtered stream, and then you can use the filtered stream instead of the output stream. This enables you to use the filtered stream's methods instead of the original stream's methods; if you choose the correct filtered stream, it will be easier for you to write your data out to the stream.

Java defines the following filtered streams:

- `BufferedInputStream`: Provides buffering input operations so that a larger quantity of data can be read into the buffer, and then you can read it out in smaller quantities. This increases efficiency because reading multiple small amounts of data is more expensive than reading one large amount of data.

- `BufferedOutputStream`: Provides buffering output operations so that you can write data in small quantities to the buffer, and then, when you are ready, you can flush the buffer to the destination; again this increases efficiency.

- `DataInputStream`: Allows you to read binary data of primitive data types. If you want to build a `double`, you would have to read in 8 bytes and construct it yourself, whereas with this filtered stream you can ask it for a double, and it takes care of reading the 8 bytes and constructing the double.

- **DataOutputStream**: Allows you to write binary data as primitive data types; similar to **DataInputStream** you can write primitive types such as **longs** and **doubles** to the stream.

- **PushbackInputStream**: Maintains a one-byte pushback buffer so that you can look at the next byte in the input stream without taking the byte. This is good when you want to read to a specific point, and then hand off the stream to another process to handle the next section of data.

- **PrintStream**: Provides methods for outputting data textually; enables you to output strings using the familiar **print()** and **println()** methods to a binary stream.

The next sections will show examples of using these streams.

Reading From and Writing to Files

Probably the most common use for input and output from most programmers' perspective is reading and writing files. This is the way that you can persist application state between executions. Four classes facility file functions:

- **FileInputStream**: Provides an **InputStream** interface to read data sequentially from a file.

- **FileOutputStream**: Provides an **OutputStream** interface to write data sequentially to a file.

- **RandomAccessFile**: Provides a proprietary mechanism to read and write data to and from a file randomly.

- **File**: Provides management functionality to learn information about files and directories.

To stay generic enough to read data from any source without knowledge of the source it is best to write your programs around interfaces, not around classes that implement those interfaces. Listing 12.1 is an example that reads a file and outputs it to the standard output as well as another file.

LISTING 12.1   FileInputOutputExample.java

```java
import java.io.InputStream;
import java.io.OutputStream;
import java.io.FileInputStream;
import java.io.FileOutputStream;

public class FileInputOutputExample
{
    public static void main( String[] args ) {
        try {
```

LISTING 12.1   Continued

```
        InputStream is = new FileInputStream( "in.txt" );
        OutputStream os = new FileOutputStream( "out.txt" );
        int c;
        while( ( c = is.read() ) != -1 ) {
    System.out.print( ( char )c );
    os.write( c );
        }
        is.close();
        os.close();        }
    catch( Exception e ) {
        e.printStackTrace();
    }
  }
}
```

Listing 12.1 opens the file `in.txt` by passing it to the constructor of the `FileInputStream` class. You can construct a `FileInputStream` from a `String` that specifies the filename, a `java.io.File` object, or a `java.io.FileDescriptor` (a handle that references the underlying physical file).

Next, it creates an instance of the `java.io.FileOutputStream` by passing `out.txt` to its constructor. You can construct a `FileOutputStream` from a string filename, a `java.io.File` object, or a `java.io.FileDescriptor`. Furthermore, if you want to append text to an existing file or simply overwrite the existing file you can specify that in the constructor—it overwrites a file if it already exists by default.

Using the `java.io.InputStream` methods, the sample reads the input stream byte-by-byte and writes it out to the output stream byte-by-byte. It also writes out each byte to the standard output by calling `System.out.print()`, but note that we must cast the integer byte to a character before writing it out to the stream (otherwise it will output the value as its string representation of the integer).

Finally, the example closes both of the streams; you must close the streams for them to be available to other applications (unless, like in this example program, execution ends, hence, releasing the file handle).

`File` **Class**

The `java.io.File` class provides you information about a file; it answers the following questions:

- Does the file exist?
- Is the file read-only or can I write to it?
- Is the file a file or a directory?
- If it is a directory, what files are in it?

It also provides you with the following management functionality:

- Delete a file

- Rename a file

- Create a directory

Furthermore, it provides you with a platform-independent abstraction for file separators. The `File.separator` and `File.separatorChar` resolve to the proper character based on the operating system you are running on:

- Windows operating systems use a backslash as the file separator \

- Unix operating systems use a forward slash as a the file separator /

When you are building filenames be sure to build it as follows:

```
String path = "files";
String filename = "myfile.txt"
String qualifiedFilename = path + File.separator + filename;
```

Listing 12.2 displays a directory of the root of the drive it is run on and it differentiates between files and directories in the output.

LISTING 12.2   `FileDirectory.java`

```
import java.io.File;

public class FileDirectory {
   public static void main( String[] args ) {
      try {
         File f = new File( File.separator );
         if( f.isDirectory() ) {
            File[] files = f.listFiles();
            for( int i=0; i<files.length; i++ ) {
               if( files[ i ].isDirectory() ) {
                  System.out.println( "<dir> " + files[ i ].getName() );
               }
               else {
                  System.out.println( files[ i ].getName() );
               }
            }
         }
      }
      catch( Exception e ) {
         e.printStackTrace();
      }
   }
}
```

Listing 12.2 creates a new `File` by passing the constructor the file separator (\ for Windows or / for Unix); this creates a reference to the root directory of the drive that the application is running on. Next, it provides a sanity check to ensure that this is a directory by calling the `isDirectory()` method.

If it is a directory, it lists all the files in the directory by calling the `listFiles()` methods. There are two categories of methods that list files in a directory:

- `listFiles()`: Returns an array of `java.io.File` objects.

- `list()`: Returns an array of `String` objects containing the filenames of the files in the directory.

The reason that we call `listFiles()` is because one of the operations in the `for` loop is a check to see whether the element is a directory or a file. If it is a directory, the code prefaces the name with the `<dir>` string.

Your output will vary from mine, but the following is a sample of what you might see:

```
<dir> Apps
AUTOEXEC.BAT
CONFIG.SYS
<dir> Documents and Settings
<dir> My Documents
<dir> Program Files
<dir> projects
<dir> RECYCLER
<dir> System Volume Information
tempfile.tmp
<dir> WINNT
```

RandomAccessFile

The `java.io.RandomAccessFile` class is used for reading files randomly, that is not sequentially from the beginning to the end; you are free to jump around to different locations in the file. It provides both input and output in one class, and it provides methods similar to the `java.io.DataInputStream` and `java.io.DataOutputStream` classes to read and write primitive types from and to the file.

To facilitate the random access to the file, the class provides the `seek( long pos )` method. This method advances a file pointer from the beginning of the file to the byte and position `pos`; wherever the file pointer is located is where reads and writes will occur. To summarize, navigating through a file is accomplished by using the following methods:

- `long getFilePointer()`: Returns the current location of the file pointer.

- `long length()`: Returns the length of the file.

- `seek( long pos )`: Moves the file pointer to the specified location (relative to the beginning of the file).

The `RandomAccessFile` class can open a file for reading or for reading and writing. The file mode is specified in the constructor:

- `RandomAccessFile(File file, String mode)`

- `RandomAccessFile(String name, String mode)`

Where the `mode` can be `r` to specify that the file is to be opened for reading only or `rw` to specify that the file is to be opened for reading and writing.

Other Byte I/O Classes

The other byte stream classes that Java provides are

- `ByteArrayInputStream`: Reads an array of bytes as though it is an InputStream object.

- `SequenceInputStream`: Concatenates data from two or more `InputStream` objects.

- `PipedInputStream`: Used for communicating between threads.

- `ByteArrayOutputStream`: Sends its output into a `byte[]` object.

- `PipedOutputStream`: Communicates with `PipedInputStream` to complete thread communication.

Character Streams

Just as Java provides a set of classes for reading and writing to and from byte streams, it also provides interfaces and classes for reading and writing to and from character streams.

The `InputStream` and `OutputStream` counterparts that read character streams are the `java.io.Reader` and `java.io.Writer` classes. These classes are responsible for properly converting each character from its encoding scheme of the native OS to Unicode; they are sensitive to different character-encoding schemes and support international applications.

Figure 12.2 shows the inheritance hierarchy for the `Reader` and `Writer` classes.

FIGURE 12.2
Reader and Writer
inheritance hierarchy.

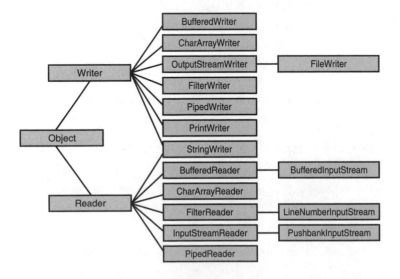

Table 12.3 shows a summary of the reader and writer classes:

TABLE 12.3   Reader and Writer Classes

Class	Description
FileReader	Character-oriented counterpart to FileInputStream.
FileWriter	Character-oriented counterpart to FileOutputStream.
InputStreamReader	Converts InputStream objects to Readers.
OutputStreamWriter	Converts OutputStream objects to Writers.
BufferedReader	Reader that uses a buffer for efficiency.
CharArrayReader	Reads an array of characters as a Reader object.
StringReader	Reads a String as a Reader object.
PipedReader	Used for communicating between threads.
BufferedWriter	Writer that uses a buffer for efficiency.
CharArrayWriter	Outputs to a char[].
StringWriter	Writes to a StringBuffer as a Writer object.
PipedWriter	Other half of thread communications.
PrintWriter	Character equivalent to PrintStream.

Table 12.4 shows the Reader methods, and Table 12.5 shows the Writer methods.

TABLE 12.4   java.io.Reader Methods

Method	Description
abstract void close()	Closes the stream
void mark(int readAheadLimit)	Marks the present position in the stream
boolean markSupported()	Tells whether this stream supports the mark() operation
int read()	Reads a single character
int read(char[] cbuf)	Reads characters into an array
abstract int read(char[] cbuf, int off, int len)	Reads characters into a portion of an array
boolean ready()	Tells whether this stream is ready to be read
void reset()	Resets the stream
long skip(long n)	Skips characters

The `Reader` class provides methods to read characters, skip over characters, set marks that you can jump back to in the stream (if they are supported), and a method to close the `Reader`.

TABLE 12.5   `java.io.Writer` Methods

Method	Description
`abstract  void close()`	Closes the stream, flushing it first
`abstract  void flush()`	Flushes the stream
`void write(char[] cbuf)`	Writes an array of characters
`abstract  void write(char[] cbuf, int off, int len)`	Writes a portion of an array of characters
`void write(int c)`	Writes a single character
`void write(String str)`	Writes a string
`void write(String str, int off, int len)`	Writes a portion of a string

The `Writer` class provides three types of methods: methods to write data to a stream, a method to flush data that has been written to the stream, and a method to close the stream.

File I/O with Readers/Writers

Java provides two classes for reading from and writing to files:

- `java.io.FileReader`

- `java.io.FileWriter`

The `FileReader` and `FileWriter` classes can be used almost identically to the `FileInputStream` and `FileOutputStream` classes. Listing 12.3 shows an example using these classes.

LISTING 12.3   `FileReaderWriterExample.java`

```
import java.io.Reader;
import java.io.Writer;
import java.io.FileReader;
import java.io.FileWriter;

public class FileReaderWriterExample
{
    public static void main( String[] args ) {
        try {
            Reader r = new FileReader( "in.txt" );
```

LISTING 12.3   Continued

```
        Writer w = new FileWriter( "out.txt" );
        int c;
        while( ( c = r.read() ) != -1 ) {
    System.out.print( ( char )c );
    w.write( c );
        }
        r.close();
        w.close();
    }
    catch( Exception e ) {
        e.printStackTrace();
    }
  }
}
```

As you can see this class is almost identical to the stream version except that it uses the reader and writer classes. This example uses the `Reader` and `Writer` base classes to read from and write to the `FileReader` and `FileWriter` instances.

Byte and Character I/O Classes

Java provides some helper classes for reading input stream classes as readers and writing to output streams as writers. These two classes are

- `java.io.InputStreamReader`

- `java.io.OutputStreamWriter`

You can use these classes by passing existing streams to their constructors. For example:

```
InputStream is = new FileInputStream( "in.txt" );
Reader r = new InputStreamReader( is );
...use r...
```

Other Character I/O Reader and Writer Classes

Similar to the `BufferedInputStream` and `BufferedOutputStream`, character readers have a `BufferedReader` class and a `BufferedWriter` class. The `BufferedReader` class not only provides a more efficient mechanism for reading data from a stream, it also provides a very useful method for reading text: `readLine()`. This method returns a new line delimited String from the stream. So, you can read an entire stream line by line as follows:

```
BufferedReader br = new BufferedReader( new FileReader( "in.txt" ) );
String line = br.readLine();
while( line != null ) {
  System.out.println( line );
  line = br.readLine();
}
```

Java provides two readers and two writers that are helpful for reading and writing existing data from and to Readers and Writers:

- **CharArrayReader**: Allows you to read a character array (**char[]**) as a Reader.

- **CharArrayWriter**: Allows you to write Writers to a character array (**char[]**).

- **StringReader**: Allows you to read a String as a Reader.

- **StringWriter**: Allows you to write a Writer to a String.

To help write **Writer** data using **print()** and **println()** methods, Java provides the **java.io.PrintWriter** class.

Most commonly, text files are read using the **BufferedReader** class because you can read one line at a time and text files are written to using the **PrintWriter** class because it has the familiar **print()** and **println()** methods.

The last category of readers and writers are the **java.io.PipedReader** and **java.io.PipedWriter** classes. These are used for communicating between two processes.

StreamTokenizer

The **java.io.StreamTokenizer** class is a utility class to help you parse **Readers** by dividing them into tokens; you can ask for each white-space delimited String to be returned to you from the **Reader**. You can think of this as returning the **Reader** word by word.

The **StreamTokenizer** is a somewhat different to use than most of the classes you have seen thus far. It parses tokens one by one returning a status to tell you if you are at the end of the **Reader**, and then makes the value available as a public attribute of the **StreamTokenizer** class (**sval**).

Listing 12.4 shows an example using the **StreamTokenizer** class to read the **in.txt** file word by word.

LISTING 12.4   StreamTokenizerExample.java

```java
import java.io.Reader;
import java.io.FileReader;
import java.io.StreamTokenizer;

public class StreamTokenizerExample
{
    public static void main( String[] args ) {
        try {
            Reader r = new FileReader( "in.txt" );
            StreamTokenizer st = new StreamTokenizer( r );
            while( st.nextToken() != StreamTokenizer.TT_EOF ) {
                System.out.println( st.sval );
            }
            r.close();
        }
        catch( Exception e ) {
            e.printStackTrace();
        }
    }
}
```

Notice from Listing 12.4 that the `StreamTokenizer` class gets the next token by calling the `nextToken()` method. This method returns one of the following status values:

- `TT_EOF`: Indicates that the end of the stream has been read
- `TT_EOL`: Indicates that the end of the line has been read
- `TT_NUMBER`: Indicates that a number token has been read
- `TT_WORD`: Indicates that a word token has been read

Thus, the example reads each token until it reaches the end of the stream (`TT_EOF`).

Accessing the `StreamTokenizer`'s `sval` public attribute retrieves the String value retrieved by the `StreamTokenizer`.

Chaining Streams For Ease of Use

You might have noticed that many of the I/O classes take as an argument to their constructors another stream type. The term for building streams from streams is referred to as *chaining*. The idea is that you will read each stream in the best manner depending on the type of data. If the data is text, the best way to read it is through a `BufferedReader`, but if the data is a collection of primitive types, it is best read using a `DataInputStream`.

Summary

This chapter introduced you to the input and output classes provided by Java's I/O class library. Specific classes are defined for reading byte-oriented data based on the `InputStream` and `OutputStream` classes, whereas specific classes are defined for reading text-based data based on the `Reader` and `Writer` classes.

You can chain streams together to ensure that you are using the best stream for the data that you are reading and writing.

Review Questions

1. What are the base classes for reading byte-oriented data?
2. What are the base classes for reading text-based data?
3. What type of data would you read from the `java.io.DataInputStream` class?
4. What is the easiest stream class for reading text-based data?
5. What type of class is `System.out`?
6. Define chaining and why is it useful?
7. What is the `java.io.StreamTokenizer` class and what does it offer you?

Exercises

1. Use the stream classes to copy a text file.

2. Read data from the standard input and echo it to the standard output and to a file called `output.txt`.

3. Use the `java.io.StreamTokenizer` class to read a text document word-by-word and display each word on a separate line.

PART III

GRAPHICAL USER INTERFACES

CHAPTER 13

ABSTRACT WINDOWS TOOLKIT

In this chapter you will learn:

- What the Abstract Windows Toolkit is
- How to create AWT Containers
- How to place AWT components in Containers
- How to use Layout Managers to control the look and feel of your GUI

reating Graphical User Interfaces using Java is fairly straightforward. This simplicity is hampered somewhat by the fact that there are two different, but related, sets of graphics classes: the Abstract Windows Toolkit (AWT) and the Java Foundation Classes (JFC), which are collectively known as Swing.

When Java 1.0 was released circa 1995, it shipped with a set of classes called the Abstract Windows Toolkit 1.0. Later, this toolkit was upgraded to AWT 1.1, which improved it considerably. This version is the one that we will discuss in this chapter. The JFC, or Swing Toolkit, will be the topic of Chapter 16, "Swing."

The AWT is built on the native graphics system of each platform that it is ported to. For example, when you create a button on the Windows platform, AWT creates a peer control in the native Windows graphics library. Whenever your users communicate with your button, it passes the information on to the peer to do the heavy lifting.

Several problems are inherent in this approach. The first problem is that these components are considered heavyweight because they cause a potentially large object to be created under the covers. This object might have considerable functionality that is never used by the AWT button, but the JVM cannot instantiate half of the peer. It must all be instantiated.

The second problem is that every graphics subsystem differs in the objects that it supports and also in the features each object provides. This forced the AWT development team to use a "least common denominator" approach, where only the object types that all platforms support could be used. This guaranteed that the AWT would be mired permanently in mediocrity.

Regretting what they had done, the AWT development team abandoned the peer approach and reimplemented the graphical objects in native Java code. They renamed it the Java Foundation Classes (Swing). AWT was not replaced, however, for reasons of backward compatibility.

Java application developers quickly noticed the superiority of the Swing classes and moved quickly to use them. Applet developers, however, were hampered by the unwillingness of browser vendors to support the new libraries.

The Java development team responded by providing a plug-in for both Internet Explorer and Netscape Navigator. This plug-in replaces the default version 1.1 JVM with Java 2 code. Even though the newer versions of the browser support Swing via the plug-in, not all users update their browsers regularly.

Finally, we have the problem of users turning off all Java functionality in their browsers. They do this based on the occurrence of some security problems associated with applets years ago. Power-user types who write in magazines made the sweeping recommendation that Java always be disabled.

The resulting situation is that you have three categories of browsers that you have to consider when writing applets: the browser with Java disabled, the browser with Java 1.1 enabled, and the browser with Java 2 enabled using a plug-in. Many Web-page developers avoid this situation by avoiding Java Applets and implementing all their functionality by using HTML only. This is a very limiting practice given the weakness of HTML as a programming language.

Another group programs applets using Swing and requires that the users install the Java plug-in. This only works where the programmer has considerable control over the browser on his users' desktops. For the other 90% of the Web applications that are trying to reach all Internet users, the programmer cannot control what the user is running. For this reason, most Java programmers still write their applets using AWT.

In this chapter, we will cover the Abstract Windows Toolkit (AWT) only. First, you will learn how to create and run AWT container classes. Following that, you will learn about the different types of controls that are available in the AWT. Finally, you will study the management of page layout using the Layout Manager classes.

Containers

A container class is one that can host other graphical objects. In this chapter, you will learn how to use the major AWT containers. (You will learn how to use the other major container classes, the Swing containers, in Chapter 16, "Swing.") Containers are interesting because they can be placed inside other containers recursively. The primary container classes are

- **Applet**—An applet is a container that runs Java in a browser.
- **Frame**—A frame is a top-level window with a title and a border.

- **Panel**—A panel is a rectangular space where you can attach other components, including other panels.

- **ScrollPane**—This is a Panel class that automatically implements both a horizontal and a vertical scrollbar.

- **Dialog**—A dialog is a window that pops up and enables the user to receive a warning or confirm an action such as an exit.

We will cover these containers first, and then use them in later examples to learn about the components that they can host.

Applets

In the age of Web Services and Java 2 Enterprise Edition (J2EE), it is hard to remember that Java was originally intended to be an applet-centric language. The ability to create applets using Java was not nearly as interesting to the developer community as some of Java's other qualities. Java is a simple, portable, object-oriented programming language. These features appealed to programmers who were tired of having to make major modifications to their programs when porting them to another platform. In the last few years, server-side Java development has grown so much that there are many Java developers who have never written a production applet.

There are some good things about applets though. For example, they are more powerful than HTML alone. In addition, they are distributed automatically with the HTML document, so there is no need to store them on a client machine.

On the downside, the security manager that ships with the JVM limits applet access to the user's machine severely. This reduces the number of useful things that an applet can do on the client machine. In addition, because applets are downloaded every time the HTML is downloaded, they must be kept fairly small in size to keep from slowing the user's download time too much.

Applet development might seem a little strange to you at first because you don't actually write applets; you extend them. The `java.applet.Applet` class provides all the functionality necessary to communicate with the browser's Java Virtual Machine (JVM). Your job is to override certain key methods to add behavior that meets your requirements.

The combination of these parts is shown if Figure 13.1.

The `java.applet.Applet` class is installed in the JVM, which is part of the browser. When the browser receives the HTML file from your Web server, it notices the applet tag and downloads the `.class` file for your applet also. Your applet will contain one or more overrides to the Applet class's method calls. The JVM will call your versions of these methods instead of the Applet class versions while it is loading and running your applet.

FIGURE 13.1
The Applet class provides all the communication between the applet code, the JVM, and the browser.

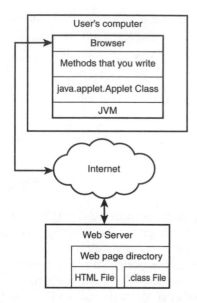

Running Applets

It is possible to write a simple applet in a very few lines of code. Listing 13.1 shows a trivial example.

LISTING 13.1   The HelloApplet Class

```java
import java.awt.*;
import java.applet.Applet;

public class HelloApplet extends Applet
{
    public void paint(Graphics g)
    {
        g.drawString("Hello, Applet", 10, 10);
    }
}
import java.applet.Applet;
```

Caution
Some versions of the JDK can cause conflicts with some versions of Microsoft's Internet Explorer. If you experience difficulty, try downloading the latest released versions of both the JDK and IE or alternatively, you can run the applet in Netscape.

This is about as simple as an applet can be while still doing something. The only instruction that we are giving it is to place the string "Hello, Applet" in the applet.

Browsers expect to run HTML files, not applets. To run this applet, we need to provide an HTML file that contains a reference to this applet. Listing 13.2 shows an HTML file that contains a reference to this applet.

LISTING 13.2   The `runHelloApplet.html` File

```
This is the Hello Applet
<applet
code=HelloApplet
width=200
height=200>
</applet>
```

The applet tag tells the HTML processor in the browser that an applet has to be downloaded from the same place the HTML file came from. The width and height determine the boundary for the applet.

To run an HTML file that contains an applet you have several choices. The first is to open a browser and type the full path and filename in the address line like this:

`C:\com\samspublishing\jpp\ch13\runHelloApplet.html`

Alternatively, if your computer has a Web server running on it, you can place both the HTML and the applet's class file in the special directory that your Web server documentation specifies and type the following in your browser's address line:

`http://127.0.0.1/runHelloApplet.html`

In either case, the result of running the `runHelloApplet.html` file in a browser is shown in Figure 13.2.

FIGURE 13.2
The HTML file downloads the applet automatically.

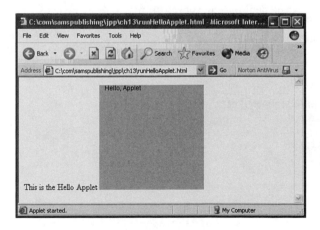

The gray section is the area covered by the applet. Gray is the default color for applets. The phrase "This is the Hello Applet" is placed in the browser window by the HTML code. The other phrase "Hello, Applet" is written in the applet area of the browser window by the applet code.

Caution

Many browser versions cache old HTML pages and applets in mysterious ways. If you make a change to an applet and recompile it, you might not see the new version of the applet when you click the refresh button. If you still see the old version, close all instances of that browser and open it again. When you type the filename or URL, the new, changed version should appear.

Although applets are not the primary focus of Java's direction at present, they can be used to create some interesting looking Web pages.

Frames

The Frame class is the container most used when creating Java applications. Even when we create Panels and ScrollPanes, we typically place them inside a Frame for display.

A Frame is an extension of the Window class that adds a title and a border for resizing. There are two ways to create a Frame object from your Java class. You can extend the Frame class, or you can declare a Frame in the `main()` method. Listing 13.3 shows how to create a Java application by extending the Frame class.

LISTING 13.3   The `FrameExtender.java` File

```
/*
 * FrameExtender.java
 *
 * Created on July 29, 2002, 3:15 PM
 */

package com.samspublishing.jpp.ch13;

import java.awt.*;
import java.awt.event.*;

/**
 *
 * @author   Stephen Potts
 * @version
 */
public class FrameExtender extends Frame
{

    /** Creates new FrameExtender */
    public FrameExtender()
    {
        addWindowListener(new WinCloser());
        setTitle("Just a Frame");
        setBounds( 100, 100, 200, 200);
        setVisible(true);
    }
```

LISTING 13.3   *Continued*

```
    public static void main(String args[])
    {
        FrameExtender fe = new FrameExtender();
    }
}

class WinCloser extends WindowAdapter
{
    public void windowClosing(WindowEvent e)
    {
        System.exit(0);
    }

}
```

The key to creating this window on the screen is extending the Frame class. The strength of object-oriented programming is that you can borrow, or inherit, functionality that performs a lot of work for you by adding the word "extends", and the name of the class that you want to borrow from.

```
public class FrameExtender extends Frame
```

Unlike an applet, applications have no `init()` method. The constructor is very similar in its function, however, and gets run when the object is created.

```
public FrameExtender()
```

Windows can close without properly cleaning up the processes that are running. To solve this problem, we have to add a Window Listener class to do this cleanup. Swing provides a more elegant solution that you will learn when we cover that GUI toolkit.

```
        addWindowListener(new WinCloser());
```

The title can be set with a method call:

```
        setTitle("Just a Frame");
```

The bounds are set which establish the initial size of the window.

```
        setBounds( 100, 100, 200, 200);
```

Finally, we tell the window to display itself.

```
        setVisible(true);
```

The `main()` method instantiates an instance of the class itself, which triggers the execution of the constructor.

```
    public static void main(String args[])
    {
        FrameExtender fe = new FrameExtender();
    }
}
```

The `WinCloser` class extends the `WindowApapter` class. The `WindowAdapter` class is an abstract class that provides a set of no-op methods. As the programmer, you then provide your own implementation by overriding the methods that you want to handle. If your program extends the WindowListener interface, an error will be thrown for every method that you don't provide an implementation for. Most programmers prefer the WindowAdapter approach. The only service that we need it to perform here is to exit the application when the window closes. We will cover events in more detail in Chapter 14, "Event Delegation Model."

```
class WinCloser extends WindowAdapter
{
    public void windowClosing(WindowEvent e)
```

The `exit()` method of the `System` class instructs the JVM to destroy the process and recover the resources whenever it chooses to.

```
        System.exit(0);
```

To run this example, compile it, and then move to the root directory of your file system (in Windows, this is most likely `c:\`) and type the following command:

`C:\>java com.samspublishing.jpp.ch13.FrameExtender`

This will open a window that looks like the one in Figure 13.3:

FIGURE 13.3
Extending the `Frame` class can create a window.

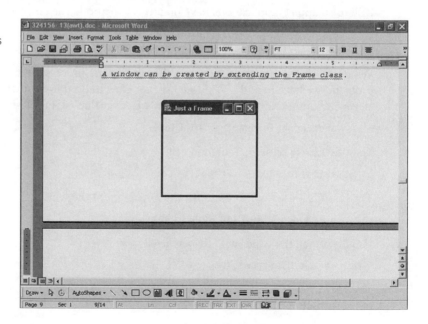

An alternative to extending the `Frame` class is to declare it in the `main()` method of the class that you are creating. Listing 13.4 shows the `FrameInstantiater` class that creates a Frame object in the `main()` method.

Listing 13.4   The `FrameInstantiater.java` File

```
/*
 * FrameInstantiater.java
 *
 * Created on July 29, 2002, 4:13 PM
 */

package com.samspublishing.jpp.ch13;

import java.awt.*;
import java.awt.event.*;

/**
 *
 * @author  Stephen Potts
 * @version
 */
public class FrameInstantiater
{
    public FrameInstantiater()
    {
    }

    public static void main(String[] args)
    {
        Frame frame1 = new Frame();

        frame1.addWindowListener(new WinCloser());
        frame1.setTitle("An Instantiated Frame");
        frame1.setBounds( 100, 100, 300, 300);
        frame1.setVisible(true);
    }
}

class WinCloser extends WindowAdapter
{
    public void windowClosing(WindowEvent e)
    {
        System.exit(0);
    }
}
```

This time the class is created without extending any other classes.

```
public class FrameInstantiater
```

The constructor is also empty.

```
    public FrameInstantiater()
    {
    }
```

All the work is done in the main method. The Frame object is created by hand.

```
        Frame frame1 = new Frame();
```

The window listener is added here.

```
frame1.addWindowListener(new WinCloser());
```

We add a title, set the bounds, and make it visible using the instance variable `frame1`.

```
frame1.setTitle("An Instantiated Frame");
frame1.setBounds( 100, 100, 300, 300);
frame1.setVisible(true);
    }
}
```

You compile and run this example in exactly the same way as you did with Listing 13.3, except for the class name, of course. The result of running this example is shown in Figure 13.4.

FIGURE 13.4

A window can be created by instantiating a Frame object.

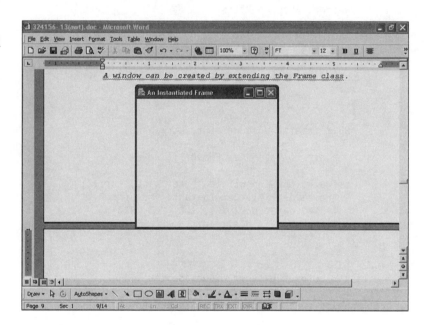

Frames would be pretty useless unless you could place objects on them. Fortunately, this is possible. The simplest way to place objects on a form is to use the Frame's `add()` method to attach GUI objects to the Frame that have been created by hand. Listing 13.5 shows this technique.

LISTING 13.5   The `TextFieldInstantiater.java` File

```
/*
 * TextFieldInstantiater.java
 *
 * Created on July 29, 2002, 4:13 PM
 */
```

LISTING 13.5   Continued

```java
package com.samspublishing.jpp.ch13;

import java.awt.*;
import java.awt.event.*;

/**
 *
 * @author  Stephen Potts
 * @version
 */
public class TextFieldInstantiater
{
   public TextFieldInstantiater()
   {
   }

   public static void main(String[] args)
   {
      Frame frame1 = new Frame();
      TextField tf1 = new TextField("Directly on the Frame");
      TextField tf2 = new TextField("On top of the old text");
      frame1.add(tf1);
      frame1.add(tf2);

      frame1.addWindowListener(new WinCloser());
      frame1.setTitle("An Instantiated Frame");
      frame1.setBounds( 100, 100, 300, 300);
      frame1.setVisible(true);
   }
}

class WinCloser extends WindowAdapter
{
   public void windowClosing(WindowEvent e)
   {
      System.exit(0);
   }
}
```

The unique part of this example is the creation and insertion of the text fields.

```java
      TextField tf1 = new TextField("Directly on the Frame");
      TextField tf2 = new TextField("On top of the old text");
      frame1.add(tf1);
      frame1.add(tf2);
```

Notice that there are no locations on either the `TextField` constructors or on the `Frame.add()` method. This means that the field will be placed at the top line of the frame. When we add the second `TextField` object, it overlays the first one, as shown in Figure 13.5.

FIGURE 13.5
A text field can be added
directly to the frame, but
it cannot be positioned in
the window.

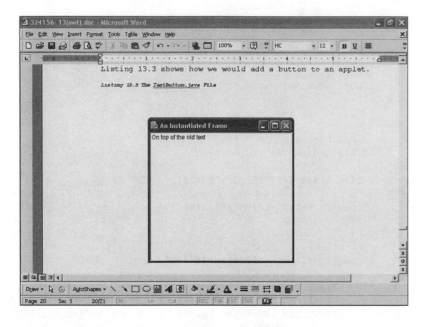

This behavior is not likely to be what you had envisioned. Normally, you don't want GUI
objects to overwrite each other. This lack of control over the placement of objects in a frame is
a primary motivation to use the **Panel** class and Layout managers to provide more control over
the appearance of your objects. Panels are the subject of the following section. We will introduce layout managers later in the chapter.

Panels

The **java.awt.Panel** class is a generic container that is rectangular, but lacks the title and border of a Frame. Its default behavior is to implement a flow of controls from left to right with
wrapping. This behavior is identical to a FlowLayout that you will learn about later in this
chapter.

Primarily, panels are used to provide several containers within a frame. This allows you greater
flexibility when laying out a screen. Listing 13.6 shows how adding a panel can change the
behavior of the layout of objects.

LISTING 13.6   The **PanelTest.java** File

```
/*
 * TestPanel.java
 *
 * Created on July 30, 2002, 11:35 AM
 */

package com.samspublishing.jpp.ch13;

import java.awt.*;
```

LISTING 13.6   *Continued*

```java
import java.awt.event.*;

/**
 *
 * @author  Stephen Potts
 * @version
 */
public class TestPanel extends Frame
{
   TextField tf1;
   TextField tf2;

   /** Creates new TestPanel */
   public TestPanel()
   {
      tf1 = new TextField("Directly on the Panel");
      tf2 = new TextField("Following the first TextField");
      Panel p1 = new Panel();
      p1.add(tf1);
      p1.add(tf2);
      add(p1);
      addWindowListener(new WinCloser());
      setTitle("Using a Panel");
      setBounds( 100, 100, 300, 300);
      setVisible(true);
   }

   public static void main(String[] args)
   {
      TestPanel tp = new TestPanel();
   }

}

class WinCloser extends WindowAdapter
{
   public void windowClosing(WindowEvent e)
   {
      System.exit(0);
   }
}
```

The important difference between this example and Listing 13.5 is that the two text fields are added to a panel, which is added to a frame, instead of being attached to the frame directly.

Two text fields are instantiated with strings.

```java
tf1 = new TextField("Directly on the Panel");
tf2 = new TextField("Following the first TextField");
```

A new panel is created and the two text strings are attached to it.

```
Panel p1 = new Panel();
p1.add(tf1);
p1.add(tf2);
```

The panel is added to the frame.

```
add(p1);
```

Running this example produces the result shown in Figure 13.6.

FIGURE 13.6
Text fields added to frames can be added directly to the panel, which lays them out flowing from left to right with line wrapping.

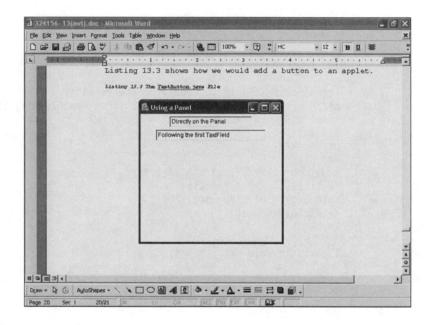

Notice the different behavior that comes from using a panel. Laying objects one after the other with wrapping is far more intuitive than overwriting one with the other.

ScrollPane

Another useful container is the `java.awt.ScrollPane` class. This container is unique in that it only allows for one object to be placed on it. This seems limiting until you realize that the object can be a panel, which can hold an arbitrary number of objects.

The big attraction of the `ScrollPane` is the optional presence of both a horizontal and a vertical scrollbar. There are three possible values that can be passed to one of the constructors:

- `ScrollPane.SCROLLBARS_AS_NEEDED`

- `ScrollPane.SCROLLBARS_ALWAYS`

- `ScrollPane.SCROLLBARS_NEVER`

The default is `ScrollPane.SCROLLBARS_AS_NEEDED`. If you create a `ScrollPane` using the default constructor, you will get scrollbars only if the size of the panel exceeds the size of the `ScrollPane`.

Note

In Java, constants are defined in the following way:

```
public static final int SCROLLBARS_AS_NEEDED = 0
```

The word `public` indicates a visibility outside the declaring class. The word `static` means that it can be referenced using the class name such as `ScrollPane`, instead of requiring an instance variable. `final` means that when set, the value can never change. Writing the name of the constant in all uppercase letters is a convention that makes constants easier to pick out in text.

Listing 13.7 shows a Panel that is added to a `ScrollPane`.

LISTING 13.7   The `TestScrollPane.java` File

```
/*
 * TestScrollPane.java
 *
 * Created on July 30, 2002, 11:35 AM
 */

package com.samspublishing.jpp.ch13;

import java.awt.*;
import java.awt.event.*;

/**
 *
 * @author  Stephen Potts
 * @version
 */
public class TestScrollPane extends Frame
{
    ScrollPane sp;
    TextField tf1;
    TextField tf2;
    TextField tf3;
    TextField tf4;
    TextField tf5;
    TextField tf6;
    TextField tf7;
    TextField tf8;

    /** Creates new TestScrollPane */
    public TestScrollPane()
    {
        //create eight text fields
```

LISTING 13.7 Continued

```java
        tf1 = new TextField("Text Field Number 1 ");
        tf2 = new TextField("Text Field Number 2 ");
        tf3 = new TextField("Text Field Number 3 ");
        tf4 = new TextField("Text Field Number 4 ");
        tf5 = new TextField("Text Field Number 5 ");
        tf6 = new TextField("Text Field Number 6 ");
        tf7 = new TextField("Text Field Number 7 ");
        tf8 = new TextField("Text Field Number 8 ");

        //add the panel
        Panel p1 = new Panel();
        p1.add(tf1);
        p1.add(tf2);
        p1.add(tf3);
        p1.add(tf4);
        p1.add(tf5);
        p1.add(tf6);
        p1.add(tf7);
        p1.add(tf8);

        //create the scroll pane
        sp = new ScrollPane();
        sp.add(p1);
        add(sp);
        addWindowListener(new WinCloser());
        setTitle("Using a ScrollPane");
        setBounds( 100, 100, 300, 300);
        setVisible(true);
    }

    public static void main(String[] args)
    {
        TestScrollPane tsp = new TestScrollPane();
    }

}

class WinCloser extends WindowAdapter
{
    public void windowClosing(WindowEvent e)
    {
        System.exit(0);
    }
}
```

All the magic in this example takes place in just a few lines of code. First, we instantiate the ScrollPane.

```java
        sp = new ScrollPane();
```

Next, we add the panel to the ScrollPane.

```java
        sp.add(p1);
```

Finally, we add the `ScrollPane`, not the `Panel` object, to the Frame.

```
add(sp);
```

The result of running this example is shown in Figure 13.7.

FIGURE 13.7
Panels added to Scroll
Panes can be accessed
using scrollbars.

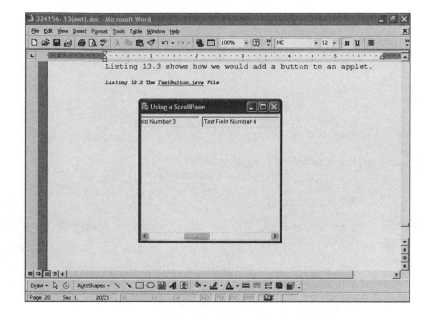

Notice that no wrapping took place, after we placed the panel in the `ScrollPane`. This gives us two choices when choosing a look and feel: a panel that wraps and one that scrolls. The reason for this is that the layout behavior of the panel is altered by the existence of the scroll-bar. Instead of wrapping, the controls are placed side-by-side. Layout managers, which are covered later in this chapter, can be used to control the look and feel of the GUI.

Programming with Dialogs

The final container type that we will cover is the `Dialog` class. A `Frame` object or another `Dialog` always contains a `Dialog` object. It might be modal, locking out other processes until the dialog is closed, or it might be modeless, allowing it to remain open while the user works in other windows.

A `Dialog` object fires window events when the state of its window changes. The `show()` method is used to bring the `Dialog` object to the front and display it.

A common use of dialogs is to confirm something. Listing 13.8 shows an example of how this works.

LISTING 13.8   The `TestDialog.java` File

```java
/*
 * TestDialog.java
 *
 * Created on July 30, 2002, 2:36 PM
 */

package com.samspublishing.jpp.ch13;
import java.awt.*;
import java.awt.event.*;

/**
 *
 * @author   Stephen Potts
 * @version
 */
public class TestDialog extends Frame
              implements ActionListener
{
    Button btnExit;
    Button btnYes;
    Button btnNo;
    Dialog dlgConfirm;

    /** Creates new TestDialog */
    public TestDialog()
    {
        btnExit = new Button("Exit");
        btnExit.addActionListener(this);

        add(btnExit);
        this.setLayout(new FlowLayout());

        dlgConfirm = new Dialog(this);
        dlgConfirm.setResizable(false);

        btnYes = new Button("Yes");
        btnYes.addActionListener(this);

        btnNo = new Button("No");
        btnNo.addActionListener(this);

        dlgConfirm.add(btnYes);
        dlgConfirm.add(btnNo);
        dlgConfirm.setTitle("Are you sure?");

        dlgConfirm.setSize(200, 100);
        dlgConfirm.setLayout(new FlowLayout());
```

LISTING 13.8   Continued

```
      addWindowListener(new WinCloser());
      setTitle("Using a Dialog");
      setBounds( 100, 100, 300, 300);
      setVisible(true);

   }


   public void actionPerformed(ActionEvent ae)
   {
      if (ae.getActionCommand().equals("Exit"))
        dlgConfirm.show();
      if (ae.getActionCommand().equals("Yes"))
        System.exit(0);
      if (ae.getActionCommand().equals("No"))
        dlgConfirm.setVisible(false);
   }

   public static void main(String[] args)
   {
      TestDialog td = new TestDialog();
   }

}

class WinCloser extends WindowAdapter
{
   public void windowClosing(WindowEvent e)
   {
      System.exit(0);
   }
}
```

This example introduces several new concepts and foreshadows several others. The **TestDialog** class implements the **ActionListener** interface. This interface handles **Action** events.

```
public class TestDialog extends Frame
             implements ActionListener
```

Most of the work that is done is in the **TestDialog** constructor.

```
   public TestDialog()
   {
```

We create an exit button and add a listener class for it.

```
      btnExit = new Button("Exit");
      btnExit.addActionListener(this);
      add(btnExit);
```

We set a different layout manager for `TestDialog` because the default border layout manager would expand the "Exit" button's size until it filled the whole window.

```
this.setLayout(new FlowLayout());
```

We create a dialog and attach it to this class.

```
dlgConfirm = new Dialog(this);
dlgConfirm.setResizable(false);
```

We add buttons for yes and no to the dialog.

```
btnYes = new Button("Yes");
btnYes.addActionListener(this);

btnNo = new Button("No");
btnNo.addActionListener(this);

dlgConfirm.add(btnYes);
dlgConfirm.add(btnNo);
```

We set the title and size of the dialog.

```
dlgConfirm.setTitle("Are you sure?");
```

```
dlgConfirm.setSize(200, 100);
```

The default `BorderLayout` is not appropriate for the dialog because it causes buttons to overlay each other.

```
dlgConfirm.setLayout(new FlowLayout());
```

The `actionPerformed()` method is required by the `ActionListener` interface. It is automatically called when any action event, such as a button click occurs.

```
public void actionPerformed(ActionEvent ae)
{
    if (ae.getActionCommand().equals("Exit"))
```

The `show()` method makes the dialog appear.

```
    dlgConfirm.show();
    if (ae.getActionCommand().equals("Yes"))
      System.exit(0);
```

The `setVisible(false)` method call causes the dialog to disappear.

```
    if (ae.getActionCommand().equals("No"))
      dlgConfirm.setVisible(false);
}
```

When we run this example, the frame appears and shows the Exit button. Clicking this will open the dialog as shown here in Figure 13.8.

FIGURE 13.8
Dialogs can be used to
confirm user actions.

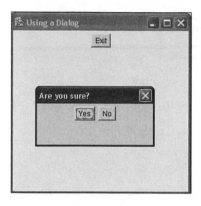

Clicking on the "Yes" button will cause the dialog and the Frame to close.

Adding AWT Components to the GUI

The AWT contains another set of graphical objects called components. Components are normally thought of as objects that you place inside of containers. You have been introduced to two types of components in the listings dealings with containers: buttons and text fields. Examples of common components include the following classes:

- TextField

- Button

- Label

- CheckBox

- Choice List

- List

- Menu Components

All these classes extend the `java.awt.component` class. This class provides a number of methods that are useful to all the graphical components. The methods `setLocation()`, `setForeground()`, `setBackground()`, `addMouseListener()`, and so on, come from this base class.

TextField

A `TextField` is a component that contains a single line of text for data entry. It can vary in length, but it can't extend for more than one line. The `TextField` class, `java.awt.TextField`, provides the following important methods:

- addActionListener()—The listener class is one that receives notification when an action event occurs.

- setColumns()—Sets the number of columns.

- setText()—Sets or modifies the text.

- removeActionListener()—Removes an action listener.

- getListeners()—Returns an array of all listeners associated with this object.

The first example simply places a TextField object in a frame. Listing 13.9 shows the code for the frame.

LISTING 13.9   The TestTextField.java File

```
/*
 * TestTextField.java
 *
 * Created on July 30, 2002, 11:35 AM
 */

package com.samspublishing.jpp.ch13;

import java.awt.*;
import java.awt.event.*;

/**
 *
 * @author  Stephen Potts
 * @version
 */
public class TestTextFields extends Frame
{
    TextField tfield1;
    TextField tfield2;

    /** Creates new TestTextField */
    public TestTextFields()
    {
        tfield1 = new TextField(15);
        tfield2 = new TextField(20);
        tfield1.setEchoChar('*');
        tfield2.setText("Some Sample Text");
        tfield2.setFont(new Font("Courier",Font.BOLD,16));
        tfield2.setEditable(false);
        tfield2.select(12,15);

        Panel p1 = new Panel();
        p1.add(tfield1);
        p1.add(tfield2);
        add(p1);
        addWindowListener(new WinCloser());
```

LISTING 13.9   Continued

```
        setTitle("Using TextFields");
        setBounds( 100, 100, 300, 300);
        setVisible(true);
    }

    public static void main(String[] args)
    {
        TestTextFields tp = new TestTextFields();
    }

}

class WinCloser extends WindowAdapter
{
    public void windowClosing(WindowEvent e)
    {
        System.exit(0);
    }
}
```

This example is designed to show some of the methods that the `TextField` class provides, as well as some of the methods that it inherits from its direct parent, the `java.awt.TextComponent` class.

Text fields can be created with a preset number of columns to show at one time.

```
        tfield1 = new TextField(15);
        tfield2 = new TextField(20);
```

We set an echo character so that sensitive information can't be viewed while it is being typed.

```
        tfield1.setEchoChar('*');
```

You can set the text programmatically to display default values.

```
        tfield2.setText("Some Sample Text");
```

You can also set the font.

```
        tfield2.setFont(new Font("Courier",Font.BOLD,16));
```

To set the field as not editable, you call this method.

```
        tfield2.setEditable(false);
```

You can also select substrings of a field programmatically.

```
        tfield2.select(12,15);
```

Running this example displays the result shown in Figure 13.9 (after you type a few characters in the first field).

FIGURE 13.9
TextFields can be manipulated manually and programmatically.

The highlighted portion of the second text field was set by the `select()` method.

Adding Buttons

One of the most popular graphical components is the button. The button class, `java.awt.Button`, class provides the following important methods:

- `addActionListener()`—The listener class is one that receives notification when the button is clicked.

- `setLabel()`—Sets the label text for the button.

- `removeActionListener()`—Removes the association between this button and the listener class.

Adding a button to a container is a fairly simple process. Listing 13.10 shows how we would add a button to a Frame.

LISTING 13.10   The `TestButton.java` File

```
/*
 * TestButton.java
 *
 * Created on July 30, 2002, 2:36 PM
 */

package com.samspublishing.jpp.ch13;
import java.awt.*;
import java.awt.event.*;

/**
 *
 * @author  Stephen Potts
 * @version
 */
public class TestButton extends Frame
                implements ActionListener
```

LISTING 13.10   Continued

```
{
   Button btnExit;

   /** Creates new TestDialog */
   public TestButton()
   {
      btnExit = new Button("Exit");
      btnExit.setFont(new Font("Courier", Font.BOLD, 24));

      btnExit.setBackground(Color.cyan);
      Cursor curs = new Cursor(Curson.HAND_CURSOR);
      btnExit.setCursor(curs);
      btnExit.addActionListener(this);

      add(btnExit);
      this.setLayout(new FlowLayout());

      addWindowListener(new WinCloser());
      setTitle("Using a Button and an ActionListener");
      setBounds( 100, 100, 300, 300);
      setVisible(true);
   }

   public void actionPerformed(ActionEvent ae)
   {
      if (ae.getActionCommand().equals("Exit"))
         System.exit(0);
   }

   public static void main(String[] args)
   {
      TestButton td = new TestButton();
   }

}

class WinCloser extends WindowAdapter
{
   public void windowClosing(WindowEvent e)
   {
      System.exit(0);
   }
}
```

This example shows some of the interesting things that you can do with a button. Buttons that don't do anything when clicked are not of very much value. For that reason, applications that contain buttons always implement the `ActionListener` interface. This interface specifies that a method called `actionPerformed()` be present.

```
public class TestButton extends Frame
               implements ActionListener
```

A `Button` variable is declared. This does not create the `Button` object, just a variable that can be assigned the address of a `Button` object.

```
Button btnExit;
```

This is where the actual object is created. The string passed into the constructor is the label that will appear on the button's face.

```
btnExit = new Button("Exit");
```

You can control the font in which the Button's label will appear.

```
btnExit.setFont(new Font("Courier", Font.BOLD, 24));
```

You can also set the background color. Here we set it to `Color.cyan`.

```
btnExit.setBackground(Color.cyan);
```

The `Cursor` class controls the shape of the cursor when the mouse is over this object. We change it from the default arrow to the hand-shaped cursor called `HAND_CURSOR`.

```
Cursor curs = new Cursor(Cursor.HAND_CURSOR);
```

The setCursor() command takes a Cursor as a parameter.

```
btnExit.setCursor(curs);
```

The connection between the button that will contain the `actionPerformed()` method is made here. The keyword `this` means that the class that we are writing code for will provide this method.

```
btnExit.addActionListener(this);
```

The `actionPerformed()` method is called whenever the button is clicked.

```
public void actionPerformed(ActionEvent ae)
{
```

The `getActionCommand()` method returns the value of the label that was given to it when it was instantiated. This is one way to determine which button in a class was clicked. Here there is only one button in the application, and it displays the string Exit. All that it does when this is clicked is terminate the application.

```
if (ae.getActionCommand().equals("Exit"))
    System.exit(0);
}
```

The result from running this example is shown in Figure 13.10.

Notice that the color of the background is a cyan (blue), the font is larger and bolded, the cursor changes back and forth to a hand shape and back to a cursor when you move the mouse over the button.

FIGURE 13.10
Buttons trigger action events.

TextArea

A `TextArea` object is a rectangular text field that can be longer than one line. It can also be set to read-only. `TextArea`s can have zero, one, or two scrollbars, which makes them useful for long pieces of text. Several methods can be used to set modify the text in a `TextArea`.

- `append`—Adds a String to the end of the text.

- `insert`—Adds the String at position x in the `TextArea` and shifts the rest of the text to the right.

- `replaceRange`—Replaces the text between a start and an end point with a String that gets passed in.

We see these methods in action in Listing 13.11.

LISTING 13.11   The `TestTextArea.java` File

```
/*
 * TestTextArea.java
 *
 * Created on July 30, 2002, 2:36 PM
 */

package com.samspublishing.jpp.ch13;
import java.awt.*;
import java.awt.event.*;

/**
 *
 * @author  Stephen Potts
 * @version
 */
public class TestTextArea extends Frame implements ActionListener
{
   Button btnExit;
   Button btnAppend;
```

LISTING 13.11   Continued

```java
Button btnInsert;
Button btnReplace;
TextArea taLetter;

public TestTextArea()
{
   btnAppend = new Button("Append");
   btnAppend.addActionListener(this);
   btnInsert = new Button("Insert");
   btnInsert.addActionListener(this);
   btnReplace = new Button("Replace");
   btnReplace.addActionListener(this);
   btnExit = new Button("Exit");
   btnExit.addActionListener(this);
   taLetter =
            new TextArea("",10,30, TextArea.SCROLLBARS_VERTICAL_ONLY);
   taLetter.append("I am writing this letter to inform you that you");
   taLetter.append(" have been drafted into the United States Army.");
   taLetter.append(" You will report to Fort Bragg, North Carolina ");
   taLetter.append("on July 20, 1966.  You will be assigned to ");
   taLetter.append("Vietnam.");


   add(btnAppend);
   add(btnInsert);
   add(btnReplace);
   add(btnExit);
   add(taLetter);

   this.setLayout(new FlowLayout());

   addWindowListener(new WinCloser());
   setTitle("Using a TextArea Object");
   setBounds( 100, 100, 400, 400);
   setVisible(true);
}

public void actionPerformed(ActionEvent ae)
{
   if (ae.getActionCommand().equals("Append"))
      taLetter.append("\n\nSincerely, \n      The Draft Board");
   if (ae.getActionCommand().equals("Insert"))
      taLetter.insert("Dear Steve,\n      ", 0);
   if (ae.getActionCommand().equals("Replace"))
      taLetter.replaceRange("Dear Jerry,\n      ", 0, 12);
   if (ae.getActionCommand().equals("Exit"))
      System.exit(0);
}
```

LISTING 13.11   Continued

```
    public static void main(String[] args)
    {
        TestTextArea tta = new TestTextArea();
    }

}

class WinCloser extends WindowAdapter
{
    public void windowClosing(WindowEvent e)
    {
        System.exit(0);
    }
}
```

The `TextArea` object is declared to be empty, with 10 rows, 30 columns, and a vertical scroll-bar.

```
    taLetter =
            new TextArea("",10,30, TextArea.SCROLLBARS_VERTICAL_ONLY);
```

The `append` command is used to create the body of the letter.

```
    taLetter.append("I am writing this letter to inform you that you");
    taLetter.append(" have been drafted into the United States Army.");
    taLetter.append(" You will report to Fort Bragg, North Carolina ");
    taLetter.append("on July 20, 1966.  You will be assigned to ");
    taLetter.append("Vietnam.");
```

Each of the buttons performs a different function. The Append button adds a Sincerely line.

```
    if (ae.getActionCommand().equals("Append"))
        taLetter.append("\n\nSincerely, \n     The Draft Board");
```

The Insert button adds a salutation.

```
    if (ae.getActionCommand().equals("Insert"))
        taLetter.insert("Dear Steve,\n     ", 0);
```

The Replace button replaces the salutation with a different name.

```
    if (ae.getActionCommand().equals("Replace"))
        taLetter.replaceRange("Dear Jerry,\n     ", 0, 12);
```

The result of running this example is shown in Figure 13.11.

Note how the `\n` causes new lines to be inserted in the text. You can use this technique to perform some crude formatting.

FIGURE 13.11
Buttons can be used to trigger method calls on the TextArea object.

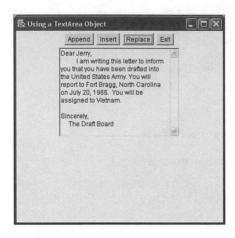

CheckBox

A Checkbox is a switch that can either be checked on or off. You can group Checkboxes together into a group where they can act like the buttons on a radio. Clicking one of them will unclick the other ones automatically.

Checkboxes are useful as toggle switches and for representing choices where only one of them would make sense, such as a choice of bread, wheat or rye.

The listener class that handles events generated by Checkboxes is the ItemListener interface. This interface requires that the itemStateChanged() method be implemented. The JVM will call this method for you whenever an item changes that has a listener registered for it. Listing 13.12 shows how this works.

LISTING 13.12   The TestCheckboxes.java File

```java
/*
 * TestCheckboxes.java
 *
 * Created on July 30, 2002, 2:36 PM
 */

package com.samspublishing.jpp.ch13;
import java.awt.*;
import java.awt.event.*;

/**
 *
 * @author  Stephen Potts
 * @version
 */
public class TestCheckboxes extends Frame
                    implements ItemListener
{
    Checkbox cbWhiteBread;
    Checkbox cbWheatBread;
```

LISTING 13.12   Continued

```
Checkbox cbRyeBread;

Checkbox cbToasted;

TextField tField;

public TestCheckboxes()
{
    cbWhiteBread = new Checkbox("White Bread");
    cbWhiteBread.setState(false);
    cbWhiteBread.addItemListener(this);

    cbWheatBread = new Checkbox("Wheat Bread");
    cbWheatBread.setState(false);
    cbWheatBread.addItemListener(this);

    cbRyeBread = new Checkbox("Rye Bread");
    cbRyeBread.setState(false);
    cbRyeBread.addItemListener(this);

    cbToasted= new Checkbox("Toasted");
    cbToasted.setState(false);
    cbToasted.addItemListener(this);

    tField = new TextField(30);


    setLayout(new FlowLayout());
    add(cbWhiteBread);
    add(cbWheatBread);
    add(cbRyeBread);

    add(cbToasted);
    add(tField);

    addWindowListener(new WinCloser());
    setTitle("Using Checkboxes");
    setBounds( 100, 100, 300, 300);
    setVisible(true);
}

public void itemStateChanged(ItemEvent ie)
{
    Checkbox cb = (Checkbox)ie.getItemSelectable();
    if( cb.getState())
       tField.setText(cb.getLabel());
    else
       tField.setText("Not " + cb.getLabel());

}

public static void main(String[] args)
{
```

LISTING 13.12   Continued

```
        TestCheckboxes tcb = new TestCheckboxes();
    }

}

class WinCloser extends WindowAdapter
{
    public void windowClosing(WindowEvent e)
    {
        System.exit(0);
    }
}
```

We implement the `ItemListener` interface to receive `ItemEvents`.

```
public class TestCheckboxes extends Frame
                    implements ItemListener
```

Each `Checkbox` is given a label, set to an unchecked state, and given an `ItemListener`.

```
        cbWhiteBread = new Checkbox("White Bread");
        cbWhiteBread.setState(false);
        cbWhiteBread.addItemListener(this);

        cbWheatBread = new Checkbox("Wheat Bread");
        cbWheatBread.setState(false);
        cbWheatBread.addItemListener(this);

        cbRyeBread = new Checkbox("Rye Bread");
        cbRyeBread.setState(false);
        cbRyeBread.addItemListener(this);

        cbToasted= new Checkbox("Toasted");
        cbToasted.setState(false);
        cbToasted.addItemListener(this);
```

The `itemStateChanged()` method is called by the JVM whenever a registered `Checkbox`'s state changes from true to false, and vice versa.

```
    public void itemStateChanged(ItemEvent ie)
    {
```

We obtain a handle to the `Checkbox` that triggered the event.

```
        Checkbox cb = (Checkbox)ie.getItemSelectable();
```

We use that object handle to determine the current state and to get the label so that we can display it.

```
        if( cb.getState())
            tField.setText(cb.getLabel());
        else
            tField.setText("Not " + cb.getLabel());

    }
```

The result of running this example is shown in Figure 13.12.

FIGURE 13.12
Checkboxes are useful for
values that are either true
or false and on or off.

Notice that multiple bread types can be checked at the same time, even though these choices
are mutually exclusive. In the following section, you will learn how to constrain them to only
one choice.

CheckboxGroup

The `CheckBoxGroup` class enables you to limit the number of check boxes that the user can
select to one at a time. Checking another will automatically uncheck the others. Listing 13.13
shows a modified version of Listing 13.12 and adds a `CheckboxGroup`.

LISTING 13.13   The `TestCheckboxGroup.java` File

```
/*
 * TestCheckboxGroups.java
 *
 * Created on July 30, 2002, 2:36 PM
 */

package com.samspublishing.jpp.ch13;
import java.awt.*;
import java.awt.event.*;

/**
 *
 * @author   Stephen Potts
 * @version
 */
public class TestCheckboxGroups extends Frame implements ItemListener
{
    Checkbox cbWhiteBread;
    Checkbox cbWheatBread;
    Checkbox cbRyeBread;

    Checkbox cbToasted;

    TextField tField;
```

LISTING 13.13   Continued

```java
/** Creates new TestCheckboxGroups */
public TestCheckboxGroups()
{
   CheckboxGroup cbgBread = new CheckboxGroup();
   cbWhiteBread = new Checkbox("White Bread", cbgBread, false);
   cbWhiteBread.addItemListener(this);

   cbWheatBread = new Checkbox("Wheat Bread", cbgBread, false);
   cbWheatBread.addItemListener(this);

   cbRyeBread = new Checkbox("Rye Bread", cbgBread, false);
   cbRyeBread.addItemListener(this);

   cbToasted= new Checkbox("Toasted");
   cbToasted.setState(false);
   cbToasted.addItemListener(this);

   tField = new TextField(30);


   setLayout(new FlowLayout());
   add(cbWhiteBread);
   add(cbWheatBread);
   add(cbRyeBread);

   add(cbToasted);
   add(tField);

   addWindowListener(new WinCloser());
   setTitle("Using Checkboxes");
   setBounds( 100, 100, 300, 300);
   setVisible(true);
}

public void itemStateChanged(ItemEvent ie)
{
   Checkbox cb = (Checkbox)ie.getItemSelectable();
   if( cb.getState())
      tField.setText(cb.getLabel());
   else
      tField.setText("Not " + cb.getLabel());

}

public static void main(String[] args)
{
   TestCheckboxGroups tcb = new TestCheckboxGroups();
}

}
```

```
class WinCloser extends WindowAdapter
{
   public void windowClosing(WindowEvent e)
   {
      System.exit(0);
   }
}
```

The `CheckboxGroup` is a class that you declare like any other. Here we declared it as a local object in the constructor.

```
CheckboxGroup cbgBread = new CheckboxGroup();
```

The work of the `CheckboxGroup` class is all done when the `Checkboxes` are being instantiated. By adding the name of the group in the `Checkbox` constructor, you associate the `Checkbox` with the group.

```
cbWhiteBread = new Checkbox("White Bread", cbgBread, false);
cbWhiteBread.addItemListener(this);

cbWheatBread = new Checkbox("Wheat Bread", cbgBread, false);
cbWheatBread.addItemListener(this);

cbRyeBread = new Checkbox("Rye Bread", cbgBread, false);
cbRyeBread.addItemListener(this);
```

This has no affect on any `Checkboxes` that are not associated with the group explicitly.

```
cbToasted= new Checkbox("Toasted");
```

The `cbToasted` checkbox functions independently of the others that were added to the group. The result of running this example is shown in Figure 13.13.

FIGURE 13.13

`CheckboxGroups` are used to associate `Checkbox` objects.

Notice that the appearance of the `Checkboxes` that were added to the group is now different from the appearance of the lone checkbox that is not a part of the group.

Programming with a `Choice` Control

The `Choice` object is a pull-down menu or list of items. It only shows the list of choices available when it has the focus, but it shows the current choice at all times.

The `Choice` object generates an `ItemEvent` when a change is made to the object. The `getSelectedItem()` method provides the information about which item was selected. Listing 13.14 shows an example that contains a `Choice` object.

LISTING 13.14   The `TestChoices.java` File

```java
/*
 * TestChoices.java
 *
 * Created on July 30, 2002, 2:36 PM
 */

package com.samspublishing.jpp.ch13;
import java.awt.*;
import java.awt.event.*;

/**
 *
 * @author  Stephen Potts
 * @version
 */
public class TestChoices extends Frame implements ItemListener
{
    Choice clBread;

    TextField tField;

    /** Creates new TestChoices*/
    public TestChoices()
    {
        clBread = new Choice();
        clBread.add("White Bread");

        clBread.add("Wheat Bread");

        clBread.add("Rye Bread");
        clBread.addItemListener(this);

        tField = new TextField(30);

        setLayout(new FlowLayout());
        add(clBread);
        add(tField);

        addWindowListener(new WinCloser());
        setTitle("Using Choices");
        setBounds( 100, 100, 300, 300);
```

LISTING 13.14   Continued

```
        setVisible(true);
    }

    public void itemStateChanged(ItemEvent ie)
    {
        Choice selBread = (Choice)ie.getItemSelectable();
        tField.setText("You selected " + selBread.getSelectedItem());
    }

    public static void main(String[] args)
    {
        TestChoices tc = new TestChoices();
    }

}

class WinCloser extends WindowAdapter
{
    public void windowClosing(WindowEvent e)
    {
        System.exit(0);
    }
}
```

The first step in using a **Choice** object is to instantiate the **Choice** class.

```
        clBread = new Choice();
```

The **add()** method places the items on the list.

```
        clBread.add("White Bread");

        clBread.add("Wheat Bread");

        clBread.add("Rye Bread");
```

An **ItemListener** interface is needed to receive the **ItemEvents** that are generated by the **Choice** object.

```
        clBread.addItemListener(this);
```

The **itemStateChange()** method provides the event handling for this object.

```
    public void itemStateChanged(ItemEvent ie)
    {
```

You first get a handle to the **Choice** object itself.

```
        Choice selBread = (Choice)ie.getItemSelectable();
```

Now you can use that handle to call the **getSelectedItem()** method.

```
        tField.setText("You selected " + selBread.getSelectedItem());
```

The result of running this example is shown in Figure 13.14.

FIGURE 13.14
`Choice` objects are useful when you want to allow users to choose one item from a list.

Notice that only one item can be chosen. If you want to allow multiple choices, you can use the `List` class, the topic of the following section.

Programming with a `List` Control

A `List` object is similar to a `Choice` object, except that the `List` allows more than one item to be displayed at a time. It also allows more than one item to be selected at the same time. Listing 13.15 shows an example of this.

LISTING 13.15   The `TextLists.java` File

```
/*
 * TestLists.java
 *
 * Created on July 30, 2002, 2:36 PM
 */

package com.samspublishing.jpp.ch13;
import java.awt.*;
import java.awt.event.*;

/**
 *
 * @author   Stephen Potts
 * @version
 */
public class TestLists extends Frame implements ItemListener
{
    List lstBread;

    TextField tField;

    /** Creates new TestLists*/
    public TestLists()
    {
        lstBread = new List(3, true);
        lstBread.add("White Bread");
```

LISTING 13.15   Continued

```java
      lstBread.add("Wheat Bread");

      lstBread.add("Rye Bread");
      lstBread.addItemListener(this);

      tField = new TextField(" ",30);

      setLayout(new FlowLayout());
      add(lstBread);
      add(tField);

      addWindowListener(new WinCloser());
      setTitle("Using Lists");
      setBounds( 100, 100, 300, 300);
      setVisible(true);
   }

   public void itemStateChanged(ItemEvent ie)
   {
      List selBread = (List)ie.getItemSelectable();
      if (selBread.getSelectedItem()!= null)
         tField.setText("You selected " + selBread.getSelectedItem());
      else
      {
         tField.setText("");
         for (int i=0; i< selBread.getItemCount() ; i++)
         {
            if (selBread.isIndexSelected(i))
            {
               String oldString = tField.getText();
               tField.setText( oldString + " " +
                                 selBread.getItem(i));
            }
         }
      }

   }

   public static void main(String[] args)
   {
      TestLists tc = new TestLists();
   }

}

class WinCloser extends WindowAdapter
{
   public void windowClosing(WindowEvent e)
   {
      System.exit(0);
   }
}
```

You instantiate the `List` with an integer for the number of rows that you want to display, and a Boolean that indicates that you want to allow multiple selections.

```
lstBread = new List(3, true);
```

The `add()` method places the items on the list

```
lstBread.add("White Bread");
```

```
lstBread.add("Wheat Bread");
```

```
lstBread.add("Rye Bread");
```

The `List` needs an implemented `ItemListener` interface to handle the events that it generates.

```
lstBread.addItemListener(this);
```

The fact that the `List` allows multiple selections complicates event handling.

```
public void itemStateChanged(ItemEvent ie)
{
```

We first get a handle to the List object.

```
    List selBread = (List)ie.getItemSelectable();
```

If one item is selected, the `getSelectedItem()` method returns it. Otherwise, it returns `null`.

```
if (selBread.getSelectedItem()!= null)
    tField.setText("You selected " + selBread.getSelectedItem());
else
{
```

We need to look at each item in the `List` to see if it is selected.

```
        tField.setText("");
        for (int i=0; i< selBread.getItemCount() ; i++)
        {
```

If it is, we need to append it to the String being displayed. Because no **append** method exists for `TextFields`, we have to do this manually.

```
        if (selBread.isIndexSelected(i))
        {
            String oldString = tField.getText();
            tField.setText( oldString + " " +
                            selBread.getItem(i));
        }
```

The result of running this is shown in Figure 13.15.

Notice that you are able to choose multiple items in the list without pressing the Ctrl key.

FIGURE 13.15

List objects are useful when you want to enable users to choose more than one item from a list.

MenuBar

One of the most useful features of a GUI is its menu system. The menu system is composed of a MenuBar. Only one MenuBar can be attached to a frame. All other menu processing must be initiated via the MenuBar.

MenuBars are containers for Menu classes. A Menu is a pull-down list that allows only one selection at a time. Listing 13.16 shows an example with a MenuBar class and three menus.

```
/*
 * TestMenuBars.java
 *
 * Created on July 30, 2002, 2:36 PM
 */

package com.samspublishing.jpp.ch13;
import java.awt.*;
import java.awt.event.*;

/**
 *
 * @author  Stephen Potts
 * @version
 */
public class TestMenuBars extends Frame
{
    MenuBar mBar;
    Menu breadMenu, toastMenu;
    Menu helpMenu;

    TextField tField;

    /** Creates new TestMenuBars*/
    public TestMenuBars()
    {
        breadMenu = new Menu("Bread");
        breadMenu.add("White");
        breadMenu.add("Wheat");
        breadMenu.add("Rye");
```

```
        toastMenu = new Menu("Toast");
        toastMenu.add("Light");
        toastMenu.add("Medium");
        toastMenu.add("Dark");

        mBar = new MenuBar();
        mBar.add(breadMenu);
        mBar.add(toastMenu);

        helpMenu = new Menu("Help");
        helpMenu.add("help");

        mBar.setHelpMenu(helpMenu);

        tField = new TextField(" ",30);

        setLayout(new FlowLayout());
        add(tField);

        setMenuBar(mBar);

        addWindowListener(new WinCloser());
        setTitle("Using Menu Bars");
        setBounds( 100, 100, 300, 300);
        setVisible(true);
    }

    public static void main(String[] args)
    {
        TestMenuBars tmb = new TestMenuBars();
    }

}

class WinCloser extends WindowAdapter
{
    public void windowClosing(WindowEvent e)
    {
        System.exit(0);
    }
}
```

We will create a menu for the bread, the toast first

```
        breadMenu = new Menu("Bread");
        breadMenu.add("White");
        breadMenu.add("Wheat");
        breadMenu.add("Rye");

        toastMenu = new Menu("Toast");
        toastMenu.add("Light");
        toastMenu.add("Medium");
        toastMenu.add("Dark");
```

We instantiate the `MenuBar` then add the `Menu` objects to it.

```
mBar = new MenuBar();
mBar.add(breadMenu);
mBar.add(toastMenu);
```

We create the `Help` menu last.

```
helpMenu = new Menu("Help");
helpMenu.add("help");
```

The `Help` menu is a special case, so we use the `setHelpMenu()` method instead of the `add()` method to attach it to the `MenuBar`.

```
mBar.setHelpMenu(helpMenu);
```

The `setMenuBar()` method attaches the `MenuBar` to the Frame.

```
setMenuBar(mBar);
```

Running this example displays the result shown in Figure 13.16.

FIGURE 13.16

The `MenuBar` is a container for `Menu` objects.

Notice how easy it was to create menus and menu bars. The reason for this is that the AWT provides all the graphics management and behavior needed to display the menus. All that you have to provide is the specification of what you want to see. This is a very good example of object-oriented programming.

MenuItem

As you probably guessed, a `MenuItem` class represents an item on a `Menu`. The primary job of the `MenuItem` is to generate an `ActionEvent` when it is chosen. You have the option of enabling and disabling the `MenuItem` object using the `enable()` and `disable()` methods. Listing 13.17 shows an example that uses `MenuItems`.

LISTING 13.17   The `TestMenuItems.java` File

```
/*
 * TestMenuItems.java
 *
```

LISTING 13.17   Continued

```
    * Created on July 30, 2002, 2:36 PM
    */

package com.samspublishing.jpp.ch13;
import java.awt.*;
import java.awt.event.*;

/**
 *
 * @author  Stephen Potts
 * @version
 */
public class TestMenuItems extends Frame implements ActionListener
{
    MenuBar mBar;
    Menu breadMenu, toastMenu;
    Menu helpMenu;

    TextField tField;

    /** Creates new TestMenuItems*/
    public TestMenuItems()
    {
        breadMenu = new Menu("Bread");

        MenuItem tempMenuItem;

        tempMenuItem = new MenuItem("White");
        tempMenuItem.addActionListener(this);
        breadMenu.add(tempMenuItem);

        tempMenuItem = new MenuItem("Wheat");
        tempMenuItem.addActionListener(this);
        breadMenu.add(tempMenuItem);

        tempMenuItem = new MenuItem("Rye");
        tempMenuItem.addActionListener(this);
        breadMenu.add(tempMenuItem);


        toastMenu = new Menu("Toast");

        tempMenuItem = new MenuItem("Light");
        tempMenuItem.addActionListener(this);
        toastMenu.add(tempMenuItem);

        tempMenuItem = new MenuItem("Medium");
        tempMenuItem.addActionListener(this);
        toastMenu.add(tempMenuItem);

        tempMenuItem = new MenuItem("Dark");
        tempMenuItem.addActionListener(this);
        toastMenu.add(tempMenuItem);
```

LISTING 13.17   Continued

```
        mBar = new MenuBar();
        mBar.add(breadMenu);
        mBar.add(toastMenu);

        helpMenu = new Menu("Help");
        helpMenu.add(new MenuItem("help"));

        mBar.setHelpMenu(helpMenu);

        tField = new TextField(" ",30);

        setLayout(new FlowLayout());
        add(tField);

        setMenuBar(mBar);

        addWindowListener(new WinCloser());
        setTitle("Using Menu Bars");
        setBounds( 100, 100, 300, 300);
        setVisible(true);
    }

    public void actionPerformed(ActionEvent ae)
    {
        String cmd = ae.getActionCommand();
        tField.setText("you selected: " + cmd);
    }

    public static void main(String[] args)
    {
        TestMenuItems tmi = new TestMenuItems();
    }

}

class WinCloser extends WindowAdapter
{
    public void windowClosing(WindowEvent e)
    {
        System.exit(0);
    }
}
```

Adding a `MenuItem` consists of a declaration, an instantiation, and the addition of an action listener.

```
        MenuItem tempMenuItem;

        tempMenuItem = new MenuItem("White");
        tempMenuItem.addActionListener(this);
```

The item is then added to the menu.

```
        breadMenu.add(tempMenuItem);
```

The `getActionCommand()` method can also be used to discover which of the menu items was actually selected by the user.

```java
public void actionPerformed(ActionEvent ae)
{
    String cmd = ae.getActionCommand();
    tField.setText("you selected: " + cmd);
}
```

This provides you with a string that can be tested to determine the action that is appropriate. The result of running this example is shown in Figure 13.17.

FIGURE 13.17
The `MenuItems` generate events that your program can respond to. Notice how the most recently selected menu item's title is displayed in the `TextField` on the form.

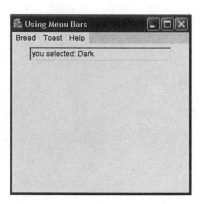

Layout Managers

Java's ancestry as an Applet-centric language manifests itself in the way that screen layout is managed. Instead of providing the programmer with method calls to produce an exact size and component layout, the Java language provides you with layout managers. These managers enable you to express opinions about where each object will be placed on the screen, but not the exact coordinates that will be used.

The reason for this indirection is to accommodate browser-based GUIs. If your GUI is going to be downloaded over the Internet and run in a browser, you have no idea of the screen resolution, window size, or even the browser brand that will run it. You must assume that (almost) every possible configuration must be supported. This is very hard to do with method calls and switch statements.

To make things easier, the Java designers have provided you with a set of layout managers that can be used either alone or in combination to provide you with the look that you want.

The layout managers provided by the `java.awt` package are not made obsolete by Swing. Swing applications can use all the layout managers mentioned in this chapter.

The layout managers that are available for you to choose from are the `BorderLayout`, `FlowLayout`, `CardLayout`, `GridLayout`, and the `GridBagLayout`.

We will look at each of these in turn and provide a summary of the advantages of each.

The `BorderLayout` Manager

The `BorderLayout` class is fairly easy to use. Normally, you create `Panel` objects and place GUI objects such as buttons and text fields on them. Next, you place these panels in one of the regions on the layout. When you display the window, each panel will appear in the region where it was assigned. Listing 13.18 shows a `BorderLayout` example.

LISTING 13.18   The `TestBorderLayout.java` File

```java
/*
 * TestBorderLayout.java
 *
 * Created on July 30, 2002, 11:35 AM
 */

package com.samspublishing.jpp.ch13;

import java.awt.*;
import java.awt.event.*;

/**
 *
 * @author  Stephen Potts
 * @version
 */
public class TestBorderLayout extends Frame
{

    TextField tfNorth;
    TextField tfCenter;
    TextField tfSouth;
    TextField tfEast;
    TextField tfWest;

    /** Creates new TestBorderLayout */
    public TestBorderLayout()
    {
        tfNorth = new TextField("North");
        tfCenter= new TextField("Center");
        tfSouth = new TextField("South");
        tfEast = new TextField("East");
        tfWest = new TextField("West");

        Panel pNorth = new Panel();
        pNorth.add(tfNorth);
```

LISTING 13.18 Continued

```java
        Panel pCenter = new Panel();
        pCenter.setBackground(Color.darkGray);
        pCenter.add(tfCenter);

        Panel pSouth = new Panel();
        pSouth.add(tfSouth);

        Panel pEast = new Panel();
        pEast.setBackground(Color.gray);
        pEast.add(tfEast);

        Panel pWest = new Panel();
        pWest.setBackground(Color.gray);
        pWest.add(tfWest);

        add(pNorth, BorderLayout.NORTH);
        add(pCenter, BorderLayout.CENTER);
        add(pSouth, BorderLayout.SOUTH);
        add(pEast, BorderLayout.EAST);
        add(pWest, BorderLayout.WEST);

        addWindowListener(new WinCloser());
        setTitle("Using a BorderLayout");
        setBounds( 100, 100, 300, 300);
        setVisible(true);
    }

    public static void main(String[] args)
    {
        TestBorderLayout tbl = new TestBorderLayout();
    }

}

class WinCloser extends WindowAdapter
{
    public void windowClosing(WindowEvent e)
    {
        System.exit(0);
    }
}
```

The Frame class defaults to a **BorderLayout** by default, so there is no need to specify it directly. We declare five text fields to place on the panels.

```java
        tfNorth = new TextField("North");
        tfCenter= new TextField("Center");
        tfSouth = new TextField("South");
        tfEast = new TextField("East");
        tfWest = new TextField("West");
```

We create a panel for each text field so that the button will have a container. If you place objects directly on the frame, strange sizing can take place.

```
Panel pCenter = new Panel();
```

We set a background color to make it clear where the boundary of each region falls.

```
pCenter.setBackground(Color.darkGray);
```

We add the text field to the panel.

```
pCenter.add(tfCenter);
```

Finally, we add the panels to the frame specifying a different region for each one.

```
add(pNorth, BorderLayout.NORTH);
add(pCenter, BorderLayout.CENTER);
add(pSouth, BorderLayout.SOUTH);
add(pEast, BorderLayout.EAST);
add(pWest, BorderLayout.WEST);
```

Running this program produces the result shown in Figure 13.18.

FIGURE 13.18
The BorderLayout enables you to place objects in five regions.

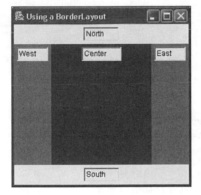

The panels are colored differently to show where one region begins and another one ends. The BorderLayout class has a mind of its own when it comes to sizing regions. You can only affect its decisions indirectly.

FlowLayout

The simplest layout of all is the FlowLayout layout manager. When a component is placed on the frame, it is placed in the left-most position. Each successive component is placed beside it until no more will fit. In that case, a new row is started and the next component is placed there. Listing 13.19 shows how this works.

LISTING 13.19   The `TestFlowLayout.java` File

```java
/*
 * TestFlowLayout.java
 *
 * Created on July 30, 2002, 11:35 AM
 */

package com.samspublishing.jpp.ch13;

import java.awt.*;
import java.awt.event.*;

/**
 *
 * @author   Stephen Potts
 * @version
 */
public class TestFlowLayout extends Frame
{

    TextField tfFirst;
    TextField tfSecond;
    TextField tfThird;
    TextField tfFourth;
    TextField tfFifth;

    /** Creates new TestFlowLayout */
    public TestFlowLayout()
    {
        setLayout(new FlowLayout());
        tfFirst = new TextField("First");
        tfSecond= new TextField("Second");
        tfThird = new TextField("Third");
        tfForth = new TextField("Fourth");
        tfFifth = new TextField("Fifth");

        add(tfFirst);
        add(tfSecond);
        add(tfThird);
        add(tfFourth);
        add(tfFifth);

        addWindowListener(new WinCloser());
        setTitle("Using a FlowLayout");
        setBounds( 100, 100, 300, 300);
        setVisible(true);
    }

    public static void main(String[] args)
    {
        TestFlowLayout tfl = new TestFlowLayout();
    }
```

LISTING 13.19 Continued

```
   }

class WinCloser extends WindowAdapter
{
   public void windowClosing(WindowEvent e)
   {
      System.exit(0);
   }
}
```

The only line in this example that is new is the declaration of the layout manager. This is necessary because a Frame's default layout is a BorderLayout, which doesn't provide the desired appearance in this example.

```
      setLayout(new FlowLayout());
```

After this is declared, the `FlowLayoutManager` class handles the placement of the components on the screen. Figure 13.19 shows the result of running this.

FIGURE 13.19
The `FlowLayout` enables you to place objects in the Frame from left to right with wrapping.

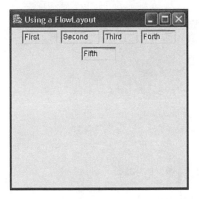

GridBagLayout

The `GridBagLayout` manager is the most powerful, but the most complicated of the Layout managers to implement. It acts a lot like a spreadsheet program by placing items in different rows and columns. It differs from an ordinary spreadsheet in that it allows the cells to differ in size, one from another.

A special helper class called `GridBagConstraints` handles the complexity of this layout manager. This class enables the programmer to specify the coordinates, dimensions, spacing, and padding. Listing 13.20 shows an example of this layout manager.

LISTING 13.20   The `TestGridBagLayout.java` File

```java
/*
 * TestGridBagLayout.java
 *
 * Created on July 30, 2002, 11:35 AM
 */

package com.samspublishing.jpp.ch13;

import java.awt.*;
import java.awt.event.*;

/**
 *
 * @author  Stephen Potts
 * @version
 */
public class TestGridBagLayout extends Frame
{

    TextField tfFirst;
    TextField tfSecond;
    TextField tfThird;
    TextField tfFourth;
    TextField tfFifth;
    GridBagConstraints gbc;
    Button saveButton;
    Label answerLabel;

    /** Creates new GridBagLayout */
    public TestGridBagLayout()
    {
        Insets i = new Insets(0, 0, 0, 0);

        saveButton = new Button("Save");
        answerLabel = new Label("Answer:");

        tfFirst = new TextField("First");
        tfSecond= new TextField("Second");
        tfThird = new TextField("Third");
        tfForth = new TextField("Forth");
        tfFifth = new TextField("Fifth");

        GridBagLayout gbl = new GridBagLayout();
        setLayout(gbl);

        gbc = new GridBagConstraints(0,0,1,1,0.0,0.0,
                                GridBagConstraints.EAST,
                                GridBagConstraints.NONE,
                                i,0,0);
        gbl.setConstraints(answerLabel, gbc);

        gbc = new GridBagConstraints(1,0,1,1,0.0,0.0,
```

LISTING 13.20   Continued

```
                                      GridBagConstraints.WEST,
                                      GridBagConstraints.NONE,
                                      i,0,0);

        gbl.setConstraints(tfFirst, gbc);
        gbc = new GridBagConstraints(1,11,1,1,0.0,0.0,
                                      GridBagConstraints.WEST,
                                      GridBagConstraints.NONE,
                                      i,0,0);
        gbl.setConstraints(tfSecond, gbc);
        gbc = new GridBagConstraints(1,8,1,1,0.0,0.0,
                                      GridBagConstraints.WEST,
                                      GridBagConstraints.NONE,
                                      i,0,0);
        gbl.setConstraints(tfThird, gbc);
        gbc = new GridBagConstraints(2,0,1,1,0.0,0.0,
                                      GridBagConstraints.WEST,
                                      GridBagConstraints.NONE,
                                      i,0,0);
        gbl.setConstraints(tfForth, gbc);
        gbc = new GridBagConstraints(2,1,1,1,0.0,0.0,
                                      GridBagConstraints.WEST,
                                      GridBagConstraints.NONE,
                                      i,0,0);
        gbl.setConstraints(tfFifth, gbc);

        gbc = new GridBagConstraints(8,1,1,1,0.0,0.0,
                                      GridBagConstraints.WEST,
                                      GridBagConstraints.NONE,
                                      i,0,0);
        gbl.setConstraints(saveButton, gbc);


        add(tfFirst);
        add(tfSecond);
        add(tfThird);
        add(tfFourth);
        add(tfFifth);
        add(answerLabel);
        add(saveButton);

        addWindowListener(new WinCloser());
        setTitle("Using a GridBagLayout");
        setBounds( 100, 100, 300, 300);
        setVisible(true);
    }

    public static void main(String[] args)
    {
        TestGridBagLayout tgbl = new TestGridBagLayout();
    }
```

LISTING 13.20   The `TestGridBagLayout.java` File

```
}

class WinCloser extends WindowAdapter
{
    public void windowClosing(WindowEvent e)
    {
        System.exit(0);
    }
}
```

We need an object that we can use to set the formatting options.

```
GridBagConstraints gbc;
```

Normally, we create a layout manager without giving it a name. In this case, we give it a name that we will use later.

```
GridBagLayout gbl = new GridBagLayout();
```

We will set the layout next.

```
setLayout(gbl);
```

Every object that is to be placed on the frame needs to have its constraints specified. The meaning of each parameter is as follows:

- `gridx`—The column location
- `gridy`—The row location
- `gridwidth`—Width of the cell
- `gridheight`—Height of the cell
- `weightx`—How extra row space will be allocated
- `weighty`—How extra column space will be allocated
- `anchor`—Where the component is anchored in the cell, as in `GridBagConstraints.NORTH`.
- `fill`—Whether and how a component will be stretched
- `insets`—The space between the component and the edge of the cell.
- `ipadx`—Padding in the x direction
- `ipady`—Padding in the y direction

```
        gbc = new GridBagConstraints(0,0,1,1,0.0,0.0,
                                     GridBagConstraints.EAST,
                                     GridBagConstraints.NONE,
                                     i,0,0);
        gbl.setConstraints(answerLabel, gbc);
```

Finally, we add each component to the Frame in the same way that we always have.

```
add(tfFirst);
```

The result of running this example is shown in Figure 13.20.

FIGURE 13.20
The `GridBagLayout` enables you to place objects in cells with quite a bit of control over the layout.

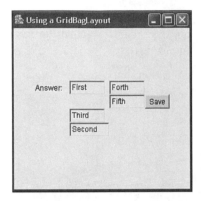

Notice that there are no blank columns or rows in the result, even though we specified high row and column numbers for some of the components. If a row or column is empty, it is ignored by the layout manager.

Summary

In this chapter, you learned how to create components using the Abstract Windows Toolkit. The first thing that you learned was how to create and manipulate containers such as panels, frames, and applets.

Following that, you were introduced to a number of components, such as buttons and lists, that can be placed inside containers.

Finally, you learned how to control the placement of components in a frame by using layout managers. You saw examples of how to use three of these managers in your code.

Review Questions

1. What is the purpose of an AWT container?

2. Why does Java have two graphics libraries?

3. What is the difference between a `Choice` and a `List`?

4. Which of the layout manager classes gives you the most control over the placement and size of components in the frame?

Exercises

1. Create an applet that contains a panel with buttons on it.

2. Create an application that contains a `Choice`, a `List`, and a `Textfield` that displays the selections that you make.

3. Create a `BorderLayout` application that uses panels for some components, but places other components in the regions directly.

4. Create a `GridBagLayout` application that places buttons in alternating cells like the black squares on a checker board.

CHAPTER 14

EVENT DELEGATION MODEL

You will learn about the following in this chapter:

- How events impact programming
- How the Java Event Model works
- What the Event Listener interfaces are and how they are used to capture events

G raphical User Interfaces (GUIs)were invented in the early 1980s, but they didn't start becoming the user interface of choice for application programmers until about 1990. Most programs that were written in the corporate world prior to that were character-based and menu-driven interfaces.

Menu-driven programming is really very simple. Your application provides a menu to the user that contains several choices. The user picks one and presses Enter. Your program tests to find out which one the user picked and responds appropriately. If there are ten items on the menu, there are exactly ten possible situations that must be handled. If the user types in a character or number that is not on the menu, your program can either ignore it or provide an error message.

GUI programming is entirely different. If you think about a modern windowing operating system like Microsoft Windows, Linux GUI, or the Mac OS, you will realize that there are hundreds of possible actions that the user can perform at any moment. He may close your application by closing the window, change the focus to another window, start a new application, minimize your application, move the mouse on and off your application, type something on the keyboard, or hit some shift-key combination. The list of possible user actions in a GUI is endless.

All GUI-based systems work on the principle of events. Events are created by the operating system whenever it notices that some signal is being generated by the hardware. This hardware is normally the keyboard or mouse, but it could also be the CPU.

In this chapter, you will learn how Java programs find out about the events that have occurred. You will also learn how to write programs that respond to these events. Finally, you will learn how to use special interfaces and classes to simplify the handling of events in Java programs.

Understanding Events

When you move the mouse, press a mouse button, release a mouse button, or strike a key on the keyboard, an electrical signal is created and sent through a wire to a hardware port on your computer. Programs called device drivers that notice that these signals have been received are monitoring these hardware ports. These drivers are responsible for translating that hardware signal into a kind of message called an event. The driver hands the event to the operating system for processing.

An operating system (OS) handles two types of events: those directed at the operating system itself, and those directed at some program running under the OS.

The OS handles any events that are directed at it. (A Windows Ctrl-Alt-Delete key sequence is an example of an instruction to the operating system.) All other events are placed in a special queue, called the event queue, where programs can look and see if anything pertaining to them has happened.

One of the programs that looks at this event queue is the Java Virtual Machine (JVM). The JVM, sometimes called the Java Interpreter, is a program written in a compiled language that can talk to the operating system directly. The JVM looks at each message that comes into the queue to see if it could potentially pertain to any of the Java programs that are currently running. When it finds one of these events, it translates it into one or more `java.awt.Event` objects and hands that event to all programs that are listening for it.

Figure 14.1 shows this process graphically.

FIGURE 14.1
The Java Virtual Machine is responsible for communicating the occurrence of events to Java programs.

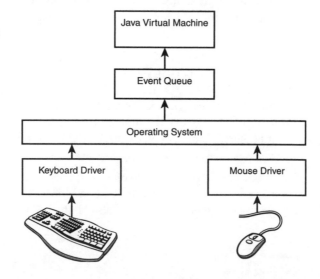

The JVM monitors the event queue to find events of interest to the Java Programs running in it. How the JVM communicates these events to these programs is the subject of the next section.

Programming with the Java Event Model

GUIs are event-generating machines. Every movement of the mouse, every keystroke, every window resizing, and every window relocation generates events that your application might be interested in knowing about. Directing your attention to the word "might" in the preceding sentence will focus your attention on the crux of the event-handling challenge.

Any single Java application or JavaBean is only going to be interested in a small subset of the events that are picked up by the JVM. If your application were notified of every event that the JVM receives, it would be overwhelmed by the overhead involved in processing them all.

Starting with Java 1.1, Sun introduced an improved event-handling strategy based on the concept of event listeners. An event listener is a class that implements the `java.awt.event.EventListener` interface, normally through one of EventListener subinterfaces. A few of these subinterfaces are listed here:

```
ActionListener, AdjustmentListener, ChangeListener, ComponentListener,
ConnectionEventListener, ContainerListener, ControllerEventListener, FocusListener,
ItemListener, KeyListener, LineListener, ListDataListener, ListSelectionListener,
MenuListener, MouseInputListener, MouseListener, MouseMotionListener,
MouseWheelListener, WindowStateListener
```

Each of these interfaces requires that one or more methods be written by any class that implements it. For example, the `MouseListener` interface requires that all five of the following methods be implemented:

```
mouseClicked(MouseEvent e)
mouseEntered(MouseEvent e)
mouseExited(MouseEvent e)
mousePressed(MouseEvent e)
mouseReleased(MouseEvent e)
```

By contrast, the `ActionListener` interface only requires one method:

```
actionPerformed(ActionEvent e)
```

Notice that each method is handed some sort of an object with Event in its name. All these methods receive an object that is derived from `java.awt.Event`. Each of these derived classes contains methods specific to its needs that enable the listener to obtain more information about the nature of the event. For example, an `ActionEvent` class contains four methods:

- `getActionCommand()` returns the command string associated with this action.
- `getModifiers()` returns the modifier keys held down during this action event.

- `getWhen()` returns the timestamp of when this event occurred.

- `paramString()` returns a parameter string for this action event.

Most of the time the JVM creates the `Event` object from the hardware event that is received. It interprets this hardware event and translates it into an object that the Java programmer will be able to handle easily.

Listing 14.1 will show how this all works:

LISTING 14.1   The `EventCreator.java` File

```java
/*
 * EventCreator.java
 *
 * Created on August 8, 2002, 12:42 PM
 */

package ch14;

import javax.swing.*;
import java.awt.event.ActionListener;
import javax.swing.border.EtchedBorder;
import java.awt.Container;
import java.awt.BorderLayout;

import java.util.*;

/**
 *
 * @author  Stephen Potts
 * @version
 */
public class EventCreator extends JFrame
{
    JButton btnBook;
    JButton btnExit;

    /** Constructors for CruiseList */
    public EventCreator() throws Exception
    {
        try
        {
            //configure the Frame
            EventConsumer ec = new EventConsumer();
            setBounds(150,200,500,250);
            setDefaultCloseOperation(JFrame.EXIT_ON_CLOSE);

            //set the layout
            BorderLayout border = new BorderLayout();
            Container content = getContentPane();
            content.setLayout(border);
            btnBook = new JButton("Book");
```

LISTING 14.1   *Continued*

```
                btnExit = new JButton("Exit");
                btnBook.addActionListener(ec);
                btnExit.addActionListener(ec);

                JPanel bottomPanel = new JPanel();
                bottomPanel.add(btnBook);
                bottomPanel.add(btnExit);
                content.add(bottomPanel, BorderLayout.SOUTH);
                setVisible(true);
            }catch(Exception e)
            {
                System.out.println("Exception thrown " + e);
            }
        }

        /**
         * @param args the command line arguments
         */
        public static void main(String args[])
        {
            //create an instance of the GUI
            try
            {
                EventCreator mainWindow = new EventCreator();
            }catch(Exception e)
            {
                System.out.println("Exception in main " + e);
            }
        }

}//class
```

The GUI objects that generated these events are two `JButtons`.

```
    JButton btnBook;
    JButton btnExit;
```

We create an instance of the event listener class here.

```
            EventConsumer ec = new EventConsumer();
```

Next, we instantiate the buttons and call the `addActionListener()` method on each button so that there will be a class to handle any Action events that these buttons generate.

```
            btnBook = new JButton("Book");
            btnExit = new JButton("Exit");
            btnBook.addActionListener(ec);
            btnExit.addActionListener(ec);
```

For this class to compile, we have to have a class called `EventConsumer.java` to handle the events.

Listing 14.2 shows this class:

LISTING 14.2   The `EventConsumer.java` File

```
/*
 * EventConsumer.java
 *
 * Created on January 24, 2002, 11:31 AM
 */

package ch14;

import javax.swing.*;
import java.awt.event.ActionListener;
import javax.swing.border.EtchedBorder;
import java.awt.Container;
import java.awt.BorderLayout;

import java.util.*;

/**
 *
 * @author  Stephen Potts
 * @version
 */
public class EventConsumer implements ActionListener
{

    JButton btnBook;
    JButton btnExit;

    /** Constructors for CruiseList */
    public EventConsumer() throws Exception
    {
    }

    public void actionPerformed(java.awt.event.ActionEvent ae)
    {
        if (ae.getActionCommand().equals("Exit"))
        {
            System.out.println("Exit was clicked");
        }

        //Try and book a ticket
        if (ae.getActionCommand().equals("Book"))
        {
            System.out.println("Book was clicked");
        }
    }
}//class
```

Several lines of code in these two listings require explanation:

- Notice that this application contains two classes instead of one. This application could have been written with the **EventCreator** class serving as its own event listener. It was written as two classes for clarity.

- Both buttons are of class `JButton`. `JButton` is derived from the class `javax.swing.AbstractButton`. One of `AbstractButton`'s methods is `addActionListener()`. `AbstractButton` extends `JComponent`. `JComponent` is an abstract class that contains a list of all the listeners of every type. Whenever an event occurs in a program, this list is searched to find the listeners to notify.

- Whenever the buttons are clicked, the `JButton` code creates an `ActionEvent` object. It then looks at the listener list to find out who the listeners are for this component. Of those listeners on the list, the `JButton` chooses the ones that implement the `ActionListener` interface. It then makes a call to each one of these listeners' `actionPerformed()` method. The code in the `actionPerformed()` method is executed.

- There is only one `actionPerformed()` method for all components that can create action events in this application. This means that the `actionPerformed()` method must use the `getActionCommand()` method of the `ActionEvent` class to figure out which button was clicked. The `getActionCommand()` returns the label of the component that caused the `Event` object to be created.

The result from running this code is shown in Figure 14.2:

FIGURE 14.2
The `EventCreator`
application uses a dialog
to communicate the event
to the `EventConsumer`
event handler.

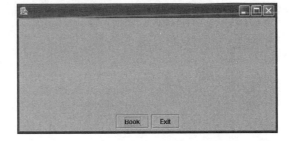

Running this program generates the following output in a console window:

```
Book was clicked
Exit was clicked
Book was clicked
Exit was clicked
```

This example showed the basic procedure that must be followed to connect the events that one component is able to generate, with the event handling code that has been written specifically for it. Many different event types and many different methods for handling each of them exist. In the end, however, they all follow the same pattern of a listener registering with an event creator.

An alternate way of listening for events is to make the single class its own event listener. All that you have to do to accomplish this is to make that class implement the listener interface itself and change the `addActionListener()` calls to pass the parameter this, indicating that this class handles its own events. Listing 14.3 shows an example of how this works.

LISTING 14.3 The `EventCreator2.java` Class

```java
/*
 * EventCreator2.java
 *
 * Created on August 8, 2002, 12:42 PM
 */

package ch14;

import javax.swing.*;
import java.awt.event.ActionListener;
import javax.swing.border.EtchedBorder;
import java.awt.Container;
import java.awt.BorderLayout;

import java.util.*;

/**
 *
 * @author  Stephen Potts
 * @version
 */
public class EventCreator2 extends JFrame implements ActionListener
{
    JButton btnBook;
    JButton btnExit;

    /** Constructors for CruiseList */
    public EventCreator2() throws Exception
    {
        try
        {
            //configure the Frame
            System.out.println("EventCreator2 executing");
            setBounds(150,200,500,250);
            setDefaultCloseOperation(JFrame.EXIT_ON_CLOSE);

            //set the layout
            BorderLayout border = new BorderLayout();
            Container content = getContentPane();
            content.setLayout(border);
            btnBook = new JButton("Book");
            btnExit = new JButton("Exit");
            btnBook.addActionListener(this);
            btnExit.addActionListener(this);

            JPanel bottomPanel = new JPanel();
            bottomPanel.add(btnBook);
            bottomPanel.add(btnExit);
            content.add(bottomPanel, BorderLayout.SOUTH);
            setVisible(true);
        }catch(Exception e)
        {
```

LISTING 14.3   Continued

```
            System.out.println("Exception thrown " + e);
        }
    }

    public void actionPerformed(java.awt.event.ActionEvent ae)
    {
        if (ae.getActionCommand().equals("Exit"))
        {
            System.out.println("Exit was clicked2");
        }

        //Try and book a ticket
        if (ae.getActionCommand().equals("Book"))
        {
            System.out.println("Book was clicked2");
        }

    }

    /**
     * @param args the command line arguments
     */
    public static void main(String args[])
    {
        //create an instance of the GUI
        try
        {
            EventCreator2 mainWindow = new EventCreator2();
        }catch(Exception e)
        {
            System.out.println("Exception in main " + e);
        }
    }

}//class
```

Now both the generation of events and their handling is done in the same class. The declaration of the class itself has to change to implement the additional interface.

```
public class EventCreator2 extends JFrame implements ActionListener
```

Instead of using a different class as the `ActionListener`, we now use this class.

```
        btnBook.addActionListener(this);
        btnExit.addActionListener(this);
```

The `actionPerformed()` method is now found in this class.

```
    public void actionPerformed(java.awt.event.ActionEvent ae)
    {
        if (ae.getActionCommand().equals("Exit"))
        {
```

```
            System.out.println("Exit was clicked2");
        }

        //Try and book a ticket
        if (ae.getActionCommand().equals("Book"))
        {
            System.out.println("Book was clicked2");
        }

    }
```

Notice that it is identical to when it was in a separate class.

The GUI for this class is identical to the one shown in Figure 14.2, but the output to the screen has changed:

```
EventCreator2 executing
Book was clicked2
Exit was clicked2
Book was clicked2
Exit was clicked2
```

This change was intentionally done so that we could distinguish between this example's output and the example in Listing 14.2. Functionally, both of these examples are equivalent.

It is more common to have the class serve as its own listener, but both approaches are considered good form. Now that we understand something about event listeners in general, we need to look at some more of the event listener classes.

Using the Other Event Listener Interfaces

Many more event-listening interfaces are supported in Java. In this section we will examine a number of the most commonly used ones.

Events can be broken down into two types, semantic or high-level events, and low-level events. The high-level events deal with meaning more than with the hardware action that caused them.

The semantic events that Java supports are

- ActionEvent—A button is clicked or a menu item is selected.
- AdjustmentEvent—A scrollbar is adjusted.
- ItemEvent—A user selected from a list of objects.
- TextEvent—A text field has been changed.

In addition, there are eight low-level event classes:

- ComponentEvent—A component was resized, moved, shown, or hidden.
- KeyEvent—A key was pressed or released.

- MouseEvent—A mouse button was pressed or released. The mouse was moved or dragged.

- FocusEvent—A component got or lost focus.

- WindowEvent—A window was iconified, activated, deactivated, and so on.

- ContainerEvent—A component was put on or removed from the container.

- PaintEvent—This event is not intended to be used with a listener, but contains methods that can be overridden.

- InputEvent—This event is mainly used to intercept events before they get to the component so that a Component event won't be thrown.

Associated with each event class is at least one event-listener interface. The following is a list of event classes, and the listener interface(s) that support it.

TABLE 14.1   The Events and Their Associated Listeners

Event	Listener
ActionEvent	ActionListener
AdjustmentEvent	AdjustmentListener
ItemEvent	ItemListener
TextEvent	TextListener
ComponentEvent	ComponentListener
KeyEvent	KeyListener
MouseEvent	MouseListener, MouseMotionListener
FocusEvent	FocusListener
WindowEvent	WindowListener
ContainerEvent	ContainerListener

Notice that the MouseEvent has two listeners associated with it. The reason for this is that the mouse moves in the x,y plane, but it also has buttons that act somewhat like keys on the keyboard.

Each of these interfaces has one or more methods associated with it. The WindowListener has the most methods, with seven. The ActionListener, AdjustmentListener, ItemListener, and TextListener have only one each.

Some of the listeners that have several methods also have a special class called an adapter class provided for it. These classes implement the interface for you and provide dummy calls to each of the methods. You extend these classes and override the methods that you want to implement. If you don't implement them all, no error is thrown because the adapter class has already implemented it for you. The adapter classes are

- `ComponentAdapter`
- `ContainerAdapter`
- `FocusAdapter`
- `KeyAdapter`
- `MouseAdapter`
- `MouseMotionAdapter`
- `WindowAdapter`

The following examples use some of the interfaces and adapter classes to demonstrate how each works.

The `ActionListener` Interface

The `ActionListener` interface is the easiest interface to implement. It has only one method that must be created, `actionPerformed()`. The `actionPerformed()` method expects to receive a `java.awt.ActionEvent` object as a parameter.

The `ActionEvent` class has three methods that you can use to determine how to proceed after a semantic action event occurs:

- `getActionCommand()`—This returns the name associated with the command that just occurred. By retrieving this name, your program can differentiate among the different components that generate action event.

- `getModifiers()`—This tells you if a shift or control key was pressed when the action event was created.

- `paramString()`—This method returns the param string associated with this action event, if any.

See Listings 14.1, 14.2, and 14.3 for examples that implement the `ActionListener` interface. Because there is only one method in this interface, there is no need for an adapter class for it.

The `AdjustmentListener` Interface

The `AdjustmentListener` interface is another single-method interface. This interface is associated with the `Scrollbar` class. Whenever a `Scrollbar`'s elevator (little box) is moved up or down, an `AdjustmentEvent` is generated. Your program can then obtain the current value of the `Scrollbar` and react to it.

The original purpose of the `Scrollbar` class was to enable scrolling of text in both directions. The `ScrollPane` does that as well, so many programmers skip the `Scrollbar` and always use `ScrollPanes`. Listing 14.4 shows how this works.

LISTING 14.4   The `TestScrollbar.java` File

```
/*
 * TestScrollbar.java
 *
 * Created on August 9, 2002, 2:32 PM
 */

package ch14;

import java.awt.*;
import java.awt.event.*;


/**
 *
 * @author   Stephen Potts
 */
public class TestScrollbar extends Frame
implements AdjustmentListener
{
    Scrollbar sb;
    TextField tField;


    /** Creates a new instance of TestScrollbar */
    public TestScrollbar()
    {
        sb=new Scrollbar(Scrollbar.VERTICAL, 0, 1, 0, 255);
        sb.addAdjustmentListener(this);
        add(sb);
        tField = new TextField(30);
        add(tField);


        this.setLayout(new FlowLayout());

        addWindowListener(new WinCloser());
        setTitle("Using a Scrollbar Object");
        setBounds( 100, 100, 400, 400);
        setVisible(true);
    }

    public void adjustmentValueChanged(AdjustmentEvent ae)
    {
```

LISTING 14.4   Continued

```
            String newString = String.valueOf(sb.getValue());
            tField.setText(newString);
        }

        public static void main(String[] args)
        {
            TestScrollbar tsb= new TestScrollbar();
        }


}

class WinCloser extends WindowAdapter
{
    public void windowClosing(WindowEvent e)
    {
        System.exit(0);
    }
}
```

The `AdjustmentListener` interface is implemented by the class itself.

```
public class TestScrollbar extends Frame
implements AdjustmentListener
```

The Scrollbar object is created to be vertical, with an initial value of 0, an elevator of size 1, with a minimum set to 0 and a maximum set to 255.

```
        sb=new Scrollbar(Scrollbar.VERTICAL, 0, 1, 0, 255);
```

We add a listener to the scrollbar, which is this class itself.

```
        sb.addAdjustmentListener(this);
```

We add the scrollbar to the frame.

```
        add(sb);
```

This is the only method that is required by this interface.

```
    public void adjustmentValueChanged(AdjustmentEvent ae)
```

The `getValue()` method returns an `int`, so we convert it to a String before we display it.

```
        String newString = String.valueOf(sb.getValue());
        tField.setText(newString);
    }
```

The result of running this example is shown here in Figure 14.3.

Notice how smooth the operation of the scrollbar and text field is. It is hard to believe that an event is being generated each time the `Scrollbar`'s value changes.

FIGURE 14.3
The `AdjustmentListener` interface is used to process events generated by scrollbars.

The `ItemListener` Interface

The `ItemListener` interface requires only one method, `itemStateChanged()`. This method is called whenever the user changes an object such as a `List`, `Checkbox`, or `Choice`.

The most useful method that the `ItemEvent` provides is `getItemSelectable()`, which tells what item created the event. After you know which item created the event, you can cast the item to its subtype and use the subtype's methods to discover what the user intends to be changed. Listing 14.5 shows an example of how this listener works with checkboxes.

LISTING 14.5   The `TestCheckBoxes2.java` File

```
/*
 * TestCheckboxes.java
 *
 * Created on July 30, 2002, 2:36 PM
 */

package ch14;
import java.awt.*;
import java.awt.event.*;

/**
 *
 * @author   Stephen Potts
 * @version
 */
public class TestCheckboxes2 extends Frame implements ItemListener
{
    Checkbox cbWhiteBread;
    Checkbox cbWheatBread;
    Checkbox cbRyeBread;
```

Listing 14.5   Continued

```java
    Checkbox cbToasted;

    TextField tField;

    /** Creates new TestCheckboxes2*/
    public TestCheckboxes2()
    {
        cbWhiteBread = new Checkbox("White Bread");
        cbWhiteBread.setState(false);
        cbWhiteBread.addItemListener(this);

        cbWheatBread = new Checkbox("Wheat Bread");
        cbWheatBread.setState(false);
        cbWheatBread.addItemListener(this);

        cbRyeBread = new Checkbox("Rye Bread");
        cbRyeBread.setState(false);
        cbRyeBread.addItemListener(this);

        cbToasted= new Checkbox("Toasted");
        cbToasted.setState(false);
        cbToasted.addItemListener(this);

        tField = new TextField(30);


        setLayout(new FlowLayout());
        add(cbWhiteBread);
        add(cbWheatBread);
        add(cbRyeBread);

        add(cbToasted);
        add(tField);

        addWindowListener(new WinCloser());
        setTitle("Using Checkboxes");
        setBounds( 100, 100, 300, 300);
        setVisible(true);
    }

    public void itemStateChanged(ItemEvent ie)
    {
        Checkbox cb = (Checkbox)ie.getItemSelectable();
        if( cb.getState())
            tField.setText(cb.getLabel() + " was set to true");
        else
            tField.setText(cb.getLabel() + " was set to false");

    }

    public static void main(String[] args)
```

LISTING 14.5   Continued

```
    {
        TestCheckboxes2 tcb = new TestCheckboxes2();
    }

}

class WinCloser extends WindowAdapter
{
    public void windowClosing(WindowEvent e)
    {
        System.exit(0);
    }
}
```

This class implements the `ItemListener` interface itself.

```
public class TestCheckboxes2 extends Frame implements ItemListener
```

We create four `Checkboxes` and one text field to display feedback.

```
    Checkbox cbWhiteBread;
    Checkbox cbWheatBread;
    Checkbox cbRyeBread;

    Checkbox cbToasted;

    TextField tField;
```

We populate each of the checkboxes, give it a state, and add the listener.

```
        cbWhiteBread = new Checkbox("White Bread");
        cbWhiteBread.setState(false);
        cbWhiteBread.addItemListener(this);
```

The `itemStateChanged()` method is handed an `ItemEvent` object.

```
    public void itemStateChanged(ItemEvent ie)
    {
```

The `getItemSelectable()` method hands the item back that caused the event. We have to cast it to the `Checkbox` data type before we can call methods on it.

```
        Checkbox cb = (Checkbox)ie.getItemSelectable();
```

The `getState()` method returns either **true** or **false**, based on the current value of the `Checkbox`. We examine this value, and then get the text by calling the `getLabel()` method.

```
        if( cb.getState())
            tField.setText(cb.getLabel() + " was set to true");
        else
            tField.setText(cb.getLabel() + " was set to false");
```

The result of running this example is shown here in Figure 14.4.

FIGURE 14.4
The ItemListener
interface is used to
process events generated
by Lists, Checkboxes,
and Choices.

Notice that the latest change that was made is displayed. The Checkbox that you are most
interested in is the one that changed most recently.

The TextListener Interface

The TextListener is another one-method interface that has no Adapter class associated with
it. TextEvents are created by text components whenever their contents change. These events
enable your program to take action whenever a keystroke takes place inside a text component
that is being listened to. Listing 14.6 shows an example where we used the TextListener
interface to verify that a keystroke is a number before we store it in another text field.

LISTING 14.6   The TestTextListener.java File

```
/*
 * TestTextListener.java
 *
 * Created on August 9, 2002, 2:32 PM
 */

package ch14;

import java.awt.*;
import java.awt.event.*;

/**
 *
 * @author  Stephen Potts
 */
public class TestTextListener extends Frame implements TextListener
{
    TextField tField;
    TextField tField2;


    /** Creates a new instance of TestTextListener */
    public TestTextListener()
```

LISTING 14.6   Continued

```
    {
        tField = new TextField(20);
        tField2 = new TextField(20);
        tField.addTextListener(this);
        add(tField);
        add(tField2);



        this.setLayout(new FlowLayout());

        addWindowListener(new WinCloser());
        setTitle("Using a TextListener Object");
        setBounds( 100, 100, 400, 400);
        setVisible(true);
    }


    public static void main(String[] args)
    {
        TestTextListener ttl= new TestTextListener();
    }

    public void textValueChanged(java.awt.event.TextEvent te)
    {
        TextField tf = (TextField)te.getSource();
        String s1 = tf.getText();
        int strlen = s1.length();
        String lastCharString = s1.substring(strlen-1);
        try
        {
            int i = Integer.parseInt(lastCharString);
            tField2.setText(tField2.getText() + lastCharString);
        }catch (NumberFormatException nfe)
        {
            System.out.println("not a number");
        }

    }

}

class WinCloser extends WindowAdapter
{
    public void windowClosing(WindowEvent e)
    {
        System.exit(0);
    }
}
```

We implement the `TextListener` in this class instead of creating a whole different class just to hold one `method()`.

```
public class TestTextListener extends Frame implements TextListener
```

We declare two text fields: one to receive text and the other to display the filtered version.

```
    TextField tField;
    TextField tField2;
```

We instantiate both of the text fields, but we only listen to the input field.

```
        tField = new TextField(20);
        tField2 = new TextField(20);
        tField.addTextListener(this);
```

The `textValueChanged()` method is required by the `TextListener` interface. It receives a `TextEvent`, which contains information about the `TextField` that caused the event.

```
    public void textValueChanged(java.awt.event.TextEvent te)
```

We obtain a handle to the text field that caused the event to be created. We will use this handle to call methods to discover the source, contents, and so on.

```
        TextField tf = (TextField)te.getSource();
```

We get the current state of the contents of the text field.

```
        String s1 = tf.getText();
```

We are only interested in the last character entered, so we use `substring()` to obtain a string with only this character.

```
        int strlen = s1.length();
        String lastCharString = s1.substring(strlen-1);
```

We use the Java error trapping mechanism to help our program decide whether the character typed in is an integer.

```
        try
        {
```

If you try to convert a string containing a number to an integer, it works fine. If the string contains a non-number, an exception is thrown.

```
            int i = Integer.parseInt(lastCharString);
```

If the exception is thrown, this line never executes.

```
        tField2.setText(tField2.getText() + lastCharString);
```

Because we catch and handle the exception here, the program continues without interruption. The user is never aware that the exception occurred.

```
        }catch (NumberFormatException nfe)
        {
            System.out.println("not a number");
        }
```

The result of running this program is shown here in Figure 14.5.

FIGURE 14.5
The `TextListener` interface is great for filtering input.

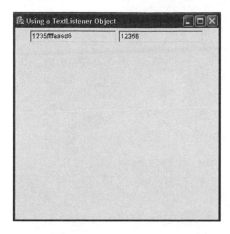

Using the Java exception handling mechanism to create program logic is very convenient, but somewhat more resource consumptive than other techniques. It should only be used in situations where CPU resources are plentiful. Normally, a GUI program is light enough that the CPU cycles needed are readily available.

The `KeyListener` and `KeyAdapter` Interfaces

The KeyListener interface requires the implementation of three methods: `keyPressed()`, `keyReleased()`, and `keyTyped()`. Whenever a key is pressed, the `keyPressed()` method is called. When that key is released, `keyReleased()` is called. When a couplet of press and release is complete, the `keyTyped()` method is called.

The `KeyAdapter` class provides dummy implementations of each of these methods. This enables you to extend this class and implement only those methods that you choose to. One complication that arises from the fact that `KeyAdapter` is a class and not an interface is that classes that already extend one class, such as `Frame`, cannot extend a second class under the rules of Java. The reason for this is that certain logical conundrums can occur when a class inherits from more than one class; if those classes share a common ancestor. To solve this problem, the Java fathers decided to outlaw multiple inheritance altogether. Some would argue that they went too far, but our job is not to redesign the language, but rather to gripe about it.

Listing 14.7 contains a class that extends the `KeyAdapter` class. This is done to add variety to the examples.

LISTING 14.7   The `TestKeyAdapter`

```
/*
 * TestKeyAdapter.java
 *
 * Created on August 9, 2002, 2:32 PM
 */
```

LISTING 14.7   Continued

```
package ch14;

import java.awt.*;
import java.awt.event.*;

/**
 *
 * @author   Stephen Potts
 */
public class TestKeyAdapter extends Frame
{
    TextField tField;
    TextField tField2;
    TextField tField3;
    TextField tField4;

    /** Creates a new instance of TestKeyAdapter */
    public TestKeyAdapter()
    {
        tField = new TextField(15);
        tField2 = new TextField(15);
        tField3 = new TextField(15);
        tField4 = new TextField(20);

        Panel testPanel = new Panel();
        testPanel.setBackground(Color.gray);

        KeyStrokeHandler ksh = new KeyStrokeHandler();
        tField.addKeyListener(ksh);
        testPanel.add(tField);
        testPanel.add(tField2);
        testPanel.add(tField3);
        testPanel.add(tField4);
        add(testPanel);

        this.setLayout(new FlowLayout());

        addWindowListener(new WinCloser());
        setTitle("Using a KeyAdapter Object");
        setBounds( 100, 100, 600, 400);
        setVisible(true);
    }

    public static void main(String[] args)
    {
        TestKeyAdapter tka= new TestKeyAdapter();
    }

    class KeyStrokeHandler extends KeyAdapter
    {
        public void keyTyped(KeyEvent ke)
        {
            String newString = String.valueOf(ke.getKeyChar());
```

LISTING 14.7   Continued

```
                tField2.setText(newString);
                tField3.setText("keyTyped() was called");
            }

        public void keyPressed(KeyEvent ke)
        {
            String newString = String.valueOf(ke.getKeyChar());
            tField2.setText(newString);
            tField4.setText("keyPressed() was called");
        }

        public void keyReleased(KeyEvent ke)
        {
            String newString = String.valueOf(ke.getKeyChar());
            tField2.setText(newString);
            tField4.setText("keyReleased() was called");
        }
    }


}

class WinCloser extends WindowAdapter
{
    public void windowClosing(WindowEvent e)
    {
        System.exit(0);
    }
}
```

Notice that this class does not extend the **KeyAdapter** class itself because it already extends the **Frame** class and a second **extends** statement or class name would generate a compiler error.

```
public class TestKeyAdapter extends Frame
{
```

We create the usual set of text fields on a panel so that we will have a place to put text on. We then declare a new handle to a class called **KeyStrokeHandler**, which we create ourselves in this same class.

```
        KeyStrokeHandler ksh = new KeyStrokeHandler();
```

We make this class the key listener for one of the text fields.

```
        tField.addKeyListener(ksh);
```

Next we create an inner class to serve as the extension of the **KeyAdapter** class. An inner class is declared inside the definition of another class. Because it is located inside the **TestKeyAdapter** class, it has visibility to the class-level variables, which are the text boxes in this example.

```
    class KeyStrokeHandler extends KeyAdapter
    {
```

We override the three methods in the `KeyAdapter` class. These methods get called whenever the key action that they represent occurs.

```
public void keyTyped(KeyEvent ke)
{
    String newString = String.valueOf(ke.getKeyChar());
    tField2.setText(newString);
    tField3.setText("keyTyped() was called");
}

public void keyPressed(KeyEvent ke)
{
    String newString = String.valueOf(ke.getKeyChar());
    tField2.setText(newString);
    tField4.setText("keyPressed() was called");
}

public void keyReleased(KeyEvent ke)
{
    String newString = String.valueOf(ke.getKeyChar());
    tField2.setText(newString);
    tField4.setText("keyReleased() was called");
}
}
```

Running this example generates the result shown in Figure 14.6.

FIGURE 14.6
The `KeyAdapter` class enables you to monitor each keystroke and differentiate between the press and the release.

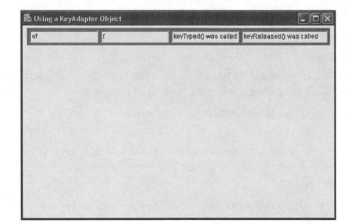

The `WindowListener` and `WindowAdapter` Interfaces

The `WindowListener` interface is used to receive notification when an event occurs that pertains to the window as a whole. We have used the `WindowAdapter` class to declare a class that handles the `windowClosing()` method in most of our AWT examples. This is required because AWT will not stop the process just because the window is closed. Listing 14.7 has the following class declared at the bottom.

```
class WinCloser extends WindowAdapter
{
    public void windowClosing(WindowEvent e)
    {
        System.exit(0);
    }
}
```

All this class does is terminate the whole process by executing the `System.exit(0)` command.

There are seven methods in this interface, however. Listing 14.8 shows these in action.

LISTING 14.8   The `TestWindowListener.java` File

```
/*
 * TestWindowListener.java
 *
 * Created on August 9, 2002, 2:32 PM
 */

package ch14;

import java.awt.*;
import java.awt.event.*;


/**
 *
 * @author  Stephen Potts
 */
public class TestWindowListener extends Frame
{
    Scrollbar sb;
    TextField tField;


    /** Creates a new instance of TestWindowListener */
    public TestWindowListener()
    {
        sb=new Scrollbar(Scrollbar.VERTICAL, 0, 1, 0, 255);
        add(sb);
        tField = new TextField(30);
        add(tField);

        this.setLayout(new FlowLayout());

        addWindowListener(new WinHandler());
        setTitle("Using a Scrollbar Object");
        setBounds( 100, 100, 400, 400);
        setVisible(true);
    }
```

LISTING 14.8   Continued

```java
    public static void main(String[] args)
    {
        TestWindowListener twl= new TestWindowListener();
    }


}

class WinHandler implements WindowListener
{
    public void windowClosing(WindowEvent e)
    {
        System.out.println("windowClosing() called");
        System.exit(0);
    }

    public void windowActivated(java.awt.event.WindowEvent windowEvent)
    {
        System.out.println("windowActivated() called");
    }

    public void windowClosed(java.awt.event.WindowEvent windowEvent)
    {
        System.out.println("windowClosed() called");
    }

    public void windowDeactivated(java.awt.event.WindowEvent windowEvent)
    {
        System.out.println("windowDeactivated() called");
    }

    public void windowDeiconified(java.awt.event.WindowEvent windowEvent)
    {
        System.out.println("windowDeiconified() called");
    }

    public void windowIconified(java.awt.event.WindowEvent windowEvent)
    {
        System.out.println("windowIconified called");
    }

    public void windowOpened(java.awt.event.WindowEvent windowEvent)
    {
        System.out.println("windowOpened() called");
    }

}
```

This class shows us another look at class structures. Instead of declaring this class to be its own listener, we declare a separate class to do it. In addition, we never created a handle to this class, we just placed the new statement inside the add listener method call as a parameter.

```
addWindowListener(new WinHandler());
```

The Windhandler class implements the WindowListener interface and provides implementations for all the methods that are required. Notice that this class is not an inner class because it is declared outside the definition of the TestWindowListener class.

```
class WinHandler implements WindowListener
{
    public void windowClosing(WindowEvent e)
    {
        System.out.println("windowClosing() called");
        System.exit(0);
    }

    public void windowActivated(java.awt.event.WindowEvent windowEvent)
    {
        System.out.println("windowActivated() called");
    }

    public void windowClosed(java.awt.event.WindowEvent windowEvent)
    {
        System.out.println("windowClosed() called");
    }

    public void windowDeactivated(java.awt.event.WindowEvent windowEvent)
    {
        System.out.println("windowDeactivated() called");
    }

    public void windowDeiconified(java.awt.event.WindowEvent windowEvent)
    {
        System.out.println("windowDeiconified() called");
    }

    public void windowIconified(java.awt.event.WindowEvent windowEvent)
    {
        System.out.println("windowIconified called");
    }

    public void windowOpened(java.awt.event.WindowEvent windowEvent)
    {
        System.out.println("windowOpened() called");
    }

}
```

When you run this program, you need the command window open so that you can see the output from System.out.println() calls. Figure 14.7 shows the result of running this example.

FIGURE 14.7
The WindowListener interface keeps your program aware of what is happening with the window.

The ComponentListener and ComponentAdapter Interfaces

The ComponentListener interface contains four methods that tell your program whenever a component is hidden, made visible, moved, or resized. The ComponentAdapter provides dummy versions of all four methods.

Listing 14.9 shows an example of this interface.

LISTING 14.9 The TestComponentListener.java File

```java
/*
 * TestComponentListener.java
 *
 * Created on July 30, 2002, 2:36 PM
 */

package ch14;
import java.awt.*;
import java.awt.event.*;

/**
 *
 * @author  Stephen Potts
 * @version
 */
public class TestComponentListener extends Frame implements ComponentListener
{
    Button btnExit;

    /** Creates new TestComponentListener*/
    public TestComponentListener()
    {
        btnExit = new Button("Exit");
        btnExit.setFont(new Font("Courier", Font.BOLD, 24));

        btnExit.setBackground(Color.cyan);
        addComponentListener(this);
```

LISTING 14.9   Continued

```
        add(btnExit);
        this.setLayout(new FlowLayout());

        addWindowListener(new WinCloser());
        setTitle("Using a ComponentListener");
        setBounds( 100, 100, 300, 300);
        setVisible(true);
    }

    public void componentResized(ComponentEvent ce)
    {
        System.out.println("Component resized");
    }
    public void componentMoved(ComponentEvent ce)
    {
        System.out.println("Component moved");
    }
    public void componentHidden(ComponentEvent ce)
    {
        System.out.println("Component hidden");
    }
    public void componentShown(ComponentEvent ce)
    {
        System.out.println("Component shown");
    }


    public static void main(String[] args)
    {
        TestComponentListener tcl = new TestComponentListener();
    }

}

class WinCloser extends WindowAdapter
{
    public void windowClosing(WindowEvent e)
    {
        System.exit(0);
    }
}
```

The class itself is the component and the implementer of the interface to handle it.

```
        addComponentListener(this);
```

We implement all four of the required methods in this class.

```
    public void componentResized(ComponentEvent ce)
    {
        System.out.println("Component resized");
    }
    public void componentMoved(ComponentEvent ce)
```

```
    {
        System.out.println("Component moved");
    }
    public void componentHidden(ComponentEvent ce)
    {
        System.out.println("Component hidden");
    }
    public void componentShown(ComponentEvent ce)
    {
        System.out.println("Component shown");
    }
```

The result is shown in Figure 14.8.

FIGURE 14.8
The `ComponentListener` interface keeps your program aware of what is happening with a registered component.

The `MouseListener` and `MouseAdapter` Interfaces

The `MouseListener` provides a high level look at the mouse. It tells you when a mouse is over a component that you are listening for, as well as when a mouse button has been clicked. The `MouseAdapter` provides the usual dummy implementations of each of the methods in this interface. Listing 14.10 shows an example of the `MouseListener` interface.

LISTING 14.10   The `TestMouseListener.java` File

```
/*
 * TestMouseListener.java
 *
 * Created on July 30, 2002, 2:36 PM
 */

package ch14;
import java.awt.*;
import java.awt.event.*;

/**
 *
```

LISTING 14.10   Continued

```
 * @author   Stephen Potts
 * @version
 */
public class TestMouseListener extends Frame implements MouseListener
{
    Button btnExit;

    /** Creates new TestComponentListener*/
    public TestMouseListener()
    {
        btnExit = new Button("Exit");
        btnExit.setFont(new Font("Courier", Font.BOLD, 24));

        btnExit.setBackground(Color.cyan);
        addMouseListener(this);

        add(btnExit);
        this.setLayout(new FlowLayout());

        addWindowListener(new WinCloser());
        setTitle("Using a ComponentListener");
        setBounds( 100, 100, 300, 300);
        setVisible(true);
    }

    public void mouseEntered(MouseEvent me)
    {
        System.out.println("Mouse Entered");
        System.out.println(me.getComponent().getName());
    }
    public void mouseExited(MouseEvent me)
    {
        System.out.println("Mouse Exited");
        System.out.println(me.getComponent().getName());
    }
    public void mousePressed(MouseEvent me)
    {
        System.out.println("Mouse Pressed");
    }
    public void mouseReleased(MouseEvent me)
    {
        System.out.println("Mouse Released");
    }

    public void mouseClicked(MouseEvent me)
    {
        System.out.println("Mouse Clicked");
    }


    public static void main(String[] args)
    {
```

LISTING 14.10   Continued

```
        TestMouseListener tml = new TestMouseListener();
    }

}

class WinCloser extends WindowAdapter
{
    public void windowClosing(WindowEvent e)
    {
        System.exit(0);
    }
}
```

This class is its own listener.

```
public class TestMouseListener extends Frame implements MouseListener
```

The whole frame is the component that we are tracking the mouse with.

```
        addMouseListener(this);
```

We provide implementation for all five methods.

```
    public void mouseEntered(MouseEvent me)
    {
        System.out.println("Mouse Entered");
        System.out.println(me.getComponent().getName());
    }
    public void mouseExited(MouseEvent me)
    {
        System.out.println("Mouse Exited");
        System.out.println(me.getComponent().getName());
    }
    public void mousePressed(MouseEvent me)
    {
        System.out.println("Mouse Pressed");
    }
    public void mouseReleased(MouseEvent me)
    {
        System.out.println("Mouse Released");
    }

    public void mouseClicked(MouseEvent me)
    {
        System.out.println("Mouse Clicked");
    }
```

When the mouse is over the Exit button, that component is consuming the event and the frame never sees it. The result of running this example is shown in Figure 14.9.

FIGURE 14.9
The `MouseListener` interface enables your program to track the movements of the mouse when it enters and exits, as well as when it is clicked.

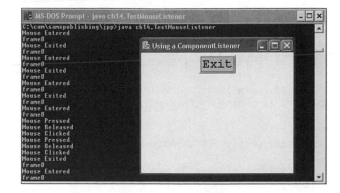

Notice that the actual coordinates of the mouse are not provided by this interface. The `MouseMotionListener` interface, which we will study in the following section, provides that functionality.

The `MouseMotionListener` and `MouseMotionAdapter` Interfaces

The final interface in this chapter is the `MouseMotionListener` interface. This interface receives a MouseEvent that it uses to determine the coordinates of the mouse and whether a mouse button is pressed to make it a dragging motion. The `MouseMotionAdapter` is also provided to make implementation simpler. Listing 14.11 shows an example.

LISTING 14.11   The `MouseMotionListener.java` File

```java
/*
 * TestMouseMotionListener.java
 *
 * Created on July 30, 2002, 2:36 PM
 */

package ch14;
import java.awt.*;
import java.awt.event.*;

/**
 *
 * @author  Stephen Potts
 * @version
 */
public class TestMouseMotionListener extends Frame
                    implements MouseMotionListener
{
    Button btnExit;

    /** Creates new TestMouseMotionListener*/
    public TestMouseMotionListener()
```

LISTING 14.11   Continued

```java
    {
        btnExit = new Button("Exit");
        btnExit.setFont(new Font("Courier", Font.BOLD, 24));

        btnExit.setBackground(Color.cyan);
        addMouseMotionListener(this);

        add(btnExit);
        this.setLayout(new FlowLayout());

        addWindowListener(new WinCloser());
        setTitle("Using a ComponentListener");
        setBounds( 100, 100, 300, 300);
        setVisible(true);
    }

    public void mouseMoved(MouseEvent me)
    {
        System.out.println("Mouse was Moved");
        System.out.println(me.getX() + "," + me.getY());
    }
    public void mouseDragged(MouseEvent me)
    {
        System.out.println("Mouse was Dragged");
        System.out.println(me.getX() + "," + me.getY());
    }

    public static void main(String[] args)
    {
        TestMouseMotionListener tmml = new TestMouseMotionListener();
    }

}

class WinCloser extends WindowAdapter
{
    public void windowClosing(WindowEvent e)
    {
        System.exit(0);
    }
}
```

This class serves as its own listener.

```java
public class TestMouseMotionListener extends Frame
                    implements MouseMotionListener
```

We add the listener to the whole frame.

```java
        addMouseMotionListener(this);
```

We provide implementations for both required methods.

```java
    public void mouseMoved(MouseEvent me)
```

```
    {
        System.out.println("Mouse was Moved");
        System.out.println(me.getX() + "," + me.getY());
    }
    public void mouseDragged(MouseEvent me)
    {
        System.out.println("Mouse was Dragged");
        System.out.println(me.getX() + "," + me.getY());
    }
```

The result of running this example is shown in Figure 14.10.

FIGURE 14.10.

The `MouseMotion Listener` interface enables your program to track the movements of the mouse at the x and y coordinate level.

Notice that every change of even one pixel causes an event to occur. This gives you the fine control needed to create smooth screen movement.

Summary

In this chapter we looked at events and event handling. We started with a generic discussion of events in Java. Following that, we looked at the basic philosophy behind Java event delegation.

Next, we looked at the semantic events and worked examples that listened for each of them. Finally, you learned how to handle low-level events. You saw examples of the most important listener interfaces and adapter classes.

Review Questions

1. Why are events represented as objects?

2. Why do you have to declare an object to be a listener to receive notifications?

3. What is the difference between a semantic event and a low-level event?

4. What is the purpose of the Adapter classes?

Exercises

1. Create an application that looks like a simple calculator.

2. Create an application with a text field that doesn't accept numbers.

3. Create a program that has components that you can drag around a frame.

4. Create a program that draws on a panel when you move the mouse around with either mouse button depressed.

CHAPTER 15

JAVABEANS

You will learn about the following in this chapter:

- What makes a class a JavaBean

- How to develop a Simple JavaBean

- How to deploy JavaBeans in Forte

- How to add custom methods to your Bean

- How to define a bound property

For software developers, software components are the equivalent to Ponce de Leon's Fountain of Youth. If software can be componentized like silicon chips, developers can drag and drop them into their applications thereby saving time and money.

In Java 1.01, there was no easy way to add components to the AWT Toolkit. The reason this was so hard was the existence of the operating system peer component. This peer component had to be one of the widgets or controls that was native to the operating system. When a Java GUI object was created, the JVM would create the native GUI object and place it on the Frame or Panel. This peer was unique to every platform, preventing the programmer from implementing a "write once, run anywhere" component.

When Sun introduced the Swing library as a download in Java 1.1, it provided not only a set of new components, but also an entire architecture—the JavaBean Architecture—for implementing components. In fact, the Swing library is composed entirely of JavaBeans.

Enormous amounts of time and energy have been spent in the past few years trying to devise schemes so that a developer can assemble an application from components. Developing an architecture to support widespread code reuse has proven elusive, but a lot of good software has resulted from the effort.

One of these successes has been the JavaBean architecture. This architecture has proved useful in producing software rapidly in certain cases. These cases tend to be in the area of creating Graphical User Interfaces (GUI).

JavaBeans are Java's version of the ActiveX controls (formerly known as Visual Basic Extensions (VBXs), and later OLE Control Extensions (OCXs). These controls, introduced around 1990, found a valuable niche in hiding the complexity of the Windows operating system from the programmers. VBXs could be used to build graphical interfaces using Visual Basic or included in source code using Visual C++. One senior developer was heard saying, "The day that Visual Basic was released, the high school student next door became a better Windows programmer than me!"

Beyond just hiding the Windows API from programmers (and it did need hiding), Visual Basic showed that far more programming could be done using drag–and-drop components than previously thought possible. It created a new category of development products now known as Rapid Application Development (RAD) tools. Although RAD products still require quite a bit of hand coding, they speed up the development of a certain category of application-GUI front ends that access and modify database tables. Attempts to go beyond these applications into game development, communications, and distributed object programming have met with mixed results.

JavaBeans are the Java version of VBX/OCX/ActiveX. They are pieces of code that are often represented visually as icons in an Integrated Development Environment (IDE). They may or may not have a visual representation at runtime.

In this chapter, you will learn how to create JavaBeans, add custom events, and test and deploy them in a commercial product.

Understanding JavaBeans

JavaBeans have made it possible for Visual Basic–like tools such as Visual Café, JBuilder, Visual Age for Java, and Forte to succeed in the market. These tools all provided a GUI-builder interface where you can drag-and-drop components from a toolbox onto a form, and then add code to define its behavior.

Developing applications using the graphical software development features that these tools provide has not proved as popular with hard-core Java programmers as they have with business-oriented programmers. (We do, however, love these tools for their nice source code editors, project management, and single-step debugging environments.) Many programmers who are comfortable working with classes and APIs don't see the need for graphical software development.

There might be some protectionism in these programmers' attitudes, but there is also some reality in these statements. It is hard to develop code faster than a computer scientist with an IQ over 140 and 10 years of professional programming experience. Unfortunately, the world is not populated with many people who fit into this category. The majority of the computing world is staffed by mere mortals, who often know more about the business of their company than they do about programming.

Many of these people are very bright and more than willing to write their own programs if they don't have to get into the world of polymorphism, serialization, and remote method invocation, and so on. They have no trouble seeing the value of programming tools that enable them to keep their heads on the business at hand.

It is a paradox that most programmers who are capable of creating JavaBeans are not capable of appreciating them. We create these components to accomplish the following goals:

- Hide some complexity so that more junior programmers can create applications.

- Package business domain–specific information so that nonprogrammers can build simple applications.

- Promote software reuse.

- Integrate with Rapid Development Environments.

- Create a division of labor where programmers who understand certain specialties develop code that others who lack their expertise can use.

Another place where components are popular is in companies that have large investments in legacy databases. These companies extend the useful life of the old systems by wrapping the old technology in a Bean wrapper.

It is true that many of these same goals can be accomplished using a traditional Java API. Rather than trying to think of JavaBeans as a replacement for traditional Java classes, try to think of them as an alternative methodology or pattern that is useful for a certain group of classes.

A JavaBean is just another Java class, but it is created to a tighter specification. This specification requires that some methods exist, and what names they can have.

The purpose of this specification is to ensure that every JavaBean can interface with the GUI tools that are available on the market. The following is a list of the features that are required:

- Support for introspection—Beans must either follow the JavaBean naming conventions, or they must implement the `BeanInfo` interface and provide a method that describes the Bean.

- Must be serializable—The Bean instances that are included in a project must be able to be saved and retrieved without any loss of state information.

- Must be usable in a visual application builder tool—This requirement implies that a toolbox icon and a design-time visual representation must exist.

- If a Bean has a runtime appearance, it must extend `java.awt.Component` (via a subclass like Canvas).

Note

Java Server Pages (JSP) documentation also make use of objects that are called JavaBeans. JSP uses a very limited subset of the JavaBeans specification to provide a simple way of creating classes that JSPs can call directly. In essence, these JavaBeans are simply Java classes with `get()` and `set()` methods for all the property values.

Beyond these requirements, a JavaBean is not limited in what actions it can perform. It can contain virtually any processing logic that can be put into other Java classes.

Developing a Simple JavaBean

Armed with an understanding of the basics, we are ready to create a simple JavaBean. The program that we will create is going to be a progress bar, which grows and shrinks to indicate progress and regress. The code for this class is shown here in Listing 15.1:

LISTING 15.1   The `ProgressBar.java`

```
/*
 * ProgressBar.java
 *
 * Created on August 27, 2002, 11:18 AM
 */

package com.samspublishing.jpp.ch15;

import java.awt.*;
import java.awt.event.*;
import java.beans.*;
import java.io.Serializable;

/**
 *
 * @author  Stephen Potts
 */
public class ProgressBar extends Canvas implements Serializable
{
    private float scaleSize;
    private float currentValue;

    //Default constructor
    public ProgressBar()
    {
        this(100, 50);
    }


    //Constructor
    public ProgressBar(float scaleSize, float currentValue)
    {
        super();

        this.scaleSize = scaleSize;
        this.currentValue = currentValue;

        setBackground(Color.lightGray);
        setForeground(Color.magenta);
```

LISTING 15.1   Continued

```java
        //sets the initial size of the bean on a canvas
        setSize(100, 25);
    }

    public float getScaleSize()
    {
        return scaleSize;
    }

    public void setScaleSize(float sSize)
    {
        //The scale size can never set to a value lower than
        //the current value
        this.scaleSize = Math.max(0.0f, sSize);
        if (this.scaleSize < this.currentValue)
        {
            this.scaleSize = this.currentValue;
        }
    }

    public float getCurrentValue()
    {
        return currentValue;
    }

    public void setCurrentValue(float cVal)
    {
        //The current value can not be set negative
        //nor can it be set greater than the scale size
        this.currentValue = Math.max(0.0f, cVal);
        if (this.currentValue > this.scaleSize)
        {
            this.currentValue = this.scaleSize;
        }
    }

    //The paint method is called by the container
    public synchronized void paint(Graphics g)
    {
        int width = getSize().width;
        int height = getSize().height;

        g.setColor(getBackground());
        g.fillRect(1, 1, width-2, height-2);
        g.draw3DRect(0,0, width-1, height-1, true);

        g.setColor(getForeground());
        g.fillRect(3,3,(int)((currentValue * (width-6))/scaleSize),
        height-6);
    }

    //The grow method makes the current value larger
```

LISTING 15.1 Continued

```
    public void grow()
    {
        setCurrentValue( this.currentValue + 1.0f);
    }


    //The shrink method makes the current value smaller
    public void shrink()
    {
        setCurrentValue( this.currentValue - 1.0f);
    }
}//class
```

The ProgressBar class extends Canvas, which is a simple rectangular area with a paint() method that can be overridden to create the appearance of the JavaBean. The Serializable interface is a marker with no methods to implement. It simply marks this class as one that can store and retrieve its state properly, in the opinion of the programmer.

```
public class ProgressBar extends Canvas implements Serializable
```

This Bean has only two unique class-level variables (properties) and about a dozen more that it inherits by extending the Canvas class. (foreground and background colors, height, width, and so on). The scaleSize property shows the value that will fill the progress bar to the max. The currentValue represents how much progress has been achieved thus far. If a gas tank holds 20 gallons, and you fill it half way, the scaleSize would be set to 20 and the currentValue would be set to 10.

```
    private float scaleSize;
    private float currentValue;
```

The default constructor is the constructor that contains no parameters. In this instance, it calls another constructor via the this() method, and passes it the values of 100 and 50. These values are the scaleSize and currentValue parameters. Most GUI tools use this constructor when you first drag and drop a component onto a form.

```
    //Default constructor

    public ProgressBar()
    {
        this(100, 50);
    }
```

The other constructor sets some unique property values, and then sets some of the inherited properties also. Note that the initial size of the Bean is set using the setSize() method. This size is the height and width of the Bean itself, not to be confused with the scaleSize and currentValue of the progress bar.

```
        setBackground(Color.lightGray);
        setForeground(Color.magenta);

        //sets the initial size of the bean on a canvas
        setSize(100, 25);
    }
```

The `paint()` method is used to create the appearance of the Bean. A Canvas object is just a rectangle with a background color of gray displayed. The word **synchronized** means that this method is threadsafe. Thread safety is important when you are creating multiple instances of the same object at the same time because GUI screens often contain multiple instances of the same JavaBean.

```
//The paint method is called by the container
public synchronized void paint(Graphics g)
{
    int width = getSize().width;
    int height = getSize().height;

    g.setColor(getBackground());
    g.fillRect(1, 1, width-2, height-2);
    g.draw3DRect(0,0, width-1, height-1, true);

    g.setColor(getForeground());
    g.fillRect(3,3,(int)((currentValue * (width-6))/scaleSize),
    height-6);
}
```

Two methods exist that other classes and components can use to cause the progress bar to grow gracefully or to shrink. The only increments and decrements are by 1 to make the growth smooth.

```
public void grow()
{
    setCurrentValue( this.currentValue + 1.0f);
}
```

JavaBean classes do explicitly inherit from the Canvas class. They also inherit implicitly from the Component class, however.

This inherited functionality does not provide everything that GUI builder tools need to manage the component, however. They still need some toolbox icons so that the users can drag and drop the component into an application. The `SimpleBeanInfo` class provides these icons.

In Listing 15.2, we extend the `SimpleBeanInfo` class and override the `getIcon` method as shown here:

LISTING 15.2   The `ProgressBarBeanInfo.java` File

```
/*
 * ProgressBarBeanInfo.java
 *
 * Created on August 27, 2002, 11:54 AM
 */

package com.samspublishing.jpp.ch15;

import java.beans.*;
import java.awt.*;
```

LISTING 15.2   Continued

```
/**
 *
 * @author   Stephen Potts
 * @version
 */
public class ProgressBarBeanInfo extends SimpleBeanInfo
{

  public Image getIcon(int iconKind)
  {
      if(iconKind == BeanInfo.ICON_COLOR_16x16)
      {
          Image img = loadImage("ProgressBarIcon16.gif");
          return img;
      }

      if(iconKind == BeanInfo.ICON_COLOR_32x32)
      {
          Image img = loadImage("ProgressBarIcon32.gif");
          return img;
      }
      return null;
  }


}
```

Because JavaBeans are programmed to a careful specification, GUI builder tools can figure out which properties a Bean exposes to programs by looking at the structure of the class file. This is called introspection. Because of introspection, we don't need to write any special code to handle properties. The reason that we have two different sizes of icons is that some GUI tools prefer one size and some the other.

Deploying JavaBeans

The whole strategy of writing Bean classes is very logical and straightforward. You just package up the classes and icons into a jar file and place the jar file in a special directory with a special document called a manifest. We will work an example to show you how to do this. This example will be deployed using the Bean Development Kit (BDK) that is available from `java.sun.com`. The BDK is a testing environment that enables programmers to test their JavaBeans before deploying them to other environments such as Forte or JBuilder.

Let's step through the deployment of the `ProgressBar` example on a Windows machine. The process for Unix is identical except for the directory names. Follow these steps:

1. Create a directory called `c:\com\samspublishing\jpp\ch15`.

2. Copy the following files from the Web site to this directory:

   `ProgressBar.java`

```
ProgressBarIcon32.gif
ProgressBarIcon16.gif
ProgressBarBeanInfo.java
```

3. Compile the two `.java` files.

4. Create a file called `ProgressBar.mf` that contains the following lines:

```
Manifest-Version: 1.0
Created-By: 1.4.0 (Sun Microsystems Inc.)

Name: com/samspublishing/jpp/ch15/ProgressBar.class
Java-Bean: True
```

5. `cd` up to `c:\`.

6. Type the following command:

   **jar cfm com\samspublishing\jpp\ch15\ProgressBar.jar [ic:ccc]
   com\samspublishing\jpp\ch15\ProgressBar.mf [ic:ccc]
   com\samspublishing\jpp\ch15*.class com\samspublishing\jpp\ch15*.gif**

7. Look in `c:\com\samspublishing\jpp\ch15` and see that a file named `ProgressBar.jar` exists. Open it with a zip program and verify that it contains the files shown in Figure 15.1:

FIGURE 15.1

The `ProgressBar.jar` file contains all the code needed to add this JavaBean to a GUI development tool.

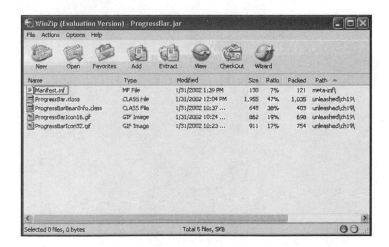

8. Download the Bean Development Kit, the BDK from the `http://java.sun.com/` Web site. (Type **BDK** in the search box, and it will take you to the download page.) You will find instructions on how to install this product on the Web site. During installation, specify `c:\BDK` as the location in which to install.

9. Copy the `ProgressBar.jar` file into the `C:\BDK\jars` directory.

10. Move to the `c:\BDK\beanbox` directory, and type **run**. This will open four windows. The first window is the ToolBox window that is shown in Figure 15.2:

FIGURE 15.2

The ToolBox contains all the Beans that have `jar` files in `c:\BDK\jars`.

11. Notice that one of the Beans in the ToolBox is our very own **ProgressBar**.

12. Click the ProgressBar icon in the ToolBox. Next, click the middle of the BeanBox window. An instance of the ProgressBar Bean appears in the window, as shown in Figure 15.3:

FIGURE 15.3

The BeanBox application allows programmers to test their Beans before placing them into other, more complex, development tools.

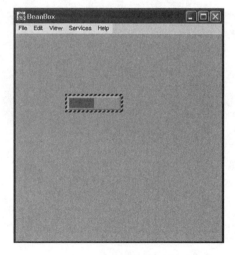

13. Next, examine the contents of the Properties window that is shown in Figure 15.4:

14. Notice that all the properties are listed, including the inherited ones. Click the colored rectangle and notice the dialog box that appears in Figure 15.5:

FIGURE 15.4
The Properties window provides a user interface for changing the bean-specific set of properties.

FIGURE 15.5
The foreground property takes a Color object as its value. A built-in property dialog exists for changing the Color object.

15. Observe that the color of the rectangle in the Properties dialog has changed along with the color of the ProgressBar that is being displayed in the BeanBox. This dialog appears automatically because the return type of the `setForgroundColor()` method is of class Color. Automatic property change dialogs exist for the intrinsic types, Strings, Fonts, and other common return types. If you return an object that you have defined, you will be responsible for implementing this.

The Bean Development Kit is a good way to start the development process. Eventually you will need to learn how to deploy JavaBeans in commercial development tools.

Deployment in Forte

Every GUI tool has its own procedure for deploying JavaBeans in their environment. Their processes do resemble each other to a degree, so we will show you how to deploy the ProgressBar Bean in the Forte development environment. To install the ProgressBar example in the Forte environment, follow this procedure:

1. Open the Forte IDE.

2. Select Tools, Install New JavaBean. The dialog shown here in Figure 15.6 will appear:

3. Move to the directory where you created the `.jar` file, select the `ProgressBar.jar` file, and click OK. This will open the Select JavaBean dialog that is shown in Figure 15.7:

FIGURE 15.6
The Install JavaBean dialog enables you to specify the location of the `.jar` file that holds your Bean.

FIGURE 15.7
The Select JavaBean dialog enables you to specify the Bean that you want to install.

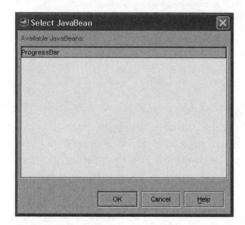

4. A single `.jar` file can contain more than one JavaBean. Select the ProgressBar and click OK. This will open the Palette Category Dialog Box shown in Figure 15.8:

FIGURE 15.8
The Palette Category dialog enables you to specify the palette in which your Bean will reside.

5. Select the Swing(Other) Palette and select OK. The ProgressBar's icon is now in the Swing(Other) palette, as shown in Figure 15.9:

FIGURE 15.9
The Swing(Other) palette now contains the ProgressBar Bean.

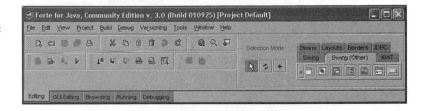

6. To use this Bean, it is necessary to create a class. Choose File, New, and then Frame. Name the new class `TestProgressBar`.

7. Choose the GUI Editing tab and add a `JPanel` to the frame from the Swing palette. This will give the ProgressBar a container.

8. Go to the Swing(Other) palette and click the ProgressBar icon.

9. Now click the panel and see the ProgressBar appear as shown in Figure 15.10:

FIGURE 15.10.
The `TestProgressBar` application now contains an instance of the ProgressBar.

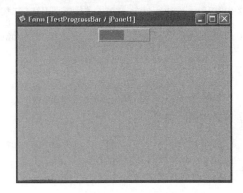

If we look at the code generated by this process you will see an instance of the Progress bar in the application as shown here in Listing 15.3:

LISTING 15.3   The `Form1.java` File

```
/*
Form1.java
 *
 * Created on August 27, 2002, 4:17 PM
 */

/**
 *
 * @author   Stephen Potts
```

LISTING 15.3   Continued

```
    */
public class Form1 extends javax.swing.JFrame
{

    /** Creates new form Form1 */
    public Form1()
    {
        initComponents();
    }

    /** This method is called from within the constructor to
     * initialize the form.
     * WARNING: Do NOT modify this code. The content of this method is
     * always regenerated by the Form Editor.
     */

    private void initComponents()
    {
        jPanel1 = new javax.swing.JPanel();
        progressBar1 = new com.samspublishing.jpp.ch15.ProgressBar();

        addWindowListener(new java.awt.event.WindowAdapter()
        {
            public void windowClosing(java.awt.event.WindowEvent evt)
            {
                exitForm(evt);
            }
        });

        jPanel1.add(progressBar1);

        getContentPane().add(jPanel1, java.awt.BorderLayout.CENTER);

        pack();
    }

    /** Exit the Application */
    private void exitForm(java.awt.event.WindowEvent evt)
    {
        System.exit(0);
    }

    /**
     * @param args the command line arguments
     */
    public static void main(String args[])
    {
        new Form1().show();
    }


    // Variables declaration - do not modify
```

LISTING 15.3   Continued

```
        private javax.swing.JPanel jPanel1;
        private com.samspublishing.jpp.ch15.ProgressBar progressBar1;
        // End of variables declaration

}
```

This is a good example of how visual programming works. We were able to create a simple application in Forte that used a progress bar built by hand and integrated into the Forte IDE using tools that Forte provided.

Properties, Methods, and Events

A JavaBean that only contains properties is a poor excuse for a component. The JavaBeans specification states that the three most important features of a JavaBean are the set of properties it exposes, the set of methods it allows other components to call, and the set of events it fires. We have already seen how to get and set simple properties. Next, we will focus on ways to take advantage of the methods and events that a JavaBean can define.

Creating New Methods

The getter and setter methods enable you to get and set the properties of the JavaBean. It is possible to define methods that perform other tasks, however. Listing 15.4 shows a class that contains a method that is neither a get nor a set:

LISTING 15.4   The GreenBean Class

```
/*
 * GreenBean.java
 *
 * Created on August 28, 2002, 10:41 AM
 */

package com.samspublishing.jpp.ch15;

import java.io.Serializable;
import java.awt.*;
import java.beans.*;


/**
 *
 * @author  Stephen Potts
 * @version
 */
public class GreenBean extends Canvas implements Serializable

{
```

LISTING 15.4   Continued

```java
    private Color color = Color.green;

    public Color getColor()
    {
        return color;
    }

    public void setColor(Color col)
    {
        this.color = col;
    }

    /** Creates new GreenBean */
    public GreenBean()
    {
        setSize(60,40);
        setBackground(Color.green);
    }

    public void paint (Graphics g)
    {
        g.setColor(color);
        g.fillRect(20,5,20,30);
    }

    public void printoutChange(PropertyChangeEvent evt)
    {
        String changeText = evt.getPropertyName() + " := "
                + evt.getNewValue();
        System.out.println(changeText);
    }
}//class
```

In addition to the usual methods such as **paint()**, **getColor()**, and **setColor()**, this Bean contains an additional method called **printoutChange()**. This method accepts a **PropertyChangeEvent** object as input. It examines the event object and obtains the information that it contains. It then prints this information to the console:

```java
        String changeText = evt.getPropertyName() + " := "
                + evt.getNewValue();
        System.out.println(changeText);
```

This method is **public**, meaning that it can be called from other classes. Both the **getXXX()** and **setXXX()** methods are called whenever the user changes the property's value using the GUI. With custom methods, however, you have to provide explicit calls to this method from the other classes.

We will wait to build and deploy the **GreenBean** class until we have created one additional class, **ButtonBean**, in the following section.

Events

Another important part of the JavaBean specification is the ability to define your own custom events. The two basic categories of events are standard and custom. A *standard event* is one that is generated by one of the classes that compose the JDK. These events can be low-level, such as mouse events, or they can be high-level, or semantic, such as ActionEvent. *Custom events* are those that you can create yourself by extending either the EventObject class or the AWTEvent class. In the next section, you will see how one very interesting type of event, the PropertyChangeEvent, is communicated between JavaBeans.

The PropertyChangeEvent

The `getXXX()` and `setXXX()` methods provide ways for development tools such as Forte to manipulate the Beans in their user interfaces. There are two special types of properties: bound properties and constrained properties.

A *Bound property* is a property that has the built-in functionality to notify another JavaBean when it changes. One good use of this feature is to manage appearance properties like the font property. If a container Bean held six Beans with text on them, it would be nice to be able to change the font on all six of them by changing the font of the container. You could do this by binding a method in each Bean to the font property of the container.

A *Constrained Property* goes even further. In addition to notifying the other Beans when a property changes, the Bean that is being notified can veto the change. This could be useful if a container Bean wanted to maintain a consistent font in all the contained Beans. If any Bean wanted to change its font, the container Bean could veto it.

An example that makes use of the `printoutChange()` method that we created in the GreenBean class can be used to show how this works. Recall that GreenBean contains a method called `printoutChange()` that accepts a PropertyChangeEvent as its parameter:

```
public void printoutChange(PropertyChangeEvent evt)
{
    String changeText = evt.getPropertyName() + " := "
            + evt.getNewValue();
    System.out.println(changeText);
}
```

This method will be called automatically when this event occurs once the event listener is defined. It will accept the Event, get the values in its variables that pertain to the name of the property that was changed, and then get the new value of the property.

When this method gets called, the information contained in the Event object will be printed to the console. JavaBeans that contain bound properties must be written in a special way so that PropertyChangeEvents can be sent whenever a bound property changes. Listing 15.5 shows a Bean that is capable of sending PropertyChangedEvents:

LISTING 15.5   The ButtonBean Class

```java
/*
 * ButtonBean.java
 *
 * Created on August 28, 2002, 11:38 AM
 */

package com.samspublishing.jpp.ch15;

import java.awt.*;
import java.awt.event.*;
import java.beans.*;
import java.io.Serializable;
import java.util.Vector;

/**
 *
 * @author  Stephen Potts
 * @version
 */
public class ButtonBean extends Component implements Serializable
{
    private boolean debug;
    private PropertyChangeSupport pcs=
        new PropertyChangeSupport(this);
    private String label;

    /** Creates new ButtonBean */
    public ButtonBean()
    {
        this("ButtonBean");
    }

    public ButtonBean(String label)
    {
        super();
        this.label = label;
        setFont(new Font("Dialog", Font.PLAIN, 12));
        setBackground(Color.lightGray);
    }

    public synchronized void paint(Graphics g)
    {
        int width = getSize().width;
        int height = getSize().height;

        g.setColor(getBackground());
        g.fill3DRect(0, 0, width-1, height-1, false);

        g.setColor(getForeground());
        g.setFont(getFont());

        g.drawRect(2, 2, width-4, height-4);
```

LISTING 15.5   Continued

```
        g.drawString(label, 10, 18);
    }

    public void addPropertyChangeListener(PropertyChangeListener pcl)
    {
        pcs.addPropertyChangeListener(pcl);
    }

    public void removePropertyChangeListener(PropertyChangeListener pcl)
    {
        pcs.addPropertyChangeListener(pcl);
    }

    public void setDebug(boolean x)
    {
        boolean old = debug;
        debug = x;
        pcs.firePropertyChange("debug", new Boolean(old),
        new Boolean(x));
    }

    public boolean getDebug()
    {
        return debug;
    }

    public void setFontSize(int x)
    {
        Font old = getFont();
        setFont(new Font(old.getName(), old.getStyle(), x));
        pcs.firePropertyChange("fontSize",
        new Integer(old.getSize()), new Integer(x));
    }

    public int getFontSize()
    {
        return getFont().getSize();
    }

    public void setFont(Font f)
    {
        Font old = getFont();
        super.setFont(f);
        pcs.firePropertyChange("font", old, f);
    }

    public void setLabel(String lab)
    {
        String oldLabel = label;
        label = lab;
        pcs.firePropertyChange("label", oldLabel, lab);
    }
```

LISTING 15.5   Continued

```java
public String getLabel()
{
    return label;
}

public Dimension getPreferredSize()
{
    FontMetrics fm = getFontMetrics(getFont());
    return new Dimension(fm.stringWidth(label) + 12,
    fm.getMaxAscent() + fm.getMaxDescent() + 8);
}

public void setForeground(Color c)
{
    Color old = getForeground();;
    super.setForeground(c);
    pcs.firePropertyChange("foreground", old, c);
    repaint();
}

public void setBackground(Color c)
{
    Color old = getBackground();;
    super.setBackground(c);
    pcs.firePropertyChange("background", old, c);
    repaint();
}
}//class
```

The PropertyChangeEvent is part of the JavaBeans package:

```java
import java.beans.*;
```

The PropertyChangeSupport is a utility class for bound properties. It will be used to hold the list of classes that are listening for this class' PropertyChangeEvents.

```java
private PropertyChangeSupport pcs=
    new PropertyChangeSupport(this);
```

The following two methods allow other Beans to register and remove their interest in being notified of changes to bound properties:

```java
public void addPropertyChangeListener(PropertyChangeListener pcl)
{
    pcs.addPropertyChangeListener(pcl);
}

public void removePropertyChangeListener(PropertyChangeListener pcl)
{
    pcs.addPropertyChangeListener(pcl);
}
```

Notice that all the set methods for the bound properties have to include an additional line of code to fire the property change event by calling the `firePropertyChange()` method. The `firePropertyChange()` method takes three parameters: the name of the property to be changed, the old value being sent, and the new value.

```
public void setFontSize(int x)
    {
        Font old = getFont();
        setFont(new Font(old.getName(), old.getStyle(), x));
        pcs.firePropertyChange("fontSize",
        new Integer(old.getSize()), new Integer(x));
    }
```

Caution

All the parameters in the `firePropertyChange()` method are sent as objects. Intrinsic types, such as `int`, must be sent using the object version like Integer.

The only task that remains is the connecting of the two Beans together. This is normally done using the development tool's user interface. In this case, we will use the BeanBox application.

The process for adding these Beans to the BeanBox is identical to the procedure described in the "Deploying JavaBeans" section earlier in this chapter.

1. Create a directory called `c:\com\samspublishing\jpp\ch15`.

2. Copy the following files from the Sams Web site to this directory:

   ```
   GreenBean.java
   ButtonBean.java
   ```

3. Compile the two `.java` files.

4. Create a file called `GreenBean.mf` in this directory that contains the following lines:

   ```
   Manifest-Version: 1.0
   Created-By: 1.4.0 (Sun Microsystems Inc.)

   Name: com/samspublishing/jpp/ch15/GreenBean.class
   Java-Bean: True
   ```

5. Create a file called `ButtonBean.mf` in this directory that contains the following lines:

   ```
   Manifest-Version: 1.0
   Created-By: 1.4.0 (Sun Microsystems Inc.)

   Name: com/samspublishing/jpp/ch15/ButtonBean.class
   Java-Bean: True
   ```

6. `cd` up to `c:\`.

7. Type the following command:

```
jar cfm com\samspublishing\jpp\ch15\ButtonBean.jar
➥com\samspublishing\jpp\ch15\ButtonBean.mf
➥com\samspublishing\jpp\ch15\ButtonBean.class
```

8. Type the following command:

```
jar cfm com\samspublishing\jpp\ch15\GreenBean.jar
➥com\samspublishing\jpp\ch15\GreenBean.mf
➥com\samspublishing\jpp\ch15\GreenBean.class
```

9. Look in `c:\com\samspublishing\jpp\ch15` and see that two files named `ButtonBean.jar` and `GreenBean.jar` exist. Open them with a zip program and verify that they contain one class file and one manifest file.

10. Copy the `ButtonBean.jar` and `GreenBean.jar` files into the `C:\BDK\jars` directory.

Next, start the BeanBox and place one instance of ButtonBean in the BeanBox along with one instance of GreenBean. Following that, highlight the ButtonBean instance, then, choose Events from the Edit menu, then propertyChange, then propertyChange again as shown in Figure 15.11.

FIGURE 15.11
The GreenBean listens for changes to the ButtonBean's properties and prints them to the console.

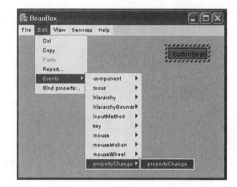

A red line will be attached to your mouse cursor. Move your mouse cursor over the GreenBean and click. This signifies that you want the GreenBean to listen to the bound property changes generated by the ButtonBean. After clicking you will see a dialog box appear as shown in Figure 15.12.

You will see quite a few methods that are inherited from GreenBean's superclasses. You will also see the `printoutChange()` method. Choose this one. Make the BeanBox console visible and change the properties of the ButtonBean using the BeanBox's Properties window. You will see output for every change you make appear on the console, similar to what is shown here:

```
debug := true
font := java.awt.Font[family=dialog.italic,name=Dialog,style=italic,size=12]
font := java.awt.Font[family=dialog.italic,name=Dialog,style=italic,size=14]
foreground := java.awt.Color[r=255,g=175,b=175]
label := Java Primer Plus
```

FIGURE 15.12
The `printoutChanges` method is the `GreenBean` method that handles bound changes.

One interesting modification that you can make to this example is to remove the `println()` statements in the `printoutChange()` method and replace them with methods that perform some task on your system, such as a database access.

Summary

In this chapter, you learned about JavaBeans and how they can be used to improve your programming. You learned how to create your own JavaBeans complete with events and custom methods. In addition, you learned how to create bound and constrained variables.

Next, we examined the anatomy of a JavaBean, and we learned what makes it different from an ordinary Java class. We then created a fairly simple Bean to illustrate these principles. We deployed the Bean using the BeanBox application that Sun distributes to assist in the verification that the Bean is correctly created.

Following that, we put our Bean into the Forte IDE and placed it in the Swing(Other) palette. Finally, we created a simple application visually to see how our code was integrated into a Forte-created application.

Finally, we created a JavaBean that fires property changes to another Bean that is a listener.

Review Questions

1. What characteristics make a Java class a JavaBean?

2. What is the purpose of the `SimpleBeanInfo` class?

3. What is a bound property?

4. What is a constrained property?

Exercises

1. Create a JavaBean that is composed of a button with your name on it.

2. Add your JavaBean to the Forte IDE, or another similar IDE.

3. Create another JavaBean that declares one of its properties as bound.

4. Using BeanBox, connect the two Beans together so that your first Bean is notified when the bound property changes on the second Bean.

CHAPTER 16

THE SWING LIBRARY

You will learn about the following in this chapter:

- What Swing is

- How Swing applications are
  Structured

- The role of the JComponent class

- How the basic Swing components
  work

In Chapter 13, "Abstract Windows Toolkit," we discussed the limitations of the AWT. To summarize the discussion, we concluded that the AWT was a good first try at developing a Graphical User Interface (GUI), but that several enhancements were needed before the Java GUI toolkit would be a really valuable tool.

The Java doctrine of "write once, run anywhere" has a corollary that states "write once, run it forever." In other words, new releases of the JVM are not supposed to break existing applications and applets. This doctrine placed so many constraints on the GUI team that the decision was made to create an entirely new toolkit that would coexist with the AWT, but would not deprecate it. This decision freed up the team to make huge changes in the new GUI system that would have broken the AWT if it were retrofitted.

The result is that we now have two sets of GUI classes, the original AWT, and the newer GUI called the Java Foundation Classes (JFC), or Swing. Swing originated as a 100% Java GUI called the Netscape Internet Foundation Classes (IFC). Netscape was able to convince Sun Microsystems that the Java vendor needed to drive this new interface. Sun agreed, took over the development of the IFC, and renamed the product the Java Foundation Classes (JFC). Some of the early demos of the JFC featured swing music from Duke Ellington. This led to the nickname "Swing." This nickname stuck and Swing is the name that you normally hear when the GUI is discussed.

In this chapter we are going to introduce you to the Swing library. We will start with a discussion of the additional features that Swing brings to your development efforts. Following that, we will look at the architecture of a Swing component. Finally, we will work examples that show you how to use the Swing version of components that you are already familiar with from the AWT. In Chapter 17, "Advanced Swing," you will learn how to use the components that were introduced with Swing that have no AWT counterpart.

Understanding Swing

Swing is really two complementary products rolled into one. On one hand, Swing is like a rearchitected version of the AWT. On the other hand, Swing is the next logical version of the Java GUI classes.

The AWT implements its components using the native GUI toolkit on each platform. It creates a peer, which is similar to an object in that GUI. This approach, called the heavyweight approach, has several drawbacks. Because AWT uses different components on each operating system, it can only use the features that they have in common. The peer object in the OS might have tons of additional features that AWT must instantiate, but not use. This causes the AWT component to be heavier than it should be, which keeps it from performing well.

The second problem with this approach is the "least-common denominator" problem. If the Java team wanted to add an xxxBox to Java, it had to identify a peer component on each platform for this widget. If even one platform is missing this component, the widget can't be added. The ambition of Java developers to implement trees, tables, and tabbed panes caused dissatisfaction with the heavyweight approach.

The third problem with the peer approach is that it is very difficult to create custom components such as JavaBeans under the AWT because they have to be written for each OS on which the JVM runs. There is no intermediate, platform-independent layer in AWT to program with.

Swing approaches the problem of component creation differently. It limits its use of heavyweight (AWT) components to just the Window, Dialog, Applet, and Frame classes. You never see the AWT classes, however, because the Swing class equivalents hides them from you. In addition, Swing makes use of low-level AWT objects such as Color, Font, Graphics, Toolkit, and Event.

By limiting the use of native windowing code to just the basic containers, Swing reduces the weight of its objects. By only using low-level libraries, it eliminates the least-common denominator problem. By creating a framework for JavaBean creation, Swing solves the problem of GUI extensibility. In fact, the Swing components that we will study in this book are implemented as JavaBeans. Chapter 15, "Creating JavaBeans," covers the process of creating and deploying custom components in commercial GUI development products such as Forte.

As we stated earlier, Swing is the next logical release of the Java windowing system. In addition to providing replacements for all the AWT components, Swing provides a whole new set of components for your use:

- JOptionPane—This enables you to create message boxes by specifying a few parameters.

- BoxLayout—A nonwrapping layout manager that lays out components either horizontally or vertically.

- Floating Toolbars—These toolbars can be moved to locations other than the top of the window.

- ToolTips—Sometimes called balloon help, these little yellow messages appear when you leave the cursor over a component for a few seconds.

- Drag and Drop—This allows for the intuitive moving of components and dropping them on to others.

- JTable—A JTable is a kind of a spreadsheet/Grid component.

- JTree—A JTree is a tree view of data like the one that MS Windows Explorer uses in the left panel. It can be expanded and contracted.

- JLayeredPane—A container that enables you to assign a permanent layer to an object to keep objects at the same depths relative to one another.

- JInternalFrame—This enables you to create a window within a window.

We will look at the new Swing components in detail in Chapter 17, "Advanced Swing."

Swing Application Structure

Beneath the surface, Swing components differ greatly from AWT components. For one thing, they are written entirely in Java. Another difference is in the way that they are implemented. Swing is built on the concept of the Model, View, and Controller (MVC) design pattern.

The MVC design pattern suggests that all the logic that is needed to make a component work be divided into three separate classes that work together to provide the behavior that you want.

- Model—Contains the actual data that describes the state of a component. That state might include whether a button is pushed or what text is currently in a text field. This layer talks to the database if the GUI is a database front-end.

- View—Displays the component on the screen. Controls colors, cell dimensions, fonts, and so on. A single Model can have several views. For example, an HTML file can be shown as a text file with the tags visible for edit. Alternatively, it can be rendered to the screen with the tags interpreted and rendered in the correct color, font, and so on.

- Controller—Responds to user input. If a user clicks on save, this class receives the event and calls the Model class's save-to-file methods to store the data.

All the Swing components are built using this division of labor, although you may or may not have to use some of the layers. For example, the JButton class is the controller, but it contains a `DefaultButtonModel` object, some state information, and a `DefaultButtonUI` object that provides the view. Because of its simplicity, a JButton's underlying MVC structure is rarely visible to the programmer. It can be made visible, however, if you choose to program with it. Listing 16.1 shows an example of this.

LISTING 16.1   The `TestButtonModel.java` File

```
/*
 * TestButtonModel.java
 *
```

LISTING 16.1   Continued

```java
 * Created on July 30, 2002, 2:36 PM
 */

package ch16;
import javax.swing.*;
import javax.swing.plaf.*;
import java.awt.FlowLayout;
import java.awt.event.*;

/**
 *
 * @author   Stephen Potts
 * @version
 */
public class TestButtonModel extends JFrame implements ActionListener
{
    JButton btnTest;

    /** Creates new TestButtonModel */
    public TestButtonModel()
    {
        btnTest = new JButton("Test");
        btnTest.addActionListener(this);

        getContentPane().add(btnTest);
        this.getContentPane().setLayout(new FlowLayout());

        addWindowListener(new WinCloser());
        setTitle("Using a JButton Model");
        setBounds( 100, 100, 300, 300);
        setVisible(true);
    }

    public void actionPerformed(ActionEvent ae)
    {
        if (ae.getActionCommand().equals("Test"))
        {
            ButtonModel bm = btnTest.getModel();
            System.out.println("The ButtonModel class is " + bm);
            System.out.println(bm.getMnemonic());
            System.out.println(bm.isArmed());
            System.out.println(bm.isEnabled());
            System.out.println(bm.isPressed());
            System.out.println(bm.isRollover());
            System.out.println(bm.isSelected());

            ButtonUI bu = btnTest.getUI();
            System.out.println("The ButtonUI class is " + bu);
        }
    }

    public static void main(String[] args)
```

LISTING 16.1   Continued

```
    {
        TestButtonModel tbm = new TestButtonModel();
    }

}

class WinCloser extends WindowAdapter
{
    public void windowClosing(WindowEvent e)
    {
        System.exit(0);
    }
}
```

We declare a JButton instead of a Button object.

```
    JButton btnTest;
```

The button is instantiated, and the **actionListener** is added in the same way as an AWT button.

```
        btnTest = new JButton("Test");
        btnTest.addActionListener(this);
```

The rules of Swing forbid operations directly on the JFrame itself. A method call to **getContentPane()** returns a handle to a Pane object that covers the JFrame. You use this object to access the JFrame.

```
        getContentPane().add(btnTest);
        this.getContentPane().setLayout(new FlowLayout());
```

The event listener is the controller for this application. It gets a handle to the Model, and then uses it to make several calls to the Model class's methods.

```
            ButtonModel bm = btnTest.getModel();
            System.out.println("The ButtonModel class is " + bm);
            System.out.println(bm.getMnemonic());
            System.out.println(bm.isArmed());
            System.out.println(bm.isEnabled());
            System.out.println(bm.isPressed());
            System.out.println(bm.isRollover());
            System.out.println(bm.isSelected());
```

We can also obtain a handle to the UI object for JButton, but all that we can do with it is print the object to the screen. The **ButtonUI** class has methods that it inherits from **ComponentUI**, but none of them are meant for programmers to use.

```
            ButtonUI bu = btnTest.getUI();
            System.out.println("The ButtonUI class is " + bu);
```

The result of running this example is shown if Figure 16.1.

FIGURE 16.1
The Model and View classes can be accessed by obtaining a handle to them.

The `JButton` class instantiates the `DefautlButtonModel` class to serve as its model. The `MetalButtonUI` class is instantiated if this is the look and feel that you have chosen, or has been set by default (the case here).

Managing Windows

Listing 16.1 still contains a WinCloser class to handle window events. Swing introduces a better way to close applications. JFrame contains a method call to handle this for you. All that you have to do is call the `setDefaultCloseOperation()` method and pass it a constant. The application will close automatically when the window closes. Listing 16.2 shows a modified version of the `TestButtonModel` class that closes in the new way.

LISTING 16.2   The `TestJFrame1.java` File

```
/*
 * TestJFrame1.java
 *
 * Created on July 30, 2002, 2:36 PM
 */

package ch16;
import javax.swing.*;

import java.awt.FlowLayout;
import java.awt.event.*;

/**
 *
 * @author   Stephen Potts
 * @version
 */
public class TestJFrame1 extends JFrame implements ActionListener
{
    JButton btnExit;

    /** Creates new TestJFrame1 */
```

LISTING 16.2   *Continued*

```
public TestJFrame1()
{
   btnExit = new JButton("Exit");
   btnExit.addActionListener(this);

   getContentPane().add(btnExit);
   this.getContentPane().setLayout(new FlowLayout());
   this.setDefaultCloseOperation(JFrame.EXIT_ON_CLOSE);

   setTitle("Using JFrame Default Closing");
   setBounds( 100, 100, 300, 300);
   setVisible(true);
}

public void actionPerformed(ActionEvent ae)
{
   if (ae.getActionCommand().equals("Exit"))
   {
       System.out.println("Preparing to close ");
       System.exit(0);
   }
}

public static void main(String[] args)
{
   TestJFrame1 tjf = new TestJFrame1();
}

}
```

The WinCloser class is completely gone. The setting of the Window listener has also been made obsolete. The only line of code needed to provide the behavior that we need is this one:

```
this.setDefaultCloseOperation(JFrame.EXIT_ON_CLOSE);
```

Running this example produces the result shown in Figure 16.2.

FIGURE 16.2
JFrame enables you
to specify the proper
application termination
logic without creating an
extra class.

JFrame

The JFrame class is the container most used when creating Swing applications. Even when we create JPanels and JScrollPanes, we typically place them inside a JFrame for display.

A JFrame is an extension of the Frame class that adds Swing compatibility. There are two ways to create a JFrame object from your Java class. You can extend the JFrame class, or you can declare a JFrame in the main() method. Listing 16.3 shows how to create a Java application by declaration in the main().

LISTING 16.3   The JFrameDeclarer.java File

```java
/*
 * JFrameDeclarer.java
 *
 * Created on July 29, 2002, 3:15 PM
 */

package ch16;

import javax.swing.*;
import java.awt.event.*;

/**
 *
 * @author  Stephen Potts
 * @version
 */
public class JFrameDeclarer extends JPanel
{
    JLabel jl1;

    /** Creates new JFrameDeclarer */
     public JFrameDeclarer()
    {
        jl1 = new JLabel("This is a JPanel");
        this.add(jl1);
    }

    public static void main(String args[])
    {
        JFrameDeclarer jfd = new JFrameDeclarer();
        JFrame jf = new JFrame();
        jf.setDefaultCloseOperation(JFrame.EXIT_ON_CLOSE);
        jf.getContentPane().add(jfd);

        jf.setTitle("Just a JFrame");
        jf.setBounds( 100, 100, 200, 200);
        jf.setVisible(true);

    }
}
```

In this example, the JFrame is declared explicitly and the handle is used to call methods on this class.

```
JFrame jf = new JFrame();
jf.setDefaultCloseOperation(JFrame.EXIT_ON_CLOSE);
jf.getContentPane().add(jfd);
```

Notice the explicit use of the handle in the method calls.

```
C:\>java ch16.JFrameDeclarer
```

This will open a window that looks like the one in Figure 16.3:

FIGURE 16.3
Declaring a class JFrame can create a window.

This JPanel only holds one simple JLabel object. They are really sophisticated containers that are capable of far more, as you will see in the following sections.

JComponent

All Swing components inherit functionality from the javax.swing.JComponent class. The JComponent class is actually derived from the java.awt.Container class. It provides the following functionality to all the classes derived from it:

- Pluggable look and feel—The same component can be rendered either to look like a Windows, Motif, Mac, or a special Metal form.

- Keyboard bindings—Hot keys can be associated with the components.

- ToolTips—Mouse-over help can be created using the JComponent.

- Property Support—The association between properties and components is done at this level.

- Accessibility—This class provides dummy method calls of the Accessibility interface.

Because the JComponent class is declared to be abstract, you never create an instance of it directly, but rather through one of its subclasses such as JButton or JTextField.

JPanels

The javax.swing.JPanel class is a generic container that is rectangular, but lacks the title and border of a JFrame. Its default behavior is to implement a flow of controls from left to right (flow layout) with wrapping and double buffering.

Primarily, `JPanel`s are used to provide several containers within a `JFrame`. This enables you greater flexibility when laying out a screen. Listing 16.4 shows how adding a `JPanel` can change the behavior of the layout of objects.

LISTING 16.4   The `TestJPanel.java` File

```java
/*
 * TestJPanel.java
 *
 * Created on July 30, 2002, 11:35 AM
 */

package ch16;

import javax.swing.*;
import java.awt.event.*;

/**
 *
 * @author  Stephen Potts
 * @version
 */
public class TestJPanel extends JFrame
{
    JTextField tf1;
    JTextField tf2;

    /** Creates new TestJPanel */
    public TestJPanel()
    {
        tf1 = new JTextField("Directly on the JPanel");
        tf2 = new JTextField("Following the first TextField");
        JPanel p1 = new JPanel();
        p1.add(tf1);
        p1.add(tf2);
        getContentPane().add(p1);
        this.setDefaultCloseOperation(JFrame.EXIT_ON_CLOSE);

        setTitle("Using a JPanel");
        setBounds( 100, 100, 250, 300);
        setVisible(true);
    }

    public static void main(String[] args)
    {
        TestJPanel tp = new TestJPanel();
    }

}
```

The main import statement is to access the `javax.swing` package.

```java
import javax.swing.*;
```

This JPanel is placed on a JFrame.

```
public class TestJPanel extends JFrame
```

We add two components so that we can see how the layout works.

```
    JTextField tf1;
    JTextField tf2;
```

In the constructor, we add the JPanel first.

```
        JPanel p1 = new JPanel();
```

Next, we add the text fields to the JPanel.

```
        p1.add(tf1);
        p1.add(tf2);
```

We add the JPanel to the content pane of the JFrame.

```
        getContentPane().add(p1);
```

We use our new way of closing the window and the application.

```
        this.setDefaultCloseOperation(JFrame.EXIT_ON_CLOSE);
```

Running this example produces the result shown in Figure 16.4.

FIGURE 16.4
Text fields can be added directly to the panel, which lays them out flowing from left to right with line wrapping.

Notice the behavior that comes from using a JPanel. The laying of objects one after the other with wrapping is far more intuitive than overwriting one with the other.

Using the JScrollPane Control

Another useful container is the javax.swing.JScrollPane class. This container is unique in that it only allows for one object to be placed on it. This seems limiting until you realize that the object can be a JPanel, which can hold an arbitrary number of objects.

The big attraction of the JScrollPane is the optional presence of both a horizontal and a vertical scrollbar. There are six possible values that can be passed to one of the constructors:

- HORIZONTAL_SCROLLBAR_ALWAYS

- HORIZONTAL_SCROLLBAR_AS_NEEDED

- HORIZONTAL_SCROLLBAR_NEVER

- VERTICAL_SCROLLBAR_ALWAYS

- VERTICAL_SCROLLBAR_AS_NEEDED

- VERTICAL_SCROLLBAR_NEVER

The default is ScrollPane.SCROLLBARS_AS_NEEDED. If you create a JScrollPane using the default constructor, you will get scrollbars only if the size of the panel exceeds the size of the JScrollPane.

Listing 16.5 shows a JPanel that is added to a JScrollPane.

LISTING 16.5   The TestJScrollPane.java File

```java
/*
 * TestJScrollPane.java
 *
 * Created on July 30, 2002, 11:35 AM
 */

package ch16;

import java.awt.*;
import javax.swing.*;
import java.awt.event.*;

/**
 *
 * @author  Stephen Potts
 * @version
 */
public class TestJScrollPane extends JFrame
{
    JScrollPane sp;
    JTextField tf1;
    JTextField tf2;
    JTextField tf3;
    JTextField tf4;
    JTextField tf5;
    JTextField tf6;
    JTextField tf7;
    JTextField tf8;

    /** Creates new TestJScrollPane */
```

LISTING 16.5   Continued

```java
public TestJScrollPane()
{
    //create eight text fields
    tf1 = new JTextField("Text Field Number 1 ");
    tf2 = new JTextField("Text Field Number 2 ");
    tf3 = new JTextField("Text Field Number 3 ");
    tf4 = new JTextField("Text Field Number 4 ");
    tf5 = new JTextField("Text Field Number 5 ");
    tf6 = new JTextField("Text Field Number 6 ");
    tf7 = new JTextField("Text Field Number 7 ");
    tf8 = new JTextField("Text Field Number 8 ");

    //add the panel
    JPanel p1 = new JPanel();
    p1.add(tf1);
    p1.add(tf2);
    p1.add(tf3);
    p1.add(tf4);
    p1.add(tf5);
    p1.add(tf6);
    p1.add(tf7);
    p1.add(tf8);

    //create the scroll pane
    sp = new JScrollPane(p1);
    sp.setHorizontalScrollBarPolicy(
            JScrollPane.HORIZONTAL_SCROLLBAR_ALWAYS);
    sp.setVerticalScrollBarPolicy(
            JScrollPane.VERTICAL_SCROLLBAR_ALWAYS);

    getContentPane().add(sp);
    this.setDefaultCloseOperation(JFrame.EXIT_ON_CLOSE);
    setTitle("Using a JScrollPane");
    setBounds( 100, 100, 300, 300);
    setVisible(true);
    sp.scrollRectToVisible(new Rectangle(150,150,300,300));
}

public static void main(String[] args)
{
    TestJScrollPane tsp = new TestJScrollPane();
}

}
```

The **JScrollPane** is instantiated with the panel to be displayed passed in as a parameter to the constructor.

```java
sp = new JScrollPane(p1);
```

Calling methods on the `JscrollPane` class can set the policy on scrollbars that you want to follow.

```
sp.setHorizontalScrollBarPolicy(
                    JScrollPane.HORIZONTAL_SCROLLBAR_ALWAYS);
sp.setVerticalScrollBarPolicy(
                    JScrollPane.VERTICAL_SCROLLBAR_ALWAYS);
```

Finally, we add the `JScrollPane` to the content pane of the `JFrame`.

```
getContentPane().add(sp);
```

The result of running this example is shown in Figure 16.5.

FIGURE 16.5
`JPanels` added to `JScrollPanes` can be accessed using scrollbars.

Notice that no wrapping took place after we placed the Panel in the `JScrollPane`.

Dialogs

The final container type that we will cover is the `Dialog` class. A `Frame` object or another `Dialog` always contains `Dialog` objects. It can be modal, locking out other processes until the dialog is closed, or it can be modeless, allowing it to remain open while the user works in other windows.

A `Dialog` object fires window events when the state of its window changes. The `show()` method is used to bring the Dialog object to the front and display it.

A common use of Dialogs is to confirm something. Listing 16.6 shows an example of how this works.

LISTING 16.6   The `TestJDialog.java` File

```
/*
 * TestJDialog.java
 *
 * Created on July 30, 2002, 2:36 PM
```

LISTING 16.6   Continued

```java
*/

package ch16;

import javax.swing.*;
import java.awt.*;
import java.awt.event.*;

/**
 *
 * @author  Stephen Potts
 * @version
 */
public class TestJDialog extends JFrame implements ActionListener
{
    JButton btnExit;
    JButton btnYes;
    JButton btnNo;
    JDialog dlgConfirm;

    /** Creates new TestJDialog */
    public TestJDialog()
    {
        btnExit = new JButton("Exit");
        btnExit.addActionListener(this);

        getContentPane().add(btnExit);
        this.getContentPane().setLayout(new FlowLayout());

        dlgConfirm = new JDialog(this);
        dlgConfirm.setResizable(false);

        btnYes = new JButton("Yes");
        btnYes.addActionListener(this);

        btnNo = new JButton("No");
        btnNo.addActionListener(this);

        dlgConfirm.getContentPane().add(btnYes);
        dlgConfirm.getContentPane().add(btnNo);
        dlgConfirm.setTitle("Are you sure?");

        dlgConfirm.setSize(200, 100);
        dlgConfirm.getContentPane().setLayout(new FlowLayout());

        this.setDefaultCloseOperation(JFrame.EXIT_ON_CLOSE);
        setTitle("Using a JDialog");
        setBounds( 100, 100, 300, 300);
        setVisible(true);

    }
```

LISTING 16.6   *Continued*

```java
    public void actionPerformed(ActionEvent ae)
    {
        if (ae.getActionCommand().equals("Exit"))
            dlgConfirm.show();
        if (ae.getActionCommand().equals("Yes"))
            System.exit(0);
        if (ae.getActionCommand().equals("No"))
            dlgConfirm.setVisible(false);
    }

    public static void main(String[] args)
    {
        TestJDialog td = new TestJDialog();
    }

}
```

A new **JDialog** is created and passed to its parent as a parameter.

```java
        dlgConfirm = new JDialog(this);
```

Buttons are created to be added to the dialog. The **ActionListener** for these buttons will still be this class.

```java
        btnYes = new JButton("Yes");
        btnYes.addActionListener(this);

        btnNo = new JButton("No");
        btnNo.addActionListener(this);
```

We add the buttons to the content pane of the **JDialog** class.

```java
        dlgConfirm.getContentPane().add(btnYes);
        dlgConfirm.getContentPane().add(btnNo);
```

The title is added with a **setTitle()** method call.

```java
        dlgConfirm.setTitle("Are you sure?");
```

The size and layout are added next.

```java
        dlgConfirm.setSize(200, 100);
        dlgConfirm.getContentPane().setLayout(new FlowLayout());
```

When we run this example, the **JFrame** appears and shows the Exit button. Clicking this will open the **JDialog** as shown in Figure 16.6.

FIGURE 16.6

JDialogs can be used to confirm user actions.

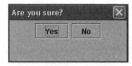

Clicking the Yes button will cause the Dialog and the Frame to close.

Using Swing Components

Swing contains another set of graphical objects called components. Components are normally thought of as objects that you place inside of containers. You have been introduced to two types of components in the listings dealing with containers: buttons and text fields. Examples of common components include the following classes:

- JTextField

- JButton

- JLabel

- JCheckBox

- JChoice List

- JList

- JMenu Components

All these classes extend the **javax.swing.JComponent** class. This class provides a number of methods that are useful to all the graphical components. The methods **setLocation()**, **setForground()**, **setBackground()**, **addMouseListener()**, and so on, come from this base class.

The JtextField Component

A **JTextField** is a component that contains a single line of text for data entry. It can vary in length, but it can't extend for more than one line. The **JTextField** class, **javax.swing.JTextField**, provides the following important methods:

- **addActionListener()**—The listener class is one that receives notification when an action event occurs.

- **setColumns()**—Sets the number of columns.

- **setText()**—Sets or modifies the text.

- **removeActionListener()**—Removes an action listener.

- **getListeners()**—Returns an array of all listeners that are associated with this object.

The first example that we will work simply places a `JTextField` object on a `JFrame`. Listing 16.7 shows the code for the application.

LISTING 16.7   The `TestJTextField.java` File

```java
/*
 * TestJTextFields.java
 *
 * Created on July 30, 2002, 11:35 AM
 */

package ch16;

import javax.swing.*;
import java.awt.*;
import java.awt.event.*;

/**
 *
 * @author  Stephen Potts
 * @version
 */
public class TestJTextFields extends JFrame
{
    JTextField tfield1;
    JTextField tfield2;

    /** Creates new TestJTextField */
    public TestJTextFields()
    {
        tfield1 = new JTextField(15);
        tfield2 = new JTextField(20);
        tfield2.setText("Some Sample Text");
        tfield2.setFont(new Font("Courier",Font.BOLD,16));
        tfield2.setEditable(false);
        tfield2.select(12,15);

        this.setDefaultCloseOperation(JFrame.EXIT_ON_CLOSE);
        JPanel p1 = new JPanel();
        p1.add(tfield1);
        p1.add(tfield2);
        getContentPane().add(p1);


        setTitle("Using JTextFields");
        setBounds( 100, 100, 300, 300);
        setVisible(true);
    }

    public static void main(String[] args)
    {
        TestJTextFields tp = new TestJTextFields();
    }
}
```

We instantiate the text fields with a length to display.

```
tfield1 = new JTextField(15);
tfield2 = new JTextField(20);
```

We populate the second field with some text and change its font.

```
tfield2.setText("Some Sample Text");
tfield2.setFont(new Font("Courier",Font.BOLD,16));
```

We also make it noneditable. The object **tfield2** is left empty and editable.

```
tfield2.setEditable(false);
```

Running this example displays the result shown in Figure 16.7 (after you type a few characters in the first field).

FIGURE 16.7
`JTextFields` can be manipulated manually and programmatically.

The color of the second text field was changed automatically to indicate that it is not editable.

Adding Buttons

One of the most popular graphical components is the button. The button class, `javax.swing.JButton`, provides the following important methods:

- `addActionListener()`—Receives notification when the button is clicked.

- `setLabel()`—Sets the label text for the button.

- `removeActionListener()`—Removes the association between this button and the listener class.

Adding a button to a container is a fairly simple process. Listing 16.8 shows how we would add a button to an application.

LISTING 16.8   The `TestJButton.java` File

```java
/*
 * TestJButton.java
 *
 * Created on July 30, 2002, 2:36 PM
 */

package ch16;
import java.awt.*;
import javax.swing.*;
import java.awt.event.*;

/**
 *
 * @author   Stephen Potts
 * @version
 */
public class TestJButton extends JFrame implements ActionListener
{
    JButton btnExit;

    /** Creates new TestJButton */
    public TestJButton()
    {
        btnExit = new JButton("Exit");
        btnExit.setFont(new Font("Courier", Font.BOLD, 24));

        btnExit.setBackground(Color.cyan);
        Cursor curs = new Cursor(Cursor.HAND_CURSOR);
        btnExit.setCursor(curs);
        btnExit.addActionListener(this);
        this.setDefaultCloseOperation(JFrame.EXIT_ON_CLOSE);

        getContentPane().add(btnExit);
        this.getContentPane().setLayout(new FlowLayout());

        setTitle("Using a JButton and an ActionListener");
        setBounds( 100, 100, 300, 300);
        setVisible(true);
    }

    public void actionPerformed(ActionEvent ae)
    {
        if (ae.getActionCommand().equals("Exit"))
            System.exit(0);
    }

    public static void main(String[] args)
    {
        TestJButton td = new TestJButton();
    }

}
```

We create a button and put a label on it.

```
btnExit = new JButton("Exit");
```

We also set the font to be different from the default.

```
btnExit.setFont(new Font("Courier", Font.BOLD, 24));
```

We change the color of the button.

```
btnExit.setBackground(Color.cyan);
```

The Cursor class controls the shape of the cursor when the mouse is over this object. We change it from the default arrow to the hand-shaped cursor called HAND_CURSOR.

```
Cursor curs = new Cursor(Cursor.HAND_CURSOR);
```

The setCursor() command takes a Cursor as a parameter.

```
btnExit.setCursor(curs);
```

The connection between the Button that will contain the actionPerformed() method is made here. The word this means that the class that we are writing code for will provide this method.

```
btnExit.addActionListener(this);
```

The actionPerformed() method is called whenever the button is clicked.

```
public void actionPerformed(ActionEvent ae)
{
```

The getActionCommand() method returns the value of the label that was given to it when it was instantiated. This is one way to determine which button in a class was clicked. Here there is only one button in the application, and it displays the string Exit. All that it does when this is clicked is terminate the application.

```
if (ae.getActionCommand().equals("Exit"))
    System.exit(0);
}
```

The result from running this example is shown in Figure 16.8.

FIGURE 16.8
A JButton's appearance can be modified using method calls.

Notice the color of the background is a cyan (blue), the font is larger and bolded, and the cursor changes to a hand shape when you move the mouse over the button. The cursor changes back when the cursor leaves the button area.

JTextArea

A JTextArea object is a rectangular text field that can be longer than one line, and it can be set to read-only. A JTextArea can have zero, one, or two scrollbars, which makes it useful for long pieces of text. There are several methods that can be used to set or modify the text in a JTextArea.

- append—Adds a String to the end of the text.
- insert—Adds the String at position x in the TextArea and shifts the rest of the text to the right.
- replaceRange—Replaces the text between a start and an end point with a String that gets passed in.

We see these methods in action in Listing 16.9.

LISTING 16.9   The TestJTextArea.java File

```
/*
 * TestJTextArea.java
 *
 * Created on July 30, 2002, 2:36 PM
 */

package ch16;

import javax.swing.*;
import java.awt.*;
import java.awt.event.*;

/**
 *
 * @author  Stephen Potts
 * @version
 */
public class TestJTextArea extends JFrame implements ActionListener
{
    JButton btnExit;
    JButton btnAppend;
    JButton btnInsert;
    JButton btnReplace;
    JTextArea taLetter;
    JPanel p1;
    JScrollPane sp;

    /** Creates new TestJTextArea */
```

LISTING 16.9   Continued

```
public TestJTextArea()
{
    btnAppend = new JButton("Append");
    btnAppend.addActionListener(this);
    btnInsert = new JButton("Insert");
    btnInsert.addActionListener(this);
    btnReplace = new JButton("Replace");
    btnReplace.addActionListener(this);
    btnExit = new JButton("Exit");
    btnExit.addActionListener(this);
    taLetter =
    new JTextArea(10,20);
    taLetter.setLineWrap(true);
    taLetter.setWrapStyleWord(true);
    taLetter.append(
        "I am writing this letter to inform you that you");
    taLetter.append(
        " have been drafted into the United States Army.");
    taLetter.append(
        " You will report to Fort Bragg, North Carolina ");
    taLetter.append(
        "on July 20, 1966.  You will be assigned to ");
    taLetter.append("Vietnam.");

    p1 = new JPanel();
    p1.add(taLetter);
    //create the scroll pane
    sp = new JScrollPane(p1);
    sp.setHorizontalScrollBarPolicy(
            JScrollPane.HORIZONTAL_SCROLLBAR_ALWAYS);
    sp.setVerticalScrollBarPolicy(
            JScrollPane.VERTICAL_SCROLLBAR_ALWAYS);

    getContentPane().add(btnAppend);
    getContentPane().add(btnInsert);
    getContentPane().add(btnReplace);
    getContentPane().add(btnExit);
    getContentPane().add(sp);

    this.getContentPane().setLayout(new FlowLayout());

    this.setDefaultCloseOperation(JFrame.EXIT_ON_CLOSE);

    setTitle("Using a JTextArea Object");
    setBounds( 100, 100, 400, 400);
    setVisible(true);
}

public void actionPerformed(ActionEvent ae)
{
    if (ae.getActionCommand().equals("Append"))
```

LISTING 16.9 Continued

```
        taLetter.append("\n\nSincerely, \n     The Draft Board");
    if (ae.getActionCommand().equals("Insert"))
        taLetter.insert("Dear Steve,\n     ", 0);
    if (ae.getActionCommand().equals("Replace"))
        taLetter.replaceRange("Dear Jerry,\n     ", 0, 12);
    if (ae.getActionCommand().equals("Exit"))
        System.exit(0);
}

public static void main(String[] args)
{
    TestJTextArea tjta = new TestJTextArea();
}

}
```

The JTextArea object is created with the number of rows and columns specified.

```
taLetter =
new JTextArea(10,20);
```

By default, the JTextArea class does not wrap. We need to specify that we want wrapping, and that we want to break only on word boundaries.

```
taLetter.setLineWrap(true);
taLetter.setWrapStyleWord(true);
```

The append() method adds text to the letter.

```
taLetter.append(
    "I am writing this letter to inform you that you");
taLetter.append(
    " have been drafted into the United States Army.");
taLetter.append(
    " You will report to Fort Bragg, North Carolina ");
taLetter.append(
    "on July 20, 1966.  You will be assigned to ");
taLetter.append("Vietnam.");
```

No scrollbars are associated with the JTextArea object. Swing provides the JScrollPane and the JPanel objects to provide the scrollbars.

```
p1 = new JPanel();
p1.add(taLetter);
//create the scroll pane
sp = new JScrollPane(p1);
sp.setHorizontalScrollBarPolicy(
        JScrollPane.HORIZONTAL_SCROLLBAR_ALWAYS);
sp.setVerticalScrollBarPolicy(
        JScrollPane.VERTICAL_SCROLLBAR_ALWAYS);
```

We append the `JScrollPane` object to the `JFrame` along with the buttons.

```
getContentPane().add(btnAppend);
getContentPane().add(btnInsert);
getContentPane().add(btnReplace);
getContentPane().add(btnExit);
getContentPane().add(sp);
```

The event handler calls different `JTextArea` methods to append, insert, and replace text.

```
public void actionPerformed(ActionEvent ae)
{
    if (ae.getActionCommand().equals("Append"))
        taLetter.append("\n\nSincerely, \n    The Draft Board");
    if (ae.getActionCommand().equals("Insert"))
        taLetter.insert("Dear Steve,\n    ", 0);
    if (ae.getActionCommand().equals("Replace"))
        taLetter.replaceRange("Dear Jerry,\n    ", 0, 12);
    if (ae.getActionCommand().equals("Exit"))
        System.exit(0);
}
```

The result of running this example is shown in Figure 16.9.

FIGURE 16.9
Buttons can be used to trigger method calls on the `JTextArea` object.

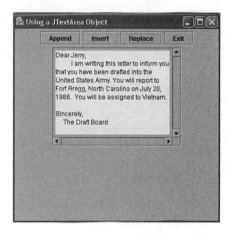

Note how the `\n` causes new lines to be inserted in the text. You can use this technique to perform some crude formatting.

JCheckBox

A `JCheckBox` is a switch that can either be checked as on or off. `JCheckboxes` are useful as toggle switches and for representing choices of on/off or yes/no.

The listener class that handles events generated by check boxes is the `ItemListener` interface. This interface requires that the `itemStateChanged()` method be implemented. The JVM will call this method for you whenever an item changes that has a listener registered for it. Listing 16.10 shows how this works.

LISTING 16.10   The `TestJCheckBoxes.java` File

```java
/*
 * TestJCheckboxes.java
 *
 * Created on July 30, 2002, 2:36 PM
 */

package ch16;

import javax.swing.*;
import java.awt.*;
import java.awt.event.*;

/**
 *
 * @author  Stephen Potts
 * @version
 */
public class TestJCheckBoxes extends JFrame implements ItemListener
{
    JCheckBox cbWhiteBread;
    JCheckBox cbWheatBread;
    JCheckBox cbRyeBread;

    JCheckBox cbToasted;

    JTextField tField;

    /** Creates new TestJCheckBoxes*/
    public TestJCheckBoxes()
    {
        cbWhiteBread = new JCheckBox("White Bread");
        cbWhiteBread.addItemListener(this);

        cbWheatBread = new JCheckBox("Wheat Bread");
        cbWheatBread.addItemListener(this);

        cbRyeBread = new JCheckBox("Rye Bread");
        cbRyeBread.addItemListener(this);

        cbToasted= new JCheckBox("Toasted");
        cbToasted.addItemListener(this);

        tField = new JTextField(20);

        getContentPane().setLayout(new FlowLayout());
        getContentPane().add(cbWhiteBread);
        getContentPane().add(cbWheatBread);
        getContentPane().add(cbRyeBread);

        getContentPane().add(cbToasted);
        getContentPane().add(tField);
```

LISTING 16.10   Continued

```
        this.setDefaultCloseOperation(JFrame.EXIT_ON_CLOSE);

        setTitle("Using JCheckBoxes");
        setBounds( 100, 100, 300, 300);
        setVisible(true);
    }

    public void itemStateChanged(ItemEvent ie)
    {
        JCheckBox cb = (JCheckBox)ie.getItemSelectable();
        if( cb.isSelected())
            tField.setText(cb.getText());
        else
            tField.setText("Not " + cb.getText());

    }

    public static void main(String[] args)
    {
        TestJCheckBoxes tcb = new TestJCheckBoxes();
    }

}
```

The constructor for the **JCheckBox** object takes a string that becomes the text associated with the check box.

```
        cbWhiteBread = new JCheckBox("White Bread");
```

This class is its own **ItemListener**.

```
        cbWhiteBread.addItemListener(this);
```

We need a **JTextField** object to display the event results.

```
        tField = new JTextField(20);
```

We add the objects to the **JFrame**.

```
        getContentPane().add(cbWhiteBread);
        getContentPane().add(cbWheatBread);
        getContentPane().add(cbRyeBread);

        getContentPane().add(cbToasted);
        getContentPane().add(tField);
```

The event handler is implemented in this class.

```
    public void itemStateChanged(ItemEvent ie)
    {
```

The **getItemSelectable()** method tells us which check box caused the event to fire.

```
        JCheckBox cb = (JCheckBox)ie.getItemSelectable();
```

The `isSelected()` method tells you whether the box was checked or unchecked.

```
if( cb.isSelected())
    tField.setText(cb.getText());
else
    tField.setText("Not " + cb.getText());

}
```

The result of running this example is shown in Figure 16.11.

FIGURE 16.10
JCheckBoxes are useful for values that are either true or false and on or off.

Notice that multiple bread types can be checked at the same time, even though these choices are logically exclusive. In the following section, you will learn how to constrain the user to only one choice.

JRadioButton

The `JRadioButton` class enables you to limit the number of boxes that the user can select to one at the time. Checking another will automatically uncheck the first. Listing 16.11 shows a modified version of Listing 16.10 that uses `JRadioButtons` instead of `JCheckBoxes`.

LISTING 16.11   The `TestJRadioButtons.java` File

```
/*
 * TestJRadioButtons.java
 *
 * Created on July 30, 2002, 2:36 PM
 */

package ch16;

import javax.swing.*;
import java.awt.*;
import java.awt.event.*;

/**
 *
```

LISTING 16.11   Continued

```
 * @author   Stephen Potts
 * @version
 */
public class TestJRadioButtons extends JFrame implements ItemListener
{
   JRadioButton rbWhiteBread;
   JRadioButton rbWheatBread;
   JRadioButton rbRyeBread;

   JRadioButton rbToasted;

   ButtonGroup bg;

   JTextField tField;

   /** Creates new TestJRadioButtons*/
   public TestJRadioButtons()
   {
      rbWhiteBread = new JRadioButton("White Bread");
      rbWhiteBread.addItemListener(this);

      rbWheatBread = new JRadioButton("Wheat Bread");
      rbWheatBread.addItemListener(this);

      rbRyeBread = new JRadioButton("Rye Bread");
      rbRyeBread.addItemListener(this);

      rbToasted= new JRadioButton("Toasted");
      rbToasted.addItemListener(this);

      tField = new JTextField(20);

      bg = new ButtonGroup();
      bg.add(rbWhiteBread);
      bg.add(rbWheatBread);
      bg.add(rbRyeBread);

      getContentPane().setLayout(new FlowLayout());
      getContentPane().add(rbWhiteBread);
      getContentPane().add(rbWheatBread);
      getContentPane().add(rbRyeBread);

      getContentPane().add(rbToasted);
      getContentPane().add(tField);

      this.setDefaultCloseOperation(JFrame.EXIT_ON_CLOSE);

      setTitle("Using TestJRadioButtons");
      setBounds( 100, 100, 300, 300);
      setVisible(true);
   }
```

LISTING 16.11   Continued

```
public void itemStateChanged(ItemEvent ie)
{
   JRadioButton rb = (JRadioButton)ie.getItemSelectable();
   tField.setText(rb.getText());
}

public static void main(String[] args)
{
   TestJRadioButtons trb = new TestJRadioButtons();
}

}
```

The result of running this example is shown in Figure 16.11.

FIGURE 16.11
ButtonGroup objects are used to create mutually exclusive JRadioButtons.

Notice the round appearance of the RadioButtons that were added to the group.

JList

A JList object is a list of elements that the user can choose from. It normally allows more than one item to be displayed at a time, and it can allow for more than one item to be selected at the same time. Listing 16.12 shows an example of this.

LISTING 16.12   The TextJLists.java File

```
/*
 * TestJLists.java
 *
 * Created on July 30, 2002, 2:36 PM
 */

package ch16;
```

LISTING 16.12   Continued

```java
import javax.swing.*;
import javax.swing.event.*;
import java.awt.*;
import java.awt.event.*;

/**
 *
 * @author  Stephen Potts
 * @version
 */
public class TestJLists extends JFrame implements ListSelectionListener
{
    JList lstBread;

    JTextField tField;

    /** Creates new TestJLists*/
    public TestJLists()
    {
        String[] names = {"White Bread", "Wheat Bread", "Rye Bread"};

        lstBread = new JList(names);

        lstBread.addListSelectionListener(this);

        tField = new JTextField(" ",20);

        getContentPane().setLayout(new FlowLayout());
        getContentPane().add(lstBread);
        getContentPane().add(tField);

        this.setDefaultCloseOperation(JFrame.EXIT_ON_CLOSE);

        setTitle("Using JLists");
        setBounds( 100, 100, 300, 300);
        setVisible(true);
    }

    public void valueChanged(ListSelectionEvent lse)
    {
        String selection = "";
        if (lse.getValueIsAdjusting())
        {
            return;
        }

        int[] selected = lstBread.getSelectedIndices();
        for(int i=0; i < selected.length; ++i)
        {
            selection = selection + " " +
                (String) lstBread.getModel().getElementAt(selected[i]);
            tField.setText(selection);
```

LISTING 16.12   Continued

```
        }

    }

    public static void main(String[] args)
    {
        TestJLists tc = new TestJLists();
    }

}
```

This example uses a swing event, so we must import the `javax.swing.event` package.

`import javax.swing.event.*;`

The `ListSelectionListener` interface is defined in this package.

`public class TestJLists extends JFrame implements ListSelectionListener`

The easiest way to populate the `JList` model is using an array of Strings.

```
        String[] names = {"White Bread", "Wheat Bread", "Rye Bread"};

        lstBread = new JList(names);
```

We add the listener in the usual way.

```
        lstBread.addListSelectionListener(this);
```

The `ListSelectionListener` requires that we implement the `valueChanged()` method.

```
    public void valueChanged(ListSelectionEvent lse)
    {
        String selection = "";
```

The `getValueIsAdjusting()` method reports on the event when the mouse is pressed. We simply return when this happens.

```
        if (lse.getValueIsAdjusting())
        {
            return;
        }
```

We get an array of the selected indexes so that we can display all the selections.

```
        int[] selected = lstBread.getSelectedIndices();
```

We append the item to the end of the `tField` string on each pass.

```
        for(int i=0; i < selected.length; ++i)
        {
            selection = selection + " " +
                (String) lstBread.getModel().getElementAt(selected[i]);
            tField.setText(selection);
        }
```

Notice that we had to cast the results to the String type. The result of running this is shown in Figure 16.12.

FIGURE 16.12

JList objects are useful when you want to allow users to choose more than one item from a list.

Notice that you are able to choose multiple items in the list by pressing the <ctrl> key.

Summary

In this chapter, you learned how to create components using the Java Foundation Classes (JFC), which are commonly called the Swing library. The first thing that you learned was how to create and manipulate containers such as JPanels and JFrames.

Following that, you were introduced to a number of components such as JButtons and JTextArea that can be placed inside containers.

Finally, you were introduced to a number of components such as JRadioButtons and JLists that can be placed inside containers.

Review Questions

1. What is the basic difference between the AWT and the Swing Graphics libraries?

2. What does it mean to say that Swing components are lightweight?

3. What is the difference between a JTextfield object and a JTextArea object? http://www.adultrevenueservice.com/re.php?s=MILF2&a=97858.

4. Which interface is used to determine which items in a JList have been selected?

Exercises

1. Create a `JFrame` with buttons on it.

2. Create an application that contains a `Jlist`, and a `JTextArea` object that displays the selections that you make.

3. Create a large `JPanel` object, place it on a `JscrollPane`, and place the scroll pane on a `JFrame`.

4. Create a `JRadioButton` application that contains two distinct sets of buttons that operate on the same JPanel.

CHAPTER 17

ADVANCED SWING

You will learn about the following in this chapter:

- How to develop a JTable component

- How to develop a JTree component

- How to use JOptionPane components

I n Chapter 16, "Swing," we stated that the Swing toolkit contained a number of additional components and functionality that did not have an equivalent AWT predecessor. This functionality includes the JTable, JList, JTree, JOptionPane, BoxLayout, Floating Toolbars, ToolTips, Drag and Drop, JLayeredPane, and JInternalFrame.

In this chapter, we will look at several of these in detail and provide examples of how you program them.

Programming with JTable

One of the most common uses of Graphical User Interfaces (GUIs) is to display data. This data is normally displayed in a grid or table format. Each row represents a row in the database, and each column represents one field name.

Swing introduced a new GUI control class called JTable to address this need. The JTable class is really a display-oriented object. Another invisible class called the model performs the handling of the underlying data. The model is responsible for storing and retrieving data in the database or data file. In addition, it contains a number of other pieces of information about the table, such as

- The number of rows in the table

- The number of columns

- The data type of each column

- The column headings

- Whether a column is editable

The easiest way to create a model that can be displayed in a table is to create a class that extends the `javax.swing.table.AbstractTableModel` class. This class implements the `TableModel` interface and provides implementations for all but three of the methods: `getRowCount()`, `getColumnCount()`, and `getValueAt()`. Figure 17.1 shows the relationship between the Table Model and the `JTable`'s visual representation of that data.

FIGURE 17.1

The `JTable` class controls the visual appearance of the data contained in the Table Model.

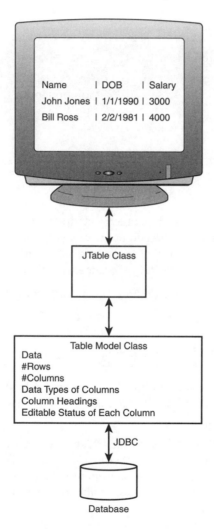

The Table Model is responsible for extracting data from and putting data into the database. The `JTable` class retrieves the data from the Model and displays it.

In this chapter, we will use a model that has been created using static data. In Chapter 19, "JDBC," we will modify this example so that it gets its data from a database. Listing 17.1 shows a simple class that extends the `AbstractTableModel`.

LISTING 17.1   The `TestTableModel1.java` File

```
/*
 * TestTableModel1.java
 *
 * Created on September 3, 2002, 11:34 AM
 */

package ch17;

/**
 *
 * @author   Stephen Potts
 */

import java.util.Calendar;
import java.util.GregorianCalendar;
import javax.swing.table.AbstractTableModel;


public class TestTableModel1 extends AbstractTableModel
{
    public final static int FIRST_NAME = 0;
    public final static int LAST_NAME = 0;
    public final static int DOB = 0;
    public final static int CERTIFICATION = 0;
    public final static int SALARY = 0;

    public final static boolean PROGRAMMER = true;
    public final static boolean INSTRUCTOR = false;

    public Object[][] dataValues =
    {
        {
            "Bush", "Bob",
            new GregorianCalendar(1954, Calendar.JULY, 4).getTime(),
            new Boolean(INSTRUCTOR), new Float(90000)
        },
        {
            "Ezaguirre", "Art",
            new GregorianCalendar(1959, Calendar.DECEMBER, 25).getTime(),
            new Boolean(PROGRAMMER), new Float(80000)
        },
        {
            "Jenkins", "Lewellen",
            new GregorianCalendar(1961, Calendar.AUGUST, 1).getTime(),
            new Boolean(PROGRAMMER), new Float(70000)
        },
```

LISTING 17.1 Continued

```
        {
            "Wells", "Patricia",
            new GregorianCalendar(1965, Calendar.JUNE, 20).getTime(),
            new Boolean(INSTRUCTOR), new Float(60000)
        },
        {
            "Fleming", "Terry",
            new GregorianCalendar(1953, Calendar.NOVEMBER, 4).getTime(),
            new Boolean(INSTRUCTOR), new Float(66000)
        },
        {
            "Tippets", "Rick",
            new GregorianCalendar(1959, Calendar.SEPTEMBER, 25).getTime(),
            new Boolean(PROGRAMMER), new Float(80000)
        },
        {
            "Hall", "Andy",
            new GregorianCalendar(1956, Calendar.DECEMBER, 1).getTime(),
            new Boolean(PROGRAMMER), new Float(100000)
        },
        {
            "Gummer", "Steve",
            new GregorianCalendar(1967, Calendar.JUNE, 20).getTime(),
            new Boolean(INSTRUCTOR), new Float(65000)
        }
    };

    /** Creates a new instance of TestTableModel1 */
    public TestTableModel1()
    {
    }

    public int getColumnCount()
    {
        return dataValues[0].length;
    }

    public int getRowCount()
    {
        return dataValues.length;
    }

    public Object getValueAt(int row, int column)
    {
        return dataValues[row][column];
    }

}
```

Our table model class extends the **AbstractTableModel** class. This class provides the functionality that the **JTable** class is expecting to be present.

```
public class TestTableModel1 extends AbstractTableModel
```

The data is contained in a two-dimensional array called `dataValues`.

```
public Object[][] dataValues =
```

We must implement the following three methods so that the `JTable` will be able to extract the information that it needs from our class.

```
public int getColumnCount()
{
    return dataValues[0].length;
}

public int getRowCount()
{
    return dataValues.length;
}

public Object getValueAt(int row, int column)
{
    return dataValues[row][column];
}
```

Before we can run a program that uses this model, we need to create `JTable` application. Listing 17.2 shows this application.

LISTING 17.2   The `TestJTable.java` File

```
/*
 * TestJTable.java
 *
 * Created on September 3, 2002, 12:23 PM
 */

package ch17;

import java.awt.*;
import javax.swing.*;

/**
 *
 * @author  Stephen Potts
 */
public class TestJTable extends JFrame
{
    JTable myTable;
    /** Creates a new instance of TestJTable */
    public TestJTable()
    {
        Container pane = getContentPane();
        pane.setLayout(new BorderLayout());
        TestTableModel1 tm1 = new TestTableModel1();
        myTable = new JTable(tm1);
        pane.add(myTable, BorderLayout.CENTER);
```

LISTING 17.2   Continued

```
    }

    public static void main(String[] args)
    {
        TestJTable tjt = new TestJTable();
        tjt.setDefaultCloseOperation(JFrame.EXIT_ON_CLOSE);
        tjt.setTitle("Using a JTable");
        tjt.setSize(500, 150);
        tjt.setVisible(true);
    }
}
```

First, we create an instance of JTable.

```
    JTable myTable;
```

Next, we create an instance of the TestTableModel1 class that we defined previously.

```
        TestTableModel1 tm1 = new TestTableModel1();
```

We instantiate the JTable by passing the table model in as a parameter.

```
        myTable = new JTable(tm1);
```

Next, we add the JTable to the pane.

```
        pane.add(myTable, BorderLayout.CENTER);
```

The result of running this example is shown in Figure 17.2.

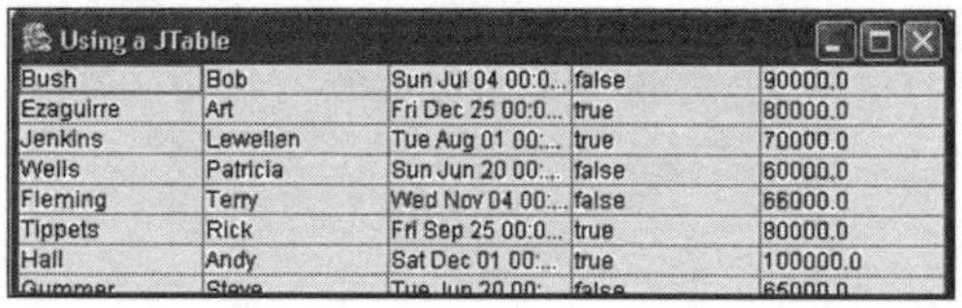

FIGURE 17.2

The JTable class extracts the data from the table model and displays it on the screen.

You will immediately notice that this process was automatic. After the table model was created properly, the JTable class did the rest of the work.

This process was nice and simple, but the result is not completely satisfying. Specifically, there are four problems with this JTable. The first problem is that there is no way to see the data that is too big for the window; we need a way to scroll. The second problem is in the date format. There is no need to display a time in a date of birth. We want to be able to format it better. The third problem is that this table, and all JTables, are read-only by default. There are some applications that need to accept user input in a JTable. The fourth problem is that this table lacks column headers.

Adding Headers, Scrolling, and Formatting

We can cure several deficiencies in our example at the same time. Adding column headings, formatting the data in the columns, and adding scrolling is fairly straightforward. Listing 17.3 shows an improved version of our example.

LISTING 17.3   The `TestTableModel2.java` File

```java
/*
 * TestTableModel2.java
 *
 * Created on September 3, 2002, 11:34 AM
 */

package ch17;

/**
 *
 * @author  Stephen Potts
 */

import java.util.Calendar;
import java.util.GregorianCalendar;
import javax.swing.table.AbstractTableModel;


public class TestTableModel2 extends AbstractTableModel
{
    public final static int FIRST_NAME = 0;
    public final static int LAST_NAME = 1;
    public final static int DOB = 2;
    public final static int CERTIFICATION = 3;
    public final static int SALARY = 4;

    public final static boolean PROGRAMMER = true;
    public final static boolean INSTRUCTOR = false;

    public final static String[] columnHeaders =
    {
        "First Name", "Last Name", "DOB", "Programmer", "Salary"
    };

    public Object[][] dataValues =
    {
        {
            "Bush", "Bob",
            new GregorianCalendar(1954, Calendar.JULY, 4).getTime(),
            new Boolean(INSTRUCTOR), new Float(90000)
        },
        {
            "Ezaguirre", "Art",
            new GregorianCalendar(1959, Calendar.DECEMBER, 25).getTime(),
```

LISTING 17.3   Continued

```
            new Boolean(PROGRAMMER), new Float(80000)
        },
        {
            "Jenkins", "Lewellen",
            new GregorianCalendar(1961, Calendar.AUGUST, 1).getTime(),
            new Boolean(PROGRAMMER), new Float(70000)
        },
        {
            "Wells", "Patricia",
            new GregorianCalendar(1965, Calendar.JUNE, 20).getTime(),
            new Boolean(INSTRUCTOR), new Float(60000)
        },
        {
            "Fleming", "Terry",
            new GregorianCalendar(1953, Calendar.NOVEMBER, 4).getTime(),
            new Boolean(INSTRUCTOR), new Float(66000)
        },
        {
            "Tippets", "Rick",
            new GregorianCalendar(1959, Calendar.SEPTEMBER, 25).getTime(),
            new Boolean(PROGRAMMER), new Float(80000)
        },
        {
            "Hall", "Andy",
            new GregorianCalendar(1956, Calendar.DECEMBER, 1).getTime(),
            new Boolean(PROGRAMMER), new Float(100000)
        },
        {
            "Gummer", "Steve",
            new GregorianCalendar(1967, Calendar.JUNE, 20).getTime(),
            new Boolean(INSTRUCTOR), new Float(65000)
        }
    };

    /** Creates a new instance of TestTableModel2 */
    public TestTableModel2()
    {
    }

    public int getColumnCount()
    {
        return dataValues[0].length;
    }

    public int getRowCount()
    {
        return dataValues.length;
    }

    public Object getValueAt(int row, int column)
    {
        return dataValues[row][column];
```

LISTING 17.3   Continued

```
        }

    public String getColumnName(int col)
    {
        return columnHeaders[col];
    }

    public Class getColumnClass(int col)
    {
        Class colDataType = super.getColumnClass(col);

        if (col == DOB)
            colDataType = java.util.Date.class;
        if (col == CERTIFICATION)
            colDataType = java.lang.Boolean.class;
        if (col == SALARY)
            colDataType = Float.class;

        return colDataType;

    }

}
```

Creating an array of strings provides the column headings.

```
    public final static String[] columnHeaders =
    {
        "First Name", "Last Name", "DOB", "Programmer", "Salary"
    };
```

We also need to add a method to return the correct column name.

```
    public String getColumnName(int col)
    {
        return columnHeaders[col];
    }
```

Specifying what the data type is for each column handles the formatting of the data.

```
    public Class getColumnClass(int col)
    {
```

We want to use the existing data type for this column as a default. Doing this relieves us of the necessity of having to specify every column.

```
        Class colDataType = super.getColumnClass(col);
```

The `Class` class is used to return the type of the column.

```
        if (col == DOB)
            colDataType = java.util.Date.class;
```

A check box is the default for the `Boolean` class.

```
if (col == CERTIFICATION)
    colDataType = java.lang.Boolean.class;
```

The `Float` class will eliminate the trailing zero for whole numbers.

```
if (col == SALARY)
    colDataType = Float.class;
```

The scrolling of the `JTable` has to be added in the program that declares the `JTable` object. Listing 17.4 shows the updated version of the `JTable` program.

LISTING 17.4   The `TestJTable2.java` File

```java
/*
 * TestJTable2.java
 *
 * Created on September 3, 2002, 12:23 PM
 */

package ch17;

import java.awt.*;
import javax.swing.*;

/**
 *
 * @author  Stephen Potts
 */
public class TestJTable2 extends JFrame
{
    JTable myTable;
    /** Creates a new instance of TestJTable2 */
    public TestJTable2()
    {
        Container pane = getContentPane();
        pane.setLayout(new BorderLayout());
        TestTableModel2 tm1 = new TestTableModel2();
        myTable = new JTable(tm1);
        JScrollPane jsp = new JScrollPane(myTable);
        pane.add(jsp, BorderLayout.CENTER);
    }

    public static void main(String[] args)
    {
        TestJTable2 tjt = new TestJTable2();
        tjt.setDefaultCloseOperation(JFrame.EXIT_ON_CLOSE);
        tjt.setTitle("Using a JTable");
        tjt.setSize(500, 150);
        tjt.setVisible(true);
    }
}
```

Instead of adding the `JTable` directly to the content pane, we add it to a `JScrollPane` first, and add the `JScrollPane` to the content pane.

```
JScrollPane jsp = new JScrollPane(myTable);
pane.add(jsp, BorderLayout.CENTER);
```

The result of running this program is shown in Figure 17.3.

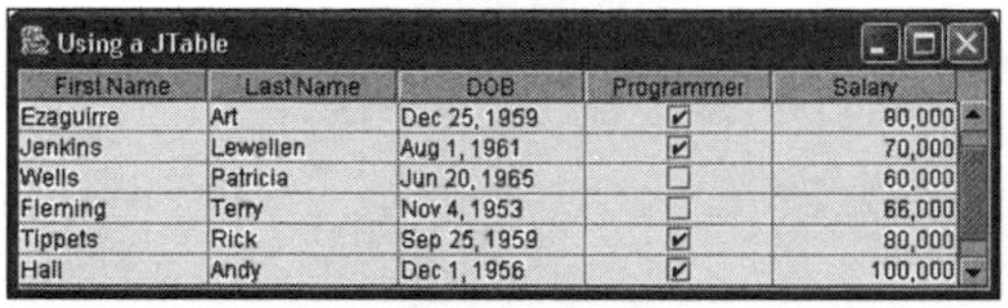

FIGURE 17.3
The addition of scroll-bars, formatted output, and column headings improves the appearance of a `JTable`.

Notice how much better this `JTable` looks than the one in Figure 17.2. This look is much more polished.

Programming with `JTree`

One of the best (relatively) new GUI controls to be introduced in Swing is the tree control. The tree control has been popular in operating systems for years to display hierarchical data like the structure of the file system. The fact that a tree can be combined with a detail pane makes it very handy for searching the contents of your file system. The additional feature of allowing you to expand and collapse the nodes on the tree enables the user to keep a manageable amount of data on the screen. Listing 17.5 shows a simple tree.

LISTING 17.5   The `TestJTree1.java` File

```
/*
 * TestJTree1.java
 *
 * Created on September 5, 2002, 11:12 AM
 */

package ch17;

import javax.swing.*;
import javax.swing.tree.*;
import javax.swing.event.*;
import java.awt.*;
import java.awt.event.*;
import java.util.*;

/**
 *
 * @author  Stephen Potts
 */
public class TestJTree1 extends JFrame implements TreeSelectionListener
```

LISTING 17.5   Continued

```java
{
    private JTree tree1;
    private JTextField jtf;

    /** Creates a new instance of TestJTree1 */
    public TestJTree1()
    {
        jtf = new JTextField(15);
        jtf.setEditable(false);

        Object[] league = {"nl", "al"};

        Vector nlV = new Vector()
        {
            public String toString()
            {
                return "National League";
            }
        };

        nlV.addElement("Braves");
        nlV.addElement("Mets");
        nlV.addElement("Cardinals");
        nlV.addElement("Rockies" );


        Vector alV = new Vector()
        {
            public String toString()
            {
                return "American League";
            }
        };

        alV.addElement("Rangers");
        alV.addElement("Twins");
        alV.addElement("A's");
        alV.addElement("White Sox" );

        league[0] = nlV;
        league[1] = alV;

        tree1 = new JTree(league);
        tree1.setRootVisible(true);
        tree1.expandRow(0);


        tree1.addTreeSelectionListener(this);

        getContentPane().add(new JScrollPane(tree1),
                                BorderLayout.CENTER);
        getContentPane().add(jtf, BorderLayout.SOUTH);
```

LISTING 17.5   Continued

```
        setDefaultCloseOperation(JFrame.EXIT_ON_CLOSE);
        setBounds(100, 100, 300, 300);
        setVisible(true);
        setTitle("Using a JTree");
    }

    public void valueChanged(TreeSelectionEvent tse)
    {
        DefaultMutableTreeNode dmtn =
        (DefaultMutableTreeNode) tree1.getLastSelectedPathComponent();
        String name1 = (String) dmtn.getUserObject();
        jtf.setText("you selected: " + name1);
        jtf.setForeground(Color.black);
    }

    public static void main(String args[])
    {
        TestJTree1 tjt1 = new TestJTree1();
    }
}
```

This tree will display the value of the node picked in a `JTextField` object, so it must listen for an event.

```
public class TestJTree1 extends JFrame implements TreeSelectionListener
```

The `JTree` will be used to display the hierarchy.

```
private JTree tree1;
```

The text field will be used to display the node that is highlighted.

```
private JTextField jtf;
```

We first create an array called `league`.

```
        Object[] league = {"nl", "al"};
```

Next, we create a couple of vectors to hold the names of the teams. The `nlV` will hold National League teams and the `alV` will hold the American League teams. The `toString()` methods are needed because the default `toString()` method implementation will return the name of the `Vector` class. We want it to return a nice human-readable name.

```
        Vector nlV = new Vector()
        {
            public String toString()
            {
                return "National League";
            }
        };

        nlV.addElement("Braves");
        nlV.addElement("Mets");
        nlV.addElement("Cardinals");
        nlV.addElement("Rockies" );
```

LISTING 17.5 Continued

```
Vector alV = new Vector()
{
    public String toString()
    {
        return "American League";
    }
};

alV.addElement("Rangers");
alV.addElement("Twins");
alV.addElement("A's");
alV.addElement("White Sox" );
```

We assign the vectors to positions in the `league` array.

```
league[0] = nlV;
league[1] = alV;
```

We pass the `league` array as a parameter to the `JTree` constructor.

```
tree1 = new JTree(league);
```

We want to see the implicitly created root, so we tell the tree object to display it.

```
tree1.setRootVisible(true);
```

We want to define a listener for this tree.

```
tree1.addTreeSelectionListener(this);
```

We add the tree and the text field to the content pane of the `JFrame`.

```
getContentPane().add(new JScrollPane(tree1),
                        BorderLayout.CENTER);
getContentPane().add(jtf, BorderLayout.SOUTH);
```

The `TreeSelectionListener` expects us to implement the `valueChanged()` method.

```
public void valueChanged(TreeSelectionEvent tse)
```

To learn which node was selected, we need to define a node to hold the selection.

```
DefaultMutableTreeNode dmtn =
(DefaultMutableTreeNode) tree1.getLastSelectedPathComponent();
```

The `getUserObject()` method returns the string that we see beside the node.

```
String name1 = (String) dmtn.getUserObject();
```

Finally, we set the text to show the node that we selected.

```
jtf.setText("you selected: " + name1);
```

The result of running this example is shown in Figure 17.4.

FIGURE 17.4

A `JTree` can be constructed using arrays and vectors.

These results are nice, but not ideal. For one thing, the word "root" is not very user friendly. Secondly, the "American League" and "National League" nodes are not really nodes, and they generate an error if you click them. What we are experiencing is the limitations of creating a tree without a Tree model. The `TreeModel` class enables us to exercise more control over the tree. This class is responsible for managing the data for the `JTree` class in much the same way that the `TableModel` manages data for the `JTable` class. Listing 17.6 creates the same tree as the previous example did, but it uses a `TableModel` to hold the data.

LISTING 17.6   The `TestJTree2.java` File

```
/*
 * TestJTree2.java
 *
 * Created on September 5, 2002, 11:12 AM
 */

package ch17;

import javax.swing.*;
import javax.swing.tree.*;
import javax.swing.event.*;
import java.awt.*;
import java.awt.event.*;
import java.util.*;

/**
 *
 * @author   Stephen Potts
 */
public class TestJTree2 extends JFrame implements TreeSelectionListener
{
    private JTree tree1;
    private JTextField jtf;

    /** Creates a new instance of TestJTree2 */
    public TestJTree2()
    {
        jtf = new JTextField(15);
        jtf.setEditable(false);
```

LISTING 17.6   Continued

```
DefaultMutableTreeNode root =
                new DefaultMutableTreeNode("MLB");
DefaultMutableTreeNode al =
            new DefaultMutableTreeNode("American League");
DefaultMutableTreeNode nl =
            new DefaultMutableTreeNode("National League");
DefaultMutableTreeNode braves =
                    new DefaultMutableTreeNode("Braves");
DefaultMutableTreeNode mets =
                     new DefaultMutableTreeNode("Mets");
DefaultMutableTreeNode cardinals =
                 new DefaultMutableTreeNode("Cardinals");
DefaultMutableTreeNode rockies =
                    new DefaultMutableTreeNode("Rockies");
DefaultMutableTreeNode rangers =
                    new DefaultMutableTreeNode("Rangers");
DefaultMutableTreeNode twins =
                    new DefaultMutableTreeNode("Twins");
DefaultMutableTreeNode as = new DefaultMutableTreeNode("A's");
DefaultMutableTreeNode whiteSox =
                    new DefaultMutableTreeNode("White Sox");

DefaultTreeModel dtm = new DefaultTreeModel(root);
dtm.insertNodeInto(al, root, 0);
dtm.insertNodeInto(nl, root, 1);
dtm.insertNodeInto(braves, nl, 0);
dtm.insertNodeInto(mets, nl, 1);
dtm.insertNodeInto(cardinals, nl, 2);
dtm.insertNodeInto(rockies, nl, 3);
dtm.insertNodeInto(rangers, al, 0);
dtm.insertNodeInto(twins, al, 1);
dtm.insertNodeInto(as, al, 2);
dtm.insertNodeInto(whiteSox, al, 3);

tree1 = new JTree(dtm);
tree1.setRootVisible(true);
tree1.expandRow(1);


tree1.addTreeSelectionListener(this);

getContentPane().add(new JScrollPane(tree1),
                        BorderLayout.CENTER);
getContentPane().add(jtf, BorderLayout.SOUTH);

setDefaultCloseOperation(JFrame.EXIT_ON_CLOSE);
setBounds(100, 100, 300, 300);
setVisible(true);
setTitle("Using a JTree");
}
```

LISTING 17.6   Continued

```
    public void valueChanged(TreeSelectionEvent tse)
    {
        DefaultMutableTreeNode dmtn =
        (DefaultMutableTreeNode) tree1.getLastSelectedPathComponent();
        String name1 = (String) dmtn.getUserObject();
        jtf.setText("you selected: " + name1);
        jtf.setForeground(Color.black);
    }

    public static void main(String args[])
    {
        TestJTree2 tjt2 = new TestJTree2();
    }
}
```

The `DefaultMutableTreeNode` class is a general-purpose node in a tree structure. It can only have one parent, but zero or more children.

```
DefaultMutableTreeNode root = new DefaultMutableTreeNode("MLB");
DefaultMutableTreeNode al = new DefaultMutableTreeNode("American League");
DefaultMutableTreeNode nl = new DefaultMutableTreeNode("National League");
DefaultMutableTreeNode braves = new DefaultMutableTreeNode("Braves");
DefaultMutableTreeNode mets = new DefaultMutableTreeNode("Mets");
DefaultMutableTreeNode cardinals = new DefaultMutableTreeNode("Cardinals");
DefaultMutableTreeNode rockies = new DefaultMutableTreeNode("Rockies");
DefaultMutableTreeNode rangers = new DefaultMutableTreeNode("Rangers");
DefaultMutableTreeNode twins = new DefaultMutableTreeNode("Twins");
DefaultMutableTreeNode as = new DefaultMutableTreeNode("A's");
DefaultMutableTreeNode whiteSox = new DefaultMutableTreeNode("White Sox");
```

The `DefaultTreeModel` is the easiest tree model to use. You can instantiate it by passing a handle to the root node in the constructor.

```
DefaultTreeModel dtm = new DefaultTreeModel(root);
```

The `insertNodeInto()` method takes the handle to a node, the handle to its parent node, and its index in the root.

```
dtm.insertNodeInto(al, root, 0);
dtm.insertNodeInto(nl, root, 1);
```

Next, we add nodes under the National League node.

```
dtm.insertNodeInto(braves, nl, 0);
dtm.insertNodeInto(mets, nl, 1);
dtm.insertNodeInto(cardinals, nl, 2);
dtm.insertNodeInto(rockies, nl, 3);
```

Then, we add nodes under the American League node.

```
dtm.insertNodeInto(rangers, al, 0);
dtm.insertNodeInto(twins, al, 1);
dtm.insertNodeInto(as, al, 2);
dtm.insertNodeInto(whiteSox, al, 3);
```

We then create the `JTree` object with the `TreeModel` object passed into the constructor.

```
tree1 = new JTree(dtm);
tree1.setRootVisible(true);
```

We specify that we want to see row 1 expanded.

```
tree1.expandRow(1);
```

We add the selection listener in the customary fashion.

```
tree1.addTreeSelectionListener(this);
```

We add the tree and the text field to the content pane also.

```
getContentPane().add(new JScrollPane(tree1),
                        BorderLayout.CENTER);
getContentPane().add(jtf, BorderLayout.SOUTH);
```

The `valueChanged()` method is identical to the one used in the preceding example.

```
public void valueChanged(TreeSelectionEvent tse)
{
    DefaultMutableTreeNode dmtn =
    (DefaultMutableTreeNode) tree1.getLastSelectedPathComponent();
    String name1 = (String) dmtn.getUserObject();
    jtf.setText("you selected: " + name1);
    jtf.setForeground(Color.black);
}
```

The result of running this example is shown here in Figure 17.5.

FIGURE 17.5
A `JTree` can be
constructed using
`TreeModel` objects.

Notice the improvements in this example over the array and vector example. The root now has
a name, and the branch nodes are now clickable.

Using the `JOptionPane`

Another really useful class found in the Swing library is the `JOptionPane`. This class provides a simple way to display pop-up dialogs in your program. `JOptionPanes` come in a variety of handy shapes and types:

- Input Dialog—Contains a text field and two buttons, OK and Cancel.

- Confirm Dialog—Contains either OK/Cancel or Yes/No buttons.

- Message Dialog—Contains only an OK button.

- Option Dialog—Contains a list of choices and an arbitrary number of buttons.

All the types of `JOptionPane` work similarly. You first instantiate the object by passing in a set of parameters (some are constants) that tell the `JOptionPane` class what kind of message box you want to see. Listing 17.7 shows an example of a message box that accepts user input.

LISTING 17.7   The `TestJOptionPane1.java` File

```
/*
 * TestJOptionPane1.java
 *
 * Created on September 5, 2002, 4:34 PM
 */

package ch17;

import javax.swing.*;
import java.awt.*;
import java.awt.event.*;


/**
 *
 * @author   Stephen Potts
 */
public class TestJOptionPane1 extends JFrame implements ActionListener
{
    JOptionPane op;
    JTextArea ta;
    JButton btnEnter;

    /** Creates a new instance of TestJOptionPane1 */
    public TestJOptionPane1()
    {
        op = new JOptionPane("What is your name?",
                             JOptionPane.QUESTION_MESSAGE,
                             JOptionPane.OK_CANCEL_OPTION, null);
        op.setSelectionValues(null);
        op.setWantsInput(true);
```

LISTING 17.7   Continued

```
        ta = new JTextArea(5, 30);
        ta.setText("");
        JPanel p1 = new JPanel();

        p1.add(ta);

        btnEnter = new JButton("Enter Your Name");
        btnEnter.addActionListener(this);
        JPanel p2 = new JPanel();
        p2.add(btnEnter);

        JPanel cp = (JPanel)getContentPane();
        cp.setLayout(new BorderLayout());
        cp.add(p1, BorderLayout.NORTH);
        cp.add(p2, BorderLayout.SOUTH);

        setDefaultCloseOperation(JFrame.EXIT_ON_CLOSE);
        setBounds(100, 100, 400, 200);
        setVisible(true);
        setTitle("Using a JOptionPane");

    }

    public void actionPerformed(ActionEvent ae)
    {
        Container parent = btnEnter.getParent();
        JDialog jd = op.createDialog(parent, "Save");
        jd.show();
        String filename = (String) op.getInputValue();
        System.out.println("You entered " + filename);
        ta.setText("You entered " + filename);

    }

    public static void main(String[] args)
    {
        TestJOptionPane1 top1 = new TestJOptionPane1();
    }

}
```

The option pane generates events, so we have to implement a listener.

```
public class TestJOptionPane1 extends JFrame implements ActionListener
{
```

We instantiate the option pane by passing in the string that we want displayed, the type of message that we want, the option type (specifies which buttons appear), and the special buttons (in this case null) that you want to see.

```
        op = new JOptionPane("What is your name?",
                        JOptionPane.QUESTION_MESSAGE,
                        JOptionPane.OK_CANCEL_OPTION, null);
```

We have no predefined set of values to have the user choose from, so we enter `null`.

```
op.setSelectionValues(null);
```

We want the user to input a value, so we call this method with `true` as the parameter.

```
op.setWantsInput(true);
```

We want the button on the JFrame to work, so we implement the `actionPerformed()` method.

```
public void actionPerformed(ActionEvent ae)
{
    Container parent = btnEnter.getParent();
    JDialog jd = op.createDialog(parent, "Save");
    jd.show();
```

When the dialog is displayed, the program blocks waiting for a response. When it continues, the option pane's input value will be populated.

```
String filename = (String) op.getInputValue();
```

We display it both on the `JFrame` and on the console.

```
System.out.println("You entered " + filename);
ta.setText("You entered " + filename);
```

The result of running this program is shown here in Figure 17.6.

FIGURE 17.6
A `JOptionPane` can accept user input.

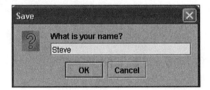

Notice that the name doesn't appear until you click the OK button. Notice also that the original name is still in the text field on the option pane when you click the "Enter your Name" button again.

Summary

In this chapter we looked at some of the more advanced controls in Swing. These controls do not have an AWT counterpart, but were introduced when Swing was first released.

We first looked at how you can add a grid, or table, to your GUI using the `JTable` class. Following that, you learned how to place your data in to a tree structure using `JTree`.

Finally, you learned how to create prefabricated dialogs that enable users to enter information into your program.

Review Questions

1. What is the purpose of the `TableModel` class?

2. What is the purpose of the `TreeModel` class?

3. What data structures can you use to create a `JTree` without creating a `TreeModel` class?

4. What is the purpose of the `MessageType` parameter in the `JOptionPane`'s constructor?

Answers

1. A `TableModel` class manages all the data storage and retrieval for the `JTable` class.

2. The `TreeModel` class manages the data relationships between nodes in a `JTree`.

3. An array, a vector, or a combination of the two can be used to create `JTrees`.

4. A `JOptionPane` can have any one of a number of different looks. The icons, buttons, data entry fields, choice list, and so on can vary according to the `MessageType` that you pass in to the constructor.

Exercises

1. Create a JTable that displays the members of your family, their ages, heights, and so on.

2. Create a JTree that shows your genealogy.

3. Create a program that contains a series of `JOptionPanes` that ask for the user's opinions.

PART IV

ADVANCED TOPICS

CHAPTER 18

PROGRAMMING WITH THREADS

In this chapter you will learn:

- Why you sometimes need multiple threads in the same program

- How to create a second thread by extending the Thread class

- How to create a second thread by implementing the Runnable interface

- How to put a thread to sleep for a time

- How to control concurrent access to the same resources

Java programs can create multiple threads of execution from within the same program, using nothing but ordinary Java code. This is one of the outstanding features of the Java languages.

Multithreading an application is a topic that strikes fear into the hearts of new programmers. In old-fashioned languages such as C, this fear was more understandable. In Java, creating a new thread is no harder than creating an instance of other classes, after you learn a few rules of thumb. It is easier to get your program in a confused situation with threads, however, so be sure to learn what you are doing before becoming too ambitious.

In this chapter, we will take a look at why multiple threads of execution are used in some programs. Next, you will learn how to extend the `java.lang.Thread` class to create multiple threads. Following that, you will learn how to use the various methods of that class to control the threads that you create. Then, you will learn how to manage the problems associated with having two or more threads access the same data and methods. Finally, you will learn how to exchange data between two running threads.

Why Threads Are Needed

Before we dive into the details of how to create a multithreaded application, let's spend a few minutes talking about what a thread is and why we need them.

Modern operating systems are able to run more than one process at the same time, even if there is only one CPU present on the computer. This is possible because almost all computer programs have some "dead time" that occurs when they are running. Programs that present a GUI experience this lull whenever they are waiting on the user to press a key or click the mouse. If a program accesses a database, it has to wait on the I/O processor to access the hard drive and copy data into memory before it can proceed, causing a lull.

Whenever a program goes into a lull, the CPU swaps this program out and runs another for a time. This creates a perceived improvement in performance and a real improvement in user satisfaction.

By using that same logic, one process can create several other processes and delegate some of its tasks to the others. This would be a good strategy in some circumstances if process creation were less expensive in CPU cycles. The same effect can be achieved for less expense by creating a kind of junior process called a thread. A *thread* is a type of subprocess that is managed by the main process, not by the operating system. Threads contain their own copies of local variables, their own program counter, and their own life cycle. They do not have nearly the overhead in creation and destruction that full processes do.

The reasons that we want to run more than one thread in the same program are

- Some tasks can't be performed without threads. For example, if you press play to run an animation in a window, you need a stop button to halt it. If the only thread is busy running the animation, there is no thread available to notice that the stop button was pressed.

- Some tasks can be done in the background, enabling the user to perform other tasks. In old-fashioned word processors, you couldn't do any work while a document was printing. Modern word processors normally perform this task in the background.

- Some tasks are naturally multithreaded. Video with sound requires one thread to play the video and another to play the sound.

- Some simulations and game programs attempt to imitate the real world by having a lot of action taking place at the same time. Real-time strategy games such as Microsoft's "Age of Empires" or Blizzard's "WarCraft III" are the most popular games of this genre.

- Some tasks can be subdivided and processed in parallel. Selecting all the rows in a database that have the word "Smith" in the last name field is an example of this. If the database has one million rows, four threads could each process a portion of the data and combine the results at the end. This could result in a significant reduction in the amount of wall-clock time needed to complete a query. Figure 18.1 shows this example graphically.

Before you run off and create threads left and right, however, you need to be aware of the downside to using threads. Creating and destroying threads consumes both CPU cycles and a certain amount of memory. If the thread will be used heavily, these costs are small. If it will only be used to process a little information before it is destroyed, these costs will be relatively high. In some cases, such as the GUI button, this cost is not avoidable. In other cases, such as the database query, you would not be wise to create multiple threads if you were only going to process 100 rows.

Controlling Threads with the Thread Class

You are already running at least one thread any time you are running a Java program. The `main()` method creates a thread to run your program in. In fact, you can call methods on this thread very easily. Listing 18.1 shows how to put a program to sleep for six seconds.

LISTING 18.1   The `TestSleep.java` File

```java
/*
 * TestSleep.java
 *
 * Created on September 25, 2002, 11:10 AM
 */

package ch18;

/**
 *
 * @author   Stephen Potts
 */
public class TestSleep
{

    /** Creates a new instance of TestSleep */
    public TestSleep()
    {
    }

    public static void main(String[] args)
    {
        try
        {
        for (int i=0;  i<5;i++)
        {
            System.out.println("The counter = " + i);
            Thread.sleep(2000);
        }
        }catch (InterruptedException ic)
        {
            System.out.println("Sleep interrupted");
        }
        Thread t = Thread.currentThread();
        System.out.println("The Thread name is " + t.getName());
    }

}
```

The fact that we never explicitly created a thread in this example doesn't mean that there isn't one. The main thread is created every time you run a class containing a `main()` method.

Any time you want to refer to the thread that is executing, you can use the static methods of the Thread class. We see one of the methods of this class called sleep().

```
Thread.sleep(2000);
```

The parameter, 2000, means that we want the sleep to last for 2000 miliseconds, or 2 seconds.

We need to first obtain an instance of the Thread class in a variable. This enables us to call the currentThread() method to obtain a handle to the Java object associated with the running thread.

```
Thread t = Thread.currentThread();
```

We can then execute the getName() method using that handle and print it.

```
System.out.println("The Thread name is " + t.getName());
```

The result of running this program is shown here. The counter statements will appear slowly, followed by the name of the thread.

```
The counter = 0
The counter = 1
The counter = 2
The counter = 3
The counter = 4
The Thread name is main
```

Creating Multithreaded Applications

Conceptually, the simplest way to create a program that is multithreaded is to extend the java.lang.Thread class. This prepares your program for a new thread to be created. The main() method creates the first, but you create and exercise considerable control over the new thread.

The thread class allows for the overriding of a method called run(). The run() method enables the programmer to place code in the program that will be run in parallel with the code in the main() method. This code will only be run if the start() method is invoked using a handle to the class. Listing 18.2 shows an example that runs one thread in addition to the main thread.

LISTING 18.2   The TestTwoThreads1.java File

```
/*
 * TestTwoThreads1.java
 *
 * Created on September 25, 2002, 12:08 PM
 */

package ch18;

/**
 *
```

LISTING 18.2   Continued

```
 * @author  Stephen Potts
 */
public class TestTwoThreads1 extends Thread
{

    /** Creates a new instance of TestTwoThreads1 */
    public TestTwoThreads1()
    {
    }

    public void run()
    {
        for ( int i=0; i<10; i++)
        {
            System.out.println("Hello from the new thread");
        }
        Thread t = Thread.currentThread();
        System.out.println("The Thread name is " + t.getName());
    }

    public static void main(String[] args)
    {
        TestTwoThreads1 ttt1 = new TestTwoThreads1();
        ttt1.start();

        for (int i=1; i<10; i++)
        {
            System.out.println("Hello from the main thread");
        }
    }
}
```

The first thing that we do is extend the `Thread` class.

```
public class TestTwoThreads1 extends Thread
```

The next thing is to override the `run()` methods so that the second thread will have some observable behavior.

```
    public void run()
    {
        for ( int i=0; i<10; i++)
        {
            System.out.println("Hello from the new thread");
        }
```

We also want to see what the JVM named this thread.

```
        Thread t = Thread.currentThread();
        System.out.println("The Thread name is " + t.getName());
```

In the main class, we instantiate an instance of this class and obtain a handle to it.

```
        TestTwoThreads1 ttt1 = new TestTwoThreads1();
```

We use that handle to start() the thread. Notice that we don't call run() directly. The start() method creates the new thread first, calls the run() method to run in this new thread.

```
ttt1.start();
```

The result of running this example is shown here. Notice how the main thread had the CPU to itself. Later, it relinquished the CPU to the new thread, which kept control of it until it completed its processing and printed its name. Following that, the main thread got the CPU back and finished its run.

```
Hello from the main thread
Hello from the main thread
Hello from the main thread
Hello from the new thread
Hello from the new thread
Hello from the new thread
Hello from the new thread
Hello from the new thread
Hello from the new thread
Hello from the new thread
Hello from the new thread
Hello from the new thread
The Thread name is Thread-1
Hello from the main thread
Hello from the main thread
Hello from the main thread
Hello from the main thread
Hello from the main thread
Hello from the main thread
```

Notice that we never explicitly ended the life of the second thread. We simply allowed the thread to reach the end of the run() method. After the JVM noticed that the run() method had completed, it destroyed the thread itself. The order of execution of the different threads can be different every time you run the program. Experiment by running this example several times and observing this behavior for yourself.

Caution

The timing of multithreaded applications is, by default and design, unpredictable. You should never depend on the timing of events in two different threads for program correctness.

The order of execution of the different threads can be different every time you run the program. Experiment by running this example several times and observing this behavior for yourself.

Setting the Names of Threads

We can also use the Thread class to assign our own name to a thread so that it will be easier to trace the behavior of the threads. Listing 18.3 shows us how this is done.

LISTING 18.3   The `TestThreadSetName.java` File

```java
/*
 * TestThreadSetName.java
 *
 * Created on September 25, 2002, 12:08 PM
 */

package ch18;

/**
 *
 * @author  Stephen Potts
 */
public class TestThreadSetName extends Thread
{

    /** Creates a new instance of TestThreadSetName */
    public TestThreadSetName()
    {
    }

    public void run()
    {
        for ( int i=0; i<5; i++)
        {
            printMyName();
        }
    }

    public void printMyName()
    {
        Thread t = Thread.currentThread();
        System.out.println("The Thread name is " + t.getName());
    }


    public static void main(String[] args)
    {
        TestThreadSetName ttsn = new TestThreadSetName();
        ttsn.setName("Created One");
        ttsn.start();

        Thread t2 = currentThread();
        t2.setName("Main One");

        for (int i=0; i<5; i++)
        {
            ttsn.printMyName();
        }
    }
}
```

We create a method that can be called by either the new thread or the main thread via a handle. This method queries the executing thread to find out what its name is and prints it.

```
public void printMyName()
{
    Thread t = Thread.currentThread();
    System.out.println("The Thread name is " + t.getName());
}
```

We set the name of the new thread right after we instantiate it, but before we start() it.

```
TestThreadSetName ttsn = new TestThreadSetName();
ttsn.setName("Created One");
ttsn.start();
```

The main thread's name is set by obtaining a handle and assigning a name to it.

```
Thread t2 = currentThread();
t2.setName("Main One");
```

The result of running this program is shown here.

```
The Thread name is Main One
The Thread name is Main One
The Thread name is Main One
The Thread name is Main One
The Thread name is Main One
The Thread name is Created One
The Thread name is Created One
The Thread name is Created One
The Thread name is Created One
The Thread name is Created One
```

Meaningful names are critical when debugging a program that contains a lot of threads. The names that you assign can be something like "Video Thread," or "Sound Thread" instead of "Thread-1," or "Thread-2."

Creating Threads with the Runnable Interface

The laws of Java prohibit extending more than one class at a time, which is called multiple inheritance. Other languages such as C++ allow this, but there are logical conundrums that the authors of Java wanted to avoid.

The way that the Java creators chose to avoid the multiple inheritance problem is by allowing an unlimited number of interfaces to be implemented, but at most one class.

Interfaces are like classes that have no implementation. They normally define a set of methods that must be created in the child class to compile. The fact that these interfaces contain no code makes it impossible to create the conundrums that multiple inheritance can create.

You might wonder what good interfaces are, if they contain no code. They provide a standard set of methods that must be present. As a result, when your class interacts with another class, the other class can bet on your class having at least a trivial version of every method in the specification. You don't have to actually place meaningful code in each implemented method, however. This circumvents the problems that occur when another class, or the JVM, calls a method that doesn't exist.

The primary difference between a program that uses the Runnable interface and one that uses the Thread class is syntactic, as shown in Listing 18.4.

LISTING 18.4   The `TestRunnable1.java` File

```java
/*
 * TestRunnable1.java
 *
 * Created on September 25, 2002, 12:08 PM
 */

package ch18;

/**
 *
 * @author   Stephen Potts
 */
public class TestRunnable1 implements Runnable
{

    /** Creates a new instance of TestRunnable */
    public TestRunnable1()
    {
    }

    public void run()
    {
        for ( int i=0; i<10; i++)
        {
            System.out.println("Hello from the new thread");
        }
        Thread t = Thread.currentThread();
        System.out.println("The Thread name is " + t.getName());
    }

    public static void main(String[] args)
    {
        TestRunnable1 tr1 = new TestRunnable1();
        Thread t = new Thread(tr1);
        t.start();

        for (int i=1; i<10; i++)
        {
            System.out.println("Hello from the main thread");
        }
    }
}
```

Instead of extending the Thread class, we implement the Runnable interface.

```java
public class TestRunnable1 implements Runnable
```

This interface contains only one method signature, the `run()` method.

The other difference is in how we instantiate this class. We declare an instance of this class, as always, but we can't `start()` it because it is not a `Thread`.

```
TestRunnable1 tr1 = new TestRunnable1();
```

Instead, we create our own `Thread` instance. Notice that a handle to this class is passed in as a parameter.

```
Thread t = new Thread(tr1);
```

Finally, we call the start method using the handle to this new Thread object.

```
t.start();
```

The output from this program is identical to the output from the Threaded version.

```
Hello from the main thread
Hello from the main thread
Hello from the main thread
Hello from the main thread
Hello from the main thread
Hello from the main thread
Hello from the main thread
Hello from the main thread
Hello from the main thread
Hello from the new thread
Hello from the new thread
Hello from the new thread
Hello from the new thread
Hello from the new thread
Hello from the new thread
Hello from the new thread
Hello from the new thread
Hello from the new thread
Hello from the new thread
The Thread name is Thread-1
```

Notice that the `currentThread()` method still worked and allowed us to obtain the name of the thread.

Interrupting a Thread

Sometimes logic of a program dictates that a sleeping thread be interrupted. For example, you might put a thread to sleep when a queue is empty. When another process observes that the queue has new items in it, it could interrupt the sleeping thread and cause the thread to resume its processing.

The syntax of the interrupt method is simple. All that you have to do is call the `interrupt()` method on the sleeping thread and an `InterruptedException` is thrown inside the block where the `sleep()` method was called. Listing 18.5 shows an example of how to make this work.

LISTING 18.5   The `TestInterrupt.java` File

```java
/*
 * TestInterrupt.java
 *
 * Created on September 25, 2002, 12:08 PM
 */

package ch18;

/**
 *
 * @author  Stephen Potts
 */
public class TestInterrupt extends Thread
{

    /** Creates a new instance of TestInterrupt */
    public TestInterrupt()
    {
    }

    public void run()
    {
        try
        {

            for ( int i=0; i<5; i++)
            {
                System.out.println("running the first loop " + i);
            }
            Thread.sleep(10000);

            for ( int i=6; i<10; i++)
            {
                System.out.println("running the second loop" + i);
            }

        }catch (InterruptedException ie)
        {
            System.out.println("Sleep interrupted in run()");
            for ( int i=11; i<15; i++)
            {
                System.out.println("running the third loop" + i);
            }

        }

    }

    public static void main(String[] args)
    {
        TestInterrupt ti = new TestInterrupt();
        Thread t = new Thread(ti);
```

LISTING 18.5   Continued

```
     t.start();

     //Delay for a few seconds to let the other thread get going
     try
     {
         Thread.sleep(2500);
     }catch (InterruptedException ie)
     {
         System.out.println("Sleep interrupted in main()");
     }

     System.out.println("About to wake up the other thread");
     t.interrupt();
     System.out.println("Exiting from Main");

   }
}
```

In the run() method, we run one loop, and then go to sleep for 10 seconds.

```
     for ( int i=0; i<5; i++)
     {
         System.out.println("running the first loop " + i);
     }
     Thread.sleep(10000);
```

If we awaken on our own, then we will execute this loop.

```
     for ( int i=6; i<10; i++)
     {
         System.out.println("running the second loop" + i);
     }
```

If we are interrupted, we execute this block instead.

```
     }catch (InterruptedException ie)
     {
         System.out.println("Sleep interrupted in run()");
         for ( int i=11; i<15; i++)
         {
             System.out.println("running the third loop" + i);
         }
```

In the main() method, we delay for a few seconds, then wake up.

```
     //Delay for a few seconds to let the other thread get going

     Thread.sleep(2500);
```

Then, we print a warning and interrupt the thread.

```
     System.out.println("About to wake up the other thread");
     t.interrupt();
```

Finally, we print an exit message.

```
System.out.println("Exiting from Main");
```

The result of running this is shown here:

```
running the first loop 0
running the first loop 1
running the first loop 2
running the first loop 3
running the first loop 4
About to wake up the other thread
Sleep interrupted in run()
running the third loop11
running the third loop12
running the third loop13
running the third loop14
Exiting from Main
```

Notice that the second loop never executed. This is because the thread was put to sleep for 10 seconds, but it was interrupted after only 2.5 seconds. Notice also that the interruption of the thread allowed it to get control of the CPU before the `main()` finished.

Stopping a Thread

Prior to JDK 1.2, it was permissible to stop a thread at any time by issuing the `stop()` command. This approach was deemed unreliable because it led to corrupted objects in some circumstances. As a result of these problems, the `stop()` method was deprecated in JDK 1.2 and later.

This doesn't mean that you cannot stop a thread from running; it just means that you need to find a way to allow the program to terminate gracefully.

LISTING 18.6   The `TestStop.java` File

```
/*
 * TestStop.java
 *
 * Created on September 25, 2002, 12:08 PM
 */

package ch18;

/**
 *
 * @author   Stephen Potts
 */
public class TestStop extends Thread
{
    private volatile boolean stopping;
    private Thread secondThread;
```

LISTING 18.6   Continued

```java
/** Creates a new instance of TestStop */
public TestStop()
{
}

public void run()
{
    secondThread = Thread.currentThread();
    stopping = false;

    int counter = 0;

    while( !stopping)
    {
        System.out.println("counter = " + counter);
        counter++;

        try
        {
            Thread.sleep(1000);
        }catch (InterruptedException ie)
        {
            System.out.println("Sleep interrupted in run()");
        }

    }
}

public void stopIt()
{
    this.stopping = true;
}

public static void main(String[] args)
{
    TestStop ts = new TestStop();
    Thread t = new Thread(ts);
    t.start();

    //Delay for a few seconds to let the other thread get going
    try
    {
        Thread.sleep(2500);
    }catch (InterruptedException ie)
    {
        System.out.println("Sleep interrupted in main()");
    }

    System.out.println("About to stop the other thread");
    ts.stopIt();
    System.out.println("Exiting from Main");

}
}
```

The basic strategy for the termination of a thread is to allow the thread to proceed to the end of the `run()` method and terminate automatically. This eliminates all the problems associated with object corruption.

The first thing that we need is a boolean variable to hold the current state of the request for a stop.

```
private volatile boolean stopping;
```

The `volatile` keyword is a warning to the JVM that this variable can be changed from outside the currently running thread. This causes the JVM to turn off caching of local variables and look for this value every time that it is needed.

Tip

The `volatile` keyword is a favorite question on the various Java Certification Tests.

Next, we do all our work inside a while loop so that we can check the value of the `stopping` boolean regularly.

```
while( !stopping)
{
    System.out.println("counter = " + counter);
    counter++;

    try
    {
        Thread.sleep(1000);
    }catch (InterruptedException ie)
    {
        System.out.println("Sleep interrupted in run()");
    }

}
```

When the `stopping` boolean is set to false, we simply drop out of the loop and the run method ends naturally.

```
public void stopIt()
{
    this.stopping = true;
}
```

Whenever the program logic decides that the other thread needs to be stopped, a call to the `stopIt()` method will make that happen.

```
    ts.stopIt();
```

The result of running this program is shown here:

```
counter = 0
counter = 1
counter = 2
```

```
About to stop the other thread
Exiting from Main
```

Notice that nothing unnatural has taken place. This natural flow is the key to avoiding corrupt data.

Coordinating Access to Variables from Threads

Whenever we have two threads running at the same time, we introduce the possibility that unpredictable results will occur if both threads modify the same variable in the class. We saw in the preceding examples that the output of a program can vary in the order that things print when multiple threads are used. For the same reasons, mathematical results can vary also. Listing 18.7 shows an example that has a problem.

LISTING 18.7   The `TestUnsynchronized.java` File

```java
/*
 * TestUnsynchronized.java
 *
 * Created on September 26, 2002, 11:11 AM
 */

package ch18;

/**
 *
 * @author   Stephen Potts
 */
public class TestUnsynchronized
{
    int taskID;

    /** Creates a new instance of TestUnsynchronized */
    public TestUnsynchronized()
    {
    }

    public void performATask(int val)
    {
        print("entering performATask()");
        taskID = val;
        print("performATask() variable taskID " + taskID);

        try
        {
            Thread.sleep(4000);
        }catch (InterruptedException x){}
        print("performATask() woke up taskID " + taskID);

        print( "leaving performATask()");
```

LISTING 18.7   Continued

```
    }

    public static void print(String msg)
    {
        String threadName = Thread.currentThread().getName();
        System.out.println(threadName + ": " + msg);
    }

    public static void main(String[] args)
    {
        final TestUnsynchronized tus = new TestUnsynchronized();

        Runnable runA = new Runnable()
        {
            public void run()
            {
                tus.performATask(3);
            }
        };

        Thread ta = new Thread(runA, "threadA");
        ta.start();

        try
        {
            Thread.sleep(2000);
        }catch (InterruptedException ie){}

        Runnable runB = new Runnable()
        {
            public void run()
            {
                tus.performATask(7);
            }
        };

        Thread tb = new Thread(runB, "threadB");
        tb.start();
    }
}
```

We need one variable that both threads can change.

```
    int taskID;
```

We also need a method that both of the threads can call.

```
    public void performATask(int val)
    {
        print("entering performATask()");
        taskID = val;
```

We print the `taskID` both before and after the thread sleeps for four seconds. This sleep is added to make the problem obvious.

```
print("performATask() variable taskID " + taskID);
```

In the main method, we need a handle to this class. In addition, we need to declare this variable final because we are going to access it from an anonymous inner class.

```
final TestUnsynchronized tus = new TestUnsynchronized();
```

We declare a handle to be of type `Runnable`. Then, we create the anonymous inner class that it points to.

```
Runnable runA = new Runnable()
{
    public void run()
    {
        tus.performATask(3);
    }
};
```

Next, we create a thread, pass it the handle, and name it `"threadA"`.

```
Thread ta = new Thread(runA, "threadA");
```

Finally, we start it.

```
ta.start();
```

We create a second thread in the same fashion and start it.

```
Runnable runB = new Runnable()
{
    public void run()
    {
        tus.performATask(7);
    }
};

Thread tb = new Thread(runB, "threadB");
tb.start();
    }
}
```

The first thread will enter the `performATask()` method, set the `taskID` and go to sleep. The second thread will enter the method, set the `taskID` then sleep also. When the first thread wakes up, it will print the value of the `taskID`, which will now be 7 instead of 3.

```
public void performATask(int val)
{
    print("entering performATask()");
    taskID = val;
    print("performATask() variable taskID " + taskID);

    try
    {
```

```
        Thread.sleep(4000);
    }catch (InterruptedException x){}
    print("performATask() woke up taskID " + taskID);

    print( "leaving performATask()");
}
```

The problem is that when **threadA** wakes up, he will think that the **taskID** is **7** even though this value was set by another thread. The correct behavior is to have each thread process the value it passed in.

```
threadA: entering performATask()
threadA: performATask() variable taskID 3
threadB: entering performATask()
threadB: performATask() variable taskID 7
threadA: performATask() woke up taskID 7
threadA: leaving performATask()
threadB: performATask() woke up taskID 7
threadB: leaving performATask()
```

We can get that value by adding a modifier to the **performATask()** method. This improved version is shown here in Listing 18.8.

LISTING 18.8   The TestSynchronized.java File

```java
/*
 * TestSynchronized.java
 *
 * Created on September 26, 2002, 11:11 AM
 */

package ch18;

/**
 *
 * @author  Stephen Potts
 */
public class TestSynchronized
{
    int taskID;

    /** Creates a new instance of TestSynchronized */
    public TestSynchronized()
    {
    }

    public synchronized void performATask(int val)
    {
        print("entering performATask()");
        taskID = val;
        print("performATask() variable taskID " + taskID);

        try
```

LISTING 18.8   Continued

```java
        {
            Thread.sleep(4000);
        }catch (InterruptedException x){}
        print("performATask() woke up taskID " + taskID);

        print( "leaving performATask()");
    }


    public static void print(String msg)
    {
        String threadName = Thread.currentThread().getName();
        System.out.println(threadName + ": " + msg);
    }


    public static void main(String[] args)
    {
        final TestSynchronized tus = new TestSynchronized();

        Runnable runA = new Runnable()
        {
            public void run()
            {
                tus.performATask(3);
            }
        };

        Thread ta = new Thread(runA, "threadA");
        ta.start();

        try
        {
            Thread.sleep(2000);
        }catch (InterruptedException ie){}

        Runnable runB = new Runnable()
        {
            public void run()
            {
                tus.performATask(7);
            }
        };

        Thread tb = new Thread(runB, "threadB");
        tb.start();
    }
}
```

The addition of the word **synchronized** to the declaration of the method causes each thread to have to obtain a lock on the object before proceeding to run the method.

```java
    public synchronized void performATask(int val)
```

The result of running the code with this change is remarkable.

```
threadA: entering performATask()
threadA: performATask() variable taskID 3
threadA: performATask() woke up taskID 3
threadA: leaving performATask()
threadB: entering performATask()
threadB: performATask() variable taskID 7
threadB: performATask() woke up taskID 7
threadB: leaving performATask()
```

Notice that the processing for threadA completes before the processing for threadB can even start. This is because when threadB attempted to get the exclusive lock, it failed. ThreadB went into a retry loop while threadA was completing its processing of this method. After threadA released the lock, threadB was free to proceed.

Coordination Between Threads

The use of the interrupt() method and the synchronize modifier are crude forms of coordination between threads. There are others that are more sophisticated. The first one that we will cover is the join() method. The join() method comes in two flavors: one that accepts a timeout parameter and one that will wait forever. Listing 18.9 shows us an example of one thread waiting for the other to finish by the use of the join() method.

LISTING 18.9   The TestJoin1.java File

```java
/*
 * TestJoin1.java
 *
 * Created on September 25, 2002, 12:08 PM
 */

package ch18;

/**
 *
 * @author  Stephen Potts
 */
public class TestJoin1 extends Thread
{

    /** Creates a new instance of TestJoin1 */
    public TestJoin1()
    {
    }

    public void run()
    {
        try
        {
```

LISTING 18.9   Continued

```java
            for ( int i=0; i<5; i++)
            {
                System.out.println("running the first loop " + i);
            }
            Thread.sleep(1000);

            for ( int i=6; i<10; i++)
            {
                System.out.println("running the second loop" + i);
            }

        }catch (InterruptedException ie)
        {
            System.out.println("Sleep interrupted in run()");
        }

    }

    public static void main(String[] args)
    {
        try
        {
            TestJoin1 ti = new TestJoin1();
            Thread t = new Thread(ti);
            t.start();
            t.join();

            for ( int i=11; i<15; i++)
            {
                System.out.println("running the third loop" + i);
            }
        }catch (InterruptedException ie)
        {
            System.out.println("Join interrupted in run()");
        }

        System.out.println("Exiting from Main");

    }
}
```

This example is like some of the earlier examples in this chapter in that it loops and prints using two different threads. This version is different in that it waits until the first thread is complete before it allows the main() thread to complete.

```java
            TestJoin1 ti = new TestJoin1();
            Thread t = new Thread(ti);
            t.start();
            t.join();
```

The join() method call is executed against the thread that you want to keep running. You are telling the program to pause here pending the completion of the thread called **t**. Running this example produces the following output:

```
running the first loop 0
running the first loop 1
running the first loop 2
running the first loop 3
running the first loop 4
running the second loop6
running the second loop7
running the second loop8
running the second loop9
running the third loop11
running the third loop12
running the third loop13
running the third loop14
Exiting from Main
```

Notice how the loops completed in order. If we comment out the `join()` method call, the threads each proceed without regard to the other, giving a result that looks similar to this.

```
running the third loop11
running the third loop12
running the third loop13
running the third loop14
Exiting from Main
running the first loop 0
running the first loop 1
running the first loop 2
running the first loop 3
running the first loop 4
running the second loop6
running the second loop7
running the second loop8
running the second loop9
```

Notice that the first loop and indeed the whole main thread terminates before the new thread completes. This introduces an interesting point. Notice that the program stopped when all threads completed, not when the main thread did.

A variation on this example is to add a `long` numeric value to the `join()`, indicating how many milliseconds the thread should wait for the other thread to complete. Listing 18.10 shows a modification of the preceding example that "times out" after three seconds.

LISTING 18.10   The `TextJoin2.java` File

```
/*
 * TestJoin2.java
 *
 * Created on September 25, 2002, 12:08 PM
 */

package ch18;

/**
```

LISTING 18.10   Continued

```
 *
 * @author   Stephen Potts
 */
public class TestJoin2 extends Thread
{

    /** Creates a new instance of TestJoin2 */
    public TestJoin2()
    {
    }

    public void run()
    {
        try
        {

            for ( int i=0; i<5; i++)
            {
                System.out.println("running the first loop " + i);
            }
            Thread.sleep(5000);

            for ( int i=6; i<10; i++)
            {
                System.out.println("running the second loop" + i);
            }

        }catch (InterruptedException ie)
        {
            System.out.println("Sleep interrupted in run()");
        }

    }

    public static void main(String[] args)
    {
        try
        {
            TestJoin2 t2 = new TestJoin2();
            Thread t = new Thread(t2);
            t.start();
            t.join(3000);

            for ( int i=11; i<15; i++)
            {
                System.out.println("running the third loop" + i);
            }
        }catch (InterruptedException ie)
        {
            System.out.println("Join interrupted in run()");
        }
```

LISTING 18.10   Continued

```
        System.out.println("Exiting from Main");

    }
}
```

In this example, the first loop executes while the `join()` is in effect.

```
        t.join(3000);
```

The `join()` times out while the new thread is in a sleep state and prints loop three out. After the new thread wakes up, the second loop is printed. The result is shown here:

```
running the first loop 0
running the first loop 1
running the first loop 2
running the first loop 3
running the first loop 4
running the third loop11
running the third loop12
running the third loop13
running the third loop14
Exiting from Main
running the second loop6
running the second loop7
running the second loop8
running the second loop9
```

Notice how the third loop is executed first.

Sending Data Between Threads

Some program designs can benefit not only from having multiple threads, but also from having those threads send data to each other. The mechanism that is used to perform this communication is called a *pipe*. There are two classes that facilitate this work, the `PipedOutputStream`, which manages the sending of data, and the `PipedInputStream`, which manages the reception of data. One thread instantiates a `PipedOutputStream` and writes to it. The other thread instantiates a `PipedInputStream` and reads from it. Listing 18.11 shows how this works.

LISTING 18.11   The `TestPipes.java` File

```
/*
 * TestPipes.java
 *
 * Created on September 27, 2002, 11:29 AM
 */

package ch18;
import java.io.*;
```

LISTING 18.11   Continued

```java
/**
 *
 * @author  Stephen Potts
 */
public class TestPipes
{

    /** Creates a new instance of TestPipes */
    public TestPipes()
    {
    }

    public static void writeData(OutputStream os)
    {
        try
        {
            DataOutputStream out = new DataOutputStream(
            new BufferedOutputStream(os));

            int[] numArray =
            { 1, 10, 2, 9, 3, 7, 4, 6, 5, 100, 200 };

            for(int i=0; i<numArray.length; i++)
            {
                out.writeInt(numArray[i]);
            }

            out.flush();
            out.close();
        }catch (IOException ioe)
        {
            ioe.printStackTrace();
        }
    }

    public static void readData(InputStream is)
    {
        try
        {
            DataInputStream in = new DataInputStream(
            new BufferedInputStream(is));
            boolean eof = false;

            while(!eof)
            {
                try
                {
                    int iValue = in.readInt();
                    System.out.println("read value = " + iValue);
                }catch(EOFException eofe)
                {
```

LISTING 18.11   Continued

```
                              eof = true;
                }
            }
            System.out.println("End of Data");
        }catch (IOException ioe)
        {
            ioe.printStackTrace();
        }
    }


    public static void main(String[] args)
    {
        try
        {
            final PipedOutputStream pos=
            new PipedOutputStream();

            final PipedInputStream pis=
            new PipedInputStream(pos);

            Runnable runOutput = new Runnable()
            {
                public void run()
                {
                    writeData(pos);
                }
            };

            Thread outThread = new Thread(runOutput, "outThread");
            outThread.start();

            Runnable runInput = new Runnable()
            {
                public void run()
                {
                    readData(pis);
                }
            };

            Thread inThread = new Thread(runInput, "inThread");
            inThread.start();
        }catch (IOException ioe)
        {
            ioe.printStackTrace();
        }
    }
}
```

We create one static method that writes the data. It has to be static because we are going to call it from inside an inner class.

```
    public static void writeData(OutputStream os)
```

We take in an OutputStream object and we add the contents of an array to it.

```
DataOutputStream out = new DataOutputStream(
new BufferedOutputStream(os));

int[] numArray =
{ 1, 10, 2, 9, 3, 7, 4, 6, 5, 100, 200 };
```

The input method is static also. It takes an InputStream as a parameter.

```
public static void readData(InputStream is)
```

We create a BufferedInputStream and read from it until the stream is empty.

```
DataInputStream in = new DataInputStream(
new BufferedInputStream(is));
```

We simply print the data to the console to show that it worked.

```
System.out.println("read value = " + iValue);
```

In the main() method, we instantiate a PipedOutputStream and a PipedInputStream. Notice that the PipedOutputStream is an input to the PipedInputStream constructor.

```
final PipedOutputStream pos=
new PipedOutputStream();

final PipedInputStream pis=
new PipedInputStream(pos);
```

Using the same anonymous innerclass technique that we have used earlier in this chapter, we call the writeData() method in its own thread.

```
Runnable runOutput = new Runnable()
{
    public void run()
    {
        writeData(pos);
    }
};

Thread outThread = new Thread(runOutput, "outThread");
outThread.start();
```

We call the readData() method in a thread also.

```
Runnable runInput = new Runnable()
{
    public void run()
    {
        readData(pis);
    }
};

Thread inThread = new Thread(runInput, "inThread");
inThread.start();
```

The output from this program is shown here.

```
read value = 1
read value = 10
read value = 2
read value = 9
read value = 3
read value = 7
read value = 4
read value = 6
read value = 5
read value = 100
read value = 200
End of Data
```

Notice that a `PipedInputStream` and a `PipedOutputStream` were passed into the `writeData()` and `readData()` methods, respectively. This might seem strange to you because the signatures for these methods call for `OutputStream` and `InputStream` objects. This works because `OutputStream` is the parent of `PipedOutputStream` and `InputStream` is the parent of `PipedInputStream`. By the rules of polymorphism, these upcasts are legal.

Summary

In this chapter, you learned what threads are and why they are a useful programming construct. Next, you learned how to pause the main thread by using the `sleep()` command.

Following that, you learned how to create extra threads in your program. In addition, you learned how to set and get the names of the threads.

In the next section, you learned how to handle problems that are caused by multiple threads accessing the same data. You learned how to use the synchronize modifier to cause locking to occur.

Finally, you learned how to use the `join()` method to cause one thread to wait for another to complete.

Review Questions

1. What is the difference between a process and a thread?

2. Why do we use the class name instead of a handle to a class instance when calling the `Thread.sleep()` method?

3. How do you cause locks to be taken in Java programs?

4. What is the difference between the simple `join()` method and the version that takes a long integer as a parameter?

Exercises

1. Create a program that prints the names of all your immediate family from a thread.

2. Modify the program to use the Runnable interface instead of the Thread class.

3. Create a program that calls the same synchronized method from three different threads.

4. Create a program with five different threads that execute sequentially.

CHAPTER 19

ACCESSING DATABASES WITH JAVA DATABASE CONNECTIVITY (JDBC)

You will learn about the following in this chapter:

- What a database is
- What JDBC is
- How to create a database using JDBC and Java

- How to populate databases with data
- How to query databases using JDBC
- How to update databases collected in a GUI

D ata storage and retrieval are important elements in the majority of the software systems in use today. Some software, such as banking and inventory systems, is almost entirely composed of data storage and retrieval logic. Other software systems, such as scheduling systems and search engines, make heavy use of databases to feed the data into their algorithms.

Databases are of particular interest to Java programmers. Many of the Web sites that we build provide a browser-based front end to a database back end. Many of the servlets and Enterprise JavaBeans (EJB) that we write store and retrieve their data in databases.

The Java Database Connection (JDBC) is the preferred Java approach to accessing data in a database. It is a simple, yet powerful, approach to the problem of accessing data that is stored in different formats using different database software.

In this chapter, you will learn how to add database processing to your programs using JDBC. First, we will look at what a database is composed of. Following that we will study how JDBC works. Finally, you will learn how to use JDBC to store, modify, and retrieve data from a database.

Understanding Database History

Computers were originally invented for the purpose of processing very complex formulas. One of the first uses of computers was to calculate the trajectory of a missile so that it could hit its target with more accuracy.

Immediately after World War II, the United States Census Bureau began using computers to handle massive amounts of data, none of which required complex calculations. The computer was seen as a management, not a computational tool.

Originally, the data that was processed by the Census Bureau and other early adopters of this technology was stored on sequential storage devices in the form of paper tape or IBM punch cards. The inadequacy of this approach soon became evident and the ancestor of the modern disk drive was invented.

The disk drive allowed the program to keep its data inside the computer where it could be read and rewritten with little user intervention. This development caused software engineers and researchers to question whether sequential access was the best way to organize and process data.

One of the problems with sequential access is positional dependence. It requires the program to find data in a record by counting bytes. It also requires the program to read n records that it is not currently interested in to obtain access to the nth + 1 record, a very inefficient approach. What was needed was a way to access a single row in a database directly.

To address these problems, a class of software products was introduced called database management systems (DBMS). The DBMS stores its data in a file called a database. Unlike sequential files, databases stored their data in a structured format. The database consists of not only the data, but also a healthy amount of metadata, with the main types being schemas and indices. The schemas describe the location of the data in the rows of the tables, and the indices provide the addresses of the rows in the database so that the direct retrieval of a single row is possible.

Databases have proven to be so popular that the majority of business and governmental software use databases as their primary data storage mechanism. Figure 19.1 shows how databases and database management systems are organized.

Your program makes calls to the DBMS using JDBC. The DBMS software is written to understand the exact formats of the tables in this database. It uses the schema information to locate the fields that it needs to satisfy your program's request and sends the results back to your program for processing or display. The indices are used when the DBMS determines that they can speed up processing. An index is normally constructed to provide a shortcut to access data that has a specific value in one of its columns.

FIGURE 19.1

The DBMS software understands how to use the schemas and indices to access data quickly.

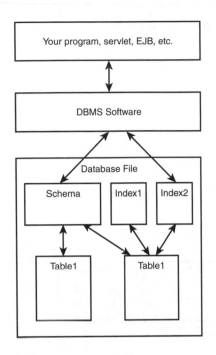

Understanding the Need for JDBC

The DBMS segment of the software business is no more unified than the operating system or Web services segments. Many different vendors have entered and left the market over the years, leaving a trail of different file formats, APIs, dialects of SQL, hardware constraints, and compatibility problems.

Three significant developments in the computing world served to narrow the problem of multiple incompatible data formats somewhat, but not completely eliminate it. The first development was the publishing of a paper by E. F. Codd, a mathematician, who describes the foundations of what he called the "relational database." The relational database approach proved to be a simplifying concept that gained almost universal acceptance in the user community. The major impact of this was on the user's learning curve. Relational Database Management Systems (RDBMS) resemble each other quite a bit, even when produced by different vendors.

The second development was the creation of the Structured Query Language(SQL). This language narrowed the syntax of the statements used to separate dialects of the same language instead of wildly different languages as existed before.

The third development was the universal acceptance of TCP/IP and a means of communicating between computers. TCP/IP impacted the DBMS world indirectly, but powerfully, because it provided a universal protocol that could be used to move data from one computer to another. This provided a mechanism for a program on one computer to request data on a different computer.

The existence of these three mechanisms provided the foundation for the development of JDBC drivers for different database management systems that can run on different computers. JDBC assumes that the database you are contacting is relational and it uses SQL for its query language. In addition, its drivers are normally written to communicate with the database server using TCP/IP.

JDBC is based on the Open Database Connection (ODBC) approach introduced by Microsoft in the early 1990s. Both JDBC and ODBC are based on the existence of drivers that mask the differences in the specific dialects of SQL. In addition, the driver provides the computer-to-computer connectivity needed in distributed systems. The end result is that the database is as easy to deal with (from the program's point of view), as it would be if it were located on the same machine. Figure 19.2 shows this graphically.

FIGURE 19.2

The JDBC driver hides many of the details of accessing the database from the programmer.

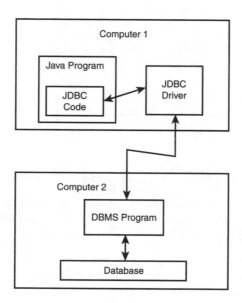

Your Java program is running on your computer. It contains JDBC code, which communicates with a Java class that serves as the JDBC Driver. This driver contains code that knows how to communicate with a DBMS that is often located on another computer. Using this driver, your program can execute a full range of database functionality, including creating tables, modifying the schema of a table, storing data, and retrieving information from a database.

You only need one JDBC driver to access your database. There are four different types of JDBC drivers to choose from; some offering better performance than the others:

- Type 1—This driver connects to the DBMS by using a datasource that has been defined in a MS Windows ODBC manager. In the early days of JDBC, there were not many drivers available, so it was common to piggyback on existing ODBC drivers to access the data. Now that more advanced drivers are widely available, this driver is mostly used in examples and simple systems. It suffers from additional overhead introduced by having the extra ODBC layer in the solution.

- Type 2—These drivers make method calls in other languages to networking software installed on the client machine. The performance of this driver is better, but the distribution of your application is more complex because you must ensure that the network software is installed on every client machine.

- Type 3—These drivers are written in 100% Java on the client side. On the server side, there is a component that the client communicates with. This removes the requirement that every client have an extra piece of software and moves that requirement to the server.

- Type 4—This is the easiest type of driver to install and use. It is written in Java and contains networking code right inside its classes. No additional installation is necessary on either the client or server.

After you have followed the instructions for installing any of the driver types, they all look the same to your program. The JDBC code uses the same SQL dialect regardless of the driver or driver type used. You need only enter the correct connection URL for the database that you want to access, and the driver does the heavy lifting for you.

It is a common practice for programmers to develop using whatever JDBC driver is readily available, and then change the driver to one whose performance is better suited to a production system.

Normally, you can obtain a JDBC driver from the vendor of your DBMS. In addition, third-party software companies often sell drivers that outperform the vendor's driver.

In this chapter, the Type 1 driver will be used in all examples. This driver ships with the Windows version of the JDK.

Programming with Java Database Connectivity

Programming with JDBC is reasonably simple. All you have to do is include a few lines of code to establish your connection and you are ready to start executing SQL statements. Listing 19.1 shows a simple example.

LISTING 19.1   The `JDBCConnection.java` File

```
package ch19;
import java.sql.*;

/**
 *
 * @author  Stephen Potts
 * @version 1.0
 */
public class JDBCConnection
{
```

LISTING 19.1   Continued

```
/** Default Constructor */
public JDBCConnection()
{
}

public static void main(String[] args)
{
    try
    {
        //load the driver class
        Class.forName("sun.jdbc.odbc.JdbcOdbcDriver");

        //Specify the ODBC data source
        String sourceURL = "jdbc:odbc:TicketRequest";

        //get a connection to the database
        Connection databaseConnection =
            DriverManager.getConnection(sourceURL);

        //If we get to here, no exception was thrown
        System.out.println("The database connection is " +
                                        databaseConnection);

    }catch(ClassNotFoundException cnfe)
    {
        System.err.println(cnfe);
    }
    catch (SQLException sqle)
    {
        System.err.println(sqle);
    }
}
}
```

The first step in using the driver is to specify which one that you want to use. In this case, we have specified the JDBC-ODBC bridge driver that ships with the JDK. This driver was chosen because it is always available.

```
Class.forName("sun.jdbc.odbc.JdbcOdbcDriver");
```

The next step is to specify the name of the datasource that you want to use. When using the bridge driver, you specify JDBC as the protocol, and ODBC as the subprotocol. The TicketRequest is the name of the data source that you defined using the ODBC manager which we will show later in the chapter.

```
String sourceURL = "jdbc:odbc:TicketRequest";
```

The goal of this program is to obtain an instance of the class Connection.

```
Connection databaseConnection =
    DriverManager.getConnection(sourceURL);
```

We will just print the connection, which will give us the name of the instance. If this executes without an exception, the program was successful.

```
System.out.println("The database connection is " +
                                databaseConnection);
```

Before we can run this program, we have to set up an ODBC datasource. A datasource roughly corresponds to a table in a database. In our case, the DBMS is MS Access. The database is located in a file called `c:\com\samspublishing\jpp\TicketRequest.mdb`. You can copy this file to that directory from the Internet site for this book, `www.samspublishing.com`.

Open the Control Panel on your Windows computer, and then the Administrative Tools folder (XP only). You will see an icon labeled Data Sources (ODBC). Double-clicking this icon will bring up the window shown in Figure 19.3.

FIGURE 19.3

The ODBC Manager enables you to specify data sources that can be used by JDBC.

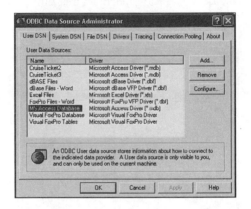

Click the Add button. It will open the window shown in Figure 19.4.

FIGURE 19.4

You specify the type of database that the data is stored in.

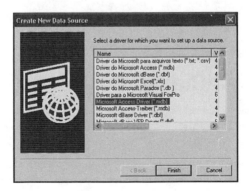

In this case, the database is MS Access, so you have to pick that driver and click the Finish button. This will open the window shown in Figure 19.5.

FIGURE 19.5
Next, you specify the
location of the database
that the data is stored in.

You type the name that you want the datasource to be known by in your code, and you use the browser to locate the database. On our test machine, that directory is called `c:\com\samspublishing\jpp`. You click the OK button, which opens the window shown in Figure 19.6.

FIGURE 19.6
The name that you chose,
`TicketRequest`, is now
the name that the data-
source is known by in
your programs.

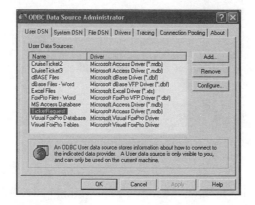

There is nothing magic about the name `TicketRequest`. You could have named it `XYZ` and it would have worked.

Querying the Database

Now that we have a database and an ODBC datasource defined, we are in a position to extract data from it and display it. Listing 19.2 shows an example that does just that.

LISTING 19.2   The `TestTicketRequest.java` File

```
/*
 * TestTicketRequest.java
 *
 * Created on July 9, 2002, 11:22 AM
 */
```

LISTING 19.2 *Continued*

```java
package ch19;

import java.sql.*;
import java.util.*;

/**
 *
 * @author   Stephen Potts
 * @version
 */
public class TestTicketRequest implements java.io.Serializable
{
    //information about the customer
    private int custID;
    private String lastName;
    private String firstName;

    //information about the cruise
    private int cruiseID;
    private String destination;
    private String port;
    private String sailing;

    private int numberOfTickets;

    public TestTicketRequest()
    {
    }


    public String toString()
    {
        String outString;
        outString = "-----------------------------------------" + "\n";

        //information about the customer
        outString += "custID = " + this.custID + "\n";
        outString += "lastName = " + this.lastName + "\n";
        outString += "firstName = " + this.firstName + "\n";
        outString += "-----------------------------------------" + "\n";

        //information about the cruise
        outString += "cruiseID = " + this.cruiseID + "\n";
        outString += "destination = " + this.destination + "\n";
        outString += "port = " + this.port + "\n";
        outString += "sailing = " + this.sailing + "\n";
        outString += "numberOfTickets = " + this.numberOfTickets + "\n";

        outString += "-----------------------------------------" + "\n";
        return outString;
    }
```

LISTING 19.2 Continued

```java
public String retrieveFromDB()
{
   java.sql.Connection dbConn = null;
   Statement statement1 = null;
   String createStatement;
   String insertStatement;

   try
   {
      // ============== Make connection to database ==================

      //load the driver class
      Class.forName("sun.jdbc.odbc.JdbcOdbcDriver");

      //Specify the ODBC data source
      String sourceURL = "jdbc:odbc:TicketRequest";

      //get a connection to the database
      dbConn = DriverManager.getConnection(sourceURL);

      //If we get to here, no exception was thrown
      System.out.println("The database connection is " + dbConn);
      System.out.println("Making connection...\n");

      //Create the statement
      statement1 = dbConn.createStatement();


      //Populate
      String getString =
      "SELECT * FROM TicketRequest ";

      ResultSet results = statement1.executeQuery(getString);

      while (results.next())
      {
           custID = results.getInt("custID");
           lastName = results.getString("lastName");
           firstName = results.getString("firstName");
           cruiseID = results.getInt("cruiseID");
           destination = results.getString("destination");
           port = results.getString("port");
           sailing = results.getString("sailing");
           numberOfTickets = results.getInt("numberOfTickets");
           System.out.println(this);
      }
      return "Successful Retrieval";
   } catch (Exception e)
   {
      System.out.println("Exception was thrown: " + e.getMessage());
      return "UnSuccessful Retrieval";
   } finally
```

LISTING 19.2   Continued

```
    {
        try
        {
            if (statement1 != null)
                statement1.close();
            if (dbConn != null)
                dbConn.close();
        } catch (SQLException sqle)
        {
            System.out.println("SQLException during close(): " +
            sqle.getMessage());
        }
    }

}

public static void main(String[] args)
{
    TestTicketRequest ttr = new TestTicketRequest();
    System.out.println("The contents of the database:");
    System.out.println(ttr.retrieveFromDB());

}
}
```

The interesting part of this example is the retrieval from the database. The first step is to connect to the datasource in exactly the same fashion as we did in the preceding example.

```
dbConn = DriverManager.getConnection(sourceURL);
```

The Connection object is used to create a Statement object.

```
//Create the statement
statement1 = dbConn.createStatement();
```

We first create the SQL as a String.

```
//Populate the bean
String getString =
"SELECT * FROM TicketRequest ";
```

Next, we create the result set by executing the query.

```
ResultSet results = statement1.executeQuery(getString);
```

For each row in the result set, we assign it to a variable and then call the **toString()** method defined previously to print out the contents of "this" class at the moment.

```
while (results.next())
{
    custID = results.getInt("custID");
    lastName = results.getString("lastName");
    firstName = results.getString("firstName");
    cruiseID = results.getInt("cruiseID");
```

```
            destination = results.getString("destination");
            port = results.getString("port");
            sailing = results.getString("sailing");
            numberOfTickets = results.getInt("numberOfTickets");
            System.out.println(this);
```

The result of running this example is sent to standard output:

```
The contents of the database:

The database connection is sun.jdbc.odbc.JdbcOdbcConnection@befab0
Making connection...
----------------------------------------
custID = 1001
lastName = Carter
firstName = Joseph
----------------------------------------
cruiseID = 2001
destination = Alaska
port = Vancouver
sailing = 1/1/1993
numberOfTickets = 3
----------------------------------------
----------------------------------------
custID = 12345
lastName = Joe
firstName = Cocomo
----------------------------------------
cruiseID = 3001
destination = Caribbean
port = Miami
sailing = 1/1/2004
numberOfTickets = 3
----------------------------------------
----------------------------------------
custID = 13
lastName = Beasley
firstName = Demarcus
----------------------------------------
cruiseID = 3001
destination = Caribbean
port = Miami
sailing = 1/1/2004
numberOfTickets = 3
----------------------------------------
----------------------------------------
custID = 17
lastName = Glance
firstName = Harvey
----------------------------------------
cruiseID = 3001
destination = Caribbean
port = Miami
sailing = 1/1/2004
numberOfTickets = 3
----------------------------------------
```

```
-----------------------------------------
custID = 29
lastName = White
firstName = Byron
-----------------------------------------
cruiseID = 20010
destination = South America
port = San Juan
sailing = 10/3/02
numberOfTickets = 3
-----------------------------------------
Successful Retrieval
```

Notice that the data is sent to output as soon as it is extracted from the result set.

If we want to extract just one row from the database, we have to modify our program to be more selective. Listing 19.3 shows an example that retrieves only a single row based on a customer ID.

LISTING 19.3   The `TestTicketRequest.java` File

```java
/*
 * TestTicketRequest2.java
 *
 * Created on July 9, 2002, 11:22 AM
 */

package ch19;

import java.sql.*;
import java.util.*;

/**
 *
 * @author   Stephen Potts
 * @version
 */
public class TestTicketRequest2 implements java.io.Serializable
{
    //information about the customer
    private int custID;
    private String lastName;
    private String firstName;

    //information about the cruise
    private int cruiseID;
    private String destination;
    private String port;
    private String sailing;

    private int numberOfTickets;
```

LISTING 19.3   Continued

```java
public TestTicketRequest2()
{
}

public String toString()
{
    String outString;
    outString = "-----------------------------------------" + "\n";

    //information about the customer
    outString += "custID = " + this.custID + "\n";
    outString += "lastName = " + this.lastName + "\n";
    outString += "firstName = " + this.firstName + "\n";
    outString += "-----------------------------------------" + "\n";

    //information about the cruise
    outString += "cruiseID = " + this.cruiseID + "\n";
    outString += "destination = " + this.destination + "\n";
    outString += "port = " + this.port + "\n";
    outString += "sailing = " + this.sailing + "\n";
    outString += "numberOfTickets = " + this.numberOfTickets + "\n";

    outString += "-----------------------------------------" + "\n";
    return outString;
}

public String retrieveFromDB()
{
    java.sql.Connection dbConn = null;
    Statement statement1 = null;
    String createStatement;
    String insertStatement;

    try
    {
        // ============== Make connection to database ==================

        //load the driver class
        Class.forName("sun.jdbc.odbc.JdbcOdbcDriver");

        //Specify the ODBC data source
        String sourceURL = "jdbc:odbc:TicketRequest";

        //get a connection to the database
        dbConn = DriverManager.getConnection(sourceURL);

        //If we get to here, no exception was thrown
        System.out.println("The database connection is " + dbConn);
        System.out.println("Making connection...\n");

        //Create the statement
```

LISTING 19.3   Continued

```
            statement1 = dbConn.createStatement();

            custID = 17;

            //Populate the bean
            String getBeanString =
            "SELECT * FROM TicketRequest " +
            "WHERE CustID = " + custID;

            ResultSet results = statement1.executeQuery(getBeanString);

            while (results.next())
            {
                custID = results.getInt("custID");
                lastName = results.getString("lastName");
                firstName = results.getString("firstName");
                cruiseID = results.getInt("cruiseID");
                destination = results.getString("destination");
                port = results.getString("port");
                sailing = results.getString("sailing");
                numberOfTickets = results.getInt("numberOfTickets");
                System.out.println(this);
            }
            return "Successful Retrieval";
        } catch (Exception e)
        {
            System.out.println("Exception was thrown: " + e.getMessage());
            return "UnSuccessful Retrieval";
        } finally
        {
            try
            {
                if (statement1 != null)
                    statement1.close();
                if (dbConn != null)
                    dbConn.close();
            } catch (SQLException sqle)
            {
                System.out.println("SQLException during close(): " +
                sqle.getMessage());
            }
        }

    }

    public static void main(String[] args)
    {
        TestTicketRequest2 ttr = new TestTicketRequest2();
        System.out.println("The contents of the database:");
        System.out.println(ttr.retrieveFromDB());

    }
}
```

This example opens the database using the JDBC-ODBC driver in the same way. Instead of allowing the `getString` to request all the rows, it limits it to only the rows that match the custID.

```
custID = 17;

//Populate the bean
String getString =
"SELECT * FROM TicketRequest " +
"WHERE CustID = " + custID;
```

Notice that we still use the `while` statement even though we only expect one row to be returned. The reason for this is that the `while` statement handles the case of zero or n rows that match this criteria. If no rows are returned, no error is thrown. If multiple rows are returned, only the last one retrieved is processed. This simplifies the error-handling code and prevents the user from getting error messages. The result of running this program is shown here:

```
The contents of the database:
The database connection is sun.jdbc.odbc.JdbcOdbcConnection@befab0
Making connection...
------------------------------------------
custID = 17
lastName = Glance
firstName = Harvey
------------------------------------------
cruiseID = 3001
destination = Caribbean
port = Miami
sailing = 1/1/2004
numberOfTickets = 3
------------------------------------------
Successful Retrieval
```

Note that only one row was retrieved.

Creating Tables with JDBC

Now that you understand how to create simple examples, we can move on to more challenging tasks. One of these tasks is using JDBC to create new tables and specify the columns in that table. We are often tempted to use the GUI provided by the DBMS vendor to create tables. This will work, but it creates a burden for the person installing your software and a potential source of errors.

A better approach is to create a Java program that deletes and adds back the table to the database automatically. This enables you to ship the program with the software and run it as part of the installation script. Listing 19.4 shows how to use JDBC to create the `TicketRequest` table in the `TicketRequest` database.

LISTING 19.4   The `TestTableCreation.java` File

```java
/*
 * TestTableCreation.java
 *
 * Created on December 27, 2001, 10:25 AM
 */

package ch19;
import java.sql.*;

/**
 *
 * @author  Stephen Potts
 * @version
 */
public class TestTableCreation
{

    /** Creates new TestTableCreation */
    public TestTableCreation()
    {
    }

    public static void main(String[] args)
    {
        String createStatement;
        try
        {
            //load the driver class
            Class.forName("sun.jdbc.odbc.JdbcOdbcDriver");

            //Specify the ODBC data source
            String sourceURL = "jdbc:odbc:TicketRequest";

            //get a connection to the database
            Connection dbConn =
            DriverManager.getConnection(sourceURL);

            //If we get to here, no exception was thrown
            System.out.println("The database connection is " + dbConn);

            //Create the statement
            Statement statement1 = dbConn.createStatement();

            /////////////////////////////////////////////////////////////
            //   Create the table in the database                      //
            /////////////////////////////////////////////////////////////
            try
            {
                statement1.execute("drop table TicketRequest");
            } catch (SQLException e)
            {
                System.out.println("table doesn't need to be dropped.");
```

LISTING 19.4   Continued

```
        }

        //Add the table
        createStatement =
        "CREATE TABLE TicketRequest(CustID int PRIMARY KEY, "
        + "LastName VARCHAR(30), FirstName VARCHAR(30), "
        + "CruiseID int, destination VARCHAR(30), port VARCHAR(30), "
        + "sailing VARCHAR(30), numberOfTickets VARCHAR(30))";

        System.out.println(createStatement);
        statement1.executeUpdate(createStatement);
        System.out.println("Table TicketRequest created.");
        //Flush and close
        dbConn.close();

    }catch(ClassNotFoundException cnfe)
    {
        System.err.println(cnfe);
    }
    catch (SQLException sqle)
    {
        System.err.println(sqle);
    }
    catch (Exception e)
    {
        System.err.println(e);
    }
    }//main
}//class
```

This example shows a little different style where the JDBC code is placed in the `main()` method. Our first task is to drop any tables that already have that name in our database. We place this statement in its own try/catch block because we don't really care whether or not the table already exists. We do note in the output window that the table doesn't need to be dropped if it does not exist.

```
        try
        {
            statement1.execute("drop table TicketRequest");
        } catch (SQLException e)
        {
            System.out.println("table doesn't need to be dropped.");
        }
```

We create a string that contains the SQL that we want to execute.

```
        createStatement =
        "CREATE TABLE TicketRequest(CustID int PRIMARY KEY, "
        + "LastName VARCHAR(30), FirstName VARCHAR(30), "
        + "CruiseID int, destination VARCHAR(30), port VARCHAR(30), "
        + "sailing VARCHAR(30), numberOfTickets VARCHAR(30))";
```

Next, we execute that statement.

```
statement1.executeUpdate(createStatement);
System.out.println("Table TicketRequest created.");
```

Finally, we close the connection.

```
dbConn.close();
```

We use the user interface provided by MS Access to verify that the table was really created. Figure 19.7 shows the result:

FIGURE 19.7

You can create and drop tables using JDBC.

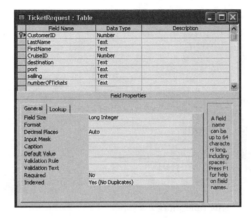

Notice that the data types are different, although similar, to the ones that we requested. We asked for integer and Access created a field that is a long integer. We asked for a **VARCHAR(30)**, and we were given a field of type **"text"**. It is the JDBC driver's responsibility to translate the JDBC SQL into the exact instructions that the DBMS receives so that it will be able to process the commands.

Populating a Database

Now that we have a table created, we can start adding data to it. The approach that we will use is to open the database connection, create statements that contain the data, and then execute them one at the time until all the rows have been added. Listing 19.5 shows an example of this.

LISTING 19.5   The `TestTablePopulate.java` File

```
/*
 * TestTablePopulate.java
 *
 * Created on December 27, 2001, 10:25 AM
 */
```

LISTING 19.5   Continued

```java
package ch19;
import java.sql.*;

/**
 *
 * @author  Stephen Potts
 * @version
 */
public class TestTablePopulate
{

    /** Creates new TestTablePopulate */
    public TestTablePopulate()
    {
    }

    public static void main(String[] args)
    {
        String createStatement;
        try
        {
            //load the driver class
            Class.forName("sun.jdbc.odbc.JdbcOdbcDriver");

            //Specify the ODBC data source
            String sourceURL = "jdbc:odbc:TicketRequest";

            //get a connection to the database
            Connection dbConn =
            DriverManager.getConnection(sourceURL);

            //If we get to here, no exception was thrown
            System.out.println("The database connection is " + dbConn);

            //Create the statement
            Statement statement1 = dbConn.createStatement();
            String insertStatement;


             //Add the information
            insertStatement = "INSERT INTO TicketRequest VALUES(" +
                    " 13, 'Beasley', 'Demarcus', 3001, "
            + "'Caribbean', 'Miami', '1/1/2004', '3')";
            statement1.executeUpdate(insertStatement);

             //Add the information
            insertStatement = "INSERT INTO TicketRequest VALUES(" +
                    " 17, 'Glance', 'Harvey', 3001, "
            + "'Caribbean', 'Miami', '1/1/2004', '3')";
            statement1.executeUpdate(insertStatement);
```

LISTING 19.5   *Continued*

```
                //Add the information
                insertStatement = "INSERT INTO TicketRequest VALUES(" +
                        " 29, 'White', 'Byron', 20010, "
                + "'South America', 'San Juan', '10/3/02', '3')";
                statement1.executeUpdate(insertStatement);

                //Add the information
                insertStatement = "INSERT INTO TicketRequest VALUES(" +
                        " 1001, 'Carter', 'Joesph', 2001, "
                + "'Alaska', 'Vancouver', '1/1/1993', '3')";
                statement1.executeUpdate(insertStatement);

                //Add the information
                insertStatement = "INSERT INTO TicketRequest VALUES(" +
                        " 12345, 'Cocomo', 'Joe', 3001, "
                + "'Caribbean', 'Miami', '1/1/2004', '3')";
                statement1.executeUpdate(insertStatement);

                System.out.println("Table TicketRequest populated");
                //Flush and close
                dbConn.close();

        }catch(ClassNotFoundException cnfe)
        {
                System.err.println(cnfe);
        }
        catch (SQLException sqle)
        {
                System.err.println(sqle);
        }
        catch (Exception e)
        {
                System.err.println(e);
        }
    }//main
}//class
```

The only difference in the creation of new rows in the table is in the syntax of the SQL statement that gets executed.

```
                insertStatement = "INSERT INTO TicketRequest VALUES(" +
                        " 13, 'Beasley', 'Demarcus', 3001, "
                + "'Caribbean', 'Miami', '1/1/2004', '3')";
```

We have to be very careful to create data that is of the exact type of the columns in the database. Next, we execute the update in the customary fashion.

```
                statement1.executeUpdate(insertStatement);
```

The opening and closing of the JDBC connection is identical, regardless of whether you are going to insert, update, or delete rows. We can use the MS Access GUI to see if the table was populated correctly. Figure 19.8 shows this data.

FIGURE 19.8
You can populate the
database using JDBC and
SQL Insert statements.

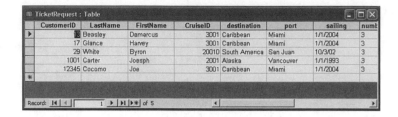

Notice that all the data is stored using the data types that we specified when we created the table. This technique of populating the database with a program is very useful when developing software. You can create a set of database tables and rows that contain test data. If your testing consumes or alters the values in the rows, you can simply drop the tables, then re-create and populate them in a few seconds.

Altering the Data Using JDBC and a GUI

Another common JDBC task is altering or updating the data in a table. Most of the systems that you will write will require that the user not only be able to insert and query data, but make changes to it as well. In addition, it is very useful if these changes can be made using a GUI. Listing 19.6 shows a program where a user can do this.

LISTING 19.6   The `TestTableAlteration.java` File

```
/*
 * TestTableAlteration.java
 *
 * Created on July 30, 2002, 11:35 AM
 */

package ch19;

import javax.swing.*;
import java.awt.*;
import java.awt.event.*;
import java.sql.*;

/**
 *
 * @author   Stephen Potts
 * @version
 */
public class TestTableAlteration extends JFrame implements ActionListener
{
    //information about the customer
    private int custID;
    private String lastName;
    private String firstName;
```

LISTING 19.6   Continued

```java
        //information about the cruise
        private int cruiseID;
        private String destination;
        private String port;
        private String sailing;

        private int numberOfTickets;

        JTextField tfCustID;
        JTextField tfLastName;
        JTextField tfFirstName;
        JTextField tfCruiseID;
        JTextField tfDestination;
        JTextField tfPort;
        JTextField tfSailing;
        JTextField tfNumberOfTickets;

        JLabel lCustID = new JLabel("CustID");
        JLabel lLastName = new JLabel("LastName");
        JLabel lFirstName = new JLabel("FirstName");
        JLabel lCruiseID = new JLabel("CruiseID");
        JLabel lDestination = new JLabel("Destination");
        JLabel lPort = new JLabel("Port      ");
        JLabel lSailing = new JLabel("Sailing");
        JLabel lNumberOfTickets = new JLabel("Number of Tickets");

        JButton btnRetrieve;
        JButton btnStore;

        java.sql.Connection dbConn = null;
        Statement statement1 = null;
        String createStatement;
        String insertStatement;


        /** Creates new TestTableAlteration */
        public TestTableAlteration()
        {
            tfCustID = new JTextField(20);
            tfLastName = new JTextField(20);
            tfFirstName = new JTextField(20);
            tfCruiseID = new JTextField(20);
            tfDestination = new JTextField(20);
            tfPort = new JTextField(20);
            tfSailing = new JTextField(20);
            tfNumberOfTickets = new JTextField(15);

            btnRetrieve = new JButton("Retrieve");
            btnStore = new JButton("Store");

            this.setDefaultCloseOperation(JFrame.EXIT_ON_CLOSE);
```

LISTING 19.6   Continued

```java
            JPanel p1 = new JPanel();

            p1.add(lCustID);
            p1.add(tfCustID);
            p1.add(lLastName);
            p1.add(tfLastName);
            p1.add(lFirstName);
            p1.add(tfFirstName);
            p1.add(lCruiseID);
            p1.add(tfCruiseID);
            p1.add(lDestination);
            p1.add(tfDestination);
            p1.add(lPort);
            p1.add(tfPort);
            p1.add(lSailing);
            p1.add(tfSailing);
            p1.add(lNumberOfTickets);
            p1.add(tfNumberOfTickets);
            p1.add(btnRetrieve);
            p1.add(btnStore);

            btnRetrieve.addActionListener(this);
            btnStore.addActionListener(this);

            getContentPane().add(p1);

            setTitle("Altering Table Data");
            setBounds( 100, 100, 315, 300);
            setVisible(true);
        }

        public void actionPerformed(ActionEvent ae)
        {
            if (ae.getActionCommand().equals("Retrieve"))
            {
                System.out.println("btnRetrieve clicked");
                if (tfCustID.getText().equals(""))
                    System.out.println("please enter a CustID");
                else
                {
                    System.out.println("CustID = " + tfCustID.getText());
                    this.custID = Integer.parseInt(tfCustID.getText());
                    retrieveFromDB();
                    tfLastName.setText(lastName);
                    tfFirstName.setText(firstName);
                    tfCruiseID.setText(Integer.toString(cruiseID));
                    tfDestination.setText(destination);
                    tfPort.setText(port);
                    tfSailing.setText(sailing);
                    tfNumberOfTickets.setText(Integer.toString(numberOfTickets));
                }
            }
```

LISTING 19.6 Continued

```java
        if (ae.getActionCommand().equals("Store"))
        {
            System.out.println("btnStore clicked");
            if (tfCustID.getText().equals(""))
                System.out.println("please enter a CustID");
            else
            {
                updateDB();
            }

        }
    }

    public String updateDB()
    {
        try
        {
            // ============== Make connection to database ==================
            connectToDB();

            lastName = tfLastName.getText();
            firstName = tfFirstName.getText();
            String strCruiseID = tfCruiseID.getText();
            destination = tfDestination.getText();
            port = tfPort.getText();
            sailing = tfSailing.getText();
            String strNumberOfTickets = tfNumberOfTickets.getText();

            //Update Last Name
            String updateString =
            "Update TicketRequest " +
            "SET lastName = '" + lastName + "' " +
            "WHERE CustID = " + custID;
            System.out.println(updateString);
            statement1.executeUpdate(updateString);

            //Update First Name
            updateString =
            "Update TicketRequest " +
            "SET firstName = '" + firstName + "' " +
            "WHERE CustID = " + custID;
            System.out.println(updateString);
            statement1.executeUpdate(updateString);

            //Update Cruise ID
            updateString =
            "Update TicketRequest " +
            "SET cruiseID= " + strCruiseID + " " +
            "WHERE CustID = " + custID;
            System.out.println(updateString);
            statement1.executeUpdate(updateString);
```

LISTING 19.6   Continued

```
            //Update destination
            updateString =
            "Update TicketRequest " +
            "SET destination = '" + destination + "' " +
            "WHERE CustID = " + custID;
            System.out.println(updateString);
            statement1.executeUpdate(updateString);

            //Update port
            updateString =
            "Update TicketRequest " +
            "SET port = '" + port + "' " +
            "WHERE CustID = " + custID;
            System.out.println(updateString);
            statement1.executeUpdate(updateString);

            //Update sailing
            updateString =
            "Update TicketRequest " +
            "SET sailing = '" + sailing + "' " +
            "WHERE CustID = " + custID;
            System.out.println(updateString);
            statement1.executeUpdate(updateString);

            //Update number of tickts
             updateString =
            "Update TicketRequest " +
            "SET numberOfTickets = " + strNumberOfTickets + " " +
            "WHERE CustID = " + custID;
            System.out.println(updateString);
            statement1.executeUpdate(updateString);

            return "Successful Update";
        } catch (Exception e)
        {
            System.out.println("Exception was thrown: " + e.getMessage());
            return "UnSuccessful Retrieval";
        } finally
        {
            try
            {
                if (statement1 != null)
                    statement1.close();
                if (dbConn != null)
                    dbConn.close();
            } catch (SQLException sqle)
            {
                System.out.println("SQLException during close(): " +
                sqle.getMessage());
            }
        }
```

LISTING 19.6   Continued

```
        }

        public String retrieveFromDB()
        {

            try
            {
                // ============== Make connection to database ==================
                connectToDB();

                //Populate
                String getString =
                "SELECT * FROM TicketRequest " +
                "WHERE CustID = " + custID;

                ResultSet results = statement1.executeQuery(getString);
                lastName = "record not found";
                firstName = "";
                cruiseID = 0;
                destination = "";
                port = "";
                sailing = "";
                numberOfTickets = 0;

                while (results.next())
                {
                    lastName = results.getString("lastName");
                    firstName = results.getString("firstName");
                    cruiseID = results.getInt("cruiseID");
                    destination = results.getString("destination");
                    port = results.getString("port");
                    sailing = results.getString("sailing");
                    numberOfTickets = results.getInt("numberOfTickets");
                }
                return "Successful Retrieval";
            } catch (Exception e)
            {
                System.out.println("Exception was thrown: " + e.getMessage());
                return "UnSuccessful Retrieval";
            } finally
            {
                try
                {
                    if (statement1 != null)
                        statement1.close();
                    if (dbConn != null)
                        dbConn.close();
                } catch (SQLException sqle)
                {
                    System.out.println("SQLException during close(): " +
                    sqle.getMessage());
                }
```

LISTING 19.6   Continued

```
            }

        }

        private void connectToDB()
        {
            try
            {
                // ============== Make connection to database ==================

                //load the driver class
                Class.forName("sun.jdbc.odbc.JdbcOdbcDriver");

                //Specify the ODBC data source
                String sourceURL = "jdbc:odbc:TicketRequest";

                //get a connection to the database
                dbConn = DriverManager.getConnection(sourceURL);

                //If we get to here, no exception was thrown
                System.out.println("The database connection is " + dbConn);
                System.out.println("Making connection...\n");

                //Create the statement
                statement1 = dbConn.createStatement();
            } catch (Exception e)
            {
                System.out.println("Exception was thrown: " + e.getMessage());
            }
        }


        public static void main(String[] args)
        {
            TestTableAlteration tta = new TestTableAlteration();
        }
    }

}
```

This example has a GUI, so we need to implement a listener interface.

```
public class TestTableAlteration extends JFrame implements ActionListener
```

We define two buttons to trigger action.

```
    JButton btnRetrieve;
    JButton btnStore;
```

The `actionPerformed()` method is where the JDBC processing is called from.

```
    public void actionPerformed(ActionEvent ae)
    {
```

The "`Retrieve`" button loads the `custID`, and then calls the `retrieveFromDB()` method to get the data.

```
if (ae.getActionCommand().equals("Retrieve"))
{
    System.out.println("btnRetrieve clicked");
    if (tfCustID.getText().equals(""))
        System.out.println("please enter a CustID");
    else
    {
        System.out.println("CustID = " + tfCustID.getText());
        this.custID = Integer.parseInt(tfCustID.getText());
        retrieveFromDB();
```

After this method returns, we load the data from the class-level variables into the text fields.

```
tfLastName.setText(lastName);
tfFirstName.setText(firstName);
tfCruiseID.setText(Integer.toString(cruiseID));
tfDestination.setText(destination);
tfPort.setText(port);
tfSailing.setText(sailing);
tfNumberOfTickets.setText(Integer.toString(numberOfTickets));
```

The "Store" button causes the `updateDB()` method to be called.

```
if (ae.getActionCommand().equals("Store"))
{
    System.out.println("btnStore clicked");
    if (tfCustID.getText().equals(""))
        System.out.println("please enter a CustID");
    else
    {
        updateDB();
    }

}
}
```

The `updateDB()` method is where the data is stored to the DB.

```
public String updateDB()
```

First, we connect to the database.

```
connectToDB();
```

Next, we update each of the class variables with the data from the text fields.

```
lastName = tfLastName.getText();
firstName = tfFirstName.getText();
String strCruiseID = tfCruiseID.getText();
destination = tfDestination.getText();
port = tfPort.getText();
sailing = tfSailing.getText();
String strNumberOfTickets = tfNumberOfTickets.getText();
```

Next, we update every column because we don't know which of them contains changes. If the table was large, we would want to determine whether a field has been changed, but for a small table, this is not necessary.

```
//Update Last Name
String updateString =
"Update TicketRequest " +
"SET lastName = '" + lastName + "' " +
"WHERE CustID = " + custID;
System.out.println(updateString);
statement1.executeUpdate(updateString);
  .
  .
  .

//Update number of tickts
 updateString =
"Update TicketRequest " +
"SET numberOfTickets = " + strNumberOfTickets + " " +
"WHERE CustID = " + custID;
System.out.println(updateString);
statement1.executeUpdate(updateString);
```

The result of running this program is shown here in Figure 19.9.

FIGURE 19.9
You can update the data-base using JDBC and the SQL Update statement.

Notice that the values for the Last Name and the number of tickets are changed.

Summary

In this chapter we looked at the subject of databases from a Java-centric point of view. The first thing we learned was what a database is. Following that the Java approach to database management, JDBC, was introduced.

Next, you learned how to create a table within a database using JDBC and Java. Following that you were shown how to populate databases with data. Next, you learned how to query databases using JDBC. Finally, you learned how to create a graphical user interface that can query and update a database table.

Review Questions

1. How is a database different from a sequential file?

2. What is JDBC?

3. What SQL command is used to add rows of data to a table?

4. What methods in a GUI contain the code that controls access to the database?

Exercises

1. Create a table in a database that contains automobile information.

2. Populate that table with information about your cars.

3. Create a GUI that enables you to query and change that data.

CHAPTER 20

NETWORK PROGRAMMING

In this chapter you will learn:

- How TCP/IP came to be

- How to transfer data using sockets

- How to set up two-way communication with sockets

- How to send complex objects over sockets

- How to download the contents of a Web site into your program

A s Java programmers, we live our lives on the network. It seems that everything we do involves servers, sockets, protocols, URLs, and the dozens of networking concepts and tools that make up our programming environment. In this chapter, we will attempt to provide an overview of the technology that provides the underpinnings of the network products and APIs that we use every day. The goal of this approach is to help the reader see the dozens of technologies in the Java-programming world as parts of a whole, with a little history sprinkled in.

The History of TCP/IP

When the history of the Internet is written, in a hundred years or so, what development will be remembered as the most important? A writer living now might say that the World Wide Web (WWW) is what put the Internet on the map. Although trying to ignore the WWW is like ignoring the proverbial elephant in the living room, there is a good chance that future historians will cite TCP/IP as the obvious winner.

In 1969, the Defense Advanced Research Projects (DARPA), later renamed to ARPA, was searching for a way to facilitate communications between their agency and the contractors who bid on and fulfilled research contracts. An ARPA employee named Larry Roberts was pondering this question when he came on the idea of creating a network of computers that could use phone lines to communicate with each other across distances of hundreds of miles. This had never been done before, and there was no hardware available to interconnect the computers.

Roberts created a specification for a special computer that would connect multiple other computers by taking information off a wire connected to one computer and placing it on a wire connected to another. This special computer was called an Interface Message Processor (IMP).

A contract was signed with a company called Bolt, Baranek, and Newman, which delivered the first IMP in 1969. Four sites were chosen to install these IMPs: UCLA, University of California at Santa Barbara, the University of Utah, and the Stanford Research Institute. By the end of 1969, all four sites were connected and accessing each other's computers.

At first, a Telnet application coordinated this access, but a program called the Network Control Protocol (NCP) soon replaced it. By 1971, 19 other sites had joined the network.

In 1974, two engineers, Bob Kahn and Vinton Cerf, wrote a paper that described an improved protocol that they called the Transfer Control Protocol (TCP). It was later combined with another lower-level protocol called the Internet Protocol (IP) and renamed TCP/IP.

Over the next several years, software written to this design began to replace NCP until 1983 when ARPA decreed that no other protocol would be allowed to connect to the ARPANET, as it had come to be called. After much weeping and gnashing of teeth, all the nodes on the ARPANET standardized on TCP/IP as their communication protocol.

By 1983, the computers on the ARPANET were exchanging quite a bit of data that was not related to the U.S. Department of Defense. Because of this, the Defense Communications Agency split the ARPANET in two parts. They called one of them the Internet, and the other MILNET. MILNET was reserved for military-related sites, and the Internet was used for everything else.

In the 1980s, TCP/IP was far from being the only, or even the dominant, protocol for interconnecting computers. It had an advantage over competing technologies in that day, however, because it was in the public domain. Before long, implementations of TCP/IP were written for every popular hardware platform. As a result, TCP/IP became the most common way to interconnect heterogeneous computers because it did not require hardware vendors to license each other's software.

TCP/IP Internals

Sometimes we think of TCP/IP as a protocol, but it is really a suite of protocols. Combinations of these protocols work together to transfer data from one computer to another. The name, TCP/IP, comes from two of the most frequently used protocols in the suite, the Transmission Control Protocol(TCP) and the Internet Protocol(IP).

To understand how TCP/IP works, you can think of the different protocols as separate APIs, or more commonly, layers. The layered diagrams sometimes confuse programmers. If you think of them as different level APIs, you will come closer to understanding them. Each layer, except the Network Access Layer, makes calls to the services provided by the layer below it. (The Network Access Layer makes calls to the hardware.) Each layer, except the application layer, returns data to the layer above it.

Another point of confusion comes by thinking that the Network Access Layer is made up of a single product or protocol. In reality, many different technologies are combined to perform the duties of this layer. Network cards have drivers that are called by routing software, and so forth.

The Application Layer can also be very complicated. Some application layers contain hundreds of servlets, JSPs, EJBs, and just about every other technology on the market. Figure 20.1 shows the layers of a typical TCP/IP model.

FIGURE 20.1
The Internet protocol model.

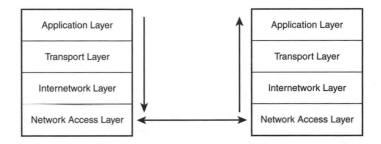

The layers in this model are

- Application layer—This layer can be as simple as a file transfer program, or it can as complex as an B2B application.

- Transport layer—This layer sends a set of data from one machine to another with data integrity and high reliability.

- Internetwork layer—This layer makes calls to pass "buckets" of data called datagrams from one computer to another and another and another until the final destination computer is reached.

- Network Access layer—This layer exchanges frames of data with other computers or routing devices on the same network.

The layers work together to create the effect of sending data reliably from one computer to one or more other computers.

The Application Layer

The top layer in the model is called the Application layer. This layer normally provides services such as encryption, compression, decryption, and decompression. You might hear this layer discussed in generic terms as the TCP/IP client or the TCP/IP server.

When TCP/IP was first created, the applications tended to be very simple. Over the years, clients have grown in sophistication so that now an Enterprise JavaBean (EJB) server resides completely in this layer. Figure 20.2 shows the layered architecture of an EJB server and an EJB client.

FIGURE 20.2

The EJB architecture.

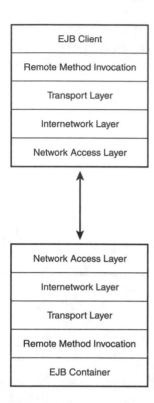

The EJB clients and servers normally talk to each other using sockets. The client makes a request by opening a socket and placing a stream of data onto it. The server receives the request, processes it, and sends a stream containing the response back to the client.

In reality, most EJB servers and clients communicate using the Remote Method Invocation (RMI) facilities that are built into Java.

The Transport Layer

The primary responsibility of the Transport layer is to make sure that all the data gets to the other computer. This is done by numbering each packet sequentially before sending it. The Transport software on the other computer takes an inventory of the packets as they arrive. If any of them get lost in transit, it requests that the missing packet be resent.

The Application layer hands the data to the Transport layer as a stream. The Transport layer subdivides the data into packets and its counterpart on the other machine turns it back into a stream.

The Internetwork Layer

The Internetwork (IP) layer is responsible for the delivery of the packets to the computer whose address they contain. It does this by talking to its IP layer counterparts on every computer that the data passes through on the way. The addressing scheme in the form 121.14.27.1 tells each computer what computer to send the data to next. At each hop along the way, the IP layer has to decide whether the packet was intended for this computer. If not, it has to decide which other computer that it is directly connected to will provide the best route to the packet's final destination.

The packet is broken into datagrams, which are a kind of minipacket. Each datagram contains part of the packet. When all the datagrams for one packet arrive at the destination computer, they are reassembled into a packet and handed to the transport layer.

A datagram is a string of characters that is made up of a header, the data, and a trailer. The header contains the IP addresses of both the source and the destination along with some security information. The trailer normally contains a checksum that is used to verify that accidental corruption has not occurred.

This layer has no concept of a session. To the IP layer, a datagram is forgotten once it is sent. If a broken datagram arrives, it is discarded and the packet that it belongs to will be broken, too. The Transport layer will notice the broken packet and request a resend.

The Network Access Layer

Network Access occupies the bottom layer of the diagram. The software in this layer talks to the hardware indirectly using the drivers that are provided (normally) by the network card manufacturer.

The basic unit of transfer at this level is the frame. Frames contain the information needed to move the data from one physical network card to another. This layer uses the physical address that identifies the card to transfer the data. This layer also knows how to handle the physical characteristics of the hardware, including the maximum frame size and the hardware-addressing scheme.

Figure 20.3 shows this encapsulation and decapsulation strategy diagrammatically.

Each layer adds its own header and trailer. Its peer layer on the other stack peels off the header and trailer that were added by that layer on the sending side. It then hands the slimmed-down message to the previous layer.

TCP/IP applications can be programmed in any language that can open a socket. Many languages require that you use an operating system utility to do this. For portability reasons, Java doesn't allow operating system calls from within programs. Instead, network functionality is provided by the classes in the `java.net` package. The Java Virtual Machine is responsible for providing the actual connection to the operating system.

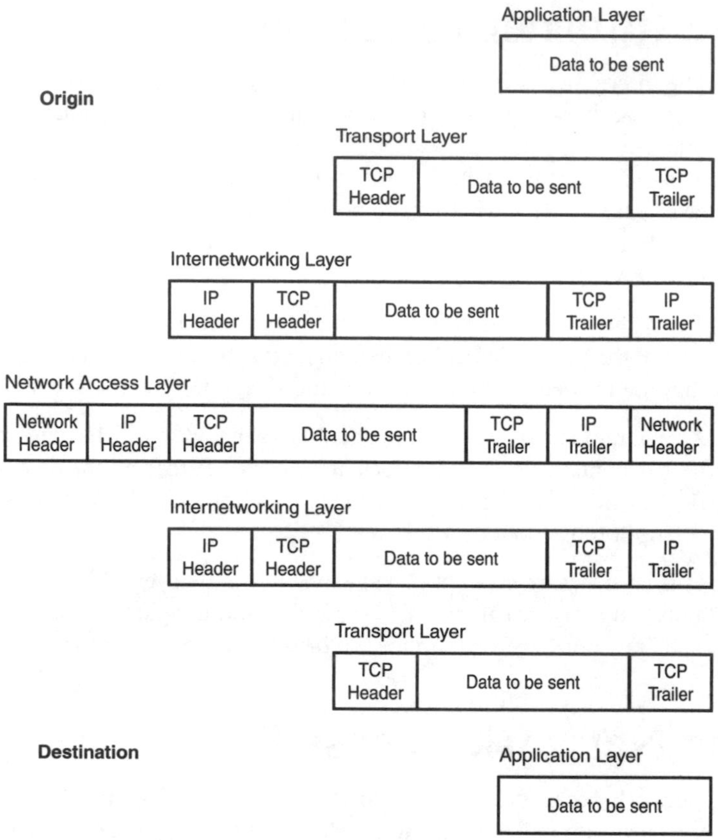

FIGURE 20.3
TCP/IP Data encapsulation and decapsulation.

The `java.net` package includes the following important classes:

- Socket class—Sends TCP messages

- ServerSocket class—Creates servers

- URL class—An object representing a Uniform Resource Locator

- URLConnection—The superclass of all classes that represent a communications link between the application and a URL

Programming Simple Sockets

The Socket and SocketServer classes are the most frequently used classes in the package. A socket is really just a numbered connection on a computer. This number is called the socket's port. If the sending and receiving computers agree on what port they want to use, they can communicate. The TCP/IP software on one computer sends messages containing the port number to the other computer. The receiving computer's TCP/IP software receives the message and checks to see if any program that it knows of is accepting messages on this port. If the answer is yes, it hands the message to that program.

For a program to work, you need to have both a client and a server. Listing 20.1 shows the code for a socket server.

LISTING 20.1   The `SimpleSocketClient.java` File

```
*
* SimpleSocketClient.java
*
* Created on October 2, 2002, 5:34 PM
*/

package ch20;


import java.net.*;
import java.io.*;


/**
 *
 * @author  Stephen Potts
 */
public class SimpleSocketClient
{
    Socket socket;
    int portNumber = 1777;
    String str = "";

    /** Creates a new instance of SimpleSocketClient */
    public SimpleSocketClient()
    {

        try
        {
            socket = new Socket(InetAddress.getLocalHost(),
            portNumber);

            ObjectInputStream ois =
            new ObjectInputStream(socket.getInputStream());
            str = (String) ois.readObject();
            System.out.println(str);

        } catch (Exception e)
        {
            System.out.println("Exception " + e);
        }
    }

    public static void main(String args[])
    {
        SimpleSocketClient ssp = new SimpleSocketClient();
    }

}
```

We import the `java.net` package because it contains the Socket class. The `java.io` package provides input and output classes that we will use to extract the data from the response.

```
import java.net.*;
import java.io.*;
```

We can choose just about any port number that we want, but some of them might already be in use. If you have a Web server running on your machine, it is likely set to use port 80, so you wouldn't want to use that number.

```
    int portNumber = 1777;
```

We instantiate the socket using the address of this computer and the port number.

```
        socket = new Socket(InetAddress.getLocalHost(),
        portNumber);
```

The program will try to open this socket on this machine. If there is no server running on that port, an Exception will be thrown. The `getInputStream()` method obtains a handle to the socket's stream.

```
            ObjectInputStream ois =
            new ObjectInputStream(socket.getInputStream());
```

The `readObject()` method reads from the stream and places it in the `str` variable.

```
            str = (String) ois.readObject();
```

Finally, we print the contents of the `str` variable so that we can see what was sent.

```
            System.out.println(str);
```

Unlike other programs, TCP programs are useless unless there is a corresponding server to connect to. The server uses the same port number as the client.

Listing 20.2 shows a server that communicates with the client in Listing 20.1:

LISTING 20.2   The `SimpleSocketServer.java` File

```
/*
 * SimpleSocketServer.java
 *
 * Created on October 2, 2002, 5:24 PM
 */

package ch20;

import java.net.*;
import java.io.*;

/**
 *
 * @author   Stephen Potts
 */
public class SimpleSocketServer
{
    ServerSocket serverSocket;
```

LISTING 20.1   Continued

```java
        int portNumber = 1777;
        Socket socket;
        String str;


    /** Creates a new instance of SimpleSocketServer */
    public SimpleSocketServer()
    {       str = " <?xml version=\"1.0\" encoding=\"UTF-8\"?>";
            str += "<ticketRequest><customer custID=\"2030\">";
            str += "<lastName>Smith</lastName>";
            str += "<firstName>Klay</firstName>";
            str += "</customer>";
            str += "<cruise cruiseID=\"3009\">";
            str += "<destination>Caribbean</destination>";
            str += "<port>San Juan</port>";
            str += "<sailing>4/30/02</sailing>";
            str += "<numberOfTickets>5</numberOfTickets>";
            str += "</cruise>";
            str += "</ticketRequest>";

            // Create ServerSocket to listen for connections
            try
            {
                serverSocket = new ServerSocket(portNumber);

                // Wait for client to connnect, then get Socket
                System.out.println("ServerSocket created");
                System.out.println("Waiting for a connection on " +
                                                    portNumber);

                socket = serverSocket.accept();

                // Use ObjectOutputStream to send String to the client
                ObjectOutputStream oos =
                new ObjectOutputStream(socket.getOutputStream());

                oos.writeObject(str);

                oos.close();

                // Close Socket
                socket.close();
            } catch (Exception e)
            {
                System.out.println("Exception " + e);
            }
    }

    public static void main(String args[])
    {
        SimpleSocketServer sss = new SimpleSocketServer();
    }


}
```

Instead of declaring a Socket, we declare an instance of a `ServerSocket`. `ServerSocket`s are sockets that are able to wait for a communication from anther process or computer. Normal sockets throw an error if they can't find their counterpart.

```
ServerSocket serverSocket;
```

Notice that we use the same port number as the client program did.

```
int portNumber = 1777;
```

We build up a String with the data that we want to send.

```
str = " <?xml version=\"1.0\" encoding=\"UTF-8\"?>";
str += "<ticketRequest><customer custID=\"2030\">";
     .
     .
     .
str += "</cruise>";
str += "</ticketRequest>";
```

The `ServerSocket` passes a port number in its constructor.

```
serverSocket = new ServerSocket(portNumber);
```

We print out some messages so that we can obtain a visual confirmation that the server has started up.

```
System.out.println("ServerSocket created");
System.out.println("Waiting for a connection on " +
                                        portNumber);
```

The `accept()` method tells the TCP/IP software that this program would like to wait until a request comes in on the previously specified port, and to accept the connection when it is requested.

```
socket = serverSocket.accept();
```

We use an `ObjectOutputStream` to send the data out. In this case, we always send the same message regardless of which process connects.

```
ObjectOutputStream oos =
new ObjectOutputStream(socket.getOutputStream());
```

We write the String out using the stream handle that was obtained from the socket.

```
oos.writeObject(str);
```

We close the stream now that we are done with it.

```
oos.close();
```

We also close the socket.

```
socket.close();
```

The result is a string that contains an XML document as shown here.

```
<?xml version="1.0" encoding="UTF-8"?><ticketRequest>
<customer custID="1001"><lastName>Carter</lastName>
```

```
<firstName>Joey</firstName></customer><cruise cruiseID="3005">
<destination>Alaska</destination><port>Vancouver</port>
<sailing>4/15/02</sailing><numberOfTickets>4</numberOfTickets>
</cruise></ticketRequest>
```

Sending XML documents over sockets is a very convenient way to transfer complex data between computers. This is especially true when the two computers are running different operating systems because every operating system can run TCP/IP.

Two-Way Communication Using Sockets

There is no reason that the communication between the client and the server can't be two-way. In the preceding example, both programs ended as soon as they processed one message. You can modify the program to accept a message and respond to it just as easily. Listing 20.3 shows a client that stays alive until the client indicates that he wants to end it.

LISTING 20.3   The `LoopingSocketClient.java` File

```java
/*
 * LoopingSocketClient.java
 *
 * Created on October 2, 2002, 5:34 PM
 */

package ch20;

import java.net.*;
import java.io.*;

/**
 *
 * @author  Stephen Potts
 */
public class LoopingSocketClient
{
    Socket socket1;
    int portNumber = 1777;
    String str = "";

    /** Creates a new instance of LoopingSocketClient */
    public LoopingSocketClient()
    {
        try
        {
            socket1 = new Socket(InetAddress.getLocalHost(),
            portNumber);

            ObjectInputStream ois =
            new ObjectInputStream(socket1.getInputStream());

            ObjectOutputStream oos =
```

LISTING 20.3 Continued

```
            new ObjectOutputStream(socket1.getOutputStream());

        str = "initialize";
        oos.writeObject(str);


        while ((str = (String) ois.readObject()) != null)
        {
            System.out.println(str);
            oos.writeObject("bye");

            if (str.equals("bye bye"))
                break;
        }

        ois.close();
        oos.close();
        socket1.close();

    } catch (Exception e)
    {
        System.out.println("Exception " + e);
    }
}

public static void main(String args[])
{
    LoopingSocketClient lsp = new LoopingSocketClient();
}

}
```

We first instantiate a single socket class by giving it the name of a computer and the port number that we want to use. This example uses the same computer to run the client and the server.

```
        socket1 = new Socket(InetAddress.getLocalHost(),
        portNumber);
```

If you replace the call to **getLocalHost()** with a string such as "Pogo," this example would attempt to contact a **SocketServer** object running on a machine known as "Pogo" on your local network:

```
        socket1 = new Socket("localhost",
        portNumber);
```

You could also use the IP address such as "123.35.67.8" of the machine instead:

```
        socket1 = new Socket("127.0.0.1",
        portNumber);
```

Most programmers prefer to use the name because IP addresses can change from time to time.

Tip

Java provides five ways to address your own machine from within a program. The first way is to call the static method getLocalHost() in the InetAddress class. The second way is to use the String "127.0.0.1", which always means this machine. The third way is to put the real IP address of your machine in a String as in "123.35.67.8"; this only works if you have a static IP address. The fourth way is to use the String "localhost" where the name would be placed. The fifth way is to enter the actual name of your machine on the local area network as in "Speedracer."

There are several different objects that you can use to put data onto a socket and get data off of one. In this example, we used the `ObjectInputStream` and the `ObjectOutputStream`. The `ObjectOutputStream` class can only be used with Objects that are serializable. Serializable classes are those that can be written to a file or socket and reconstituted on another computer properly. In our example, we use String objects to pass the data. Because the String class is serializable, this works.

```
ObjectInputStream ois =
          new ObjectInputStream(socket1.getInputStream());
```

The `ObjectOutputStream` can be used to place objects on the stream. This class is not only associated with sockets, but it can be used for files as well. For that reason, we have to use the `getOutputStream()` class to get an object that it can accept.

```
          ObjectOutputStream oos =
          new ObjectOutputStream(socket1.getOutputStream());
```

When we start the client, we want to send some sort of an initialization string to make sure that we are up and running. If there is no **ServerSocket** listening on the specified port, an Exception will be thrown.

```
          str = "initialize";
```

The actual writing of the String object is accomplished by calling the `writeObject()` method.

```
          oos.writeObject(str);
```

We don't want this program to terminate after only one pass through it, so we create a `while` loop that will perform our read also. Notice that the `readOject()` method needs an explicit cast to type String. This method returns an object of type Object. The cast turns it into a String. There are restrictions on what kind of cast is allowed, but you are safe here because both programs are only using Strings to pass the data.

```
          while ((str = (String) ois.readObject()) != null)
          {
              System.out.println(str);
```

In this example, we send the initialization string first. The next string that we send is the "bye" string. This indicates to our program that the client wants the server to shutdown.

```
          oos.writeObject("bye");
```

The message that the server sends when it is shutting down is a similar string that contains the words "bye bye". When the program sees this, it issues a **break** command to exit the loop.

```
if (str.equals("bye bye"))
        break;
```

When the process ends, all the streams and sockets will be closed automatically. It is considered good form to close them yourself, however, because explicit calls are easier for the JVM to deal with. In some situations, this might improve performance slightly.

```
ois.close();
oos.close();
socket1.close();
```

The other half of the program is the server. The server in a two-way conversation is not much different from the client. It too uses the socket to create both an **ObjectInputStream** and an **ObjectOutputStream**. The main difference is that the server contains an instance of the **ServerSocket**. This special class waits for another program to contact it. Listing 20.4 shows a socket server that communicates both ways.

LISTING 20.4   The LoopingSocketServer.java File

```
/*
 * LoopingSocketServer.java
 *
 * Created on October 2, 2002, 5:24 PM
 */

package ch20;

import java.net.*;
import java.io.*;

/**
 *
 * @author   Stephen Potts
 */
public class LoopingSocketServer
{
    ServerSocket servSocket;
    Socket fromClientSocket;
    int cTosPortNumber = 1777;
    String str;


    /** Creates a new instance of LoopingSocketServer */
    public LoopingSocketServer()
    {
        // Create ServerSocket to listen for connections
        try
        {
            servSocket = new ServerSocket(cTosPortNumber);
```

LISTING 20.4   Continued

```java
            // Wait for client to connnect, then get Socket
            System.out.println("ServerSocket created");
            System.out.println("Waiting for a connection on " +
            cTosPortNumber);

            fromClientSocket = servSocket.accept();
            System.out.println("fromClientSocket accepted");

            // Use ObjectOutputStream to send String to the client
            ObjectOutputStream oos =
            new ObjectOutputStream(fromClientSocket.getOutputStream());

            //Use ObjectInputStream to get String from client
            ObjectInputStream ois =
            new ObjectInputStream(fromClientSocket.getInputStream());

            while ((str = (String) ois.readObject()) != null)
            {
                System.out.println("The message from client is *** " +
                                                            str);

                if (str.equals("bye"))
                {
                    oos.writeObject("bye bye");
                    break;
                }
                else
                {
                    str = "Server returns " + str;
                    oos.writeObject(str);
                }

            }
            oos.close();

            // Close Sockets
            fromClientSocket.close();
        } catch (Exception e)
        {
            System.out.println("Exception " + e);
        }
    }

    public static void main(String args[])
    {
        LoopingSocketServer lss = new LoopingSocketServer();
    }


}
```

The primary difference between the server and the client is that the server contains a ServerSocket object, which is used to make the connection to the client.

```
servSocket = new ServerSocket(cTosPortNumber);
```

The accept command will provide us with a handle to the socket that the client requested. If no client is available when the server is started, the server just waits for it. It does not throw an Exception the way the client does.

```
fromClientSocket = servSocket.accept();
System.out.println("fromClientSocket accepted");
```

We instantiate an ObjectOutputStream object so that we can send data to the ObjectInputStream on the client.

```
ObjectOutputStream oos =
new ObjectOutputStream(fromClientSocket.getOutputStream());

//Use ObjectInputStream to get String from client
ObjectInputStream ois =
new ObjectInputStream(fromClientSocket.getInputStream());
```

We also use a while loop on the server to keep this program alive until we are ready to shut it down.

```
while ((str = (String) ois.readObject()) != null)
{
```

We print the message to standard output.

```
System.out.println("The message from client is *** " +
                                                   str);
```

We test for the "bye" message first. When we receive it, we send the "bye bye" message, then break.

```
if (str.equals("bye"))
{
    oos.writeObject("bye bye");
    break;
}
```

Otherwise, this is a valid message that needs to be processed.

```
else
{
    str = "Server returns " + str;
```

Writing to the server's ObjectOutputStream will send data to the ObjectInputStream of the client.

```
oos.writeObject(str);
```

You must start the server program first. These two programs interact with each other until the "bye" command is sent. The results of running these program are shown here:

The server output looks like this:

```
ServerSocket created
Waiting for a connection on 1777
fromClientSocket accepted
The message from client is *** initialize
The message from client is *** bye
```

The client output looks like this:

```
Server returns initialize
bye bye
```

FIGURE 20.4
The Socket
communication
process.

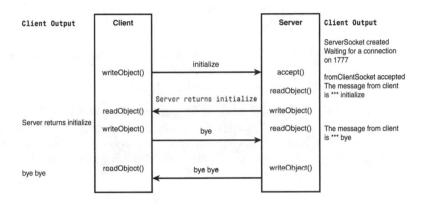

The following sequence of events takes place in this diagram.

1. The **ServerSocket** object is created on the server. The created and waiting messages are issued.

2. The **ServerSocket** object calls the **accept()** method.

3. The client opens a socket and writes the word "initialize" to it.

4. The **accept()** method returns the socket handle.

5. The server uses the socket handle to call **readObject()**.

6. The server prints the information to output and calls **writeObject()**, which contains a String that says "Server returns initialize."

7. The client makes a call to **readObject()** and retrieves the String object.

8. The client prints the "Server returns initialize" string.

9. The client calls **writeObject()**, and sends the string "bye."

10. The server calls **readObject()** and gets the String "bye."

11. The server prints out the String "bye."

12. The server calls **writeObject()** and sends the string "bye bye."

13. The server breaks out of the loop, closes the streams and socket, then exits.

14. The client calls `readObject()` to get the string "bye bye."

15. The client prints the string "bye bye."

16. The client breaks out of the loop, closes the streams and socket, then exits.

Don't be surprised if it takes a while to understand this example. It contains some processing that is not trivial to understand.

Transferring Complex Objects with Sockets

Sometimes we are given requirements to create a system that needs to have objects move from one computer to the other. One way to do this would be to turn the objects into String objects, send them via the socket to the other computer, then re-create the object on the other machine. This will work, but there is a better way.

Listings 20.3 and 20.4 used the `ObjectInputStream` and the `ObjectOutputStream` classes to transfer objects back and forth. The object being sent was just a String, however. You might be wondering how you would send a complex object using sockets. Listings 20.5, 20.6, and 20.7 show you a fairly complex set of objects that can be sent using these same streams.

LISTING 20.5   The `ComplexEmployee.java` File

```java
/*
 * ComplexEmployee.java
 *
 * Created on October 3, 2002, 3:42 PM
 */

package ch20;

import java.io.*;
import java.util.*;
/**
 *
 * @author   Stephen Potts
 */
public class ComplexEmployee implements Serializable
{
    private String name;
    private int salary;

    /** Creates a new instance of ComplexEmployee */
    public ComplexEmployee(String name, int salary)
    {
        this.name = name;
        this.salary = salary;
    }
```

LISTING 20.5   The `ComplexEmployee.java` File

```
    public String getName()
    {
        return name;
    }

    public int getSalary()
    {
        return this.salary;
    }
}
```

This class is ordinary except for the fact that it is declared to be serializable. The serializability of this class is not hard to understand; its data consists of one String and one int, both of which are serializable. The Serializable interface does not require us to implement any special methods. It is what is called a marker interface. By implementing this interface, we are stating that moving this class from one machine to another will not break it because it contains no machine-specific data. An example of machine-specific data would be a handle to a Socket. The data in the Socket object pertains to addresses on this specific machine. Moving it to another machine would render the values in the object useless.

```
public class ComplexEmployee implements Serializable
```

Listing 20.6 contains the code for the `ComplexDepartment` class.

LISTING 20.6   The `ComplexDepartment.java` File

```
/*
 * ComplexDepartment.java
 *
 * Created on October 3, 2002, 3:54 PM
 */

package ch20;

import java.io.Serializable;

/**
 *
 * @author  Stephen Potts
 */
public class ComplexDepartment implements Serializable
{
    private String name;
    private ComplexEmployee manager;

    public ComplexDepartment(String name)
    {
        this.name = name;
    }
```

LISTING 20.6   Continued

```java
        public String getName()
        {
            return this.name;
        }
        public ComplexEmployee getManager()
        {
            return this.manager;
        }

        public void addManager(ComplexEmployee e)
        {
            manager = e;
        }
}
```

The only really interesting feature of this class is the fact that one of its private class-level variables is of type `ComplexEmployee`.

```java
        private String name;
        private ComplexEmployee manager;
```

This was done to make the situation more difficult for the Java serialization mechanism to handle.

The third class that we will need for this experiment is called ComplexCompany. It is shown here in Listing 20.7.

LISTING 20.7   The `ComplexCompany` Example

```java
/*
 * ComplexCompany.java
 *
 * Created on October 3, 2002, 3:39 PM
 */

package ch20;

/**
 *
 * @author   Stephen Potts
 */
import java.util.Vector;
import java.util.Iterator;
import java.util.Set;
import java.io.Serializable;


public class ComplexCompany implements Serializable
{
    private String name;
    private ComplexEmployee president;
    private Vector departments;
```

LISTING 20.7   Continued

```
/** Creates new Company */
public ComplexCompany(String name)
{
    this.name = name;
    departments = new Vector();
}

public String getName()
{
    return this.name;
}

public void addDepartment(ComplexDepartment dept)
{
    departments.addElement(dept);
}

public ComplexEmployee getPresident()
{
    return this.president;
}

public void addPresident(ComplexEmployee e)
{
    this.president = e;
}

public Iterator getDepartmentIterator()
{
    return departments.iterator();
}

public void printCompanyObject()
{
    System.out.println("The company name is " + getName());
    System.out.println("The company president is " +
    getPresident().getName());
    System.out.println(" ");

    Iterator i = getDepartmentIterator();
    while (i.hasNext())
    {
        ComplexDepartment d = (ComplexDepartment)i.next();
        System.out.println("   The department name is " +
        d.getName());
        System.out.println("   The department manager is " +
        d.getManager().getName());
        System.out.println(" ");
    }
}

}
```

This class is designed specifically as a brain buster. It contains three different variables. The first one is a `String`, the second one is a `ComplexEmployee`, and the third is a Vector of `ComplexDepartments`.

```
private String name;
private ComplexEmployee president;
private Vector departments;
```

The Vector is the most interesting. We have placed it here to show how well the serialization mechanism in the JVM works. If it can serialize a Vector of class objects that is a member variable of another class properly, we can be duly impressed. Add to that the fact that the classes in the vector each contain a member variable that is a class, and you have a very good test of the strength of the serialization mechanism.

```
/** Creates new Company */
public ComplexCompany(String name)
{
    this.name = name;
    departments = new Vector();
}
```

The `addElement()` method is how you add objects to the vector.

```
public void addDepartment(ComplexDepartment dept)
{
    departments.addElement(dept);
}
```

The recommended way to step through a Vector is by using the methods of the Iterator class. The responsibility for returning the Iterator is placed on the class that contains the vector.

```
public Iterator getDepartmentIterator()
{
    return departments.iterator();
}
```

The `ComplexCompany` class knows how to print itself out to standard output for us to inspect.

```
public void printCompanyObject()
{
    System.out.println("The company name is " + getName());
    System.out.println("The company president is " +
    getPresident().getName());
    System.out.println(" ");
```

The department Vector must be stepped through and each item read to make sure that we have all the departments printed out.

```
    Iterator i = getDepartmentIterator();
    while (i.hasNext())
    {
```

Notice the explicit cast that is done here. The Vector stored its members as being of type Object. You must perform a downcast to the correct datatype.

```
        ComplexDepartment d = (ComplexDepartment)i.next();
        System.out.println("   The department name is " +
        d.getName());
        System.out.println("   The department manager is " +
        d.getManager().getName())
```

The client class creates the object, opens a socket, and writes the object to the socket. Listing 20.8 shows this class.

LISTING 20.8   The `ComplexSocketClient.java` File

```java
/*
 * ComplexSocketClient.java
 *
 * Created on October 2, 2002, 5:34 PM
 */

package ch20;

import java.net.*;
import java.io.*;

/**
 *
 * @author   Stephen Potts
 */
public class ComplexSocketClient
{
    Socket socket1;
    int portNumber = 1777;
    String str = "";

    /** Creates a new instance of ComplexSocketClient */
    public ComplexSocketClient()
    {
        try
        {
            socket1 = new Socket(InetAddress.getLocalHost(),
            portNumber);

            ObjectInputStream ois =
            new ObjectInputStream(socket1.getInputStream());

            ObjectOutputStream oos =
            new ObjectOutputStream(socket1.getOutputStream());

            ComplexCompany comp =
                    new ComplexCompany("The Blazer Company");
            ComplexEmployee emp0 =
                    new ComplexEmployee("Leslie Waller", 1000);
            comp.addPresident(emp0);
```

LISTING 20.8   Continued

```
            ComplexDepartment sales =
                            new ComplexDepartment("Sales");
            ComplexEmployee emp1 =
                        new ComplexEmployee("Grant Jackson", 1200);
            sales.addManager(emp1);
            comp.addDepartment(sales);

            ComplexDepartment accounting =
                            new ComplexDepartment("Accounting");
            ComplexEmployee emp2 =
                        new ComplexEmployee("Clay Cain", 1230);
            accounting.addManager(emp2);
            comp.addDepartment(accounting);

            ComplexDepartment maintenance =
                            new ComplexDepartment("Maintenance");
            ComplexEmployee emp3 =
                        new ComplexEmployee("Greg Hladlick", 1020);
            maintenance.addManager(emp3);
            comp.addDepartment(maintenance);

            oos.writeObject(comp);

            while ((str = (String) ois.readObject()) != null)
            {
                System.out.println(str);
                oos.writeObject("bye");

                if (str.equals("bye bye"))
                    break;
            }

            ois.close();
            oos.close();
            socket1.close();

        } catch (Exception e)
        {
            System.out.println("Exception " + e);
        }
    }

    public static void main(String args[])
    {
        ComplexSocketClient lsp = new ComplexSocketClient();
    }

}
```

We first create the `ComplexCompany` object.

```
            ComplexCompany comp =
                        new ComplexCompany("The Blazer Company");
```

Next, we add the president.

```
ComplexEmployee emp0 =
                new ComplexEmployee("Leslie Waller", 1000);
comp.addPresident(emp0);
```

Next, we add a department.

```
ComplexDepartment sales =
                new ComplexDepartment("Sales");
ComplexEmployee emp1 =
                new ComplexEmployee("Grant Jackson", 1200);
```

We add the department manager.

```
sales.addManager(emp1);
```

Then, we add the department to the company object. Following that, we add two more departments in the same fashion. Then, we write the object to the stream that is connected to the Socket.

```
oos.writeObject(comp);
```

Finally, we wait in a while loop for a response.

```
while ((str = (String) ois.readObject()) != null)
{
    System.out.println(str);
    oos.writeObject("bye");

    if (str.equals("bye bye"))
        break;
}
```

The server is fairly simple also. Listing 20.9 shows the code for this application.

LISTING 20.9 The `ComplexSocketServer.java` File

```
/*
 * ComplexSocketServer.java
 *
 * Created on October 2, 2002, 5:24 PM
 */

package ch20;

import java.net.*;
import java.io.*;
import java.util.*;

/**
 *
 * @author  Stephen Potts
 */
public class ComplexSocketServer
```

LISTING 20.9 Continued

```java
{
    ServerSocket servSocket;
    Socket fromClientSocket;
    int cTosPortNumber = 1777;
    String str;
    ComplexCompany comp;


    /** Creates a new instance of ComplexSocketServer */
    public ComplexSocketServer()
    {
        // Create ServerSocket to listen for connections
        try
        {
            servSocket = new ServerSocket(cTosPortNumber);

            // Wait for client to connnect, then get Socket
            System.out.println("ServerSocket created");
            System.out.println("Waiting for a connection on " +
            cTosPortNumber);

            fromClientSocket = servSocket.accept();
            System.out.println("fromClientSocket accepted");

            // Use ObjectOutputStream to send String to the client
            ObjectOutputStream oos =
            new ObjectOutputStream(fromClientSocket.getOutputStream());

            //Use ObjectInputStream to get String from client
            ObjectInputStream ois =
            new ObjectInputStream(fromClientSocket.getInputStream());


            while ((comp = (ComplexCompany) ois.readObject()) != null)
            {
                comp.printCompanyObject();

                oos.writeObject("bye bye");
                break;
            }
            oos.close();

            // Close Sockets
            fromClientSocket.close();
        } catch (Exception e)
        {
            System.out.println("Exception " + e);
        }
    }
```

LISTING 20.9   Continued

```
public static void main(String args[])
{
    ComplexSocketServer css = new ComplexSocketServer();
}


}
```

The really amazing thing about this application is how little it does. All the work of turning the object into a stream, and then turning it back into an object again is done by the JVM.

After reading the object, it is cast to a handle of type `ComplexCompany`.

```
while ((comp = (ComplexCompany) ois.readObject()) != null)
{
```

We then use this handle to call the `printCompanyObject()` method. In a real-world application, we would obviously do more with this object.

```
comp.printCompanyObject();
```

Following that, we write a message back to the client so that it will know that we got the objects and processed them.

The output from running client is shown here:

```
Server returns initialize
bye bye
```

The output from running the server is shown here.

```
ServerSocket created
Waiting for a connection on 1777
fromClientSocket accepted
The company name is The Blazer Company
The company president is Leslie Waller

    The department name is Sales
    The department manager is Grant Jackson

    The department name is Accounting
    The department manager is Clay Cain

    The department name is Maintenance
    The department manager is Greg Hladlick
```

Notice that the object contained all the information, including what was stored in the Vector.

Transferring Streams with Sockets

The preceding example showed how we can use the `ObjectOutputStream` and `ObjectInputStream` classes to send serializable objects via sockets. Another common need is to send streams via sockets. You can package streams as objects and send them using `ObjectOutputStreams` as demonstrated earlier in this chapter. This might not be the best-performing solution, however, especially when sending large quantities of streaming data.

A better choice in these cases is to use the `PrintWriter` and `BufferedReader` classes. Listing 20.10 shows a modified version of the `LoopingSocketClient` that uses these new I/O classes.

LISTING 20.10   The `BufferedSocketClient.java` File

```java
/*
 * BufferedSocketClient.java
 *
 * Created on October 2, 2002, 5:34 PM
 */

package ch20;

import java.net.*;
import java.io.*;

/**
 *
 * @author   Stephen Potts
 */
public class BufferedSocketClient
{
    Socket socket1;
    int portNumber = 1777;
    String str = "";

    /** Creates a new instance of BufferedSocketClient */
    public BufferedSocketClient()
    {
        try
        {
            socket1 = new Socket(InetAddress.getLocalHost(),
            portNumber);

            BufferedReader br =  new BufferedReader(
                    new InputStreamReader(socket1.getInputStream()));

            PrintWriter pw =
            new PrintWriter(socket1.getOutputStream(), true);

            str = "initialize";
            pw.println(str);


            while ((str = br.readLine()) != null)
            {
                System.out.println(str);
                pw.println("bye");
```

LISTING 20.10   Continued

```
                    if (str.equals("bye bye"))
                        break;
                }

                br.close();
                pw.close();
                socket1.close();

            } catch (Exception e)
            {
                System.out.println("Exception " + e);
            }
        }

        public static void main(String args[])
        {
            BufferedSocketClient bsc = new BufferedSocketClient();
        }

}
```

This client uses the same logic flow as the LoopingSocketClient example, except that it uses different classes to handle the input and the output. The BufferedReader class provides a more efficient way to read characters. Unbuffered readers, like the InputStreamReader class, tend to be inefficient because they tend to trigger an actual read to the underlying stream every time a read method is invoked. BufferedReaders, on the other hand, read larger amounts of data when, a read method call is made. It buffers the extra data that was retrieved and hands it over to the program if and when it is requested by a subsequent read method call.

```
            BufferedReader br =  new BufferedReader(
                        new InputStreamReader(socket1.getInputStream()));
```

The PrintWriter class prints objects to an output stream in text form. The second parameter indicates that we want autoflushing to occur whenever a println() method is invoked.

```
            PrintWriter pw =
            new PrintWriter(socket1.getOutputStream(), true);
```

The PrintWriter uses the println() method to place the String into the stream in text form.

```
            str = "initialize";
            pw.println(str);
```

The BufferedReader class uses the readLine() method to get data from the stream. Notice that this method places the data directly into a String object and that no explicit casting had to be done by the programmer.

```
            while ((str = br.readLine()) != null)
            {
                System.out.println(str);
                pw.println("bye");

                if (str.equals("bye bye"))
                    break;
```

The server portion of this example also needs to have its `ObjectInputStream` and `ObjectOutputStream` classes replaced by the `BufferedReader` and the `PrintWriter` classes. Listing 20.11 shows this class.

LISTING 20.11   The `BufferedSocketServer.java` File

```java
/*
 * BufferedSocketServer.java
 *
 * Created on October 2, 2002, 5:24 PM
 */

package ch20;

import java.net.*;
import java.io.*;

/**
 *
 * @author   Stephen Potts
 */
public class BufferedSocketServer
{
    ServerSocket servSocket;
    Socket fromClientSocket;
    int cTosPortNumber = 1777;
    String str;


    /** Creates a new instance of BufferedSocketServer */
    public BufferedSocketServer()
    {
        // Create ServerSocket to listen for connections
        try
        {
            servSocket = new ServerSocket(cTosPortNumber);

            // Wait for client to connnect, then get Socket
            System.out.println("ServerSocket created");
            System.out.println("Waiting for a connection on " +
            cTosPortNumber);

            fromClientSocket = servSocket.accept();
            System.out.println("fromClientSocket accepted");

            PrintWriter pw =
            new PrintWriter(fromClientSocket.getOutputStream(), true);

            BufferedReader br = new BufferedReader(
              new InputStreamReader(fromClientSocket.getInputStream()));
```

LISTING 20.11 Continued

```
            while ((str = br.readLine()) != null)
            {
                System.out.println("The message from client is *** " +
                                                                str);

                if (str.equals("bye"))
                {
                    pw.println("bye bye");
                    break;
                }
                else
                {
                    str = "Server returns " + str;
                    pw.println(str);
                }

            }
            pw.close();
            br.close();

            // Close Sockets
            fromClientSocket.close();
        } catch (Exception e)
        {
            System.out.println("Exception " + e);
        }
    }

    public static void main(String args[])
    {
        BufferedSocketServer bss = new BufferedSocketServer();
    }


}
```

We obtain a handle to the socket in exactly the same way as before.

```
            fromClientSocket = servSocket.accept();
            System.out.println("fromClientSocket accepted");
```

```
The PrintWriter object is used on the server side also.
```

```
            PrintWriter pw =
            new PrintWriter(fromClientSocket.getOutputStream(), true);
```

The BufferedReader is used to communicate back to the client also. Notice that Sockets are bidirectional, allowing a program to send information back using the same socket that it is reading from.

```
            BufferedReader br = new BufferedReader(
              new InputStreamReader(fromClientSocket.getInputStream()));
```

We use the `readLine()` method without having to perform an explicit cast and place the result in a String object.

```
while ((str = br.readLine()) != null)
{
    System.out.println("The message from client is *** " +
                                                str);
```

We also use the `println()` method to place data onto the socket.

```
    str = "Server returns " + str;
    pw.println(str);
}
```

You start the `BufferedSocketServer` first, and then the `BufferedSocketClient`. The output from the client is shown here:

```
Server returns initialize
bye bye
```

The output from the server is shown here:

```
ServerSocket created
Waiting for a connection on 1777
fromClientSocket accepted
The message from client is *** initialize
The message from client is *** bye
```

Notice that the output from running this program is identical to the output we received when we ran the `ObjectStream` versions of the same program. This suggests that both approaches are valid, and that your decision should be based on the kind of data that you are sending, and what the normal volume of data is.

The URL Class

Another useful class in the `java.net` package is the URL class. A URL (Uniform Resource Locator) is a pointer or handle to a resource on the network. Sometimes this resource is a simple HTML file, and other times it can be a servlet, a Web Service, or a database.

The format of the URL is

`protocol:hostname:port:filename`

In addition, there can also be an optional reference appended to the end.

The URL class can be used to retrieve a resource from the Internet using a program instead of a browser. In fact, you could use this class to write your own browser. Listing 20.12 shows how to use the URL class to download an HTML page.

LISTING 20.12   The `TextFromURL.java` File

```java
/*
 * TextFromURL.java
 *
 * Created on October 4, 2002, 12:38 PM
 */

package ch20;

import java.net.*;
import java.io.*;

/**
 *
 * @author   Stephen Potts
 */
public class TextFromURL
{
    int rawData;

    /** Creates a new instance of TextFromURL */
    public TextFromURL()
    {
        try
        {
            URL myURL = new URL("http://java.sun.com");

            URLConnection uc = myURL.openConnection();

            System.out.println("the host is " + myURL.getHost());
            System.out.println("****************************");
            System.out.println("Here is the HTML for this page");

            InputStream is = myURL.openStream();

            while((rawData = is.read()) != -1)
            {
                System.out.print((char)rawData);
            }

            is.close();
        }catch (MalformedURLException mue)
        {
            System.out.println("Exception " + mue);
        }catch (Exception e)
        {
            System.out.println("Exception " + e);
        }
    }

    /**
     * @param args the command line arguments
     */
```

LISTING 20.12   Continued

```
     public static void main(String[] args)
     {
         TextFromURL tfu = new TextFromURL();
     }

}
```

The data will be read in as an integer and converted to a character.

```
     int rawData;
```

The URL class is constructed with the address of the Java Web site at Sun Microsystems.

```
         URL myURL = new URL("http://java.sun.com");
```

The class that opens the connection is called `URLConnection`.

```
         URLConnection uc = myURL.openConnection();
```

The `getHost()` method returns the name of the host computer for this URL.

```
         System.out.println("the host is " + myURL.getHost());
         System.out.println("****************************");
         System.out.println("Here is the HTML for this page");
```

We will use a stream to access this data.

```
         InputStream is = myURL.openStream();
```

We read the `rawData`, then cast it to a char before printing it out.

```
         while((rawData = is.read()) != -1)
         {
             System.out.print((char)rawData);
         }
```

If there is a problem with the URL, a `MalFormedURLException` is thrown.

```
         }catch (MalformedURLException mue)
         {
             System.out.println("Exception " + mue);
         }catch (Exception e)
```

The output from this program is shown here:

```
the host is java.sun.com
****************************
Here is the HTML for this page
<!DOCTYPE HTML PUBLIC "-//W3C//DTD HTML 4.01 Transitional//EN">
<HTML>
<HEAD>
<TITLE>The Source for Java(TM) Technology</TITLE>
<META http-equiv="Content-Type" content="text/html; charset=iso-8859-1">
<META NAME="description" value="Sun Microsystems'
Java Technology Home Page - Visit this site to get the latest Java
 technologies, news, and products.">
.
```

```
        .
        .

</tr>
<tr>
<td colspan="7" height="1" bgcolor="#cccccc"><img src="/images/v3_pixel.gif"
width="1" height="1"></td>
</tr>
</table>
</span>
        </BODY>
        </HTML>
```

The dots in the middle of this listing indicate that only the beginning and the end of the listing is shown. The entire listing was about 25 pages long.

Summary

In this chapter, you learned about the TCP/IP suite of protocols. The first thing we covered was where TCP/IP came from and how it works. Following that, you saw a simple program that allowed two different processes to exchange data using the `Socket` and `ServerSocket` classes.

Following that, you learned how to get two different Socket-based programs to communicate with each other in a two-way conversation. Next, we worked an example of how complex serialized classes can be sent from one computer to another with very little programming beyond the basic socket handling.

Next, you learned how to write programs that use the `BufferedReader` and the `PrintWriter` classes instead of the `ObjectStreamReader` and the `ObjectStreamWriter` classes. Finally, we learned how to use the URL and `URLConnection` classes to download the HTML from a Web site into our program.

Review Questions

1. What do TCP and IP stand for?

2. What package contains the Java networking classes?

3. What does serializable mean?

4. What is a URL?

Exercises

1. Create a program that sends your address and telephone number over a socket from a client to a server. Use the `ObjectStream` classes.

2. Create a program where the server adds 10 to a number that it is passed via a socket. Return the new value to the client program.

3. Modify Exercise 1 to use the `PrintWriter` and `BufferedReader` classes for I/O.

4. Create a program to download the HTML code from your favorite Web site.

PART V

WEB TECHNOLOGIES

CHAPTER 21

SERVLETS

You will learn about the following in this chapter:

- What servlets are why you need them

- How servlets work

- How to set up a Jakarta Web server to run servlets

- How to program servlets in Java

- How to call other Java classes from inside servlets

- How to maintain the state of a servlet using cookies in the user's browser

- How to maintain the state of a servlet using a session on the server

When Java 1.01 was released, it was heavily oriented toward the development of applications that can run in a browser. The Applet architecture had received a lot of consideration and most of that release supported the GUI classes that facilitated their creation. Almost immediately, the question was asked, "What about developing for the server?"

The Java language offers much more to the developer than cool Internet graphics. It is a robust, highly object-oriented language that is easy to learn. It has a small footprint, and it can run on almost any computer that you can name. It is supported by a host of standard extensions that enables you to perform tasks, such as managing sound and video, without making you learn a host of proprietary command sets and scripting languages. It was only natural for Java to become popular on the server as well.

Java's presence on the server side was initially through programs called servlets. Servlets, like applets, are intended to run in a container. The servlet's engine is not called a browser, however, but a servlet container. Both applets and servlets have to be written to a pretty exact specification, but the servlets cannot have graphical user interfaces. They can, however, extract data from HTML forms, and they can create HTML and send it to the client to provide visual feedback.

With the introduction of the Java 2 Enterprise Edition (J2EE), servlets became only one of many server-side technologies available to programmers. Enterprise JavaBeans (EJB) have become popular for complex applications, but servlets remain as popular as ever.

In this chapter, we are going to cover servlets from the developer's standpoint. First, you will learn how to obtain and install a servlet container on your machine. Next, you will learn how to develop, deploy, and run servlets. Following that, you will learn how to write servlets that maintain user information across transactions.

What Servlets Are and Are Not

Servlets are miniature programs that must be run inside another program called a container. The container is responsible for brokering communication between the servlet and the outside world. Beyond that, servlets are like every Java application. They can import packages, write to the hard drive, and even install viruses on your machine. By default, servlets are trusted code. The reason is that if someone has enough permission on your computer to install a servlet, he already has enough power to tie the whole machine in knots anyway. The thought is that this installer is a trusted person, so the work that he does should be trusted, too.

Servlets are not Java applications. They must be run inside a container instead of from a command line. That being said, you can add almost any functionality available to a Java application to a servlet also.

Servlets are not the only way for the server to communicate with a browser. A Web server is an HTTP application. It receives communication via the HTTP protocol and it communicates with the browser via HTTP also. You can write your own HTTP server-side application that processes its own requests, bypassing both servlets and the servlet container. This chapter contains a simple example of how that is done.

Why Do I Need Servlets?

Servlets are here to make your life easier. If the only option available was to write HTTP applications from scratch every time new functionality was needed, not much development would take place on the Web. Not many organizations could afford to write HTTP programs from scratch. The existence of the servlet container avoids the cost of having to include the entire HTTP header processing code in every program. Servlets extend classes that take care of all that work behind the scenes.

Another advantage of servlets is that they scale nicely. The servlet container is responsible for instantiating your servlet whenever it is needed. If it is needed a lot, the servlet container has the option of creating as many threads or instances of your servlet as its load-balancing algorithms indicates it needs.

Servlets make good use of machine resources. They run in threads that are created by the servlet container. Each individual HTTP application program runs in its own process.

Processes are far more expensive to create than threads, so the servlet approach is more efficient. Servlet containers can also pool connections so that the threads already created are reused instead of discarded. The ancestor of the servlet, the CGI program, lacked these features and has faded in popularity as a result.

How Servlets Work

Servlets are really parts of an application and require a servlet container to run. This servlet container is responsible for instantiating your servlet and calling the appropriate methods in the servlet at the appropriate times.

When you type the name of a servlet, you are really making a call to a program that is located on a server and not on your machine. At first, this process seems like magic, but after a little study you will see that this process only requires that each piece of software in the process perform a fairly simple set of tasks. Figure 21.1 shows this process graphically.

FIGURE 21.1.

The servlet container is responsible for instantiating your servlets.

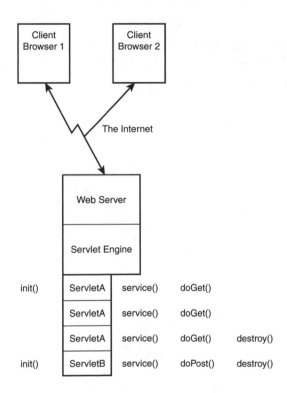

1. You type in the URL of a servlet that you want to call.

2. The browser creates a request that contains the servlet and the name of your machine so that the server will know who to send feedback to.

3. The server receives the request and hands it to the servlet container. The servlet container is a program that knows how to run servlets.

4. The servlet container checks to see if any instances of this servlet are already in memory. If not, it loads an instance and runs the servlet's `init()` method.

5. The servlet container waits for the `init()` method to finish. It then calls the `service()` method in your servlet from a new thread.

6. The `service()` method calls the `doGet()` or `doPost()` method depending on what the request type is.

7. A second user's browser requests that the same servlet be run on its behalf.

8. The servlet container notices that an instance of the servlet is already in memory. So, it creates a new thread and starts running the same servlet that you are running.

9. This new thread calls the `service()` method.

10. If this is an HTTP servlet, the `service()` method calls the `doGet()` or `doPost()` methods.

11. The first thread finishes and a response is sent to the Web server, which forwards it to your browser.

12. The second thread finishes and a response is sent to the Web server, which forwards it to the second user's browser.

13. At a certain point in the future, the servlet container decides to deinstantiate the servlet. At that point it calls the `destroy()` method once for each instance in memory.

> ### Caution
> Whether more than one instance of a single servlet is in memory depends on whether it is declared to be thread-safe. A servlet is assumed to be thread-safe unless it implements the `SingleThreadModel` interface. If it implements this interface, a new instance will be created for each simultaneous access. This has serious performance penalties associated with it, so it should only be done if absolutely necessary.

Setting Up a Web Environment

Before you can develop and test servlets, you need to set up a Web development environment. You will need several pieces of software to accomplish this. The first one is a recent version of Java, which you probably already have installed on your machine. In case you don't, however, you can obtain the Java Software Development Kit (SDK) from Sun Microsystems at `http://www.java.sun.com`.

You most likely have a browser installed on your machine also. You will want to make sure that you have an up-to-date browser version, so it would be a good idea to check this version against the latest release that is available on the Microsoft and Netscape Web sites. There are times when the two leading browsers behave differently, so it is also a good idea to install both of them on your machine for testing.

In addition, you need some way to compose and edit programs. All the examples in this chapter can be typed in using Notepad or vi and run from a command line.

Note

Java-specific editors are available, and you might find that it is worth your while to learn how to use one. Forte has a version that is available for free at `http://www.java.sun.com`. JBuilder and Visual Café are two commercial products that are popular with developers also.

The third piece of the servlet puzzle is the servlet container itself. If you are currently running a Web server that provides servlet support, you can skip this step. If you don't have a servlet container running already, you will need to follow the instructions in the next section to set up the Tomcat server on your machine. Tomcat contains a light version of a Web server that is complete with a servlet container.

Installing Jakarta Tomcat

Jakarta Tomcat is available at no cost from the Apache Web site at `http://www.apache.org/`.

The link for Tomcat 4.0.4 is

`http://jakarta.apache.org/builds/jakarta-tomcat-4.0/release/v4.0.4/bin/`.

Choose a release that is right for your needs. If you are running Java 1.4, the following self-extracting `.exe` file will be correct for you:

`jakarta-tomcat-4.0.4-LE-jdk14.exe`

Caution

As new versions of Tomcat are released, the links that lead to them will differ from those shown previously. In these cases, you will need to go to the `http://jakarta.apache.org/` Web site and navigate to the newest release.

You will then be prompted to enter the location where you want this `.exe` file stored. Next, open Windows Explorer and double-click the name of the `.exe` file. This will open an installation wizard that will guide you through the installation. After you answer a few questions, you will be told that the installation is complete.

If you are running under Unix, you can download the tar version and follow the instructions on the Apache Web site on how to install Tomcat on your machine.

Caution

Vendor Web sites change from time to time. If the previous steps don't work exactly, look for similar links at each step, and you should be able to succeed in getting Tomcat installed.

Starting Tomcat

You start Tomcat by opening a command window and typing the following command.

```
java -jar -Duser.dir="C:\Program Files\Apache Tomcat 4.0"
"C:\Program Files\Apache Tomcat 4.0\bin\bootstrap.jar" start
```

Tomcat will output several lines of responses like these, which provide feedback that the server is really running.

```
Starting service Tomcat-Standalone
Apache Tomcat/4.0.4
Starting service Tomcat-Apache
Apache Tomcat/4.0.4
```

On some operating systems, the installation script places some shortcuts in your file system to make the task of starting Tomcat easier. On our test machine, Windows XP, these shortcuts were placed in a directory called:

```
C:\Documents and Settings\Your Name\Start Menu\Programs\Apache Tomcat 4.0
```

`Your Name` will be replaced by the login name of the machine that you are using.

Another link on that page opens a browser that contains the root page for the copy of the Tomcat documentation that is stored on your local hard drive. Figure 21.2 shows this page.

FIGURE 21.2
The Tomcat documentation provides detailed instructions about how to get the server and keep it running.

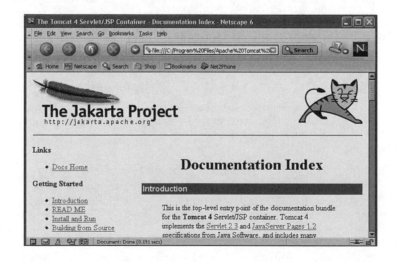

> **Note**
>
> You can find answers to many of your questions with these pages, so it would be a good idea to bookmark the root page in your browser.

Most of the work that you will do with Tomcat will involve four of the directories located under the root Tomcat directory. These directories are

- `C:\Program Files\Apache Tomcat 4.0\bin`—This directory contains scripts to perform functions such as startup, shutdown, and so on. Under Windows, these scripts are `.bat` files, and under Unix, they are `.sh` files.

- `C:\Program Files\Apache Tomcat 4.0\conf`—This directory contains configuration files, which control the behavior of the server. Most of these files are in XML format. The most important file in here is called `server.xml`, the main configuration file for the server.

- `C:\Program Files\Apache Tomcat 4.0\logs`—This directory contains the logs that are created by the Tomcat server. You inspect these logs to discover clues about why certain problems are occurring with the installation and/or your programs.

- `C:\Program Files\Apache Tomcat 4.0\webapps`—This directory is where you put your programs. Web servers don't like to access files all over your computer because of the security risks. They prefer to allow clients to access only files that are stored in one place and its subdirectories.

Testing the Installation

After you have finished the installation, you will want to test the server using servlets provided by Apache before writing your own. The reason for this is that any problem you have running their servlets is certainly a configuration problem. If you run your own servlets without first verifying that the installation is correct, the problem could be either in the installation or with your servlet.

Testing the installation is easy. First, start Tomcat by following the procedure described previously. Next, type the following command in a browser address box:

`http://localhost:8080`

You should immediately see a screen that looks like Figure 21.3.

If you do not see this page immediately, the most likely reason is that you have another program listening to port 8080. In that case, edit the file called `server.xml` in the `C:\Program Files\Apache Tomcat 4.0\conf` directory. Look for the following lines:

```
<!-- Define a non-SSL HTTP/1.1 Connector on port 8080 -->
<Connector
        className="org.apache.catalina.connector.http.HttpConnector"
            port="8080" minProcessors="5" maxProcessors="75"
            enableLookups="true" redirectPort="8443"
```

```
                        acceptCount="10" debug="0" connectionTimeout="60000"/>
```

Edit the fourth line and change it to some value more than 1024, like 1776. It will look like this:

```
<!-- Define a non-SSL HTTP/1.1 Connector on port 8080 -->
  <Connector className=
            "org.apache.catalina.connector.http.HttpConnector"
            port="1776" minProcessors="5" maxProcessors="75"
            enableLookups="true" redirectPort="8443"
            acceptCount="10" debug="0" connectionTimeout="60000"/>
```

FIGURE 21.3
The Tomcat localhost home page will display when the server is running properly.

Save this file and restart the Tomcat server. Repeat the test by opening a browser, but this time type

`http://localhost:1776`

If this doesn't open the magic Web page shown in Figure 21.3, consult the troubleshooting documentation that Tomcat installed on your hard drive.

Note

This chapter uses port 1776 for all the examples. The reason for this is that port 8080, the default Tomcat port, was already in use on our test machine.

Programming Servlets

Servlet programming is built on a solid foundation of prewritten Java classes. Instead of creating servlets as Java classes that are started by calling a main method, servlets are extensions of other classes that already know how to interact with Web servers and servlet containers.

The following classes and interfaces are the most important ones to understand when programming servlets:

- **Servlet**—This interface defines the `init()`, `service()`, and `destroy()` methods. It also defines two more methods that implementing classes must provide, `getServletConfig()` and `getServletInfo()`, which allow you to query the servlet for information about the servlet itself (author, version, copyright, and so on). The servlet container is programmed to expect a servlet to implement these five methods. This is how code that you write can be plugged into a framework such as the servlet container so easily. Advanced programmers might want to implement this interface directly in a new class instead of using either the `GenericServlet` class or `HttpServlet` class. This would require you to write quite a bit of code, however, and it is not needed to satisfy ordinary requirements.

- **GenericServlet**—The `GenericServlet` class provides a simple implementation of the `Servlet` interface. It is called "Generic" because it does not assume that the protocol it will process will be HTTP. If you were writing your own protocol, you would extend this class. Normally, you override the `service()` method.

- HttpServlet—This is the class that is most often extended when servlets are written. It extends `GenericServlet` to provide HTTP-specific processing. Because HTTP is so common, servlets that extend this class tend to be the easiest to write. Normally, you override the `doGet()`, `doPost()`, or both methods of this class. This class contains a default implementation of `service()` that calls the appropriate `doXXX()` method, depending on the type of request that is received.

- **ServletRequest**—This interface defines an object that contains the information that the client has provided, along with his request to run the servlet. A concrete implementation of this object is `ServletRequestWrapper` class.

- **HttpServletRequestWrapper**—This is an extension of the `ServletRequestWrapper` that contains information specifically assuming that the request will be in HTTP format. In most servlets, this class is accessed polymorphically via a handle to the `ServletRequest` interface. See Chapter 7, "Inheritance," for information on how this works.

- **ServletResponse**—This interface defines a convenient way for a servlet to communicate the information that it wants to send to the client to the servlet container. A concrete implementation of this object is `ServletResponseWrapper` class.

- **HttpServletResponseWrapper**—This is an extension of the `ServletResponseWrapper` that assumes that the response will be in HTTP format. In most servlets, this class is accessed polymorphically via a handle to the `ServletResponse` interface.

Programming Generic Servlets

Even though most of this chapter will deal with HTTP-based servlets, it is useful to understand how a servlet can be created that is not tied to this protocol. Listing 21.1 shows a simple generic servlet.

LISTING 21.1   The `GenericHello` Class

```java
/*
 * GenericHello.java
 *
 * Created on June 21, 2002, 5:28 PM
 */


import javax.servlet.*;
import java.io.*;

/**
 *
 * @author  Stephen Potts
 * @version
 */
public class GenericHello extends GenericServlet
{

    /** Initializes the servlet.
     */
    public void init(ServletConfig config) throws ServletException
    {
        super.init(config);

    }

    /** Destroys the servlet.
     */
    public void destroy()
    {

    }

    public void service(ServletRequest req, ServletResponse resp)
    throws ServletException, java.io.IOException
    {
        resp.setContentType("text/html");
        java.io.PrintWriter out = resp.getWriter();
        out.println("Hello from the GenericHello Servlet");
        out.close();
    }

    /** Returns a short description of the servlet.
     */
    public String getServletInfo()
    {
        return "This servlet tests the GenericServlet class";
    }

}
```

Notice that this class extends the `GenericServlet` class. As discussed previously, this is a protocol-neutral servlet class.

```
public class GenericHello extends GenericServlet
```

The `init()` method is overridden here. Notice that it is passed a `ServletConfig` class, which it passes along to the `super(GenericServlet)` class's `init()` method. The `ServletConfig` class contains references to the servlet name and the `ServletContext` object. For now, we can ignore these objects.

```
public void init(ServletConfig config) throws ServletException
{
    super.init(config);
}
```

We override the `destroy()` method just for show.

```
public void destroy()
{

}
```

We also override the `getServletInfo()` method so that you will have an example of how this is done.

```
public String getServletInfo()
{
    return "This servlet tests the GenericServlet class";
}
```

Finally, the `service()` routine is where the action is, what little there is in this example.

```
public void service(ServletRequest req, ServletResponse resp)
throws ServletException, java.io.IOException
{
    java.io.PrintWriter out = resp.getWriter();
    out.println("Hello from the GenericHello Servlet");
    out.close();
}
```

We create a handle to the response object's `PrintWriter` object so that we can send some information to the client. We are not interested in any of the information available from the client in this simple example. We print a string to this object, and then close it. The servlet container is responsible for actually getting the string to the client.

Deploying the Servlet

Under JDK 1.4, all the classes needed to compile this program are automatically installed. This makes it simple to compile the program. You just type the following at a command line:

```
javac GenericHello.java
```

The servlet is now compiled into a `.class` file in this same directory. If this were a garden-variety Java application, we could run it by typing the following:

```
java GenericHello
Exception in thread "main" java.lang.NoSuchMethodError: main
```

Being a servlet, this class has no `main()` method, and the Java runtime engine points that out to you by throwing an exception.

We could just go and type the name of this servlet in the address line of our browser, but that will give us an error message stating that the servlet container doesn't know anything about this servlet as shown in Figure 21.4.

FIGURE 21.4.
The Tomcat server doesn't know anything about this servlet, so it provides a polite error message.

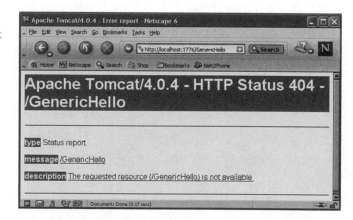

We have a servlet container running, and we have a servlet that compiles. What we need is a way to tell the servlet container about this servlet. A good quick-hitter approach to this is to place the servlet in the `...\webapps\examples\WEB-INF\classes` directory. After that is done, we can type the following URL in your browser's address field (with Tomcat running):

`http://localhost:1776/examples/servlet/GenericHello`

If you installed Tomcat using the default port of 8080, you would substitute "8080" for the "1776."

The examples string indicates that the `GenericHello` class is a servlet, and that its class file can be found under the `examples` subdirectory. Figure 21.5 shows the result of running `GenericHello`.

Notice that the message is output to the screen in whatever font the browser chooses. This is done because we provided no input to the browser on how to format the results. This desire to have more control over the layout is the motivation for creating the `HTTPServlet` class.

Next, let's modify our example to use the `HTTPServlet` class so that we can have more control over the output. Listing 21.2 shows the code for the new servlet.

FIGURE 21.5.
The `GenericServlet`'s output contains no formatting information.

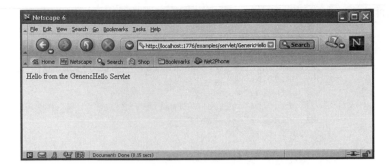

LISTING 21.2 The `HTTPHello` Example

```java
/*
 * HTTPHello.java
 *
 * Created on June 21, 2002, 9:59 AM
 */

import javax.servlet.*;
import javax.servlet.http.*;

/**
 *
 * @author   Stephen Potts
 * @version
 */
public class HTTPHello extends HttpServlet
{

    /** Initializes the servlet.
     */
    public void init(ServletConfig config) throws ServletException
    {
        super.init(config);

    }

    /** Destroys the servlet.
     */
    public void destroy()
    {

    }

    /** Processes requests for both HTTP <code>GET</code>
     *   and <code>POST</code> methods.
     * @param request servlet request
     * @param response servlet response
     */
    protected void processRequest(HttpServletRequest request,
                                  HttpServletResponse response)
```

LISTING 21.2   Continued

```java
    throws ServletException, java.io.IOException {
        response.setContentType("text/html");
        java.io.PrintWriter out = response.getWriter();
        out.println("<html>");
        out.println("<head>");
        out.println("<title>HTTPHello</title>");
        out.println("</head>");
        out.println("<body>");

        //Make the font large
        out.println("<H1>");
        //Make the font bold
        out.println("<B>");

        out.println("Hello from the HTTPHello Servlet");
        out.println("</H1>");
        out.println("</B>");

        out.println("</body>");
        out.println("</html>");
        out.close();
    }

    /** Handles the HTTP <code>GET</code> method.
     * @param request servlet request
     * @param response servlet response
     */
    protected void doGet(HttpServletRequest request,
                             HttpServletResponse response)
    throws ServletException, java.io.IOException {
        processRequest(request, response);
    }

    /** Handles the HTTP <code>POST</code> method.
     * @param request servlet request
     * @param response servlet response
     */
    protected void doPost(HttpServletRequest request,
                             HttpServletResponse response)
    throws ServletException, java.io.IOException {
        processRequest(request, response);
    }

    /** Returns a short description of the servlet.
     */
    public String getServletInfo() {
        return "This is the HTTPHello Servlet";
    }

}
```

This servlet was created using the Forte for Java code editor, which generates an empty `HTTPServlet` for you. This can save you time when writing servlets, but it can retard learning. Until you become familiar with the purpose of every line of code in this example, any tools will hamper learning. After you can write servlets in your sleep, the tools will speed up your coding a little.

Notice that we now have an extra import statement. This package will give us HTTP processing.

```
import javax.servlet.http.*;
```

This servlet extends `HTTPServlet`. This will impact us because we will be overriding `doGet()` and `doPost()` instead of `service()`.

```
public class HTTPHello extends HttpServlet
```

We have overridden the `doGet()` and `doPost()` methods in a unique fashion.

```
    protected void doGet(HttpServletRequest request,
                              HttpServletResponse response)
    throws ServletException, java.io.IOException
    {
        processRequest(request, response);
    }

    protected void doPost(HttpServletRequest request,
                              HttpServletResponse response)
    throws ServletException, java.io.IOException
    {
        processRequest(request, response);
    }
```

In both cases we simply made a call to a method that we named `processRequest()` and passed the request and response objects to it. There is nothing special about the name `processRequest()`. We could have called it `xyz()`. Later in this chapter we will look at the HTTP protocol and the difference between the `Get` and `Post` commands.

The real work in our example is now done in the `processRequest()` method. This method is passed in both an `HttpServletRequest` object and an `HTTPServletResponse` object.

```
    protected void processRequest(HttpServletRequest request,
                                    HttpServletResponse response)
    throws ServletException, java.io.IOException {
```

These will be used extensively in future examples, but for now, we only use the response object.

```
        response.setContentType("text/html");
        java.io.PrintWriter out = response.getWriter();
```

We use the `PrintWriter` object to put data into the response object for transmission back to the client. Notice that HTML code makes up the contents of the string.

```
        out.println("<html>");
        out.println("<head>");
```

```
out.println("<title>HTTPHello</title>");
out.println("</head>");
out.println("<body>");
```

We add this line to make the font large.

```
out.println("<H1>");
```

This line makes the font bold.

```
out.println("<B>");
```

This line contains the contents of what we want displayed.

```
out.println("Hello from the HTTPHello Servlet");
```

The result of running this is similar to when we ran the `GenericHello` servlet, as shown here in Figure 21.6.

FIGURE 21.6
The `HTTPServlet` enables us to format our output by using HTML commands.

Understanding HTTP

Because you will be using `HttpServlet` class to implement most of the servlets that you will ever write, it is important for you to understand what HTTP is. HTTP stands for Hypertext Transfer Protocol. A protocol is simply a published agreement between clients and servers that specifies what data, and its syntax, will be passed from one party to the other.

HTTP is an application layer protocol, which means that it depends on lower-layer protocols to do much of the work. In the case of HTTP, this lower-layer protocol is TCP/IP. The information in HTTP is transferred as plain ASCII characters. Plain text is convenient for programmers because the instructions are human-readable. By contrast, binary protocols like those used in RMI and CORBA are much more difficult to decipher when searching for the cause of a programming error.

HTTP is a stateless and connectionless protocol. Stateless means that each request and response pair constitutes an entire conversation. There is no memory of one transaction available to the next transaction. It is kind of like computerized amnesia. Connectionless means that there is no concept of a logon or logoff in HTTP, as there is in FTP. In fact, the requester is anonymous from the protocol's point of view.

Being stateless is both good and bad. It is good from a performance standpoint because there is no need for the program that accepts HTTP requests (the Web server) to remember any state information. This greatly reduces the server's workload and makes it possible for one server to process thousands of clients. On the other hand, being stateless limits the usefulness of the protocol. If you want to create an application that does some work, asks the user some questions, then does some more work, you have to manage this in the code that you write. We will cover this problem of saving state later in the chapter.

A connectionless protocol also has positives and negatives. If no time is spent establishing a connection, the server can service more requests per unit of time. This also limits the usefulness of the protocol. If you want a user to logon, do some stuff, then logoff, you will have to write your own code to do that. Fortunately, the servlet classes support this requirement pretty well.

HTTP is a request and response protocol. This means that it is composed of pairs of requests and responses, as shown in Figure 21.7.

FIGURE 21.7.
The HTTP protocol is based on the assumption that every request will be answered with one response.

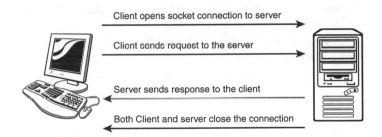

Client opens socket connection to server

Client sends request to the server

Server sends response to the client

Both Client and server close the connection

The format of the request is all done in plain text and is sent as a string from the client to the server. The server reads the message and performs the task that it has been instructed to do. In some cases, this task is to retrieve a static document and send it back to the client's browser for display. In other cases, this request is for a servlet to be run and the results of that, if any, to be sent to the client.

The GET Command

The most frequently used HTTP command is the GET command. This command states that the browser is to ask the server to send back a copy of a document. If that document has already been cached, the browser might use that one instead of retrieving it again. Listing 21.3 shows a simple HTTP GET request for a document.

LISTING 21.3 A Request for xyz.html

```
GET /xyz.html HTTP/1.0
User-Agent: Mozilla/4.51   (WinNT; I)
Accept: image/gif, image/jpeg, image/pjpeg, */*
```

- The GET means that we want to retrieve a result. Also those parameters, if any, will be appended to the name of the document or servlet.

- The User-Agent tag tells the server what version of the browser the client is running. This gives the server a chance to tailor the response to suit this browser.

- The Accept tag tells the server what kind of replies, in addition to text, the browser can process.

The job of the Web server is to parse this text and decide how to handle the results. If you want to pass parameters to the server, you can do that by appending them to the name of the document, as shown in Listing 21.4.

LISTING 21.4   Passing Parameters with GET

```
GET /xyz.html?myparm=hello&myotherparm=world HTTP/1.0
User-Agent: Mozilla/4.51    (WinNT; I)
Accept: image/gif, image/jpeg, image/pjpeg, */*
```

In this listing, we are telling the server to return that HTML page modified by the values in the parameters. The special syntax using the ? tells the server that parameters start here. A parameter/value pair is indicated by the =. The & indicates that another parameter follows this. Notice that there are no quotes around the strings. If numbers are placed on the line, they are sent as strings also, and it is up to the server or servlet to do any conversion or casting to another data type.

The parameters modify the behavior of the document or servlet. The nature of the modification is a decision of the page designer or servlet programmer. The names of the parameters are important because they will be used to extract the value for this parameter from the request object in the servlet.

There is a limit of 255 characters that can be used to pass parameters appended in this way. The reason for this is that some Web servers store this string in an environment variable that is rather small. If you use a length greater than 255, it may or may not work, depending on the client. In practice, if there is a parameter list that long, the programmer will use the POST command instead.

Another drawback of passing the parameters this way is that they appear in the address bar of the browser. If your password is one of the data items, this could be a problem because the history kept by your browser now contains your password in plain text.

Calling a servlet is very similar. Listing 21.5 contains the HTTP message to invoke a servlet:

LISTING 21.5   Calling a Servlet

```
GET /xyz.html?myparm=hello&myotherparm=world HTTP/1.0
User-Agent: Mozilla/4.51    (WinNT; I)
Accept: image/gif, image/jpeg, image/pjpeg, */*
```

Notice that we don't specify the name of the server in this command. This is because a socket to this machine has already been opened before this message is sent. Notice also that there is no special syntax to indicate that this is a servlet. It is the responsibility of the Web server to figure out what kind of request it has been given.

The POST Command

The POST command is used to send data to the Web server. By convention, POST requests are not answered out of cache, but rather sent to the server every time. Listing 21.6 contains an example of a post command.

LISTING 21.6   The POST Command

```
POST /xyz.html HTTP/1.0
User-Agent: Mozilla/4.51   (WinNT; I)
Accept: image/gif, image/jpeg, image/pjpeg, */*
Content-Length: 34
Content-Type:application/x-www-form-urlencoded

myparm=hello&myotherparm=world
```

Notice that there is a blank line between the header and the contents of the message; this is required. The length must also be passed as well as a content type. There is no stated limit to the length of the parameters to be passed using the POST command. In addition, the values of the parameters are not displayed on the command line of the browser. Aside from these differences, the behavior of the GET and the POST commands are identical.

The Other Commands

The HEAD command is like a GET command that returns only the header, but not the contents of the response. This can be useful if the browser wants only information about the document, but it doesn't have much practical value for servlet development. Other commands such as PUT, DELETE, LINK, and UNLINK are in the specification, but because they have little or no value to the servlet developer, we will not cover them here.

HTTP 1.1

A new version, HTTP 1.1, has been proposed and published by the Internet Engineering Task Group (IETF). This new version will add quite a few improvements to the HTTP 1.0 standard, but none that directly impact servlet developers. One improvement that indirectly impacts developers is the fact that connections are now kept alive by default. This means that the server will discontinue its conversation with the client, but without actually closing the connection. This connection can be reused, but it is not associated with the client that used it last. This behavior changes the performance, but not the syntax, of the HTTP commands.

Programming HTTP

The browser is a program that processes HTTP commands, among other things. The Web server is also an HTTP processing program. Both of these programs fill a place in our programming world, but they are not the only ways to process HTTP commands.

You can write a fairly simple pair of Java programs that communicate with each other, with browsers, and with servers using HTTP. Understanding how they work will clarify many points that are sometimes fuzzy when dealing with browsers and Web servers. Listing 21.7 shows a simple Java program that is able to talk to the Tomcat server using port 1776.

LISTING 21.7   The HTTPFetch Class

```
/*
 * HTTPFetch.java
 *
 * Created on June 18, 2002, 2:54 PM
 */


import java.io.*;
import java.net.*;

/**
 *
 * @author  Stephen Potts
 * @version
 */
public class HTTPFetch
{

   /** Creates new HTTPFetch */
    public HTTPFetch()
    {
    }

    public static void main (String[] args)
    {
       try
       {
          URL url = new URL(
          "http://localhost:1776");
          BufferedReader in = new BufferedReader(
                    new InputStreamReader(url.openStream()));
          String line;
          while ((line = in.readLine()) != null)
          {
             System.out.println(line);
          }
          in.close();
       }catch(Exception e)
       {
```

LISTING 21.7   Continued

```
            e.printStackTrace();
        }
    }
}
```

This program simply initiates communication with the Tomcat server and receives the default home page. This is the page that was shown in Figure 21.3.

This program makes heavy use of the HTTP processing built into Java. We first declare a new URL object and pass in the address of the Tomcat server as a parameter to the constructor.

```
        URL url = new URL(
        "http://localhost:1776");
```

Next, we open the URL's `inputStream` in a Buffered reader.

```
        BufferedReader in = new BufferedReader(
                    new InputStreamReader(url.openStream()));
        String line;
```

Finally, we look through it and write each line to the screen.

```
        while ((line = in.readLine()) != null)
        {
            System.out.println(line);
    }
```

To run this program, you type the following at the command line, not in a browser:

```
    java HTTPFetch
```

Instead of displaying this page in a nice graphical format, as a browser would, this program just writes the code to standard output as shown here.

```
<!doctype html public "-//w3c//dtd html 4.0 transitional//en"
 "http://www.w3.org/TR/REC-html40/strict.dtd">
<html>
    <head>
    <meta http-equiv="Content-Type" content="text/html; charset=iso-8859-1">
    <title>Jakarta Project - Tomcat</title>
    <style type="text/css">
      <!--
        body {
            color: #000000;
            background-color: #FFFFFF;
            font-family: Arial, "Times New Roman", Times;
            font-size: 16px;
        }

        A:link {
            color: blue
        }

        A:visited {
```

```
                color: blue
            }

            td {
                color: #000000;
                font-family: Arial, "Times New Roman", Times;
                font-size: 16px;
            }

            .code {
                color: #000000;
                font-family: "Courier New", Courier;
                font-size: 16px;
            }
        -->
    </style>
</head>

<body>

<!-- Header -->
<table width="100%">
    <tr>
        <td align="left" width="130"><a href=
"http://jakarta.apache.org/tomcat/index.html"><img src=
"tomcat.gif" height="92" width="130" border="0" alt=
"The Mighty Tomcat - MEOW!"></td>
        .
        .
        .
```

Because of its length, only the first part of the output is displayed here, and that part is formatted to fit on this page. This program is similar to a browser's view source command.

The second part of this example is the HTTPServer program shown here in Listing 21.8.

LISTING 21.8   The HTTPServer Class

```
/*
 * HTTPServer.java
 *
 * Created on June 18, 2002, 3:07 PM
 */


import java.io.*;
import java.net.*;

/**
 *
 * @author  Stephen Potts
 * @version
 */
```

LISTING 21.8 Continued

```java
public class HTTPServer
{

   /** Creates new HTTPServer */
   public HTTPServer()
   {
   }

   public static void main(String[] args)
   {
      try
      {
         ServerSocket sSocket = new ServerSocket(1777);
         System.out.println("Created the socket");

         while (true)
         {
            System.out.println("Waiting for a client...");
            Socket newSocket = sSocket.accept();
            System.out.println("accepted the socket");

            OutputStream os = newSocket.getOutputStream();
            BufferedReader br = new BufferedReader(
            new InputStreamReader(newSocket.getInputStream()));

            String inLine = null;
            while (((inLine = br.readLine()) != null)
            && (!(inLine.equals(""))))
            {
               System.out.println(inLine);
            }
            System.out.println("");

            StringBuffer sb = new StringBuffer();
            sb.append("<html>\n");
            sb.append("<head>\n");
            sb.append("<title>Java Primer Plus\n");
            sb.append("</title>\n");
            sb.append("</head>\n");
            sb.append("<body>\n");
            sb.append("<H1>HTTPServer Works!</H1>\n");
            sb.append("</body>\n");
            sb.append("</html>\n");

            String string = sb.toString();

            //Put the output into a byte array
            byte[] byteArray = string.getBytes();

            //add some header information
            os.write("HTTP/1.0 200 OK\n".getBytes());
            os.write(new String(
```

LISTING 21.8   Continued

```
                "Content-Length: "+ byteArray.length + "\n").getBytes());
            os.write("Content-Type: text/html\n\n".getBytes());
            //add the output
            os.write(byteArray);
            os.flush();

            //close it up
            os.close();
            br.close();
            newSocket.close();
        }//while

    }catch(Exception e)
    {
        e.printStackTrace();
    }

  }//main
}//class
```

This program is another very simple TCP/IP sockets program. The first thing that we do is create the socket:

```
        ServerSocket sSocket = new ServerSocket(1777);
        System.out.println("Created the socket");
```

Notice that we used a different port number because we have Tomcat on 1776, and we don't want a conflict. We loop and wait for a communication from a client on port 1777.

```
        while (true)
        {
            System.out.println("Waiting for a client...");
            Socket newSocket = sSocket.accept();
            System.out.println("accepted the socket");
```

When we get a communication from that port, we will create a handle to the socket that the client has handed us, and call it `newSocket`. We will use it to send information back to the client.

```
        OutputStream os = newSocket.getOutputStream();
```

From this point on, the program acts like any other Java IO program. We get the `InputStream` from the client.

```
        BufferedReader br = new BufferedReader(
        new InputStreamReader(newSocket.getInputStream()));
```

We echo the information that the client sends us to standard output.

```
        String inLine = null;
        while (((inLine = br.readLine()) != null)
        && (!(inLine.equals(""))))
        {
            System.out.println(inLine);
        }
        System.out.println("");
```

We then create some HTML code and put it in a `StringBuffer`.

```
StringBuffer sb = new StringBuffer();
sb.append("<html>\n");
sb.append("<head>\n");
sb.append("<title>Java Primer Plus\n");
sb.append("</title>\n");
sb.append("</head>\n");
sb.append("<body>\n");
sb.append("<H1>HTTPServer Works!</H1>\n");
sb.append("</body>\n");
sb.append("</html>\n");
```

We transform it to a `String` object, and then to a `byteArray` so that the `OutputStream` can accept it.

```
String string = sb.toString();

//Put the output into a byte array
byte[] byteArray = string.getBytes();
```

Next, we add the HTTP header information.

```
os.write("HTTP/1.0 200 OK\n".getBytes());
```

We add the `Content-Length`.

```
os.write(new String(
"Content-Length: "+ byteArray.length + "\n").getBytes());
```

We add the `Content-Type`.

```
os.write("Content-Type: text/html\n\n".getBytes());
```

Next, we add the HTML that we wrote earlier.

```
os.write(byteArray);
os.flush();
```

Finally, we close up shop.

```
//close it up
os.close();
br.close();
newSocket.close();
```

Run this server by typing the following:

`java HTTPServer`

It pauses at the `Waiting for a client ...` until a client tries to connect. Open a browser and type the following:

`http://localhost:1777/`

Note that a Web server doesn't need to be running for this to work. This program is its own server.

```
Created the socket
Waiting for a client...
```

Action by the browser causes this server to receive the following communication:

```
accepted the socket
GET / HTTP/1.1
Host: localhost:1777
User-Agent: Mozilla/5.0 (Windows; U; Windows NT 5.1; en-US; rv:0.9.4.1)
 Gecko/20020508 Netscape6/6.2.3
Accept: text/xml, application/xml, application/xhtml+xml,
 text/html;q=0.9, image/png, image/jpeg, image/gif;q=0.2,
 text/plain;q=0.8, text/css, */*;q=0.1
Accept-Language: en-us
Accept-Encoding: gzip, deflate, compress;q=0.9
Accept-Charset: ISO-8859-1, utf-8;q=0.66, *;q=0.66
Keep-Alive: 300
Connection: keep-alive

Waiting for a client...
```

You end this program by typing Ctrl-c.

We see that the browser issued a GET. We also see that the browser didn't stipulate which document to return. The server has to decide what to do in this case. Normally, commercial servers return index.html.

We see that the browser message is in HTTP 1.1. We also see that it was a Netscape 6.2.3 browser. We also see several more pieces of information that we could make use of if we were writing a fancy server. At the end, it loops back and waits for a client. The server responds to this request by stuffing the HTTP commands that we created into the OutputStream that the client sent to us. The result is displayed on the screen, as shown in Figure 21.8.

FIGURE 21.8

The HTTP protocol is sent to the browser that displays it.

We can see that the browser had no trouble receiving and understanding this communication. If we run the `HTTPFetch` command against the `HTTPServer` command, we can see the details of what the `HTTPServer` returned. All that we have to do is change the port number in the `HTTPFetch` program to 1777, and we are ready.

```
URL url = new URL("http://localhost:1777");
```

Open a second command window and type

```
java HTTPFetch
```

The result will now be output to the screen.

```
<html>
<head>
<title>Java Primer Plus
</title>
</head>
<body>
<H1>HTTPServer Works!</H1>
</body>
</html>
```

Note

If you understand this section on HTTP, you will be in a great position to comprehend what is happening behind the scenes when your servlets are running.

HTML Forms and Servlets

Servlets that don't accept input from the client are of very little practical value outside of testing. Real-world servlets often receive data and additional instructions from clients in the form of parameters. The most common way for these parameters to be entered by the user is by using HTML forms.

Numerous HTML books are on the market, so I won't try to replace them here. You will, however, learn just enough HTML to be able to do data entry so that you can pass it to your servlets. Listing 21.9 shows an HTML page that enables the user to enter data bound for a servlet.

LISTING 21.9   The `DataEntry.html` File

```
<!DOCTYPE HTML PUBLIC "-//W3C//DTD HTML 4.01 Transitional//EN">

<HTML>
  <HEAD>
    <TITLE>Passing Parameters to Java Servlets</TITLE>
  </HEAD>
  <BODY BGCOLOR-"#FDF5E6">
  <H1 align="CENTER">
```

LISTING 21.9   Continued

```
Enter Values for all three Parameters
</H1>

<FORM action='/examples/servlet/PassParam'>
   Name:           <INPUT TYPE="TEXT" NAME="UserName"><BR><BR>
   Age:            <INPUT TYPE="TEXT" NAME="UserAge"><BR><BR>
   Favorite Sport: <INPUT TYPE="TEXT" NAME="UserSport"><BR><BR>
   <CENTER>
      <INPUT TYPE="SUBMIT">
   </CENTER>
</FORM>

</BODY>
</HTML>
```

The most interesting part of this HTML file is the `<FORM>` tag. The design of this feature pre-dates Java servlets by several years. In the formative years of Web development, forms were heavily used with CGI and Perl on the server. The basic flow is fairly intuitive. The `FORM` tag contains an action value that tells which script the Web server is to run when the SUBMIT but-ton is clicked. In this case, the action is to run a servlet stored in the examples application, called PassParam. On Tomcat, this means that this servlet will be stored in a classes directory immediately under the `WEB-INF` directory. Other Web servers use other naming conventions.

```
<FORM action='/examples/servlet/PassParam'>
```

This form tag contains three data entry boxes, along with some text that tells you what belongs in each box.

```
   Name:           <INPUT TYPE="TEXT" NAME="UserName"><BR><BR>
   Age:            <INPUT TYPE="TEXT" NAME="UserAge"><BR><BR>
   Favorite Sport: <INPUT TYPE="TEXT" NAME="UserSport"><BR><BR>
```

Following these, a SUBMIT button is defined. When the user clicks on this button, the action is to be triggered. The browser processes this form and creates the HTTP containing the request.

```
   <CENTER>
      <INPUT TYPE="SUBMIT">
   </CENTER>
```

To execute this example, store this file in the `webapps\examples\` directory and type the fol-lowing line in the address box of a browser:

```
http://localhost:1776/examples/DataEntry.html
```

The browser will look like Figure 21.9.

When you enter the data into the form and click the SUBMIT button, the following line will appear in the address line of the browser:

```
http://localhost:1776/examples/servlet/PassParam?
[ic:ccc]UserName=Joe&UserAge=15&UserSport=Soccer
```

FIGURE 21.9.
The Form tag causes data entry fields to be created on a Web page.

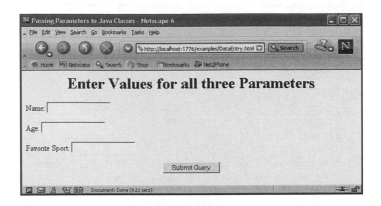

Notice that the parameters are passed right on the command line, providing proof that a GET HTTP command has been issued. We could have written this HTML page with the following FORM tag:

```
<FORM action='/examples/servlet/PassParam' method='GET'>
```

The result would have been the same, however, because GET is the default form-handling method. The syntax of the method says that we want to call a servlet in the examples application called PassParam. As mentioned earlier in this section, the Web server will look for the file ...\webapps\examples\WEB_INF\classes\PassParam.class. Listing 21.10 shows the .java file that was used to create the PassParam.class file.

LISTING 21.10   The PassParam.java Class

```java
/*
 * PassParam.java
 *
 * Created on June 21, 2002, 5:25 PM
 */


import javax.servlet.*;
import javax.servlet.http.*;

/**
 *
 * @author  Stephen Potts
 * @version
 */
public class PassParam extends HttpServlet
{

    /** Initializes the servlet.
     */
    public void init(ServletConfig config) throws ServletException
    {
        super.init(config);
```

LISTING 21.10 Continued

```
        }

        /** Destroys the servlet.
         */
        public void destroy()
        {

        }

        /** Processes requests for both HTTP <code>GET</code>
         * and <code>POST</code> methods.
         * @param request servlet request
         * @param response servlet response
         */
        protected void processRequest(HttpServletRequest request,
                                      HttpServletResponse response)
        throws ServletException, java.io.IOException
        {
            response.setContentType("text/html");
            java.io.PrintWriter out = response.getWriter();

            // output your page here
            out.println("<html>");
            out.println("<head>");
            out.println("<title>" + "Parameter Passing" +
                                        "</title>");
            out.println("</head>");
            out.println("<body BGCOLOR=\"#FDF5E6\"\n>");
            out.println("<h1 ALIGN=CENTER>");
            out.println("Here are the Parameters");
            out.println("</h1>");
            out.println("<B>The UserName is </B>");
            out.println(request.getParameter("UserName") + "<BR>");
            out.println(" ");
            out.println("<B>The UserAge is </B>");
            out.println(request.getParameter("UserAge") + "<BR>");
            out.println(" ");
            out.println("<B>The UserSport is </B>");
            out.println(request.getParameter("UserSport") + "<BR>");
            out.println(" ");
            out.println("</body>");
            out.println("</html>");

            out.close();
        }

        /** Handles the HTTP <code>GET</code> method.
         * @param request servlet request
         * @param response servlet response
         */
        protected void doGet(HttpServletRequest request,
```

LISTING 21.10   Continued

```
                                        HttpServletResponse response)
throws ServletException, java.io.IOException
{
    processRequest(request, response);
}

/** Handles the HTTP <code>POST</code> method.
 * @param request servlet request
 * @param response servlet response
 */
protected void doPost(HttpServletRequest request,
                                HttpServletResponse response)
throws ServletException, java.io.IOException
{
    processRequest(request, response);
}

/** Returns a short description of the servlet.
 */
public String getServletInfo()
{
    return "Short description";
}

}
```

This servlet looks like the simple servlets already described in this chapter, but it has some new features. As usual, the real work is done in the **processRequest()** method, which is called by both the **doGet()** and **doPost()** methods. This method is passed to the **HttpServletRequest** and **HttpServletResponse** objects.

```
protected void processRequest(HttpServletRequest request,
                                HttpServletResponse response)
throws ServletException, java.io.IOException
```

The response object is how we will communicate back to the client's browser. The Web server will magically communicate anything printed to this object back to the client's browser.

```
response.setContentType("text/html");
java.io.PrintWriter out = response.getWriter();
```

Much of the output consists of simple static HTML statements, but there are several dynamic statements. The **request** object contains quite a bit of information that has been passed to the servlet from the browser. The most important parts of this information are the values of the parameters that were passed in from the HTML.

```
out.println("<B>The UserName is </B>");
out.println(request.getParameter("UserName") + "<BR>");
out.println(" ");
```

Notice how the **request** object retrieves these values by the exact string names that were specified in the HTML. The HTML line for the age was

```
Age:            <INPUT TYPE="TEXT" NAME="UserAge"><BR><BR>
```

The parameter that the `getParameter()` passed is the same name, `"UserAge"`. The value that it returns will be a String containing exactly what the user entered into the browser.

```
out.println("<B>The UserAge is </B>");
out.println(request.getParameter("UserAge") + "<BR>");
out.println(" ");
out.println("<B>The UserSport is </B>");
out.println(request.getParameter("UserSport") + "<BR>");
```

The result of running the `DataEntry.HTML` page and clicking SUBMIT is shown in Figure 21.10.

FIGURE 21.10
The `HttpServletRequest` contains information that is being passed from the browser to the servlet.

The `DataEntry.HTML` page used the default `HTTP GET` command to communicate with the server. We can change that very easily to use the `POST` command instead. All that we have to do is modify the HTML as shown in Listing 21.11.

LISTING 21.11   The `DataEntryPost.HTML` File

```
<!DOCTYPE HTML PUBLIC "-//W3C//DTD HTML 4.01 Transitional//EN">

<HTML>
  <HEAD>
    <TITLE>Posting Parameters to Java Servlets</TITLE>
  </HEAD>
  <BODY BGCOLOR="#FDF5E6">
  <H1 align="CENTER">
  Enter Values for all three Parameters
  </H1>

  <FORM action='/examples/servlet/PassParam' method='post'>
    Name:           <INPUT TYPE="TEXT" NAME="UserName"><BR><BR>
    Age:            <INPUT TYPE="TEXT" NAME="UserAge"><BR><BR>
    Favorite Sport: <INPUT TYPE="TEXT" NAME="UserSport"><BR><BR>
```

LISTING 21.11   Continued

```
    <CENTER>
        <INPUT TYPE="SUBMIT">
    </CENTER>
  </FORM>

  </BODY>
</HTML>
```

Notice that only one line has changed:

```
<FORM action='/examples/servlet/PassParam' method='post'>
```

The **post** method is telling the browser to generate a different set of HTTP commands to send to the server. This new version passes the parameters in the content of the HTTP communication, not in the address as we saw earlier. The URL being sent to the server now looks like the following:

```
http://localhost:1776/examples/servlet/PassParam
```

Notice that no changes were made to the servlet. The reason for this is that the Web server prepares the same request object regardless of which method is specified. A second reason is that we wrote the servlet with the same processing for both the **doGet()** and the **doPost()** methods. Be aware that the GET method will only allow 255 bytes to be passed. Anything longer will be truncated, therefore longer parameters must use the POST method.

Calling Other Classes from Servlets

The organization of servlets is a subject of some discussion among those of us who think about this kind of thing. One camp says that it is fine to place business logic in servlets, and the other says that the servlet itself should be reserved for communication purposes. There are distinct advantages to the second point of view.

- Simplicity—The communication and housekeeping portions of a servlet are complex enough without adding business logic to them.

- Object Orientation—Using classes to encapsulate functionality is the basic tenet of OO. All the benefits normally associated with OO flow from it.

- Debugging—It is far simpler to debug an ordinary Java Class than it is to debug a servlet. Single-step debuggers are much easier to set up when ordinary classes are involved. A **main()** method can be written that instantiates the class in a similar way to the servlet in production.

To illustrate the OO approach to servlets, we will modify the **PassParam** class that you were introduced to earlier in this chapter. Listing 21.12 shows this new class.

LISTING 21.12   The `PassParam2` Class

```java
/*
 * PassParam2.java
 *
 * Created on June 21, 2002, 5:25 PM
 */

import javax.servlet.*;
import javax.servlet.http.*;
import com.samspublishing.jpp.ch21;
/**
 *
 * @author  Stephen Potts
 * @version
 */
public class PassParam2 extends HttpServlet
{

    /** Initializes the servlet.
     */
    public void init(ServletConfig config) throws ServletException
    {
        super.init(config);

    }

    /** Destroys the servlet.
     */
    public void destroy()
    {

    }

    /** Processes requests for both HTTP <code>GET</code>
     * and <code>POST</code> methods.
     * @param request servlet request
     * @param response servlet response
     */
    protected void processRequest(HttpServletRequest request,
    HttpServletResponse response)
    throws ServletException, java.io.IOException
    {
        response.setContentType("text/html");
        java.io.PrintWriter out = response.getWriter();

        System.out.println("Creating the HTMLBuilder");
        HTMLBuilder hb = new HTMLBuilder();
        String htmlOutput = hb.formatResponse(request);
        out.println(htmlOutput);
        System.out.println("Response was formatted by HTMLBuilder");


        out.close();
```

LISTING 21.12   Continued

```
    }

    /** Handles the HTTP <code>GET</code> method.
     * @param request servlet request
     * @param response servlet response
     */
    protected void doGet(HttpServletRequest request,
    HttpServletResponse response)
    throws ServletException, java.io.IOException
    {
        processRequest(request, response);
    }

    /** Handles the HTTP <code>POST</code> method.
     * @param request servlet request
     * @param response servlet response
     */
    protected void doPost(HttpServletRequest request,
    HttpServletResponse response)
    throws ServletException, java.io.IOException
    {
        processRequest(request, response);
    }

    /** Returns a short description of the servlet.
     */
    public String getServletInfo()
    {
        return "Short description";
    }

}
```

Compiling this class can be tricky. This class is not part of a package (except the default package), so it can be compiled in any directory that has visibility to the `HTMLBuiler` class. `HTMLBuilder`, which this class calls, is in the `com.samspublishing.jpp.ch21` package, so move the `PassParam2.java` file to the directory just above the `com/samspublishing/jpp/ch21` class and compile it there. If you placed this chapter's code in `C:\com\samspublishing\jpp\ch21`, you would move to the `c:\` directory to compile it.

This class is identical to the `PassParam` class except for the contents of **processRequest()**. In this version, `processRequest()` does only servlet-type work, delegating the actual layout work to the `HTMLBuilder` class, which we will examine next. An instance of `HTMLBuilder` is created, and its `formatResponse()` method is called with the `HttpServletRequest` object passed in as a parameter. It returns a `String` object, which we print to the `PrintWriter` object.

```
    protected void processRequest(HttpServletRequest request,
    HttpServletResponse response)
    throws ServletException, java.io.IOException
    {
        response.setContentType("text/html");
```

```
            java.io.PrintWriter out = response.getWriter();

            System.out.println("Creating the HTMLBuilder");
            HTMLBuilder hb = new HTMLBuilder();
            String htmlOutput = hb.formatResponse(request);
            out.println(htmlOutput);
            System.out.println("Response was formatted by HTMLBuilder");


            out.close();
    }
```

Several `println()` statements were added to this class. These statements appear in the Tomcat console when the servlet runs. This is a primitive, but effective, technique for debugging servlets. The real work has now been delegated to the **HTMLBuilder** class, which is shown in Listing 21.13.

```
/*
 * HTMLBuilder.java
 *
 * Created on June 25, 2002, 9:55 AM
 */

package com.samspublishing.jpp.ch21;

import javax.servlet.*;
import javax.servlet.http.*;


/**
 *
 * @author  Stephen Potts
 * @version
 */
public class HTMLBuilder
{

    /** Creates new HTMLBuilder */
    public HTMLBuilder()
    {
    }

    public String formatResponse(HttpServletRequest request)
    throws ServletException, java.io.IOException

    {
        System.out.println("Entered into HTMLBuilder.formatResponse()");
        StringBuffer sb = new StringBuffer();

        // output your page here
        sb.append("<html>\n");
        sb.append("<head>\n");
        sb.append("<title>" + "HTML Formatting" +
```

```
              "</title>\n");
       sb.append("</head>\n");
       sb.append("<body BGCOLOR=\"#FDF5E6\"\n>\n");
       sb.append("<h1 ALIGN=CENTER>\n");
       sb.append("Here are the Parameter2");
       sb.append("</h1>\n");
       sb.append("<B>The UserName2 is </B>\n");
       sb.append(request.getParameter("UserName") + "<BR>\n");
       sb.append(" ");
       sb.append("<B>The UserAge2 is </B>\n");
       sb.append(request.getParameter("UserAge") + "<BR>\n");
       sb.append(" ");
       sb.append("<B>The UserSport2 is </B>\n");
       sb.append(request.getParameter("UserSport") + "<BR>\n");
       sb.append(" ");
       sb.append("</body>\n");
       sb.append("</html>\n");
       System.out.println("Returning from HTMLBuilder.formatResponse()");

       return sb.toString();
   }
}
```

This class is created in a package. This will impact its deployment in the Tomcat directory structure. In Java, the package name and the class name form the real name of the program or servlet. The directory structure must match the package name, according to the rules of Java.

```
package com.samspublishing.jpp.ch21;
```

The `formatResponse()` method takes the `HttpServletRequest` object as a paramater, and it returns a `String` object. The fact that this class is not a servlet does not impact its capability to make method calls on the `HttpServletRequest` object. This is an object like any other in Java and can be passed as a parameter as is done here.

```
   public String formatResponse(HttpServletRequest request)
   throws ServletException, java.io.IOException
```

We create a `StringBuffer` class because we will be appending a lot of strings to it. `StringBuffer`'s performance is so much better than the `String` class's, that it makes sense to use it here. In fact, programmers who do serial appends to `String` objects risk embarrassment during code review.

```
       StringBuffer sb = new StringBuffer();

       // output your page here
       sb.append("<html>\n");
       sb.append("<head>\n");
```

The request object's methods, such as `getParameter()`, are available inside this class also.

```
       sb.append(request.getParameter("UserName") + "<BR>\n");
```

Before returning, we transform the `StringBuffer` into a `String` object and return it to the servlet for insertion into the response object.

```
       return sb.toString();
```

To get this to work we also have to modify the `DataEntry.html` file, as shown in Listing 21.14.

LISTING 21.14   The `DataEntry2.html` File

```
<!DOCTYPE HTML PUBLIC "-//W3C//DTD HTML 4.01 Transitional//EN">

<HTML>
  <HEAD>
    <TITLE>Passing Parameters to Java Servlets</TITLE>
  </HEAD>
  <BODY BGCOLOR="#FDF5E6">
  <H1 align="CENTER">
  Enter Values DataEntry2
  </H1>

  <FORM action='/examples/servlet/PassParam2'>
     Name2:            <INPUT TYPE="TEXT" NAME="UserName"><BR><BR>
     Age2:             <INPUT TYPE="TEXT" NAME="UserAge"><BR><BR>
     Favorite Sport2: <INPUT TYPE="TEXT" NAME="UserSport"><BR><BR>
     <CENTER>
        <INPUT TYPE="SUBMIT">
     </CENTER>
  </FORM>

  </BODY>
</HTML>
```

The only major change is the calling of the `PassParam2` servlet instead of the `PassParam` servlet.

```
<FORM action='/examples/servlet/PassParam2'>
```

The deployment of this servlet and class is a bit different. The `PassParam2.class` file can be placed in the `...\webapps\examples\WEB-INF\classes` directory, and the HTML file can be placed in the `...\webapps\examples` directory as before. The `HTMLBuilder` class, however, is in a package. The rules of packages state that the class file must be stored in a directory structure that matches the package name. The package name for `HTMLBuilder` is com.samspublishing.jpp.ch21. This requires that this class be placed in the directory:

`...\webapps\examples\WEB-INF\classes\com\samspublishing\jpp\ch21`

This makes for a long subdirectory string, but Tomcat can find what it needs very easily.

You run this by entering the name of the HTML file in the address line of the browser:

`http://localhost:1776/examples/DataEntry2.html`

When you click the SUBMIT button, the URL that appears is

```
http://localhost:1776/examples/servlet/PassParam2?
➥UserName=Jake&UserAge=9&UserSport=Soccer
```

The browser output is nearly identical to Figures 21.9 and 21.10, so they won't be repeated here. This application added several `println()` statements for debugging purposes. The Tomcat console, which is shown here, is where these statements appear.

```
Creating the HTMLBuilder
Entered into HTMLBuilder.formatResponse()
Returning from HTMLBuilder.formatResponse()
Response was formatted by HTMLBuilder
```

It is often useful to add `println()` statements to your code to monitor its progress and to track down bugs.

Using Cookies to Maintain State

The fact that the HTTP protocol is stateless is one of its finest features. The simplicity of this approach makes it an ideal tool for delivering content quickly.

This statelessness is also a hindrance when you need to perform a task that has to span several Web pages. It would be nice if you could identify yourself to the server so that it could pick up where it left off in the previous transaction, instead of having to start over every time.

The browser writers addressed this issue first when they introduced the idea of cookies. Cookies are small files that live on the client's hard drive, which identify the user to a specific Web application. The server sends the cookie to the browser in response to the initial request. Subsequent requests send the same cookie back to the server, which enables the server to identify these requests as being from the same requester.

Java supports the creation and manipulation of cookies via the `javax.servlet.http.Cookie` class. About a dozen methods are defined by this class, but the constructor, `setValue()` and `getValue()`, are the most commonly used. Listing 21.15 shows how cookies are used to store the state of an application.

LISTING 21.15   The `SpecialDiet.java` Class

```java
/*
 * SpecialDiet.java
 *
 * Created on June 25, 2002, 1:27 PM
 */

import javax.servlet.*;
import javax.servlet.http.*;
import java.util.*;
import java.io.*;

/**
 *
 * @author   Stephen Potts
 * @version
```

LISTING 21.15   Continued

```java
 */
public class SpecialDiet extends HttpServlet
{

    /** Initializes the servlet.
     */
    public void init(ServletConfig config) throws ServletException
    {
        super.init(config);

    }

    /** Destroys the servlet.
     */
    public void destroy()
    {

    }


    /** Handles the HTTP <code>GET</code> method.
     * @param request servlet request
     * @param response servlet response
     */
    protected void doGet(HttpServletRequest request,
                                    HttpServletResponse response)
    throws ServletException, java.io.IOException
    {

    }

    /** Handles the HTTP <code>POST</code> method.
     * @param request servlet request
     * @param response servlet response
     */
    protected void doPost(HttpServletRequest request,
                                     HttpServletResponse response)
    throws ServletException, java.io.IOException
    {
        response.setContentType("text/html");
        Cookie myCookie = new Cookie("null", "null");

        Enumeration keys;
        String key, value;
        keys = request.getParameterNames();
        while (keys.hasMoreElements())
        {
            key = (String)keys.nextElement();
            value = request.getParameter(key);
            if(!key.equals("btnSubmit"))
            {
```

LISTING 21.15 *Continued*

```
            System.out.println("value= " + value + " key= " + key);
            myCookie = new Cookie(value,key);
            response.addCookie(myCookie);
        }
    }
    response.sendRedirect(
            "http://localhost:1776/examples/servlet/SpecialDiet2");
}


    /** Returns a short description of the servlet.
     */
    public String getServletInfo()
    {
        return "Short description";
    }

}
```

This is a typical servlet until you get into the `doPost()` method. A `Cookie` object is declared and used to store several cookies.

```
Cookie myCookie = new Cookie("null", "null");
```

We step through each parameter and create a cookie that stores the current value.

```
Enumeration keys;
String key, value;
keys = request.getParameterNames();
while (keys.hasMoreElements())
{
    key = (String)keys.nextElement();
```

We get the parameters from the `request` object.

```
value = request.getParameter(key);
```

The only key that we don't want to create a cookie for is the OK button.

```
if(!key.equals("btnSubmit"))
{
    System.out.println("value= " + value + " key= " + key);
```

We store the value and the key in the cookie and add it to the response object.

```
myCookie = new Cookie(value,key);
response.addCookie(myCookie);
```

Finally, we call the `sendRedirect()` method to another servlet that displays all the cookies.

```
response.sendRedirect(
        "http://localhost:1776/examples/servlet/SpecialDiet2");
```

This line causes a different servlet, `SpecialDiet2`, to be called. Because we don't specify a method, `doGet()` will be called. Listing 21.16 shows this program.

LISTING 21.16   The SpecialDiet2 Class

```java
/*
 * SpecialDiet2.java
 *
 * Created on June 25, 2002, 1:27 PM
 */

import javax.servlet.*;
import javax.servlet.http.*;
import java.util.*;
import java.io.*;

/**
 *
 * @author  Stephen Potts
 * @version
 */
public class SpecialDiet2 extends HttpServlet
{

    /** Initializes the servlet.
     */
    public void init(ServletConfig config) throws ServletException
    {
        super.init(config);

    }

    /** Destroys the servlet.
     */
    public void destroy()
    {

    }


    /** Handles the HTTP <code>GET</code> method.
     * @param request servlet request
     * @param response servlet response
     */
    protected void doGet(HttpServletRequest request,
                                HttpServletResponse response)
    throws ServletException, java.io.IOException
    {
        response.setContentType("text/html");
        PrintWriter out = response.getWriter();

        Cookie cookies[];
        cookies = request.getCookies();

        System.out.println("Creating the SpecialDiet HTML");

        // output your page here
```

LISTING 21.16   Continued

```java
        out.println("<html>");
        out.println("<head>");
        out.println("<title>" + "Your Diet Choices" +
        "</title>");
        out.println("</head>");
        out.println("<body BGCOLOR=\"#FDF5E6\"\n>");
        out.println("<h1 ALIGN=CENTER>");
        out.println("Here are your choices");
        out.println("</h1>");
        for (int i=0; i< cookies.length; i++)
        {
            System.out.println(cookies[i].getName()+
                            "   " + cookies[i].getValue() + "<BR>");
            out.println(cookies[i].getName()+
                            "   " + cookies[i].getValue() + "<BR>");
            out.println(" ");
        }
        out.println("</body>");
        out.println("</html>");

        out.close();

    }

    /** Handles the HTTP <code>POST</code> method.
     * @param request servlet request
     * @param response servlet response
     */
    protected void doPost(HttpServletRequest request,
                                    HttpServletResponse response)
    throws ServletException, java.io.IOException
    {

    }


    /** Returns a short description of the servlet.
     */
    public String getServletInfo()
    {
        return "Short description";
    }

}
```

This servlet is ordinary also, except for the cookie-handling code. We declared an array of
Cookie objects called cookies, and then called the **HttpServletRequest** class's **getCookies()**
method.

```java
        Cookie cookies[];
        cookies = request.getCookies();
```

In the midst of creating the HTML code, we loop through and print every cookie that was sent.

```
for (int i=0; i< cookies.length; i++)
{
    System.out.println(cookies[i].getName()+
                    "   " + cookies[i].getValue() + "<BR>");
    out.println(cookies[i].getName()+
                    "   " + cookies[i].getValue() + "<BR>");
    out.println(" ");
}
```

The HTML that is used to gather the user input is shown in Listing 21.17.

LISTING 21.17   The ChooseDiet.HTML File

```
<!DOCTYPE HTML PUBLIC "-//W3C//DTD HTML 4.01 Transitional//EN">

<HTML>
  <HEAD>
    <TITLE>Choose Your Dietary Preference</TITLE>
  </HEAD>
  <BODY BGCOLOR="#FDF5E6">
  <H1 align="CENTER">
  Do you have special dietary needs?:
  </H1>

  <FORM action='/examples/servlet/SpecialDiet' method='post'>
  <TABLE cellspacing='5' cellpadding='5'>
  <TR>
      <TD align='center'><B>Choose one or more</B></TD>
      <TD align='center'><B></B></TD>
      <TD align='center'><B></B></TD>
  </TR>
  <TR>
      <TD align='center'><INPUT TYPE='Checkbox'
                        NAME="losodium" VALUE="loso117"></TD>
      <TD align='center'>Delicious Low-Sodium Pizza</TD>
  </TR>
  <TR>
      <TD align='center'><INPUT TYPE='Checkbox'
                        NAME="lofat" VALUE="lofat118"></TD>
      <TD align='center'>Delicious Lo-Fat Chicken</TD>
  </TR>
  <TR>
      <TD align='center'><INPUT TYPE='Checkbox'
                        NAME="vegan" VALUE="vegan119"></TD>
      <TD align='center'>Delicious Vegetarian Lasagna</TD>
  </TR>
```

LISTING 21.17   Continued

```
</TABLE>
<HR><BR>
<CENTER>
<INPUT type='SUBMIT' name='btnSubmit' value='OK'>
<BR><BR>
<A href='/examples/servlet/SpecialDiet2'>View Current Choices</A>
</CENTER>
</FORM>
</BODY>
</HTML>
```

Notice that the method on the `Form` is `Post`. This is so that `doPost()` will be called on the servlet.

```
<FORM action='/examples/servlet/SpecialDiet' method='post'>
```

We also included a link to the output servlet from this page:

```
<A href='/examples/servlet/SpecialDiet2'>View Current Choices</A>
```

The result of running the `ChooseDiet.html` is shown here in Figure 21.11.

FIGURE 21.11
The `ChooseDiet.html` form uses check boxes to gather user input.

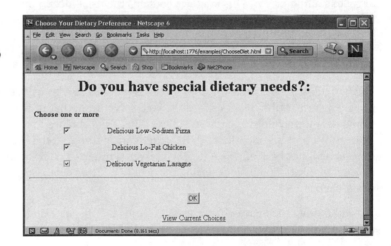

The `SpecialDiet` servlet has no visible result. It calls the `SpeciaDiet2` servlet, which displays the values and the keys that were stored in the cookies.

Cookies provide a simple way to store small amounts of data using the browser. You can see how this approach might become unmanageable if the amount of state data were to become large. The `Session` object uses cookies to provide a more elegant solution for larger amounts of data.

FIGURE 21.12
The `SpecialDiet2` servlet
displays the contents of
the cookies.

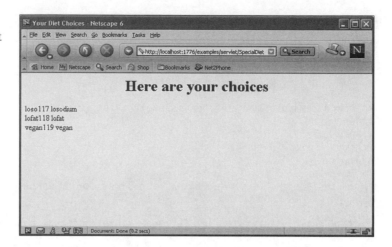

Using Session Objects to Maintain State

The Java servlet API gives us a way to manage state on the server side through the use of the `HttpSession` interface. This interface contains the usual dozen methods, but the most important ones are the constructor, `getAttribute()`, and `setAttribute()`. Internally, the Web server uses cookies to determine which of all the potentially active session objects is the one to provide to a particular servlet, but this processing is invisible to the programmer for security reasons.

The basic flow of a session-oriented servlet is that one servlet will create the session object and place data in it. Subsequent calls to the Web server from that browser will have access to that stored data if they need it. Session objects differ from cookies in that they use the cookie to store only a browser identifier. All the other data is stored in the Web server. This means that the data will not be available if the Web server is restarted. If restarting could cause problems in your application, consider storing the data to a file or database periodically and reloading it when needed.

We will modify the `SpecialDiet` servlet to use sessions instead of cookies and call it `SpecialDietSession`. This servlet is shown in Listing 21.18.

LISTING 21.18   The `SpecialDietSession` Servlet

```
/*
 * SpecialDietSession.java
 *
 * Created on June 25, 2002, 1:27 PM
 */

import javax.servlet.*;
import javax.servlet.http.*;
```

LISTING 21.18   Continued

```java
import java.util.*;
import java.io.*;

/**
 *
 * @author  Stephen Potts
 * @version
 */
public class SpecialDietSession extends HttpServlet
{

    /** Initializes the servlet.
     */
    public void init(ServletConfig config) throws ServletException
    {
        super.init(config);

    }

    /** Destroys the servlet.
     */
    public void destroy()
    {

    }


    /** Handles the HTTP <code>GET</code> method.
     * @param request servlet request
     * @param response servlet response
     */
    protected void doGet(HttpServletRequest request,
                                  HttpServletResponse response)
    throws ServletException, java.io.IOException
    {

    }

    /** Handles the HTTP <code>POST</code> method.
     * @param request servlet request
     * @param response servlet response
     */
    protected void doPost(HttpServletRequest request,
                                  HttpServletResponse response)
    throws ServletException, java.io.IOException
    {
        //Get the Session Object
        HttpSession httpSess = request.getSession(true);
        Integer numItems = (Integer) httpSess.getAttribute("numItems");
        if (numItems== null)
        {
            numItems = new Integer(0);
```

LISTING 21.18   Continued

```
      }
      response.setContentType("text/html");
      PrintWriter out = response.getWriter();

      Enumeration keys;
      String key, value;
      keys = request.getParameterNames();
      while (keys.hasMoreElements())
      {
         key = (String)keys.nextElement();
         value = request.getParameter(key);
         if(!key.equals("btnSubmit"))
         {
            System.out.println("SDS value= " + numItems +
                                          " " + value + " key= " + key);
            httpSess.setAttribute("Item" + numItems , key + " " + value);
            numItems = new Integer(numItems.intValue()+ 1);
         }
      }
      httpSess.setAttribute("numItems", numItems);
               // output your page here
        out.println("<html>");
        out.println("<head>");
        out.println("<title>" + "SpecialDietSession" +
                                        "</title>");
        out.println("</head>");
        out.println("<body BGCOLOR=\"#FDF5E6\"\n>");
        out.println("<h1 ALIGN=CENTER>");
        out.println("Session Object Populated");

        out.println("<CENTER>");
        out.println("<BR><BR>");
        out.println("<A href=[ic:ccc]
         '/examples/servlet/SpecialDietSession2'>View Your Choices</A>");
        out.println("</CENTER>");

        out.println("</body>");
        out.println("</html>");

      out.close();


    }


   /** Returns a short description of the servlet.
    */
   public String getServletInfo()
   {
      return "Short description";
   }

 }
```

This servlet is fairly normal with the exception of the `HttpSession` processing. We use the `HttpServletRequest` object to get a handle to the `HttpSession` object. The Boolean value in the parameter to the `getSession()` method call states that a new session object is to be created if none exists for this client.

```
HttpSession httpSess = request.getSession(true);
```

We declare an attribute that will be used to track the number of attributes in the session object.

```
Integer numItems = (Integer) httpSess.getAttribute("numItems");
```

We use an enumeration to process all the parameters in the request object.

```
Enumeration keys;
String key, value;
keys = request.getParameterNames();
while (keys.hasMoreElements())
{
   key = (String)keys.nextElement();
   value = request.getParameter(key);
```

We want to store every parameter except `btnSubmit`.

```
if(!key.equals("btnSubmit"))
{
   System.out.println("SDS value= " + numItems +
                      " " + value + " key= " + key);
```

The `setAttribute()` method is the one that adds the parameters to the session object. We are adding an artificial name for each key-value pair called `Itemx`, where `x` is an increasing number. This is for convenience when retrieving all the attributes later.

```
httpSess.setAttribute("Item" + numItems , key + " " + value);
```

We increment a counter that we will store after the loop is complete.

```
numItems = new Integer(numItems.intValue()+ 1);
   }
}
httpSess.setAttribute("numItems", numItems);
```

The servlet is called by the `ChooseDietSession.html` file, which is shown in Listing 21.19.

LISTING 21.19   The `ChooseDietSession.html` File

```
<!DOCTYPE HTML PUBLIC "-//W3C//DTD HTML 4.01 Transitional//EN">

<HTML>
  <HEAD>
    <TITLE>Choose Your Dietary Preference</TITLE>
  </HEAD>
  <BODY BGCOLOR="#FDF5E6">
  <H1 align="CENTER">
  Do you have special dietary needs?:
```

LISTING 21.19   Continued

```
    </H1>

    <FORM action='/examples/servlet/SpecialDietSession' method='post'>
    <TABLE cellspacing='5' cellpadding='5'>
    <TR>
        <TD align='center'><B>Choose one or more</B></TD>
        <TD align='center'><B></B></TD>
        <TD align='center'><B></B></TD>
    </TR>
    <TR>
        <TD align='center'><INPUT TYPE='Checkbox'
                        NAME="losodium" VALUE="loso117"></TD>
        <TD align='center'>Delicious Low-Sodium Pizza</TD>
    </TR>
    <TR>
        <TD align='center'><INPUT TYPE='Checkbox'
                          NAME="lofat" VALUE="lofat118"></TD>
        <TD align='center'>Delicious Lo-Fat Chicken</TD>
    </TR>
    <TR>
        <TD align='center'><INPUT TYPE='Checkbox'
                          NAME="vegan" VALUE="vegan119"></TD>
        <TD align='center'>Delicious Vegetarian Lasagna</TD>
    </TR>
</TABLE>
<HR><BR>
<CENTER>
<INPUT type='SUBMIT' name='btnSubmit' value='OK'>
<BR><BR>
<A href='/examples/servlet/SpecialDietSession2'>View Current Choices</A>
</CENTER>
</FORM>
</BODY>
</HTML>
```

Figure 21.13 shows what the `ChooseDietSession.html` file looks like when displayed.

At the end of the `SpecialDietSession` servlet, a message is displayed back to the user that contains a hyperlink to the `SpecialDietSession2` servlet.

```
out.println(
"<A href='/examples/servlet/SpecialDietSession2'>View Your Choices</A>");
```

Listing 21.20 shows this display-oriented servlet.

FIGURE 21.13

The `ChooseDietSession` HTML file gives the user the choices and calls `SpecialDietSession`.

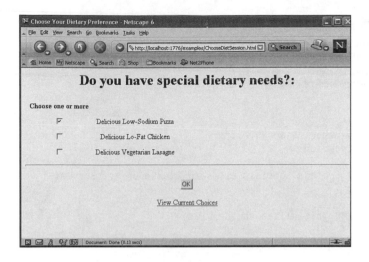

After the OK button is clicked, you will be taken to a confirmation screen as shown in Figure 21.14.

FIGURE 21.14

The `SpecialDietSession` servlet displays a confirmation page that contains a hyperlink to view the results.

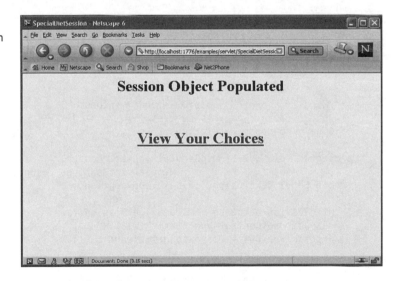

LISTING 21.20 The `SpecialDietSession2` Servlet

```
/*
 * SpecialDietSession2.java
 *
 * Created on June 25, 2002, 1:27 PM
 */
```

LISTING 21.20   Continued

```java
import javax.servlet.*;
import javax.servlet.http.*;
import java.util.*;
import java.io.*;

/**
 *
 * @author  Stephen Potts
 * @version
 */
public class SpecialDietSession2 extends HttpServlet
{

    /** Initializes the servlet.
     */
    public void init(ServletConfig config) throws ServletException
    {
        super.init(config);

    }

    /** Destroys the servlet.
     */
    public void destroy()
    {

    }


    /** Handles the HTTP <code>GET</code> method.
     * @param request servlet request
     * @param response servlet response
     */
    protected void doGet(HttpServletRequest request,
                            HttpServletResponse response)
    throws ServletException, java.io.IOException
    {
        HttpSession httpSess = request.getSession(true);
        response.setContentType("text/html");
        PrintWriter out = response.getWriter();


        System.out.println("Creating the SpecialDiet HTML");

        // output your page here
        out.println("<html>");
        out.println("<head>");
        out.println("<title>" + "Your Diet Choices" +
        "</title>");
        out.println("</head>");
        out.println("<body BGCOLOR=\"#FDF5E6\"\n>");
        out.println("<h1 ALIGN=CENTER>");
```

LISTING 21.20   Continued

```java
        out.println("Here are your choices");
        out.println("</h1>");
        Integer numItems = (Integer) httpSess.getAttribute("numItems");

        for (int i=0; i< numItems.intValue(); i++)
        {
            String itemContents = (String)httpSess.getAttribute("Item" + i);
            System.out.println(itemContents + "<BR>");
            out.println("Item" + i + "= " + itemContents + "<BR>");
            out.println(" ");
        }
        out.println("</body>");
        out.println("</html>");

        httpSess.invalidate();

        out.close();

    }


    /** Handles the HTTP <code>POST</code> method.
     * @param request servlet request
     * @param response servlet response
     */
    protected void doPost(HttpServletRequest request,
                                        HttpServletResponse response)
    throws ServletException, java.io.IOException
    {

    }



    /** Returns a short description of the servlet.
     */
    public String getServletInfo()
    {
        return "Short description";
    }


}
```

This servlet mostly displays code. Its main feature is that it steps through the entries of the session object and outputs them to the browser.

```java
        Integer numItems = (Integer) httpSess.getAttribute("numItems");

        for (int i=0; i< numItems.intValue(); i++)
        {
            String itemContents = (String)httpSess.getAttribute("Item" + i);
            System.out.println(itemContents + "<BR>");
            out.println("Item" + i + "= " + itemContents + "<BR>");
            out.println(" ");
        }
```

The `getAttribute()` method is the main player here. The contents of the session object are referenced by name and printed.

At the end, we invalidated the session object, which causes the information in it to be purged. If we didn't do this, the entries would continue to be added each time we ran the servlets, which is not the desired result. Figure 21.15 shows the result of running the `SpecialDietSession2`.

FIGURE 21.15
The `SpecialDietSession2` servlet displays the results.

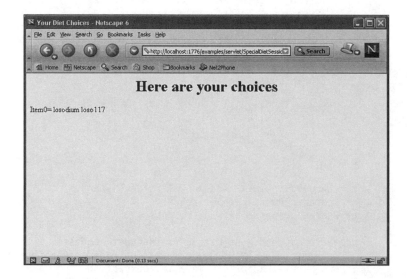

The contents of the session object are displayed both for you to inspect and to prove that they retained their values across different servlet calls.

Summary

This chapter has introduced you to the world of servlet development. We started with a discussion of how servlets worked. Following that, you learned how to set up your development environment.

You learned how the HTTP protocol, the language of servlets, works. Following that, you learned how to create servlets using both the `GenericServlet` class and the `HttpServlet` class.

We covered how to create servlets that called other classes and how to deploy those classes. Then you learned how to preserve servlet state in the browser using cookies. Finally, you learned how to use the `HTTPSession` interface to store data on the server between servlet calls by the same browser.

Review Questions

1. What is the difference between a servlet and a Java application running on the server?

2. What is servlet container?

3. What is the difference between the `HTTPServlet` class and the `GenericServlet` class?

4. What is a session object?

5. What is the difference between a cookie and a session object?

Exercises

1. Create a servlet that echoes your name when called.

2. Create a servlet that lets you choose toppings on a pizza.

3. Expand the pizza servlet to use cookies to remember your last order and ask you if you want the same toppings this time.

4. Modify the pizza servlet to use a session to accomplish this.

5. Move the creation of the HTML to be returned by the pizza servlet to a class in a package.

CHAPTER 22

JAVASERVER PAGES (JSP)

You will learn about the following in this chapter:

- Setting up a Java Web environment
- What JSP is and is not
- How JSPs work
- How to program JSPs
- Deploy and run JSPs

J ava servlets were a hit from day one. The ability to use Java code on the server released the programmer from having to use three or four different technologies to get a Web application up and running.

Not every aspect of the servlet's architecture was well received, however. Programmers had to use the `out.println()` method on every line of HTML code that was to be output, which proved to be very tedious. True, programmers could write classes that allowed the HTML text to be passed in as a parameter, but this was only slightly better than the `println()` methods.

Another problem with servlets was that they tended to grow to amazing lengths. One servlet would contain code to communicate with the browser, mixed with code to provide presentation logic, which was also mixed with business logic.

What was needed was a way to write some sort of scripts inside the HTML statements themselves, in a manner similar to Microsoft's Active Server Pages (ASP), but vendor-neutral and integrated with the servlet and class architecture that was already on the server. The solution that Sun's engineers came up with was called JavaServer Pages (JSP).

What JSP Is and Is Not

JavaServer Pages are just text files filled with standard HTML code that is interspersed with nuggets of Java-like code. This code is interpreted by a JSP translator and turned into Java code, along with the HTML that it modified. This architecture provides a script language that integrates well with the JVM, but that is simple enough to be learned by anyone capable of writing HTML. You can think of JSP as adding logical constructs to HTML.

The JSP page is translated into a servlet prior to being run. The servlet's output is HTML statements, so authoring JSP pages can be thought of as a fancy form of HTML authoring.

JSP can make calls to Java classes on the server. This is the subject of Chapter 23, "Component-Based JSP Pages." In addition, a programmer can write custom tags to extend JSP functionality. This is the subject of Chapter 24, "Custom Tag Libraries."

JavaServer Pages are not servlets or Java programs, although the syntax resembles Java syntax. They aren't JavaScript programs, which run in the browser instead of the server. JSP can be thought of as shorthand versions of servlets that must be translated into real Java servlets before execution.

Advantages of JSP

The advantages of JSP compared to servlets are shown in Table 22.1.

TABLE 22.1 Advantage of JSP Compared to Servlets

JSP is simpler to read and understand. The JSP syntax is a small subset of the Java language that you find in most Java programs.
JSP removes the presentation logic from the communication logic. Servlets contain logic to manage the communication as well as that of the presentation. Normally, JSP contains only presentation logic.
JSP can separate the presentation from the business logic if component-based techniques are used.
JSP supports a division of labor between the presentation person and the Web server programmer. An HTML programmer can become proficient in JSP in less than half the time that it would take to learn how to program servlets. This enables the team to be separated into the presentation programmers using JSP, and the business-layer programmers who write components in Java to be used by the JSP programmers.

The only disadvantage of JSP versus Java is that JSP syntax is a dialect of Java, but not the entire language. This introduces a learning curve for the heavyweight Java developer. The advantages of JSP over other Web languages are shown in Table 22.2.

TABLE 22.2   Advantages of JSP over ASP, ColdFusion, and PHP Tools

JSP is a dialect of Java, which means that the entire solution from presentation and business logic to database access can be done using only one programming language.
JSP is operating system neutral. It is not tied to one tool vendor or operating system vendor.

These advantages are primarily responsible for the tremendous popularity that JSP has enjoyed since its introduction. The primary disadvantage of JSP compared to the proprietary languages such as ASP and ColdFusion is that JSP tools might not be as rich as the ones available for the single-vendor tools.

How JavaServer Pages Works

You, the programmer, create JSP using your editor of choice. Anything from vi to Forte will work. You place JSP in a special directory where the Web server can find it. The user types in the name of the JSP just like he would type the name of a servlet.

When the request arrives at the Web server, the server translates the JSP page into a servlet and runs that servlet. From that point forward until the server is shut down, the server will submit subsequent requests directly to the servlet and bypass the JSP.

If the JSP has been modified, or if the server unloaded it because of lack of use, the translation step is repeated. Concurrent access to the JSP-generated servlet is handled by threading the requests just as it is in ordinary servlets. Figure 22.1 shows this process graphically.

FIGURE 22.1

The JSP is translated into a servlet prior to being run by the Web server.

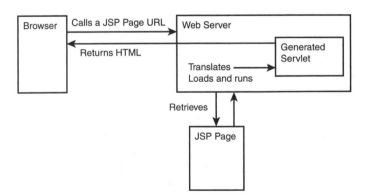

The end result of this process is HTML being displayed on a browser.

Programming with JSP

Every programming language has special syntax that must be understood before you can program with it. JSP uses Java syntax wrapped in special character delimiters so that the servlet generator can differentiate between code that you have written to provide logic and the HTML code that is to be sent to the browser verbatim.

Expressions

The first special syntax is called the expression. Expressions are statements that are to be reduced to a literal value that will be included in the HTML document being created. The delimiting characters are <%= and "%>. In a JSP, you might find the following line:

```
Hello, <b><%= request.getparameter("firstName") %></b>
```

If the parameter value is Joe, the following would be what the user would see in his browser:

```
Hello, Joe
```

Adding Scriptlets to JSP Pages

Scriptlets are like expressions in that after they are run HTML commands are the result. They are less restrictive than expressions in that they enable arbitrary Java code to be used.

The syntax for scriptlets is simply:

```
<% some Java code %>
```

A typical use of scriptlet code is shown in this fragment:

```
<%
    for (int i=0; i<10; i++)
    {
%>
        <b>
        <%= i %>
        </b>
<%
    }
%>
```

Declarations

Declarations are for declaring servlet-level variables that will appear in the servlet outside of any methods. Code that is in a scriptlet can contain variable declarations, but these declarations will be placed in the _jspService() method, which will be called by the service() method. As such, their scope will be limited to that method.

The syntax for a declaration is

```
<%! Declarative code %>
```

A fragment that uses this syntax is shown here:

```
<%! char c1 = 0; %>
```

Adding Comments

There are two types of comments in JSP. The first type is the HTML comment, which takes the form:

```
<!-- This is an HTML comment -->
```

Like any other HTML expression, it appears outside of all scriptlets in the page and is passed through to the browser just like any other piece of HTML.

The second type of comment is a JSP comment. These comments are never intended to appear in the output, but are included for the benefit of the JSP's programmers, both current and future. This comment's syntax is

```
<%-- This is a JSP comment --%>
```

Directives

Directives are commands that modify the resulting servlet in a major way. The three types of directives are page, include, and taglib. The `page` directive enables you to import classes, specify the servlet's superclass, set the content type, and so on. The `include` directive enables you to insert an external file into a JSP page at a certain point. This allows a modular approach to creating JSP pages. The taglib directive can be used to describe custom markup tags. Chapter 24, "Custom Tag Libraries," will provide further explanation of this directive.

The syntax for a directive is

```
<%@ directive text %>
```

An example of a directive is shown here:

```
<%@ page import="mypackage.myclass" %>
```

Implicit Objects

Servlets have access to the request and response objects via the passing of these parameters in the `doGet()`, and the `doPost()` methods. These objects are accessible to JSP not as parameters passed in, but as implicit objects. From the standpoint of the JSP author, eight objects just exist and they are available for your use. These objects are

- request—The `request` object is the `HttpServletRequest` object from which you extract parameter and browser data in servlets.

- response—The `response` object is the `HttpServletResponse` object that you send data to for transmission to the browser.

- out—The out object is a buffered version of the PrintWriter object that you are used to declaring and printing to in servlets. JSP expressions use this object without naming it explicitly, whereas scriptlets make explicit reference to it.

- session—The session object is the HttpSession object that servlet writers use to preserve and retrieve state variables across different servlets called by the same browser.

- application—The application object is the ServletContext object that contains attributes that are available to all servlets in the servlet engine, independent of the browser that invoked them.

- config—This is the ServletConfig object for this page. The servlet container places information to this object during initialization.

- pageContext—The PageContext object is unique to JSP. Many of the page attributes are stored in this object. It can also be used to store shared data.

- page—The page object is a synonym for this, but it is not often used.

These objects enable the JSP programmer to have access to information about the environment that he is programming.

Deploying and Running JSP

The cheapest way to deploy and run JSPs on your computer is to download the Apache Tomcat Web server.

Jakarta Tomcat is available at no cost from the Apache Web site at http://www.apache.org/.

The link for Tomcat 4.0.4 is http://jakarta.apache.org/builds/jakarta-tomcat-4.0/release/v4.0.4/bin/.

Choose a release that is right for your needs. If you are running Java 1.4, the following self-extracting .exe file will be correct for you.

```
jakarta-tomcat-4.0.4-LE-jdk14.exe
```

Caution

As new versions of Tomcat are released, the links that lead to them will differ from those shown previously. In these cases, you will need to go to the http://jakarta.apache.org/ Web site and navigate to the newest release.

Chapter 21, "Servlets," provides detailed instructions on how to install and verify Tomcat on your computer.

It is easy to deploy JSP on Tomcat. All you have to do is create a folder of your own under the
...\webapps\examples\jsp\ directory. For this chapter, we have created a directory called
jpp. Whenever we write a servlet, we can place it in this directory and call it by using the following URI:

http://localhost:1776/examples/jsp/jpp/xyz.jsp

In this case, xyz.jsp is the name of the file that contains the JSP code. Listing 22.1 shows a
simple JSP page that we can use to prove to ourselves that JSPs placed in this new directory
will run on the server.

LISTING 22.1   The requestExamination.jsp Page

```
<html>

<!--
  The requestExamination.jsp File.  This JSP uses expressions to do
  all of the Java work. This is an HTML comment
-->
<%--
  The requestExamination.jsp File.  This JSP uses expressions to do
  all of the Java work. This is a JSP comment
--@>

<body bgcolor="white">
<h1> Request Examination </h1>
<font size="4">
JSP Request Method: <%= request.getMethod() %>
<br>
Server: <%= request.getServerName() %>
<br>
port: <%= request.getServerPort() %>
<br>
address: <%= request.getRemoteAddr() %>
<br>
host: <%= request.getRemoteHost() %>
<br>
Locale: <%= request.getLocale() %>
<hr>
Request URI: <%= request.getRequestURI() %>
<br>
Request Protocol: <%= request.getProtocol() %>
<br>
Servlet path: <%= request.getServletPath() %>
<br>
Browser version <%= request.getHeader("User-Agent") %>
<hr>
</font>
</body>
</html>
```

We see the usual HTML tags in this code along with some of the new JSP syntax that you have been introduced to in this chapter. The first things we notice are the JSP comment and the HTML comment. The first comment will show up in the result, but the second one is only for the JSP programmer's eyes.

```
<!--
  The requestExamination.jsp File.  This JSP uses expressions to do
  all of the Java work. This is an HTML comment
-->
<%--
  The requestExamination.jsp File.  This JSP uses expressions to do
  all of the Java work. This is a JSP comment
-->
```

The next nugget of JSP that we see is an expression. This expression is using the request object that we mentioned previously as always being available in JSP. The `getMethod()` method returns whether the request was a `Get` or a `Post`.

```
JSP Request Method: <%= request.getMethod() %>
```

The server name for our example is `localhost`. The `localhost` machine name always means this machine, regardless of the machine's real `ServerName`.

```
Server: <%= request.getServerName() %>
```

The port is 1776 because the test machine for this chapter chooses to run Tomcat on that port to avoid conflicts with other products that were using the default port 8080.

```
port: <%= request.getServerPort() %>
```

The `getRemoteAddr()` method returns the IP address of the server running the JSP. `127.0.0.1` is a magic IP address that always means "this machine," regardless of the true IP address of the machine.

```
address: <%= request.getRemoteAddr() %>
```

The `getRemoteHost()` method returns the name of the machine running the browser that called the JSP page. In this example's case, the same machine is running both the browser and the server.

```
host: <%= request.getRemoteHost() %>
```

The `getLocale()` is used to internationalize the JSP. This value is set when you install Java on your computer. It is initially based on settings in your operating system that the installation program reads. It has two parts; the first is the language, and the second is the locality. This machine returns `en_US`, indicating English as spoken in the United States instead of English as spoken in England.

```
Locale: <%= request.getLocale() %>
```

The `getRequestURI()` returns the relative path entered into the address line on the browser. It is the directory location in relation to the Web server's root.

```
Request URI: <%= request.getRequestURI() %>
```

The `getProtocol()` method will return the version of HTTP that was submitted with the request.

`Request Protocol: <%= request.getProtocol() %>`

The servlet path is the path relative to the name of the application, which in our case is a directory called `<install-dir>\webapps\examples`.

`Servlet path: <%= request.getServletPath() %>`

The `getHeader("User-Agent")` method returns the precise name and version number of the browser that was used.

`Browser version <%= request.getHeader("User-Agent") %>`

To run this example, type the following in the address line of your browser:

`http://localhost:1776/examples/jsp/jpp/requestExamination.jsp`

This will result in the display of the Web page shown in Figure 22.2.

FIGURE 22.2
The result of running this JSP program is a formatted HTML page.

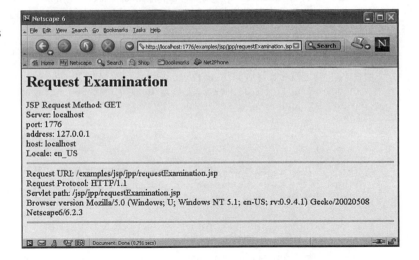

We can view the HTML source that was generated by selecting Page Source from the View menu when running Netscape Navigator, or by selecting Source from the View menu when running Microsoft Internet Explorer. The generated HTML for `requestExamination.jsp` is shown in Listing 22.2.

LISTING 22.2   The `requestExamination.jsp`-Generated HTML

```
<html>

<!--
  The requestExamination.jsp File.  This JSP uses expressions to do
  all of the Java work. This is an HTML comment
-->
```

LISTING 22.2   Continued

```
<body bgcolor="white">
<h1> Request Examination </h1>
<font size="4">
JSP Request Method: GET
<br>
Server: localhost
<br>
port: 1776
<br>
address: 127.0.0.1
<br>
host: localhost
<br>
Locale: en_US
<hr>
Request URI: /examples/jsp/jpp/requestExamination.jsp
<br>
Request Protocol: HTTP/1.1
<br>
Servlet path: /jsp/jpp/requestExamination.jsp
<br>
Browser version Mozilla/5.0 (Windows; U;
 Windows NT 5.1; en-US; rv:0.9.4.1) Gecko/20020508 Netscape6/6.2.3
<hr>
</font>
</body>
</html>
```

Notice that no <% characters are left in the code by the time that it arrives in the server. You can think of the <% as the **remove me** command. Every bit of JSP that falls inside of this delimiter is to be resolved and removed. This includes the Java comment delimiters /**, */, and //.

The JSP is translated into an ordinary servlet before being run. You might notice an unusual delay, caused by the translation step, the first time you run a large servlet. Each JSP is translated only once and will be run without retranslation until it is modified. Fortunately, in Tomcat 4.x, this retranslation is automatic, saving the programmer much time and aggravation. Listing 22.3 shows the servlet that was created for the requestExamination.jsp file.

LISTING 22.3   The requestExamination$jsp.java Servlet

```
package org.apache.jsp;

import javax.servlet.*;
import javax.servlet.http.*;
import javax.servlet.jsp.*;
import org.apache.jasper.runtime.*;
```

LISTING 22.3 Continued

```java
public class requestExamination$jsp extends HttpJspBase
{
    static
    {
    }
    public requestExamination$jsp( )
    {
    }

    private static boolean _jspx_inited = false;

    public final void _jspx_init()
    throws org.apache.jasper.runtime.JspException
    {
    }

    public void _jspService(HttpServletRequest request,
                        HttpServletResponse  response)
        throws java.io.IOException, ServletException
    {

        JspFactory _jspxFactory = null;
        PageContext pageContext = null;
        HttpSession session = null;
        ServletContext application = null;
        ServletConfig config = null;
        JspWriter out = null;
        Object page = this;
        String  _value = null;
        try
        {

            if (_jspx_inited == false)
            {
                synchronized (this)
                {
                    if (_jspx_inited == false)
                    {
                        _jspx_init();
                        _jspx_inited = true;
                    }
                }
            }
            _jspxFactory = JspFactory.getDefaultFactory();
            response.setContentType("text/html;ISO-8859-1");
            pageContext = _jspxFactory.getPageContext(this,
            request, response,        "", true, 8192, true);

            application = pageContext.getServletContext();
            config = pageContext.getServletConfig();
            session = pageContext.getSession();
            out = pageContext.getOut();
```

LISTING 22.3   Continued

```
// HTML // begin [file="/jsp/jpp/requestExamination.jsp";
//from=(0,0);to=(6,0)]
out.write("<html>\r\n\r\n<!—\r\n  The requestExamination.jsp
   File.  This JSP uses expressions to do\r\n  all of the
   Java work. This is an HTML comment\r\n—>\r\n");

// end
// HTML // begin [file="/jsp/jpp/requestExamination.jsp";
      //from=(9,4);to=(14,20)]
out.write("\r\n\r\n<body bgcolor=\"white\">\r\n<h1>
         Request Examination </h1>\r\n<font size=\"4\">\r\nJSP
         Request Method: ");

// end
// begin [file="/jsp/jpp/requestExamination.jsp";
         //from=(14,23);to=(14,44)]
out.print( request.getMethod() );
// end
// HTML // begin [file="/jsp/jpp/requestExamination.jsp";
         //from=(14,46);to=(16,8)]
out.write("\r\n<br>\r\nServer: ");

// end
// begin [file="/jsp/jpp/requestExamination.jsp";
//from=(16,11);to=(16,36)]
out.print( request.getServerName() );
// end
// HTML // begin [file="/jsp/jpp/requestExamination.jsp";
//from=(16,38);to=(18,6)]
out.write("\r\n<br>\r\nport: ");

// end
// begin [file="/jsp/jpp/requestExamination.jsp";
//from=(18,9);to=(18,34)]
out.print( request.getServerPort() );
// end
// HTML // begin [file="/jsp/jpp/requestExamination.jsp";
//from=(18,36);to=(20,9)]
out.write("\r\n<br>\r\naddress: ");

// end
// begin [file="/jsp/jpp/requestExamination.jsp";
//from=(20,12);to=(20,37)]
out.print( request.getRemoteAddr() );
// end
// HTML // begin [file="/jsp/jpp/requestExamination.jsp";
//from=(20,39);to=(22,6)]
out.write("\r\n<br>\r\nhost: ");

// end
// begin [file="/jsp/jpp/requestExamination.jsp";
//from=(22,9);to=(22,34)]
```

LISTING 22.3   Continued

```
out.print( request.getRemoteHost() );
// end
// HTML // begin [file="/jsp/jpp/requestExamination.jsp";
//from=(22,36);to=(24,8)]
out.write("\r\n<br>\r\nLocale: ");

// end
// begin [file="/jsp/jpp/requestExamination.jsp";
//from=(24,11);to=(24,32)]
out.print( request.getLocale() );
// end
// HTML // begin [file="/jsp/jpp/requestExamination.jsp";
//from=(24,34);to=(26,13)]
out.write("\r\n<hr>\r\nRequest URI: ");

// end
// begin [file="/jsp/jpp/requestExamination.jsp";
//from=(26,16);to=(26,41)]
out.print( request.getRequestURI() );
// end
// HTML // begin [file="/jsp/jpp/requestExamination.jsp";
//from=(26,43);to=(28,18)]
out.write("\r\n<br>\r\nRequest Protocol: ");

// end
// begin [file="/jsp/jpp/requestExamination.jsp";
//from=(28,21);to=(28,44)]
out.print( request.getProtocol() );
// end
// HTML // begin [file="/jsp/jpp/requestExamination.jsp";
//from=(28,46);to=(30,14)]
out.write("\r\n<br>\r\nServlet path: ");

// end
// begin [file="/jsp/jpp/requestExamination.jsp";
//from=(30,17);to=(30,43)]
out.print( request.getServletPath() );
// end
// HTML // begin [file="/jsp/jpp/requestExamination.jsp";
//from=(30,45);to=(32,16)]
out.write("\r\n<br>\r\nBrowser version ");

// end
// begin [file="/jsp/jpp/requestExamination.jsp";
//from=(32,19);to=(32,52)]
out.print( request.getHeader("User-Agent") );
// end
// HTML // begin [file="/jsp/jpp/requestExamination.jsp";
//from=(32,54);to=(37,0)]
out.write("\r\n<hr>\r\n</font>\r\n</body>\r\n</html>\r\n");

// end
```

LISTING 22.3   Continued

```
        } catch (Throwable t)
        {
          if (out != null && out.getBufferSize() != 0)
             out.clearBuffer();
          if (pageContext != null) pageContext.handlePageException(t);
        } finally
        {
          if (_jspxFactory != null)
             _jspxFactory.releasePageContext(pageContext);
        }
     }
}
```

This listing is a bit long, but understanding it is critical if you are going to be a JSP programmer instead of a JSP page developer. This servlet is placed in a package and in a special directory that differs from Web server to Web server. On Tomcat 4.x, it was found in the directory ...\ work\Standalone\localhost\examples\jsp\jpp. The package the class file is moved to be run is `package org.apache.jsp;`.

This servlet imports the usual group of servlet packages along with the `org.apache.jasper.runtime` package. Jasper is the name of the Apache JSP engine.

```
import javax.servlet.*;
import javax.servlet.http.*;
import javax.servlet.jsp.*;
import org.apache.jasper.runtime.*;
```

Notice that the JSP file has been renamed during the translation process.

```
public class requestExamination$jsp extends HttpJspBase
```

The work of the servlet is done in the `_jspService()` method, which looks a lot like the service method from the `GenericServlet` class.

```
    public void _jspService(HttpServletRequest request,
                            HttpServletResponse  response)
        throws java.io.IOException, ServletException
     {
```

Apache uses its own `JspFactory` object to obtain contexts and such. These objects are the intrinsic objects from earlier in the chapter.

```
        JspFactory _jspxFactory = null;
        PageContext pageContext = null;
        HttpSession session = null;
        ServletContext application = null;
        ServletConfig config = null;
        JspWriter out = null;
        Object page = this;
```

Here the servlet obtains the values to all the intrinsic objects that you can access in the JSP page.

```
_jspxFactory = JspFactory.getDefaultFactory();
response.setContentType("text/html;ISO-8859-1");
pageContext = _jspxFactory.getPageContext(this,
request, response,        "", true, 8192, true);

application = pageContext.getServletContext();
config = pageContext.getServletConfig();
session = pageContext.getSession();
out = pageContext.getOut();
```

Finally, the generated HTML is written to out. Notice that the origin of each statement is listed in the comments. This is to aid debugging, especially when JSP gets large and complex. The coordinates are in units of characters that are counted with 0,0 at the origin, with the x-coordinate increasing downward and the y-coordinate increasing from left to right.

```
// HTML // begin [file="/jsp/jpp/requestExamination.jsp";
//from=(0,0);to=(6,0)]
out.write("<html>\r\n\r\n<!—\r\n  The requestExamination.jsp
    File. This JSP uses expressions to do\r\n  all of
    the Java work. This is an HTML comment\r\n—>\r\n");

// end
```

Static HTML is just written out in a formatted fashion.

```
// HTML // begin [file="/jsp/jpp/requestExamination.jsp";
       //from=(9,4);to=(14,20)]
out.write("\r\n\r\n<body bgcolor=\"white\">\r\n<h1>
           Request Examination </h1>\r\n<font size=\"4\">\r\nJSP
           Request Method: ");
```

The dynamic values are extracted or calculated using normal servlet logic. Here a call to an HttpServletRequest object's getMethod() method is employed.

```
// begin [file="/jsp/jpp/requestExamination.jsp";
           //from=(14,23);to=(14,44)]
out.print( request.getMethod() );
// end
```

In the end, the servlet is run and gets the illusion that the JSP is really a program that can be run directly. This mindset is productive as long as everything works. When bugs arise, peel back the cover and look at the intermediate servlet to find the problem.

Defining Methods in JSP

Many experienced Java programmers want to include modularity in their JSP. One of the best ways to preserve some order is to create methods to perform specific functions. These methods can then be called from within the scriptlet code in the JSP. The value returned can then be displayed. Listing 22.4 shows an example of this.

LISTING 22.4   The `MethodCaller` JSP

```
<%!
    private java.util.Date sinceDate = new java.util.Date();

    private java.util.Date getSinceDate()
    {
        return sinceDate;
    }
%>

<html>
<head>
<title>Method Caller</title>
<body>
<h2>The Startup Date</h2>
This page was first run on <%= getSinceDate() %>.
</body>
</html>
```

This short example shows some interesting code. The first section starts with a `<%!`, which tells the JSP engine that everything in here is a declaration. The first thing that we do in this section is create a variable of type **Date** that will hold the date that this JSP was first run.

```
<%!
    private java.util.Date sinceDate = new java.util.Date();
```

We could have referred to the **sinceDate** directly, using an expression, but we use a method call so that you can see how this is done.

```
    private java.util.Date getSinceDate()
    {
        return sinceDate;
    }
%>
```

The syntax of the call is an expression. Because this method returns the **Date** object, it is a simple thing to place it inside an expression and display it.

```
This page was first run on <%= getSinceDate() %>.
```

The result of running this program is shown here in Figure 22.3:

Run this same page several times; notice how the time doesn't change. Restart the Tomcat server, and then run this JSP again. Notice now how the date has changed. What we have discovered is that the JSP and the servlet that is generated to run it both remain in memory between calls. This means that all class level servlet variables are static by nature because there is only one instance of the servlet in memory. Whenever a browser runs a page, a new thread of the same servlet is created.

This fact will be clearer after we run the next example. This example shows the classic counter application where the number of hits that the page has received is shown. Listing 22.4 shows this example.

FIGURE 22.3
The method call is made, and the resulting date is displayed.

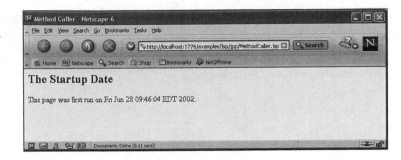

LISTING 22.4   The MethodCounter JSP

```
<%!
    private int hits = 1;

    private int getHits()
    {
        return hits++;
    }
%>

<html>
<head>
<title>Method Counter</title>
<body>
<h2>The Hit Count</h2>
This page has been accessed <%= getHits() %> times.
</body>
</html>
```

The declaration of the variable hits is not stated to be static, but its behavior is as if it were.

```
    private int hits = 1;
```

The method body returns the current value of the counter before incrementing it.

```
    private int getHits()
    {
        return hits++;
    }
```

The result is displayed using an expression:

```
This page has been accessed <%= getHits() %> times.
```

The result is shown in Figure 22.4.

FIGURE 22.4
The page counter behaves like a static variable.

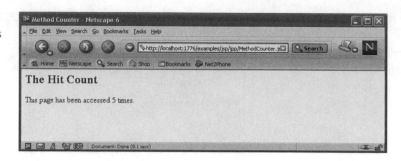

Again, if you restart the Web server, the number will reset to one.

Conditional Output

One of the most common dynamic HTML activities is to selectively display content, based on some condition. This condition could be tied to the time of day or month of the year, but typically it is tied to a parameter that is passed in. The example shown in Listing 22.5 shows a parameter-based JSP.

LISTING 22.5   The Temperature JSP

```
<html>
<head>
<title>Temperature Translator</title>
<body>
<% float fTemp;
   float cTemp;
   String sTemp = request.getParameter("temp");
   cTemp = Integer.parseInt(sTemp);
   fTemp = (cTemp*9/5)+32;
%>
The Fahrenheit Temperature is <%=fTemp %> <br>

<%if (fTemp < 60) %>
<b>It's chilly </b>

<%if (fTemp > 85) %>
<b>It's Hot </b>

<%if ((fTemp >= 60) && (fTemp <= 85)) %>
<b>It's Nice </b>

</body>
</html>
```

This example demonstrates how a value can be calculated based on user input, and then that value used to make a conditional choice.

The parameters that are retrieved from a browser are of type `String`. Before you can do any math with them, you have to convert them to either integer or float values. The Integer class contains a static method called `parseInt()` that performs this conversion and returns an integer value.

```
<% float fTemp;
   float cTemp;
   String sTemp = request.getParameter("temp");
   cTemp = Integer.parseInt(sTemp);
   fTemp = (cTemp*9/5)+32;
%>
```

After displaying the temperature in the Fahrenheit scale, a conditional test is made to give the user some idea of the quality of the current temperature.

```
<%if (fTemp < 60) %>
<b>It's chilly </b>

<%if (fTemp > 85) %>
<b>It's Hot </b>

<%if ((fTemp >= 60) && (fTemp <= 85)) %>
<b>It's Nice </b>
```

Notice how the scriptlets start and end on every line. The line following each scriptlet is simple HTML. The conditional statement applies to all lines following the condition until the next scriptlet line is encountered.

The result is shown in Figure 22.5.

FIGURE 22.5
The conditional statements control what is displayed.

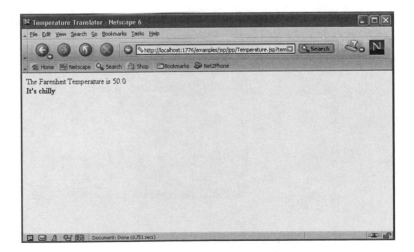

Calling JSP from HTML Forms

Rather than entering the temperature as part of the URL, it would be more realistic to have the user enter it into an HTML form. Listing 22.5 shows the HTML for this form.

LISTING 22.5   The `Temp.HTML` File

```
<!DOCTYPE HTML PUBLIC "-//W3C//DTD HTML 4.01 Transitional//EN">

<HTML>
  <HEAD>
    <TITLE>Passing Parameters to JSPs</TITLE>
  </HEAD>
  <H1 align="CENTER">
  Enter the Temperature in Celcius
  </H1>

  <FORM action="/examples/jsp/jpp/Temperature.jsp">

    Temperature:    <INPUT TYPE="TEXT" NAME="temp"><BR><BR>
    <CENTER>
       <INPUT TYPE="SUBMIT">
    </CENTER>
  </FORM>

  </BODY>
</HTML>
```

JSP references inside the HTML file are identical to the references to servlets, except that the path is normally more logically stated. Servlets are often stored in special directories that don't match the path that you enter on the command line, where JSP references do.

```
<FORM action="/examples/jsp/jpp/Temperature.jsp">
```

The HTML form is displayed on the screen, as shown in Figure 22.6.

FIGURE 22.6
The HTML form can call a JSP directly.

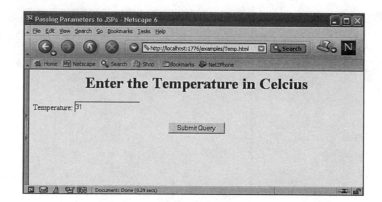

Error Handling

If the user enters in a letter instead of a number in the `Temp.HTML` form, an ugly, programmer-oriented error message will result. If Grandma is viewing this page, she will not find much help in resolving her problem. You can include `try/catch` logic to address this. Listing 22.6 is a modified version of the `Temperature.jsp` that handles invalid formats.

LISTING 22.6   The Temperature2.jsp

```
<html>
<head>
<title>Temperature Translator</title>
<body>
<%
    try
    {
        float fTemp;
        float cTemp;
        String sTemp = request.getParameter("temp");
        System.out.println("The temp is " + sTemp);
        cTemp = Integer.parseInt(sTemp);
        fTemp = (cTemp*9/5)+32;
%>
The Fahrenheit Temperature is <%=fTemp %> <br>

<%if (fTemp < 60) %>
<b>It's chilly </b>

<%if (fTemp > 85) %>
<b>It's Hot </b>

<%if ((fTemp >= 60) && (fTemp <= 85)) %>
<b>It's Nice </b>

<%
}
 catch (NumberFormatException e)
{
%>
<H2>Invalid Number</H2>
Please make sure that the temperature is a number
<% } %>

</body>
</html>
```

The **try** is placed before the input is retrieved from the request object.

```
<%
    try
    {
        float fTemp;
```

The **catch** could have been placed in the same scriptlet, or it could be placed near the end of the JSP as we did here.

```
}
 catch (NumberFormatException e)
{
%>
<H2>Invalid Number</H2>
Please make sure that the temperature is a number
```

LISTING 22.6   Continued

```
<% } %>

</body>
</html>
```

The result of entering the data incorrectly is a nice error page as shown here in Figure 22.7.

FIGURE 22.7
Try/catch logic can be used in a JSP also.

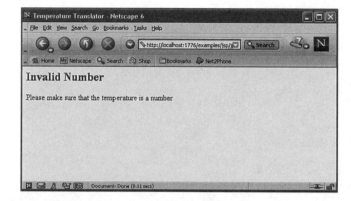

This error message is much more likely to provide real information to end users than the stack-trace information that appears by default.

Summary

This chapter introduced you to JavaServer Pages (JSP). We started out with a discussion of what JSP is. That was followed by an analysis of the advantages of JSP versus both servlets and other technologies such as Microsoft ASP.

Then, we looked at the meaning of the special syntax that JSP employs. Following that, you learned about the intrinsic objects that JSP has access to.

You saw an example dissected and analyzed by looking at the servlet that it generated, and the HTML that was the result. You learned where the intrinsic objects get instantiated.

Finally, we created a series of interesting JSP that showed you how to use methods, conditions, class-level variables, and so on.

Review Questions

1. What is the difference between a servlet and a JSP?

2. What advantages does JSP provide over servlets?

3. What are the differences between an expression and a scriptlet?

4. What is an intrinsic object?

Exercises

1. Create a JSP that echoes your name when called.

2. Create a JSP that lets you choose toppings on a pizza.

3. Create a JSP that assigns a letter grade when a numeric grade is entered.

4. Modify the letter grade JSP to output a special error page when a non-number or negative number is entered.

COMPONENT-BASED JAVASERVER PAGES

You will learn about the following in this chapter:

- The purpose of JSP actions
- How to include other JSPs in your page
- How to access JavaBeans from your JSP
- How to use JavaBeans to access databases

JavaServer Pages (JSP) simplify the task of creating HTML-based Web pages programmatically. They enable you to create scriptlets that give you far more control over the appearance of the output than you can achieve using HTML alone, and with far less effort than using servlets.

It is possible to carry the concept of embedding Java code in scriptlets too far, however. JSP excels in providing control over the presentation of data on a Web page. If you insert too much nonpresentation logic on the page, however, it can become just as unmanageable as a huge servlet. Because of this, many system architects forbid the use of nondisplay logic in JSP. The existence of component-based development makes it possible to segregate display logic from business logic.

There are three ways to include external logic in your JSPs. You can

- Use the `include` directive to insert other JSPs into your page.
- Use the `include` action to include other servlets, JSPs, and HTML files into your JSPs.
- Create JavaBeans that contain the logic that you want to use and call them from the JSP.

Component-based development is a concept that is as old as object-oriented programming itself. The basic idea is to separate your program into three or more layers or tiers.

The presentation layer concerns itself with how information looks in a browser. What color the background is? What fonts will be displayed? Will navigation be with hyperlinks or buttons? Will there be cute little animations on the page? This layer doesn't care about the contents, just the look.

The business layer determines what data will be shown. If pricing differs based on volume, distance from the factory, date of delivery, and so on, this layer will be responsible for determining the correct information to display. This layer doesn't care anything about the look of the display, just the contents. There may be several of these layers in a complex system.

The data layer is where raw data is stored and retrieved. Normally, this layer is implemented as a database. A table of prices based on distance from the factory might be stored in the database. In addition, customer data that could be used to determine the distance from the nearest factory might be stored in another table. However, the logic that uses this data to determine the actual price to display is not the business of this layer. It lives only to store and retrieve data. Figure 23.1 shows this n-tiered architecture:

FIGURE 23.1
The JSP provides the presentation of the data that it is handed by the business-logic layer.

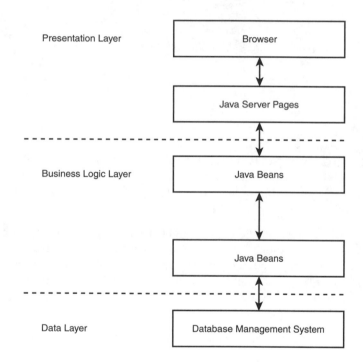

The JavaBeans in the business logic layer could be Enterprise JavaBeans (EJB). There are real benefits to this approach, but a full discussion of them is beyond the scope of this book. Please see *Sams Teach Yourself EJB in 21 Days* from Sams Publishing for a complete discussion of EJB.

Note

JSP calling components such as JavaBeans fit this n-tiered model very nicely. Normally, the JSP determines appearance. They call JavaBeans to request the data to display. The JavaBean calls the database to obtain the data that it needs to calculate the data to display.

In this chapter, you will learn how to add components to your JSP. We start by using the `include` directive. Following that, you will learn how to use JSP `actions` to do a more sophisticated "including" of other components such as servlets and other JSPs. Finally, you will learn how to create JavaBeans that provide information to the JSP for display. Some of these JavaBeans will get their data from databases, showing you how an n-tiered application can be built using JSPs.

Understanding JSP Actions

JSP actions are special tags that perform functions such as transferring control from one JSP to anther, including external HTML into a JSP, generating output, and manipulating JavaBeans.

The syntax of an action is strictly XML, which means that it is more restrictive than HTML. The additional strictness is in the following areas:

- All names used in actions are case sensitive.

- All tags must be terminated with a `/>`.

- Quotes must be used around values.

The simplest action is `forward`. When a forward is encountered, the JSP translator discards all information obtained from this JSP and transfers control to another URL, which may or may not be a JSP. Listing 23.1 shows a JSP that contains a forward action.

LISTING 23.1   The `ForwardTest.jsp` File

```
<html>
<head>
<title>Forward Test</title>
<body>
This is a forward test
<jsp:forward page="ForwardTest2.jsp" />
</body>
</html>
```

When this JSP is called, all the normal processing begins, but it is interrupted and never displayed after the forward tag is encountered. The directory that searched for this new JSP is, by default, the same directory where the original JSP is located. Listing 23.2 shows the JSP page that was the object of the forward command.

LISTING 23.2   The `ForwardTest2.jsp` File

```
<%!
    private java.util.Date sinceDate = new java.util.Date();

    private java.util.Date getSinceDate()
    {
        return sinceDate;
```

LISTING 23.2   Continued

```
        }
%>

<html>
<head>
<title>Forward Test2</title>
<body>
<h2>Forward Test2</h2>
This page was first run on <%= getSinceDate() %>.
</body>
</html>
```

This listing is just a simple date display, as shown here in Figure 23.2.

FIGURE 23.2

The JSP forward action transfers control immediately to another JSP.

Notice that the URL in the address box of the browser didn't change, only the contents did.

There are four more actions that we will use in this chapter to provide the logical separation of the applications logic into layers:

- include—This action performs a text substitution that accepts parameters.
- usebean—This action instantiates a JavaBean (if not yet instantiated) and assigns it a name.
- setProperty—This action is used to set the values of a property in a JavaBean.
- getProperty—This action is used to get the value of a property in a JavaBean.

These actions will be used to support the inclusion of components in the JSPs covered in this chapter.

How to include Other JSPs in Your JSP

One of the simplest forms of component software is the simple include. There are actually two different inclusion mechanisms that can be used in JSPs, the include directive and the include action.

The `include` Directive

The `include` directive can be used to insert the contents of another file into the JSP before the page is translated into a servlet. The JSP `include` is analogous to the `#include` that you find in C and C++ programs.

The syntax for this directive is very simple:

```
<%@ include file="includes/heading.jsp" %>
```

Listing 23.3 shows the `include` directive used in an example.

LISTING 23.3   The `IncludeDirectiveTest.jsp` File

```
<html>
<head>
<title>Include Directive Test</title>
<body>
<h2>Include Directive Test</h2>
This is the header
<%@ include file="includes/IncludeDirectiveHeader.jsp" %>
This is the body of the page.
<br>
This is the footer
<%@ include file="includes/IncludeDirectiveFooter.jsp" %>
</body>
</html>
```

The `include` directive is expecting a URL that is relative to the location of the first JSP. It included the file in the exact location where the directive is found:

```
<%@ include file="includes/IncludeDirectiveHeader.jsp" %>
```

The contents of the two included files are very simple. The first one is shown in Listing 23.4.

LISTING 23.4   The `IncludeDirectiveHeader.jsp` File

```
<center>
<font size=10>
<b>
Include Directive Header
</b>
</font>
</center>
```

The footer is very similar. It is shown in Listing 23.5.

LISTING 23.5   The IncludeDirectiveFooter.jsp File

```
<center>
<font size=10>
<b>
Include Directive Footer
</b>
</font>
</center>
```

Both of these files must be stored in a directory called `includes`, which is a subdirectory of the current directory. Running this page generates the result shown in Figure 23.3.

FIGURE 23.3
The JSP `include` directive copies the contents of other files into this JSP before translation takes place.

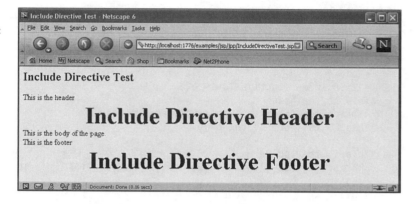

Notice that a different font size was used for the header and footer so that they would stand out.

The `include` Action

The `include` action resembles the `include` directive superficially in that both of them cause information from an external source to be included into the current JSP page. They differ in other aspects of their processing in the following ways:

- The `include` action inserts the contents of the other file into the JSP at runtime. This information is reloaded every time the page is run. The `include` directive only inserts the information at translation time.

- The `include` action can dynamically insert the name of the page to `include`. This enables the actual page to be selected based on user input.

- The `include` action can accept parameters.

- The `include` directive is a textual substitution that can reference variables local to the page. The `include` action transfers control to the other JSP or servlet that does not have access to the local variables of the calling JSP.

Because the processing done to support the `include` action is so much more complex than that done to support the `include` directive, the performance of the `include` directive is superior. If you have a situation where only static HTML or JSP is to be included, you should use the directive. If, however, you need the features mentioned previously in the bulleted list, you must use the `include` action.

You can think of the include action as a type of subroutine call. Your program (JSP) runs to a certain point. It then transfers control to another JSP that runs to completion. Upon completion, control is passed back to the calling program (JSP), which resumes processing at the line following the call (the `include` line).

The syntax of the `include` action is as follows:

```
<jsp:include page='xyz.jsp' flush="true" />
```

The page is the name of the page relative to the location of the calling JSP. The normal double quotes can be used instead of the single quotes, if you prefer. The flush attribute is required, although it must always be set to true. This indicates the programmer's desire to flush the buffer prior to transferring control to the included program. Listing 23.6 shows how the `include` action can be used to include another JSP at runtime.

LISTING 23.6   The `IncludeAction.jsp` File

```
<html>
<head>
<title>Include Action Test</title>
<body>
<h2>Include Action Test</h2>
This is before the included page.
<jsp:include page='includes/IncludedPage1.jsp' />
This is after the included page.
<br>
</body>
</html>
```

Notice that the `include` action uses the page attribute to designate the page to transfer control to temporarily. The page's location is calculated relative to the location of the calling page. The result of running this program is shown in Figure 23.4.

Listing 23.4 showed how the `include` action can be used to insert the contents of a static JSP file into another. The result was correct, but unexciting because you could have accomplished the same thing using the `include` directive. Listing 23.5 shows a more sophisticated use of the `include` action where user input is used to determine which JSP to include.

FIGURE 23.4
The JSP `include` action transfers control to another JSP or servlet, and then returns control after it completes.

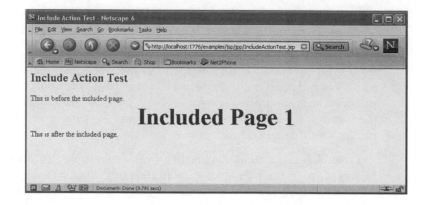

LISTING 23.5   The IncludeActionTest2.jsp File

```
<html>
<head>
<title>Include Action Test2</title>
<body>
<h2>Include Action Test2</h2>
This is before the included page.
<%
    String pageNum;
    pageNum = request.getParameter("pageNum");
 %>
<jsp:include page='<%= "includes/IncludedPage" + pageNum +".jsp" %>' />
This is after the included page.
<br>
</body>
</html>
```

In this example, the page number to be included is retrieved by a call to the request object.

```
pageNum = request.getParameter("pageNum");
```

The page attribute of the **include** action is created dynamically using a JSP expression.

```
<jsp:include page='<%= "includes/IncludedPage" + pageNum +".jsp" %>' />
```

The HTML file that displays the form is shown in Listing 23.6.

LISTING 23.6   The PageNum.html File

```
<!DOCTYPE HTML PUBLIC "-//W3C//DTD HTML 4.01 Transitional//EN">

<HTML>
  <HEAD>
    <TITLE>Passing Parameters to JSPs</TITLE>
  </HEAD>
  <H1 align="CENTER">
  Enter the Page that you want to see
  </H1>
```

LISTING 23.6   Continued

```
<FORM action='/examples/jsp/jpp/IncludeActionTest2.jsp'>

    Page Number:     <INPUT TYPE="TEXT" NAME="pageNum"><BR><BR>
    <CENTER>
        <INPUT TYPE="SUBMIT">
    </CENTER>
</FORM>

</BODY>
</HTML>
```

The parameter named **pageNum** is the one that is accessed via the request object. The JSP pages to be displayed are very simple. Listing 23.7 shows one of them. The others are nearly identical, so only one of them needs to be shown.

LISTING 23.7   The `IncludedPage3.jsp` File

```
<center>
<font size=10>
<b>
Included Page 3
</b>
</font>
</center>
```

This file is kept simple to make the use of the **include** easy to understand. Your included files can be of arbitrary complexity, which may take several forms, and can contain their own **include** actions. Listing 23.8 shows an example that has a number of additional features beyond simple insertion of static HTML.

LISTING 23.8   The `IncludeActionTest3.jsp` File

```
<html>
<head>
<title>Include Action Test3</title>
<body>
<h2>Include Action Test3</h2>
This is before the included page.
<%
    String newPageNum;
    newPageNum = request.getParameter("pageNum");
%>
<jsp:include page="IncludeActionTest4.jsp" flush="true" >
    <jsp:param name ="forwardedPageNum" value="<%= newPageNum %>" />
</jsp:include>
This is after the included page.
<br>
</body>
</html>
```

The purpose of this JSP is to show the passing of the parameter from a form to an included JSP. The first step in doing this is to retrieve the **pageNum** variable from the request object and store it in a local variable.

```
<%
    String newPageNum;
    newPageNum = request.getParameter("pageNum");
 %>
```

The next step is to add the jsp:param action to the jsp:include tag.

```
<jsp:include page="IncludeActionTest4.jsp" flush="true" >
    <jsp:param name ="forwardedPageNum" value="<%= newPageNum %>" />
</jsp:include>
```

Notice that the nature of the closing tag </jsp:include> is different from the /> that we used when there were no params being passed. The /> ending doesn't work when you have nested tags. The "flush" attribute indicates that the output buffer should be flushed before the include is executed. As of JSP 1.1, this value must always be "true." The HTML that calls this JSP is included here in Listing 23.9 to show the complete example.

LISTING 23.9   The PageNum3.HTML File

```
<!DOCTYPE HTML PUBLIC "-//W3C//DTD HTML 4.01 Transitional//EN">

<HTML>
  <HEAD>
    <TITLE>Passing Parameters to JSPs</TITLE>
  </HEAD>
  <H1 align="CENTER">
  Enter the Page that you want to see
  </H1>

  <FORM action='/examples/jsp/jpp/IncludeActionTest3.jsp'>

    Page Number:     <INPUT TYPE="TEXT" NAME="pageNum"><BR><BR>
    <CENTER>
      <INPUT TYPE="SUBMIT">
    </CENTER>
  </FORM>

  </BODY>
</HTML>
```

Note that the original parameter name is **"pageNum"**. The IncludeActionTest4.jsp file is the most interesting part of this example. It is shown here in Listing 23.10.

LISTING 23.10   The IncludeActionTest4.jsp File

```
<center>
<font size=10>
<b>
IncludeActionTest4
<br>
<%
    String fpn = request.getParameter("forwardedPageNum");
    if (fpn.equals("1"))
    {
%>
    <jsp:include page='includes/IncludedPage1.jsp' />
<%
    }
    if (fpn.equals("2"))
    {
%>
    <jsp:include page='includes/IncludedPage2.jsp' />
<%
    }
    if (fpn.equals("3"))
    {
%>
    <jsp:include page='includes/IncludedPage3.jsp' />
<%
    }
%>
The pageNum parameter =
<%= request.getParameter("pageNum") %>
</b>
</font>
</center>
```

The parameter `forwardedPageNum` was declared in `IncludedActionTest3` and passed as a parameter. This program gains access to it by using the same request object as always.

```
String fpn = request.getParameter("forwardedPageNum");
```

The local variable `fpn` now contains a string value that can be tested and branched off of.

```
    if (fpn.equals("1"))
    {
%>
    <jsp:include page='includes/IncludedPage1.jsp' />
<%
```

Notice that we had to terminate the scriptlet and start another one after the `include` action line. Notice also that the fact that this file was included by `IncludeActionTest3.jsp` does not prevent it from doing its own `jsp:include` actions. The included files are the same ones that we showed in Listing 23.7.

The fact that we have added a parameter to the request object doesn't interfere with the other fields that it already contains.

```
The pageNum parameter =
<%= request.getParameter("pageNum") %>
```

The `pageNum` parameter is the one that was declared in the HTML form shown earlier in Listing 23.9. It continues to exist as we move down into the included files. The result of running this is shown here in Figure 23.5.

FIGURE 23.5

The JSP `include` action can make up parameters and pass them to the included page.

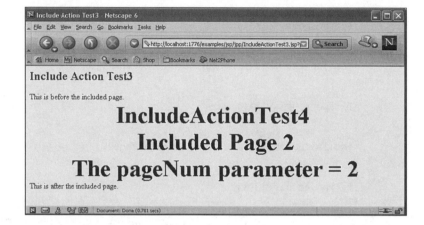

This figure shows output from three different JSPs. The `IncludeAction3.jsp` generated the `Include Action Test 3` line, as well as the `before` and `after` lines. `IncludeAction4.jsp` generated the `IncludedActionTest4` line as well as the `The pageNum parameter = 2` line. The line that reads `Included Page 2` was generated by the `IncludedPage2.jsp` file.

Including other files with or without parameter passing is a powerful capability. In the next section you will learn another way to use components that don't involve the `include` action at all.

Accessing JavaBeans from JSPs

The most powerful way to use component programming in JSPs is to call JavaBeans from within them. JavaBeans are normal Java classes that can be created using any editing tools. They don't extend any special classes or implement any particular interfaces. What makes JavaBeans different from ordinary Java classes is that they are designed according to a specific pattern.

Normally, JavaBeans are associated with Graphical User Interfaces (GUIs). If the JavaBean pattern is followed, visual tools such as Forte, JBuilder, and Visual Cafe can place these Beans on the toolbar and allow users to drag them into their applications.

On the server side, the requirements are not as strict because these JavaBeans don't have a GUI representation. The rules for creating server-side JavaBeans are fairly simple:

- A JavaBean must have an empty constructor, which is a constructor that takes no arguments. It might have other constructors as well, but one constructor must accept no arguments. If no constructors are declared, the empty constructor that is automatically generated by the JVM satisfies this requirement.

- A JavaBean can have no variables declared as `public`. You probably follow this rule already because the declaration of public variables in a class definition is considered bad form.

- A JavaBean may have properties. These properties are private variables that are accessed via `get` and `set` methods. If a variable has only a `get`, but not a `set` method associated with it, it is considered a read-only property. If a variable has only a `set` method, it would be a write-only property. If it has neither, it is not a property at all, but only a private variable of the class.

Using JavaBeans in your JSPs has a number of advantages over using `include` files. The primary advantage comes from the division of labor that is possible using JSPs and JavaBeans in combination.

JavaBean development is virtually identical to ordinary Java class development. JavaBeans can extend any superclass and implement any interface that you want it to. This means that a Bean can be multithreaded, it can access a database via JDBC, it can use the Java Cryptography Extension (JCE), and any other standard extension that you know how to program.

Programmers who are capable of programming with all these extensions are expensive and hard to find and hire. To make the best use of their time, it is wise to give them the responsibility of developing the JavaBeans that contain the nondisplay-oriented logic of your application.

JSP developers are often more junior and, in some cases, are not programmers at all. Many JSP developers are Web page designers who have migrated to JSP to gain more power over their content. They describe their needs to the JavaBean developers who provide them with the Beans that they need as well as instructions on how to use them.

Creating JavaBeans and calling them from within a JSP is fairly simple. The complexity of the task comes from the challenge of trying to program a Bean to solve your business problems, not from the structure of the Bean itself. Listing 23.11 shows a simple server-side JavaBean.

LISTING 23.11   The `TicketRequestBean` Class

```
/*
 * TicketRequestBean.java
 *
 * Created on July 9, 2002, 11:22 AM
 */

package com.samspublishing.jpp.ch23;

import java.sql.*;
```

LISTING 23.11   Continued

```java
import java.util.*;



/**
 *
 * @author  Stephen Potts
 * @version
 */
public class TicketRequestBean implements java.io.Serializable
{
    //information about the customer
    private int custID;
    private String lastName;
    private String firstName;


    public TicketRequestBean()
    {
    }

    /** Constructor */
    public TicketRequestBean(int custID, String lastName, String firstName,
    int cruiseID, String destination,
    String port, String sailing, int numberOfTickets,
    boolean isCommissionable)
    {
        //set the information about the customer
        this.custID = custID;
        this.lastName = lastName;
        this.firstName = firstName;

    }

    public int getCustID()
    {
        return this.custID = custID;
    }

    public String getLastName()
    {
        return this.lastName = lastName;
    }

    public String getFirstName()
    {
        return this.firstName = firstName;
    }


    public void setCustID(int custID)
    {
```

LISTING 23.11   Continued

```
        this.custID = custID;
    }

    public void setLastName(String lastName)
    {
        this.lastName = lastName;
    }

    public void setFirstName(String firstName)
    {
        this.firstName = firstName;
    }

    public String toString()
    {
        String outString;
        outString = "-----------------------------------------" + "\n";

        //information about the customer
        outString += "custID = " + this.custID + "\n";
        outString += "lastName = " + this.lastName + "\n";
        outString += "firstName = " + this.firstName + "\n";
        outString += "-----------------------------------------" + "\n";

        return outString;
    }

}
```

This class contains the usual complement of getters and setters, as well as the required empty constructor. In addition, it contains a nonempty constructor and a `toString()` method to dump the contents for debugging purposes.

This class will give you some fields to learn with. Conceptually, this Bean is very simple. The definition of the fields is shown here:

- `custID`—The customer's ID in our system.

- `lastName`—The last name of the customer.

- `firstName`—The first name of the customer.

Making calls to this JavaBean from within a JSP is fairly simple. A special action, called `jsp:useBean`, provides us with a way of instantiating a JavaBean inside our JSP. The syntax of the `useBean` action is shown here:

```
<jsp:useBean
id="MyTicketBean"
class="com.samspublishing.jpp.ch23.TicketRequestBean"
scope="page"
/>
```

The id is the name of this instance in your JSP and it is used to reference the bean within the page. The class is the full name of the class, including the package. The scope specifies what pages will be able to access this instance. (Page, the default, specifies that only this page will see this instance.)

This JavaBean can be populated by a JSP. Listing 23.12 shows the form that we will use to do this.

LISTING 23.12   The `AddCustomertForm.html` File

```
<!DOCTYPE HTML PUBLIC "-//W3C//DTD HTML 4.01 Transitional//EN">

<HTML>
  <HEAD>
    <TITLE>Add a Customer</TITLE>
  </HEAD>
  <H1 align="CENTER">
  Enter the new customer's information
  </H1>

  <FORM action='/examples/jsp/jpp/TicketRequestProcessor.jsp'>

    Customer ID:    <INPUT TYPE="TEXT" NAME="custID"><BR><BR>
    Customer Last Name:     <INPUT TYPE="TEXT" NAME="lastName"><BR><BR>
    Customer First Name:    <INPUT TYPE="TEXT" NAME="firstName"><BR><BR>
    <CENTER>
      <INPUT TYPE="SUBMIT">
    </CENTER>
  </FORM>

  </BODY>
</HTML>
```

There is nothing special about this form. It gives the user a place to enter information about the customer, and then calls the `TicketRequestProcessor.jsp` page when the SUBMIT button is clicked.

```
<FORM action='/examples/jsp/jpp/TicketRequestProcessor.jsp'>
```

The `TicketRequestProcessor.jsp` fileis shown in Listing 23.13.

LISTING 23.13   The `TicketRequestProcessor.jsp` File

```
<jsp:useBean id="trb"
    class="com.samspublishing.jpp.ch23.TicketRequestBean"
    scope="page" />
<html>
<head>
<title>Ticket Request Processor</title>
<body>
<h2>Ticket Request Processor</h2>
```

LISTING 23.13   Continued

```
<br>
Customer ID: <%= request.getParameter("custID") %>
<br>
Customer First Name: <%= request.getParameter("firstName") %>
<br>
Customer Last Name: <%= request.getParameter("lastName") %>
<br>
<jsp:setProperty name="trb" property="firstName"
     value='<%= request.getParameter("firstName") %>' />
<jsp:setProperty name="trb" property="lastName"
     value='<%= request.getParameter("lastName") %>' />

Now get the property to see if it is there
<br>
<jsp:getProperty name="trb" property="firstName"/>
<br>
<jsp:getProperty name="trb" property="lastName"/>

</body>
</html>
```

It is customary to place the `jsp:usebean` tag first in a JSP. The `id` field is the name that this Bean will be known by in this scope. The class name is the full name of the class, complete with the package. The scope tells the translator whether this `id` will exist outside of this page. The `scope="page"` parameter indicates that the scope is limited to this page.

```
<jsp:useBean id="trb"
    class="com.samspublishing.jpp.ch23.TicketRequestBean"
    scope="page" />
```

First, we display the values in the request using JSP expressions. Then, we set the name properties in the JavaBean using the `jsp:setProperty` action.

```
<jsp:setProperty name="trb" property="firstName"
     value='<%= request.getParameter("firstName") %>' />
<jsp:setProperty name="trb" property="lastName"
     value='<%= request.getParameter("lastName") %>' />
```

Following that we use the `jsp:getProperty` action to retrieve the values from the JavaBean for display. We do this to prove that the setProperty action worked.

```
<jsp:getProperty name="trb" property="firstName"/>
<br>
<jsp:getProperty name="trb" property="lastName"/>
```

The only tricky part of this example is the location of the JavaBean's class file. Because this application is part of the **examples** application, Apache Tomcat requires that the file be placed in the `...\webapps\examples\WEB-INF\classes` directory. However, because this class is part of a package, according to the rules of Java it must be placed in the directory that matches the package name. Therefore, in this example, the `.class` file must be placed in a directory named

`...\webapps\examples\WEB-INF\classes\com\samspublishing\jpp\ch23`

To run this example, place the JavaBean's .class file in this directory. Place the `TicketRequestProcessor.jsp` file in the `...\webapps\examples\jsp\jpp` directory and the `AddCustomerForm.html` file in the `...\webapps\examples` directory. Type the following URL in the address bar of your browser:

`http://localhost:1776/examples/AddCustomerForm.html`

The result that you see should resemble Figure 23.6:

FIGURE 23.6
The JSP `useBean` action gives a JSP page access to Java code stored in a JavaBean.

Notice that we avoided processing the `custID` field in the previous example. We separated out this field because the type of the `custID` in the JavaBean is not `String`, but `int`. This complicates things because we will get a type-mismatch message if we try to store the string into an integer field. To solve this problem, we need to do a conversion on the numeric field before performing the `setProperty` action. Listing 23.14 shows the HTML code for an example that performs this conversion.

LISTING 23.14   The `AddCustomerForm2.html` File

```
<!DOCTYPE HTML PUBLIC "-//W3C//DTD HTML 4.01 Transitional//EN">

<HTML>
  <HEAD>
    <TITLE>Add a Customer 2</TITLE>
  </HEAD>
  <H1 align="CENTER">
  Enter the new customer's information
  </H1>

  <FORM action='/examples/jsp/jpp/TicketRequestProcessor2.jsp'>

    Customer ID:      <INPUT TYPE="TEXT" NAME="custID"><BR><BR>
    Customer Last Name:      <INPUT TYPE="TEXT" NAME="lastName"><BR><BR>
    Customer First Name:      <INPUT TYPE="TEXT" NAME="firstName"><BR><BR>
    <CENTER>
```

LISTING 23.14   Continued

```
            <INPUT TYPE="SUBMIT">
        </CENTER>
    </FORM>

    </BODY>
</HTML>
```

The only difference in this file is the name of the JSP page.

```
<FORM action='/examples/jsp/jpp/TicketRequestProcessor2.jsp'>
```

Listing 23.15 shows the version of the JSP that does the conversion.

LISTING 23.15   The `TicketRequestProcessor2.jsp` File

```
<jsp:useBean id="trb"
    class="com.samspublishing.jpp.ch23.TicketRequestBean"
    scope="session" />
<html>
<head>
<title>Ticket Request Processor 2</title>
<body>
<h2>Ticket Request Processor 2</h2>
<br>
Customer ID: <%= request.getParameter("custID") %>
<br>
Customer First Name: <%= request.getParameter("firstName") %>
<br>
Customer Last Name: <%= request.getParameter("lastName") %>
<br>

<%
  String custIDString = request.getParameter("custID");
  int custIDValue = Integer.parseInt(custIDString);
%>

<jsp:setProperty name="trb" property="custID"
    value='<%= custIDValue %>' />
<jsp:setProperty name="trb" property="firstName"
    value='<%= request.getParameter("firstName") %>' />
<jsp:setProperty name="trb" property="lastName"
    value='<%= request.getParameter("lastName") %>' />

Now get the property to see if it is there
<br>
<jsp:getProperty name="trb" property="custID"/>
<br>
<jsp:getProperty name="trb" property="firstName"/>
<br>
<jsp:getProperty name="trb" property="lastName"/>

</body>
</html>
```

The parameter `custID` is passed in as a `String`, so we need to assign it to a `String` in the scriptlet.

```
String custIDString = request.getParameter("custID");
```

Before we can store the `custID` value in a JavaBean, we must convert it to an `int` using the `parseInt()` static method from the `java.lang.Integer` class.

```
int custIDValue = Integer.parseInt(custIDString);
```

Now we can set the property using the `custIDValue`.

```
<jsp:setProperty name="trb" property="custID"
    value='<%= custIDValue %>' />
```

The result of running this is shown in Figure 23.7.

FIGURE 23.7
A conversion must take place before you can store a `String` value in a JavaBean using the `jsp:setProperty` action.

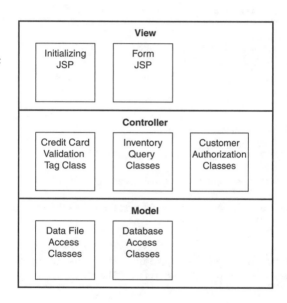

This conversion is a bit cumbersome, especially for nonprogrammers who are learning JSP. Fortunately, JSP provides an automatic way to associate a parameter with a property in a JavaBean. The `param` argument of the `setProperty` action will perform this association automatically, along with any conversion that may be needed. The syntax for this is shown here:

```
<jsp:setProperty name="trb" property="custID" param="custID" />
```

Using this new syntax, we can simplify the `TicketRequestProcessor2.jsp` file as shown here in Listing 23.16.

LISTING 23.16   The `TicketRequestProcessor3.jsp` File

```
<jsp:useBean id="trb"
    class="com.samspublishing.jpp.ch23.TicketRequestBean"
    scope="session" />
<html>
<head>
<title>Ticket Request Processor 3</title>
<body>
<h2>Ticket Request Processor 3</h2>
<br>
Customer ID: <%= request.getParameter("custID") %>
<br>
Customer First Name: <%= request.getParameter("firstName") %>
<br>
Customer Last Name: <%= request.getParameter("lastName") %>
<br>


<jsp:setProperty name="trb" property="custID"
    param="custID" />
<jsp:setProperty name="trb" property="firstName"
    param="firstName" />
<jsp:setProperty name="trb" property="lastName"
    param="lastName" />

Now get the property to see if it is there
<br>
<jsp:getProperty name="trb" property="custID"/>
<br>
<jsp:getProperty name="trb" property="firstName"/>
<br>
<jsp:getProperty name="trb" property="lastName"/>

</body>
</html>
```

This JSP is identical to `TicketRequestProcessor`, except for the method of associating a value with a property.

```
<jsp:setProperty name="trb" property="custID"
    param="custID" />
<jsp:setProperty name="trb" property="firstName"
    param="firstName" />
<jsp:setProperty name="trb" property="lastName"
    param="lastName" />
```

In this JSP, the parameter names are passed in directly to the `setProperty` actions, and the type conversions are done automatically.

Using JavaBeans to Access Databases

A very common use of JavaBeans is to provide the JSP page with access to database information. This includes both updates and queries. In this section, we will enhance the JavaBean to include methods that both store data in database tables and retrieve it from those tables for display in a browser.

The `TicketRequestBean` needs to be enhanced to add the Java DataBase Connection (JDBC) code. This code is needed to access a database, to insert and retrieve data from it. We will use MS Access for the DBMS.

The schema of this single table database is shown in Figure 23.8.

FIGURE 23.8
An MS Access database will store the data from the JavaBean.

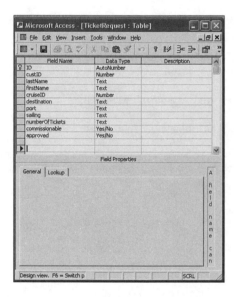

To use the Access database from Java, we need to define an ODBC data source for it. In Windows XP, we do this by clicking the `DataSources(ODBC)` icon in the Administrative tools folder in the Control Panel.

This will open the dialog box shown in Figure 23.9.

Name the datasource TicketRequest and click the Select button. This gives you a dialog that will enable you to locate the database file that you created earlier in this section. Choose OK, and then OK again on the other dialog. Your datasource is now ready to use.

FIGURE 23.9
An ODBC datasource can be defined for this database.

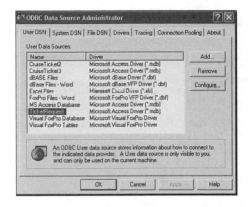

Click the Add button to display the dialog shown in Figure 23.10.

FIGURE 23.10
Select a driver for this database.

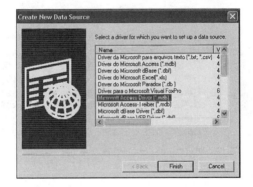

Select the Microsoft Access Driver and click the Finish button. This opens the dialog shown in Figure 23.11.

FIGURE 23.11.
Select the database file associated with this data-source using a dialog.

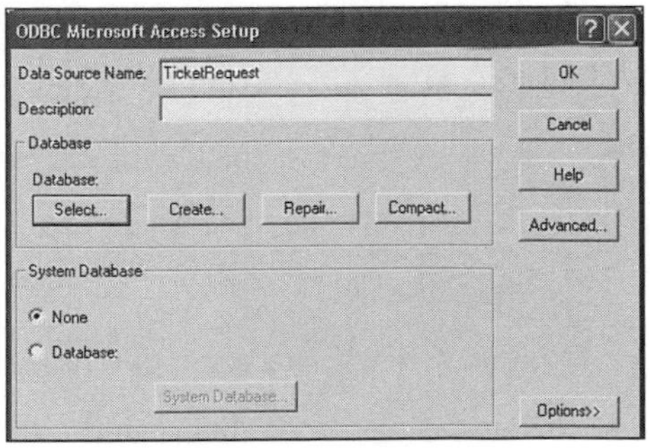

Updating the Database

We need an HTML page that gathers more information than the old ones. Listing 23.17 shows the HTML code for this page.

LISTING 23.17   The `RequestTicketForm.html` File

```
<!DOCTYPE HTML PUBLIC "-//W3C//DTD HTML 4.01 Transitional//EN">

<HTML>
  <HEAD>
    <TITLE>Add a Customer 4</TITLE>
  </HEAD>
  <H1 align="CENTER">
  Enter the new customer's information
  </H1>

  <FORM action='/examples/jsp/jpp/TicketRequestProcessor4.jsp'>

     Customer ID:            <INPUT TYPE="TEXT" NAME="custID"><BR><BR>
     Customer Last Name:   <INPUT TYPE="TEXT" NAME="lastName"><BR><BR>
     Customer First Name: <INPUT TYPE="TEXT" NAME="firstName"><BR><BR>
     Cruise ID:              <INPUT TYPE="TEXT" NAME="cruiseID"><BR><BR>
     Destination:            <INPUT TYPE="TEXT" NAME="destination"><BR><BR>
     Port:                   <INPUT TYPE="TEXT" NAME="port"><BR><BR>
     Sailing:                <INPUT TYPE="TEXT" NAME="sailing"><BR><BR>
     Number Of Tickets:    <INPUT TYPE="TEXT" NAME="numberOfTickets">
     <BR><BR>
     <CENTER>
        <INPUT TYPE="SUBMIT">
     </CENTER>
  </FORM>

  </BODY>
</HTML>
```

We have added the following fields to our form:

- `cruiseID`   The cruise's ID in our system. We have dozens of cruises available.

- `destination`   Where the cruise is going: the Caribbean, Alaska, Europe, and so on

- `port`   The port of embarkation: Miami or San Juan.

- `sailing`   The date that the ship sails.

- `numberOfTickets`   How many tickets are being purchased.

The JSP now has to update the JavaBean for more fields, and it must tell the Bean to store the information in the database. Listing 23.18 shows this file.

LISTING 23.18   The `TicketRequestProcessor4.jsp` File

```jsp
<jsp:useBean id="trb2"
    class="com.samspublishing.jpp.ch23.TicketRequestBean2"
    scope="session" />
<html>
<head>
<title>Ticket Request Processor 4</title>
<body>
<h2>Ticket Request Processor 4</h2>
<br>

<jsp:setProperty name="trb2" property="custID"
    param="custID" />
<jsp:setProperty name="trb2" property="firstName"
    param="firstName" />
<jsp:setProperty name="trb2" property="lastName"
    param="lastName" />
<jsp:setProperty name="trb2" property="cruiseID"
    param="cruiseID" />
<jsp:setProperty name="trb2" property="destination"
    param="destination" />
<jsp:setProperty name="trb2" property="port"
    param="port" />
<jsp:setProperty name="trb2" property="sailing"
    param="sailing" />
<jsp:setProperty name="trb2" property="numberOfTickets"
    param="numberOfTickets" />

Here is the data that you entered
<br>
<br>
<jsp:getProperty name="trb2" property="custID"/>
<br>
<jsp:getProperty name="trb2" property="firstName"/>
<br>
<jsp:getProperty name="trb2" property="lastName"/>
<br>
<jsp:getProperty name="trb2" property="cruiseID"/>
<br>
<jsp:getProperty name="trb2" property="destination"/>
<br>
<jsp:getProperty name="trb2" property="port"/>
<br>
<jsp:getProperty name="trb2" property="sailing"/>
<br>
<jsp:getProperty name="trb2" property="numberOfTickets"/>
<br>
<br>
Here is the result of the update attempt
<br>
<%=
    trb2.updateDB()
%>
</body>
</html>
```

Notice that we are now referencing a new JavaBean, called `TicketRequestBean2`.

```
<jsp:useBean id="trb2"
    class="com.samspublishing.jpp.ch23.TicketRequestBean2"
    scope="session" />
```

We add more fields to the Bean using the same syntax that you have already seen. The final step is new, however. We make a call to a method in the JavaBean called `updateDB()`. This method is shown here in Listing 23.19.

LISTING 23.19   The `updateDB()` Method

```java
public String updateDB()
{
    java.sql.Connection dbConn = null;
    Statement statement1 = null;
    String createStatement;
    String insertStatement;

    try
    {
        // ============== Make connection to database ==================

        //load the driver class
        Class.forName("sun.jdbc.odbc.JdbcOdbcDriver");

        //Specify the ODBC data source
        String sourceURL = "jdbc:odbc:TicketRequest";

        //get a connection to the database
        dbConn = DriverManager.getConnection(sourceURL);

        //If we get to here, no exception was thrown
        System.out.println("The database connection is " + dbConn);
        System.out.println("Making connection...\n");

        //Create the statement
        statement1 = dbConn.createStatement();

        /////////////////////////////////////////////////////////////
        //          Create the row in the database                 //
        /////////////////////////////////////////////////////////////

        insertStatement = "INSERT INTO TicketRequest VALUES(" +
        custID + "," +
        "'" + lastName + "'," +
        "'" + firstName + "'," +
        cruiseID + "," +
        "'" + destination + "'," +
        "'" + port + "'," +
        "'" + sailing + "'," +
        numberOfTickets + ")";
        System.out.println(insertStatement);
```

LISTING 23.19   Continued

```
      statement1.executeUpdate(insertStatement);
      return "Successful Update";
} catch (Exception e)
{
   System.out.println("Exception was thrown: " + e.getMessage());
   return "UnSuccessful Update";
} finally
{
   try
   {
      if (statement1 != null)
         statement1.close();
      if (dbConn != null)
         dbConn.close();
   } catch (SQLException sqle)
   {
      System.out.println("SQLException during close(): "
                                       + sqle.getMessage());
   }
}

}
```

This method does some standard JDBC processing to access the database. It first loads the ODBC processing class.

```
Class.forName("sun.jdbc.odbc.JdbcOdbcDriver");
```

Next, it names the `TicketRequest` data source that we created earlier in the chapter.

```
String sourceURL = "jdbc:odbc:TicketRequest";
```

Finally, it creates a connection to the datasource via the driver class.

```
//get a connection to the database
dbConn = DriverManager.getConnection(sourceURL);
```

This connection will be used to process the data. We use it to create a Statement object.

```
statement1 = dbConn.createStatement();

///////////////////////////////////////////////////////////////
//         Create the rowin the database                     //
///////////////////////////////////////////////////////////////
```

Next, we create a string that represents the SQL statement that we want to execute.

```
insertStatement = "INSERT INTO TicketRequest VALUES(" +
custID + "," +
"'" + lastName + "'," +
"'" + firstName + "'," +
cruiseID + "," +
"'" + destination + "'," +
"'" + port + "'," +
"'" + sailing + "'," +
numberOfTickets + ")";
```

Finally, we do an `executeUpdate()` method to run the SQL.

```
statement1.executeUpdate(insertStatement);
```

To run the program, open a browser and type the address of the `RequestTicketForm.html` file:

```
http://localhost:1776/examples/RequestTicketForm.html
```

The result from running this HTML file is shown here in Figure 23.12.

FIGURE 23.12
You update the database by calling a method in the JavaBean.

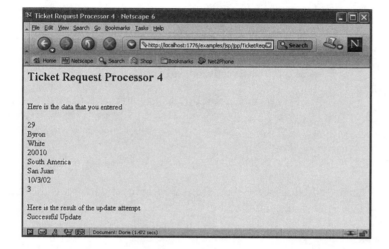

Retrieving the Data from the Database

Now that we have the data in the database, we need to retrieve and look at it. To do this, we need to enhance our JavaBean again by adding a method called `retrieveFromDB()`. Listing 23.20 shows this method.

LISTING 23.20   The `retrieve FromDB()` Method

```java
public String retrieveFromDB()
{
   java.sql.Connection dbConn = null;
   Statement statement1 = null;
   String createStatement;
   String insertStatement;

   try
   {
      // ============== Make connection to database ==================

      //load the driver class
      Class.forName("sun.jdbc.odbc.JdbcOdbcDriver");

      //Specify the ODBC data source
      String sourceURL = "jdbc:odbc:TicketRequest";
```

LISTING 23.20   Continued

```java
        //get a connection to the database
        dbConn = DriverManager.getConnection(sourceURL);

        //If we get to here, no exception was thrown
        System.out.println("The database connection is " + dbConn);
        System.out.println("Making connection...\n");

        //Create the statement
        statement1 = dbConn.createStatement();

        //        Create the tables in the database

        //Populate the bean
        String getBeanString =
        "SELECT * FROM TicketRequest " +
        "WHERE CustID = " + custID;

        ResultSet results = statement1.executeQuery(getBeanString);

        while (results.next())
        {
            lastName = results.getString("lastName");
            firstName = results.getString("firstName");
            cruiseID = results.getInt("cruiseID");
            destination = results.getString("destination");
            port = results.getString("port");
            sailing = results.getString("sailing");
            numberOfTickets = results.getInt("numberOfTickets");
        }
        return "Successful Retrieval";
    } catch (Exception e)
    {
        System.out.println("Exception was thrown: " + e.getMessage());
        return "UnSuccessful Retrieval";
    } finally
    {
        try
        {
            if (statement1 != null)
                statement1.close();
            if (dbConn != null)
                dbConn.close();
        } catch (SQLException sqle)
        {
            System.out.println("SQLException during close(): " +
                                        sqle.getMessage());
        }
    }

}
```

This method presumes that the Bean has already been updated with the request `custID`. It uses that `custID` to do a `SELECT` on the `TicketRequest` table.

```
String getBeanString =
"SELECT * FROM TicketRequest " +
"WHERE CustID = " + custID;

ResultSet results = statement1.executeQuery(getBeanString);
```

The `ResultSet` object contains all the data that was retrieved. We need to step through it and get the data fields for this record.

```
while (results.next())
{
    lastName = results.getString("lastName");
    firstName = results.getString("firstName");
    cruiseID = results.getInt("cruiseID");
    destination = results.getString("destination");
    port = results.getString("port");
    sailing = results.getString("sailing");
    numberOfTickets = results.getInt("numberOfTickets");
}
return "Successful Retrieval";
```

We use a `while` loop even though there should be only one row that matches this `custID`. This is done commonly with JDBC retrievals to avoid an error message if more than one row or zero rows are returned. After running this, a string containing `"Successful Retrieval"` is returned.

We need an HTML form that asks for the `custID` that the user wants to see. Listing 23.21 shows this file.

LISTING 23.21   The `RetrieveTicketForm.html` File

```
<!DOCTYPE HTML PUBLIC "-//W3C//DTD HTML 4.01 Transitional//EN">

<HTML>
  <HEAD>
    <TITLE>Retrieve a Ticket</TITLE>
  </HEAD>
  <H1 align="CENTER">
  Enter the customer ID
  </H1>

  <FORM action='/examples/jsp/jpp/TicketRetrievalProcessor.jsp'>

    Customer ID:          <INPUT TYPE="TEXT" NAME="custID"><BR><BR>
    <CENTER>
      <INPUT TYPE="SUBMIT">
    </CENTER>
  </FORM>

  </BODY>
</HTML>
```

This form calls the action named `TicketRetrievalProcessor.jsp`, which is shown in Listing 23.22.

LISTING 23.22   The `TicketRetrievalProcessor.jsp` File

```
<jsp:useBean id="trb2"
    class="com.samspublishing.jpp.ch23.TicketRequestBean2"
    scope="session" />
<html>
<head>
<title>Ticket Retrieval Processor </title>
<body>
<h2>Ticket Retrieval Processor </h2>
<br>

<jsp:setProperty name="trb2" property="custID"
    param="custID" />

Here is the data that you entered
<br>
<br>
<jsp:getProperty name="trb2" property="custID"/>
<br>

Here is the result of the retrieval attempt
<br>
<%=
    trb2.retrieveFromDB()
%>

<br>
<br>
Here is the data that was retrieved
<br>
<br>
<jsp:getProperty name="trb2" property="firstName"/>
<br>
<jsp:getProperty name="trb2" property="lastName"/>
<br>
<jsp:getProperty name="trb2" property="cruiseID"/>
<br>
<jsp:getProperty name="trb2" property="destination"/>
<br>
<jsp:getProperty name="trb2" property="port"/>
<br>
<jsp:getProperty name="trb2" property="sailing"/>
<br>
<jsp:getProperty name="trb2" property="numberOfTickets"/>
<br>
<br>

</body>
</html>
```

The first action is to set property:

```
<jsp:setProperty name="trb2" property="custID"
    param="custID" />
```

Following that, a call is made to the `retrieveFromDB()` method in the JavaBean.

```
Here is the result of the retrieval attempt
<br>
<%=
   trb2.retrieveFromDB()
%>
```

Finally, the data is displayed.

```
<jsp:getProperty name="trb2" property="firstName"/>
<br>
<jsp:getProperty name="trb2" property="lastName"/>
<br>
  …
```

You run this program by typing the following in your browser's address box:

```
http://localhost:1776/examples/RetrieveTicketForm.html
```

The result of running this program is shown in Figure 23.13.

FIGURE 23.13
You can retrieve data
from a database using
JavaBeans and JSP.

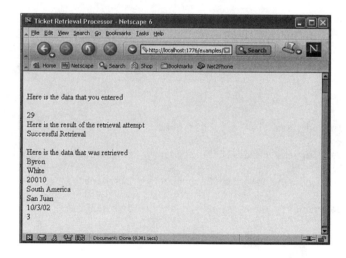

Notice that the data that appears is identical to that which you entered earlier in the chapter. Listing 23.23 shows the entire listing for the `TicketRequestBean2`.

LISTING 23.23   The `TicketRequestBean2.java` File

```java
/*
 * TicketRequestBean2.java
 *
 * Created on July 9, 2002, 11:22 AM
 */

package com.samspublishing.jpp.ch23;

import java.sql.*;
import java.util.*;

/**
 *
 * @author  Stephen Potts
 * @version
 */
public class TicketRequestBean2 implements java.io.Serializable
{
    //information about the customer
    private int custID;
    private String lastName;
    private String firstName;

    //information about the cruise
    private int cruiseID;
    private String destination;
    private String port;
    private String sailing;

    private int numberOfTickets;

    public TicketRequestBean2()
    {
    }

    /** Constructor */
    public TicketRequestBean2(int custID, String lastName,
                String firstName, int cruiseID, String destination,
                String port, String sailing, int numberOfTickets,
                                        boolean isCommissionable)
    {
        //set the information about the customer
        this.custID = custID;
        this.lastName = lastName;
        this.firstName = firstName;

        //set the information about the cruise
        this.cruiseID = cruiseID;
        this.destination = destination;
        this.port = port;
        this.sailing = sailing;
```

LISTING 23.23 Continued

```java
        this.numberOfTickets = numberOfTickets;
    }

    public int getCustID()
    {
        return this.custID = custID;
    }

    public String getLastName()
    {
        return this.lastName = lastName;
    }

    public String getFirstName()
    {
        return this.firstName = firstName;
    }

    public int getCruiseID()
    {
        return this.cruiseID;
    }

    public String getDestination()
    {
        return this.destination;
    }

    public String getPort()
    {
        return this.port;
    }

    public String getSailing()
    {
        return this.sailing;
    }

    public int getNumberOfTickets()
    {
        return this.numberOfTickets;
    }


    public void setCustID(int custID)
    {
        this.custID = custID;
    }

    public void setLastName(String lastName)
    {
        this.lastName = lastName;
```

LISTING 23.23   Continued

```java
   }

   public void setFirstName(String firstName)
   {
      this.firstName = firstName;
   }

   public void setCruiseID(int cruiseID)
   {
      this.cruiseID = cruiseID;
   }

   public void setDestination(String destination)
   {
      this.destination = destination;
   }

   public void setPort(String port)
   {
      this.port = port;
   }

   public void setSailing(String sailing)
   {
      this.sailing = sailing;
   }

   public void setNumberOfTickets(int numberOfTickets)
   {
      this.numberOfTickets = numberOfTickets;
   }

   public String toString()
   {
      String outString;
      outString = "------------------------------------------" + "\n";

      //information about the customer
      outString += "custID = " + this.custID + "\n";
      outString += "lastName = " + this.lastName + "\n";
      outString += "firstName = " + this.firstName + "\n";
      outString += "------------------------------------------" + "\n";

      //information about the cruise
      outString += "cruiseID = " + this.cruiseID + "\n";
      outString += "destination = " + this.destination + "\n";
      outString += "port = " + this.port + "\n";
      outString += "sailing = " + this.sailing + "\n";
      outString += "numberOfTickets = " + this.numberOfTickets + "\n";

      outString += "------------------------------------------" + "\n";
      return outString;
```

LISTING 23.23   Continued

```
    }

    public String updateDB()
    {
        java.sql.Connection dbConn = null;
        Statement statement1 = null;
        String createStatement;
        String insertStatement;

        try
        {
            // ============== Make connection to database ==================

            //load the driver class
            Class.forName("sun.jdbc.odbc.JdbcOdbcDriver");

            //Specify the ODBC data source
            String sourceURL = "jdbc:odbc:TicketRequest";

            //get a connection to the database
            dbConn = DriverManager.getConnection(sourceURL);

            //If we get to here, no exception was thrown
            System.out.println("The database connection is " + dbConn);
            System.out.println("Making connection...\n");

            //Create the statement
            statement1 = dbConn.createStatement();

            //                            Create the tables in the database

            insertStatement = "INSERT INTO TicketRequest VALUES(" +
            custID + "," +
            "'" + lastName + "'," +
            "'" + firstName + "'," +
            cruiseID + "," +
            "'" + destination + "'," +
            "'" + port + "'," +
            "'" + sailing + "'," +
            numberOfTickets + ")";
            System.out.println(insertStatement);
            statement1.executeUpdate(insertStatement);
            return "Successful Update";
        } catch (Exception e)
        {
            System.out.println("Exception was thrown: " + e.getMessage());
            return "UnSuccessful Update";
        } finally
        {
            try
            {
                if (statement1 != null)
```

LISTING 23.23   Continued

```
                   statement1.close();
              if (dbConn != null)
                 dbConn.close();
          } catch (SQLException sqle)
          {
             System.out.println("SQLException during close(): " +
                                                 sqle.getMessage());
          }
       }

   }

   public String retrieveFromDB()
   {
      java.sql.Connection dbConn = null;
      Statement statement1 = null;
      String createStatement;
      String insertStatement;

      try
      {
         // ============== Make connection to database ==================

         //load the driver class
         Class.forName("sun.jdbc.odbc.JdbcOdbcDriver");

         //Specify the ODBC data source
         String sourceURL = "jdbc:odbc:TicketRequest";

         //get a connection to the database
         dbConn = DriverManager.getConnection(sourceURL);

         //If we get to here, no exception was thrown
         System.out.println("The database connection is " + dbConn);
         System.out.println("Making connection...\n");

         //Create the statement
         statement1 = dbConn.createStatement();

         //                        Create the tables in the database

         //Populate the bean
         String getBeanString =
         "SELECT * FROM TicketRequest " +
         "WHERE CustID = " + custID;

         ResultSet results = statement1.executeQuery(getBeanString);

         while (results.next())
         {
             lastName = results.getString("lastName");
             firstName = results.getString("firstName");
```

LISTING 23.23   Continued

```
              cruiseID = results.getInt("cruiseID");
              destination = results.getString("destination");
              port = results.getString("port");
              sailing = results.getString("sailing");
              numberOfTickets = results.getInt("numberOfTickets");
        }
      return "Successful Retrieval";
    } catch (Exception e)
    {
      System.out.println("Exception was thrown: " + e.getMessage());
      return "UnSuccessful Retrieval";
    } finally
    {
      try
      {
        if (statement1 != null)
          statement1.close();
        if (dbConn != null)
          dbConn.close();
      } catch (SQLException sqle)
      {
        System.out.println("SQLException during close(): " +
                                         sqle.getMessage());
      }
    }

  }
}
```

This version of the JavaBean contains the code to update the database, as well as the code to retrieve the data from the database. Notice the simplicity of the JSP and HTML for this example. All the complexity of hitting the database is delegated to the Bean where it belongs.

Summary

This chapter introduced the concept of component development for use in JSP. The first thing that you learned how to do was use the `include` directive to insert static text into your JSPs. Following that, we covered how to use the `include` action to add dynamic processing to the inclusion of external logic in a JSP.

We then discussed the mechanics of using JavaBeans to supply component processing to JSP. You learned how to retrieve data from a form, convert it to the correct data type, and store it in a JavaBean for later retrieval.

Finally, you learned how to store and retrieve data from a database using a JavaBean that was called from inside a JSP page. This is a very common use of component processing in JSP.

Review Questions

1. What is the difference between the `include` directive and the `include` action?

2. What advantages do JavaBeans provide over included files?

3. How does the `jsp:useBean` action know where to find the class file for that Bean?

4. How do you perform automatic conversion of data types using the `setParameter()` action?

5. Why do we place all the database access logic in a Bean instead of in scriptlets?

Exercises

1. Create a JSP that includes another JSP that contains your name.

2. Create a JSP that passes your name to another JSP as a parameter. Make that JSP display the name.

3. Create a JSP and JavaBean that updates a database with your personal information.

4. Create another JSP that retrieves this information and displays it on the screen. Use a JavaBean to access the database.

CHAPTER 24

CUSTOM TAG LIBRARIES

You will learn about the following in this chapter:

- What custom tags are
- Why you need custom tags
- How custom tags work
- How to use the tag body
- How to pass parameters

The final JSP topic that we will cover in this book is custom tag libraries, hereafter it will be referred to simply as tag libraries. Tag libraries are programmer-defined XML tags that enable the JSP writer to include component functionality inside the JSP file.

In this chapter, you will learn how tag libraries and JavaBeans are similar and how they differ. You will also learn how to create custom tags, program the implementation classes, and tie the tag to the class using a taglib. In addition, you will learn how to write a JSP file that makes use of these new tags.

Following that, you will learn how to pass parameters to a tag, and how to use tags to access data stored in a database.

What Custom Tags Are and Are Not

In Chapter 23, "Component-Based JSP Pages," you were introduced to the concept of JSP actions. Actions are special tags that tell the JSP page to do something, for instance, like use a JavaBean, include an external file, or set the value of a property. These actions greatly increase the usefulness of JSP pages. All the tags that we have studied thus far are built into the JSP engine.

Custom tags are similar to the action tags that you have already encountered, except that you define them yourself. There are subtle differences between the capabilities of custom tags and JavaBeans, but the primary difference is syntactic. For many JSP developers, the XML syntax of the action tags is more intuitive than the syntax for using JavaBeans, especially after you get beyond simple get() and set() methods.

Hard-core Java programmers usually prefer the JavaBean/scriptlet syntax. Web page developers often prefer the XML-style actions because its syntax is more similar to HTML than scriptlet code.

The similarities between JavaBeans and custom tags are summarized here:

- JavaBeans and custom tags are both implemented as Java classes.

- Both encapsulate complex behavior.

- Both can be invoked from within JSPs.

In many situations, but not all, you can think of custom tags as an alternate syntax for calling methods in JavaBeans.

Custom tags are not identical to JavaBeans, but they resemble them. The following list shows some important differences:

- Custom tags can manipulate JSP content, but JavaBeans cannot.

- JSPs can pass parameters into the custom tags.

- Custom tags require the existence of a Tag Library Descriptor File (`.tld`) that associates a tag name with a Java class.

- The class that implements a tag must implement the `javax.servlet.jsp.tagext.Tag` interface directly, or through either the `TagSupport` or `BodyTagSupport` helper classes. JavaBeans do not require any class to be extended.

The primary impact of this list is felt during tag definition. In practical terms, you can fulfill almost any conceivable JSP requirement with either technical approach.

How Custom Tags Work

You embed the custom tag into a JSP using syntax that is similar to other actions.

```
<%@ taglib uri="xyz-taglib.tld" prefix="xyz" %>
```

This associates the tags in the taglib with the name (prefix) `xyz`. If you had a tag called `myTag` defined in the `.tld` file, you would add it to your JSP using the following syntax:

```
...
<body>
<xyz:myTag />
</body>
...
```

The meaning of the tag is defined in the Tag Library Definition file (`.tld`). The `.tld` file will contain a number of lines of boilerplate code followed by the definition of one or more tags using the following syntax:

```
...
<tag>
<name>myTag</name>
<tagclass>com.samspublishing.jpp.ch25.MyTag</tagclass>
```

```
<info>This tag does xyz</info>
<bodycontent>EMPTY</bodycontent>
</tag>
...
```

The `tagclass` is the name of the class in the classpath of the server. It will be a normal Java class that extends one of the helper classes mentioned previously. It provides an implementation of the `doStartTag()` method, which is required by the Tag interface. The basic structure of this class file is shown here:

```
package com.samspublishing.jpp.ch25;
import javax.servlet.jsp.tagext.*;
.
.
.
public class MyTag extends TagSupport
{
    public int doStartTag()
    {
      create some interesting output
    }
    return(SKIP_BODY)
}
```

The combination of these three parts is shown in Figure 24.1.

The JSP file uses the name of the tag. The JSP engine looks up the `tagclass` at runtime and runs the `doStartTag()` method in this class that provides the output that will be inserted in the JSP.

A simple example will illustrate how this works. We need to create a tag that can be included in a JSP. We'll call this tag `stringTag`. Before we can start using `stringTag`, we have to create a tag library, or taglib, to define the behavior of the tag. Listing 24.1 shows the contents of a taglib.

LISTING 24.1   The `jpptaglib.tld` File

```
<?xml version="1.0" encoding="ISO-8859-1" ?>
<!DOCTYPE taglib
 PUBLIC "-//Sun Microsystems, Inc.//DTD JSP Tag Library 1.1//EN"
 "http://java.sun.com/j2ee/dtds/web-jsptaglibrary_1_1.dtd">

<!— a tag library descriptor —>

<taglib>
<!— after this the default space is
        "http://java.sun.com/j2ee/dtds/jsptaglibrary_1_2.dtd"
   —>

<tlibversion>1.0</tlibversion>
<jspversion>1.1</jspversion>
<shortname>jpptaglib</shortname>
<info>
```

LISTING 24.1   Continued

```
    A tag library from Java Primer Plus
</info>

<tag>
<name>stringTag</name>
<tagclass>com.samspublishing.jpp.ch25.StringTag</tagclass>
<info>a Hello World custom tag example</info>
<bodycontent>EMPTY</bodycontent>
</tag>

</taglib>
```

FIGURE 24.1

The three components of the custom tag are the JSP file, the Tag Library Descriptor (`.tld`) file, and the class file.

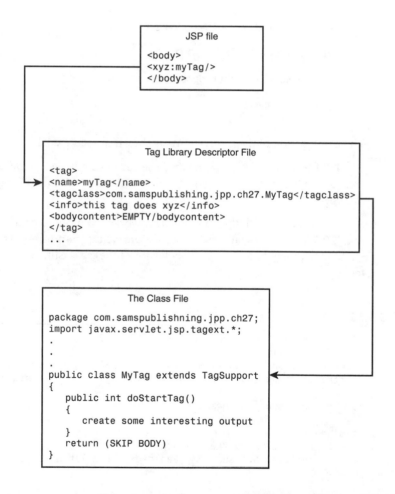

The lines preceding `<shortname>` tag will be the same for every `.tlb` file that you create. This file is an XML file, so the version of XML used, as well as the Document Type Definition(DTD), for this file type are listed. See Chapter 25, "XML," for a more complete discussion of XML particulars.

```
<?xml version="1.0" encoding="ISO-8859-1" ?>
<!DOCTYPE taglib
 PUBLIC "-//Sun Microsystems, Inc.//DTD JSP Tag Library 1.1//EN"
 "http://java.sun.com/j2ee/dtds/web-jsptaglibrary_1_1.dtd">
```

Following this, the version of the taglib and JSP are listed.

```
<tlibversion>1.0</tlibversion>
<jspversion>1.1</jspversion>
```

Following that, a short name for this taglib is declared.

```
<shortname>jpptaglib</shortname>
```

The real work of this `.tlb` is found between the `<tag>` and `</tag>` tabs.

```
<tag>
```

The name of the custom tag is the name that it will be known by inside JSPs.

```
<name>stringTag</name>
```

The `tagclass` is the name of the class in the classpath of the Web server. This includes the package in which it is located.

```
<tagclass>com.samspublishing.jpp.ch25.StringTag</tagclass>
```

Info tags provide information to the reader in a manner similar to comments.

```
<info>a Hello World custom tag example</info>
```

The `bodycontent` tag will be used later when we create a more full-featured tag.

```
<bodycontent>EMPTY</bodycontent>
</tag>
```

Now that we have a tag defined, we need a Java class to provide its implementation. This is the class that was named previously in the `tagclass` tag. Listing 24.2 shows this class.

LISTING 24.2   The `StringTag.java` File

```
/*
 * StringTag.java
 *
 * Created on July 13, 2002, 12:38 PM
 */

package com.samspublishing.jpp.ch25;

import javax.servlet.jsp.*;
import javax.servlet.jsp.tagext.*;
import java.io.*;

/**
 *
 * @author   Stephen Potts
```

LISTING 24.2   Continued

```
 * @version
 */
public class StringTag extends TagSupport
{
   public int doStartTag()
   {
      try
      {
         JspWriter out = pageContext.getOut();
         out.print("Hello, String tag example ");
      }catch (Exception e)
      {
         System.out.println("Error in StringTag class" + e);
      }
      return(SKIP_BODY);
   }
}
```

Notice that the package name is the first item in the listing. This package name must match the directory structure under the rules of Java.

```
package com.samspublishing.jpp.ch25;
```

There are several import files required.

```
import javax.servlet.jsp.*;
import javax.servlet.jsp.tagext.*;
import java.io.*;
```

This class extends `TagSupport`, which implements the `javax.servlet.jsp.tagext.Tag` interface for us.

```
public class StringTag extends TagSupport
```

The `doStartTag()` method must be overridden to use the `TagSupport` class. This method is called automatically when the JSP engine is loading the custom tag into the page.

```
   public int doStartTag()
   {
```

The only actual work that is done is performed here. A simple string is written out.

```
      JspWriter out = pageContext.getOut();
      out.print("Hello, String tag example ");
```

The return is a constant that tells the JSP there is no body to process.

```
      return(SKIP_BODY);
```

Now the custom tag is ready to use. Listing 24.3 shows a JSP page that uses this tag.

LISTING 24.3   The StringTag.jsp File

```
<!DOCTYPE HTML PUBLIC "-//W3C//DTD HTML 4.0 Transitional//EN">
<html>
<head>

<%@ taglib uri="jpptaglib.tld" prefix="jpp" %>

<title>A Simple Custom Tag</title>
</head>

<body>
<h1>A Simple Custom Tag</h1>
<br>
<b><jpp:stringTag /> <b>

</body>
</html>
```

This JSP file is ordinary in every respect with the exception of the use of the **stringTag**. The first step is to tell the JSP engine which taglib that you want to use.

```
<%@ taglib uri="jpptaglib.tld" prefix="jpp" %>
```

Now we can refer to the **stringTag** wherever we want.

```
<b><jpp:stringTag /> <b>
```

Whenever this string is encountered, the JSP engine runs the methods in the Java class. This is the class that was associated with this tag in the taglib file. The result is inserted in place and displayed along with the output from this JSP.

To run this example, place both the JSP and the **.tlb** files in the same directory where you have been placing JSPs. Place the class file in the same directory where you have been placing class files, allowing for the package name, of course. On our test machine, these locations were as follows:

Class file:

```
install-dir\webapps\examples\WEB-INF\classes\com\samspublishing\jpp\ch25
```

JSP and **.tlb**:

```
Install-dir\webapps\examples\jsp\jpp
```

Figure 24.2 shows the result of running this JSP.

This example uses custom tags to do something that could easily be done without them, but it does illustrate the plumbing that is needed to get these tags to work.

FIGURE 24.2
The tag is translated at runtime, and the results are included in the response.

Using the Custom Tag Body

In the preceding section, we added the custom tag using the XML syntax:

```
<jpp:stringTag />
```

This syntax states that this tag has no body and, therefore, no need for an explicit end tag. Custom tags are allowed to have bodies, however, as shown in the following snippet:

```
<jpp:stringTag>
This is the body of the tag.  It will only show up if the implementing
class instructs it to.
</jpp:stringTag>
```

The primary use of this is to provide a small amount of conditional processing in the tag. Small changes are needed to the example to accommodate the inclusion of the body. Listing 24.4 shows the taglib for a tag that contains a body.

LISTING 24.4   The `jpptaglib2.tlb` File

```
<?xml version="1.0" encoding="UTF-8" ?>

<!DOCTYPE taglib
        PUBLIC "-//Sun Microsystems, Inc.//DTD JSP Tag Library 1.1//EN"
        "http://java.sun.com/j2ee/dtds/web-jsptaglibrary_1_1.dtd">
<!-- a tag library descriptor -->

<taglib>
<!-- after this the default space is
        "http://java.sun.com/j2ee/dtds/jsptaglibrary_1_2.dtd"
   -->

<tlibversion>1.0</tlibversion>
<jspversion>1.1</jspversion>
<shortname>jpptaglib2</shortname>
<info>
   A tag library from Java Primer Plus
</info>
```

LISTING 24.4   Continued

```
<tag>
<name>stringTag2</name>
<tagclass>com.samspublishing.jpp.ch25.StringTag2</tagclass>
<bodycontent>JSP</bodycontent>
<info>a Hello World custom tag example</info>
</tag>

</taglib>
```

The primary difference in this file is the changing of the **bodycontent** from EMPTY to JSP.

```
<bodycontent>JSP</bodycontent>
```

This tells the JSP engine to process the body of the JSP.

Listing 24.5 shows the implementation class file for this example.

LISTING 24.5   The `StringTag2.class` File

```
/*
 * StringTag2.java
 *
 * Created on July 13, 2002, 12:38 PM
 */

package com.samspublishing.jpp.ch25;

import javax.servlet.jsp.*;
import javax.servlet.jsp.tagext.*;
import java.io.*;

/**
 *
 * @author   Stephen Potts
 * @version
 */
public class StringTag2 extends TagSupport
{
    public int doStartTag()
    {
        try
        {
            JspWriter out = pageContext.getOut();
            out.print("Hello, String tag2 example ");
        }catch (Exception e)
        {
            System.out.println("Error in StringTag2 class" + e);
        }
        return(EVAL_BODY_INCLUDE);
    }

    public int doEndTag()
```

LISTING 24.5 Continued

```
    {
      try
      {
        JspWriter out = pageContext.getOut();
        out.print("<br>");
        out.print("<br>");
        out.print("Hello from doEndTag() ");
      }catch (Exception e)
      {
        System.out.println("Error in doEndTag()" + e);
      }
      return(EVAL_PAGE);
    }

  }
```

There are several changes in this class. The return value has changed from **SKIP_BODY** to **EVAL_BODY_INCLUDE**, which, as you might guess, tells the JSP engine to process the body also.

In addition to including the body, changing from **SKIP_BODY** to **EVAL_BODY_INCLUDE** causes the **doEndTag()** method to be processed as well.

```
    public int doEndTag()
    {
      try
      {
        JspWriter out = pageContext.getOut();
        out.print("<br>");
        out.print("<br>");
        out.print("Hello from doEndTag() ");
      }catch (Exception e)
      {
        System.out.println("Error in doEndTag()" + e);
      }
      return(EVAL_PAGE);
    }
```

This method is similar to the **doStartTag()** method except that it runs at the end of the tag processing phase. It contains mostly **print()** method calls.

The JSP file has to be altered to add a body to the tag as well. Listing 24.6 contains this JSP file.

LISTING 24.6 The **StringTag2.jsp** File

```
<!DOCTYPE HTML PUBLIC "-//W3C//DTD HTML 4.0 Transitional//EN">
<html>
<head>

<%@ taglib uri="jpptaglib2.tld" prefix="jpp" %>
```

LISTING 24.6   *Continued*

```
<title>A Simple Custom Tag2</title>
</head>

<body>
<h1>A Simple Custom Tag2</h1>
<br>
<b>
<jpp:stringTag2>
<br>
This is the body of the tag.  It will only show up if the implementing
class instructs it to.
<br>
</jpp:stringTag2>
<b>

</body>
</html>
```

The tag now has a separate start and end tag.

```
<jpp:stringTag2>
<br>
This is the body of the tag.  It will only show up if the implementing
class instructs it to.
<br>
</jpp:stringTag2>
```

Figure 24.3 shows the result of running this example:

FIGURE 24.3
The tag body is only displayed if the implementing class instructs it to.

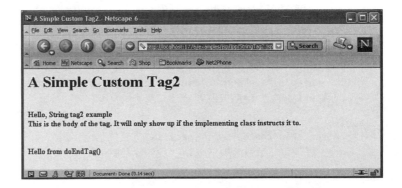

As you can see, the body of the tag, as well as the information in the `doEndTag()` method, are displayed following the information from the `doStartTag()` method.

Passing Parameters with Custom Tags

One of the areas where custom tags have an advantage over JavaBeans is in passing parameters. With JavaBeans, you normally set the values of the bean's class variables before invoking the method that you want to call. This is an effective, if somewhat cumbersome, way to pass parameters.

Custom tags, on the other hand, are allowed to pass parameters in a more direct fashion. The basic syntax for passing parameters to custom tags is

```
<jpp:stringTag2 attr1="val1" attr2="val2" \>
```

The name of the attribute is followed by the =, and then the value of the attribute in quotes. Providing support for these attributes is simple also. All you have to do is add methods to the implementing class in the form:

```
public void setAttr1(String value1)
{
    ... do something with this attribute's value ...
}
```

Note

The name of the attribute is normally lowercase in the tag. The set() method name will always include a capitalized version of this name following the word "set."

The taglib must also reflect the existence of the attribute. It must provide a name, whether it is a required field, and whether it can be an expression.

Listing 24.7 shows a taglib that contains attributes.

LISTING 24.7   The `jppticket-taglib.tld`

```
<?xml version="1.0" encoding="UTF-8" ?>

<!DOCTYPE taglib
        PUBLIC "-//Sun Microsystems, Inc.//DTD JSP Tag Library 1.1//EN"
        "http://java.sun.com/j2ee/dtds/web-jsptaglibrary_1_1.dtd">
<!-- a tag library descriptor -->

<taglib>
<!-- after this the default space is
        "http://java.sun.com/j2ee/dtds/jsptaglibrary_1_2.dtd"
    -->

<tlibversion>1.0</tlibversion>
<jspversion>1.1</jspversion>
<shortname>jpptaglib</shortname>
<info>
    A tag library from Java Primer Plus
</info>

<tag>
<name>ticketTag</name>
<tagclass>com.samspublishing.jpp.ch25.TicketTag</tagclass>
```

LISTING 24.7   Continued

```
<bodycontent>empty</bodycontent>
<info>a Hello World custom tag example</info>

<attribute>
   <name>param1</name>
   <required>true</required>
</attribute>
</tag>
</taglib>
```

In most ways, this taglib is identical to the others that we have created. The only difference is in the addition of the attribute. To process an attribute, the attribute tag must be added.

```
<attribute>
   <name>param1</name>
   <required>true</required>
</attribute>
```

The implementing class must contain a method to handle the parameter **param1** when it is passed in. Listing 24.8 shows the Java class file for this example.

LISTING 24.8   The TicketTag.java Class

```
/*
 * TicketTag.java
 *
 * Created on July 13, 2002, 12:38 PM
 */

package com.samspublishing.jpp.ch25;

import javax.servlet.jsp.*;
import javax.servlet.jsp.tagext.*;
import java.io.*;

/**
 *
 * @author  Stephen Potts
 * @version
 */
public class TicketTag extends TagSupport
{
    private String param1;
    public int doStartTag()
    {
        try
        {
            JspWriter out = pageContext.getOut();
            out.print("The parameter that you entered = " + param1);
        }catch (Exception e)
        {
```

LISTING 24.8 Continued

```
            System.out.println("Error in TicketTag class" + e);
        }
        return(SKIP_BODY);
    }

    public void setParam1(String id)
    {
        this.param1=id;
    }

}
```

We added a set method for the parameter. The name of the method will be **setXXX()** where **XXX** is the name of the parameter. In this case, the name of the parameter is **setParam1()** because our parameter name is **param1**.

```
    public void setParam1(String id)
    {
        this.param1=id;
    }
```

This populates the private member variable called **param1**. Then, we use this variable in the output for this tag.

```
            out.print("The parameter that you entered = " + param1);
```

The JSP file for this example is shown in Listing 24.9.

LISTING 24.9 The `TicketTag.jsp` File

```
<!DOCTYPE HTML PUBLIC "-//W3C//DTD HTML 4.0 Transitional//EN">
<html>
<head>

<%@ taglib uri="jppticket-taglib.tld" prefix="jpp" %>

<title>Parameter Passing</title>
</head>

<body>
<h1>Parameter passing</h1>
<br>
<b>
<jpp:ticketTag param1="13" />
<b>

</body>
</html>
```

The only type of parameter we can pass here is a literal because this taglib doesn't contain the proper instructions to allow a dynamic attribute value.

If we change the taglib, we can then take this parameter from a form. If we can take a parameter from a form, we can use a taglib to do a database access. Listing 24.10 shows a form that calls a JSP that accepts a dynamic value.

LISTING 24.10 The `RetrieveTicketTagForm.html` File

```html
<!DOCTYPE HTML PUBLIC "-//W3C//DTD HTML 4.01 Transitional//EN">

<HTML>
  <HEAD>
    <TITLE>Retrieve a Ticket</TITLE>
  </HEAD>
  <H1 align="CENTER">
  Enter the customer ID
  </H1>

  <FORM action='/examples/jsp/jpp/TicketTag2.jsp'>

      Customer ID:         <INPUT TYPE="TEXT" NAME="custID"><BR><BR>
      <CENTER>
         <INPUT TYPE="SUBMIT">
      </CENTER>
  </FORM>

  </BODY>
</HTML>
```

This form's action calls the `TicketTag2.jsp` file.

```html
<FORM action='/examples/jsp/jpp/TicketTag2.jsp'>
```

Listing 24.11 shows this JSP file.

LISTING 24.11 The `TicketTag2.jsp` File

```jsp
<!DOCTYPE HTML PUBLIC "-//W3C//DTD HTML 4.0 Transitional//EN">
<html>
<head>

<%@ taglib uri="jppticket-taglib2.tld" prefix="jpp" %>

<title>Ticket Selection</title>
</head>

<body>
<h1>Ticket Selected</h1>
<br>
<b>
<%
   String custIDString =  request.getParameter("custID");
%>
```

LISTING 24.11   Continued

```
<jpp:ticketTag custID= '<%= custIDString %>' />
<b>

</body>
</html>
```

Notice that the `custID` is now extracted from the request object.

```
String custIDString =  request.getParameter("custID");
```

This `custIDString` is used as the parameter passed to the implementing class file.

```
<jpp:ticketTag custID= '<%= custIDString %>' />
```

The taglib must also be changed to accept dynamic attributes. Listing 24.12 shows this new taglib.

LISTING 24.12   The `jppticket-taglib2.tld` File

```
<?xml version="1.0" encoding="UTF-8" ?>

<!DOCTYPE taglib
        PUBLIC "-//Sun Microsystems, Inc.//DTD JSP Tag Library 1.1//EN"
        "http://java.sun.com/j2ee/dtds/web-jsptaglibrary_1_1.dtd">
<!-- a tag library descriptor -->

<taglib>
<!-- after this the default space is
        "http://java.sun.com/j2ee/dtds/jsptaglibrary_1_2.dtd"
    -->

<tlibversion>1.0</tlibversion>
<jspversion>1.1</jspversion>
<shortname>jpptaglib</shortname>
<info>
   A tag library from Java Primer Plus
</info>

<tag>
<name>ticketTag</name>
<tagclass>com.samspublishing.jpp.ch25.TicketTag2</tagclass>
<bodycontent>empty</bodycontent>
<info>a Hello World custom tag example</info>

<attribute>
   <name>custID</name>
   <required>true</required>
   <rtexprvalue>true</rtexprvalue>
</attribute>
</tag>
</taglib>
```

The `custID` attribute must be told explicitly that a dynamic parameter can be used. The `<rtexprvalue>` tag stands for runtime expression value. Setting it to `true` tells the JSP engine that runtime expressions are allowed. By default, this value is `false`.

Listing 24.13 shows the class file associated with this example.

LISTING 24.13   The `TicketTag2.java` File

```
/*
 * TicketTag2.java
 *
 * Created on July 13, 2002, 12:38 PM
 */

package com.samspublishing.jpp.ch25;

import javax.servlet.jsp.*;
import javax.servlet.jsp.tagext.*;
import java.io.*;
import java.sql.*;
import java.util.*;

/**
 *
 * @author  Stephen Potts
 * @version
 */
public class TicketTag2 extends TagSupport
{
    private String custIDString;
    //information about the customer
    private int custID;
    private String lastName;
    private String firstName;

    //information about the cruise
    private int cruiseID;
    private String destination;
    private String port;
    private String sailing;

    private int numberOfTickets;

    public int doStartTag()
    {
        retrieveFromDB();

        /*lastName = "Joe";
        firstName = "Burns";

        //information about the cruise
        cruiseID = 1001;
```

LISTING 24.13 Continued

```
            destination = "Cuba";
            port = "Tampa";
            sailing = "1/1/03";
            numberOfTickets = 4;
             **/

        try
        {
            JspWriter out = pageContext.getOut();
            out.print("The custID that you entered = " + custID);
            out.print("<br>" );
            out.print("The Last Name = " + lastName);
            out.print("<br>" );
            out.print("The First Name = " + firstName);
            out.print("<br>" );
            out.print("The cruiseID = " + cruiseID);
            out.print("<br>" );
            out.print("The destination = " + destination);
            out.print("<br>" );
            out.print("The port = " + port);
            out.print("<br>" );
            out.print("The sailing = " + sailing);
            out.print("<br>" );
            out.print("The number of tickets = " + numberOfTickets);
        }catch (Exception e)
        {
            System.out.println("Error in TicketTag2 class" + e);
        }
        return(SKIP_BODY);
    }

    public void setCustID(String id)
    {
        this.custIDString=id;
        this.custID = Integer.parseInt(custIDString);
    }

    public String retrieveFromDB()
    {
        java.sql.Connection dbConn = null;
        Statement statement1 = null;
        String createStatement;
        String insertStatement;

        try
        {
            // =============== Make connection to database ==================

            //load the driver class
            Class.forName("sun.jdbc.odbc.JdbcOdbcDriver");

            //Specify the ODBC data source
            String sourceURL = "jdbc:odbc:TicketRequest";
```

LISTING 24.13   *Continued*

```
        //get a connection to the database
        dbConn = DriverManager.getConnection(sourceURL);

        //If we get to here, no exception was thrown
        System.out.println("The database connection is " + dbConn);
        System.out.println("Making connection...\n");

        //Create the statement
        statement1 = dbConn.createStatement();


        //Populate the bean
        String getBeanString =
        "SELECT * FROM TicketRequest " +
        "WHERE CustID = " + custID;

        ResultSet results = statement1.executeQuery(getBeanString);

        while (results.next())
        {
           lastName = results.getString("lastName");
           firstName = results.getString("firstName");
           cruiseID = results.getInt("cruiseID");
           destination = results.getString("destination");
           port = results.getString("port");
           sailing = results.getString("sailing");
           numberOfTickets = results.getInt("numberOfTickets");
        }
        return "Successful Retrieval";
    } catch (Exception e)
    {
        System.out.println("Exception was thrown: " + e.getMessage());
        return "UnSuccessful Retrieval";
    } finally
    {
        try
        {
           if (statement1 != null)
               statement1.close();
           if (dbConn != null)
               dbConn.close();
        } catch (SQLException sqle)
        {
           System.out.println("SQLException during close(): " +
                                       sqle.getMessage());
        }
    }

  }


  }
```

The support for the parameter passing is provided by the addition of the `setCustID()` method.

```
public void setCustID(String id)
{
   this.custIDString=id;
   this.custID = Integer.parseInt(custIDString);
}
```

Accessing the database is done using JDBC in the `retrieveFromDB()` method.

```
public String retrieveFromDB()
{
```

We connect to the database in typical JDBC fashion. See Chapter 19, "Accessing Databases with Java Database Connectivity (JDBC)," for a detailed explanation of JDBC connection code.

```
//load the driver class
Class.forName("sun.jdbc.odbc.JdbcOdbcDriver");

//Specify the ODBC data source
String sourceURL = "jdbc:odbc:TicketRequest";

//get a connection to the database
dbConn = DriverManager.getConnection(sourceURL);

//If we get to here, no exception was thrown
System.out.println("The database connection is " + dbConn);
System.out.println("Making connection...\n");

//Create the statement
statement1 = dbConn.createStatement();
```

We create the SQL string.

```
//Populate the class
String getBeanString =
"SELECT * FROM TicketRequest " +
"WHERE CustID = " + custID;
```

Next, we execute the query and obtain the `ResultSet`. The `ResultSet` object contains all of the information that was returned by the execution of the query.

```
ResultSet results = statement1.executeQuery(getBeanString);
```

We extract the parameters from the `ResultSet` object by making a series of `get` calls. Each `get` call is tailored to the data type of the data in the database. In this way, we move data from the database into class-level variables that can be manipulated or displayed.

```
while (results.next())
{
   lastName = results.getString("lastName");
   firstName = results.getString("firstName");
   cruiseID = results.getInt("cruiseID");
   destination = results.getString("destination");
```

```
        port = results.getString("port");
        sailing = results.getString("sailing");
        numberOfTickets = results.getInt("numberOfTickets");
    }
```

The final step is to return these values to the JSP using the **JspWriter** object. The **out.print()** method is the easiest way to send information to the JSP for display.

```
        JspWriter out = pageContext.getOut();
        out.print("The custID that you entered = " + custID);
        out.print("<br>" );
        out.print("The Last Name = " + lastName);
        out.print("<br>" );
        out.print("The First Name = " + firstName);
        out.print("<br>" );
        out.print("The cruiseID = " + cruiseID);
        out.print("<br>" );
        out.print("The destination = " + destination);
        out.print("<br>" );
        out.print("The port = " + port);
        out.print("<br>" );
        out.print("The sailing = " + sailing);
        out.print("<br>" );
        out.print("The number of tickets = " + numberOfTickets);
```

To run this program, type the following line in the address bar on your browser and enter a value:

`http://localhost:1776/examples/RetrieveTicketTagForm.html`

The result of running this program is shown in Figure 24.4.

FIGURE 24.4

A tag can be used to retrieve data from a database.

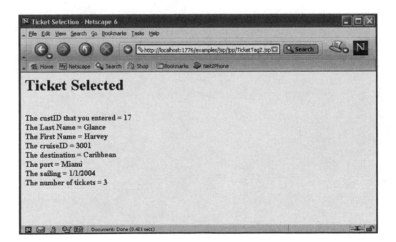

All the data extracted from the database is displayed in the browser.

Summary

This chapter has introduced you to the concept of custom tag development in JSPs. You learned what custom tags are, and how to create them. Following that, you learned how to process the bodies of the tags.

Next, you learned how to pass parameters, both static and dynamic, to the implementation class. Finally, you learned how to use these parameters to access data in a database.

Review Questions

1. What is the purpose of custom tags?

2. What role does the taglib play?

3. How does the implementation class obtain the value of an attribute?

4. What special tag do you add to an attribute to allow it to accept dynamic values?

Exercises

1. Create a custom tag that displays your personal information on the screen.

2. Modify the tag to accept a parameter that displays your age.

3. Enhance the tag's implementation class to retrieve that personal information from a database.

4. Create a tag that enables you to update a database.

XML

You will learn about the following in this chapter:

- Purpose of XML

- How to read XML documents using the Simple API for XML (SAX) parsing

- How to read and manipulate XML documents using the Document Object Model (DOM)

- How to use style sheets and an XSLT processor to transform XML documents to other forms

- How to read and manipulate XML documents using the open source JDOM project

The Importance of XML

As software programs evolve from standalone singular applications to distributed enterprise systems, developers are faced with a new set of challenges. No longer are applications running on a single machine, but on multiple machines with potentially different operating systems on different hardware architectures. Thus, the developer is challenged with the task of defining a communication mechanism between applications written in different programming languages and running on different operating systems.

If all applications were written in Java, your job would be easy. Java was designed to run in a consistent virtual machine on any supported operating system, and it is the virtual machine's responsibility to translate the "Java" representation of data to the operating system. Java uses 4 bytes to represent an Integer, whereas some implementations of programming languages use 2 bytes, so how do you account for the missing two bytes? The underlying interpretation of the byte order of data varies between Windows and Unix operating systems: if you have a 4-byte Integer, the exact same bits are interpreted differently on the two operating systems, generating a different value.

As I said, if all programs were written in Java there would be no problem, but the practicality is that all programs cannot be written in Java. Consider the class of applications that talk directly to hardware—these applications need to see the underlying operating system and understand the computer architecture hosting the hardware. This is just one case where Java cannot be used; another class of software that is running on an operating system for which a Java virtual machine has not been developed.

Now that you understand some of the challenges you face, how might you consider passing data unambiguously between two applications? Consider passing the variable speed with the value 65. You are trying to convey two pieces of information: the value 65, and its associated meaning speed. As I have mentioned, passing the Integer value as a collection of bits does not work. How about sending the data as the character 6 followed by the character 5? Regardless of operating system and programming language, the character 5 is the same.

That works, so now we need to identify that 65 represents the speed of something, so how about passing the string speed along with the value 65? We could send the following string across operating systems and programming languages:

```
speed=65
```

This works to pass a primitive type, but what about sending an object (or the state of an object so that it can be re-created on the other side)? This is a little more complicated. Let's consider passing a `Car` from a Java program running on Windows (again the operating system does not matter to Java) to a C++ program running on Sun Solaris. Consider the following `Car` class:

```java
public class Car {
  private Color color = Color.red;
  private String make = "Porsche";
  private String model = "Carerra 911";

  private int gas = 15; // in gallons
  private int speed = 0; // in mph
  private int oil = 5; // in quarts

  private boolean running = false;

  ... methods ...
}
```

You have learned that we can send strings between applications to solve our problems, so now the question is how do we persist this `Car` class to a string and one that is self describing so that application on the other end can easily identify all the car's attributes? Consider passing the following variable to another program:

```java
Car myCar = new Car();
```

So, we want to attach the variable `myCar` with all the data represented in the particular Car instance. Because all the car's attributes are owned by the car itself, it would be nice to preserve that relationship when describing the car to another application. Thus, the solution is to create a string that is hierarchical: the car object contains (or is the parent of) its attributes. Rather than reinvent the wheel, we can borrow the notation used in HTML tags for two reasons:

1. They have defined a nice hierarchical model

2. HTML works across operating systems and programming languages, so it is a good place to start

The root of an HTML document is the `<html>` tag, its children can include a `<head>` element and a `<body>` element. The `<head>` can contain a `<title>` element or a `<script>` element. The `<body>` element can contain a `bgcolor` attribute that changes the background color of the page, a `<table>` element that can contain `<tr>` elements, and so on. Each element begins with a start tag that is a tag name enclosed between less than and greater than signs: `<tag-name>`. Each element is terminated by using the same tag name prepended with a less than sign followed by a forward slash and terminated by a greater than sign: `</tag-name>`. For example:

```
<html>
  <head>
    <title>My Page</title>
  </head>
  <body bgcolor="black">
    ... body content ...
  </body>
</html>
```

Although HTML documents have specific HTML tags, they don't quite fit when describing a car, but the structure is nice. How about borrowing the structure (tag notation and notion that an element can contain attributes and other elements), but replacing the tag names with ones that are more meaningful when describing a car? Consider the following:

```
<car name="myCar">
  <color>yellow</color>
  <make>Porsche</make>
  <model>Carerra 911</model>
  <gas>15</gas>
  <oil>5</oil>
  <speed>95</speed>
  <running>true</running>
</car>
```

This description of a car has the following characteristics:

- It is self describing: You can easily see that the `<car>` object is named `myCar` and has a `<speed>` element with the value `95`.

- It is possible to send this representation of a car between operating systems and programming languages.

- It preserves the hierarchical nature of object-oriented programming.

This is the essence of XML: It follows a tagging structure similar to HTML, but with tag names that describe the data they represent, as well as a hoard of other features, including rules that allow you to define the structure of your specific data. For example, a `<car>` can contain a `<speed>` element, but a `<speed>` element cannot contain a `<car>` element, a `<speed>` element may be optional and assumed to be 0 if not present, and so forth.

XML Components

Before we dive into manipulating XML files, let's define the components that comprise XML documents.

The XML Document

The core of an XML document is the document itself. It is comprised of the following components:

- Prolog: Contains version information, comments, and references to Documenet Type Definition (DTD) files.

- Body: Contains a document root and subelements.

- Epilog: Contains comments and processing instructions.

Listing 25.1 shows a simple XML file that might be used in a bookstore to define a set of books.

LISTING 25.1   books.xml

```
1:   <?xml version="1.0"?>
2:   <!DOCTYPE books SYSTEM "Books.dtd">
3:   <books>
4:     <book category="computer-programming">
5:       <author>Steven Haines</author>
6:       <title>Java 2 From Scratch</title>
7:       <price>39.95</price>
8:     </book>
9:     <book category="fiction">
10:      <author>Tim LaHaye</author>
11:      <title>Left Behind</title>
12:    </book>
13: </books>
```

Lines 1 and 2 define the header. Line 1 notes that this XML document is written against the 1.0 version of the XML specification; line 2 references a Document Type Definition (DTD) file that defines the syntax rules for this XML file.

Lines 3 through 13 define the body of the XML document. Most XML documents that you will encounter, as well as this one, will not have an epilog, but the specification allows for it.

Document Type Definition (DTD)

Document Type Definition files, or DTD for short, define the syntactical rules by which XML files are written. It defines things such as:

- The name of the root element in the document (for example, `<books>`).

- The elements that can be contained inside of other elements (for example, `<book>` can be contained by `<books>`).

- The multiplicity of elements (for example, <book> can appear multiple times).

- The order of elements (for example, <author> must precede <title>, which must precede <price>).

- Optional elements (for example, <price> appears in the first <book>, but not in the second <book>).

- The type of data that is contained in the content of the element (for example, all elements are text elements).

- The attributes that can appear in an element (<book> contains the attribute category—and it is a text string).

The origin of DTD files dates back to XML's forefather markup language: SGML, so it might initially appear cryptic, but its conventions are pretty straightforward. Listing 25.2 shows the DTD that defines the **books.xml** file in Listing 25.1.

LISTING 25.2   books.dtd

```
1:  <!ELEMENT books (book*)>
2:  <!ELEMENT book (author, title, price?)>
3:  <!ATTLIST book category CDATA>
4:  <!ELEMENT author (#PCDATA)>
5:  <!ELEMENT title (#PCDATA)>
6:  <!ELEMENT price (#PCDATA)>
```

Line 1 defines the element <books> as containing zero or more <book> elements:

```
1:  <!ELEMENT books (book*)>
```

The <books> element is defined as an element, denoted by the <!ELEMENT prefix. The parentheses contain a comma-separated list of subelements that the <books> element can contain. In this case it can only contain the element <book>, but because there is an asterisk following book, it denotes that it can contain zero or more instances of the <book> element. Note that if book was followed by a plus sign it would denote that <books> could contain one or more <book> elements (but it must contain at least one).

```
2:  <!ELEMENT book (author, title, price?)>
```

Similarly, line 2 defines the subelements that the <book> element can contain; that is <author>, followed by <title>, followed by an optional <price> element. The question mark following price notes that price is optional and can appear zero or one time as a subelement of the <book> element. Note that the order is enforced by the DTD; if <price> appears, it must be after <title>, which must be after <author>.

```
3: <!ATTLIST book category CDATA>
```

Line 3 defines one of the attributes of the <book> element as category and notes its type: **CDATA**. **CDATA** (character data) and its counterpart **PCDATA** (parsed character data) both refer to character data or text.

Lines 4–6 define the elements `<author>`, `<title>`, and `<price>` as containing character data. Note that if you were to consider an XML document as a tree, the `<book>` element would be a branch that contained other elements and the `<author>`, `<title>`, and `<price>` elements would be considered leaf nodes (they do not have any children of their own).

Document Validation

Why all these rules? The answer lies in document validation. When an XML document is parsed (or read) the parser (process that is responsible for reading the document) can validate the XML document's syntax against its DTD file and report back whether the document is well formed. If it is well formed you can trust that you will be able to extract its data according to the rules in the DTD file; if not you can reject the document. This is a valuable asset to you as the programmer.

Parsing Techniques

Sun, through the Java API for XML Parsing (JAXP), provides two mechanisms for reading XML documents:

- An event model
- A tree model

The JDOM open-source project provides a solution to manipulating XML documents using Java-familiar Collection classes.

The Simple API for XML (SAX) Parser is event driven: the program registers a listener with the parser, and the parser streams through the file, firing notifications when it encounters XML elements. The Document Object Model (DOM) constructs a tree representation of the XML document and provides an Application Programmers Interface (API) for accessing and manipulating the data in the tree.

SAX and DOM both exist for different application purposes and both have their advantages and disadvantages. The SAX parser maintains a very small memory footprint because it does not save any information, but simply streams through the document and fires notifications of what it finds. It is extremely fast, but it requires the developer to build his own data-structure representation of the document for in-memory use of the data. The DOM is slow to build and consumes a lot of memory, but it maintains an in-memory representation of the data, provides an API to access and manipulate that data, and even allows for complex searching and reporting based off of that data.

If you are reading an XML file to load data into your own data structures, you should use SAX. If need a subset of the information or are simply trying to compute a value based on what is contained in the XML file (for example, how many books are in my document), you should use SAX.

On the other hand, if you want to access the entire document in memory, you should use DOM. If you want to manipulate the document, and then output the modified document to a destination (for example, save it to a file), you should use DOM.

The choice is all a matter of how you are going to use the data obtained from the XML document.

Before we get started you are going to have to obtain a copy of JAXP from Sun's Web site `http://java.sun.com/xml/jaxp`.

When you download JAXP simply decompress it to a directory on your computer and you're ready to go. The files of interest in the distribution are

- docs subdirectory: This contains all the `javadocs` for all the classes provided in the JAXP. It is the resource that you are going to make the most use of in your XML development.

- `crimson.jar`: This archive contains all the World Wide Web Consortium (W3C) DOM and SAX classes along with the Apache Crimson JAXP implementation classes.

- `jaxp.jar`: This archive contains all the JAXP interfaces.

You will need to add these two archives to your **CLASSPATH** when compiling and running Java applications that make use of the JAXP.

Although both SAX and DOM are standard interfaces defined by the World Wide Web Consortium (`www.w3c.org`), and implementations are available for a variety of programming languages, JDOM is a proprietary solution that is only usable in the Java programming language. Then why use it? If you are a Java programmer and familiar with the Java Collection classes (as you are now), it is extremely easy to use! As we get into the examples later in the chapter you will see the difference, and why I personally use JDOM over both SAX and DOM whenever I am developing in Java.

You are going to need to obtain a copy of JDOM, which is available as a free download at `http://www.jdom.org`.

Download and decompress the latest version of JDOM to your local computer. The following files must be in your **CLASSPATH** when you compile programs that use JDOM:

- `build/jdom.jar`: This is the implementation JDOM API.

- `lib/xerces.jar`: This is the open source Xerces Java XML libraries that JDOM is built on top of.

- `build/apidocs/index.html`: This is the root of the JavaDoc that describes the JDOM API.

Reading XML Documents Using the Simple API for XML (SAX) Parser

The main advantages of the SAX parser over the DOM include

- It can parse documents of any size

- Useful when you want to build your own data structures

- Useful when you only want a small subset of information contained in the XML document

- It is simple

- It is fast

Its main disadvantages include

- It does not provide random access to the document; it starts at the beginning and reads through serially to the end

- Complex searches can be difficult to implement

- Lexical information is not available

- It is read-only

Using a SAX parser to read an XML document requires a SAX parser to read the document and a document handler to make meaningful use of the data the SAX parser reads.

JAXP provides a SAX parser in its distribution: `javax.xml.parsers.SAXParser`; the SAX parser is made available to you through the SAX parser factory: `javax.xml.parsers.SAXParserFactory`. The `SAXParserFactory` class is an API for obtaining SAX-based parsers. Call its `newSAXParser()` method to obtain a preconfigured SAX parser (based on the settings you define in the factory). Note that both of these classes are abstract and are provided as base classes so that you, the developer, have a consistent programming interface irrespective of the underlying implementation.

Your job now is to create a document handler. A document handler is defined by the class `org.xml.sax.helpers.DefaultHandler`. It implements several interfaces, but the one that you will be most interested in is the `org.xml.sax.ContentHandler` interface, see Table 25.1.

TABLE 25.1 `ContentHandler` Interface

Method	Description
`void characters(char[] ch, int start, int length)`	Receive notification of character data
`void endDocument()`	Receive notification of the end of a document
`void endElement(String namespaceURI, String localName, String qName)`	Receive notification of the end of an element
`void endPrefixMapping (String prefix)`	End the scope of a prefix-URI mapping
`void ignorableWhitespace(char[] ch, int start, int length)`	Receive notification of ignorable whitespace in element content

TABLE 25.1   Continued

Method	Description
void processingInstruction (String target, String data)	Receive notification of a processing instruction
void setDocumentLocator (Locator locator)	Receive an object for locating the origin of SAX document events
void skippedEntity(String name)	Receive notification of a skipped entity
void startDocument()	Receive notification of the beginning of a document
void startElement (String namespaceURI, String localName, String qName, Attributes atts)	Receive notification of the beginning of an element
void startPrefixMapping (String prefix, String uri)	Begin the scope of a prefix-URI Namespace mapping

Table 25.1 displays all the methods defined in the `org.xml.sax.ContentHandler` interface. The document parser calls these methods on the class that implements this interface; for example, when the document starts the `startDocument()` methods is called, when the `<books>` element is found, the `startElement()` method is called and the `qName` is book.

The `DefaultHandler` class also implements the `org.xml.sax.DTDHandler`, `org.xml.sax.EntityHandler`, and `org.xml.sax.ErrorHandler` interfaces to help the SAX parser resolve symbols it does not understand and to handle errors. When creating a handler it is best to extend the `DefaultHandler`.

With that said, here are the steps to parsing and handling the content of an XML document using the SAX parser:

1. Import the SAX classes, handler class, and parser classes into your Java program.
2. Get an instance of the `org.xml.sax.SAXParserFactory` by calling its static method `newInstance()`.
3. Configure the `SAXParserFactory`'s options (whether it is aware of namespaces and whether it is validating).
4. Obtain an `org.xml.sax.SAXParser` by calling the `SAXParserFactory`'s `newSAXParser()` method.
5. Create an instance of your `org.xml.sax.helpers.DefaultHandler` class.
6. Open a stream to your XML source.
7. Ask the SAX parser to parse your XML stream by calling one of its `parse()` methods, see Table 25.2.
8. Handle all the SAX parser notifications in your `DefaultHandler` class.

TABLE 25.2   SAX Parser `parse()` Methods

Method	Description
`void parse(java.io.File f, DefaultHandler dh)`	Parse the content of the file specified as XML using the specified `DefaultHandler`.
`void parse(org.xml.sax. InputSource is, DefaultHandler dh)`	Parse the content given `InputSource` as XML using the specified `DefaultHandler`.
`void parse(java.io. InputStream is, DefaultHandler dh)`	Parse the content of the given `InputStream` instance as XML using the specified `DefaultHandler`.
`void parse(java.io. InputStream is, DefaultHandler dh, String systemId)`	Parse the content of the given `InputStream` instance as XML using the specified `DefaultHandler`.
`void parse(String uri, DefaultHandler dh)`	Parse the content described by the giving Uniform Resource Identifier (URI) as XML using the specified `DefaultHandler`.

Table 25.2 shows the `SAXParser`'s various `parse()` methods; the basic variation is that the source can be a file, a stream, a URI pointing to the file, or an `InputSource` (which can be an `InputStream` or a Reader—see the `javadoc` that accompanies the JAXP for more information). When looking at the `javadoc` for the `SAXParser` class, you might notice reference to the deprecated `HandlerBase` class in addition to the `DefaultHandler` class. This is a remnant of the original SAX implementation, but with the advent of SAX2, which is what we are studying, it is no longer supported.

As an example, consider the aforementioned `books.xml` file in Listing 25.1. To read that XML file and do something meaningful with it, we will need to create a couple classes to represent an individual book and a collection of books. To realize this in software we will create two helper classes: `SAXBook` and `SAXBooks`; see Figure 25.1.

FIGURE 25.1
`SAXBook` and `SAXBooks` class diagram.

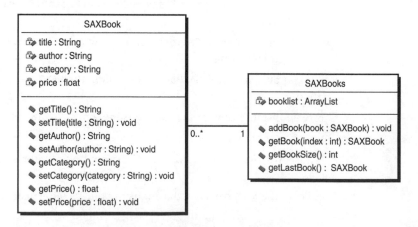

Listings 25.3 and 25.4 show the code for the **SAXBook** and **SAXBooks** classes.

LISTING 25.3   SAXBook.java

```
001: public class SAXBook {
002:     private String title;
003:     private String author;
004:     private String category;
005:     private float price;
006:
007:     public SAXBook() {
008:     }
009:
010:     public SAXBook( String title,
011:                     String author,
012:                     String category,
013:                     float price ) {
014:         this.title = title;
015:         this.author = author;
016:         this.category = category;
017:         this.price = price;
018:     }
019:
020:     public String getTitle() {
021:         return this.title;
022:     }
023:
024:     public void setTitle( String title ) {
025:         this.title = title;
026:     }
027:
028:     public String getAuthor() {
029:         return this.author;
030:     }
031:
032:     public void setAuthor( String author ) {
033:         this.author = author;
034:     }
035:
036:     public String getCategory() {
037:         return this.category;
038:     }
039:
040:     public void setCategory( String category ) {
041:         this.category = category;
042:     }
043:
044:     public float getPrice() {
045:         return this.price;
046:     }
047:
048:     public void setPrice( float price ) {
```

LISTING 25.3   Continued

```
049:        this.price = price;
050:    }
051:
052:    public String toString() {
053:        return "Book: " + title + ", " + category + ", " +
                    author + ", " + price;
054:    }
055:}
```

Listing 25.3 has simple code to provide standard JavaBean-esque access to the four fields
defined in the class: title, author, category, and price. It also overloads the toString() method
to return the values contained in all the fields.

LISTING 25.4   SAXBooks.java

```
001:import java.util.ArrayList;
002:
003:public class SAXBooks {
004:    private ArrayList bookList = new ArrayList();
005:
006:    public SAXBooks() {
007:    }
008:
009:    public void addBook( SAXBook book ) {
010:        this.bookList.add( book );
011:    }
012:
013:    public SAXBook getBook( int index ) {
014:        if( index >= bookList.size() ) {
015:            return null;
016:        }
017:        return( SAXBook )bookList.get( index );
018:    }
019:
020:    public SAXBook getLastBook() {
021:        return this.getBook( this.getBookSize() - 1 );
022:    }
023:
024:    public int getBookSize() {
025:        return bookList.size();
026:    }
027:}
```

Listing 25.4 shows that the SAXBooks class maintains its collection of SAXBook objects in a
java.util.ArrayList and provides methods to add a book, retrieve a book, and retrieve the
total number of books in the ArrayList. There is one additional method, getLastBook(),
that returns the last book in the ArrayList; the reason for that will become apparent in the
MyHandler.java file in Listing 25.6. When you run this example be sure that the DTD
file is in the same directory as the XML file or you may inadvertently receive a
FileNotFoundException.

LISTING 25.5   SAXSample.java

```
001:import java.io.*;
002:import org.xml.sax.*;
003:import org.xml.sax.helpers.DefaultHandler;
004:import javax.xml.parsers.SAXParserFactory;
005:import javax.xml.parsers.ParserConfigurationException;
006:import javax.xml.parsers.SAXParser;
007:
008:public class SAXSample {
009:    public static void main( String[] args ) {
010:        try {
011:            File file = new File( "book.xml" );
012:            if( !file.exists() ) {
013:                System.out.println( "Couldn't find file..." );
014:                return;
015:            }
016:
017:            // Use the default (non-validating) parser
018:            SAXParserFactory factory = SAXParserFactory.newInstance();
019:
020:            // Create an instance of our handler
021:            MyHandler handler = new MyHandler();
022:
023:            // Parse the file
024:            SAXParser saxParser = factory.newSAXParser();
025:            saxParser.parse( file, handler );
026:            SAXBooks books = handler.getBooks();
027:
028:            for( int i=0; i<books.getBookSize(); i++ ) {
029:                SAXBook book = books.getBook( i );
030:                System.out.println( book );
031:            }
032:
033:        }
034:        catch( Throwable t ) {
035:            t.printStackTrace();
036:        }
037:    }
038:}
```

Listing 25.6 shows the code for the SAXSample class; this is the main class that opens our XML file, creates a parser, and asks the parser to notify our handler.

Lines 11–15 create a java.io.File object that points to the book.xml file that it is expecting to be in the same directory that this program is launched from. It validates that the file exists and quits out of the program if it does not exist.

```
018:            SAXParserFactory factory = SAXParserFactory.newInstance();
```

Line 18 creates a new instance of the SAXParserFactory class by calling the SAXParserFactory class's static newInstance() method; recall that the SAXParserFactory is responsible for configuring a SAXParser and returning it upon request.

```
021:            MyHandler handler = new MyHandler();
```

Line 21 creates an instance of the MyHandler class that will be described in Listing 25.6.

```
024:            SAXParser saxParser = factory.newSAXParser();
```

Line 24 asks the SAXParserFactory to create a new SAXParser by calling its newSAXParser() method.

```
025:            saxParser.parse( file, handler );
```

Line 25 uses the SAXParser to parse the book.xml file and provide notifications to the MyHandler instance.

Lines 26–31 retrieve the SAXBooks from the MyHandler instance, and then iterate over all the SAXBook instances it contains, displaying the books to the screen (passing the SAXBook instance to System.out.println invokes the toString() that was overridden in Listing 25.3).

LISTING 25.6   MyHandler.java

```
001:import org.xml.sax.*;
002:import org.xml.sax.helpers.DefaultHandler;
003:
004:public class MyHandler extends DefaultHandler {
005:    private SAXBooks books;
006:    private boolean readingAuthor;
007:    private boolean readingTitle;
008:    private boolean readingPrice;
009:
010:    public SAXBooks getBooks() {
011:        return this.books;
012:    }
013:
014:    public void startElement( String uri,
015:                              String localName,
016:                              String qName,
017:                              Attributes attributes ) {
018:        System.out.println( "Found element: " + qName );
019:        if( qName.equalsIgnoreCase( "books" ) ) {
020:            books = new SAXBooks();
021:        }
022:        else if( qName.equalsIgnoreCase( "book" ) ) {
023:            SAXBook book = new SAXBook();
024:            for( int i=0; i<attributes.getLength(); i++ ) {
025:                if( attributes.getQName( i ).equalsIgnoreCase( "category" ) ) {
026:                    book.setCategory( attributes.getValue( i ) );
027:                }
028:            }
029:            books.addBook( book );
030:        }
031:        else if( qName.equalsIgnoreCase( "author" ) ) {
032:            this.readingAuthor = true;
033:        }
034:        else if( qName.equalsIgnoreCase( "title" ) ) {
```

LISTING 25.6   Continued

```
035:                    this.readingTitle = true;
036:                }
037:                else if( qName.equalsIgnoreCase( "price" ) ) {
038:                    this.readingPrice = true;
039:                }
040:                else {
041:                    System.out.println( "Unknown element: " + qName );
042:                }
043:        }
044:
045:        public void startDocument() {
046:            System.out.println( "Starting..." );
047:        }
048:
049:        public void endDocument() {
050:            System.out.println( "Done..." );
051:        }
052:
053:        public void characters( char[] ch,
054:                                int start,
055:                                int length ) {
056:            String chars = new String( ch, start, length).trim();
057:            if( chars.length() == 0 ) {
058:                return;
059:            }
060:
061:            SAXBook book = books.getLastBook();
062:            if( readingAuthor ) {
063:                book.setAuthor( chars );
064:            }
065:            else if( readingTitle ) {
066:                book.setTitle( chars );
067:            }
068:            else if( readingPrice ) {
069:                book.setPrice( Float.parseFloat( chars ) );
070:            }
071:        }
072:
073:        public void endElement( String uri,
074:                                String localName,
075:                                String qName ) {
076:            System.out.println( "End Element: " + qName );
077:            if( qName.equalsIgnoreCase( "author" ) ) {
078:                this.readingAuthor = false;
079:            }
080:            else if( qName.equalsIgnoreCase( "title" ) ) {
081:                this.readingTitle = false;
082:            }
083:            else if( qName.equalsIgnoreCase( "price" ) ) {
084:                this.readingPrice = false;
085:            }
086:        }
087:}
```

Listing 25.6 defines the `MyHandler` class; it is the most complicated class in the sample and is responsible for handling all the `SAXParser` notifications and building our data structures from those notifications.

```
004:public class MyHandler extends DefaultHandler {
```

Line 4 shows that the `MyHandler` class extends the `org.xml.sax.helpers.DefaultHandler` class; this class has methods that can be overloaded to respond to `SAXParser` notifications. The notifications that we will be interested in are

- `startDocument()`

- `endDocument()`

- `startElement()`

- `endElement()`

- `characters()`

The `startDocument()` and `endDocument()` methods in the `MyHandler` class simply print out debug statements; all the real work happens in the `startElement()`, `endElement()`, and `characters()` methods. Because the SAX model is dealing with message notifications, the handler cannot run serially, it must instead run as a state machine.

The order of events in the SAX model is that the handler will receive a `startElement()` notification for the `book` element, at which time we can get its attributes (category), then a `startElement()` for the `author` element, then a `characters()` call containing the text for the `author` element, and then an `endElement()` for `authors`. The process continues through `title` and `price` and finally we will get an `endElement()` call on `book`; at this point we have a complete book.

When the `MyHandler` class gets a `startElement()` call for `book`, it creates a new book, retrieves its `category` attribute, and adds it to the `SAXBooks` class (lines 19–30).

The `MyHandler` class maintains three variables to help it keep track of what element it is reading (lines 6–8); invocations of `startElement()` for `author`, `title`, and `price` modify these variables to note what element a subsequent `characters()` method can be applied to (lines 31–42); in a larger example you might want to use one integer variable and define some constant states in which that variable could be. When the `endElement()` method is called for each of these elements, the handler resets the appropriate variable (lines 77–85).

Lines 53–71 define the `characters()` method. This method retrieves the last book added (which is the reason why the `SAXBooks` class has the `getLastBook()` method), which was added in the `startElement()` for the `book` element and is the book for which this `characters()` method is applicable. The `characters()` method has three parameters: a character array containing the entire contents of the XML file and the start index and length into that character array that this element's character text is applicable to. The method builds a new

String from this subsection of the character array, trimming off white space, and then ensuring that it has some characters. The reason we check the length is that elements such as book, which contain other elements, still might have some white space between the end of the <book> tag and the beginning of the <author> tag, and so on. After it verifies that it has data, it checks the state variables defined earlier, accesses the last book added to the SAXBooks instance, and updates the appropriate book property (author, title, or price).

It took a fair amount of work, but the end result is that the MyHandler instance has a complete SAXBooks property that maintains an in-memory representation of the XML file that can now be used elsewhere in the application.

Manipulating XML Documents Using the Document Object Model (DOM)

The Document Object Model presents a tree representation of an XML document through a standards-based API maintained by the World Wide Web Consortium (W3C). The DOM is better suited for applications that want to read information from an XML file, manipulate the XML data, and then eventually write the data out to a destination. Additionally, it offers the benefit over the SAX that the document can be accessed randomly (the program does not have to read through the document sequentially).

The DOM does have a serious limitation in the fact that is must read the entire XML document into memory. This isn't a problem for the small example we've been working through in the chapter, but in some real-world applications, such as B2B e-commerce, XML files can get considerably larger (in B2B e-commerce applications that mapped EDI to XML we saw XML files that were over 100MB in size). But, if your application's architecture can make use of the DOM, it does not require all the code that we saw to build an in-memory representation of an XML file using the SAX.

Building an XML Tree in Memory

Building a DOM XML tree in memory is actually a fairly trivial task. Similar to the SAX model, the DOM model has a factory that creates parsers: javax.xml.parsers.DocumentBuilderFactory. This class enables the programmer to define the parser parameters that he would like the parser to present (see the javadoc documentation for more information). A DocumentBuilderFactory can be obtained by calling its static newInstance() method. After the DocumentBuilderFactory is configured, its newDocumentBuilder() method will return an instance of the javax.xml.parsers.DocumentBuilder class—this is the DOM parser. The DocumentBuilder class has several parse() methods that will construct a DOM document, shown in Table 25.3.

TABLE 25.3 DocumentBuilder parse() Methods

Method	Description
Document parse(java.io.File f)	Parse the content of the given file as an XML document and return a new DOM Document object.
Document parse(org.xml.sax. InputSource is)	Parse the content of the given input source as an XML document and return a new DOM Document object.
Document parse(java.io. InputStream is)	Parse the content of the given InputStream as an XML document and return a new DOM Document object.
Document parse(java.io. InputStream is, String systemId)	Parse the content of the given InputStream as an XML document and return a new DOM Document object.
Document parse(String uri)	Parse the content of the given URI as an XML document and return a new DOM Document object.

These parse() methods are very similar to their SAX counterparts, but the bottom line is that they build an org.w3c.dom.Document object from varying input sources. For example, consider building a DOM document from a file:

```
File f = new File( "myfile.xml" );
DocumentBuilderFactory factory = DocumentBuilderFactory.newInstance();
DocumentBuilder builder = factory.newDocumentBuilder();
Document doc = builder.parse( f );
```

Reading from the XML Tree

A DOM tree is an in-memory representation of an XML file; and just as it sounds it is in the form of a tree. Figure 25.2 shows how the book.xml file might appear in a DOM.

FIGURE 25.2
A sample DOM
tree diagram.

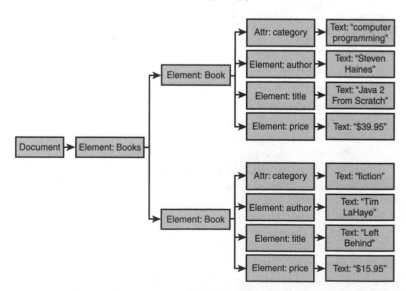

Observe from Figure 25.2 that the <books> root element contains two <book> elements. Each <book> element has an attribute node named category, and has three elements: <author>, <title>, and <price>. Each of these elements has a child text node that contains the element's value.

After a Document object is obtained from the DocumentBuilder, its root node can be accessed through the DocumentBuilder's getDocumentElement() method; this method returns an instance of a class implementing the org.w3c.com.Element interface. Table 25.4 describes some of the more useful retrieval methods of the Document class.

TABLE 25.4 Document Retrieval Methods

Method	Description
DocumentType getDoctype()	The Document Type Declaration (see org.w3c.dom.DocumentType) associated with this document.
Element getDocumentElement()	This is a convenience attribute that allows direct access to the child node that is the root element of the document.
NodeList getElementsByTagName (String tagname)	Returns a NodeList of all the Elements with a given tag name in the order in which they are encountered in a preorder traversal of the Document tree.

The org.w3x.dom.Element interface defines a set of methods for traversing the DOM tree. Table 25.5 shows some of the more useful Element retrieval methods.

TABLE 25.5 Element Retrieval Methods

Method	Description
String getAttribute(String name)	Retrieves an attribute value by name
Attr getAttributeNode(String name)	Retrieves an attribute node by name
NodeList getElementsByTagName (String name)	Returns a NodeList of all descendant Elements with a given tag name in the order in which they are encountered in a preorder traversal of this Element tree
String getTagName()	The name of the element

The Element interface is derived from the org.w3c.dom.Node interface that offers the addition methods shown in Table 25.6.

TABLE 25.6   Element Retrieval Methods

Method	Description
NamedNodeMap getAttributes()	A NamedNodeMap containing the attributes of this node (if it is an Element) or null otherwise
NodeList getChildNodes()	A NodeList that contains all children of this node
Node getFirstChild()	The first child of this node
Node getLastChild()	The last child of this node
String getNodeName()	The name of this node, depending on its type
short getNodeType()	A code representing the type of the underlying object
String getNodeValue()	The value of this node, depending on its type

Together, the Element methods and the Node methods offer the capability to discover the node's type (element node, text node, attribute node, and so on—see the javadoc for the org.w3c.dom.Node interface), retrieve a list of child nodes, retrieve a list of attributes, retrieve the name of the node, and retrieve its value. Listing 25.7 shows a sample application that reads the same book.xml file into a DOM object and traverses it using the methods just discussed.

LISTING 25.7   DOMSample.java

```
001:import javax.xml.parsers.DocumentBuilder;
002:import javax.xml.parsers.DocumentBuilderFactory;
003:import javax.xml.parsers.FactoryConfigurationError;
004:import javax.xml.parsers.ParserConfigurationException;
005:
006:import org.xml.sax.SAXException;
007:import org.xml.sax.SAXParseException;
008:
009:import java.io.FileInputStream;
010:import java.io.File;
011:import java.io.IOException;
012:
013:import org.w3c.dom.Document;
014:import org.w3c.dom.Element;
015:import org.w3c.dom.NodeList;
016:import org.w3c.dom.Node;
017:import org.w3c.dom.DOMException;
018:
019:public class DOMSample
020:{
021:    public static void main( String[] args )
022:    {
023:        try
024:        {
025:            File file = new File( "book.xml" );
026:            if( !file.exists() )
027:            {
```

LISTING 25.7   Continued

```
028:                      System.out.println( "Couldn't find file..." );
029:                      return;
030:                  }
031:
032:              // Parse the document
033:              DocumentBuilderFactory factory =
                              DocumentBuilderFactory.newInstance();
034:              DocumentBuilder builder = factory.newDocumentBuilder();
035:              Document document = builder.parse( file );
036:
037:              // Walk the document
038:              Element root = document.getDocumentElement();
039:              System.out.println( "root=" + root.getTagName() );
040:
041:              // List the children of <books>; a set of <book> elements
042:              NodeList list = root.getChildNodes();
043:              for( int i=0; i<list.getLength(); i++ )
044:              {
045:                  Node node = list.item( i );
046:                  if( node.getNodeType() == node.ELEMENT_NODE )
047:                  {
048:              // Found a <book> element
049:              System.out.println( "Handling node: " + node.getNodeName() );
050:              Element element = ( Element )node;
051:              System.out.println( "\tCategory Attribute: " +
                          element.getAttribute( "category" ) );
052:
053:              // Get its children: <author>, <title>, <price>
054:              NodeList childList = element.getChildNodes();
055:                  for( int j=0; j<childList.getLength(); j++ )
056:                  {
057:              // Once we have one of these nodes we need to find its
058:              // text element
059:                      Node childNode = childList.item( j );
060:              if( childNode.getNodeType() == childNode.ELEMENT_NODE )
061:              {
062:                  NodeList childNodeList = childNode.getChildNodes();
063:                  for( int k=0; k<childNodeList.getLength(); k++ )
064:                  {
065:                  Node innerChildNode = childNodeList.item( k );
066:                  System.out.println( "\t\tNode=" +
                                  innerChildNode.getNodeValue() );
067:                  }
068:              }
069:                  }
070:                  }
071:              }
072:          } catch( Exception e )
073:          {
074:              e.printStackTrace();
075:          }
076:      }
077:}
```

Lines 25–30 obtain a reference to the `book.xml` file and verify that it exists.

```
033:             DocumentBuilderFactory factory =
DocumentBuilderFactory.newInstance();
034:             DocumentBuilder builder = factory.newDocumentBuilder();
035:             Document document = builder.parse( file );
```

Lines 33–35 use the `DocumentBuilderFactory` to obtain a `DocumentBuilder`, and then have the `DocumentBuilder` parse the XML file. The return value is an instance a class implementing the `org.w3c.dom.Document` interface.

```
038:             Element root = document.getDocumentElement();
```

Line 38 gets the root element of the document as an `org.w3c.dom.Element`; this is the `<books>` element.

```
042:             NodeList list = root.getChildNodes();
```

Line 42 gets all the child nodes of the `<books>` element; this contains the `<book>` elements as well as a set of empty text elements (which we ignore). The result is an instance of a class implementing the `org.w3c.dom.NodeList` interface. This interface defines two methods, as shown in Table 25.7.

TABLE 25.7   `NodeList` Methods

Method	Description
int getLength()	The number of nodes in the list
Node item(int index)	Returns the item at the "index" zero-based index in the collection

Line 46 takes the node from the child-node list and determines if it is an element node (in this case it is the `<book>` node). If it is then lines 50–51 extract the category attribute.

Lines 53–69 iterate over all the `<book>` nodes children: `<author>`, `<title>`, and `<price>`. Remember that these nodes do not contain the value of the aforementioned tags, but they instead contain text nodes that contain the values, which is extracted in lines 59–67.

As you experiment with the DOM, you will notice that every node that has children also has a set of text nodes containing only white space. The reason for this is that unless the elements in the document do not have spaces between them, the DOM builds a node to hold them. The example carefully avoided printing blank text nodes because it understood the nature of the XML document. The results of this sample application should resemble the following:

```
root=books
Handling node: book
        Category Attribute: fiction
                Node=Left Behind
                Node=Tim Lahaye
                Node=14.95
Handling node: book
```

```
Category Attribute: Computer Programming
        Node=Java 2 From Scratch
        Node=Steven Haines
        Node=39.95
```

Outputting the XML Tree

After all the work involved in parsing through the DOM tree, outputting the DOM tree to a stream is a very simple thing. The DOM implementation of the Element interface in the JAXP has overridden the `toString()` method to display the tree in XML form. Therefore, to display the entire DOM tree to the screen:

```
System.out.println( root );
```

Manipulating the XML Tree

After a DOM tree is constructed in memory, you might want to modify the tree by adding nodes, changing values, or deleting nodes.

Adding an Element to the XML Tree

When adding nodes to a DOM tree recall the internal structure of the DOM tree (refer to Figure 25.2). An element in the DOM tree is a node that is the composition of other nodes, including attribute nodes, text nodes, and other element nodes. Therefore, to add a new `<book>` to the `<books>` root element node, `<author>`, `<title>`, and `<price>` nodes must be created that contain text nodes with their respective values and added to a new `<book>` node.

The Document class offers some helpful methods that create new nodes, see Table 25.8.

TABLE 25.8 Document Node Creation Methods

Method	Description
Attr createAttribute(String name)	Creates an Attr of the given name
CDATASection createCDATASection (String data)	Creates a CDATASection node whose value is the specified string
Comment createComment(String data)	Creates a Comment node given the specified string
DocumentFragment createDocumentFragment()	Creates an empty DocumentFragment object
Element createElement(String tagName)	Creates an element of the type specified
EntityReference createEntityReference(String name)	Creates an EntityReference object

TABLE 25.8   Continued

Method	Description
ProcessingInstruction createProcessingInstruction (String target, String data)	Creates a ProcessingInstruction node given the specified name and data strings
Text createTextNode(String data)	Creates a Text node given the specified string

The Element and Node interfaces offer additional help in document creation through the methods described in Table 25.9.

TABLE 25.9   Element and Node Document Creation Methods

Method	Description
Node appendChild(Node newChild)	Adds the node newChild to the end of the list of children of this node
void setAttribute(String name, String value)	Adds a new attribute
Attr setAttributeNode(Attr newAttr)	Adds a new attribute node

Listing 25.8 shows a sample application that adds a new book to the DOM, and then displays the new document to the standard output.

LISTING 25.8   DOMSample2.java

```
001:import javax.xml.parsers.DocumentBuilder;
002:import javax.xml.parsers.DocumentBuilderFactory;
003:import javax.xml.parsers.FactoryConfigurationError;
004:import javax.xml.parsers.ParserConfigurationException;
005:
006:import org.xml.sax.SAXException;
007:import org.xml.sax.SAXParseException;
008:
009:import java.io.FileInputStream;
010:import java.io.File;
011:import java.io.IOException;
012:
013:import org.w3c.dom.Document;
014:import org.w3c.dom.Element;
015:import org.w3c.dom.NodeList;
016:import org.w3c.dom.Node;
017:import org.w3c.dom.DOMException;
018:import org.w3c.dom.Text;
```

LISTING 25.8   Continued

```
019:
020:public class DOMSample2
021:{
022:    public static void main( String[] args )
023:    {
024:        try
025:        {
026:            File file = new File( "book.xml" );
027:            if( !file.exists() )
028:            {
029:                System.out.println( "Couldn't find file..." );
030:                return;
031:            }
032:
033:            // Parse the document
034:            DocumentBuilderFactory factory =
DocumentBuilderFactory.newInstance();
035:            DocumentBuilder builder = factory.newDocumentBuilder();
036:            Document document = builder.parse( file );
037:
038:            // Get the root of the document
039:            Element root = document.getDocumentElement();
040:
041:        // Build a new book
042:        Element newAuthor = document.createElement( "author" );
043:        Text authorText = document.createTextNode( "Tim Lahaye" );
044:        newAuthor.appendChild( authorText );
045:        Element newTitle = document.createElement( "title" );
046:        Text titleText = document.createTextNode( "Desecration" );
047:        newTitle.appendChild( titleText );
048:        Element newPrice = document.createElement( "price" );
049:        Text priceText = document.createTextNode( "19.95" );
050:        newPrice.appendChild( priceText );
051:        Element newBook = document.createElement( "book" );
052:        newBook.setAttribute( "category", "fiction" );
053:        newBook.appendChild( newAuthor );
054:        newBook.appendChild( newTitle );
055:        newBook.appendChild( newPrice );
056:
057:        // Add the book to the root
058:        root.appendChild( newBook );
059:
060:        // Display the document
061:        System.out.println( root );
062:        } catch( Exception e )
063:        {
064:            e.printStackTrace();
065:        }
066:    }
067:}
```

The output from Listing 25.8 should appear similar to the following:

```
<books>

    <book category="fiction">
        <title>Left Behind</title>
        <author>Tim Lahaye</author>
        <price>14.95</price>
    </book>

    <book category="Computer Programming">
        <title>Java 2 From Scratch</title>
        <author>Steven Haines</author>
        <price>39.95</price>
    </book>

<book category="fiction"><author>Tim
Lahaye</author><title>Desecration</title><price>19.95</price></book></books>
```

Notice that the XML content is correct, but why is the added node formatted so poorly? Remember all those aforementioned text nodes? Without those nodes this is how the output looks.

Removing an Element from the XML Tree

Removing an element from the DOM tree is a simple operation:

1. Obtain a reference to the node to delete

2. Call the Node interface's `removeChild( Node node )` method from the parent node, passing it the child to delete

For example:

```
// Get document root into variable books
// Find the book we are looking for: oldBook
books.removeChild( oldBook );
```

Modifying an Element in the XML Tree

Modifying an element involves retrieving the element and calling one of the Element or Node document modification methods, see Table 25.10.

TABLE 25.10 Element and Node Document Modification Methods

Method	Description
void removeAttribute(String name)	Removes an attribute by name
Attr removeAttributeNode(Attr oldAttr)	Removes the specified attribute node
void setAttribute(String name, String value)	Adds a new attribute

TABLE 25.10   Element and Node Document Modification Methods

Method	Description
`Attr setAttributeNode(Attr newAttr)`	Adds a new attribute node
`void setNodeValue(String nodeValue)`	Sets the value of a node

From the Element interface, there are methods to remove and set attributes and the Node interface offers a method that sets or replaces the value of a node.

XSLT

The XML Style Sheet Language Transformation (XSLT) API is used for transforming an XML document into any other form. The most common use of XSLT for Web development is transforming XML documents into HTML for presentation in a Web browser.

The JAXP defines an XSLT Transformer that reads an XML document and applies the rules specified in a style sheet to it to produce a resultant document. Figure 25.3 shows this graphically.

FIGURE 25.3
XSLT process.

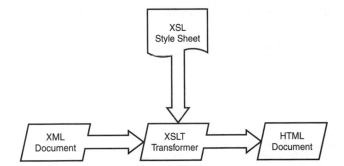

The JAXP provides XSLT support through the `javax.xml.transform` package. The `javax.xml.Transformer` class performs the actual transformation and similar to obtaining a SAX parser or a DOM document builder, a Transformer is obtained through a factory, or more specifically a `javax.xml.TransformerFactory`. An instance of the `TransformerFactory` class can be obtained by calling the `TransformerFactory`'s `newInstance()` method:

```
TransformerFactory factory = TransformerFactory.newInstance();
```

From the `TransformerFactory`, a Transformer can be obtained by calling one of its `newTransformer()` methods, see Table 25.11.

TABLE 25.11 `TransformerFactory newTransformer()` Methods

Method	Description
`Transformer newTransformer()`	Create a new Transformer object that performs a copy of the source to the result.
`Transformer newTransformer (javax.xml.transform.Source source)`	Process the Source into a Transformer object.

The latter of the `newTransformer()` methods is used when transforming an XML document into another form. It accepts a stylesheet in the form of a class implementing the `javax.xml.transform.Source` interface; three classes are provided as sources in the JAXP:

- `javax.xml.transform.SAXSource`

- `javax.xml.transform.DOMSource`

- `javax.xml.transform.StreamSource`

Together these source objects allow a Transformer to be built with an XML stylesheet from an existing DOM document, a SAX parser, or a stream, which includes a file, a `java.io.InputStream`, or a `java.io.Reader`.

The Transformer is then used by calling its `transform()` method to transform a source document to a result document:

```
void transform( Source xmlSource, Result outputTarget )
```

The XML source document is another instance of a class implementing the `javax.xml.transform.Source` interface, which includes SAX, DOM, or Stream inputs) and the output target is an instance of a class implementing the `javax.xml.transform.Result` interface. Similar to the Source interface, the Result interface has three implementations:

- `javax.xml.transform.SAXResult`

- `javax.xml.transform.DOMResult`

- `javax.xml.transform.StreamResult`

The resultant transformation can be in the form of SAX events, a DOM document, or any `java.io.OutputStream`, `java.io.File`, or `java.io.Writer` variation.

To summarize the steps in transforming an XML document to another form using XSLT:

1. Get an instance of the `TransformerFactory` by calling its static `newInstance()` method.

2. Create a `javax.xml.transform.Source` reference to the stylesheet used in the transformation by building a `SAXSource`, `DOMSource`, or `StreamSource`.

3. Get a Transformer from the `TransformerFactory` using the XSL source by calling the `newTransformer()` method.

4. Create a `javax.xml.transform.Source` reference to the source XML document.

5. Create a `javax.xml.transform.Result` reference to the output target.

6. Call the Transformer's `transform()` method.

XSL Stylesheets

The Java code to apply a stylesheet to an XML document to produce an output document is trivial; the real work is in defining the stylesheet. Exhaustive references to XSL and the corresponding XPath specification can be found both in print (see *Special Edition Using XSLT*, by Que Publishing) and on the World Wide Web at `http://www.w3c.org`.

At its core, XSL files contain processing instructions that are organized by XPath expressions; the XSLT processor traverses the source XML document looking for matching XPath expressions defined in the stylesheet. An XSL stylesheet always starts by defining the XSL namespace and version:

```
<xsl:stylesheet version="1.0" xmlns:xsl="http://www.w3.org/1999/XSL/Transform">
```

This header defines the XSL stylesheet language and fully qualifies the `xsl` prefix that will be used later in the document with the qualifying URL:

```
http://www.w3.org/1999/XSL/Transform
```

From this point forward, XSL-specific tags will be represented with the XSL prefix: `<xsl:command>`.

The most common XSL command is the `match` command; this is used to match patterns in the XML file. For example, the following statement matches the root of the XML file:

```
<xsl:template match="/">
  ...
</xsl:template>
```

The statements enclosed between the `<xsl:template>` start and end tags will be written to the result document. Another common tag is the `<xsl:apply-templates>` tag, which tells the XSLT transformer to execute the other template match expressions and place their output at the location of the `<xsl:apply-templates>` tag. For example:

```
<xsl:template match="/">
  <HTML>
    <BODY>
      <table>
        <xsl:apply-templates/>
      </table>
    </BODY>
  </HTML>
</xsl:template>

<xsl:template match="books/book">
  <tr><td>...</td></tr>
</xsl:template>
```

This example creates a new HTML document that contains a table when it sees the root of the XML document. The contents of the table are handled by other patterns, in this case the pattern **books/book**, or in XML terms this looks for all **<book>** tags that appear inside of a **<books>** tag. The **books/book** handler creates table rows and table cells that presumably describe a book. For more information on XPath, XSL, and XSLT fundamentals, please refer to the World Wide Web Consortium Web Site at `http://www.w3c.org`.

An Example Using XSLT

This example transforms the **book.xml** file that we've been working with throughout this chapter and generates an HTML representation of it. The HTML is purposely simple so as not to confuse the technical issues. Listing 25.9 shows the contents of the XSL file that contains the instructions for the transformation, and Listing 25.10 shows the Java code that performs the transformation.

LISTING 25.9   book.xsl

```
001:<xsl:stylesheet version="1.0"
      xmlns:xsl="http://www.w3.org/1999/XSL/Transform">
002:
003:<xsl:template match="/">
004:   <HTML>
005:     <HEAD>
006:       <TITLE>My Books</TITLE>
007:     </HEAD>
008:     <BODY>
009:       <TABLE>
010:         <TR>
011:        <TH>Category</TH>
012:        <TH>Title</TH>
013:          <TH>Author</TH>
014:        <TH>Price</TH>
015:         </TR>
016:         <xsl:apply-templates select="books/book">
017:           <xsl:sort select="@category"/>
018:         </xsl:apply-templates>
019:       </TABLE>
020:     </BODY>
021:   </HTML>
022:</xsl:template>
023:
024:<xsl:template match="books/book">
025:   <TR>
026:     <TD><xsl:value-of select="@category" /></TD>
027:     <TD><xsl:value-of select="./title" /></TD>
028:     <TD><xsl:value-of select="./author" /></TD>
029:     <TD><xsl:value-of select="./price" /></TD>
030:   </TR>
031:</xsl:template>
032:
033:</xsl:stylesheet>
```

Line 1 defines the version of XSL stylesheet that this stylesheet is using and it defines the `xsl` namespace.

Lines 3–22 handle the root element: It creates an HTML document with a table, a table header, and then it delegates the contents of the table to the `books/book` element. The select clause in the `<xsl:apply-template>` tag tells the XSLT transformer what patterns to match; if it is omitted, it matches all patterns. Line 17 tells the transformer to sort the results by the `<book>` element's `category` attribute (the at sign @ denotes category).

Lines 24–31 handle the `<book>` nodes by creating a table record and four table rows. It obtains the value of the category attribute by using the `<xsl:value-of>` tag and passing its select clause `@category` (again the @ means attribute). Similarly, it uses the `<xsl:value-of>` tag passing its select clause of the child nodes to get the title, author, and price.

LISTING 25.10   XSLTTest.java

```
001:import javax.xml.transform.*;
002:import javax.xml.transform.stream.*;
003:import java.io.File;
004:
005:public class XSLTTest
006:{
007:    public static void main( String[] args )
008:    {
009:        try
010:        {
011:            StreamSource source - new StreamSource( new File( "book.xml" ) );
012:            StreamResult result = new StreamResult( System.out );
013:            TransformerFactory factory = TransformerFactory.newInstance();
014:            Transformer transformer = factory.newTransformer(
                    new StreamSource( new File( "books.xsl" ) ) );
015:            transformer.transform( source, result );
016:        }
017:        catch( Exception e )
018:        {
019:            e.printStackTrace();
020:        }
021:    }
022:}
```

Line 11 creates a `StreamSource` to the file `book.xml` and line 12 creates a `StreamResult` to the standard output; this application will transform the `book.xml` file to the screen.

Line 13 obtains a new instance of the `TransformerFactory` and Line 14 uses it to create a new Transformer for the `books.xsl` file (as a StreamSource).

Finally, line 15 transforms the source document to the result (screen). The output should look something like the following:

```
<HTML>
<HEAD>
<META http-equiv="Content-Type" content="text/html; charset=UTF-8">
```

```
<TITLE>My Books</TITLE>
</HEAD>
<BODY>
<TABLE>
<TR>
<TH>Category</TH><TH>Title</TH><TH>Author</TH><TH>Price</TH>
</TR>
<TR>
<TD>Computer Programming</TD><TD>Java 2 From Scratch</TD><TD>Steven
Haines</TD><TD>39.95</TD>
</TR>
<TR>
<TD>fiction</TD><TD>Left Behind</TD><TD>Tim Lahaye</TD><TD>14.95</TD>
</TR>
</TABLE>
</BODY>
</HTML>
```

Manipulation XML Documents Using JDOM

As a Java-centric alternative to SAX and DOM, JDOM was developed. JDOM was designed with the following philosophy (taken from www.jdom.org):

- JDOM should be straightforward for Java programmers

- JDOM should support easy and efficient document modification

- JDOM should hide the complexities of XML wherever possible, while remaining true to the XML specification

- JDOM should integrate with DOM and SAX

- JDOM should be lightweight and fast

- JDOM should solve 80% (or more) of Java/XML problems with 20% (or less) of the effort

After using JDOM for the last 18+ months I have to say I think the JDOM programmers have met these requirements. Being Java programmers, we are very familiar with using Java's Collections API. All throughout Java's class libraries and components the underlying data structures are all members of Java's collections API. Because of this intimate familiarity it is only natural that we should deal with XML data similarly. The creators of JDOM understood this and, thus, created a collections API-based representation of XML data.

JDOM uses the SAX parser that yields the best performance when reading documents and uses far less memory-representing data than the DOM because of the difference between the DOM overhead and the Collections API overhead. Because JDOM does hold all the XML data in memory, it is not ideal for all purposes; in some business-to-business XML transactions the sheer amount of data requires that you use SAX to avoid keeping all the data in memory.

The core functionality of the JDOM API is provided in three packages, each with a distinct purpose:

- `org.jdom`: Classes to manage and create XML documents

- `org.jdom.input`: Classes to read XML documents

- `org.jdom.output`: Classes to write XML documents

Reading an XML Document

The first step in reading an XML document using JDOM is parsing the document. JDOM provides the `org.jdom.input.SAXBuilder` class to parse XML documents.

TABLE 25.12   `org.jdom.input.SAXBuilder` Constructors

Constructor	Description
SAXBuilder()	Creates a new SAXBuilder that will attempt to first locate a parser via JAXP, then will try to use a set of default SAX Drivers.
SAXBuilder(boolean validate)	Creates a new SAXBuilder that will attempt to first locate a parser via JAXP, then will try to use a set of default SAX Drivers.
SAXBuilder(java.lang. String saxDriverClass)	Creates a new SAXBuilder using the specified SAX parser.
SAXBuilder(java.lang.String saxDriverClass, boolean validate)	Creates a new SAXBuilder using the specified SAX parser.

Table 25.12 shows two variations of constructors: one that does not validate and one that gives to you the option to validate. If you have a SAX parser that you want to use you can specify it; otherwise, one is provided for you.

Table 25.13 shows some of more useful methods of the SAXBuilder class.

TABLE 25.13   `org.jdom.input.SAXBuilder` Methods

Method	Description
Document build(java.io.File file)	This builds a document from the supplied filename.
Document build (org.xml.sax.InputSource in)	This builds a document from the supplied input source.
Document build(java.io.InputStream in)	This builds a document from the supplied input stream.

TABLE 25.13   Continued

Method	Description
`Document build(java.io.InputStream in, java.lang.String systemId)`	This builds a document from the supplied input stream.
`Document build (java.io.Reader characterStream)`	This builds a document from the supplied Reader.
`Document build(java.io.Reader characterStream, java.lang. String SystemId)`	This builds a document from the supplied Reader.
`Document build(java.lang. String systemId)`	This builds a document from the supplied URI.
`Document build(java.net.URL url)`	This builds a document from the supplied URL.
`void setValidation(boolean validate)`	This sets validation for the builder.

From Table 25.13 you can see that the `SAXBuilder` class has a plethora of `build()` methods that can build an XML document from almost any source. The class also provides a `setValidation()` method that enables you to modify the validation mode.

The `build()` method returns an `org.jdom.Document` instance. The `Document` class represents the XML document; its constructors are shown in Table 25.14, and its methods are shown in Table 25.15.

TABLE 25.14   `org.jdom.Document` Constructors

Constructor	Description
`Document()`	Creates a new empty document.
`Document(Element rootElement)`	This will create a new Document, with the supplied Element as the root element, and no `DocType` declaration.
`Document(Element rootElement, DocType docType)`	This will create a new Document, with the supplied Element as the root element and the supplied `DocType` declaration.
`Document (java.util.List content)`	This will create a new Document, with the supplied list of content, and no `DocType` declaration.
`Document(java.util.List newContent, DocType docType)`	This will create a new Document, with the supplied list of content, and the supplied `DocType` declaration.

TABLE 25.15 `org.jdom.Document` Methods

Method	Description
`DocType getDocType()`	This will return the `DocType` declaration for this Document, or null if none exists.
`Element getRootElement()`	This will return the root Element for this Document.
`boolean hasRootElement()`	This will return true if this document has a root element, false otherwise.
`Document setContent` `(java.util.List newContent)`	This sets the content of the Document.
`Document setDocType(DocType docType)`	This will set the DocType declaration for this Document.
`Document setRootElement` `(Element rootElement)`	This sets the root Element for the Document.

The `Document` constructors in Table 25.14 enable you to create a new XML document from an `org.jdom.Element` object, and its methods in Table 25.15 enable you to modify the `Document` and obtain the `Element`. The `org.jdom.Element` object is the core of the JDOM API; its constructors are shown in Table 25.16, and its methods are shown in Table 25.17.

TABLE 25.16 `org.jdom.Element` Constructors

Constructor	Description
`Element(java.lang.String name)`	This will create an Element in no Namespace.
`Element(java.lang.String name,` `Namespace namespace)`	This will create a new Element with the supplied (local) name, and define the Namespace to be used.
`Element(java.lang.String name,` `java.lang.String uri)`	This will create a new Element with the supplied (local) name, and specifies the URI of the Namespace the Element should be in, resulting it being unprefixed (in the default namespace).

`Element(java.lang.String name,`
`java.lang.String prefix,`
`java.lang.String uri)`
	This will create a new Element with the supplied (local) name, and specifies the prefix and URI of the Namespace the Element should be in.

TABLE 25.17   `org.jdom.Element` Methods

Method	Description
`Attribute getAttribute(String name)`	This returns the attribute for this element with the given name or null if no such attribute exists.
`java.util.List getAttributes()`	This returns the complete set of attributes for this element, as a List of Attribute objects in no particular order, or an empty list if there are none.
`String getAttributeValue(String name)`	This returns the attribute value for the attribute with the given name, null if there is no such attribute, and the empty string if the attribute value is empty.
`Element getChild(String name)`	This returns the first child element within this element with the given local name
`java.util.List getChildren()`	This returns a List of all the child elements nested directly (one level deep) within this element, as Element objects.
`java.util.List getChildren(String name)`	This returns a List of all the child elements nested directly (one level deep) within this element with the given local name returned as Element objects.
`String getChildText(String name)`	This convenience method returns the textual content of the named child element, or returns an empty String ("") if the child has no textual content.
`String getChildTextTrim(String name)`	This convenience method returns the trimmed textual content of the named child element, or returns null if there's no such child.
`java.util.List getContent()`	This returns the full content of the element as a List that might contain objects of type Text, Element, Comment, ProcessingInstruction, CDATA, and EntityRef.
`Document getDocument()`	This retrieves the owning Document for this Element, or null if not currently a member of a Document.
`String getText()`	This returns the textual content directly held under this element.
`String getTextTrim()`	This returns the textual content of this element with all surrounding whitespace removed.
`boolean hasChildren()`	Test whether this element has a child element.
`boolean isRootElement()`	This returns a Boolean value indicating whether this Element is a root Element for a JDOM Document.

TABLE 25.17 `org.jdom.Element` Methods

Method	Description
`boolean removeAttribute` `(Attribute attribute)`	This removes the supplied Attribute should it exist.
`boolean removeAttribute(String name)`	This removes the attribute with the given name
`boolean removeChild(String name)`	This removes the first child element (one level deep) with the given local name
`boolean removeChildren()`	This removes all child elements.
`boolean removeChildren(String name)`	This removes all child elements (one level deep) with the given local name
`Element setAttribute` `(Attribute attribute)`	This sets an attribute value for this element.
`Element setAttribute` `(String name, String value)`	This sets an attribute value for this element.
`Element setAttributes` `(java.util.List newAttributes)`	This sets the attributes of the element.
`Element setName(String name)`	This sets the (local) name of the element.
`Element setText(String text)`	This sets the content of the element to be the text given.

The main components of XML nodes are

- Node name
- Node attributes
- Node text
- Node children

From Table 25.17 you can modify any of these values. Pay particular attention to the use of Collections classes, such as the `List` returned by `getChildren()`. Refer to www.jdom.org for more detailed information.

To summarize the steps in reading an XML document:

1. Create a parser.
2. Parse the document and obtain a `Document` object.
3. Get the root `Element` of the `Document` by calling the `getRootElement` method.
4. Use the `Element` methods to read through the document.

In code that is

```
SAXBuilder builder = new SAXBuilder();
Document doc = builder.build( "book.xml" );
Element root = doc.getRootElement();
List books = root.getChildren( "book" );
for( Iterator i=books.iterator(); i.hasNext(); ) {
  Element book = ( Element )i.next();
  System.out.println( "Book: " + book.getAttributeValue( "category" ) + ", " +
                      book.getChildTextTrim( "title" ) + ", " +
                      book.getChildTextTrim( "author" ) + ", " +
                      book.getChildTextTrim( "price" ) );
}
```

This code snippet reads through the book.xml file and displays all its books.

JDOM Example

The following example shows how to open an XML document, parse it, display its contents to the screen, modify its contents, and then display the complete XML document. See Listing 25.11.

LISTING 25.11   JDOMTest.java

```
import org.jdom.*;
import org.jdom.input.*;
import org.jdom.output.*;

import java.util.*;
import java.io.*;

public class JDOMTest {

  public static void showBooks( Element root ) {
      List books = root.getChildren( "book" );
      for( Iterator i=books.iterator(); i.hasNext(); ) {
        Element book = ( Element )i.next();
        System.out.println( "Book: " + book.getAttributeValue(
                            "category" ) + ", " +
                            book.getChildTextTrim( "title" ) + ", " +
                            book.getChildTextTrim( "author" ) + ", " +
                            book.getChildTextTrim( "price" ) );
      }
  }

  public static void main( String[] args ) {
    try {
      SAXBuilder builder = new SAXBuilder();
      Document doc = builder.build( "book.xml" );
```

LISTING 25.11   Continued

```java
            Element root = doc.getRootElement();
            System.out.println( "Book List Before: " );
            showBooks( root );

            // Add a new book
            Element newBook = new Element( "book" );
            newBook.setAttribute( "category", "fiction" );
            Element newTitle = new Element( "title" );
            newTitle.addContent( "Desecration" );
            Element newAuthor = new Element( "author" );
            newAuthor.addContent( "Tim LaHaye" );
            Element newPrice = new Element( "price" );
            newPrice.addContent( "19.95" );
            newBook.addContent( newTitle );
            newBook.addContent( newAuthor );
            newBook.addContent( newPrice );
            root.addContent( newBook );

            System.out.println( "Book List After: " );
            showBooks( root );

            XMLOutputter out = new XMLOutputter( "  ", true );
            out.output( root, System.out );

        }
        catch( Exception e ) {
            e.printStackTrace();
        }
    }
}
```

Listing 25.11 shows the code for the `JDOMTest.java` class. It uses the `SAXBuilder` class to open the *book.xml* file, parse it, get a `Document`, and the get the root of the document.

Next the program calls the `showBooks()` method that traverses through the contents of the root `Element` and displays all `book` elements.

It then creates a new `book Element` and adds it to the root element by calling the `addContent()` method. After a subsequent call to `showBooks()`, it displays the contents of the XML file using the `org.jdom.output.XMLOutputter` class. This class has various `output()` methods that write out a JDOM object to an `OutputStream` or `Writer`.

Table 25.18 shows the constructors for the `XMLOutputter` class and Table 25.19 shows some of its useful methods.

TABLE 25.18   `org.jdom.output.XMLOutputter` Constructors

Constructor	Description
`XMLOutputter()`	This will create an `XMLOutputter` with no additional whitespace (indent or newlines) added; the whitespace from the element text content is fully preserved.
`XMLOutputter (java.lang.String indent)`	This will create an `XMLOutputter` with the given indent added, but no new lines added; all whitespace from the element text content is included as well.
`XMLOutputter(java.lang. String indent, boolean newlines)`	This will create an `XMLOutputter` with the given indent that prints newlines only if newlines is true; all whitespace from the element text content is included as well.
`XMLOutputter(java.lang. String indent, boolean newlines, java.lang.String encoding)`	This will create an XMLOutputter with the given indent and new lines printing only if newlines is true, and encoding format encoding.
`XMLOutputter(XMLOutputter that)`	This will create an `XMLOutputter` with all the options as set in the given `XMLOutputter`.

TABLE 25.19   `org.jdom.Element` Methods

Method	Description
`void output(Document doc, java.io.OutputStream out)`	This will print the Document to the given output stream.
`void output(Document doc, java.io.Writer out)`	This will print the Document to the given Writer.
`void output(Element element, java.io.OutputStream out)`	Print out an Element, including its Attributes, and all contained (child) elements, and so on.
`void output(Element element, java.io.Writer out)`	Print out an Element, including its Attributes, and all contained (child) elements, and so on.

This section gave a good overview and introduction to using JDOM, but I would strongly encourage you to download it from the Web site and try using it in your own projects.

Summary

This chapter discussed the Java API for XML Parsing (JAXP) as well as the open source JDOM API. The JAXP provides two models for reading XML documents: Simple API for XML (SAX) parser and the Document Object Model (DOM). The SAX parser is event-driven, and the DOM maintains an in-memory tree representation of the XML document. Each has its advantages, depending on the application being developed. This chapter discussed the XML Stylesheet Language Transformation (XSLT) API that is used for transforming an XML document into any form; in Web applications the most dominant use for XSLT is the transformation of XML data into an HTML presentation. Finally, this chapter discussed the JDOM API and provided a sample program to get you started.

Review Questions

1. Why is XML a good choice for transferring data between operating systems and programming languages?

2. What is the difference between SAX and DOM?

3. Which implementation parses documents faster, SAX or DOM?

4. Does a SAX parser maintain an entire XML document in memory?

5. When would you be forced to use SAX over DOM?

6. What is XSLT?

7. Describe the purpose of a style sheet.

8. Why is JDOM intuitive to Java programmer?

9. How do you read an XML document using JDOM?

10. How do you print an XML document to the screen using JDOM?

Exercises

1. Following the book DTD in this chapter, create a 100 record XML file and compare the performance of using SAX, DOM, and JDOM (hint: parse the document with each, recording the start time and end time, and compare them). Your tests should involve reading the document and displaying each book title and author on a single line to the standard output.

2. Advanced: Do the same thing using a stylesheet and XSLT.

CHAPTER 26

WEB ARCHITECTURE

You will learn about the following in this chapter:

- How Web sites are organized

- Common pitfalls in Web site design

- How Web sites are designed with servlets

- How Web sites are designed with JavaServer pages

- How Web sites are designed with Enterprise JavaBeans (EJB)

- How Web sites are designed with Web services

*I*nternet access is considered to be a vital tool in the toolbox of the modern-knowledge worker. Many of us spend a portion of every day using a browser to access Web sites that may be internal to our company or external. We post project status, download software, order supplies, make airline reservations, find articles about new technology, check on the activities of the competition, and so on.

One of the miracles of the Web is that it doesn't matter to us, as users, whether Microsoft Internet Information Server (IIS) or Apache Tomcat powered the Web site that we just accessed. It also makes no difference whether the language that was used to program the site was Java or CGI, and it makes no difference whether Compaq or Sun Microsystems made the server. We also don't care whether the Web site is a well-organized set of programming layers and elements, or a monolithic mass of confusion. The only thing that we care about is whether we were able to book the flight or access the documents that we needed.

As programmers of Web sites, however, we cannot afford to be so cavalier about the design of our sites The choice of server, language, and architecture can seriously impact the cost of creating the site, and the satisfaction that the users are able to derive from it.

In this chapter, we will look at how Web sites have been architected in the past, how they are currently being built, and how they will likely be built in the future. We will start off by covering the basics of how Web sites work. Following that, we will look at the most important ways to measure the "goodness" of a design. Finally, we will cover the most common architectural approaches used in site design.

Organizing a Web Site

The modern, interactive, full-color Web site is really just a milepost in a long list of computer interconnection technologies. It was not the first technology used to connect computers and it won't be the last.

In the earliest days of computing, circa 1955, computers were huge, single program devices that were used to crunch large numbers or manipulate large amounts of text data. The only network available in those days was the proverbial "SneakerNet," where a programmer or graduate student would output data to a tape drive, remove the reel and walk to the site of the second computer and mount the tape on a drive connect to this computer. It didn't take long for programmers and researchers to become dissatisfied with this approach.

In the early 1960s, the Advanced Research Projects Agency (ARPA) started a project with the purpose of finding a way to connect these mainframe computers so that data could be shared between them.

ARPA's first step was to create the hardware necessary to transfer electrical signals from one end of the computer to the other. The second step was to create the software that sits on each computer and controls the flow and interpretation of the data from the other machine. The result of this research effort was the TCP/IP protocol. In the early days TCP/IP was only one of several popular protocols. Because it was developed by a research project instead of by a company, there was no license fee for using it. That factor, combined with the fact that the fee-based technologies were not that much better, led to its near-universal adoption in the decades that followed.

The TCP/IP Level of the Web Site

All the technologies that we will describe in this chapter run on top of TCP/IP. That is to say that the other programs contain calls to the TCP/IP application-programming interface (API) somewhere in the lower layers of their systems. The reason for this is that every computer that runs TCP/IP software can communicate with every other computer that runs this software.

TCP/IP is not really a protocol, but rather a suite consisting of dozens of protocols. It is named for two of the most important protocols, Transmission Control Protocol (TCP) and the Internet Protocol (IP). TCP/IP is composed of four layers:

- Application layer—This layer can be a simple chat program or a complete online store such as Amazon.com. It conducts its business by making calls to transport a layer's API.

- Transport layer—This layer sends chunks of data from one computer to another with guaranteed delivery by making calls to the internetwork layer's API.

- Internetwork layer—This layer breaks the chunks of data into small pieces called datagrams and sends them to the other computer by calling the network access layer's API.

- Network access layer—This layer controls the hardware that sends bits and bytes to other computers.

The layers were created to separate low-level functionality from higher-level functionality. This organization of functions enables you to remove a product that provides one layer and replace it with one that performs better, is easier to use, and so on. Figure 26.1 shows an illustration of this interaction between layers.

FIGURE 26.1
The various layers in the TCP/IP protocol work together to provide reliable intercomputer communications.

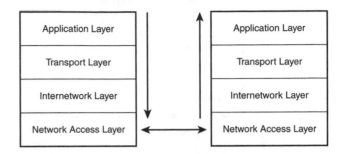

Each layer calls the API of the layer beneath it to make requests for service. The end result is reliable communication between two computers.

The TCP and IP protocols take care of the movement of the data from one computer to the next. When the data gets there, however, the application layer must take over and process the data. A key part of that processing is the HTTP protocol, which is covered in the next section.

Hypertext Transport Protocol (HTTP)

A *protocol* is simply a published agreement between clients and servers that specifies what data will be passed from one party to the other and what syntax it will be in.

HTTP is an application layer protocol, which means that it depends on lower-layer protocols to do much of the work. In the case of HTTP, this lower-layer protocol is TCP/IP. The information in HTTP is transferred as plain ASCII characters. This is convenient for programmers because the instructions are human-readable, making debugging easier.

HTTP is a request and response protocol. This means that it is composed of pairs of requests and responses. Each of the request-and-response pairs is independent of every other pair. This kind of communication is called connectionless. If you want to string together requests to form a larger transaction, you must do this yourself in the programs that you write; HTTP will not do it for you. Figure 26.2 shows where HTTP fits into the layer diagram that we drew in Figure 26.1.

The format of the HTTP request is a plain-text message. The server reads the message and performs the task that it has been instructed to perform in the message. In some cases, this task is to retrieve a static document and send it back to the client's browser for display; but in other cases, this request is for a servlet to be run. The results of this transaction, if any, are sent to the client.

FIGURE 26.2
The HTTP protocol runs as a sublayer in the application layer.

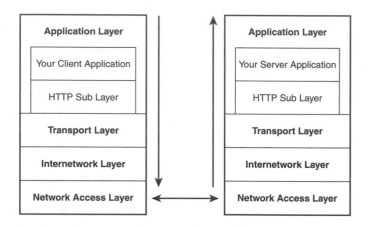

The Browser

On the left side of the Figure 26.2, you see a sublayer that is labeled "Your Client Application." In most cases, this client application is a browser. A browser is a piece of software that performs an amazing range of tasks. First, it is an HTTP application, meaning that it creates messages in that protocol for transmission to a Web server. In addition, it contains an HTTP parser that takes the messages that are returned by the Web server and translates them into a display that is pleasant, hopefully, to the human eye. This translation might require that a `.jpg` image be rendered, HTML be translated into text, XML parsed and Java Applets run, and so on.

The fact that the browser is normally a free download, or available as part of the operating system installation pack obscures the fact that it is really a sophisticated piece of software.

The Web Server

On the right side of Figure 27.2, you see a box labeled "Your Server Application." In the majority of installations, that server application is a piece of software known as the Web server. Web servers are also HTTP applications in that they both parse requests formatted in HTTP and respond by creating messages in HTTP format.

Originally, the job of the Web server was to locate documents and send them back to the requesting client computer in HTTP format. The Web servers were enhanced to add the capability to process CGI, Perl, and a host of other niche languages that composed the first generation of Web programming languages.

The modern Web server has a much more complicated task to perform. In addition to handing static documents to the client and running scripts, the Web server has to be able to call servlets, translate JSPs into servlets, and call enterprise JavaBeans (EJB). Figure 26.3 shows a newer version of Figure 26.2, which shows the browser and the Web server in the application layer.

FIGURE 26.3
The Browser and the Web server are both HTTP applications.

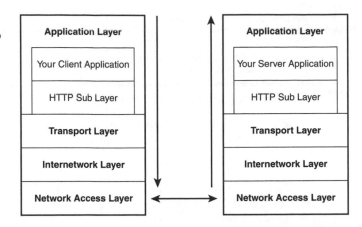

The client and the server applications are heavily dependent on the browser and the Web server's support mechanisms to run.

The Application

On the client side, the top sublayer in the application layer is unique in that it is almost always composed of an application that was downloaded from the Web server. These applications range from the simplest static HTML file to a complex Java applet. In addition, the availability of JavaScript parsers in the browsers adds the capability of doing some Java-like computing outside of the applets as well.

In reality, the amount of applet processing that a browser performs is dwarfed by the amount of HTML, both static and dynamic, that it processes. The source of the static HTML is far from constant because every server-side, application-building programming language communicates the results to the browser that made the request using HTML and HTTP. Thus, from the server side, almost every Web site seems to send it HTML.

The top sublayer in the server side is far more complex than its counterpart on the client side. There is a seemingly endless variety of programming languages that can be called by a Web server. In this chapter, we will limit our discussion to the Java varieties: JavaServer Pages (JSP), Servlets, Enterprise JavaBeans, and Web services.

Pitfalls in Web Design

Some of the pitfalls that exist in Web design are ever present, regardless of the technology used. It is this group of problems that we want to examine in this section.

There are a number of measures of "badness" that are valuable whenever we discuss software. Web design software is no exception to this rule. This list follows:

- Poor performance—Users want to receive quick responses when they interact with your Web site.

- Low availability—If your site is down too much, users will stop coming to it.

- Lack of scalability—As a business grows, it needs to be able to easily expand the volume of transactions per hour that it can handle.

- Hard to maintain—Change is inevitable. All businesses change over time and, therefore, need to update the software that runs the Web site.

- Expensive to develop—Almost no one has an unlimited budget.

- Hard to learn—Programmers must be somehow induced to work on your system if you want to keep it up to date. Obscure languages and bizarre architectures make programmers reluctant to work on a system. Just because a technology is used for Web development does not mean that the programmers you want to hire will be willing to work on it.

If attacked individually, this list might overwhelm all but the bravest of programmers. Fortunately, there is an architecture that can be applied to any Java-based Web design that will address all these problems: the Model-View-Controller (MVC) architecture.

The Model-View-Controller (MVC) Architecture

The MVC architecture is not a new design pattern that was invented to create Web sites. In fact, this architecture has been often discussed, if rarely implemented, since the early days of object-oriented programming.

The concept that underlies the architecture is the simple divide-and-conquer approach. It seems to be human nature to create giant, monolithic programs that perform every task under the sun. Less obvious, but more useful is the concept of layers where a system is subdivided into smaller functional units. Each layer is given a specific, but limited, set of tasks to perform. This approach is not unlike the division of labor principle that became popular during the industrial revolution, where workers are given a specific job to perform, instead of having everyone do every job in the plant.

In the MVC architecture, a system's tasks are subdivided into three layers:

- The Model—All the data, as well as the code that stores and retrieves it, is located in this layer.

- The View—All the processing that is concerned with appearance such as fonts, colors, and animation are handled by this layer.

- The Controller—The rest of the code goes here. This layer normally contains the logic of a program. For example, a Web site's user interface might enable you to type a price of $5000 for a new car, and the database of current inventory might contain one of these cars. But the business rules state that a car cannot be listed for less than its cost, so the controller layer generates an error message that rejects the input on business rule grounds.

The effect of this subdivision can be very positive on the behavior of your system:

- Performance—Separating your system into three logical parts enables you to measure and tune the performance of each independently. In addition, you have the option to move one or more parts to a dedicated server if necessary.

- High Availability—The separation of layers allows for unit testing to be performed. This results in fewer errors that occur during the initial days after going into production.

- Scalability—The controller and model module can be a very complex piece of code. By separating out this piece, you have made it possible to implement it as servlets or EJBs, both of which scale nicely.

- Maintainability—It is much easier to work on a small system than a large one. By dividing the system into three pieces, we gain an advantage when we go to make changes or to replace one piece. It is much easier to comprehend one logical part and make the changes correctly.

- Affordability—It is easier to track the progress and make changes to three smaller systems than one giant one.

- Learnability—The learning curve that must be traversed is cut into three parts, allowing a new person to be productive on one of the parts quickly. In addition, if the technology that was used to create one of the parts is superceded by a superior approach, that part can be replaced without much impact on the others. This reduces the chances that you will be stuck supporting a technology that the programmers hate to work on.

The level of compliance to this model varies from technology to technology. Some of the approaches in this book provide a clear separation between layers, whereas others leave the task of separation into layers to the programmer.

Servlets

The original server-side Java technology is called servlets. The name comes from a play on the word applet. Because the word means little application, it was reasoned that the word servlet would mean little server application. Strictly speaking, the name is not exactly correct because servlets can be huge. The name is convenient and useful, however, because it gives us a unique name that cannot be confused with other technical terms.

Servlets are not really programs in their own right. They cannot be run from a command line because they contain no `main()` method. They are intended to be run from a special piece of software called the servlet container. This container used to be a separate container from the Web server itself and required a separate download. Recent releases of Web server software have included the servlet engine in the base product.

The servlet container has several responsibilities:

- Loads the servlet when it is requested.

- Loads additional instances of the servlet in response to increased demand.

- Unloads servlets and copies of servlets when demand falls.

- Calls the servlet's entry point causing execution to begin.

- Receives the output from the servlet and hands it over to the Web server to be sent to the requesting client.

Servlets can be called by placing a URL in a browser's address bar as shown here:

```
http://localhost/examples/servlet/GenericHello
```

The `http` prefix tells the Web server that we want to communicate using the http protocol. The word `localhost` is the name of computer that we want to connect to. The `examples/servlet/GenericHello` tells the Web server which servlet you want to run. The physical location on disk where you place servlets that you want to make runnable varies from one Web server to anther. For example, on Apache Tomcat, the physical location of this servlet's class file is

```
C:\Program Files\Apache Tomcat 4.0\Web apps\examples\WEB -INF\classes
```

As you can see, the actual location of the class file is not easily discerned by looking at the URL used to call it. To complicate matters further, each Web server vendor seems to have different ideas about how the mapping between the logical location shown in the URL and the physical location of the servlet's class files in the server's file system.

Figure 26.4 shows the inclusion of the servlet engine in the layered software diagram of the server.

Notice that the Servlet Engine is not an HTTP application. It uses the Web server to communicate with the client. There is a call level interface between the servlet engine and the Web server software.

Calling one simple servlet from a browser is a fairly easy task. How would someone go about creating a servlet that follows the Model-View-Controller architecture, though? To do this, separate servlets are used for different parts of the application.

This servlet normally displays a welcome of some sort, and then gives the user a choice of functions to perform. When the user clicks one of these HTML buttons, a second servlet is called, which causes a screen or form to be displayed. (This form might contain JavaScript code to do browser-level error checking.) These two servlets constitute part of the View portion of this system.

FIGURE 26.4

The Web server calls the Servlet Engine.

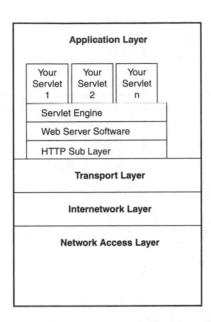

When a user fills out the form on the second screen and clicks a submit button, a third servlet is called, which applies business logic to answer questions like these:

- Is this user allowed to purchase this item?

- Do we extend credit to this user?

- Is this credit-card number valid?

- Do we have this item in the warehouse?

Notice that none of these tasks places HTML on the screen; therefore, the servlet or servlets that answer these questions are part of the Controller portion of the system. In addition, the servlets themselves might make calls to other classes to do this work. In that case, the servlets and the other classes would, as a group, be called the Controller.

The servlets in the Controller portion of the system might determine the appropriateness of the request by using logic alone, but more than likely some external data would be required. This external data could be stored in a flat file or in a database. Normally, a Controller servlet doesn't access a database directly because of our desire to provide a division of labor. The preferred approach to performing database access is to place all database access code in a regular Java class in the Model layer. The Controller servlet can then instantiate this database-centric class that contains the JDBC code. Figure 26.5 shows how this architecture looks.

Notice that each layer except the View has regular Java classes in it. Servlets can become complicated very quickly if you try to do all the processing inside of them. The strongest feature of servlets is that they can be called from a browser on the client's computer. Many system designers move as much logic as possible into regular Java classes. These classes are easier to debug because they are just ordinary Java classes. If you add a `main()` method that instantiates the class and calls the methods, you can debug the class before ever calling it from a servlet.

FIGURE 26.5
By combining servlets with regular Java classes, we can implement a system that is faithful to the MVC architecture.

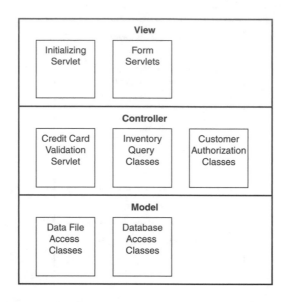

JavaServer Pages (JSP)

JSPs are text files filled with standard HTML code that is interspersed with nuggets of Java code. All this code, both the JSP and the nuggets of Java code, are interpreted by a JSP translator and turned into 100% Java code, along with any HTML that is found in the file. This architecture provides a script language (JSP) that integrates well with the Java VM, but that is simple enough to be learned by anyone capable of writing HTML well.

The JSP page is translated into a servlet prior to being run. The servlet's outputs are HTML statements, so authoring JSP pages can be thought of as a fancy form of HTML authoring, with the additional option of adding programming logic.

JavaServer Pages technology was created in response to complaints that creating HTML in servlets was too tedious and unnecessarily complicated. This complication kept Web site designers away from Java for many of their applications because they considered the learning curve associated with Java servlets to be too steep.

One of the drawbacks of JSP technology is that JSP pages can become very difficult to debug and maintain if they contain too much Java. As a result, JSPs are heavily used in creating the View layer, but not often used for heavy Java logic. That kind of logic is better suited for normal Java classes called from the JSP or for Custom Tags, the implementation of which is done in Java classes. In either case, the JSPs provide View, and Java classes provide the Controller and the Model. Figure 26.6 shows this approach.

Notice that the JSP translator never interacts directly with the Web Server except to receive a request. The requested file is translated into a servlet before it can be run. The organization of the Model-View-Controller architecture is a little different with the JSPs because of the addition of Custom Tag Libraries to the picture. Figure 26.7 shows this new arrangement.

FIGURE 26.6
JSPs are converted into servlets before they are run by a piece of software called the JSP translator.

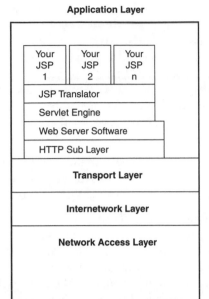

Application Layer

Your JSP 1

Your JSP 2

Your JSP n

JSP Translator

Servlet Engine

Web Server Software

HTTP Sub Layer

Transport Layer

Internetwork Layer

Network Access Layer

FIGURE 26.7
By combining JSPs with regular Java classes and custom tags, we can implement a system that is faithful to the MVC architecture.

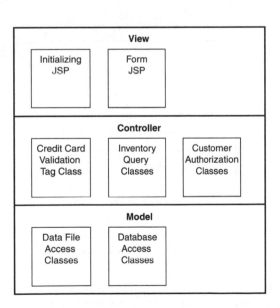

View

Initializing JSP

Form JSP

Controller

Credit Card Validation Tag Class

Inventory Query Classes

Customer Authorization Classes

Model

Data File Access Classes

Database Access Classes

Notice that there are no servlets in the picture. The servlets appear behind the scenes, but no servlet programming is required. The controller is composed of custom tags and ordinary Java classes. The Model layer is unchanged between the JSP approach and the servlet approach.

JavaScript

JavaScript is a Java-like language that runs inside the browser on the client's computer. Because JavaScript doesn't have access to the data that is stored on the server, it is limited in the types of chores that it can do for us. One task that JavaScript excels in is simple data validation. This validation is composed of two types. The first is the traditional validation, where the script is able to determine that you have entered in a wrong number or letter in an input field. The second validation approach is to place only valid choices in a list box or check boxes so that it is physically impossible for the user to enter data that is not valid.

JavaScript code is transported via HTTP along with the rest of the Web page's HTML. When the browser loads the page into memory, it notices the existence of JavaScript calls in the HTML and creates branching operations so that the Web page behaves correctly.

Because the JavaScript code is uncompiled, it can be sent as plain text, which means that it can be generated dynamically by a servlet or JSP. This provides a powerful addition, but not a substitute for, other technologies like servlets and JSP. The primary advantage of JavaScript is in the performance of the system. The ability to do some validation on the browser relieves the network of some traffic and offloads your server, too. The end result is a net speed increase from the user's point of view and a reduced cost of operation for the server. Figure 27.8 shows the software layers on the client side with JavaScript enabled.

FIGURE 26.8
JavaScript provides programming logic that runs in the browser.

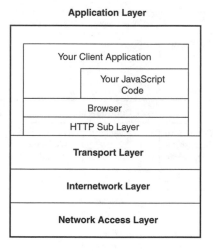

The existence of JavaScript doesn't change the layout of the server-side, however, because either servlets or JSPs can generate HTML that contains JavaScript.

Enterprise JavaBeans

The combination of HTML, JSP, JavaScript and servlets provides a number of quality options for communicating with a user's browser. This approach provides us with many of the benefits of a traditional LAN-based client/server system without the expense and limitations. This puts the View layer of our architecture in pretty good shape.

In the Controller layer, things can be improved beyond what we have explained thus far. We stated earlier in this chapter that often, Java classes are better suited for the logic that is needed by the Controller and the Model layers than either servlets or JSPs. What is the best form for these classes to take?

If an application lists scalability as a primary requirement, it is a candidate for the use of Enterprise JavaBeans (EJB). EJBs are classes that have been created according to a fairly strict pattern. They are not instantiated directly by other classes and servlets. EJBs reside in special pieces of software called Application Servers, or EJB Containers. They are instantiated by making a request to the container for an EJB to be instantiated.

These servers provide a variety of services for the classes that they host.

- Life-cycle Management—The EJB container is responsible for creating and destroying instances of your class (called an EJB), based on the demand.

- Availability—Some EJB containers can be clustered so that they can provide near 100% availability by redirecting a request to a different container if the first container is unable to respond.

- Reliability—EJB containers are capable of handling most errors without closing the container. They can retry a request that did not complete.

- Security—EJB containers can provide authorization as well as encryption/decryption services.

- Transaction Support—EJB transaction is managed at the container level, enabling you to create multi-EJB transactions.

- Distribution Services—EJB can call other EJBs, even when they are located on another server.

- Threading—EJBs run in their own threads automatically.

- Persistence—EJBs can be written so that they automatically update a database when they are changed.

There are two varieties of EJBs, Session Beans and Entity Beans. Session Beans are expected to maintain state for only one session or instantiation. Entity Beans represent databases and they are expected to maintain state across multiple sessions just like a database does.

The downside to the EJB architecture is the cost. Instead of being a free download from a vendor, you normally purchase the container. Prices vary, but it is not unusual to spend thousands or tens of thousands of dollars on license fees. By the time you pay for training, you have a sizeable amount of money invested. This investment is recouped in both the development and testing phase, however. Development is faster because the container provides so many of the programming tasks. Testing is easier because there is less code to test. Figure 26.9 shows the effect of developing with EJBs on the MVC architecture diagram.

FIGURE 26.9
EJBs occupy both the
Controller layer and the
Model layer of the MVC
architecture.

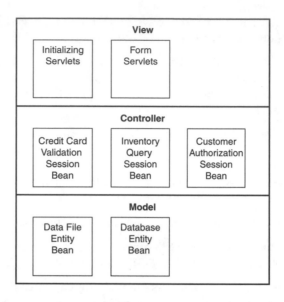

The use of EJBs instead of ordinary Java classes in the Controller and Model layers of the MVC architecture can improve your system in many ways. The cost/benefit analysis only works for fairly large systems that have a strong scalability requirement.

Web Services

The newest addition to the Web architecture field is called the Web service, or more commonly, Web services. Web services differ from other Web applications in that they normally expect to be called by another program and not by a human with a browser.

The impact of this seemingly small detail is huge. When a human is looking at a Web site, he can understand what the page is trying to convey, even if the page is formatted in one of twenty different ways. Programs, on the other hand, are very picky about the kind of data that they can accept and the manner in which it must be formatted.

Web services are the logical outgrowth of the concept of XML documents. These documents give us a way to communicate complex data in plain text. This plain text works well with the Internet, because HTTP is a plain-text protocol. In addition, many firewalls are programmed to let HTTP through removing a huge hurdle to acceptance.

Web services requests are formatted in a dialect of XML called Simple Object Access Protocol (SOAP). This format enables one programmer to create an XML document and ship it to another computer for execution.

Humans are also able to find out what Web sites are available to them by using their eyes, their voices, and their ears. Programs, on the other hand, are not as flexible. They need a way of finding out what services are available to them, and they can do this by using a Registry that has been created using the Universal Description, Discovery, and Integration (UDDI) format.

These registries form a universal repository of all the services companies, governments, and individuals are willing to allow your program to use, either free, or for a fee.

Other uses for the UDDI are the creation of a private repository. A private repository provides a place for a closed group to find out about Web services that are available inside the company or organization itself.

Humans are also able to connect to Web sites using simple URLs. Programs need more security and also more details when connecting to a Web service. What commands are legal to send? What protocols (HTTP, FTP, JMS, and so on) options does my program have? (With the human Web, the answer is normally HTTP.) Another XML document, the Web service Description Language (WSDL) document provides this information. Figure 26.10 shows how Web services can use the same layers as human Web sites use.

FIGURE 26.10
Web services are Web sites designed to be used by other programs.

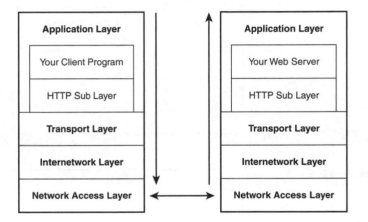

Notice that both the client and the server look like ordinary Web application components to the other layers in the model. Figure 26.11 shows the relationship between each of the three main components of the Web services architecture.

If the WSDL is already in the possession of the client, no call to the UDDI Registry needs to take place.

The Web services architecture fits into the MVC architecture with the exception that there is not always a View layer present. In some ways, the SOAP messages take the place of the View layer, but it would be a stretch to call them the View. The other layers are in play, however, as shown in Figure 26.12.

The diagram shows simple Java Classes as the implementation as Java classes. In reality, these classes could be servlets or EJBs. In fact, the Web services can be written in any language that can handle the reading and writing of text because XML is a text-based language.

FIGURE 26.11
Web services send SOAP messages to each other after communication is established.

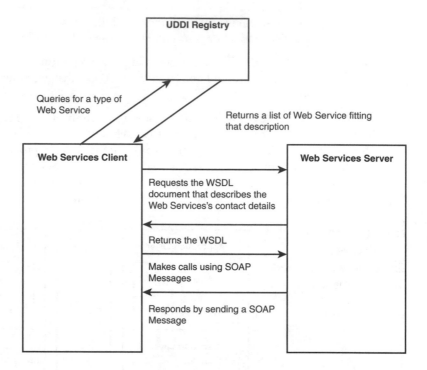

FIGURE 26.12
Web services can also be represented by the MVC architecture.

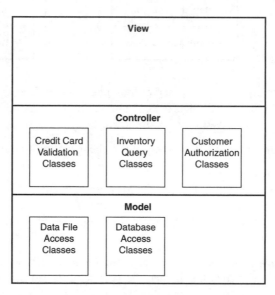

Summary

In this chapter we looked at the subject of databases from a Java-centric point of view. The first thing that we learned was what a database is. Following that, we introduced the Java approach to database management, JDBC.

Next, we looked at how Web sites have been architected in the past, how they are currently being built, and how they will likely be built in the future. We started off by covering the basics of how Web sites are organized. Following that, we looked at the most important ways to measure the goodness of a design.

Then, we then covered the most common architectural approaches used in site design: Servlets, JSPs, and JavaScript. Finally, we looked at some promising new approaches to creating Web sites with EJB, and Web services.

Review Questions

1. What is the difference between TCP/IP and HTTP?

2. What does MVC stand for?

3. What is the advantage of subdividing a system into components using the MVC pattern?

4. What layers of an MVC-based design can be created using Enterprise JavaBeans?

APPENDIXES

APPENDIX A

USING BORLAND JBUILDER

In this appendix you will learn:

- How to download and install JBuilder
- How to develop applications
- How to debug applications
- How to develop JSPs with JBuilder

Borland JBuilder is a very nice Java Integrated Development Environment. It compares favorably, featurewise, with products like Visual Café and Forte. Unlike Forte, JBuilder is a commercial product that must be purchased. A 30-day trial version of JBuilder is available for free from `http://www.borland.com/products/downloads/download_jbuilder.html`.

JBuilder is a complete environment for developing Java applications. It features editors for Java source code, JavaServer Pages, tag libraries, XML, and J2EE deployment descriptors. It also features a source code debugger that performs the full range of stepping, breaking, and watching that programmers expect from development tools.

JBuilder is useful for developing both standalone applications and Web-based applications with JSPs and servlets. In this chapter, you will learn how to obtain and install the JBuilder software on your computer. You will learn how to use JBuilder to develop and debug Java programs. Finally, you will learn how to create and debug Web-based applications using JBuilder.

Downloading JBuilder

To obtain a trial copy of JBuilder, go to the `http://www.borland.com/products/downloads/download_jbuilder.html` Web page. Choose the "Enterprise Trial" by clicking it. Before you can perform the download, you will need to provide some information to Borland about yourself and your development plans. This information will include an email address. Borland will send you an email containing an attachment that you will need during installation.

After you provide this information, you will be taken to a page where you can download a zip file containing the installation files.

The email that you will receive will instruct you to copy the attached file to a directory on your computer. The exact location will vary by operating system, but the following lists some of them:

- Windows 95/98 (single-user)—`C:\Windows`

- Windows 95/98 (multiuser)—`C:\Windows\Profiles\`

- Windows NT—`C:\WINNT\Profiles\`

- Windows 2000/XP—`C:\Documents and Settings\`

- Unix and Linux—The home directory can vary. For example, it could be `/user/` or `/home/` (when you log in, you should be in your home directory).

Because Web sites change so often, it is not likely that the step-by-step procedures used in this chapter will be identical to the ones that you will use. The procedures will probably be similar enough to be of some value to you, however.

Installing JBuilder

Before you can install JBuilder on your machine, you must extract the files from the zip. This extraction process will create a directory called `<download-dir>jbuilder7`, where `<download-dir>` is the location of the Zip file.

You begin the installation process by double-clicking the icon labeled:

`ent_trial_install.exe.`

This opens the installation wizard that you can follow to perform the installation. Follow the simple instructions that this wizard provides and JBuilder will be installed on your hard drive.

Running JBuilder

On our Windows/XP test machine the installation wizard didn't create a desktop icon. We opened the Start menu and clicked the All Programs icon. Next, we located the Borland JBuilder Enterprise Trial icon in the submenu of the same name, and dragged it onto the desktop. We chose "copy" when we were prompted, and an icon appeared on the desktop.

You can run JBuilder by double-clicking this desktop icon. Alternatively, you can type the following in a command window:

`C:\>JBuilder_jdk\JBuilder4j\bin\runidew`

In either case, the first window that you see enables you to create a project (see Figure A.1).

FIGURE A.1

The Welcome project is displayed when you first start the IDE.

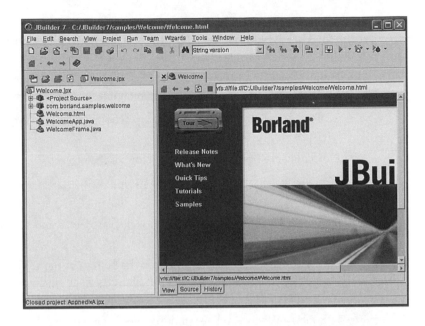

You create a project by choosing "New Project" from the "File" menu. This opens a dialog that enables you to enter a project name. You can use any project name. We used "JavaPrimerPlus" as the first project name on our test machine.

After you specify the name of the project, click the "Finish" button and you will see a screen that looks like the one in Figure A.2.

FIGURE A.2

The IDE is the control panel for managing a project.

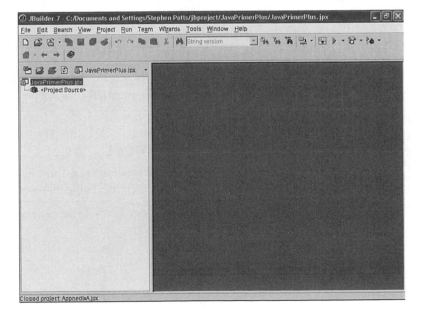

The number of buttons, tabs, and menu choices that are available in the IDE can be over-whelming. Luckily, you can learn how to use a few of them at a time until you learn your way around the IDE. The IDE is divided into different logical areas:

- Menu Bar—Contains menu picks. For many of the menu picks there is a corresponding tool in the toolbar and a hotkey combination.

- Toolbar—Contains buttons to perform actions quickly. It also contains the debugging controls.

- Project Pane—Displays the file structure of the project.

- Structure Pane—Displays the relationships between packages, methods, and classes in your project.

- Status Bars—These one-line text areas display details and statistics about what is going on in your project.

- File View Tabs—These tabs appear at the bottom of the Content pane. They are marked Source, Design, Bean, UML, Doc, and History. Each displays a different view of the information pertaining to the project in the Content Pane.

- File Tabs—When you have multiple files open, you navigate by using these tabs.

- Content Pane—This pane contains source code, control layout, and so on, depending on what the current task is.

- Message Pane—A variety of messages, including the output from `System.out.println()` statements appear here.

You will learn how to use these features as we walk through the examples in this chapter.

Developing Java Applications with the IDE

The easiest way to learn how to use the IDE is to create a project in a step-by-step fashion. The first example that we will work will be a simple Hello, World program that uses `println()` method calls to create its output.

Creating a Class in the Project

The next step in running a program is the creation of a source code file. To do this, choose New Class from the File menu. This will open the dialog that is pictured in Figure A.3.

Call the name of the class `TestIDE1` and specify the `javaprimerplus` package. Following that, add the lines shown in Listing A.1 to the class.

FIGURE A.3

The Class Wizard enables you to specify details about the class that you are creating.

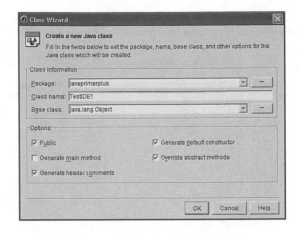

LISTING A.1   The TestIDE1.java File

```java
package javaprimerplus;

public class TestIDE1
{

    /** Creates a new instance of TestIDE1 */
    public TestIDE1()
    {
    }

    public static void main(String[] args)
    {
        int ans1 = 3;
        int ans2 = 4;
        int ans;

        String s1 = "This is ";
        String s2 = "String data";
        String s3 = s1 + s2;

        ans = ans1 + ans2;
        System.out.println("The string is " + s3);
        System.out.println("The answer is " + ans);
    }
}
```

Before we can run this program, we need to specify the class that contains the main() method. To do this, choose Project Properties from the Project menu. This will open the dialog box shown in Figure A.4.

Click the New button. When the Runtime Properties dialog appears, click the Browse button and select the javaprimerplus.TestIDE1 class, as shown in Figure A.5.

FIGURE A.4

You specify the class that contains the `main()` method in the Project Properties dialog.

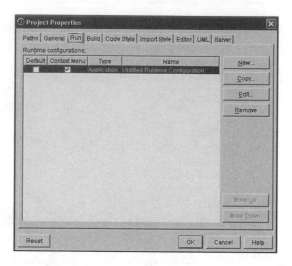

FIGURE A.5

Make your selection from the Runtime Properties dialog.

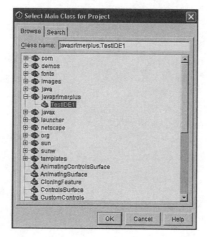

Next, click Run Project in the Run menu to execute this program. The result of running it is shown in Figure A.6.

The output that appears in the Message Pane is shown here in a reformatted version. The first block of output is the Java command, followed by classpath information, and, finally, the name of the class to be run.

```
C:\JBuilder7\jdk1.3.1\bin\javaw -classpath "C:\Documents and Settings\
Stephen Potts\jbproject\JavaPrimerPlus\classes;
C:\JBuilder7\jdk1.3.1\demo\jfc\Java2D\Java2Demo.jar;
C:\JBuilder7\jdk1.3.1\jre\lib\i18n.jar;
C:\JBuilder7\jdk1.3.1\jre\lib\jaws.jar;
C:\JBuilder7\jdk1.3.1\jre\lib\rt.jar;
C:\JBuilder7\jdk1.3.1\jre\lib\sunrsasign.jar;
```

```
C:\JBuilder7\jdk1.3.1\lib\dt.jar;
C:\JBuilder7\jdk1.3.1\lib\htmlconverter.jar;
C:\JBuilder7\jdk1.3.1\lib\tools.jar"  javaprimerplus.TestIDE1
```

The output of the program consists of a string followed by another string that displays an integer.

```
The string is This is String data.
The answer is 7.
```

This program will give us some processing that we can use to explore how to debug programs using JBuilder.

FIGURE A.6

Running the program in the IDE causes the output to be displayed in the Message Pane.

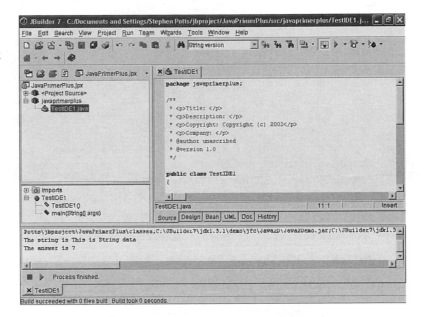

Debugging a Java Application

The IDE provides a wonderful set of tools for debugging the source code. The debugger doesn't run automatically. Before you can run the debugger, you need to tell the project what `main()` class you want to use when running in debug mode. The process to do this is similar to the process used to specify the `main()` class to be used in run mode.

The first step is to choose Project Properties from the Project menu. Next, select the same runtime configuration that you used to specify the runtime `main()` method and click the Edit button. The Runtime properties dialog appears. Click the Run tab, and then on the Test sub tab. Using the ... button, select the same class as before, `javaprimerplus.TestIDE1`, as the class containing the `main()`, as shown in Figure A.7.

FIGURE A.7
You can specify a different `main()` class in Test mode than the one that you specify in Run mode.

Next, you need to learn how to set a breakpoint. The easiest way to set a breakpoint is to click in the left margin of the Content pane when a Java source code file is open within it. The gray left margin is about a quarter of an inch wide. When you click it, a red circle appears indicating that a breakpoint is now set on that line. During program execution, the program will pause and wait for instructions from you when it encounters that line.

As an exercise, set a breakpoint in the main method on the line that reads:

```
System.out.println("The string is " + s3);
```

Next, choose Debug Project from the Run menu, or click the Debug Project button in the tool bar. The program will continue until it hits the first breakpoint. It will then pause until you give it the command to continue, as shown in Figure A.8.

The IDE takes on a much more complicated look when in debug mode. Notice the colored line that is now resting on the line with the breakpoint, line 31. The colored line and the arrow in the margin over the red dot mean that the debugger has paused at this line waiting for you to examine variables, set new breakpoints, and so forth, before resuming.

The debugging portion of the screen is located at the bottom. The red stop sign icon indicates that this is a list of all the breakpoints in the project. Clicking it changes the contents of the Message Pane, as shown in Figure A.9.

Notice that there are two breakpoints in the list. The one that we set is for line 31, and the other is for all uncaught exceptions.

FIGURE A.8
The IDE is transformed into a debugger when you run in debug mode.

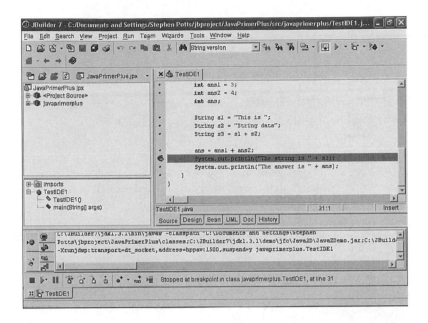

FIGURE A.9
The debugging controls are located at the bottom of the screen.

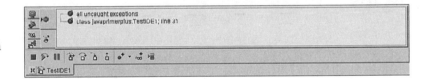

The meaning of all the other icons is shown here:

   • The Data and Code Breakpoints—Provides a list of breakpoints.

   • Console Output—Shows the `System.out.println()` output as well as other messages.

   • Threads, CallStacks, and Data—Shows the call stack and data values for each thread.

   • Data Watches—Displays the values for all the variables that are being watched.

   • Load Classes and Static Data—Lists all the classes and the values of their static variables.

- Reset Debugging Session—Ends the current session.

- Resume Program—Continues the debugging session after a break or a pause.

- Pause—Pauses the debugging session.

- Toggle Smart Step—Turns Smart Step on and off. Smart Step determines whether classes that have had tracing turned off will be stepped into.

- Step Over—Moves forward one line without entering called methods.

- Step Into—Moves forward one line entering a method if encountered.

- Step Out—Moves to the line following the call to this method.

- Add Breakpoint—Provides a GUI that enables you to add a breakpoint.

- Add Watch—Enables you to add a watched variable.

- Show Current Frame—Shows detailed information for the current stack frame.

- Tracing Disabled View—Displays an interface that enables you to specify for which classes you want to enable tracing.

These controls give you a great deal of power when searching for bugs in your projects.

Developing JSPs and Java Servlets with the IDE

The next procedure that you need to learn is how to create JSP pages and servlets using the IDE. These types of programs are different from Java applications in that they normally run as part of a set of components instead of as a single class file.

The first step to creating a JSP is to create a new project. To do this, choose New Project from the File menu and name the project **JPPJSP1**.

The next step is to specify which version of the Tomcat Server you want to use to run your JSP. You do this by selecting Project Properties from the Project menu and selecting the Server tab. Click the Single Server for All Services in Project radio button to select it. Next, choose a server from the list. Normally, the most recent release is best. Figure A.26 shows this Tabbed Pane.

FIGURE A.26
The server tab gives you an opportunity to change the server and the options.

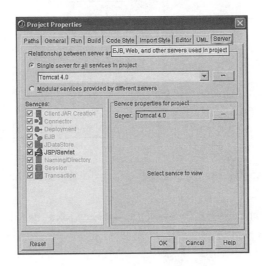

The next step is to create the WebApp for this application. The WebApp is a kind of subproject that is required for JSP and Servlet applications. The WebApp is a directory tree containing all the content used in your application. When you deploy the application, a file called `web.xml` is created based on the information contained in the WebApp. The `web.xml` file is called a deployment descriptor. It provides the metadata needed by the Web server to run your application properly. You create the WebApp by choosing New from the File menu. This will open the Object Gallery, which is shown here in Figure A.27.

FIGURE A.27
The Object Gallery will enable you to create a number of different types of Java objects.

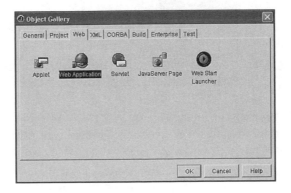

Click the Web tab, choose the Web Application icon and click the OK button. This will open the dialog shown in Figure A.28.

FIGURE A.28
The WebApp contains metadata about your Web project.

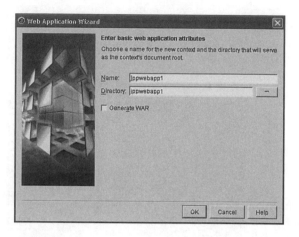

Enter the names as shown here. Leave the Generate WAR check box blank and click the OK button.

Next, we need to create the JSP. To do this, select New from the File menu again. Click the Web tab again, but this time select the JavaServer Page icon and click the OK button. This will open the wizard shown here in Figure A.29.

FIGURE A.29
The JSP Wizard leads you through the creation of your JSP.

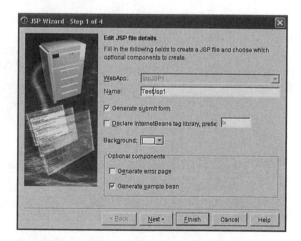

Name your JSP `TestJsp1` and make sure that the Generate Submit Form and the Generate Sample Bean check boxes are checked. This will provide you with some of the structure needed to create the project. Click the Finish button, which will generate the JSP file shown in Listing A.2.

LISTING A.2   The `TestJsp1.jsp` File

```
html>
<head>
<title>
TestJsp1
</title>
</head>
<jsp:useBean id="TestJsp1BeanId" scope="session"
                                class="jppjsp1.TestJsp1Bean" />
<jsp:setProperty name="TestJsp1BeanId" property="*" />
<body>
<h1>
JBuilder Generated JSP
</h1>
<form method="post">
<br>Enter new value    :   <input name="sample"><br>
<br><br>
<input type="submit" name="Submit" value="Submit">
<input type="reset" value="Reset">
<br>
Value of Bean property is :<jsp:getProperty
                        name="TestJsp1BeanId" property="sample" />
</form>
</body>
</html>
```

The most interesting part of this JSP is the `useBean` tag. It provides us access to the Bean that was created for this class.

```
<jsp:useBean id="TestJsp1BeanId" scope="session"
                        class="jppjsp1.TestJsp1Bean" />
```

The source code for this Bean is shown in Listing A.3.

LISTING A.3   The `TestJsp1Bean.java` File

```
package jppjsp1;
public class TestJsp1Bean {
  private String sample = "Start value";
  //Access sample property
  public String getSample() {
    return sample;
  }
  //Access sample property
  public void setSample(String newValue) {
    if (newValue!=null) {
      sample = newValue;
    }
  }
}
```

This JSP and Bean combination is ready to run without modification. All that you have to do is to expand the WebApp icon in the Project Pane until you see the Root Directory entry. Under it you will see the `TestJsp1.jsp` listing. Right click this filename and choose Web Run Using TestJsp1 from the menu. This will start up the JSP and display its screen in the Content Pane, as shown in Figure A.30.

FIGURE A.30
The JSP runs in the
Content Pane of the IDE.

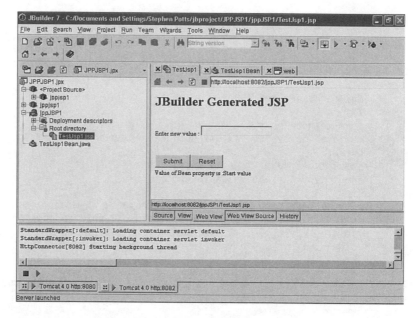

This is a fully functioning JSP. When you enter data in the Text field and click the Submit button, the data that you entered is shown beneath the buttons, as shown in Figure A.31.

FIGURE A.31
The JSP is fully functional
when it is generated by
the servlet.

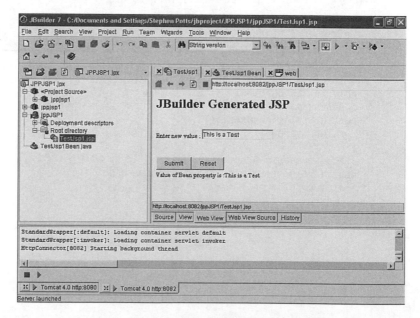

The JSP and the Bean are ready for you to add your code to. Chapter 22, "JavaServer Pages" and Chapter 23, "Component-based JSP Pages," will provide you with instructions on how to create JSPs that solve business problems.

Summary

In this appendix, you learned how to create a variety of Java programs using the Borland JBuilder IDE. First, you created an application in the IDE, and then you learned how to step through and debug it.

Following that, you learned how to create and run JSPs.

APPENDIX B

SUN ONE STUDIO 4 (FORTE), COMMUNITY EDITION

> **You will learn about the following in this appendix:**
> - How to download and install
> - How to develop applications
> - How to debug applications
> - How to develop servlets and JSPs
> - How to debugging servlets and JSPs

The Sun One Studio 4, Community Edition, also known as Forte, is a very nice Java Integrated Development Environment. It competes, feature-wise, with products such as Visual Café and JBuilder, but with one important difference; the price. The edition of Forte that we will cover in this chapter, called the Community Edition, is available for free from http://wwws.sun.com/software/download/.

Forte is a complete environment for developing Java applications. It features editors for Java source code, Java ServerPages, tag libraries, XML, and J2EE deployment descriptors. In addition, Forte contains a monitor to view HTTP messages that are sent and received by your application. It also features a source code debugger that performs the full range of stepping, breaking, and watching that programmers have come to expect from development tools.

Forte is useful for developing both standalone applications and Web-based applications with JSPs and servlets. In this chapter, you will learn how to obtain and install the Forte software on your computer. You will learn how to use Forte to develop and debug Java programs. Finally, you will learn how to create and debug Web-based applications using Forte.

Downloading Sun One Studio 4

To obtain a free copy of Forte, go to the http://wwws.sun.com/software/download/ Web page. A link to either Forte or to Sun One Studio. If not, follow the Application Development link to locate the product.

Because Web sites change so often, it is not likely that the step-by-step procedures used in this chapter will be identical to the ones that you will use. It will probably be similar enough to be of some value to you, however.

From the download page, `http://wwws.sun.com/software/download/`, choose the Application Development option. This will take you to `http://wwws.sun.com/software/sun-dev/jde/buy/index.html`. Move to the bottom of the page and choose either download or download in a bundle with J2SE 1.4. Because our test machine does not yet have J2SE 1.4, we will download the bundle.

You will be led to a page where you specify your platform and natural language preferences. Make sure that you scroll down to the section where you download both the J2SE and the Sun One Studio 4. You will then be taken to a license page. If you accept the license agreement, you will proceed to a page with a link that will enable you to start the download.

On our test machine, we downloaded a file called `j2sdk-1_4_0-forte_ce-4-bin-windows.exe` to the `c:\download` directory.

Installing Sun One Studio 4

You begin the installation process by double-clicking the icon for the installation file or by typing the following in a command window:

```
C:\>c:\downloads\j2sdk-1_4_0-forte_ce-4-bin-windows.exe
```

This opens the installation wizard. Follow the simple instructions that this wizard provides and Sun One Studio 4 will be installed on your hard drive.

Running Sun One Studio 4

You can run Sun One Studio by double-clicking the desktop icon that the installation process creates. Alternatively, you can type the following in a command window:

```
C:\>forte_jdk\forte4j\bin\runidew
```

In either case, the first window that you see will request that you specify a directory that Sun One Studio can use to store information about your projects and preferences. Figure B.1 shows this screen:

You can use any directory name, but Sun recommends that you not use the installation directory. We used `c:\ide-userdir` on our test machine.

After you specify this directory, you will be led through a series of questions about your preferences and given a chance to register. When you finish, you will see a screen that looks like the one in Figure B.2.

FIGURE B.1

The IDE stores project information and preferences in the User Directory.

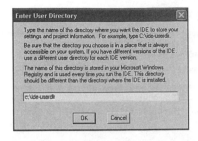

FIGURE B.2

The IDE contains more options than a Swiss Army Knife.

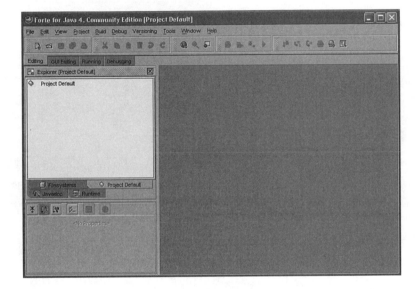

The sheer number of buttons, tabs, and menu choices available in the IDE can be overwhelming. Luckily, you can learn how to use a few of them at time until you learn your way around the IDE. There are two options for running the IDE: single-window, where different panels contain the functionality, and multiple-window mode, where different windows contain a single panel each. We will use the single-window mode in this chapter.

The IDE is divided into different logical areas, including

- Menu Bar—Contains menu picks.

- Tabbed Tool Bar—Contains buttons that change depending on the tab selected. The tabs are Editing, GUI Editing, Running, and Debugging.

- Explorer Panel—This is a set of Tabbed Dialogs that provide views of different information in the IDE. The Tabs are Filesystems, Project Default, Javadoc, and Runtime. Whenever you create a new project, it receives its own tab in the Explorer.

- Output Panel—This panel appears whenever the Tool Bar Tab is set to either Running or Debugging. It displays error messages and `println` statements.

- Debugger Panel—This window shows you current watches, call stacks, and so forth when you are debugging.

- Editing Panel—This window shows you the document that you are currently editing. Normally, you click a file or class name in the Explorer Panel to open that file in an editor.

You will learn how to use each of these panels as we walk through the examples in this chapter.

Developing Java Applications with the IDE

The easiest way to learn how to use the IDE is to create a project in a step-by-step fashion. The first example that we will work is a simple Hello, World program that uses `println()` method calls to create its output.

Creating the Project

Java development with Sun ONE Studio is easier if you organize your work into projects. A project is a set of files, possibly of different types, that comprise one programming goal. For example, a project can be used to organize all HTML, JSP, servlets, and Beans needed for a commercial site.

One big advantage of a project is your ability to view all the files associated with it at once in the Explorer Panel. This keeps your Explorer pane from becoming a jumbled mass of files.

To create a new project, choose Project Manager from the Project menu. When the Project Manager dialog appears, click the New button. You will then be given a chance to name your project whatever name you choose. Following that, you will hear the hard drive work hard for a few seconds, and a new project tab will appear in the Explorer Panel with the name that you chose.

Creating a Class in the Project

The next step in running a program is the creation of a source code file. To do this, choose the Project *xxx* tab in the Explorer Panel, where *xxx* is the name of your project. Next, right-click the name of the project on the Project Tab's content area. This will open the dialog that is pictured in Figure B.3.

You will then be led through a series of questions about the file that you want to add to the project. The first question is for the name of the class, and the package that it will belong to. Figure B.4 shows this dialog.

FIGURE B.3

The New Wizard enables you to choose a template for the type of Java entity that you want to create.

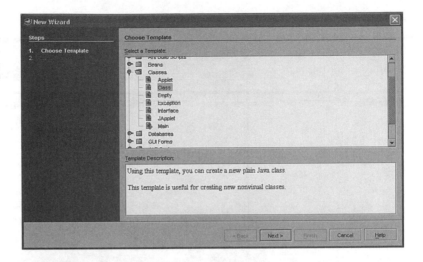

FIGURE B.4

The New Wizard enables you to specify the name and package for the new class.

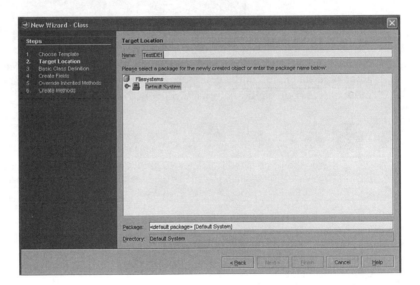

The wizard enables you to specify all types of details about the class such as field names and types, interfaces implemented, and so on. If, like many programmers, you prefer to write code to add these details, click the Finish button. Otherwise, use the dialogs to specify as many features of your class as you choose.

After you click the Finish button of the wizard, your source code will be generated. You will see it appear in the Editing Panel. In the Explorer, you will now see an icon and the name of this class under the Project icon as shown here in Figure B.5

FIGURE B.5
The new class shows up in the Explorer as an icon and in the Editing Pane as a source code file.

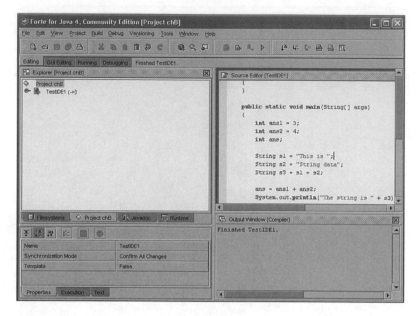

Notice how the source code file already contains certain constructs such as a Javadoc identifier, a **package** statement, and a constructor. If we had used more of the dialogs in the wizard, more of this code would have been generated.

Caution

You should resist the temptation to overuse the wizard to generate code for you until you know Java very well. These interfaces can be a timesaver for an experienced Java programmer, but they can be a crutch for a novice. Remember that your goal is to be a great Java programmer, not an IDE power user.

If you look next to the class name on the Explorer Panel you will see some tiny maroon or red marks. This handy indicator means that this class has not been compiled since the last modification was made.

Before we compile the class, we should actually make it produce some output and create some variables that we can examine using the debugger. All that you have to do to edit this source code is to place your mouse's cursor over the source code that you want to change, click, and start typing. Listing B.1 shows a class that has the additional lines that we need.

LISTING B.1   The `TestIDE1.java` File

```
/*
 * TestIDE1.java
 *
 * Created on August 6, 2002, 3:33 PM
 */
```

LISTING B.1   Continued

```java
/**
 *
 * @author  Stephen Potts
 */
public class TestIDE1
{

    /** Creates a new instance of TestIDE1 */
    public TestIDE1()
    {
    }

    public static void main(String[] args)
    {
        int ans1 = 3;
        int ans2 = 4;
        int ans;

        String s1 = "This is ";
        String s2 = "String data";
        String s3 = s1 + s2;

        ans = ans1 + ans2;
        System.out.println("The string is " + s3);
        System.out.println("The answer is " + ans);
    }

}
```

Before you can run this program, you need to learn how to use the toolbar to compile and build the class. You do this by choosing Build from the Build menu, pressing F11, or by clicking the Build icon in the toolbar. To find what each icon in the toolbar does, you can let your mouse cursor rest on top of an icon for a few seconds until a ToolTip appears.

If you have no compile errors, the output window will display the message:

`Finished TestIDE1.`

If it has compile errors, they will be displayed here also.

After the program compiles, you can run it by clicking the Execute item in the Build menu, by pressing F9, or by clicking the Execute icon in the toolbar. Running this program produces the following output:

```
The string is This is String data
The answer is 7
```

Debugging a Java Application

The IDE provides a wonderful set of tools for debugging the source code. The debugger doesn't run automatically. Regardless of the number of breakpoints that you have set, you must choose Start from the Debug menu or they will be ignored.

Debug mode behaves like normal execution mode unless you set up some debugging commands before clicking Start. The simplest command is to set a breakpoint. A break point pauses the program at a certain line that you choose. This enables you to examine the value of variables, and the state of the call stack to learn how your program is behaving.

Breakpoints can be either toggled or added. Toggling a breakpoint causes an unconditional breakpoint to be set or unset. Adding a breakpoint gives you the opportunity to attach conditions to the breakpoint. When the conditions are met, the program pauses.

Let's add a breakpoint at line number 23, the first line of the `main()` method. To do this, position your cursor anywhere on line 23 and choose Toggle Breakpoint from the Debug menu. This will cause that line to turn red.

Before we test our new breakpoint, let's set a couple of watches on the variables in the program. A watch tells you the value of a variable at the time that the code was last paused. There is an automatic watch that occurs for all variables in the program when you rest the mouse cursor over any variable currently in scope. A ToolTip will pop up and tell you its value. The second type of watch appears in the Debug pane while a program is running or paused. To add a manual watch, choose Add Watch from the Debug menu. A dialog will appear that enables you to specify which variable you want watched. In this example, let's specify that we want to watch the variable `ans1`.

Next, choose Start from the Debug menu. This will move the cursor to the first breakpoint, where it will pause. Choose Step Over from the Debug menu to move down one line. We need to do this so that our watched variable, `ans1`, will have a value. Figure B.6 shows what the IDE looks like at this point.

FIGURE B.6
The IDE changes to Debug mode showing the breakpoints, watches, and call stack in the Explorer panel.

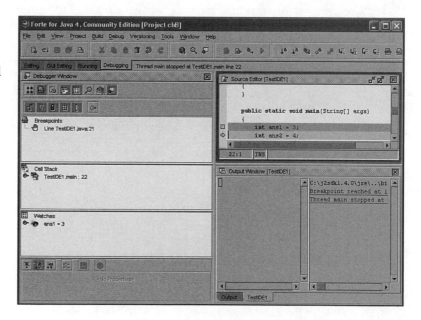

Notice in the left panel that the breakpoint, the watch, and the method calls that are on the stack are all visible. If we want to continue stepping, we can choose Step Over from the Debug menu again and again. Alternatively, we could set another breakpoint in the program and choose Continue from the Debug menu to pause when the new breakpoint is reached. If we decide that we want to just let the program terminate immediately, we choose Finish from the Debug menu. The program will terminate automatically when the last executable line, the in `main()` method, has been processed.

Developing JSPs and Java Servlets with the IDE

The next procedure that you need to learn is how to create JSPs and servlets using the IDE. These types of programs are different from Java applications in that they normally run as part of a set of components instead of as a single class file. The set of all files that make up one application is called a Web Module in Sun ONE Studio. A Web Module is a specialized file structure that contains a tree of directories that conform to the Java Servlet Specification Version 2.3.

According to this specification, the structured hierarchy consists of a root directory, which contains HTML and JSP pages that are accessed directly by the browser. A special nonpublic directory called WEB-INF is created underneath the root. This includes the deployment descriptor file, the servlets, and the utility classes used by the application.

Before we create the Web Module, let's first create a new project called `WebProject1` using the procedure that you learned earlier in this chapter. Click the Project Tab in the Explorer Pane. Next, right-click the name of this project in the Explorer Pane and choose Add New. This will start the New Wizard.

Expand the item in the New Wizard that is called JSP and Servlet. Figure B.7 shows this wizard.

FIGURE B.7

The New Wizard can be used to create JSP and Servlet projects also.

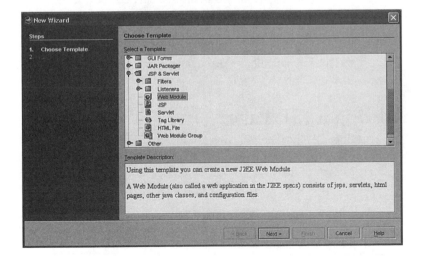

Click the Web Module option, and then click the Next button. When the Choose Target dialog appears, enter a location in the file system such as `c:\jpp`. This directory will be created automatically and the Web Module's file structure will be built under this location. Click the Finish button. Click the Filesystem Tab in the Explorer Pane and expand the WEB-INF directory. Figure B.8 shows the file structure after the Web Module is created.

FIGURE B.8
Several new files appear under the target directory.

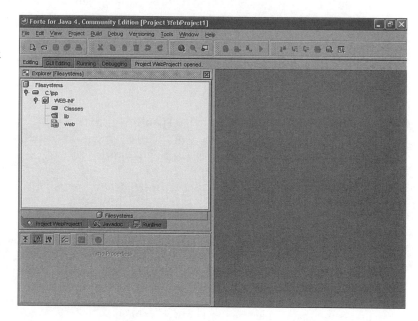

Each of these entities has a role that it plays in the project:

- The WEB-INF directory references all the items in the module.

- The Classes directory contains the servlets, Beans, and other classes that are instantiated by classes in this module.

- The `lib` folder contains tag libraries and imported JAR files.

- The `web.xml` file is a deployment descriptor for this application. It contains instructions about how this application is to be built.

Adding a JSP Page

Adding a JSP page to this Web Module is easy to do using the IDE. The first step is to create the JSP page using the New Wizard. To do this, you can right-click the project root node in the Project tab of the Explorer Pane. Choose Add New and the New Wizard will appear. Expand the JSP & Servlet item, and select the JSP item and click Next.

A dialog will appear that will give you a chance to name the JSP page. Choose the name (ours is named `FirstJSPage`), but leave the package blank. Choose the root directory, `c:\jpp` as the directory for this file as shown here in Figure B.9.

FIGURE B.9
The Add Wizard can also
be used for JSP files.

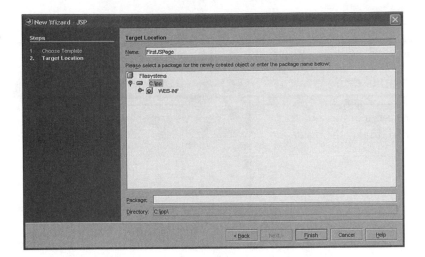

Caution

Because different versions of Forte vary slightly in appearance, there might be small differences in the way your screens look.

Click the Finish button, and you will see the JSP filename appear in the Filesystem Tab of the Explorer Panel. Double-click the filename in the Explorer to see the source code for the JSP page appear in the Editing Panel.

Edit the JSP page by adding the following line to it in the body below the tags:

```
This is the first JSP Page that we created.
```

Listing B.2 shows the source code for this simple JSP page.

LISTING B.2   The `FirstJSPage.jsp` File

```
<%@page contentType="text/html"%>
<html>
<head><title>JSP Page</title></head>
<body>

<%-- <jsp:useBean id="beanInstanceName" scope="session"
                        class="package.class" /> --%>
<%-- <jsp:getProperty name="beanInstanceName"
                        property="propertyName" /> --%>

This is the first JSP Page that we created.

</body>
</html>
```

Running this JSP page from within the IDE is simple. All that you have to do is choose Execute from the Build menu. This will start a browser and display the JSP page, which is shown here in Figure B.10.

FIGURE B.10

The JSP page execution causes a browser to open and display the result.

Notice that this JSP page is being run on a machine called `localhost` and on port 8081. This is the URL of your machine's copy of the Tomcat Web Server, which was installed along with the IDE. This server is integrated with the IDE in such a way that it is not necessary to even be aware that it is running behind the scenes.

The IDE contains several panels that all deal with this one JSP, as shown in Figure B.11.

FIGURE B.11

The IDE provides a lot of information about the JSP page being created.

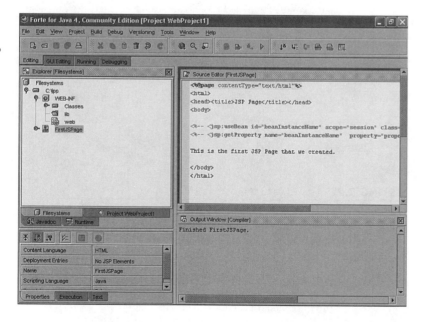

On the left is the Explorer with the JSP page highlighted. On the right is the Editing Panel with the source code displayed in editing mode. Below that, the output panel contains the compiler messages. If your page contains errors, they will appear here.

During the execution of the page, the layout of the IDE changes. The Explorer is hidden and the Execution View takes over that part of the screen. Figure B.12 shows the IDE while the JSP is running.

FIGURE B.12
The IDE changes during execution to provide runtime information.

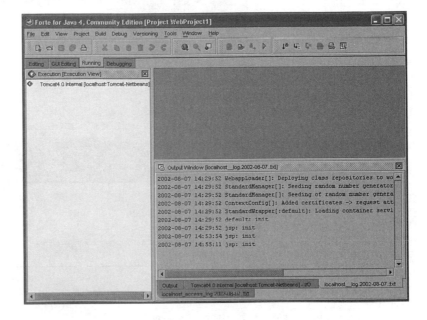

The default display in the output window changes to the localhost log. Each time you run the JSP page, a new entry is placed in this log.

Adding a Servlet

Creating a servlet with Sun ONE Studio 4 is similar to creating a JSP. You start out by right-clicking the project name and choosing Add New. When the New Wizard comes up, you choose to add a servlet and click the Next button. When the Target Location dialog appears, enter `FirstServlet` in the name field. The location of the file must be in the `WEB-INF\Classes` directory, according to the Java Servlet Specification Version 2.3. Figure B.13 shows this dialog.

Click the Finish button to generate the servlet. We need to change the servlet contents slightly so that it will generate some visible output. We do this by removing the comments surrounding the `out.println()` method calls in the `processRequest()` method. In addition, we need to add the following line under the `out.println()` statement that adds the `<body>` tag to the output:

```
out.println("This is our first Servlet");
```

FIGURE B.13
The location of servlet files is different from the location of JSP files.

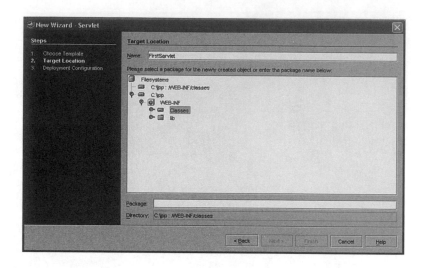

Listing B.3 shows the full listing of this servlet.

LISTING B.3   The `FirstServlet.java` File

```java
/*
 * FirstServlet.java
 *
 * Created on August 7, 2002, 5:30 PM
 */

import javax.servlet.*;
import javax.servlet.http.*;

/**
 *
 * @author  Stephen Potts
 * @version
 */
public class FirstServlet extends HttpServlet
{

    /** Initializes the servlet.
     */
    public void init(ServletConfig config) throws ServletException
    {
        super.init(config);

    }

    /** Destroys the servlet.
     */
    public void destroy()
    {
```

LISTING B.3   Continued

```java
    }

    /** Processes requests for both HTTP <code>GET</code>
     * and <code>POST</code> methods.
     * @param request servlet request
     * @param response servlet response
     */
    protected void processRequest(HttpServletRequest request,
                                  HttpServletResponse response)
    throws ServletException, java.io.IOException
    {
        response.setContentType("text/html");
        java.io.PrintWriter out = response.getWriter();
        // output your page here
        out.println("<html>");
        out.println("<head>");
        out.println("<title>Servlet</title>");
        out.println("</head>");
        out.println("<body>");
        out.println("This is our first Servlet");
        out.println("</body>");
        out.println("</html>");

        out.close();
    }

    /** Handles the HTTP <code>GET</code> method.
     * @param request servlet request
     * @param response servlet response
     */
    protected void doGet(HttpServletRequest request,
                         HttpServletResponse response)
    throws ServletException, java.io.IOException
    {
        processRequest(request, response);
    }

    /** Handles the HTTP <code>POST</code> method.
     * @param request servlet request
     * @param response servlet response
     */
    protected void doPost(HttpServletRequest request,
                          HttpServletResponse response)
    throws ServletException, java.io.IOException
    {
        processRequest(request, response);
    }

    /** Returns a short description of the servlet.
     */
    public String getServletInfo()
    {
```

LISTING B.3   Continued

```
        return "Short description";
    }

}
```

See Chapter 21, "Servlets," for an explanation of what each of the elements in the servlet adds to the total. We can run this servlet by choosing Execute from the Build menu. Running this application starts a browser and displays the result, as shown in Figure B.14.

FIGURE B.14
The servlet results are displayed in a browser also.

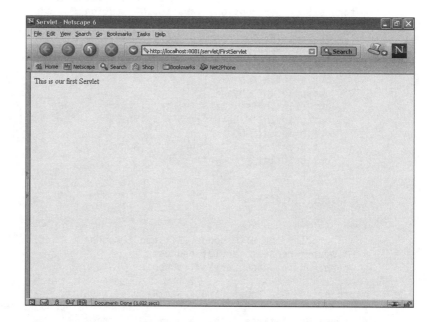

You can set breakpoints and watchpoints in servlets just like you can in Java applications. You must choose Start from the Debug menu if you want them to actually pause your program.

Summary

In this appendix, you learned how to create a variety of Java programs using the Sun ONE Studio 4 IDE. First, you created an application in the IDE, and then learned how to step through and debug it.

Following that, you learned how to create and run JSPs. Finally, you saw how you can use the IDE to create servlets also.

ANSWERS TO REVIEW QUESTIONS

Chapter 1

None

Chapter 2

1. b. label

2. Syntax defines the rules by which a program must adhere to be processed by the compiler. Semantics defines the logical rules that make a computer program do what you want it to.

3. Computers represent data as a sequence of 1s and 0s.

4. A data type is a human-readable tag that represents a specific usage of a computer's memory.

5. A short is represented by two bytes while an int is represented by four bytes.

6. The first two statements are legal but the third is not because the result of adding two shorts is automatically converted to an integer; an explicit cast to a short is required for this statement to be correct:

```
short result = ( short )( s1 + s2 );
```

7. Arithmetic promotion means that a variable of a certain data type is automatically converted to a "wider" type during an arithmetic operation.

8. You can only assign a byte or a short to a short.

9. Casting is explicitly interpreting a variable as a more narrow type; the result of this is dropping bits from the variable. It is accomplished by prefacing the variable with the type to cast the variable to enclosed in parentheses:

```
int integer = 50;
short s = ( short ) integer;
```

10. You define a variable to be a constant by prefacing its data type with the keyword *final*:

```
final int i = 50;
```

Chapter 3

1. The modulus operator (%) returns the remainder of integer division:

   10 % 3 = 1, or explicitly 10 / 3 = 3 with remainder 1

2. The && operator is the logical AND and is used in Boolean operations that compare two values, for example:

   ```
   if( a > 5 && a < 10 ) ...
   ```

   This will evaluate to true only with a value between 5 and 10.

   The & operator is the bitwise AND and is used when performing the bitwise AND of type numbers. For example:

   3 & 9 = 1, or explicitly 0000 0011 & 0000 1001 = 0000 0001

3. A truth table is a list of all possible input values and their corresponding values. For example the truth table for the AND operation is

   A B Result

   0 0 0

   0 1 0

   1 0 0

   1 1 1

4. 21 & 3 == 0001 0101 & 0000 0011 = 0000 0001 = 1 (AND)

5. 21 | 3 == 0001 0101 | 0000 0011 = 0001 0111 = 23 (OR)

6. 21 ^ 3 = 0001 0101 ^ 0000 0011 = 0001 0110 = 22 (XOR)

7. >> is right shift while >>> is right shift fill with 0s. >> fills with the left most bit.

8. 5 * 5 + 5 is equivalent to (5 * 5) + 5 = 25 + 5 = 30

9. 5 + 5 * 5 is equivalent to 5 + (5 * 5) = 5 + 25 = 30

10. Evaluate the following:

    ```
    int a = 5;
    a += 6 * ++a / 2 - 6 * 9 + 2
    a += ( ( ( 6 * ++5 ) / 2 ) - (6 * 9) ) + 2 =
    a += ( ( ( 6 * 6 ) / 2 ) - (6 * 9) ) + 2 =
    a += ( ( ( 36 ) / 2 ) - (54) ) + 2 =
    a += ( 18 - 54 ) + 2 =
    a += ( -36 ) + 2 =
    a += -34 =
    a = a - 34 =
    a = 5 - 34 =
    a = -29
    ```

Chapter 4

1. The general form of the if statement is

```
if( boolean_value ) {
    // Execute these statements
}
```

2. If the boolean value inside the if statement evaluates to false then an else block can be executed:

```
if( boolean_value ) {
    // boolean is true: Execute these statements
}
else {
    // boolean is false: Execute these statements
}
```

3. There is not a limit to the number of else if statements that can follow an if statement.

4. The switch statement only evaluates int variables or variables that can be converted to int.

5. The do-while statement assures that the body of the loop is evaluated at least once.

6. An infinite loop is a loop that does not terminate, its loop control variable never evaluates to a value that allows the loop to exit. For example:

```
int a = 10;
while( a > 0 ) {
    // Never change the value of a
}
```

7. The most popular type of loop for iterating over a variable or set of variables is the for loop.

8. You can skip the statements in the current iteration of a loop by issuing the continue statement.

9. You can stop executing the statements in a loop and continue at the first line following the loop by issuing the break statement.

10. You can break out of a multiple nested loop by defining a label and then breaking to the label, for example:

```
outer:
for( int a=0; a<10; a++ ) {
    for( int b=0; b<10; b++ ) {
        if( a * b == 25 ) break outer;
    }
```

```
        }
```

Chapter 5

1. Divide and conquer is breaking down a large problem into smaller more manageable problems.

2. A method definition looks as follows:

```
return_type method_name( parameter_list )
{
    declarations and statements...
}
```

3. A method's signature consists of the method name, return type, and parameter list.

4. You specify that a method is not going to return a value by specifying the void return type in the method signature.

5. The three types of scope are

   • Class Scope: Available to all methods in the class

   • Block Scope: Available only with the block it is declared to, or within nested blocks

   • Method Scope: Special type for labels used with break and continue statements

6. Recursion is the act of a method calling itself.

7. Any problem that can be solved using recursion can be solved using iteration and iteration has far better performance, therefore use iteration.

8. Method overloading is defining multiple methods with the same name but different signatures.

9. Both of these methods can exist because their parameter lists are different. If two methods only differ by return type then they cannot coexist, but as long as the parameter list is different there is no problem.

10. You access the `Math` methods by appending the `Math` class with a period and then specifying the method name, for example:

```
Math.tan( angle )
```

Chapter 6

1. Encapsulation is the mechanism of encapsulating data and methods into a class and providing a public mechanism for other classes to use your object; the other classes do not need to know what you are doing internally, only that they will get the result they expect.

2. get/set methods are accessor methods to your class's public attributes; set methods allow you to maintain the integrity of your class's attributes by validating the value passed to them before assigning to your internal attributes.

3. A class's constructor is a method that initializes the class; it is the first method called when instantiating the class.

4. A `public` variable is accessible from objects outside of the class while `private` variables are only accessible from within the class.

5. The `this` variable is used to dereference methods and/or variables from within a class; it represents "this" class.

6. Composition is the concept of a class containing another class instance.

7. Garbage collection is an action that the Java Virtual Machine (JVM) performs to reclaim memory no longer being used in your Java application. It is run whenever the JVM needs to reclaim memory.

8. Inner classes are classes defined inside of another class. Inner classes may be regular classes, static inner classes, or anonymous inner classes.

9. "Pass By Reference" means that when variables are passed to other objects or methods, the object being passed is not a copy of the original object but rather a reference back to the original object; modifying the object reference modifies the object itself.

10. The significance of Java's objects being passed by reference is that modifying the object reference modifies the object itself.

Chapter 7

1. Overriding a method in a subclass means that you provide a new implementation for an existing method in the super class.

2. Define the class to be abstract.

3. Define the class to be final.

4. Polymorphism literally means "many shapes" and refers to one object being used in multiple differing ways. In Java it is implemented by referencing a class instance by its base class or through an interface (next chapter) so that the specific implementation of a class does not matter when programming against it.

5. In the subclass.

6. In the super class.

7. The super classes' constructor is called first.

8. The keyword **super** allows you to reference your class's super class's methods directly from within your class.

9. The **super()** method calls the super class's constructor and is useful for calling a specific constructor that you want executed before your class is constructed.

10. If you want your super class's **finalize()** method called, you must explicitly call it from your class's **finalize()** method; note that you must call it after you have completed finalizing your class.

Chapter 8

1. No, all interfaces and their methods are both public and abstract by design.

2. No, all methods are abstract.

3. You implement an interface by using the *implements* keyword in your class definition and then providing implementations for each method in the interface.

4. Multiple inheritance is the act of deriving a class from more than one class (note that Java does not support multiple inheritance).

5. If a class is derived from two classes and those are derived from the same class (this is called diamond inheritance) then there is a question of how the object is created in memory; there must be two instances of the same class in memory that are both references as the parent of the sub class. If the two (or more) classes that the class in question extends provide different implementations of the same method, the compiler will not know which one to reference when it is called.

6. If the functionality is specific to an object, then it is best to put it in the class itself.

7. Put methods in an interface when the functionality is external to the core functionality of objects that will implement it. Put methods in an abstract class that represent functionality that will be core to the classes that will derive from the abstract base class.

8. Diamond inheritance can be a result of multiple inheritance and it is deriving a class from two or more classes that are themselves derived from a common base class. The danger of this is defined in the answer to question number 5 of this chapter.

Chapter 9

1. You throw an exception by creating an instance of the exception class and passing it to the *throw* keyword. For example:

```
MyException ex = new MyException( "This is my exception" );
throw ex;
```

Or:

```
throw new MyException( "This is my exception" );
```

2. You handle an exception by call any method that can throw an exception in a *try* block and then catching the exception in a *catch* block. If the method `accelerate()` can throw a `CarException` then you would handle it as follows:

```
try {
    accelerate();
}
catch( CarException ex ) {
  ex.printStackTrace();
}
```

3. The *try* keyword denotes the start of a *try* block; the *try* block contains method calls that can throw exceptions and it exists to handle those exceptions.

4. java.lang.Throwable

5. Exceptions that derive from the `java.lang.Exception` class.

6. Exceptions that derive from the `java.lang.RuntimeException` class.

7. A subclass method can only throw exceptions that are explicitly defined in its super class's method's signature. The only caveat is that it can throw an exception that is of a class type that subclasses one of the super class method's exceptions.

8. The *throws* method is used in a method's signature to define the list of exceptions that the method can throw.

9. These are the steps:

1.Create a class that extends the `java.lang.Exception` class.

2.In a class that will throw this exception, create a method that lists the custom exception in its *throws* clause.

3.Somewhere in the method create an instance of the custom exception and throw it using the *throw* keyword.

10. Exceptions are classes because they need to be sent from one to another, possibly in a different process. The benefit to you is that you can define your own data and methods in the exception class to help better diagnose the root cause of the problem.

Chapter 10

1. Object Wrappers are serializable classes and thus can be safely passed between classes possibly running inside different processes.

2. Use the `Integer.parseInt( String s )` method.

3. Immutability means that an object's value cannot be changed; in order to change the value of an immutable class, a new instance of the class must be created with the new value and the old value is orphaned in memory.

4. Because strings are immutable, Java has created the notion of a string table that represents all strings running in an application; this is an optimization so that only one instance of a string is represented in memory even if multiple variables are referencing it.

5. Java has created the notion of a string table that represents all strings running in an application; this is an optimization so that only one instance of a string is represented in memory even if multiple variables are referencing it.

6. The `String` class is immutable while the `StringBuffer` class is not; the `StringBuffer` class is free to change its value without having to orphan its old value in memory and create a new instance in memory as the `String` class does.

7. The `StringBuffer` class provides a `reverse()` method that reverses the contents of a string.

8. The `StringTokenizer` class is a utility class that takes a `String` and returns tokens, with delimiters defined by the caller, back to the caller.

9. A delimiter defines the characters that separate tokens.

10. Some of its uses include parsing text based documents into words or parsing comma-separated value (CSV) files into their comma-separated values.

Chapter 11

1. An array is a structure built into Java, whereas an `ArrayList` is a class. More importantly an array is a fixed size, whereas an `ArrayList` can grow and shrink as needed.

2. A `Vector` is thread-safe; meaning that multiple threads of execution can access the `Vector` at the same time without clobbering each other's data.

3. A hash table is faster at inserting and retrieving data than a tree, so if this reflects the nature of your data, a hash table is the best choice.

4. Hash table collision occurs when two objects compute the same hash code; this is resolved by applying another algorithm on one of the objects to compute a new unique hash value.

5. The search operation on a tree is fast (defined the worst case time as the natural logarithm of the number of elements in the tree) because object-insertion operations into and deletion operations from a tree take care to "balance" the tree. This ensures that there are approximately the same number of child nodes to the left of any node as there are to the right.

6. The definition of a Set precludes it from containing duplicate values.

7. A HashMap maintains its keys in a hash table while a TreeMap maintains its keys in a tree. Trees are sorted, whereas hash tables are not, so the iterated output of a TreeMap will be sorted, but the output of a HashMap most likely won't.

8. A stack is a data structure in which the first item added to the Stack is the last object removed and the last item added is the first object removed. This is explained in the acronym LIFO: Last In, First Out. It is similar in concept to piling books one on top of the other: You can only see the book on the top of your stack.

9. Although a stack defines the retrieval of its elements as last in, first out (LIFO), a queue works the opposite, it is first in, first out (FIFO). A stack is similar to a stack of books: You can only see the book on the top of your stack, whereas a queue is similar to a line in the supermarket: The first person in line checks out first.

10. An iterator is a generic interface used for traversing the values stored in one of Java's collection classes. It has three simple methods:

    hasNext(): Are there any more elements in the collection?

    next(): Returns the next element in the collection.

    remove(): Removes the last element returned by the next() method call from the underlying collection.

Chapter 12

1. java.io.InputStream and java.io.OutputStream

2. java.io.Reader and java.io.Writer

3. Primitive types

4. java.io.BufferedReader

5. java.io.PrintStream

6. Chaining is the action of wrapping an existing stream by another stream that is easier to read or write from. It is useful because streams exist to service specific types of data and depending on the data you want to read or write there is a stream that makes it easier for you.

7. The java.io.StreamTokenizer class tokenizes input, using a delimiter that you specify. This enables you to read data in a way specific to the nature of your data; e.g. you could read a document word by word or a comma-separated value (CSV) file token-by-token without reading the commas.

Chapter 13

1. AWT Containers serve as holders for other AWT objects. Java has two graphics libraries for historical reasons. The AWT was released with JDK 1.01, and when it was found to be inefficient the Swing library was added. So many applications were written with AWT that it was judged impractical to remove it.

2. A `List` object is similar to a `Choice` object, except that the `List` allows more than one item to be displayed at the time. It also allows more than one item to be selected at the same time.

3. The `GridBagLayout` is the most powerful, but also the most complex of the layout managers.

Chapter 14

1. Representing events as objects allows for a more sophisticated interaction between the object that generated the event and the event listener. Many methods can be used to query the details of the event.

2. Declaring an object to be listener registers the fact that it wants to be notified with the event-generating object. This is more efficient than the polling-type approach used in JDK 1.01.

3. A semantic event is a high-level event like a button click or a list selection. A low-level event is like a mouse movement.

4. Adapter classes are special classes in the JDK that implement an interface for you and provide a dummy version of every required method. You can extend this class and override only the methods that you really want to use.

Chapter 15

1. A JavaBean provides a get and a set method for all its publicly exposed properties. If a property is read-only, the set method is omitted. Normally, JavaBeans also have a visual representation both on the toolbar and on the screen at runtime.

2. The `SimpleBeanInfo` class provides a `getIcon()` method that can be called by GUI tool to obtain an icon for its toolbar.

3. A bound property is one that can accept a listener who will be notified when the property value changes.

4. A constrained property is one that can also accept a listener. In addition, it provides the listener with a veto over the changes.

Chapter 16

1. They are both graphics libraries. AWT is the old-fashioned library that uses the windowing system of the operating system to control its objects. Swing is the new library that is written almost entirely in Java.

2. Lightweight means that they consume fewer resources than their heavyweight AWT counterparts.

3. A **JTextField** object is limited in size and intended for use when a single piece of data is to be entered. A **JTextArea** object expects to contain many lines of text.

4. The **ListSelectionListener** interface is used to determine which item in the list was selected.

Chapter 17

1. A **TableModel** class manages all the data storage and retrieval for the **JTable** class.

2. The **TreeModel** class manages the data relationships between nodes in a **JTree**.

3. An array, a vector, or a combination of the two can be used to create **JTrees**.

4. A **JOptionPane** can have any one of a number of different looks. The icons, buttons, data entry fields, choice list, and so forth can vary according to the **MessageType** that you pass in to the constructor.

Chapter 18

1. Processes contain threads. Threads are lightweight processes that are handled by the JVM instead of by the operating system.

2. The **sleep()** method is declared to be **static**, which means that there is only one copy of this method and that it resides at the class level. As a result, you can call it with either a handle to an instance or the name of the class. The preferred approach is to call it with the name of the class.

3. The **synchronize** keyword signals that locks should be used to allow only one thread at the time to access a method.

4. The simple **join()** method will wait forever for another process to finish. The version that takes a parameter *n* will time out after *n* milliseconds and resume the thread's execution, with or without the other thread finishing.

Chapter 19

1. A database allows for random access to records, whereas a sequential file can only be read in order. In addition, databases are schema-driven, and sequential files are processed directly.

2. The Java Database Connection (JDBC) made up of a dialect of SQL and set of objects that access databases in an operating system-independent fashion.

3. The `Insert` command adds rows to a table.

4. The access to the database is either done in the Listener methods or in private methods that are called by the Listener methods.

Chapter 20

1. TCP stands for Transmission Control Protocol. IP stands for Internet Protocol.

2. The `java.net` package contains these classes.

3. An object is serializable if it implements the Serializable interface and if it can be stored for later retrieval without the loss of data.

4. A URL is a Uniform Resource Locator. This is a kind of pointer that allows a pointer to find a document or program on the Internet.

Chapter 21

1. A servlet can be run from a browser on a remote computer, whereas an application cannot.

2. A servlet container is a program that runs on a server that is capable of running servlets. Often, the servlet container is installed automatically with the Web server software.

3. The `HTTPServlet` class can only process HTTP requests. If you are using another protocol, you must use the `GenericServlet` class.

4. A session object stores the values of a servlet's variables on the server. This enables the state of the user's session to be maintained for a period of time.

5. A cookie stores the state information in the user's browser. The Session object stores the same information, but on the server itself.

Chapter 22

1. A JSP is written in a special subset of Java that is considered easier to learn. Servlets are written 100% in Java.

2. JSP pages separate out presentation logic from the business logic. JSP is easier to learn than Java.

3. Expressions are limited to the display of one value. Scriptlets can contain a variety of code constructs and are, therefore, more powerful than expressions.

4. The intrinsic objects are those that are built in to the Servlet Container and, therefore, available to JSP pages without instantiation.

Chapter 23

1. You can only use the `include` directive to insert other JSPs into your page. You can use the `include` action to include other servlets, JSPs, and HTML files into your JSPs.

2. JavaBeans are Java classes in every way. This means that they have access to every Java construct and standard extension. Included JSP files are still JSPs, and should only be used to provide view (presentation layer) logic.

3. The `class` attribute specifies the name of the class, including the package.

4. The `param` argument of the `setProperty` action will perform this association automatically.

5. Scriptlets are intended to be short pieces of code that provide logic to the presentation layer of an application. Accessing a database is a controller layer function and, therefore, belongs in a Bean.

Chapter 24

1. Custom tags allow you to add sophisticated component processing to your JSP pages.

2. The taglib ties the custom tag to the class that provides the implementation of the behavior.

3. The implementation class provides a special set method, which is called automatically when the tag is processed.

4. We add `<rtexprvalue>true</rtexprvalue>` to the tablib to indicate that expressions are allowed.

Chapter 25

1. XML is a good choice for transferring data between operating systems and programming languages because it is character-based and agnostic to the underlying operating system or programming language. Furthermore, its structure is very intuitive and can align itself very well with programming data structures.

2. SAX is an event-based parser and a DOM is a tree-based parser.

3. SAX parses data faster because it does not need to construct the in-memory tree that the DOM does.

4. The SAX parser streams through an XML file and notifies the calling process as it encounters tags and data, but does not maintain any part of the XML document in memory.

5. You would be forced to use SAX over DOM when the size of the XML document exceeds the memory limitations of your physical hardware.

6. XSLT is an engine that translates an XML document to another form based off of instructions contained in a stylesheet.

7. A stylesheet provides instructions to the XSLT processor about how to translate the source XML document to its final destination type.

8. JDOM is built on top of Java's collection classes; anyone familiar with using the Java collection classes will find reading an XML document through JDOM extremely simple.

9. You read an XML document using JDOM by creating a `SAXParser` and calling its `build()` method.

10. You can print a copy of the XML document to the screen by using the XMLOutputter class and passing it an XML document and the standard output stream (`System.out`).

Chapter 26

1. TCP/IP is a lower-level protocol whose job is to get data reliably from one computer to another. HTTP is a higher-level protocol, which is used to move requests from a client to a Web Server and responses from a Web Server to a client.

2. It stands for the Model-View-Controller architecture.

3. An MVC design subdivides the task of creating an interactive system into logical subsystems. By grouping these functions logically, you get an easier design to understand and modify.

4. Session Beans can be used for the Controller layer, and Entity Beans can be used for the Model.

INDEX

How can we make this index more useful? Email us at indexes@samspublishing.com

D

E

M

How can we make this index more useful? Email us at indexes@samspublishing.com

P

How can we make this index more useful? Email us at indexes@samspublishing.com

T

X-Y-Z